The Seven Trumpets
and
The Investigative Judgment

By
David D. Burdick

World rights reserved. You may reproduce the whole or part of this work in unaltered form for your own personal use or, if you are part of an organization, for internal use within your organization, but only if you or your organization do not use the reproduction for any commercial purpose and retain this copyright notice and all disclaimer notices as part of that reproduction. Apart from rights to use as permitted by the United States Copyright Acts or allowed by this copyright notice, all other rights are reserved and you are not allowed to reproduce the whole or any part of this work in any way (electronic or otherwise) without first being given specific written permission from the publisher.

The author assumes full responsibility for the accuracy of all facts and quotations as cited in this book. The opinions expressed in this book are the author's personal views and interpretations, and do not necessarily reflect those of the publisher.

This book is provided with the understanding that the publisher is not engaged in giving spiritual, legal, medical, or other professional advice. If authoritative advice is needed, the reader should seek the counsel of a competent professional.

Copyright © 2017 David D. Burdick

Copyright © 2017 ASPECT Books, Inc.

ISBN-13: 978-1-4796-0502-6 (Paperback)

ISBN-13: 978-1-4796-0503-3 (ePub)

ISBN-13: 978-1-4796-0504-0 (Mobi)

Library of Congress Control Number: 2017900691

"Write the vision,
and make it plain upon tables,
that he may run that readeth it"
  –(Hab. 2:2).
"I set watchmen over you, saying,
Hearken to the sound of the trumpet."
  –(Jer. 6:17).

Note: The King James Version (KJV) of the Bible was used for the biblical quotes. Words added for clarity by the KJV translators have been un-italicized in this book. Therefore, all italicized scripture verses used in this book are for emphasis by the author. The Bamberg Apocalypse (11th Century) image on the cover comes from Christiansunite.com.

Table of Contents

Foreword 5
    Unconquerable Forces Waiting

Introduction 7

Chapter 1 12
    Revelation Chapter 4: In the Beginning, God

Chapter 2 15
    Revelation Chapter 5: The Controversy

Chapter 3 29
    Revelation Chapter 6: A Historical Sketch

Chapter 4 41
    Revelation Chapter 7: Adventism Appears

Chapter 5 44
    Revelation Chapter 8: The Trumpets Begin

Chapter 6 65
    Revelation Chapter 9: The Strong Delusion

Revelation Chapters 4 — 11 (KJV) 125

Chapter 7 131
    Revelation Chapter 10: Preparation for the Latter Rain

Chapter 8 184
    Revelation Chapter 11: The Final Victory

Appendix A: 250
    Comments referred to from main text 250
    Notes 303

Appendix B: 305
    Stock Market Graphs

Appendix C: 306
    Pilgrim Pastor John Robinson's scriptural honesty, a warning against rejecting new light

Conclusion 307

Foreword

Unconquerable Forces Waiting
(*Testimonies to Ministers*, pp. 216-219)

Those who eat the flesh and drink the blood of the Son of God will bring from the books of Daniel and Revelation truth that is inspired by the Holy Spirit. They will start into action forces that cannot be repressed. The lips of children will be opened to proclaim the mysteries that have been hidden from the minds of men.

We are standing on the threshold of great and solemn events. Many of the prophecies are about to be fulfilled in quick succession. Every element of power is about to be set to work. Past history will be repeated; old controversies will arouse to new life, and peril will beset God's people on every side. Intensity is taking hold of the human family. It is permeating everything upon the earth....

Study Revelation in connection with Daniel, for history will be repeated.... We, with all our religious advantages, ought to know far more today than we do know.

Angels desire to look into the truths that are revealed to the people who with contrite hearts are searching the word of God and praying for greater lengths and breadths and depths and heights of the knowledge which He alone can give.

As we near the close of this world's history, the prophecies relating to the last days especially demand our study. The last book of the New Testament Scriptures is full of truth that we need to understand. Satan has blinded the minds of many so that they have been glad of any excuse for not making the Revelation their study. But Christ through His servant John has here declared what shall be in the last days; and He says, "Blessed is he that readeth, and they that hear the words of this prophecy, and keep those things which are written therein."...

A message that will arouse the churches is to be proclaimed. Every effort is to be made to give the light, not only to our people, but to the world. I have been instructed that the prophecies of Daniel and the Revelation should be printed in small books, with the necessary explanations, and should be sent all over the world. Our own people need to have the light placed before them in clearer lines.

The vision that Christ presented to John, presenting the commandments of God and the faith of Jesus, is to be definitely proclaimed to all nations, people, and tongues. The churches, represented by Babylon, are represented as having fallen from their spiritual state to become a persecuting power against those who keep the commandments of God and have the testimony of Jesus Christ.

To John this persecuting power is represented as having horns like a lamb, but as speaking like a dragon....

As we near the close of time, there will be greater and still greater external parade of heathen power; heathen deities will manifest their signal power, and will exhibit themselves before the cities of the world; and this delineation as already begun to be fulfilled. By a variety of images the Lord Jesus represented to John the wicked character and seductive influence of those who have been distinguished for their persecution of God's people. All need wisdom carefully to search out the mystery of iniquity that figures so largely in the winding up of this earth's history.... In the very time in which we live, the Lord has called His people and has given them a message to bear. He has called them to expose the wickedness of the man of sin who has made the Sunday law a distinctive power, who has thought to change times and laws, and to oppress the people of God who stand firmly to honor Him by keeping the only true Sabbath, the Sabbath of creation, as holy unto the Lord.

The perils of the last days are upon us, and in our work we are to warn the people of the danger they are in. Let not the solemn scenes which prophecy has revealed be left untouched. If our people were half awake, if they realized the nearness of the events portrayed in the Revelation, a reformation would be wrought in our churches, and many more would believe the message. We have no time to lose; God calls upon us to watch for souls as they that must give an account. Advance new principles, and crowd in the clear-cut truth. It will be as a sword cutting both ways. But be not too ready to take a controversial attitude. There will be times when we must stand still and see the salvation of God. Let Daniel speak, let the Revelation speak, and tell what is truth. But whatever phase of the subject is presented, uplift Jesus as the center of all hope, "the Root and the Offspring of David, and the bright and morning Star."

Dig Deeper

We do not go deep enough in our search for truth. Every soul who believes present truth will be brought where he will be required to give a reason of the hope that is in him. The people of God will be called upon to stand before kings, princes, rulers, and great men of the earth, and they must know that they do know what is truth. They must be converted men and women. God can teach you more in one moment by His Holy Spirit than you could learn from the great men of the earth. The universe is looking upon the controversy that is going on upon the earth. At an infinite cost, God has provided for every man an opportunity to know that which will make him wise unto salvation. How eagerly do angels look to see who will avail himself of this opportunity! When a message is presented to God's people, they should not rise up in opposition to it; they should go to the Bible, comparing it with the law and the testimony, and if it does not bear this test, it is not true. God wants our minds to expand. He desires to put His grace upon us. We may have a feast of good things every day, for God can open the whole treasure of heaven to us.--*Review and Herald*, February 18, 1890.

Introduction

This book contains some new concepts in Revelation that are timely and urgent. The book takes a new view on the investigative judgment, overlaying it with the seven trumpets, and reaffirming the validity and importance of the investigative judgment. All age groups need to read this. I hope I have written to young and old, and not only to the mind, but also to the heart.

Maybe you feel that you are a kindergartner in the school of Christ. You aren't an authority on the Bible or on its last book. You don't know Koine Greek or Masoretic Hebrew. Neither are you a scholar or a theologian. You are *just* a Bible student. But, thankfully the Bible gives its own authoritative commentary. The Bible has no higher commentary on earth than itself. So, anyone can understand the Revelation of Jesus Christ which God gave Him, whether a young farmer who drives a plow, a shepherd boy, or even "a gatherer of sycomore fruit" (Amos 7:14). They need only surrender to God's righteousness and love, and let Him teach them.

There is no other requirement. David said, "I have more understanding than all my teachers: for *thy testimonies are my meditation*. I understand more than the ancients, because *I keep thy precepts*" (Ps. 119:99, 100). This doesn't put down schoolhouse education. Original Greek and Hebrew are helpful, and I don't mean to say I never look at them. Yet, though I am not a theologian, the Lord meant for children to understand His plain word. Spiritual things are spiritually discerned; and simple things are simply discerned. The spiritual, that is, the simplistic child, will be awed by the profound things of the Bible.

"Whom shall he teach knowledge? and whom shall he make to understand doctrine? them that are weaned from the milk, and drawn from the breasts. For precept must be upon precept, precept upon precept; line upon line, line upon line; here a little, and there a little: for with stammering lips and another tongue will he speak to this people", "that no flesh should glory in his presence" (Isa. 28:9-11; 1 Cor. 1:29).

Out of the mouth of babes and sucklings hast thou ordained strength (Ps. 8:2).

The simple farmers of 1848 through 1850 who gathered inside of barns and living rooms were desperate, deep thinking people, though commoners. Even today, God can still choose the desperate, "foolish things of the world...and base things," even "things which are despised" (1 Cor. 1:27, 28). So, don't think because you are not a diplomaed theologian that you cannot grasp the simple, yet profound lessons from Jehovah's prophecies.

As dependent children, knowing God's love and yielding to Him will teach us everything. Bible prophecy is no exception to this rule. "Little children, it is the last time….the anointing which ye have received of him abideth in you, and ye need not that any man teach you: but as the same anointing teacheth you of all things, and is truth, and is no lie, and even as it hath taught you, ye shall abide in him. And now, little children, abide in him; that, when he shall appear, we may have confidence, and not be ashamed before him at his coming" (1 John 2:18, 27, 28). "None of the wicked shall understand; but the wise shall understand" (Dan. 12:10). The humble will sit at the feet of Jesus and learn from Him.

> *The book of Revelation has a continuous storyline from chapter 4 to chapter 11, beginning before Lucifer's rebellion.*

The book of Revelation has a continuous storyline from chapter 4 to chapter 11, beginning before Lucifer's rebellion, and ending with the last call of mercy to the world and the grand finale of the controversy between Christ and Satan. In particular, those chapters have given us a view of God and of His kingdom before sin began and throughout the terrible sin calamity. The gospels and epistles show us the Son of God who laid down His life for us, His friends. But, Revelation reveals the Father who, from the start of the controversy in heaven, has been locked up and imprisoned in house arrest. The exoneration of the Father by His righteous character re-implanted and fully manifested in fallen man is the essence of Revelation chapters 4 through 11.

The Revelation first half, drama-filled section of John's prophecy draws an architecture and builds a structure before the reader for a concise chronicling of God's redeeming work. Then the last half of Revelation, chapter 12 and onward, as ancillary to the central seal/trumpet pageant, fill in details for the prophetic framework outlined by this core theme of Revelation's foundational chapters 4 through 11. These first eight especially focus on humanity's final generation — the generation of the investigative judgment period before Jesus returns.

In this book, we will look at these eight chapters from the context of the whole Bible: the Old Testament scriptures, to find their usages of figurative symbology that Revelation so much draws upon; and the New Testament gospel, to see beautiful nuances of redemption and the gospel's many warnings of eternal destruction reaffirmed in the Revelation. We will sit Old Testament next to New Testament scriptures, "comparing spiritual things with spiritual" (1 Cor. 2:13). Comprehending Revelation, then, assumes familiarity with the whole Bible and a personal encounter with Jesus. We will rest secure in the good news in order to brave the bad news. We will see that this science of salvation, which brings us good and bad news fills the last book of the Bible like it does the whole of God's powerful, life-changing word.

We will explore new perspectives of Revelation. We will seek to handle the word of God honestly and try to candidly search for the solemn message presented by the seal/trumpet drama. We will see old light in new settings, old truth in new framework. Like kids digging through a toy box, we will dig out of the Bible's treasure chest things new and old. "We may have a feast of good things every day, for God can open the whole treasure of heaven to us."

Ellen White made this incumbent upon us:

> We cannot obtain wisdom without earnest attention and prayerful study. Some portions of Scripture are indeed too plain to be misunderstood, but there are others whose meaning does not lie on the surface to be seen at a glance. Scripture must be compared with scripture. There must be careful research and prayerful reflection. And such study will be richly repaid. As the miner discovers veins of precious metal concealed beneath the surface of the earth, so will he who perseveringly searches the word of God as for hid treasure find truths of the greatest value, which are concealed from the view of the careless seeker. The words of inspiration, pondered in the heart, will be as streams flowing from the fountain of life *Steps to Christ*, p. 90.

Let the Bible speak for itself.

> Lead the minds of the youth from truth to truth, up higher and higher, showing them how scripture interprets scripture, one passage being the key to other passages *Evangelism*, p. 581.

> The Scriptures need not be read by the dim light of tradition or human speculation. As well might we try to give light to the sun with a torch, as to explain the Scriptures by human tradition or imagination. God's holy Word needs not the

torch-light glimmer of earth to make its glories distinguishable. It is light itself — the glory of God revealed; and beside it every other light is dim. But there must be earnest study and close investigation. Sharp, clear perceptions of truth will never be the reward of indolence. No earthly blessing can be obtained without earnest, patient, persevering effort *Signs of the Times*, June 6, 1906, par. 10-13.

Mrs. White also gave the following advice:

> There is no excuse for anyone in taking the position that there is no more truth to be revealed.... We are living in perilous times, and it does not become us to accept everything claimed to be truth without examining it thoroughly; neither can we afford to reject anything that bears the fruits of the Spirit of God; but we should be teachable, meek and lowly of heart. There are those who oppose everything that is not in accordance with their own ideas, and by so doing they endanger their eternal interest as verily as did the Jewish nation in their rejection of Christ *Counsels to Writers and Editors*, p. 35.

> We are to counsel together, and to be subject to one another; but at the same time we are to exercise the ability God has given us to learn what is truth. Each one of us must look to God for divine enlightenment. We must individually develop a character that will stand the test in the day of God. We must not become set in our ideas, and think that no one should interfere with our opinions *Review and Herald*, June 18, 1889, para. 6.

For,

> Our minds have become so narrow that we do not seem to understand that the Lord has a mighty work to do for us. Increasing light is to shine upon us; for "the path of the just is as the shining light, that shineth more and more unto the perfect day" *Review and Herald*, June 18, 1889, par. 4).

And she noted:

> The fact that there is no controversy or agitation among God's people, should not be regarded as conclusive evidence that they are holding fast to sound doctrine. There is reason to fear that they may not be clearly discriminating between truth and error. When no new questions are started by investigation of the Scriptures, when no difference of opinion arises which will set men to searching the Bible for themselves, to make sure that they have the truth, there will be many now, as in ancient times, who will hold to tradition, and worship they know not what *Counsels to Writers and Editors*, p. 39.

Bible prophecy our eschatological clock to the end:

> Prophecy Alone Holds the Answer to the Questions of thinking People. — The prophecies which the great I AM has given in His Word, uniting link after link in the chain of events, from eternity in the past to eternity in the future, *tell us where we are today in the procession of the ages, and what may be expected in the time to come* [emphasis mine]. All that prophecy has foretold as coming to pass, until the present time, has been traced on the pages of history, and we may be assured that all which is yet to come will be fulfilled in its order. Today the signs of the times declare that we are standing on the threshold of great and solemn events. Everything in our world is in agitation. Before our eyes is fulfilling the Saviour's prophecy of the events to precede His coming: "Ye shall hear of wars and rumors of wars.... Nation shall rise against nation, and kingdom against kingdom: and there shall be famines, and pestilences, and earthquakes, in divers places" *Prophets and Kings*, p. 537.

The intention of this study is to review, to inform, and to revive. The Bible, and especially the prophecies, need to make sense to everyone. The Bible must be seen as reputable, the living word of God that "liveth and abideth for ever" (1 Pet. 1:23). We need to know our Bibles. For this reason I supply many scripture references throughout, even for common verses with which people are familiar but may not know their whereabouts in the Holy Writ. We need to understand the original issues surrounding the Old Testament precious promises. That's what makes them precious.

Another purpose of this book is to alert the Advent movement and the Protestant denominations of the point in prophetic time where we sit today, as indicated by the seven trumpets of Revelation. For good reasons, this book doesn't follow the trumpets' traditional placement, which start at the destruction of Jerusalem or the collapse of the Roman Empire. Rather, it will show that the trumpets began in 1844. Much time has already passed and we are late to understand the trumpets prophecy. Therefore, their placement beginning in 1844 has alarming ramifications for us, by the sealing and also the mark of the Beast that Revelation shows occurring during the fifth and sixth trumpets. The trumpets force us to acknowledge the present reality of the imminent first time of trouble, and the nearness of the Latter Rain of the Holy Spirit, both of which precede the great time of trouble; and that tribulation being that which prepares us for the return of the Lord in power and glory. "Blessed is he that readeth....and keep those things which are written therein: for the time is at hand" (Rev. 1:3).

> *For good reasons, this book doesn't follow the trumpets' traditional placement, which start at the destruction of Jerusalem or the collapse of the Roman Empire. Rather, it will show that the trumpets began in 1844.*

This book is not meant to be a verse by verse commentary of the whole of Revelation, but a handbook explanation of the seal/trumpet prophecy. Thus, the reader will need to do his or her own perusal of each chapter in Revelation before reading the respective chapters of this book. Then, the reader can follow closely the scriptural interpretation of its symbols, some symbols which may be new to Christians of all persuasions, even to Adventists. As Adventists, the trumpets of chapters 8 through 11 are our final frontier. We have not understood them correctly, yet they open the door to a detailed vista of God's omniscient view down through the past 172 years.

For your convenience to more easily peruse each segment of the seal/trumpet drama, this publication contains near its center a copy of Revelation chapters 4 through 11. I believe the reader will greatly profit from this. Reading scripture for oneself has a thousand times the power of hearing it from another.

I don't apologize for using the King James Version (KJV) of the Bible in this study. It has been called the most accurate word-for-word translation. Although it has a few outdated words — some 40 in all — the rest of the thousands are perfectly understandable, once the reader gets over prejudice toward the "thee's" and the "thou's", and the "ye's", the "eth's" and "est's". Being a word-for-word translation, the construction of the KJV phraseology can at first cause a little consternation because of its close transliteration of ancient syntax and the sometimes switching of subject pronouns mid-sentence. But, God made the human mind adaptable to anything, and the KJV quirks are easily overcome.

The words supplied by the King James translators have been un-italicized. This gave me the ease of italicizing words from scripture that I felt needed emphasis without having to attach "[emphasis mine]", which would interrupt the force of the scripture messages. As the reader sees italicized words of scripture, he should assume that I italicized them for the purpose of importance. I have also added a page for notes at the end of Appendix A, in case the reader desires to jot down items of interest.

The reader may be a grownup, a teenager, or younger. Any group, any age, however, should be searching to understand the scriptures a little better every day. To study is to question. "What does this verse mean?" "Lord, why was it said like that?" "How does this verse fit into the larger context?" "Why do I believe like I do based on that scripture?" "Oh, *thank you*, Lord; now I understand!"

No truth will lose anything by close investigation. By challenging prophetic beliefs of our Adventist patriarchs, the purpose of this project is to more firmly establish faith in our forefathers' interpretation of Revelation and of the issues surrounding the great controversy, as first understood by Ellen White in 1858. This study shows how the 2,000 year old Revelation reveals God's view of our world, primarily after 1844. It also introduces a biblical reason for our sojourn here since we first said, "Jesus will come *soon*."

This review of Revelation intends to invite old and young to read *The Great Controversy* and other Spirit of Prophecy books (http://www.whiteestate.org/), and to look at passages of scripture, some brief and some lengthy, not because it was easy for me to copy and paste from *e-Sword*, but in order to interest Bible students to read the precious whole chapters and books for themselves. I desire to communicate the need to be a thoughtful, voluminous reader of scripture, and not a surface student. We must understand more than proof texts of scripture. Disjointed verses alone, removed from their context, do little to give the full picture that the Lord intended us to gain from His invaluable written word. Precious promises are scattered all about. We will take a verse here and there, line upon line, and precept upon precept. We will ply the context for clues. We will also keep in mind the most important part of all: our Father's wonderful promises of redemption.

> We should exert all the powers of the mind in the study of the Scriptures and should task the understanding to comprehend, as far as mortals can, the deep things of God; yet we must not forget that the docility and submission of a child is the true spirit of the learner *The Great Controversy*, p. 599.

May I recommend that the reader read this book in the "cool of the day", that is, the beginning of your day (whatever time of day that is), rather than in the end of it. The frustrations of the day could negatively affect the reception of the tough and distressing ramifications that come from this study. I have sought to weave the hopes and promises of the gospel in throughout the apocalyptic scenes of Revelation's gloom and doom. Revelation isn't normally seen as a devotional, but I believe that my book puts in sufficient good news to outweigh the bad news, so that the seals and trumpets pageant can be inspirational as well as instructive for these last days. What more is there to the full gospel than instruction from and inspiration by, information of and communication with Jesus?

Part of this essay concerns the "popular Protestant churches," the Roman Papacy, and even a disobedient Advent movement. The intention here is not to be divisive or bashing. However, much of the Revelation points to the failures of the church of God after the apostles passed from the scene; and, history is left as a warning from which we must learn. Nevertheless, the church's history need not be treated crassly. And, truth must always be communicated in kindness and humility, "considering thyself, lest thou also be tempted" (Gal. 6:1, cf 1 Sam. 26:11). My desire is that kindness, hope, and warmth are heard in these pages, and that I have considered all of my flaws. "God has children, many of them, in the Protestant churches, and a large number in the Catholic churches, who are more true to obey the light to the very best of their knowledge than a large number among Sabbathkeeping Adventists who do not walk in the light.... And shall no voice be raised of direct warning to arouse the churches to their danger?... God forbid" *The Ellen G. White 1888 Materials*, p. 377. Our Protestant and Catholic brethren need to hear the warnings and promises associated with Revelation, and I hope this book can play a part in that great work.

Let the point be recognized: Every revival that has ever reformed God's people — from the most ancient times to the present — has had its turn at unfaithfulness and apostasy. And, let's not think that the early church or the Reformation or the Advent movement may never be exempt from unfaithfulness. Prophecy indicates that this happened, as we will see in this study. So, we are all in the same boat together. The current Israel of God needs to admit this, because this admission is just what Heaven is waiting for. Once we admit it, then Jesus will restore to us the glorious work He originally gave us: to gather all of His scattered people the second time. We must not be satisfied with anything less than the Latter Rain work.

Finally, we will see that the message of the investigative judgment and Earth's final redemption, given to the Seventh-day Adventist church in the setting of the great controversy, is founded squarely upon Bible prophecy. We will see that the Advent patriarchs and prophet had correctly searched the scriptures for what the Spirit of Christ which was in them signified when they testified of the future sufferings of the people of God, and the glory that would follow. Cheer up, pilgrim brothers and sisters. We are almost home!

Do not delay to get onboard
You can put faith in the messenger of the Lord
Others fail integrity with the Spirit's sword
Time is too short for her to be ignored

Chapter 1
Revelation Chapter 4: In the Beginning, God

Revelation Chapter 4 gives the setting for the great events to be revealed until the end of chapter 11. In the beginning, even before time, Revelation chapter 4 opens with the Father eternally sitting on His throne. Before Him are the seven Spirits of God, similar to the seven angels lighting the seven churches. In Revelation chapter 1, Christ held seven stars in His right hand (see Revelation 1:16), just as the earthly tabernacle had the seven candlesticks on the right side of the Holy Place, as one faces out the veil of the Holy Place. Gold bands Jesus' chest like a breastplate reflecting the spotless purity that filled His heart, and His feet have the appearance of fine brass, just as the earthly tabernacle had items of pure gold inside the sanctuary and the courtyard items were made of brass. The brightness of Christ's face disabled John, and His eyes shone even brighter, just as the glorious shekinah in the Most Holy Place would mean mortal death without having a cloud of incense to obscure it. Here we can see through shadowy types that John saw Christ embodying the earthly sanctuary and its courtyard. The sanctuary is Jesus (see Hebrews 10:20; Matthew 8:17; Isaiah 53:4); the Son of God is the plan of salvation. Jesus is "greater than the temple" (Matt. 12:6), even "as he who hath builded the house hath more honour than the house" (Heb. 3:3, cf Zech. 6:13).

John sees before the Father shining lamps of fire — "the seven Spirits of God" (Rev. 4:5) — representative of the whole infinite, omnipotent, omniscient, omnipresent, and eternal Spirit of God. John sees seven Spirits not because there are literally multiple Holy Spirits, but because the numeral *seven* in Hebrew thought represented fullness to the fullest extent of divine and holy things; *seven* quantifies the epitome of infinity in power, "the utmost bound of the everlasting hills" (Gen. 49:26) in the way of holiness. The seven Spirits are "the eternal Spirit" (Heb. 9:14), the Father's Spirit without measure given to His Son (see John 3:34; Revelation 3:1), "the power of the Highest" (Luke 1:35, cf Matt. 28:18), "even his eternal power and Godhead" (Rom. 1:20). The brilliant lamps of fire sat between "him that sat on the throne…that liveth for ever and ever" (Rev. 4:10) and "a sea of glass like unto crystal" (Rev. 4:6).

An insight here from my Bible teacher, Pastor James Ayars, is that the seven Spirits describe seven attributes of Christ, six specific and one all-encompassing. "The spirit of the LORD shall rest upon him, the spirit of wisdom and understanding, the spirit of counsel and might, the spirit of knowledge and of the fear of the LORD" (Isa. 11:2). The description "seven spirits" represents every attribute of the Father, all of which He displayed through His Son (see Hebrews 1:3).

This very first scene of heaven is a peaceful one. The heart of God was happy and jubilant, as was His kingdom of peace that surrounded Him like a sea (see Ezekiel 28:2), settled and undisturbed, sitting below and stretching out before "the holy mountain of God" (Eze. 28:14, cf Isa. 11:9; 65:25). His "peace [had] been as a river," like waters "that go softly", "and [His] righteousness as the waves of the sea" (Isa. 48:18; Isa. 8:6, cf Gen. 2:10). Neither did any member of that sea "hurt nor destroy in all my holy mountain"; but the kingdom was "full of the knowledge of the LORD, as the waters cover the sea" (Isa. 11:9, cf Isa. 65:25). This vast, pacific ocean contrasts with the Revelation chapter 15 scene of the sea mingled with fire, when God's full wrath against sin is stirred up and He is about to begin His final plagues. Yet, in His judgments God will keep His people stable and they will still retain the peace of the glass sea (see Revelation 15:2-4).

We can see at this time represented by chapter 4, that the perfect peace of God reigned in His presence and throughout His kingdom of grace and truth. This calm picture also helps us peer into the mind and heart of the Prince of Peace. Like Father, like Son; with either it could be said that it was heaven to be in His presence and multitudes were happy to serve Him.

"In the heart of Christ, where reigned perfect harmony with God, there was perfect peace. He was never elated by applause, nor dejected by censure or disappointment. Amid the greatest opposition and the most cruel treatment, He was still of good courage" *The Desire of Ages*, p. 330. Christ was united with His Father and a counsel of peace was between Them both. Thus, nothing could disturb Him. Hidden with Christ in God, we, too, can have the same invincible peace (see Psalm 16:9; Colossians 3:1-3; Philippians 4:7).

Enveloping Their awesome glory were four orders of created beings, each representing aspects of character of the Godhead: a lion, dreaded and courageous; a calf, lowly and self-sacrificing; a man, omniscient and noble; and a flying eagle, ever-existent and omnipresent. Like the camp of Israel in the wilderness, laid out by tribe in ever-widening rings, the hosts of heavenly orders surrounding the throne of God were full of eyes (see Ezekiel 1:18), all happily riveted on the great Center. Like the spiral galaxies in deep space with their streams of glowing light encircling each great nucleus, the hosts of heavenly beings reverently sought a closer proximity to the sanctuary of the Creator's presence.

David instituted twenty-four priests to officiate in the tabernacle under the supervision of high priests Zadok and Ahimelech (see 1 Chronicles 24:3-9) to ensure that Israel would never be without an intercessor. Likewise, John saw that circumscribing the immediate presence of God sat twenty-four elders, angel ministers for incessant intercession for the inhabited worlds, over whom Lucifer ranked highest (see Ezekiel 28:13, 14; Ex. 28:15-21).

Cherubim appeared to Ezekiel as a living altar of incense (see Ezekiel 1:6-13, 17) and a living chariot-like ark of the covenant, all moved by whirlwind clouds of heaven (see Ezekiel 9:3; 10:2, 6-13; Daniel 7:9, 13). A cloud of witnesses following the Lamb wherever He went, all were praising the Lord of hosts. From deepest appreciation, they blessed the Father without ceasing. The innumerable hosts knew only perfect trust and obedience to their Father, and all worked together in perfect unity. The immediate throne area that John witnessed was a place of lightning and thunder intensity and ten thousand times ten thousand voices, just as Isaiah and Ezekiel had seen and heard. (See Isaiah 6:1-4; Ezekiel 1:13, 22, 24, cf Daniel 7:9.)

Lightning-like, blinding excellence shrouded the great white throne of Him from whose sight the stars fled away. Yet, in that intense, high volume environment, happiness filled the quiet God of serenity and strength. He dwelt in a purity which none could approach except the angels that guarded His majestic selflessness. "That temple, filled with the glory of the eternal throne, where seraphim, its shining guardians, veil their faces in adoration, could find, in the most magnificent structure ever reared by human hands, but a faint reflection of its vastness and glory" *The Great Controversy*, p. 414.

And the billions upon billions of heavenly beings never ceasing, found rest in exulting His worthiness, "Holy, holy, holy, Lord God Almighty, which was, and is, and is to come" (Rev. 4:8). No earthly orchestra, no human chorus can ever compete with that of heaven. And as the four orders gave glory and honor and thanks to Him that dwelt on the mount, who had lived for ever and ever, their thanksgiving gladly compelled the twenty-four elders to fall down before the Creator. They cast their brilliant crowns before the throne, crying out, "Thou art worthy, O Lord, to receive glory and honour and power: for thou hast created all things, and for thy pleasure they are and were created" (Rev. 4:11). What a beautiful scene of endless happiness in our Father's house!

The subject of their praise concerned the Father, His creative power and wisdom, and His pleasure to create. Throughout this scene, we see God's love in His creative ability; the beauty of creation alone encompassed His praises. Make note that no mention was made of the lamb of God. Note also that the heavenly hosts made no mention of the glories of *redemption*, which would later be all for which they could praise the Father *and the lamb* throughout eternity. In the next chapter we will see why this should be.

Nevertheless, as wonderful as the purity and blissful trust of heaven had been in the timeless past, it all came to a sad end. Beginning at chapter 5, a sudden change comes over the happy scene that had satiated John's wondering eyes.

Chapter 2
Revelation Chapter 5: The Controversy

Chapter 5 opens with a whole different scene in heaven. The eternal Father is still seated on His throne as He ever had been, but now He has in His right hand a book "written within and on the backside" (Rev. 5:1), bound up with seven seals. By all appearances this is a book infinitely shut, forever shut, omnipotently shut. No one can open it; no one in heaven, on earth, or under the earth; that is, no holy angel, no sinful mortal, and not even demons could open this book of doom. John understood it to be so terrible a situation that he wept inconsolably; with the hosts of heaven, he wept for the Father. The Father, His wisdom and His love, were suspected guilty of crimes against the state, His authority and justice under arrest; His reputation and character as though held in confinement without bail — the eternal Creator can no longer be trusted implicitly. For the duration of the conflict until "the hour of his judgment is come" (Rev. 14:7), the Father must live suspended without His original perfect joy, eon after eon.

This mysterious script written within and on the backside can be compared with the ones, by the same description, given to Moses and Ezekiel. "And Moses turned, and went down from the mount, and the two tables of the testimony were in his hand: the tables were written on *both their sides*; on the *one side and on the other* were they written. And the tables were the work of God, and the writing was the writing of God, graven upon the tables" (Ex. 32:15, 16). "And when I looked, behold, an hand was sent unto me; and, lo, a roll of a book was therein; and he spread it before me; and it was written *within and without*: and there was written therein lamentations, and mourning, and woe" (Eze. 2:9, 10) — the maligned holy character of God and the irreverence toward Him into which Satan would lead God's children. Judging by the descriptions of each of these communiqués, writing filled all their surfaces for awful, divine emphasis.

The book of Revelation 5 must be the archives relating to the great controversy between Satan and God that only Christ could expose and vanquish (see Revelation 5:5, 6). It represents the issues of the King's mercy, truth, and self-sacrifice versus the devil's deception and the self-seeking conquest by the work of corruption. The evil one's work of deception and conquest has spread so much lamentation, mourning, and woe. The book in God's hand represents the ultimate fate of those within whose hearts Lucifer works his wicked control (see Deuteronomy 32:32-34); and it speaks of ultimate divine retribution upon all who destroyed God's holy Law in the hearts of His children.

The book also speaks of temptation. Could Lucifer tempt God to overstep His wisdom and power before destroying the inveterate angel? Could he, in any way, move God into the trap to think that the end justifies the means? Could he drag God into a game of tit-for-tat? Could he get God to rail on him, to go beyond righteous indignation and exchange excessive judgment for Lucifer's subtle vitriol toward Him, and, thus, eternally tarnish His holy reputation? Jesus' answer to the deceiver, "Thou shalt not tempt the Lord thy God" (Matt. 4:7), was a snapshot of this conflict that occurred at the beginning of the controversy.

All three groups could not open the book. "No man in heaven, nor in earth, neither under the earth, was able to open the book, neither to look thereon" (Rev. 5:3). No man "in heaven" (see Daniel 9:21; 12:6; Acts 1:10; Genesis 18:3; 19:1) — the holy angels that excel in strength couldn't open the book, because the alleged charges that were brought against God concerned issues that were completely new to them, of which they had never before conceived. No man "in earth" could open it — Adam and his fallen offspring had been knocked out of God's defense and therefore they lost everything they had to offer His justification. Following the revolt in heaven, the special creation of man was to comfort the Father's anguish with the exemplification of His character before the kingdom. But, their acceptance of Satan's trap to be masters of their own little universe, as creator peers with their Creator, had then added to the reason that the everlasting Father was bound up so tightly as with seven unbreakable cords. The Father must tread this difficult path alone, and of His creation there was none with Him.

The third group, no man "under the earth", represented Lucifer and his hosts. They spiritually "left their own habitation…reserved in everlasting chains under darkness unto the judgment of the great day" (Jude 6); the devil and his angels metaphorically were "cast… down to hell, and delivered…into chains of darkness, to be reserved unto judgment" (2 Pet. 2:4, cf Phil. 2:10). The rebellious angels couldn't undo what they had started. False allegations are never easily removed, and allegations had been made against the great Father of all. Now there was no taking back what Lucifer had said, and neither did he want to.

"*Who can open the case I've closed? Jehovah can do nothing against Lucifer!*" trumpeted the blasphemous cherub to his armies.

But in the midst of heaven's inconsolable grief, a voice rings out, speaking immediate hope to all the multitudes around the throne: **OUR FATHER IS SAVED! HIS KINGDOM IS SECURE AGAIN! "WEEP NOT: BEHOLD, THE LION OF THE TRIBE OF JUDA, THE ROOT OF DAVID, HATH PREVAILED TO OPEN THE BOOK, AND TO LOOSE THE SEVEN SEALS THEREOF"** (Rev. 5:5).

"And I beheld, and, lo, in the midst of the throne and of the four beasts, and in the midst of the elders, stood a Lamb as it had been slain, having seven horns and seven eyes, which are the seven Spirits of God sent forth into all the earth" (Rev. 5:6). The Lord of hosts, by whom the omnipotent and omniscient and omni-gracious Holy Spirit makes its way into the minds and hearts throughout the intelligent universe, laid down His life to acquit His Father, to spare fallen man, and to restore the peace of the heavenly agencies.

Once offered, the crucified lamb of God could ascend to His Father's throne and take the book. When He had possession of it, suddenly heaven bursts into joyful relief and thankfulness, as also do the saints on earth who, by faith dwell there (see Ephesians 2:6). "The whole family in heaven and earth" (Eph. 3:15) sing "a new song, saying, Thou art worthy to take the book, and to open the seals thereof: for thou wast slain, and hast redeemed us to God by thy blood" (Rev. 5:9). "For it pleased the Father that in him [Christ] should all fulness dwell; and, having made peace through the blood of his cross, by him to reconcile all things unto himself; by him, I say, whether they be things in earth, or things in heaven" (Col. 1:19, 20, cf Eph. 1:10).

Because His sacrifice completely exonerates His Father and can make mankind acceptable in His Father's kingdom, Christ is authorized to pour out the Early Rain of His Holy Father's seven Spirits upon His disciples (see John 14:16-18, cf Revelation 1:12, 13; 5:6). "Therefore," says the Father, "will I divide him a portion with the great, and he shall divide the spoil with the strong; because he hath poured out his soul unto death: and he was numbered with the transgressors; and he bare the sin of many, and made intercession for the transgressors" (Isa. 53:12).

Now the kingdom's joy does not concern God's *creation and creative power*, as we saw in the Revelation chapter 4 heaven before sin; rather, their praise concerns Christ's *redemption and His omnipotence to redeem*. In one act of the ages, Christ redeemed three entities: humanity, fallen under the dominion of sin and Satan; the holy angels, who suffered in a heaven without the original perfect trust and the safe vulnerability that had reigned prior to Lucifer's allegations; but, most of all, He redeemed His Father of every charge Satan had laid against Him. Consequently, Lucifer's attempt to usurp God's throne utterly failed. The Father, King of all creation and King of humility foreseeing the need, condescended to advocacy which could only come through His Son, the only Begotten and His cross.

After the fall of man everything would revolve around His beloved lamb. The Ancient of days, "him that liveth for ever and ever" (Rev. 5:14) had moved off of center stage and His Son had taken over the reins of the eternal divine government in the sanctuary. Now that God's provision for our redemption was ratified by Christ's successful victory over Satan, Christ's cross would become His sword. And everything would continue to revolve around Jesus until God could step up and finalize the battle to put to flight all the armies of the alien.

> Then cometh the end, when he shall have delivered up the kingdom to God, even the Father; when he [the Father] shall have put down all rule and all authority and power. For he [Christ] must reign, till he [the Father] hath put all enemies under his [Christ's] feet.... And when all things shall be subdued unto him [Christ], then shall the Son also himself be subject unto him that put all things under him, that God may be all in all (1 Cor. 15:24, 25, 28, cf Rev. 5:14).

> Until the appearing of our Lord Jesus Christ: which in his times he shall shew, who is the blessed and only Potentate, the King of kings, and Lord of lords; who only hath immortality, dwelling in the light which no man can approach unto; whom no man hath seen, nor can see: to whom be honour and power everlasting. Amen (1 Tim. 6:14-16, vs. 13).

First, throughout the Old Testament dispensation the Son consistently, fairly, and lovingly exercised the strong justice and mercy of His Father. This prepared the human race to receive His great act for their salvation. It also prepared Himself for the day when He would assume infinitely more justice upon Himself. But, when Israel finally proved unwilling to keep His covenant, the Lord reiterated the fulfillment of His many threatening cautions through Moses, and He put them into operation.

> And he said, Go, and tell this people, Hear ye indeed, but understand not; and see ye indeed, but perceive not. Make the heart of this people fat, and make their ears heavy, and shut their eyes; lest they see with their eyes, and hear with their ears, and understand with their heart, and convert, and be healed. Then said I, Lord, how long? And he answered, Until the cities be wasted without inhabitant, and the houses without man, and the land be utterly desolate, and the LORD have removed men far away, and there be a great forsaking in the midst of the land. But yet in it shall be a tenth, and it shall return, and shall be eaten: as a teil tree, and as an oak, whose substance is in them, when they cast their leaves: so the holy seed shall be the substance thereof (Isa. 6:9-13).

The Son of God, the only true Mediator between God and man, wisely permitted Earth's 600 year descent into Babylonian corruption, bringing onto the world the harsh, violent, and sophisticated environment of Satan's lusts. Without this merciful desolation from Providence, the provisions of Christ's salvation would have been wasted upon the unbroken, self-sufficient hearts of lost mankind. During those four pagan empires ending with Imperial Rome, Satan increased his control of every mind and heart. The blended justice and mercy of God no longer seen or heard in the earth by His redemptive gospel through Israel, humanity's wicked captivity by the devil waxed all-pervasive and inescapable.

> Because God is a God of justice and terrible majesty, Satan caused them to look upon Him as severe and unforgiving. Thus he drew men to join him in rebellion against God, and the night of woe settled down upon the world *The Desire of Ages*, p. 21.

· Baal, or Beelzebub, welcomed to a world willingly ignorant of Jehovah's truth, kept them restless and buzzing with voices from below. Within every undesirable branded as a demoniac, as well as the moral caste who did the branding, devil-possession tortured minds and bodies with bitterness and anger.

> The people whom God had called to be the pillar and ground of the truth had become representatives of Satan. They were doing the work that he desired them to do, taking a course to misrepresent the character of God, and cause the world to look upon Him as a tyrant. The very priests who ministered in the temple had lost sight of the significance of the service they performed.

They had ceased to look beyond the symbol to the thing signified. In presenting the sacrificial offerings they were as actors in a play. The ordinances which God Himself had appointed were made the means of blinding the mind and hardening the heart. God could do no more for man through these channels. The whole system must be swept away.

The deception of sin had reached its height. All the agencies for depraving the souls of men had been put in operation. The Son of God, looking upon the world, beheld suffering and misery. With pity He saw how men had become victims of satanic cruelty. He looked with compassion upon those who were being corrupted, murdered, and lost. They had chosen a ruler who chained them to his car as captives. Bewildered and deceived, they were moving on in gloomy procession toward eternal ruin, — to death in which is no hope of life, toward night to which comes no morning. Satanic agencies were incorporated with men. The bodies of human beings, made for the dwelling place of God, had become the habitation of demons. The senses, the nerves, the passions, the organs of men, were worked by supernatural agencies in the indulgence of the vilest lust. The very stamp of demons was impressed upon the countenances of men. Human faces reflected the expression of the legions of evil with which they were possessed. Such was the prospect upon which the world's Redeemer looked. What a spectacle for Infinite Purity to behold!

Sin had become a science, and vice was consecrated as a part of religion. Rebellion had struck its roots deep into the heart, and the hostility of man was most violent against heaven. It was demonstrated before the universe that, apart from God, humanity could not be uplifted. A new element of life and power must be imparted by Him who made the world *Ibid.*, p. 36, 37.

At this time the systems of heathenism were losing their hold upon the people. Men were weary of pageant and fable. They longed for a religion that could satisfy the heart. While the light of truth seemed to have departed from among men, there were souls who were looking for light, and who were filled with perplexity and sorrow. They were thirsting for a knowledge of the living God, for some assurance of a life beyond the grave *Ibid.*, p. 32.

Now, at Earth's lowest depravity, needy eyes could open and yearning ears were able to hear. Now, God could prepare for His Son a body. So, powered by His Father's mercy and truth, and living amongst satanic toxicity, Messiah the Prince **ad**sorbed our rebellion day by day throughout a life that was separate from sin. Every day His soul was assaulted and abused by the slowness of heart among the sincere and by the animosity among His enemies. Hour after hour and day after day, He must witness the rebellion and lust of the multitudes, and the rampant carelessness toward His Father and toward each other. And then He gave it all to His Father in a flood of repentance night after night. "Oh, this people have sinned a great sin…. Yet now, if thou wilt forgive their sin —; and if not, blot me, I pray thee, out of thy book which thou hast written" (Ex. 32:31, 32). The Holy One found no relief for their sin until He knew that His Father again accepted the children He was rearing; and then He could sleep in perfect peace. Love, in the context of saving mankind from its enslavement to iniquity and from its sure destruction, was the motive driving every act and look and word of the Anointed. He carried their weaknesses and infirmities, and exchanged them for His Father's strength and righteousness.

> And he came down with them, and stood in the plain, and the company of his disciples, and a great multitude of people out of all Judaea and Jerusalem, and from the sea coast of Tyre and Sidon, which came to hear him, and to be healed of their diseases; and they that were vexed with unclean spirits: and they were healed. And the whole multitude sought to touch him: for there went virtue out of him, and healed them all (Luke 6:17-19).

His voice was the first sound that many had ever heard, His name the first word they had ever spoken, His face the first they had ever looked upon. Why should they not love Jesus, and sound His praise? As He passed through the towns and cities He was like a vital current, diffusing life and joy wherever He went *The Desire of Ages*, p. 350.

Behold, my servant shall deal prudently, he shall be exalted and extolled, and be very high (Isa. 52:13).

He met humbled men and women, broken and degraded by the tempter, and gave them the message of His Father's acceptance and their life of sin forgiven. He healed hearts and minds as He took the diseases from their bodies. He gave them the Holy Spirit of union with the God of peace. He brought to our crumbling world the embassage of His Father,

Comfort ye, comfort ye my people, saith your God. Speak ye comfortably to Jerusalem, and cry unto her, that her warfare is accomplished, that her iniquity is pardoned: for she hath received of the LORD's hand double for all her sins (Isa. 40:1, 2).

For God so loved the world, that he gave his only begotten Son, that whosoever believeth in him should not perish, but have everlasting life (John 3:16).

He proved God's love through a life of blessing, not only to Israel, but in them He showed His strong desire to bless the whole world. Then, after having fully gained our love and confidence, in Gethsemane all the sins for which Jesus had sought His Father's forbearance, must now be given equivalent retribution. From the perspective of God's strained balance of divine justice, it was only right (see 2 Peter 3:9, 10). Jesus must now hold in suspense, resisting all of our adsorbed toxic pollution without His Father available to take it from Him in His normal flood of grief, His Father no more adsorbing the race's sins as He had always done. If the Father could not unburden upon His Son all that He had been adsorbing and holding in suspense since Adam's fall then He must break forth in a retributive plague upon the sinful world. The ages-old plan to spare humanity said that the Son of God must absorb, not adsorb, His Father's wrath against our rebellion. In vain Jesus would seek His Father's mercy which had always been His faithful outlet for adsorbing our sins. The dependable, burden-bearing God must evade Christ, until the King's anger toward sin destroyed His one and only begotten Son, whom He loved. Like a clock that had been winded up more and more, the time had come when the Great Judge could no longer be wound. Now the King must be relieved of all the strain of adsorbing sin. The time had come that the sanctuary of the Father's soul must be cleansed. The Day of Judgment and Atonement had come, and Jesus heard loudly His Father's alarm against sin, which would echo for all eternity throughout the whole family of heaven and earth. The Father's rebuke of sin upon His Only-Begotten would never be forgotten in heaven and earth.

The chastisement of our peace was upon him (Isa. 53:5).

He took with him Peter and the two sons of Zebedee, and began to be sorrowful and very heavy. Then saith he unto them, My soul is exceeding sorrowful, even unto death: tarry ye here, and watch with me. And he went a little further, and fell on his face, and prayed, saying, O my Father, if it be possible, let this cup pass from me (Matt. 26:37-39).

There, staggering into that hill garden, Jesus collapsed to the ground mentally confused and emotionally nerve-wracked. His ever present Help in trouble had left Him. The Father's mercy could not be seen past the enormity of His justice. Now, with all of Christ's power being scattered, He struggled to deal with the horrifically darkened mercy. Spiritually uncertain, in emotional upheaval, and physically exhausted, the Son of God grappled over whether He could continue, completely and forever, losing all the measureless Spirit that He had ever known of the blissful presence of His God,

He had offered up prayers and supplications with strong crying and tears unto him that was able to save him from death (Heb. 5:7).

Without the constant, comforting, and holy atmosphere and communion of His Father's blessed Spirit, could He survive this inexorable emptiness? Would the excruciating anxietal convulsions never cease?

Under the Father's wrath and Satan's exacerbating torment, Jesus pleaded for us while in the middle of His extremity. He could request no excuses for us, but only claim His Father's mercy which endureth forever. Without His Abba near, Jesus placed Himself open to Satan who would desperately gouge and claw at Him, body, mind, and soul, in order to prevent Him from saving man and exonerating His God. "I gave my back to the smiters, and my cheeks to them that plucked off the hair: I hid not my face from shame and spitting" (Isa. 50:6). If Satan could successfully tempt Jesus to abort humanity from His heart, then he could win the issue over the character of God. If he could cause Christ enough physical agony and "contradiction of sinners against himself" (Heb. 12:3), then he could rob God of His most prized human race, and throw God's reputation back into disarray. Satan could amplify the confusion over God's nature and wisdom, confusion which he had caused heaven before earth was created. If he could overpower God with temptation, then his government of deception and selfishness would prove itself stronger than God's government of purity and love.

The Father looked upon Jesus as sin, for the Son chose to take our place in judgment. This forced God to close His ears to His Son's cries for His eternal Spirit. (See Psalm 22:1-3; Isaiah 59:2.) And God, forced by the issues of the great controversy to empty His full wrath upon His voluntary Propitiation, thus separated Himself from His Son. He left Him unprotected from Satan, who seeing the opportunity, lost his composure. Satanic hosts flew with blind rage at their only chance to mutilate and consume the Prince of heaven, like the children of Israel running upon the long lusted-for quail (see Numbers 11:32).

All of this Christ had long anticipated; therefore He had redoubled His communion with His Father during His ministry (see Luke 12:50). In Gethsemane especially so did Jesus seek God until every power was stretched to the limit, though then, for the first time, His Father would never again answer Him. He showed His Son "the back, and not the face, in the day of [His Son's] calamity" (Jer. 18:17). Christ had chosen and had prepared Himself to take the whole fire and brimstone that His Father would rain upon a wholly wicked race at the end. But, when His great God's abhorrence against sin came upon Him, it was too big. He had always known His Father's tremendous vexation from sin, but this was super-heated indignation He could never anticipate. The previous, clear plan of His ultimate resurrection instantly turned unlikely. His worm would never die nor the fire of His Father's wrath ever be quenched. The invisible disconnection from God forced His life out from every pore of His body. Living apart from God is so commonplace for us. But, this Jesus had never once known. Since His very conception the Father had always been the sun in His sky (see Psalm 22:9).

Without His Father's presence, the Prince of peace must strain every faculty to hang on to any evidence of His Father's love. All the while He was coming under an increasing cloud of Satan's furious lust to gain the victory at this last chance to win the controversy over the universe. Throughout His life until now God had rewarded His willing Son with His eternal Spirit of immeasurable truth and peace. But what would the Son do now that that holy hedge of protection was no longer present? He has experienced our hopeless experience ten billion-fold. He knows what we know. Will we not put forth the same effort to get to God as Jesus did whenever we are in the painful dark, and God's Spirit is silent to our deafened minds?

At the outset of the controversy with Lucifer, the Ancient of days had multiplied in His Anointed One His eternal Spirit when He exalted Him to His heavenly throne. Now, God who in eternity past had "put his holy Spirit within him" (Isa. 63:11, cf John 3:34), turned away from His eternal Son. "To make himself an everlasting name" (vs. 12), He took back His blessed Spirit from His Only Begotten. The contrast from infinite fullness to infinite emptiness only the Son of God has ever known. The fullness in His heart from His Father's previous presence and love became a gigantic, cavern, silent and pitch black. All the waves above the Marianas Trench were weighing inexpressibly upon Him who had previously walked above every storm. The sudden darkness was blinding with delirium, "exceeding sorrowful, even unto death" (Matt. 26:38). Now, the inseparable, only Son of Divinity must cling to an infinite, unmet yearning for His Father's faithful, soul-healing eternal Spirit. The wages of Their separation would mean death to Them both.

> And there appeared an angel unto him from heaven, strengthening him. And being in an agony he prayed more earnestly: and his sweat was as it were great drops of blood falling down to the ground (Luke 22:43, 44).
>
> Again the Son of God was seized with superhuman agony, and fainting and exhausted, He staggered back to the place of His former struggle. His suffering was even greater than before *The Desire of Ages*, p. 689.

"Being in an agony", wave after wave of His Father's wrath and depressing emptiness gripped Jesus. Certain death was imminent. Satan's temptation: one little indulgence of self, one little sip of self-pity, one little outburst of impatience, would make all the pain go away. But, Jesus knew the reality: the slightest grudge of unwillingness, one little request to leave the infinite distress would take Him down forever. His death must be perfect, or He would lose us all. However, no sin was in Him; He had no self-love. He possessed only love for His Father and for His children. Again and again, exponentially stronger and with increasing frequency, the woeful trauma of infinite anxiety assailed His soul and mind and body. He sought for some relief from His friends, but found none. "Of the people there was none with me" (Isa. 63:3). He must tread the winepress of the wrath of God alone.

Alone, so very alone, He prayed for Himself as much as He prayed for the human race. "If it be possible, let this cup pass from me" (Matt. 26:39). But, His supplications for Himself were for help to stay faithful under the agonies of our redemption, and He determinedly left Himself open to His Father's original plan. Our Prince "resisted unto blood, striving against sin" (Heb. 12:4), striving under the separation that our sins caused the King.

> *Like a trillion Hg vacuum, the Almighty cut off every beam of hope and joy from His immeasurable Spirit to His dear Son, suffocating His soul in the hell owed to every man.*

Like a trillion Hg vacuum, the Almighty cut off every beam of hope and joy from His immeasurable Spirit to His dear Son, suffocating His soul in the hell owed to every man. Though the harshest depression pressed upon His holy mind, begging His Father's forgiveness toward His human family continued to emerge from Jesus' agonizing mouth. The human race had come from His hand as His personalized model of His Father's heavenly kingdom of love. His interests had been one with Adam's, and now the Son of man clung to His desire to be forever united to His Adamic race.

> I was set up [H5258, "poured forth", as in a libation; "melted" for a cast] from everlasting, from the beginning, or ever the earth was (Prov. 8:23).
>
> The Lamb slain from the foundation of the world (Rev. 13:8).
>
> He hath poured out his soul unto death: and he was numbered with the transgressors; and he bare the sin of many, and made intercession for the transgressors (Isa. 53:12).

He poured out His soul under His Father's hellish magma. Over and over again, enclosed in darkness and agony, He used Himself to leverage our salvation. "…forgive their sin —; and if not, blot me, I pray thee, out of thy book which thou hast written" (Ex. 32:31, 32). Blinded under the wrath of the Almighty, He could see nothing of His obedience to recommend to God. He was made to be sin for us, and all He could see was His world of sin. But, through His sealed, eternal Spirit, the Son committed all judgment to His Father to decide whether His sacrificial love for humanity was sufficiently worthy and acceptable.

This sacrifice of self Christ had looked forward to before the beginning of the great controversy, and was anxious to accomplish it. He chose to take upon Himself the whole fire and brimstone that His Father would rain upon a fully wicked race at the Day of Judgment. From infinite abundance to infinite abandonment, from infinite acceptance to infinite loathing, the shivering anxiety from being cast out and fatherless enervated every fiber of Christ's being. He felt that His great God's abhorrence against Him was bottomless. The One who from eternity had been in the bosom of His Father's infinite love and grace, now sensed the hell of His infinite hatred and inviolable justice. The invisible disconnect from God pressed His eternal life out of His bleary eyes, from His swollen face and head, and from every pore of His bloating, bloody body. Even before His first humiliating facial assault and bodily flogging, Jesus' head and body were red all over because His whole frame had extruded blood prior to leaving Gethsemane's press. From the souls of His feet to the crown of His head there was no soundness, but wounds and bruises and putrefying sores. Redemption is offensive and humiliating. It would be forty days before the Son of man would shed His uncleanness and He could again stand before God (see Acts 1:3; Leviticus 12:2-4).

> …many were [astonished] at thee; his visage [countenance] was so marred more than any man, and his form [outline, conformation] more than the sons of men: so shall he sprinkle many nations; the kings shall shut their mouths at him: for that which had not been told them shall they see; and that which they had not heard shall they consider (Isa. 52:14, 15).

Christ, whose blood God's divine wrath pressed out from Him, was the great red heifer which was slain before His Father. Afterward, Himself, the new Priest officiating

His own sacrifice, would be the replacement of His less effective, but necessary, Old Testament economy of animal sacrifice. Christ's hope for eternal life was burnt *to ash* to announce His soon-coming High Priesthood (see Hebrews 9:11-15). Then His immaculate, desiccated soul could mix into the Father's new fountain of grace and truth for eternally **ad**sorbing and purifying uncleanness among Their children (see Numbers 19; Zechariah 13:1). Nothing is more immaculate than the pure ashes from a spotless heifer — Jesus Christ our Lord.

> He hath made him to be sin for us, who knew no sin; that we might be made the righteousness of God in him (2 Cor. 5:21).

His Father's abounding, ever gracious presence wholly blotted from His sight, the lamb felt the aggravated, assaulting malignity of sin. Like never before, Jesus experienced sin's dread affects upon whomever in the kingdom it diseases. He took the eternal damnation of the whole human race. Our Lord drank all the cup of His Father's woe toward us. If only He might sway His just Father and us from our destruction Christ must now willingly accept the crushing punishment due us. For serving Satan and worshiping his filth, the eternal hell made Jesus feel that He would be permanently rejected by God and cast away, as had been the ten tribes of Israel. Never before disassociated from His human race, and through all eternity never blotted from His Father's favor, He must let pour upon Himself a worse destruction than He had ever poured upon Sodom and Gomorrah. The implacable damnation of the Almighty would incinerate the soul of His only Begotten, the great Burnt Offering.

> So that the generation to come of your children that shall rise up after you, and the stranger that shall come from a far land, shall say, when they see the plagues of that [Man], and the sicknesses which the LORD hath laid upon [Him];
>
> And that the [Saviour's whole mind and heart] thereof is brimstone, and salt, and burning, that it is not sown, nor beareth, nor any [hope] groweth therein, like the overthrow of Sodom, and Gomorrah, Admah, and Zeboim, which the LORD overthrew in his anger, and in his wrath:
>
> Even all nations shall say, Wherefore hath the LORD done thus unto this [Man]? what meaneth the heat of this great anger?
>
> Then men shall say, Because [of the unreleasable tie He had with those who] have forsaken the covenant of the LORD God of their fathers, which he made with them when he [created them]:
>
> For they went and served other gods, and worshipped them, gods whom they knew not, and whom he had not given unto them:
>
> And the anger of the LORD was kindled against this [Man], to bring upon [Him] all the curses that are written in this book:
>
> And the LORD rooted [Him] out of [existence] in anger, and in wrath, and in great indignation, and cast [Him down to hell] (adapted from Deuteronomy 29:22-28, cf Psalms 16:10; 22:31).

Under the thunderous rebuke of God, "Get Thee behind ME", Jesus was made a lightning rod to save our tabernacle from burning down. Like a hundred megawatt electrocution we see God's rightful anger again and again strike His Anointed One. The Guilty One would be our Surety, forever to bear our sin, to bring us home again, and to set us before our Father (see Genesis 43:9). The agitating cutting off from the eternal Spirit of acceptance gagged His throat (see Psalm 22:15), with every nerve jangling, cellular structures dissolving, internal organs bursting (see verse 14), His blood pressure soaring. All Jesus could do was to barely hang on. Divine wrath overthrew the divine Son of man in retribution upon all the abominations that have ever characterized us, His most beloved creation. Beholding His execution in our damnation, our conscience is shocked with conviction, crucified with Christ. His unrelenting spiritual electrocution from the Judge shunts our pride to ground, our natural self-centeredness thrust into the grave. A new power jolts our mind, awakening it to holier desires and purposes. We are delivered from Satan's hold and a new nature comes to life.

The Son of God saw Himself forever giving up His paradise so that we could replace Him, He forever paying the cost for our reinstatement to His Father's kingdom. On the cross the Prince of heaven must suffer our damnation and eternal extinction, so that humanity might eternally take His exalted place and privileges as heir to the throne next to His beloved Father (see Isaiah 8:18; Romans 8:17; Revelation 3:21). By all that the Servant lamb could know from His senses was that He would be forever buried, His Holy Father's Spirit forever lost to Him. He felt that He would never ever again hold communion that had been wonderful without measure. He must lose His greatest pleasure, dwelling in the excellent Spirit of His Abba. For sin to be forever put away, He must be forever shut away. And the tempter was present to persuade Him that, just as all His disciples felt no sympathy for Him in His distress, neither would anyone of humanity take advantage of His provision for their reconciliation with His Father. Still, He never lost hold of faith in His Father's love to send His reconciled Spirit to call His children to Himself.

Jehovah purposely designed His Son's inability to see through the portals of suffering and death. Christ must take *all* of our due wrath; no pinhole of hope must come from God to encourage Him in His Father's kindness. His soul, utterly hopeless in the dark, must suffer the grinding absence of His Father's blessed comfort. The children must see what God thinks of sin, and, simultaneously He must show them that their Comforter and Consoler has been in their hopelessness and in the painful darkness of their separation from His Spirit.

"He shall see the travail of his soul, and shall be satisfied" (Isa. 53:11). God treated His endeared Son with all the abhorrence that He has for sin. He became the rebuke of God, dying alone without His Abba. It was wrath like the only Begotten had never known to exist in His Father. The angry thunders of offense against each rebellious and unclean thought, word, and act, conscious and subconscious, even the very coalescing beginnings of self-service within our nature, all forced the lamb to see Himself "as Sodom and Gomorrha, …set forth for an example, suffering the vengeance of eternal fire" (Jude 7), remaining cursed because of us and forgotten throughout perpetuity.

"I am come to send fire on the earth; and what will I, if it be already kindled? But I have a baptism to be baptized with; and how am I straitened till it be accomplished!" (Luke 12:49, 50).

Before the Lord ever pepper-sprayed us with judgment, He had Himself pepper-sprayed all over, again and again, ten billion times. Before He would ever drop a bomb of reproof on any sinner, He first accepted the hydrogen bomb from His Father's offence. The lamb damned in our stead has proven the lamb's mediatory discipline upon us to be righteous. We have a Mediator before God who is touched with the torment and plagues and sicknesses that we suffer, and who knows the smoking ruins of our lives. In all of our affliction He was afflicted; and He thus comforts us in every tribulation that He permits.

"Him that liveth for ever and ever" (Rev. 5:14) greatly multiplied His Son's sorrow (see John 16:21; 3:5). This would ensure His Son's rightful intercession in the ever perfect upbringing of His regenerated children, and it would provide for the eternal salvation of all who obey Him. Thus, we can know with certainty that God has made His acceptance and forgiveness possible for *everyone* who will come to His Son. And everyone who will suffer under the thunders seen at Christ's cross will also possess that certainty of God's acceptance.

Eve, the crowning of creation, was made in the image of the beautiful Son of God. As Adam was over Eve, so was God over His Son (see Genesis 3:16; 1 Corinthians 11:3). In the great controversy we see that Jesus is the self-sacrificing "mother of all living" (Gen. 3:20), whose sorrows God greatly multiplied for our second birth (see Genesis 3:16; Matthew 26:38). Our High Priest Jesus is the Mother of all mothers, who now wants to draw every child of Adam to Himself, "even as a hen gathereth her chickens under her wings" (Matt. 23:37).

Behold I and the children which God hath given me (Heb. 2:13).

Though a captive of wave after increasing wave of agony in an extended delivery (see Luke 22:44), Jesus does not complain in exchanging His "second death" (Rev. 21:8, cf Rev. 20:6, 14) for our second birth. Indeed, we see the Fullness of the Godhead fighting to remain conscious to ensure that He has sufficiently drunk the entire cup of wrath to cover even the most distant, offensive son and daughter of Adam. On the cross, He is extending the picture of His desire for His precious fallen race, proving His love "unto the end" (John 13:1). While agonizing under His Father's lost embrace, we see our lamb struggling to find in His Father's eyes the assurance of forgiveness for every soul captive to the wicked power of Lucifer. Both Father and Son struggled to be certain of our salvation. The universe witnessed both the inseparable hearts of Son and Father fleshed open like never before, in the convulsions of Christ for our deliverance from sin.

Did the lamb of God really know He would be resurrected after His eternal death? He knew only by a life of constantly fortifying His faith in His Father's promises. But, after being shoved and hit and flogged and hated, emaciated, dehydrated, and sleep deprived, His humanity was ground down physically, and drained mentally and spiritually. All that He would see and feel was the insatiable justice of His Father against a beloved planet in rebellion. That all-consuming fire seemed determinedly unquenchable, a judgment against Him unalterably chiseled in stone. But, He was umbilically attached to us at our creation, and He must deliver His Father from the harsh decision whether to destroy the human race in order to keep His larger kingdom safe from our rebellion. Which weighed more, Adam's children or His only-begotten Child? We will weigh that question throughout eternity.

We see that Jesus' attachment to His Father's creation, which had come from His own hand (see Ephesians 3:9), is so strong that aborting the provision for our new birth is not an option. The Mother of all living committed Himself fully to our reconciliation and redemption. Either He will reunite the severed bond between His children and their Father, or He will be pulled apart trying. No matter how harsh the combined mistreatment coming from above and from below and from around Him, He can't let go of humanity. It's an impossibility. The perfect mediator between heaven and earth, His very last waking thought before descending into unconsciousness and death is, "I won't let You go until You bless Me; and I can't let them go, until You bless them." And by the providence of God, His Son's strong body secured to iron Rome's tool of humiliating execution preaches to our world about a potentially eternal friendship. "**GREATER LOVE HATH NO MAN**" (John 15:13). "Behold these wounds…with which I was wounded in the house of my friends" (Zech. 13:6). "And I, if I be lifted up from the earth, will draw all men unto me" (John 12:32).

An end of the Son of God was the best weapon that Satan could use to bruise God. To this the Father acquiesced in order to draw out the implacable, unwarranted hostility of Satan toward Himself. But He must not let Satan officiate over the most holy sacrifice. Thus, the Father Himself strongly ruled over His Son "with his glorious arm" (Isa. 63:12, cf Gen. 3:16) and with His "right hand"; and the breach of Their eternal Spirit baptized Them both into the pangs of death. Both can say that They have seen our days of an endlessly tormented soul.

The lamb had continued to plead for His Father to pass over His outrage toward our sin. His pleas had strengthened as His physical strength weakened until He would draw His very last breath. Then He shouted His final victory claim upon His Father's love. "Jesus cried with a loud voice", "Father, into thy hands I commend my spirit"! And He "gave up the ghost" (Mark 15:37; Luke 23:46).

The mother of Ichabod testified to the Mother of all living travailing to death, when the Glory that brightens every man went dark (see 1 Samuel 4:21). Yet, the Facilitator of His darkness, in expectant and fearless silence, foresaw much seed brought to the glory of eternal day (see Isaiah 53:10).

> And about the time of her death the women that stood by her said unto her, Fear not; for *thou hast born a son*. But she answered not, neither did she regard it (1 Sam. 4:20).

> In the volume of the book it is written of me (Heb. 10:7, cf John 5:39).

The Life dead! Absolute silence in heaven while the Son rested from hard labor. To the ravaged, dying Mother of all living we had been Benoni, "son of my sorrow" (Gen. 35:18); but to His Father we were Benjamin, "son of my right hand". The dying Creators brought life to a lifeless creation. The mystery of re-creation! Their science of our eternal birth!

The Creator's death is just what lustful Lucifer wanted; but, he miscalculated God's plan. Instead of gaining all of heaven at the demonstration of his boldness and strength, the high priest of familiar spirits allowed his hatred of the Son to reveal his self-pity and true vindictiveness. Under his calculating intellect was a weak fool; his massive mental powers were no match for Infinite Love and Omniscience, whose foolishness is wiser than Lucifer (see Ezekiel 28:3, 2). Together, Father and Son saved Their children who need Their peace, and destroyed the enemy of all peace and happiness. Satan's judgment was now decided.

> Hell from beneath is moved for thee to meet thee at thy coming.… Thy pomp is brought down to the grave, and the noise of thy viols: the worm is spread under thee, and the worms cover thee.… Thou shalt be brought down to hell, to the sides of the pit (Isa. 14:9, 11, 12, 15).

> O the depth of the riches both of the wisdom and knowledge of God! how unsearchable are his judgments, and his ways past finding out! For who hath known the mind of the Lord? Or who hath been his counsellor? Or who hath first given to him, and it shall be recompensed unto him again? For of him, and through him, and to him, are all things: to whom be glory for ever. Amen (Rom. 11:33-36).

Thus, as the object of divine retribution, the lamb of God had descended into shock with only kindness and longing for peace toward Adam's race, and in complete forgetfulness of Himself. He also died with uncompromising, loving submission to His Father's will who was satisfying the inviolable Law and working out a legal, impregnable redemption for us. From eternity God had trained up His Son in the way He should go, and now Jesus would not depart from His beloved Father's counsel and character. He bore the rejection of His earthly children and prayed for those who despitefully abused Him and hated Him. Until the end, the law of kindness was in His mouth. The King and His hosts finally saw a son of Adam, even in painful anxiety and silence, beautifully exemplify the Law of God's kingdom, the Law of self-sacrifice. Adam had magnified God in a garden of glory and angelic praise; but this "seed" (Gen. 3:15) of Adam magnified God under the most aggravated, excruciating circumstances.

"For the love he had" for them (Gen. 29:20; Heb. 2:13), the Son of man endured all that Gethsemane and Golgotha brought Him to regain His children's affection to the Father they despised. "Jesus…loved his own" "as his own soul" (John 13:1; 1 Sam. 18:3).

Christ showed how surrendered He was to self-sacrificing love for His Father and for His kingdom, in order to prove to us and to the whole kingdom that He is worthy to judge the accusations of Lucifer against His Father. Through the Only Begotten, God showed how empty of self divine love is and how far it goes to protect its most precious creation. He must destroy His lamb once, and forever make His body "an ensample unto those that after should live ungodly" (2 Pet. 2:6).

Because of His infinite relinquishment of all that His holy self desired, and of even His eternal pleasure in His Father's presence, the Mother of all living honored the Father, and His excellence forever confirmed God's heart toward vile but beloved Adam and his descendants. The infinite Law was satisfied in every particular. God could legally keep this beloved race, and His turbulent soul rested. Thus, His labor also ended.

Once unconscious in death, Christ was beyond the grasp of Satan and beyond any more torturous temptation. "The dead know not any thing, neither have they any more a reward; for the memory of them is forgotten" (Ecc. 9:5, cf Job 14:20-22). This successfully sealed Lucifer's doom 4,000 years after his effort to frustrate and unsettle the angels and humanity regarding the character of the Father's love. This gospel is not just an old, old Christian story, but one reaffirmed a million times over through the millennia of sacrificial toddler animals.

The only legal redemption for the kingdom of heaven and earth must be the Father's infinite severity creating infinite tenderness in His Son; the Son submitting to infinite accountability to assure His Father of our infinite advocacy. Omnipotent justice was the Father's cause for His Son's omnipotent mercy, God and Christ working together to empty Themselves of all but love. They cooperated to ensure a perfect restoration of Their kingdom and a perfect restoration of Adam's race to Their kingdom. For three days, the Word of God was stifled; yet His obedient silencing has deliberated doctrine and will forever expound volumes. Thus, through the Father's abhorrence which inundated the Son, God made all of His enemies His footstool. No voice in heaven could henceforth doubt and no voice in hell could henceforth contest the declaration of the God-man reconciliation.

> Who shall lay any thing to the charge of God's elect? It is God that justifieth. Who is he that condemneth? It is Christ that died, yea rather, that is risen again, who is even at the right hand of God, who also maketh intercession for us…. For I am persuaded, that neither death, nor life, nor angels, nor principalities, nor powers, nor things present, nor things to come, nor height, nor depth, nor any other creature, shall be able to separate us from the love of God, which is in Christ Jesus our Lord (Rom. 8:33, 34, 38, 39).

> Seeing then that we have a great high priest, that is passed into the heavens, Jesus the Son of God, let us hold fast our profession. For we have not an high priest which cannot be touched with the feeling of our infirmities; but was in all points tempted like as we are, yet without sin. Let us therefore come boldly unto the throne of grace, that we may obtain mercy, and find grace to help in time of need (Heb. 4:14-16).

The omnipotent God powerfully, and permanently thrust His own Son to a cross, as more than a statement of mercy to us, but also a statement of justice. It was the manifestation of God's hatred of sin that hung up His Son like King Saul's body as a show of victory for all to behold (see 1 Samuel 31:10). "From the sole of [Jesus'] foot even unto the head there [was] no soundness in it; but wounds, and bruises, and putrifying sores: they [were not] closed, neither bound up, neither mollified with ointment" (Isa. 1:6).

All this torture and infinite distress upon the Father and Son because nothing less than our witnessing Their eternal suffering will bring down the crashing bedlam of Gomorrah's overthrow upon our twenty-first century arrogance. Nothing else can motivate us to hate the filth upon which we have thrived.

God proved that He, the great offended One, would accept our offensive race in entirety, *under every condition of sin, and in all of our offensive wickedness … if* we come to witness the just wrath of God and the merciful sacrifice of His lamb. At the cross *no one* is expelled, no one is excluded. At the cross *everyone,* no matter how filthy, may come and let sink in the most ancient message from the sanctuary above. But, *everyone* **must** *come to it and look.* As the serpent was lifted up in the wilderness, only those who look at the dying lamb will live eternally. "This is the will of him that sent me, that every one which seeth the Son, and believeth on him, may have everlasting life" (John 6:40). They carry their own cross when they learn all that the Mother of all living endured for them. Every person can learn only that to which he attends. Everyone must see Earth's hatred toward God's righteousness and goodness. Although counter-intuitive to modern psychology, we must witness the hatred of God and His Son toward man's sin and self-esteem. We must see Jesus who took the whole brunt of our conflict with God which pierced Him through with many sorrows. "They shall look upon me whom they have pierced" (Zech. 12:10). All must be burned by Calvary's burnt Offering before they can receive His water of life to satisfy their maddening, burning unrest.

All who ingest, utterly to their core, this holy message of severity upon their obedient Creator, but His goodness toward aberrant humanity, letting it "sink down into [their] ears" (Luke 9:44), will immediately find rest. They will transform into beloved children of holy love, *immediately worthy* of the heavenly family (see Job 33:27; Lamentations 3:35, 36; Hebrews 10:22). Sorrow, repentance, and faith spring up; they are justified by His grace. The Mother of all living has quickened them and delivered them from dead works.

Our salvation is all the Father's will; but it must be genuine. Saving grace begins with God; but, so does His offense toward our sin. If we are offended at God by a never to be forgotten, yet well deserved, accusing dispensation of justice that will ring in our conscience throughout endless ages, and we rebel against it, then this is evidence that self still refuses to accept its death sentence. Satan still controls us and God's offer of eternal life we have not yet claimed. We have yet to surrender to the crucified One, our soul forever stung with Christ, our pride stifled and burnt to soot. But, if we can accept these terms when we come to the cross because we know ourselves to be fully guilty and wretched, then God will accept us as He accepts His Son. If we will receive God's mercy and love while forever and ever living humbly under the commutation of our just obliteration upon the anointed Mother of our rebirth, then heaven is ours now. By the mercy and justice that we constantly see streaming from His flaming soul and flesh we will yearn to overcome our sin so that the Father and Son need no longer agonize over our self-orientation and meanness. Our self must die in order for the just Ones to live again.

Christ enthroned on His cross, His head was crowned with anguish and His face indelibly bore His greatly multiplied sorrows. Forever having received the bolts of God's anger toward the world's sin, "the vengeance of eternal fire" (Jude 7), is the Father's provision and humanity's only door back into His kingdom. As we meditate on this again and again, Jesus' tortured body, mind, and soul create in us surrender and repentance. And they provide for continual access into God's mercy and to the transformation of our will to His holy, just, and good Law. Only Jesus is the way to Jehovah and His peace.

> See from His head, His hands, His feet,
>
> Sorrow and love come mingled down;
>
> Did ere such love and sorrow meet,
>
> Or thorns compose so rich a crown?

When I survey the wondrous cross, Isaac Watts.

In the plainest possible pictorial, Providence thrust His Son's arms back and permanently pinned them so widely that He could beckon the whole of Earth's multitudes, nations, tongues, and peoples, Come unto ME, all ye that labour and are heavy laden, and I will give you rest. Take MY yoke upon you, and learn of ME; for I am meek and lowly in heart: and ye shall find rest unto your souls.

"God was in Christ, reconciling the world unto himself, not imputing their trespasses unto them" (2 Cor. 5:19). Shell-shocked by Heaven's almighty thunders and hanging lifeless from the cross which Providence provided, the mute Word, the loveless Beloved, the spent

Life woos us back to His Father, who pleads with humanity to love Him again. The Father calls all to repentance.

> Being justified freely by his grace through the redemption that is in Christ Jesus: whom God hath set forth to be a propitiation through faith in his blood, to declare his righteousness for the remission of sins that are past, through the forbearance of God; to declare, I say, at this time his righteousness: that he might be just, and the justifier of him which believeth in Jesus (Rom. 3:24-26).

Their infinite self-sacrifice made it legal before the court of heaven to justify the repentant children of Adam. The Son ensured that His Father could justly redeem every sinner who, falling on the propitiatory lamb, would be made so sorry for his sin that he would turn away from it.

God's execution of One equal in worth to our world's six thousands years and its billions of fallen children showed His readiness to destroy sin. The souls of both God and the participating penitents die together with the pure, sacrificed lamb of God. They both partake of the lamb's spotless sacrifice; we, because we needed the humbling, and God, though He didn't. Our labor is never good enough for God, but His Son's labor is good enough forever. His lamb with Him again, the Father forever remembers Their sacrifice for our sake. The lamb brought God and us together for one greatly needed cooperative effort. And thus, having united two alienated parties, the self-sacrificing Mother of all living achieved atonement for all Their children. His pure, lifeless body touches their "body of sin" "and death" (Rom. 6:6; 8:2, cf Rom. 7:24), charging it with life and power to yield themselves to God, and their will to His.

> And they cast the man into the sepulchre of Elisha: and when the man was let down, and touched the bones of Elisha, he revived, and stood up on his feet (2 Ki. 13:21).

The whole great controversy, with the Son of God at its beginning and end, will prove that the Godhead can maintain perfect law and order in its government without ever losing any from deceived humanity who long for Christ to disconnect their allegiance from Lucifer (see John 10:28, 29; 17:9-12). God can finally destroy Satan and his irredeemable demonic hosts without destroying any of His humbled children. The adept God of wisdom surgically strikes sin, sparing the sinners who Jesus has made sorry, and exploding the kingdom of their enslavement. Their characters reborn will restore and even improve the Father's reputation because of the labor Christ passed through from Gethsemane to Golgotha.

God's justice and self-sacrifice proved the only legal means to forgive us. We must accept self-sacrifice. Death to self is the only ground for atonement and for uplifting humanity from its ruin. Self-sacrifice, humiliation, loving-kindness are the standard to come up to for a treaty with the Father. Won't we go there and die together with the Godhead? Won't we join Them in self-denial? Won't we permit our self-sufficiency and self-will to be nailed to Their cross, slain upon Their altar?

Jesus' revelation of the justice and mercy of God was more than sufficient to be useable by God. Through the beloved Son's work in the heavenly sanctuary He could bring back to man's darkened perceptions the misapprehended love of the Unknown God. Never again could any voice have the right to dissent against Christ's authority to mediate for man, for He more fully than any other proved that He knew the issues that plague the human heart. Therefore, the Father could accept Jesus' death and bring Him out of the tomb.

> He shall see of the travail of his soul, and shall be satisfied: by his knowledge shall my righteous servant justify many; for he shall bear their iniquities. Therefore will I divide him a portion with the great, and he shall divide the spoil with the strong; because he hath poured out his soul unto death: and he was numbered with the transgressors; and he bare the sin of many, and made intercession for the transgressors (Isa. 53:11, 12).

Having successfully accomplished the mission of salvation, God highly exalted His Son. He divided to Christ all power in order to ratify what He had begun — the "restitution of all things" (Acts 3:21), "to reconcile all things" to His Father like it had been before the controversy, "having made peace through the blood of his cross, …whether they be things in earth, or things in heaven" (Col. 1:20). "Knowing this, that our old man is crucified with him, that the body of sin might be destroyed, that henceforth we should not serve sin" (Rom. 6:6). Christ ascended to finish the war against Satan that He had commenced on earth. There was a great work left to be done.

Together, Father and Son worked out "the right of a man before the face of the most High" (Lam. 3:35, cf Heb. 13:10). The labor of the Godhead proved to the universe of unfallen beings the true goodness of God, and all the libel of Lucifer. By working together with His Son in the propitiation, God declared His righteousness to rule His kingdom (see Romans 3:25; Revelation 5:6-9). The Godhead could justly deliver the human race from their confusion, and restore the Holy Spirit in them. Yet, this high privilege of the Spirit and man's "right" must be realized by man.

Thus, the Father was finally delivered from His incarceration, but still on bail until the end of a Day of Atonement judgment. Tied to God's full justification and rest must be the actual fruit of the redemption of His purchased possession; that is, His glorified character permanently enthroned in His redeemed race. "The body of sin…destroyed, …we should not serve sin. For he that is dead is freed from sin" (Rom. 6:6, 7).

The final exoneration of the Father hinges on our full recovery from rebellion to perfect appreciation of His self-forgetful love and righteousness, His zero tolerance for self-exaltation and self-preservation. Our Creator's acquittal depends upon our perfect inculcation of Christ's character into our own. That means our dependence on His justice and mercy for our obedience to all of His commandments (see John 14:21, 24; 15:10). It means our full restoration by faith into His kingdom, body, mind, and nature. For this Christ's cross accomplished the needed tool: "the heavenly gift, …the Holy Ghost, …the good word of God, and the powers of the world to come" (Heb. 6:4, 5), i.e., "the seven Spirits of God sent forth into all the earth" (Rev. 5:6). Upon departing from His heart-broken disciples He proclaimed, "All power is given unto me in heaven and in earth" (Matt. 28:18). The victory at the cross gave the Lamb that necessary full authority when "he came and took the book out of the right hand of him that sat upon the throne" (Rev. 5:7).

In anticipation of the total and complete restoration of man into the image of a vindicated, Law-giving God, a cherub and seraph cadre broke out in song when the Saviour arrived to continue His mission (see Revelation 5:9, 10). "Glory to God in the highest, and on earth peace, good will toward men" (Luke 2:14). And one day soon, everyone whose nature and body He has won back from Satan will sing together with those same cherubim and seraphim, "Worthy is the Lamb that was slain to receive power, and riches, and wisdom, and strength, and honour, and glory, and blessing" (Rev. 5:12).

John hears that song in heaven and in earth continuing on and on for ever, "even for ever and ever" (Dan. 7:18). As he describes it, "Every creature which is in heaven, and on the earth, and under the earth, and such as are in the sea, and all that are in them, heard I saying, Blessing, and honour, and glory, and power, be unto Him that sitteth upon the throne, and unto the Lamb for ever and ever" (Rev. 5:13, cf Phil. 2:10, 11; Rev. 20:10; 1 Cor. 15:25-28).

Throughout the timeless "ages to come" our thankful song to our Father will be, "The exceeding riches of his grace in his kindness toward us through Christ Jesus" (Eph. 2:7).

Chapter 3
Revelation Chapter 6: A Historical Sketch

Don't we all love good news! No one is ashamed to tell good news. But, we are only a tenth of the way through this book. And, sad to say there will be a lot of bad news in the long, difficult journey before we reach the glorious end of Revelation 11. So, I recommend the reader return to chapter 2 often to relive the exceeding cost of our redemption's exceeding riches from the Godhead as we make our way to the exceeding finale of the Day of Atonement.

In this chapter, the breaking off the first six seals to clear the Father from the libel in His mystery book will show an initially brilliant start of Christ's kingdom. But, then we will quickly see a rapid departure from the powerful salvation which Jesus worked so hard to provide Adam's race. It also acts as a countdown to God's final glorification seen through His children, especially in the end. Let Satan enjoy his heyday while he can, and let him rule like a ferocious Bengal; but, as each seal peals he will be reminded that his day is coming. The Lamb detaches six of the seven seals from the Father's book coinciding with the first six testimonies for the church in Revelation 2 and 3, each testimony reference of which I will attach in parentheses to each seal. And I here remind the reader about the Revelation chapters 4 through 11 for your reference, located in the middle section of this book.

The Lamb opened the first seal (Rev. 6:1), and John sees a white horse, whose rider wears a simple victory laurel, going out conquering the world (see Revelation 6:2). Christ made peace and war in heaven and in earth (see Revelation 12:7, 8; Matthew 21:5; Deuteronomy 32:35-43; Isaiah 45:7; Luke 12:51; Matthew 16:18; Exodus 17:16; Deuteronomy 32:35-43); and the gates of hell could not prevail against Him (see Deuteronomy 32:4). This scene presents by symbol the way the gospel dispensation began, as Paul attested,

> Blessed be the God and Father of our Lord Jesus Christ, who hath blessed us with all spiritual blessings in heavenly places in Christ: according as he hath chosen us in him before the foundation of the world, that we should be holy and without blame before him in love: having predestinated us unto the adoption of children by Jesus Christ to himself, according to the good pleasure of his will, to the praise of the glory of his grace, wherein he hath made us accepted in the beloved.... In whom ye also trusted, after that ye heard the word of truth, the gospel of your salvation: in whom also after that ye believed, ye were sealed with that holy Spirit of promise (Eph. 1:3-6, 13).

That in the dispensation of the fullness of times he might gather together in one all things in Christ, both which are in heaven, and which are on earth; even in him: in whom also we have obtained an inheritance, being predestinated according to the purpose of him who worketh all things after the counsel of his own will (vs. 10, 11).

The apostolic church was a chosen generation, a blessed movement predestinated since the great controversy began (see Genesis 3:15, cf Gal. 3:16, 19). Like Joshua the son of Nun leading the conquest of Canaan, Jesus in Spirit went out strong against Satan's kingdom, saving His people from their sins (see Romans 6-8).

"And the Lord added to the church daily such as should be saved" (Acts 2:47). All the adventures of which we read in the Acts of the Apostles describe only the work of a handful of apostles. But, the lives of the other apostles and disciples of Christ, who the book of Acts did not record, "above five hundred brethren" (1 Cor. 15:6), Christ's seven Spirits also sent out (see Revelation 5:6). And the gospel work spread around the globe. This first seal's scene refers to the period that occurs while the apostles lead the church, and it ends shortly after John passes away in 100 AD.

At the passing of beloved John's reign as "king" (Deut. 33:5) of the New Testament Jeshurun, Satan immediately began regaining his lost advantage. He failed with Christ at Calvary and with His apostles, but he vowed to succeed with their followers. (See Revelation 12:9-12.) Now, the deceiver would recover all that he had lost. He had great success with the children of Israel after Moses and Joshua had died (see Judges 2:10-23; Psalm 78:54-58; 106:34-43). Why should he not have the same again after the apostles pass away? He would accomplish this by leading the church to forget the terrible and humbling struggle and agony that their salvation had cost the world's truest Friend (see John 10:11, 3, 4). The self-exaltation from Job, because of his many wonderful works, was a forgotten lesson as the church lost its vision of the gospel in view of all their earlier successful work for the Lord (see Job 31:1-32:2; 33:9; 34:5, 7; 38:1-3; 40:7, 8; Revelation 2:2, 3).

The testimony for the church at Ephesus (see Revelation 2:2) lists their efforts to keep the church clean from apostasy while the apostles were still with them. They exposed leaders who professed Christ, but who did not preach Him. The Christians actively presented the sanctified life to the pagans, and their labor looked good. But, once losing Christ's robe of righteousness (see Revelation 2:4) they had no armor shielding them from temptation. Thus, the tantalizing world around them began to dilute their translation "into the kingdom of [God's] dear Son", their sitting "together in heavenly places in Christ Jesus", "in paradise" (Col. 1:13; Eph. 2:6; Luke 23:43, cf Rev. 2:7; 1 Cor. 13:12). They lost their reconnected communion with heaven.

Living faith suffered and the focus on the living Jesus in the heavenly sanctuary lost its appeal (see Matthew 13:15). All that Christ had done on earth to win the hearts of His church went largely for naught. Paul had emphatically pleaded with all the Christians in the region of Galatia, "I am afraid [for] you, lest I have bestowed upon you labour in vain.... Ye know how through infirmity of the flesh I preached the gospel unto you at the first. And my temptation which was in my flesh ye despised not, nor rejected; but received me as an angel of God, even as Christ Jesus. Where is then the blessedness ye spake of? for I bear you record, that, if it had been possible, ye would have plucked out your own eyes, and have given them to me" (Gal. 4:11, 13-15, 18). "It is good to be zealously affected always in a good thing, and not only when I am present with you." Yet, they did not keep his circulated warning, "If God spared not the natural branches [the nation of Israel], take heed lest he also spare not thee. Behold therefore the goodness and severity of God: on them which fell, severity; but toward thee, goodness, if thou continue in his goodness: *otherwise thou also shalt be cut off*" (Rom. 11:21, 22).

The church had had renowned disciples of Christ, upon whom they relied for spirituality. They knew the apostles, but lost sight of the warm almighty Friend of those apostles, and His Counsel of peace that could reach from heaven to earth (see Zechariah 6:13; 4:10; Revelation 5:6). Despite the late beloved apostle's written exhortation to be wary of the enemy (see Revelation 3:11), they let Satan take their crown. The church exchanged friendship with the good Shepherd who was carrying the church in His arms (see Isaiah 40:11; Exodus 19:4) for the promise of prosperity in their sin-polluted earthly empire. The Holy Ghost quietly disappeared from the hearts of the people and they made insufficient effort to bring it back. The terrifying story of King Saul's loss of the Lord's anointing should have cried out as a precedent and shocked them back into sincere reconciliation with Jesus (see 1 Samuel 10:6, 9-11; 16:14; 19:9, 10; 24:1, 2, 16-22; 26:2, 17, 21-25; 28:5-25; 31:2-6). The church, however, which had once experienced the powers of the world to come, and despite all the Bible's warnings, let it all slip away (see Hebrews 6:4-6; 2:1; Luke 19:20-26; Matthew 12:43-45). Like Saul, the church never regained the fear of the Lord or His presence. No longer possessing the fear of God, they lost all fear of Satan. Now the devil as a roaring lion could devour them.

A demonic spirit from the Lord had given King Saul endless chastisement of peace because he refused to fall on the Lord and be broken. Now, the same must vex the Christians. Due to their negligence to seek the Prince of peace while He could be found He must remain cut off from them, and thus remove His barrier against sin. The eternal rules of free choice demanded it. The wormwood and gall of Satan's presence increasingly replaced the sweet Spirit from Christ (see Revelation 5:6) and poisoned them against the Law of God until their light dimmed to a flicker. In His beloved eternal kingdom, God has never given, nor can He ever give anyone protection from consequences. Our Lord cannot protect His precious earth-bound church from the consequences of sin, as He did not protect Himself (see Galatians 4:4; Hebrews 5:8; 2:14). "Be not deceived; God is not mocked: for whatsoever a man soweth, that shall he also reap" (Gal. 6:7). Throughout the universe and through all eternity, He must and will abide by this principle.

For the greater majority of the church Christ's warning eventually fell on deaf ears. "Remember therefore from whence thou art fallen, and repent, and do the first works; or else I will come unto thee quickly, and will remove thy candlestick out of his place, except thou repent" (Rev. 2:5). Had they realized their weakness apart from their Saviour (see Isaiah 51:1) they would have awakened to their fearful condition. The "first works" were the things people do when they are dating or courting. They talk a lot together, do things together, and go places together. They love to think of each other and to be together. These first works of the first love result in permanent commitment.

If the church had rehearsed the life of the Anointed One; if they had let the truth coming from His Spirit sanctify them of all personality conflicts; had they heeded Paul's admonition to Timothy, "Wherefore I put thee in remembrance that thou stir up the gift of God, which is in thee by the putting on of my hands" (2 Tim. 1:6), then repentance and a revival would have sprung up again and the Holy Ghost would have poured down from the heavenly sanctuary with renewed revival and reformation (see Psalm 85:6-13). Had they sighed and cried for their abominable condition before the Law of God and the cross of Christ, as their apostles had done during the ten days leading to Pentecost; if they had done the first works with Jesus, they would have regained the privileged seal known in those holier days (see Acts 2:42-47; Ephesians 1:13; 4:30).

Satan eclipsed Jesus, the pinnacle of the sacred scriptures, and stole away from the church the daily preaching of Christ's sacrifice. Thus, he robbed from the church Christ's holy gift of His Spirit (see John 20:22) sent through His ministry in the heavenly Holy Place. As the love died that the first disciples had so much treasured, Christ extinguished the light of His presence among the Christians, as He had warned (see Revelation 2:5); and, faith in Him began to fade into eternity. The presumption and lust for idolatry replaced trust and disinterested love; winning an argument replaced testifying to the beauty of Christ's love; apologetics replaced pastoral preaching; laughing at men's cleverness replaced rejoicing in the Spirit. (See the first Testimony for the churches, Revelation 2:1-7.)

Certainly, the Revelation warning had come true, "The Revelation of Jesus Christ, which God gave unto him, to shew unto his servants things which must shortly come to pass.... Blessed is he that readeth, and they that hear the words of this prophecy, and keep those things which are written therein: for the time is at hand" (Rev. 1:1, 3).

The Lamb opened the second seal of the Father's book (Rev. 6:5), and John sees a rider atop a red horse who receives power to take peace from the earth. This signified an open war that Satan would bring against the gospel because the early church's failure to repent of their lost first love with Jesus. The moral church would not admit their need of righteousness, and therefore could not stir up the gift of God. They had given up the faith delivered to the saints and had despised the sacrifice of Christ. Therefore, He must give up His promised protection and provisions.

> I wrought for my name's sake, that it should not be polluted before the heathen, in whose sight I brought them out. Yet also I lifted up my hand unto them in the wilderness, that I would not bring them into the land which I had given them, flowing with milk and honey, which is the glory of all lands; because they despised my judgments, and walked not in my statutes, but polluted my sabbaths: for their heart went after

their idols. Nevertheless mine eye spared them from destroying them, neither did I make an end of them in the wilderness (Eze. 20:14-17).

For the sake of the church's health, for the sake of the souls truly dedicated to Jesus, God must allow this time of persecution as He began to hand the children of Christ over to Satan. Through a growing spiritual intrigue from within the church and martyrdom from without, Satan finally succeeded to stop the rapid spread of the holy work which God had accomplished through Jesus' mediation. The issuance of His Holy Spirit ceased and the entrance within the heavenly veil closed. The grace of Jesus can have no power without a genuine faith to receive it. Not only must we abide in Him, but His words must abide in us (see John 14:21; 15:7; Matthew 12:44; Thessalonians 2:10).

Satan's kingdom of earthly enchantment stopped the hemorrhaging that the deep gash of the sword from Christ's Spirit had given it; and the kingdom of Christ's righteousness began to hemorrhage. Yet, despite this judgment, a small holy segment would be spared. Nevertheless, the church, charmed by the idolatrous world, was repeating the apostasy of Ezra's holy revival of Israel.

> Your words have been stout against me, saith the LORD. Yet ye say, What have we spoken so much against thee?
>
> Ye have said, It is vain to serve God: and what profit is it that we have kept his ordinance, and that we have walked mournfully before the LORD of hosts?
>
> And now we call the proud happy; yea, they that work wickedness are set up; yea, they that tempt God are even delivered.
>
> Then they that feared the LORD spake often one to another: and the LORD hearkened, and heard it, and a book of remembrance was written before him for them that feared the LORD, and that thought upon his name.
>
> And they shall be mine, saith the LORD of hosts, in that day when I make up my jewels; and I will spare them, as a man spareth his own son that serveth him.
>
> Then shall ye return, and discern between the righteous and the wicked, between him that serveth God and him that serveth him not (Mal. 3:13-18).

Satan turned the contest to his advantage by leading the church to more determinedly covet the world's acceptance, and he brought into their communion men ingenious and influential, but with no interest in spirituality. Satan's unconverted men inspired the church to baptize the world's religions into Christianity. Then he steered the whole church from within.

This was the beginning of the apostasy concerning which Paul had sounded a loud alarm to the flock. "Of your own selves shall men arise, speaking perverse things, to draw away disciples after them. Therefore watch, and remember, that by the space of three years I ceased not to warn every one night and day with tears" (Acts 20:30, 31). The Greek *nikao laos* means, "Conquest of the laity". According to one interpretation of the name, the Nicolaitans (see Revelation 2:6, 15) were a Gnostic group who believed in pagan top-heavy leadership, and who were not consecrated to God through a valid, warm relationship with Jesus. Satan had placed these overlords within the church (see 1 Peter 5:2, 3). And they casually, yet deliberately, sold their flock to Satan, as Balaam had led Israel into apostasy. Politically motivated fathers with orchestrated movements centralized church power into the bishop of Rome, by colluding with the bishop of Alexandria. Politics usurped the anointing of God, as shallow and vain religious celebration replaced settled Christian sobriety and vigilance. They called themselves happy who had never been humbled by the exalted Law of God and the crucified body of Christ.

The advancing pall of spiritual death drove the new self-centered Christianity deeper into their determination to deny God's seven Spirits through Christ that He was sending into the world. Rejection of Christ led them to work for their salvation, many adopting pagan asceticism from Egypt. They beatified and fanatically worshipped John the Baptist, who they claimed to be, and wandered after as, an ascetic. Pagan asceticism was eagerly sought out to appease the gall and wormwood that vexed their souls, the church adding the drunkenness of Satan to their chastising thirst caused by the Lord's absence. They sought out asceticism instead of surrendering to the heavy hand of God's Spirit and being refreshed by His Intercessor, the only begotten Son (see Deuteronomy 29:19; Deuteronomy 32:20-25, 32-34; 1 Timothy 2:5).

Chapter 3 Revelation Chapter 6: A Historical Sketch

The church, no longer consecrated to Jesus, lost its white purity and golden Solomonic love. The epistles of every writer of the New Testament point out the work of the apostates. Paul wrote, "I press toward the mark for the prize of the high calling of God in Christ Jesus.… Brethren, be followers together of me, and mark them which walk so as ye have us for an ensample. (For many walk, of whom I have told you often, and now tell you even weeping, that they are the enemies of the cross of Christ: whose end is destruction, whose God is their belly, and whose glory is in their shame, who mind earthly things.)" (Phil. 3:14, 17-19). "What I do, that I will do, that I may cut off occasion from them which desire occasion; that wherein they glory, they may be found even as we. For such are false apostles, deceitful workers, transforming themselves into the apostles of Christ. And no marvel; for Satan himself is transformed into an angel of light. Therefore it is no great thing if his ministers also be transformed as the ministers of righteousness; whose end shall be according to their works" (2 Cor. 11:12-15).

John had written, "Little children, it is the last time: and as ye have heard that antichrist shall come, even now are there many antichrists; whereby we know that it is the last time. They went out from us, but they were not of us; for if they had been of us, they would no doubt have continued with us: but they went out, that they might be made manifest that they were not all of us" (1 John 2:18, 19, cf 2:2; 4:3). Peter had warned, "There were false prophets also among the people, even as there shall be false teachers among you, who privily shall bring in damnable heresies, even denying the Lord that bought them, and bring upon themselves swift destruction" (2 Pet. 2:1).

For two centuries, silently and subtly did the mystery of iniquity creep into the darkening church and slowly move it away from its Saviour. "His power shall be mighty, but not by his own power: and he shall destroy wonderfully, and shall prosper, and practise, and shall destroy the mighty and the holy people. Through his policy also he shall cause craft to prosper in his hand; and he shall magnify himself in his heart, and by peace shall destroy many: he shall also stand up against the Prince of princes" (Dan. 8:24, 25). "Yea, he magnified himself even to the prince of the host, and by him the daily sacrifice was taken away, and the place of his sanctuary was cast down" (Dan. 8:11). Through Satan's studied aim, "the eyes of man" (Dan. 7:8), treachery and flattery would increasingly develop under his leadership (see Daniel 8:25), as he would "practice and prosper". While the evil one deluded the Christian masses into celebrating holiness rather than maintaining sober-mindedness before the holy God, this son of perdition, this high priestly angel of familiar spirits, gradually stole the place of God in their hearts.

Although the church suffered persecution for its Christian culture, the suffering largely came not because of hearts full of faith and love for Jesus. They no longer knew Jesus because He had taken away the light of their love (see Revelation 2:5; Matthew 13:14, 15). He had disappeared from their consciences, as asceticism had replaced the convictions of His Law in their hearts. Pastors and church fathers were full of self-preservation and self-interest. Within the larger church, self-denial and self-sacrificing love through knowing the self-sacrificing love of Christ dwindled to an extremely small minority. This period culminated in the Council of Nicaea, 325 AD, over which the pagan Emperor Constantine presided. (See the second Testimony for the churches, Revelation 2:8-11.)

The Lamb opened the third seal and the Revelator sees a black horse with the rider having a balance for buying and selling. John hears, "A measure of wheat for a penny, and three measures of barley for a penny; and see thou hurt not the oil and the wine" (Rev. 6:6). This correlates directly to the message for Israel immediately prior to the long, six century Babylonian spiritual siege.

> The field is wasted, the land mourneth; for the corn is wasted: the new wine is dried up, the oil languisheth. Be ye ashamed, O ye husbandmen; howl, O ye vinedressers, for the wheat and for the barley; because the harvest of the field is perished. The vine is dried up, and the fig tree languisheth; the pomegranate tree, the palm tree also, and the apple tree, even all the trees of the field, are withered: because joy is withered away from the sons of men. Gird yourselves, and lament, ye priests: howl, ye ministers of the altar: come, lie all night in sackcloth, ye ministers of my God: for the meat offering and the drink offering is withholden from the house of our God. Sanctify ye a fast, call a solemn assembly, gather the elders and all the inhabitants of the land into the house of the LORD your God, and cry unto the LORD, Alas for the day! for the day of the LORD is at hand, and as a destruction from the Almighty shall it come (Joel 1:10-15).

To appoint unto them that mourn in Zion, to give unto them…the oil of joy for mourning (Isa. 61:3).

"Joy is withered away from the sons of men" (verse 12). Why had Israel's joy died? The glorious wheat and barley, and the new wine of joy would die on the vine because of the "northern army" (Joel 2:20) of Babylon (see also Jeremiah 1:14-16; Joel 2:1-11; Leviticus 26:16, 17; Deuteronomy 28:34). Likewise, the third seal shows that the darkened church has a mysterious parasite that had slipped in and worked its charms on the bride of Christ. The last sparkles of the church's beauty were waning in the carnal siege, even as the worldly glory of the Empire was crumbling. It was the dusking of darkness.

> And in his estate shall stand up a vile person, to whom they shall not give the honour of the kingdom: but he shall come in peaceably, and obtain the kingdom by flatteries. And with the arms of a flood shall they be overflown from before him, and shall be broken; yea, also the prince of the covenant (Dan. 11:21, 22).

Emperor Diocletian's reign of terror against Christianity having ended in 312 AD, his successor-brother, Constantine, determined to transfer the solemnity of state religion from Mithraism to a hollowed-out Christianity, gutted of fervent, pure love, unfeigned faith, and holy principles. Their condition resulted from denying God's authority to rebuke sin and awaken their conscience (see 1 Timothy 1:5; Romans 7:7-12). The new emperor arrived at the transfer of religion for uniting his empire because Christianity was growing widespread, however violently the previous emperors tried to prevent it. Now, with the church absent of the Spirit from Christ's heavenly ministry, Constantine saw that the church could just as well serve the empire as paganism had. So, Satan moved the emperor to make the transition. Secular Rome took its first step in accepting a wily theocratic Rome.

> After the league made with him he shall work deceitfully: for he shall come up, and shall become strong with a small people (Dan. 11:23).

"The great adversary now endeavored to gain by artifice what he had failed to secure by force. Persecution ceased, and in its stead were substituted the dangerous allurements of temporal prosperity and worldly honor" *The Great Controversy*, p. 42. The pagan Roman populace was enervated and its strength wasted by centuries of socially accepted self-indulgence. Satan saw that the church in comparison was physically and mentally healthy, yet spiritually unprepared to reject his proposal to serve the political world.

Suddenly, the church was moved from persecution to state favor. Satan often takes God's people from the first extreme to the second. By politicking with the pagan spiritual leaders, the church leaders usurped the pagan birthright of official state religion (see Daniel 11:25). The church's union with the state was secured by its intrigue-filled leadership. The movements to bring pagan practices and worldliness into the church, having begun two centuries earlier, now accelerated.

> A little horn…waxed exceeding great, …even to the host of heaven; and it cast down some of the host and of the stars to the ground, and stamped upon them (Dan. 8:9, 10).

Biblical doctrine came under full attack, having previously prepared the celebrating people of God to overlook the conspiracy.

> He shall destroy wonderfully, and shall prosper, and practise, and shall destroy the mighty and the holy people. And through his policy also he shall cause craft to prosper in his hand…and by peace shall destroy many (vs. 24, 25).

As the Lord had raised up the vulgar and brutal King Nebuchadnezzar because of the Jews' Babylonizing of the ancient Hebrew religion, this New Testament son of perdition rapidly spread his vulgar and brutal paganizing of Christianity by the church fathers. Ignorant of the character of God, the church was under besiegement, indicated in Revelation by the cost of a day's wage — a penny — for a small, hand-size loaf of wheat bread as a whole family's daily fare: "A measure of wheat for a penny, and three measures of barley for a penny" (Rev. 6:6). But, though surrounded by that spiritual onslaught, those who strictly held fast to the Bible would retain the conviction and comfort of the Spirit: "See thou hurt not the oil and the wine" (vs. 6). Their faith and joy would thrive and prosper. The Lord was closing up His case against the lukewarm church, but sealing His Law in His true followers.

> Bind up the testimony, seal the law among my disciples (Isa. 8:16).

Chapter 3 Revelation Chapter 6: A Historical Sketch

"Bind up" (Heb. *tsarar*, "distress", "besiege", "pangs", "shut up") for final judgment, or permanently close up the testimony to cause final decisions to be made for or against the God of heaven (see 1 Timothy 1:20). Providence was ending the merciful probation of His church, which was following after spiritualism as Israel had so many times (see Deuteronomy 29:18; Judges 2).

The gospel had long before disappeared and faith in Christ was completely lost to the great majority of the holy people (see Daniel 8:12; 11:31). The conscience of the mainline church was wholly blind to the true character of Christ and was hoping in this world. "The light of the body is the eye: if therefore thine eye be single, thy whole body shall be full of light. But if thine eye be evil [skewed], thy whole body shall be full of darkness. If therefore the light that is in thee be darkness, how great is that darkness!" (Matt. 6:22, 23, cf Isaiah 50:10, 11). This former warning to the Jews now applied to the church, and great was the darkness of the black horse prophetic period!

But, to His scant chosen ones, the Lord would be "for a sanctuary" (Isa. 8:14). Faithful to the Bible, they separated from the apostate church and escaped to the Alps, and were spared the corrupting influence of paganism that had moved in. Long had they worked as missionaries within the church before leaving it; therefore, they continued having the Holy Spirit and its missionary zeal. Their faith and love were only minimally affected by the great falling away of the majority. But, persecution would soon clothe their joy in sackcloth, their oil and wine mingled with fasting (see Revelation 11:3; Matthew 9:15).

Multitudes, multitudes were careless toward a legitimate relationship with Jesus which they should have seen in Hebrews 12:5-8 and 1 Timothy 1:5, 6, and their religious forms shared the look of consecration with the lusts of mammon. Lucifer convinced them that the world religions made people holy enough, and thus the Protestant God's voice through His Law could no longer convict them of disobedience. Therefore, the Schoolmaster could not bring anyone to His Son for pardon as Paul had taught in Galatians 3:23, 24. To these lacking diligence to have Jesus' acceptance and power to obey Him He would act as "a stone of stumbling and for a rock of offence.... And many among them shall stumble, and fall, and be broken, and be snared, and be taken" (Isa. 8:14, 15).

With the merciful thou wilt shew thyself merciful; with an upright man thou wilt shew thyself upright; with the pure thou wilt shew thyself pure; and with the froward thou wilt shew thyself froward (Ps. 18:25, 26).

The official church had committed the unpardonable sin, yet Jesus would glean from it every honest soul throughout the approaching Dark Age. This period ended at 538 AD by Rome's destruction of the Ostrogoths, the last of the three conquering Germanic tribes that kept the seventh day Sabbath and withstood primacy of the Bishop of Rome (see Daniel 11:30; 7:8). (See the third Testimony for the churches, Revelation 2:12-17.)

I considered the horns, and, behold, there came up among them another little horn, before whom there were three of the first horns plucked up by the roots: and, behold, in this horn were eyes like the eyes of man, and a mouth speaking great things (Dan. 7:8).

Lo, I raise up the Chaldeans, that bitter and hasty nation (Hab. 1:6).

Christ opened the fourth seal (Rev. 6:7) and now a pale horse comes into view, ridden by Death, with wasteness and desolation following in its wake (see Deuteronomy 29:18-24). The church was fully corrupted, enamored with the Empire's pagan sacraments and its Greek philosophy, seen in vision with great iron teeth and big brass claws (see Daniel 7:19). Gall and wormwood filled the church with superstitions and the fear of death which would enslave it in ignorance. The people would live empty and emaciated of spirituality and life from Jesus; conversion to God would be next to non-existent throughout vast, religious Europe. The Christian continent would remain beyond Christ's help for more than a thousand years of imagined "peace" (Dan. 8:25, cf 11:21, 32; Deut. 29:19). With exception of the Reformation, this was the long dry summer between Pentecost and the Feast of Trumpets, during which there would be neither dew nor rain from the Spirit of holiness.

From the days before Constantine, the church leaders had received the same "evil spirit from the LORD" (1 Sam. 16:14) that had afflicted King Saul. "Briers and thorns" (Isa. 7:24, cf Heb. 6:8, Judg. 2:1-3) of impatience and inter-personal assault, of competition and ambition, had cursed the church fathers. Because the people of God had so long loved the philosophy and worship practices of the Roman world, the Lord had to hand them over to the adversary, who was transforming them from a heavenly power into a humanistic, pagan power. They lusted for world domination, forgetting the Lord's express prohibition, "It shall not so be among you; but whosoever will be great among you, let him be your minister… even as the Son of Man came…to minister, and to give his life a ransom for many" (Matt. 20:26, 28). "My kingdom is not of this world" (John 18:36).

Their jockeying for political power resulted in the full exaltation of the bishop of Rome as high priest of a Mithraistic Christendom, home to a growing system of Babylonian mysteries. Satan could only create this toxic environment as forgetfulness of Christ, their Burnt Offering, had moved the experience of heart conversion deeper and deeper into the forgotten past. During the third seal period, that constant fighting against God's Law and Christ's mercy, in lieu of popular religion, finally turned to dull apathy in this fourth seal period. The consciences of the Church were now fully closed to God's kingdom, as Paul had warned:

> The Spirit speaketh expressly, that in the latter times some shall depart from the faith, giving heed to seducing spirits, and doctrines of devils; speaking lies in hypocrisy; having their conscience seared with a hot iron (1 Tim. 4:1, 2).

"The noon of the papacy was the midnight of the world."--J. A. Wylie, *The History of Protestantism*, b. 1, ch. 4. The Holy Scriptures were almost unknown, not only to the people, but to the priests. Like the Pharisees of old, the papal leaders hated the light which would reveal their sins. God's law, the standard of righteousness, having been removed, they exercised power without limit, and practiced vice without restraint. Fraud, avarice, and profligacy prevailed. Men shrank from no crime by which they could gain wealth or position. The palaces of popes and prelates were scenes of the vilest debauchery. Some of the reigning pontiffs were guilty of crimes so revolting that secular rulers endeavored to depose these dignitaries of the church as monsters too vile to be tolerated. For centuries Europe had made no progress in learning, arts, or civilization. A moral and intellectual paralysis had fallen upon Christendom *The Great Controversy*, p. 60.

The Spirit had spoken expressly through Daniel.

> And such as do wickedly against the covenant shall he corrupt by flatteries (Dan. 11:32).

> And an host was given him against the daily sacrifice by reason of transgression, and it cast down the truth to the ground; and it practised, and prospered (Dan. 8:12).

> But the people that do know their God shall be strong, and do exploits. And they that understand among the people shall instruct many: yet they shall fall by the sword, and by flame, by captivity, and by spoil, many days (Dan. 11:32, 33).

In the face of deadly reactions by paganized Christendom, Jesus sent His Waldensian and Albigensian Christians from the Italian and French Alps to make missionary incursions into Satan's kingdom. They brought light to the benighted and kept the gospel truth alive. The fourth letter to the churches depicts the Christian dispensation as wicked Queen Jezebel who led ancient Israel into pagan worship (see 1 Kings 16:31), and who followed the pagan standard of uniting the Israel's pagan religion and state (see 1 Kings 18:19). Satan had cast down the church of Christ and restored the pagan theocracy of the world (see Daniel 8:11; 11:31).

Nevertheless, from His heavenly throne (see Hebrews 8:1, 2), Christ alone, and no one else, can righteously unite church with state (see Zechariah 6:13; Isaiah 9:6, 7; Numbers 3:10; 2 Chronicles 26:16-21). The Lord entreats His fallen Church as to an imperious, whorish wife, punishing her and her pagan lovers (see Revelation 2:20-23; 17:1, 2; Ezekiel 16:28-30). This period of monumental departure from God did not complete its climax until Christ brought out the gospel again by the Protestant Reformation in 1517 (see Revelation 2:24-29), and freed Europe from church-imposed ignorance and despotism inspired by Satan. (See the fourth Testimony for the churches, Revelation 2:18-29.)

Jesus opened the fifth seal (Rev. 6:9) and John sees "souls" "under the altar" (Rev. 6:9) crying out to God for deliverance from persecution. The Greek word in this verse for "soul" is "*psuche*", which means a living person or his innermost yearnings. Christ's Gethsemane pouring out helps us understand this picture presented by the fifth seal. "My soul [*psuche*] is exceeding sorrowful, even unto death: tarry ye here, and watch with me" (Matt. 26:38). Isaiah's prophecy pointing to the sacrifice of Jesus uses "*nephesh*" [H5315], the Hebrew counterpart to the Greek "*psuche*".

He shall see of the travail of his soul[H5315], and shall be satisfied: by his knowledge shall my righteous servant justify many; for he shall bear their iniquities. Therefore will I divide him a portion with the great, and he shall divide the spoil with the strong; because he hath poured out his soul[H5315] unto death (Isa. 53:11, 12).

After the sacrificial animal was slain in ancient Israel, its lifeless body was laid on the grate "beneath" (Ex. 38:4), and the blood representing "the life" (Lev. 17:11, 14) which the priests were to "pour out" (vs. 13, cf Isa. 53:12) at the base of, or "the bottom of" (Ex. 29:12), "under" (Ex. 27:5) the altar of sacrifice. The altar that had looked forward to the offering of Christ here He uses to signify the sacrifices of His children of the Reformation during the Church's reaction by its Counter-Reformation. Evidence before the angelic court mounted that the Holy Roman Empire was no different than Nero's Imperial Rome.

> As it is written, For thy sake we are killed all the day long; we are accounted as sheep for the slaughter (Rom. 8:36).

Often ancient sculptures and paintings show the conquered laying under the throne or the foot of the victor. This part of the vision foretells a time of fierce persecution against Christians who poured out their souls as they laid down their lives for the gospel. Specifically, it portrays the concentrated effort by Satan to destroy the Reformation and those regenerated Christians who had picked up their cross and had followed Christ. All those during the Counter-Reformation Inquisitions who lost their lives for the gospel that they loved were special lambs in God's sight (see Matthew 10:29-31). But, as a group, we see them crying to God to spare them further martyrdom. "How long, O Lord, holy and true, dost thou not judge and avenge our blood on them that dwell on the earth?" (Rev. 6:10, cf Rom. 8:35-37).

> By the light of burning martyrs,
>
> Christ, Thy bleeding feet we track
>
> *Once to every man and nation, Seventh-day*
>
> *Adventist Hymnal,* #606.

Nevertheless, we can know by this prophecy that He who "spared not his own Son, but delivered him up for us all" (Rom. 8:32) had foreknown their torments 1,500 years before and that the great Burnt Offering Himself had experienced it all with them long before they passed through it, while they were in it, and long after they suffered and perished. His whole kingdom has grieved with Him while He "groaned in the spirit, and was troubled" (John 11:33, cf Matt. 26:29), suffering with His children. "For we know that the whole creation groaneth and travaileth in pain together until now" (Rom. 8:22).

As He did for Joshua, son of Josedech, when He justified the high priest, Jesus commands that these shining cross-bearers be dressed in the robe of His holy merits as brands that had been plucked from the fire (see Revelation 6:11; Zechariah 3). They are also told to wait patiently until their brethren also suffer; thus, not only speaking to the Reformation, but also to those in the end who will keep the faith of Jesus in the future times of trouble just before He returns (see Revelation 7:14). His counsel is sufficient for the Counter-Reformation Christians and they remain faithful (see Daniel 11:32-35). They exemplify the patience of their Early Rain forebears and also of the Latter Rain remnant of their seed. Their patient endurance throughout the Counter-Reformation persecutions is founded upon the Bible promises of a day of justice:

> All they that devour thee shall be devoured; and all thine adversaries, every one of them, shall go into captivity; and they that spoil thee shall be a spoil, and all that prey upon thee will I give for a prey (Jer. 30:16).

> He that leadeth into captivity shall go into captivity: he that killeth with the sword must be killed with the sword. Here is the patience and the faith of the saints (Rev. 13:10, cf Deut. 32:41-43; Isa. 33:1; Jer. 25:8-13; Ps. 37:1, 2).

Who among our generation will receive the same faithfulness and wear the same robe? "Ye shall be hated of all men for my name's sake: but he that endureth to the end shall be saved" (Matt. 10:22). Who among us will hear the same approbation from Jesus, "Blessed are ye, when men shall revile you, and persecute you, and shall say all manner of evil against you falsely, for my sake. Rejoice, and be exceeding glad: for great is your reward in heaven: for so persecuted they the prophets which were before you" (Matt. 5:11, 12)?

The removal of the fifth seal exposes the violent aftermath and satanic madness to retain power that dwelled in the hearts of the Roman Church leaders during the late Dark Ages. It shows "the overspreading of abominations" (Dan. 9:27) by the "Mother of…abominations of the earth" (Rev. 17:5). It reveals the depths of evil to which self-sufficient, Christless, loveless religion ultimately takes its slaves (see Revelation 13:11). This scene shows the aggravated assault against Jesus by the Jesuits (see Daniel 8:11, 25; 7:7; 11:22). Even under the very guise of His holy name, the Jesuit Order took control of the deadly Inquisitions. It shows Satan's implacable bitterness vented upon Bible Christians because they endangered his evil empire through their love of God's peace and truth. And this scene also reveals the primitive power of grace upon the Bible believers, which gave them courage to face grievous torture and death (*see Appendix A*).

To the Jesuit leaders Jesus made it clear,

> Woe unto the world because of offences! for it must needs be that offences come; but woe to that man by whom the offence cometh! (Matt. 18:7).

In God's Law, there is no such thing as "the end justifies the means." If the means for teaching church doctrine are contrary to His blended truth and grace gently distilling upon even the Jesuit soul, then the end will be as contrary. The means creates the character of the end. "The labour of the righteous tendeth to life: the fruit of the wicked to sin." (Prov. 10:16). But, the Church had no ear to hear what His Spirit of truth said to her. She was full of "the evil spirit from God" (1 Sam. 18:10).

During the fifth seal, those so-called Christian leaders were as filled with the same mind that King Saul had experienced, and were as willing to kill holy lives as Saul was to drive a spear through David's heart (see 1 Samuel 18:11; 19:10), a man following after Jesus' own Spirit (see 1 Samuel 13:14; Psalm 63:8; Romans 8:1). The victims of Church Inquisitions well knew the words that David had penned, "Yea, for thy sake are we killed all the day long; we are counted as sheep for the slaughter" (Ps. 44:22). Those true Bible Christians must learn the seemingly incomprehensible words of Christ to John the Baptist before he went to certain execution, "Blessed is he, whosoever shall not be offended in me" (Matt. 11:6).

As Cain hated Abel because he had God's blessing (see 1 John 3:10; Genesis 4:3-8), endless, relentless war by the visible, pseudo-Christian state Church raged against the true, unrecognized church in the wilderness (see Revelation 12:6, 14, 15; 13:6). This dichotomy within Christendom exposed the depth of Satan's hostility toward the Spirit of Christ, which Satan treated as a trespasser in his earthly kingdom. Satan's malignant hatred of good was seen especially as the light of the gospel dawned during and following the Protestant Reformation, as seen in the fifth seal. All the while, a biblically ignorant populace accepted the war as a necessary work for God. This terrorism-ridden period finally ended around 1798, not because the fanatical blood-thirst was quenched in the Vatican and her Jesuits, but because Providence made it so by the initiation of free, popular governments that would force the separation of church from state and would vote down religious intolerance. The faithfulness of the Protestants during the Counter-Reformation gave power to Christ in the angelic court to send relief and to institute protection for the wasted church, providentially unveiling the hidden continent of America for a refuge (see Revelation 12:16). Yet, in spite of all the Protestant self-sacrifice, later generations would show a slackening fervor for the holy religion that their holy Reformation fathers died to give them (see Deuteronomy 31:11-32:47). (See the fifth Testimony for the churches, Revelation 2:24-29; 3:1-6.)

The Lamb opens the sixth seal (Rev. 6:12). Per the prophecy, there was a great earthquake, the sun went dark, the moon turned scarlet, and the stars fell from heaven. The massive 8.7 magnitude Lisbon earthquake of 1755 warned Catholic Europe of coming judgment. This prophecy later foretells of a strange darkness that sought to awaken a sleeping Protestantism through a natural phenomenon which went down in American history as "The Dark Day". The Dark Day caused, as many witnesses described it, the dimness of night at noon time. During daytime, candles created distinct silhouettes. It was impossible to read black ink on white paper.

Especially so was this the case after the sun had set. At that time they couldn't see their hand directly in front of their face, due to the inky blackness. Lateral sources of light from candles was darkened, although everyone did not claim that smoke was clouding their vision, stinging their eyes, or making it hard to breathe. Their testimonies indicate no fears of an approaching conflagration. It was not an "advection inversion" over New England from an immense Canadian forest fire. And, no one called it fog. The Dark Day was like the "darkness over the land of Egypt, even darkness which may be felt" (Ex. 10:21).

> "'Nor was the darkness of the night less uncommon and terrifying than that of the day; notwithstanding there was almost a full moon, no object was discernible but by the help of

some artificial light, which, when seen from the neighboring houses and other places at a distance, appeared through a kind of Egyptian darkness which seemed almost impervious to the rays.'--Isaiah Thomas, Massachusetts Spy; or, American Oracle of Liberty, vol. 10, No. 472 (May 25, 1780). Said an eyewitness of the scene: 'I could not help conceiving at the time, that if every luminous body in the universe had been shrouded in impenetrable shades, or struck out of existence, the darkness could not have been more complete.'"--Letter by Dr. Samuel Tenney, of Exeter, New Hampshire, December, 1785 (in Massachusetts Historical Society Collections, 1792, 1st series, vol. 1, p. 97) *The Great Controversy*, p. 307.

Concerning the inability of science to assign a satisfactory cause for this manifestation, Herschel the astronomer declares: "The dark day in North America was one of those wonderful phenomena of nature which philosophy is at a loss to explain" *The Great Controversy (1888)*, p. 306.

The Dark Day was not a solar eclipse that lasted 8 hours and caused a deep red, gibbous moon that night. It was supernatural darkness. Neither was the gibbous moon a lunar eclipse after the fearful darkness disappeared. The moon was supernaturally red like blood.

> Nineteenth of May, a gloomy day,
>
> When darkness veil'd the sky;
>
> The sun's decline may be a sign,
>
> Some great event is nigh.
>
> Let us remark, how black and dark,
>
> Was the ensuing night;
>
> And for a time the moon decline,
>
> And did not give her light.
>
> Can mortal man, their wonder skan?
>
> Or tell a second cause?
>
> Did not our God, then shake his rod,
>
> And alter nature's laws?...
>
> Anonymous

Then, in November of 1833, after the start of William Miller's preaching, a unique and extraordinary meteor shower filled the sky, lasting many hours of the night — no typical autumn Leonid event. All these sixth seal oddities of nature announced the close of the 1,260 year reign of Satan in Christ's church and the return of Jesus to take His people to His Father's throne. All of this in fulfillment of the sixth seal prophecy, "I beheld when he had opened the sixth seal, and, lo, there was a great earthquake; and the sun became black as sackcloth of hair, and the moon became as blood; and the stars of heaven fell unto the earth, even as a fig tree casteth her untimely figs, when she is shaken of a mighty wind" (Rev. 6:12, 13).

John then sees the fearful scenes of the Day of Judgment when will fall great balls of fire from the sky. Then will "all the tribes of the earth mourn, and they shall see the Son of man coming in the clouds of heaven with power and great glory" (Matt. 24:30). John sees Earth's atmosphere peal back at the presence of the Lamb. He witnesses everyone running for the mountains to bury them, crying out, "Fall on us, and hide us from the face of him that sitteth on the throne, and from the wrath of the Lamb: for the great day of his wrath is come; and who shall be able to stand?" (Rev. 6:16, 17).

But, the Second Advent does not happen in the sixth seal. Providence pauses the seven seal pageant that will end in Judgment Day.

But, the Second Advent does not happen in the sixth seal. Providence pauses the seven seal pageant that will end in Judgment Day (see Revelation 11:18; 14:7). The literal winds of strife are held back (see Revelation 7:1); the Millerite descendants of the Reformation are yet in their sins and unable to go with Jesus should He come. He cannot return until after the prophecy's seventh seal is opened when the book of the great controversy is dealt with during the succeeding series of trumpets from Revelation 8 through Revelation 11. God's people must yet be sealed; the heavenly sanctuary must yet be cleansed. Therefore, like the message from Jeremiah, (see Jeremiah 4:20-29), this scene must indicate *only the merciful warning message* by the Millerite movement that would awaken the world to the day when the Lamb actually will return, "sitting on the right hand of power, and coming in the clouds of heaven" (Matt. 26:64). This period ended at the Great Disappointment of October 22, 1844. (See the sixth Testimony for the churches, Revelation 3:7-13.)

Thus, the fearful question remains, "The great day of his wrath is come; and who shall be able to stand?" (Rev. 6:17). And that question demands an answer because the means for its answer will be the necessary preparation for Jesus' actual return.

> Through the grace of God and their own diligent effort they must be conquerors in the battle with evil.... When this work shall have been accomplished, the followers of Christ will be ready for His appearing *The Great Controversy*, p. 425.

At this time, new light from Christ was needed to instruct the church in the science of salvation. Their many misconceptions of God's character and His requirements needed to be corrected before they could live with Him forever, all which comes to them during the next five chapters.

Chapter 4
Revelation Chapter 7: Adventism Appears

Revelation chapter 7 is a preview that gives the answer to the big question of chapter 6 — *who shall be able to stand when the heavens fall at the Lamb's day of great wrath.*

As seen in Revelation 7:1, the closing troubles on earth would have quickly brought the world to Judgment Day. This work of global destruction would have preceded the explosive entrance of Jesus in power. But, in mercy to the world, these troubles and the great day of the Lord are held back because no one, even among the Millerites, would have survived. One very involved Millerite later wrote,

> The people were not yet ready to meet their Lord. There was still a work of preparation to be accomplished for them. Light was to be given, directing their minds to the temple of God in heaven; and as they should by faith follow their High Priest in His ministration there, new duties would be revealed *The Great Controversy*, p. 424.

Therefore, the next scenes of Revelation chapters 7 through 11 indicate a grace period, a necessary time of preparation which alone can prevent the fearful wails of Revelation 6:17, and satisfy the question — Who will stand when Jesus returns?

Revelation 7 shows who does stand at that last world-wide conflagration. John sees an angel ascending from the east having the seal of the living God. This seal — the Law of God indelibly stamped into hearts, and the faith of Jesus deeply settled into minds — will be the cause of God's power to protect His people throughout the up-coming seventh seal period. Especially during its last three trumpets would this be the case, when Satan's forces are let loose to destroy faith until the day when Jesus returns to do battle with His ancient enemy.

John hears, "Hurt not the earth, neither the sea, nor the trees, till we have sealed the servants of our God in their foreheads" (Rev. 7:3). Then listed is the mustering of God's final army of evangelists who fight against Baal, the god of this world, and his earthly system. The symbolism of this muster takes its meaning from the Exodus numbering of Israel:

> And the LORD spake unto Moses in the wilderness of Sinai, in the tabernacle of the congregation, on the first day of the second month, in the second year after they were come out of the land of Egypt, saying, Take ye the sum of all the congregation of the children of Israel, after their families, by the house of their fathers, with the number of their names, every male by their

polls; from twenty years old and upward, *all that are able to go forth to war in Israel* (Num. 1:1-3).

Revelation 7:4-8 is the first of two numberings of the 144,000 before a time of wandering — a merciful delay given to prepare them for Christ's return. "Hurt not the earth, neither the sea, nor the trees, **till**...." Revelation 14:1-5 is the second numbering that occurs at the end of the wandering delay and after the abomination of desolation in Revelation 13:12-18. Likewise Israel wandered, while preparing to enter the earthly land of promise (see Number 14:29-33), and was numbered before and at the end of their delay in the desert (see Numbers 1 and 26), "that great and terrible wilderness, wherein were fiery serpents, and scorpions" (Deut. 8:15, cf Num. 21:4-9; Rev. 9:5-11, 16-19), enemy armies (see Numbers 21:1, 23, 33), and finally, harlots at Baalpeor (see Numbers 25:1-26; Revelation 9:8).

This enlisting of a sealed army is comprehended in the seventh testimony for a dismal church, Revelation 3:14-22. Despite their initial unworthiness, after the delay the 144,000 are shaken, surrendered, stablished, strengthened, settled into the truth, and sealed so that they cannot be moved from it. They stand in the battle of the Lamb (see Revelation 14:1-5; Revelation 6:17; 1 Peter 5:10; Revelation 3:21), for their character is perfectly tuned to Christ. No one can do battle with the sword of the Spirit in the worst troubles that Earth has ever seen until they know perfect surrender to their Creator — and this deep lesson must necessarily take time to learn. Then, they undauntedly wear the whole armor of God, "an exceeding great army" (Eze. 37:10) "having done all, to stand" (Eph. 6:13).

Revelation 7:9-17, which ends with a scene of the church's victorious redemption, skips over the wandering delay. And, therefore, the Revelation 7 sealing scene presents one redeemed generation, when in reality there are two actual generations separated by a wandering, testing, sealing. The precedent for the 144,000 two-generations-in-one was already set by Daniel and Paul (see Daniel 2:41-43; 8:23-25 and 2 Thessalonians 2:4-12) where the prophecies that they each first presented as one event later would be seen divided into two distinct, more detailed phases (see Daniel 11:21-39, 40-45; Revelation 13:1-10, 11-17).

Finally, beyond all the troubles of earth, and safely past the greatest tribulation that ever was, the specially privileged 144,000 and great multitude together experience the holy, sacred joy of their restoration to Adam's original peaceful image of God. Heaven bursts into a praise before unknown (see Revelation 7:10-12) since the day Christ originally took the mystery book from His Father at His ascension (see Revelation 5:7). God promises that all the tribulation through which His people have passed they will never see again (see Exodus 14:13). They have laid down their lives for the King of heaven, and He duly rewards them with special privileges in His eternal kingdom (see Matthew 19:28-30; John 14:2, 3). Instead of danger, they will forever dwell peacefully in the King's presence and in the presence of Jesus, their Commander and Good Shepherd. Everyone in that kingdom will have suffered because of sin; and they will know the suffering they have caused Jesus. Therefore, they will know to never allow sin and suffering to arise a second time. (See Nahum 1:9; Revelation 7:15-17.)

Thou shalt bring them in, and plant them in the mountain of thine inheritance, in the place, O LORD, which thou hast made for thee to dwell in (Ex. 15:17).

I will set up one shepherd over them, and he shall feed them, even my servant David [Jesus]; he shall feed them, and he shall be their shepherd.

And I the LORD will be their God, and my servant David [Jesus] a prince among them; I the LORD have spoken it.

And I will make with them a covenant of peace, and will cause the evil beasts to cease out of the land: and they shall dwell safely in the wilderness, and sleep in the woods.

And I will make them and the places round about my hill a blessing; and I will cause the shower to come down in his season; there shall be showers of blessing.

And the tree of the field shall yield her fruit, and the earth shall yield her increase, and they shall be safe in their land, and shall know that I am the LORD, when I have broken the bands of their yoke, and delivered them out of the hand of those that served themselves of them.

And they shall no more be a prey to the heathen, neither shall the beast of the land devour them; but they shall dwell safely, and none shall make them afraid.

And I will raise up for them a plant of renown, and they shall be no more consumed with hunger in the land, neither bear the shame of the heathen any more.

Thus shall they know that I the LORD their God am with them, and that they, even the house of Israel, are my people, saith the Lord GOD.

And ye my flock, the flock of my pasture, are men, and I am your God, saith the Lord GOD (Eze. 34:23-31).

Chapter 5
Revelation Chapter 8: The Trumpets Begin

This Revelation chapter ends the scene of all the future excitement in heaven, the victorious church of chapter 7 upon which John, like Jeremiah, so pleasantly lingered (see Jeremiah 31). With Jeremiah John could say, "My sleep was sweet unto me" (Jer. 31:26). John, like Jeremiah, was viewing the redemption of another humbled Israel. John must, however, leave those restful scenes of redemption and revert to the mustering church still earth-bound and marching against Satan. The scene of Revelation 7's celebration must close in patient hope. The future celebration must cease from John's sight, for he must review the most solemn period of all Earth's history, the final examination that decides who will be part of Revelation 7's joyful, eternal kingdom of God, or who will refuse the war with self in order to gain it. On October 22, 1844, the seventh seal opens and there is a solemn silence in heaven for about a half hour (one week on earth). Revelation chapter 7 provides the hope and encouragement that would be needed for the reader prior to continuing on to the distressing scenes of the seventh seal's seven trumpets. Christ's chapter 7 vision does for the reader what Christ did for His disciples when He gave them a break from their public labors. "Come ye yourselves apart into a desert place, and rest a while" (Mark 6:31). Now, in chapter 8 the reader must hear His words to move forward in battle. "Ye have compassed this mountain long enough: turn you northward" (Deut. 2:3) to fight for the church's home in the heavenly land of promise, "in the Sanctuary, O Lord, which thy hands have established" (Ex. 15:17, cf Ps. 77:13; Heb. 8:1, 2).

The chapter 8 silence intentionally divides chapter 7's celebrating by the church *victorious* at Jesus' coming (see Acts 3:19-21; Isaiah 13:12, 13) from the next scenes of the church *militant* which precede that final redemption. The silence separates the final reward from the struggles which will culminate in that final reward. That day of reward will condemn Satan and his hosts (see Leviticus 16:12; Daniel 8:9-14, 23-25), and will cleanse the memory of sin from the heavenly sanctuary (see Leviticus 16:16, 19, 30). Since the days of Adam, all who sought God's love and grace, and obtained it, were recorded in the book of life (see Psalm 56:8). Jesus tells in His parable, however, that not every soul fights to keep His grace all the way to the very end of life. (See Matthew 13:20-22 cf, Matthew 24:13; Revelation 1:3; 2:25, 26; 16:15; Hebrews 2:1-3; 3:6; 6:4-8, 15; Romans 4:17-22; John 8:31.)

Jesus said that most do not strive for full surrender (see Matthew 7:13; Revelation 2:11; Hebrews 10:36, 38). They do not put their whole heart and will toward pleasing God or toward wrestling with His Law. They become indolent, temptation engulfs them, and they end up with an abrasive heart and character, and a religious experience of thorns and briers (see Isaiah 32:13, 16; 33:11-14; Matthew 7:15-17; 12:43-45). They miss the fullness of redemption, not doing as Abraham who continued pressing to the mark of the high calling of God in Christ Jesus (see Romans 4:18-22).

Therefore, an investigation by Jesus must ensue (see Ezekiel 34:17; Isaiah 40:10) and be recorded by all the angelic hosts (see Revelation 3:5; 14:6, 10). It must judge all whose hearts had confessed the Son of God, from Adam until the end of the judgment. Heaven must examine all who initially surrendered to the condemnation and goodness of God, who trusted in the pouring out of Christ's soul for them, and ultimately whose candlestick Satan was or was not able to take away (see Revelation 2:5; Matthew 13:38-43; 22:12-14; Revelation 17:14). If their trust and obedience remained to the end, then the heavenly court will not blot out their names from the book of life.

> He that overcometh, the same shall be clothed in white raiment; and I will not blot out his name out of the book of life, but I will confess his name before my Father, and before his angels (Rev. 3:5, cf Heb. 10:39).

This infers that Jesus must blot out of His book people who will not keep His word and remain surrendered to the will of God, enduring (see John 8:33; 14:21-23; Rev. 3:11) until the end in the battle against their sins. The sanctuary cleansing infers that there will be punishment on those who failed in that investigation (see 1 Corinthians 3:13; 2 Peter 2:18-22; 1 Peter 4:17; Psalm 73:17) by their rejoining Satan's hosts (see 1 Timothy 5:11-13; 2 Timothy 4:10). But thankfully, the promise means blessing on everyone who, like their Master, patiently held the beginning of their confidence in God to the very last moment of life (see Hebrews 3:14; 2 Timothy 4:7, 8). It promises that through His continued, abundant grace from above, many do overcome. The great cleansing of the heavenly sanctuary determines who of the final generation will stand when Jesus returns and who will be destroyed by the brightness of His coming (see 2 Thessalonians 2:8, 9). When Jesus returns, He delivers those who, after the investigation and tribulation, are still "found written in the book" (Dan. 12:1, cf Rev. 13:8; 17:8).

The Revelation chapter 8 sanctuary scene is a solemn event because it begins the preliminary investigative judgment. This period must require soul-searching from everyone on earth. Is my mind fortified with truth so that I can stand in the day of battle, and ultimately on the day of destruction? Does the love of God so control my heart that Satan cannot inspire me with hate toward even one enemy in the persecutions? Can I accept correction; can I be reproved? Can my appetites survive "the loss of all things", "to be abased", to be "hungry", and "to suffer need" (Phil. 3:8; 4:12) during the time of trouble and Jesus' return? Am I experiencing the Early Rain's justification and sanctification by faith so that I can take part in the Latter Rain's sealing and glorification by faith? Am I reconciling with the work of losing personal idols; do I "count them but dung, that I may win Christ" (Phil. 3:8)? Are the heavenly agencies putting in me a love of the truth and giving me the Early Rain's promised sprinkling from a cursed, evil conscience, giving me relief from the hounding of Satan for my past shame? Are the heavenly agencies perfectly reproducing in me the character of Jesus? Am I being sanctified by the truth that I preach, or am I a castaway? Am I understanding and experiencing the science of salvation, so that I will be among the 144,000 who correctly preach the everlasting gospel "in all the world for a witness unto all nations" (Matt. 24:14)?

Per the Old Testament atonement guideline, the investigation mandates such self-examination. "Whatsoever soul it be that shall not be afflicted in that same day [during the Day of Atonement], he shall be cut off from among his people. And whatsoever soul it be that doeth any work in that same day, the same soul will I destroy from among his people. Ye shall do no manner of work: it shall be a statute for ever throughout your generations in all your dwellings. It shall be unto you a sabbath of rest, and ye shall afflict your souls" (Lev. 23:29-32). Thus, examining our character and conscience in the light of the Law of God demands our special attention today. Trusting in Christ's redemptive suffering for us to give rest and victory over sin has not become obsolete in the investigative judgment. Trusting Christ will be a current requirement all the way to the end; the investigative judgment *amplifies* our need of the Son (see 1 John 3:2, 3).

John sees a high priestly Angel standing at a golden altar before God (see Revelation 8:3). This altar can be none other than the altar of incense which guards the "second veil" (Heb. 9:3, cf Heb. 9:4) that had been set up at the entrance to both Most Holy Places of the earthly and heavenly sanctuaries (see Hebrews 8:2, 5). There Christ intercedes His Father for our heaven-borne requests and communion, giving us groans that we could not of ourselves utter (see Romans 8:26). This scene of Revelation chapter 8 indicates a preparation to cleanse the heavenly sanctuary. The Angel is carrying a censer, officiating at the altar of incense. Thus, He is ready to enter the Most Holy on the Day of Atonement of October 22, 1844. Like ancient Israel crowding around the tent sanctuary in the wilderness, Christ is surrounded by "all saints" (Rev. 8:3, cf Lev. 23:29) — His people are praying for God's grace to remain firm during that dark time of their desire to see Jesus.

Gary, a Bible student acquaintance, made this seventh seal introduction more concretely connected to the cleansing of the sanctuary and to the investigative judgment. He showed the comparison of this scene's over-abundant incense with its type.

> Aaron shall bring the bullock of the sin offering, which is for himself, and shall make an atonement for himself, and for his house, and shall kill the bullock of the sin offering which is for himself: and he shall take a censer full of burning coals of fire from off the altar before the LORD, and his *hands full* of sweet incense beaten small, and bring it within the vail (Lev. 16:11, 12).

The "much" incense of the angelic High Priest in Revelation 8 is the antitype of the two hands-full of incense that Aaron needed to enter the earthly Most Holy Place on the Day of Atonement. Everything in Revelation 8:3 speaks of the typical fifteenth day of the seventh month Day of Atonement, and thus speaks of the literal, antitypical commencement of the heavenly sanctuary cleansing in the seventh seal.

The seventh seal picks up the storyline where the sixth seal left off after its pause in Revelation 6:17-7:3. The sixth seal finished with the close of the Millerite movement which initiated the proclamation of Christ's return. Also, all of Revelation chapter 8 and its sanctuary scene are connected to the Revelation 7 glorious tangent by picking up again the seven seal storyline (from Revelation 7:3) at Revelation 8:1. Chapter 7's inspired intermission bridges the sixth and seventh seals, and then it ends in order for the prophecy to transition into the somber seventh seal's seven trumpet activities. And, it is a given that both Revelation chapter 6 ended and chapter 7 began at the Great Disappointment of 1844, the conclusion of God's sixth seal merciful warning by the Millerite movement. So, the seventh seal begins on October 22, 1844, followed by a week of heavenly silence.

Judgment Day could have come on October 22, 1844 or shortly thereafter. And God had every right to terminate the church dispensation by His appearing, though no one alive would have been ready for that terrifying day. He didn't come, not because the human race merited another 170 years of existence in its sins; but due to God's enduring forbearance and grace to produce a group which will perfectly vindicate His ability to attract sinful humanity away from their lustful idols to His righteousness and love.

So, to begin the seventh seal Christ, "the angel of his [Father's] presence" (Isa. 63:9, cf Ex. 23:20) stands before the altar of incense. He is about to enter the Most Holy Place to blot out of the heavenly sanctuary all the sin of the saints since Adam. "Into the second went the high priest alone once every year, not without blood, which he offered for himself, and for the errors of the people" (Heb. 9:7).

But before He goes in to His Father in order to prepare the world for His return, Jesus must first be cleansed of the open shame with which His Protestants have sullied His name. Then He must also prepare them for ministry. This He can accomplish only by purifying His Protestant church; then He can cleanse the greater bulk of His people sprinkled throughout the other world religions.

Jesus casts His censer to the heavenly floor; and, as the first trumpet blows, out of the sky on earth fall the coals from His censer.

Jesus casts His censer to the heavenly floor; and, as the first trumpet blows, out of the sky on earth fall the coals from His censer, "burning coals of fire from off the altar before the LORD" (Lev. 16:12), and "his own blood" (Heb. 9:12, cf vs. 7).

> It is he that sitteth upon the circle of the earth, and the inhabitants thereof are as grasshoppers; that stretcheth out the heavens as a curtain, and spreadeth them out as a tent to dwell in: that bringeth the princes to nothing; he maketh the judges of the earth as vanity (Isa. 40:22, 23).

Since the first trumpet involved the contents of the Angel's censer and His blood, then the first trumpet is integral to this sanctuary cleansing scene at the opening

Chapter 5 Revelation Chapter 8: The Trumpets Begin

of the seventh seal. The combination opening sanctuary scene and following trumpets are one whole act within the seventh seal drama. The seven trumpets of Revelation 8 and 9 result from Christ's ministry in the heavenly sanctuary.

Therefore, the commencement of the seventh seal sanctuary cleansing and the seventh seal's first trumpet both happened at the 1844 Great Disappointment. And, therefore, all the subsequent six trumpets are blown after 1844. Thus, the seven trumpets span the final period of Earth's history before Jesus returns, rather than spanning the whole church dispensation, as many have mistakenly believed. And it makes sense that all the seven trumpets' fulfillment should be placed in the prophetic timetable just prior to the cleansing of the heavenly sanctuary and the return of Christ. Their apocalyptic placement during the investigative judgment must be correct since the typical feast of trumpets immediately prefaced the earthly sanctuary cleansing at each ceremonial year's end. The antitypical seven trumpets of Revelation mirror the typical Feast of trumpets. (See Leviticus 23:23-32.) Scripture must interpret scripture.

At that time, our angelic High Priest must first cleanse and prepare His final Adventist generation; then He can cleanse the whole sanctuary for the saints throughout the world. The Old Testament type showed this in the requirement for Aaron to first cleanse *himself and his family* prior to cleansing the sanctuary for the nation. (See Leviticus 16:11, 29.) "Behold, I and the children whom the LORD hath given me are for signs and for wonders in Israel from the LORD of hosts, which dwelleth in mount Zion" (Isa. 8:18). The last generation is God's special group of children who will demonstrate for Him the true sacrifice of praise (see Revelation 7:10).

Therefore, not the first Most Holy entrance in 1844 by Jesus for His Adventist family, but the second and great Most Holy Place appearance of Jesus for the heavenly sanctuary's cleansing will not occur anti-typically until the end of the trumpets period. This should grow clearer to the reader as we study the fifth and sixth trumpet events. But, Christ can enter the Most Holy Place the second time only after first cleansing His remnant Adventist and Protestant peoples as Aaron did his family. Then Jesus can enter to cleanse the heavenly sanctuary, give the Latter Rain to the world, and bring all of His redeemed home.

Mr. Miller and those who were in union with him supposed that the cleansing of the sanctuary spoken of in Daniel 8:14 meant the purifying of the earth by fire prior to its becoming the abode of the saints. This was to take place at the advent of Christ; therefore we looked for that event at the end of the 2300 days, or years. But after our disappointment the Scriptures were carefully searched with prayer and earnest thought, and after a period of suspense, light poured in upon our darkness; doubt and uncertainty were swept away.

Instead of the prophecy of Daniel 8:14 referring to the purifying of the earth, it was now plain that it pointed to the closing work of our High Priest in heaven, the finishing of the atonement, and the preparing of the people to abide the day of His coming *Testimonies for the Church*, vol. 1, p. 58.

We will see, as both the Holy Place sanctuary scene described in Revelation 8 and the trumpets demonstrate, that the great Judge of all the earth has paralleled the investigative judgment in heaven with a world-wide judgment gathering strength on the earth, "the hour of temptation, which shall come upon all the world, to try them that dwell upon the earth" (Rev. 3:10). The core pageant of Revelation, chapters 4 through 11, very tersely treats the great controversy from the beginning before time until the start of the Advent movement (chapters 4 through 6). Then, after 1844 the core Revelation vision slows down and gives us much greater detail until the very end of time (chapters 7 through 11). As most of the Old Testament concerned Israel and its dealing with the nations surrounding them, most of Revelation is about the Advent movement and the world around it. As salvation had been of the Jews, and later through the church in the wilderness, in their respective eras, salvation would be through the Seventh-day Adventist Church during the time of the end.

The first trumpet sounds and the Angel's coals, fire, and blood fall from the sky. "The first angel sounded, and there followed hail and fire mingled with blood, and they were cast upon the earth: and the third part of trees was burnt up, and all green grass was burnt up" (Rev. 8:7, cf Eze. 10:2; 9:9; Deut. 29:24-27). This symbolism, commonly used elsewhere, is against the enemies of God's holiness.

Behold, I will kindle a fire in thee, and it shall devour every green tree in thee, and every dry tree: the flaming flame shall not be quenched, and all faces from the south to the north shall be burned therein. And all flesh shall see that I the LORD have kindled it: it shall not be quenched (Eze. 20:47, 48).

So there was hail, and fire mingled with the hail, very grievous, such as there was none like it in all the land of Egypt since it became a nation. And the hail smote throughout all the land of Egypt all that was in the field, both man and beast; and the hail smote every herb of the field, and brake every tree of the field. Only in the land of Goshen, where the children of Israel were, was there no hail (Ex. 9:24-26).

And the light of Israel shall be for a fire, and his Holy One for a flame: and it shall burn and devour his thorns and his briers in one day; and shall consume *the glory of his forest, and of his fruitful field, both soul and body*.... And the rest of the trees of his forest shall be few, that a child may write them.... For though thy people Israel be as the sand of the sea, yet a remnant of them shall return: the consumption decreed shall overflow with righteousness. For the Lord GOD of hosts shall make a consumption, even determined, in the midst of all the land (Isa. 10:17-19, 22, 23).

The coals and fire from the Angel's censer, with "the blood of Christ, who through the eternal Spirit offered himself without spot to God" (Heb. 9:14) fall on the trees. The coals burn the proudest and most resistant of the leaders of Protestantism, who heard the message of William Miller, but who heckled and denounced it. The coals also burn the fields of grain that clothe the earth, the Protestant multitudes who knew God's pointed conviction to their conscience, but heeded the wisdom of men instead.

The denominations' continued rejection of the blessed hope of the literal return of Jesus, caused their consciences to be burned up by the word of God. The truth of Christ's destructive return had been a central theme of their Bible, a book which they professed to whole-heartedly believe. The falling hail was the judgment of God's Spirit of truth upon all the Protestants and their high profession of serving Him. A religion empty of real substance could no longer abide His presence, as the preparation for His final judgment must begin. The coals falling on the faithful among the Millerites was also a trial very difficult to bear — the Great Disappointment and all the rejection and ridicule that came with it.

Trees symbolize leaders and those of the highest religious profession.

Behold, the Lord, the LORD of hosts, shall lop the bough with terror: and the high ones of stature shall be hewn down, and the haughty shall be humbled. And he shall cut down the thickets of the forest with iron, and Lebanon shall fall by a mighty one (Isa. 10:33-34).

Beware of false prophets.... Every tree that bringeth not forth good fruit is hewn down, and cast into the fire (Matt. 7:15, 19).

The "third" is not a mathematical fraction, but the last of descending moral worth. The "third" is the *proudest*, the *most rebellious*. The third group that could not open the book of God were those "under the earth" (see Revelation 5:3) — that is, the angels that fell, and were like Ham, the rebellious third son of Noah. The "third" infers that, during the scattering and gathering time of the trumpets before human probation closes (see Luke 13:24-28), our merciful God does not at this time judge all the Protestants worthy of receiving the burning punishment. Christ's door of mercy remains open for the group. He does, however, judge the third part, those who stood in the way of His Advent testing truth for the Protestants. They refused to believe that Jesus would ever return to destroy the world, and influenced many others to doubt (see Luke 11:52). The less than total divine retribution upon the church also serves as a warning of a future similar judgment to all who will presume upon this final investigative period of grace. "For the time is come that judgment must begin at the house of God: and if it first begin at us, what shall the end be of them that obey not the gospel of God?" (1 Pet. 4:17). When those same angels return for the last plagues, their plagues will bring a misery on the unprepared which then the Spirit of God will not blend with the trumpets' compassion and probation.

The trees symbolize the denominational leadership. The "third part" of the trees burnt up represents the many Protestant religious leaders in 1844 who had already lost the power of faith in God's grace. They had not kept their glorious new continent and the freedoms of their wonderful new Constitution subservient to the beauty of the gospel and to the authority of God's Law. They attempted

Chapter 5 Revelation Chapter 8: The Trumpets Begin

to serve God and mammon. This diluted their love for God with a love for this world, a mixture which dissolved their ardor for Christ. The cares of this world and the deceitfulness of riches choked the convictions of God's word, and the Protestants could not repent. Their profession of grace created apathy toward the Bible's holy and just and good Law (see Romans 7:9-12), and toward its condemnation of sin. Thus, they had not prepared for the delusive idolatry with which Satan subtly charmed them. They had lost the Reformation's first love and Jesus was soon to remove their candlestick from its place, except for those who would repent. Their lack of readiness for the completed first phase of the "times of the Gentiles" (Luke 21:24, cf Rev. 11:2, 7) led them to refuse the unarguable prophetic preaching which the Spirit of God had moved upon Elder Miller, Dr. Joseph Wolff, and many others to give the Protestant world in the 1830s and '40s.

> As the spirit of humility and devotion in the church had given place to pride and formalism, love for Christ and faith in his coming had grown cold. Absorbed in worldliness and pleasure-seeking, the professed people of God were blinded to the Saviour's instructions concerning the signs of his appearing.... Especially was this the case in the churches of America. The freedom and comfort enjoyed by all classes of society, the ambitious desire for wealth and luxury, begetting an absorbing devotion to money-making, the eager rush for popularity and power, which seemed to be within the reach of all, led men to center their interests and hopes on the things of this life, and to put far in the future that solemn day when the present order of things should pass away *The Great Controversy (1888)*, p. 308.

The grass, or the fields of grain (see Matthew 6:30), symbolize the people. "The grass withereth, the flower fadeth: because the spirit of the LORD bloweth upon it: *surely the people is grass*. The grass withereth, the flower fadeth: but the word of our God shall stand for ever" (Isa. 40:7, 8). The Protestant multitudes were judged, because they were only following the preachers instead of listening to the Lord Himself.

It has been the case throughout human history that people look to a creature instead of to Christ in heaven. The Protestants no longer walked by the faith of their Reformation fathers. For them, the Reformation had ended. A new reform from Jesus would burn them up.

> Behold, I will make my words in thy mouth fire, and this people wood, and it shall devour them (Jer. 5:14).

The fire from the censor was God's convicting message of a literal Second Coming to our Protestant brethren that would lead to the denominations' full acceptance or complete rejection of Him.

> If a man abide not in me, he is cast forth as a branch, and is withered; and men gather them, and cast them into the fire, and they are burned (John 15:6).

> For the earth which drinketh in the rain that cometh oft upon it, and bringeth forth herbs meet for them by whom it is dressed, receiveth blessing from God: but that which beareth thorns and briers is rejected, and is nigh unto cursing; whose end is to be burned (Heb. 6:7, 8).

That burning test came from Miller's biblically accurate message concerning the nearness of Christ's return in power and glory. (See 1 Thessalonians 2:19; 2 Thessalonians 1:7-10; 2 Peter 3:10-13.) But this test through plain and understandable prophecies the denominations could not accept. His message did not square with their understanding because they did not study the Bible and examine themselves in its light. Many suffered under a dangerous daze. The word of God was not to them as they should have sought it to be, "quick, and powerful, and sharper than any twoedged sword, piercing even to the dividing asunder of soul and spirit" (Heb. 4:12).

The churches stopped their ears to God's appointed childlike messenger, William Miller. Thus, they turned away from God. We reject God Himself when we reject His designated representatives. Israel rejected the Lord when they rejected Samuel: "They have not rejected thee, but they have rejected me, that I should not reign over them" (1 Sam. 8:7). The Lord said, "Whosoever shall receive one of such children in my name, receiveth me: and whosoever shall receive me, receiveth not me, but him that sent me" (Mark 9:37). Like the people of Israel who rejected the Messiah (see Luke 19:14; John 7:48; 19:15), once the Protestant leadership rejected the Second Advent message and had departed from the God of the Bible, all their followers, "the grass" departed with them (see 1 Kings 12:15, 16).

Therefore say I unto you, The kingdom of God shall be taken from you, and given to a nation bringing forth the fruits thereof (Matt. 21:43).

The Protestants who stood through the Great Disappointment, and who received the coals from off the altar that fell from heaven, were transformed into an unstoppable Advent body.

When the Lord touches your lips with a live coal from off His altar, then the trumpet of every true watchman will give a certain sound....

God has a living testimony, not a tame, lifeless, sermonizing. Men in responsible positions are not to study to meet the world's plans, to cater to the world's ideas, to speak smooth words and prophesy deceit. The Comforter — the Holy Spirit of God whom Christ said the Father would send in His name — with unsparing lips reproves the world of sin, and of righteousness, and of judgment. "Reprove, rebuke, exhort, with all longsuffering and doctrine." 2 Timothy 4:2 *The Ellen G. White 1888 Materials*, p. 947.

There were, however, many among the Millerite Adventists who were in the movement only to save themselves from judgment. They had never surrendered their hearts to Jesus before He was to enter into His new and final phase of the plan of redemption. These unconverted ones didn't receive the Spirit from Christ that had warmed the hearts and compelled the minds of those who were following Christ into His new ministry to cleanse the heavenly sanctuary. The unconverted Millerites failed out of the movement at the disappointment and claimed that they never believed He was coming, though they had intently listened to William Miller. These could accept no more light from Jesus. The door went shut on them forever also as it had on the bitterest opponents of the Millerite message.

Another group within the Millerite movement, blinded by pride, continued to resituate the 2,300 day prophecy with more dates for the Second Advent, until they turned into burning bundles of briers. Others not of the Millerite movement, but of that era of religion in American history added confusion to the Adventists, even competing with their own prophet. But, they never believed *Sola Scriptura*, nor were they ever Protestant.

The burning conviction from Christ divided the Reformation children between the few who desired to live by every word of God, and the rest of the descendants who only professed it or who simply would not take God seriously. The first trumpet's heat borrows from other similar symbolism of the Old Testament gospel.

Blessed is the man that trusteth in the LORD, and whose hope the LORD is. For he shall be as a tree planted by the waters, and that spreadeth out her roots by the river, and shall not see when heat cometh, but her leaf shall be green; and shall not be careful in the year of drought, neither shall cease from yielding fruit (Jer. 17:7, 8).

Cursed be the man that trusteth in man, and maketh flesh his arm, and whose heart departeth from the LORD. For he shall be like the heath [dry bush, a tumbleweed] in the desert, and shall not see when good cometh; but shall inhabit the parched places in the wilderness, in a salt land and not inhabited (Jer. 17:5, 6).

The Angel's coals "from off the altar" (Isa. 6:6, cf 8:5) that gave new life to the Adventists, who accepted the sanctuary present truth in 1844, was the same heaven-ordained hail that brought down divine retribution on our Protestant brothers and sisters who had long disregarded the authority of the Bible. Now that they rejected God's present truth message a great separation took place. As Jeroboam had cut off the many northern tribes of Israel from the sanctuary in Jerusalem (see 1 Kings 12:25-33), and just as those tribes' mindset, without communion with Jehovah, transformed more and more into that of the Canaanite peoples surrounding them (see Jeremiah 3:6-9), likewise did the mainline churches after 1844. Isaiah's warning to apostate Israel was, "Bind up [shut up] the testimony" (Isa. 8:16, cf Isa. 6:9-12; 29:9-14).

The falling away, which happened in ancient Israel and Judah, and later to the apostolic church, was being repeated in the Reformation church. "Bind up" (Heb. *tsarar*, "distress", "besiege", "pangs", "shut up") for final judgment upon final decisions to be made for or against the God of heaven. The fourth trumpet will show that their cutting off from heaven's grace would soon follow. When the deadline for decisions arrives after He has for so long waited patiently, God sends a very strong message that causes decided "victory that overcometh the world" (1 John 5:4) or decided "madness, and blindness" (Deut. 28:28).

The many popular Protestant denominations lost their spirituality when they separated themselves from the God-given light shining out of the Bible that had

Chapter 5 Revelation Chapter 8: The Trumpets Begin

graciously pointed them to His heavenly sanctuary. And the door went permanently shut on those denominations as it had to the unrepentant Jewish nation (see Luke 13:24-28; Matthew 12:31; 21:43). Like the papists who rejected and fought the Protestant Reformation, the Protestant descendants of the Reformation have continued until this day to fight or ignore that providentially given new light to the Adventists. And the denominations, having rejected the 1840s scriptural truth from the Advent movement, by and large have returned to Rome, even leaving their name of Protestant and accepting the subtle, non-protesting gift of Rome, Evangelical. Even if they keep the look of Protestantism, they have gone to worship with the ancient Canaanite religion and God has removed them from His promised blessedness.

The Reformation exalted the whole Bible, both Law and gospel. "Do we then make void the law through faith? God forbid: yea, we establish the law" (Rom. 3:31). Why do the Protestants today claim only the New Testament gospel? "Because the carnal mind is enmity against God: for it is not subject to the law of God, neither indeed can be" (Rom. 8:7). They have made amends with the ancient Beast of the Dark Ages to trample the authority of God to condemn sin; and God has taken them out of His promised land.

> For though thy people Israel be as the sand of the sea, yet a remnant of them shall return: the consumption decreed shall overflow with righteousness. For the Lord GOD of hosts shall make a consumption, even determined, in the midst of all the land (Isa. 10:22, 23).

> Now the just shall live by faith: but if any man draw back, my soul shall have no pleasure in him (Heb. 10:38).

> Therefore we ought to give the more earnest heed to the things which we have heard, lest at any time we should let them slip (Heb. 2:1).

However, the Lord has not left the Protestants without hope.

> But yet in it shall be a tenth, and it shall return, and shall be eaten: as a teil tree, and as an oak, whose substance is in them, when they cast their leaves: so the holy seed shall be the substance thereof (Isa. 6:13, cf Isa. 51:11).

"Notwithstanding the widespread declension of faith and piety, there are true followers of Christ in these churches" *The Great Controversy*, p. 464. "Notwithstanding the spiritual darkness and alienation from God that exist in the churches which constitute Babylon, the great body of Christ's true followers are still to be found in their communion. There are many of these who have never seen the special truths for this time. Not a few are dissatisfied with their present condition and are longing for clearer light" *The Great Controversy*, p. 390. "There are now true Christians in every church, not excepting the Roman Catholic communion, who honestly believe that Sunday is the Sabbath of divine appointment. God accepts their sincerity of purpose and their integrity before Him" *The Great Controversy*, p. 449. "It is true that there are real Christians in the Roman Catholic communion. Thousands in that church are serving God according to the best light they have. They are not allowed access to His word, and therefore they do not discern the truth" *The Great Controversy*, p. 565. One day, many among those groups will look at the Bible and see more clearly that everything their Adventist brethren have been saying was true. That will be a day of "light, and gladness, and joy, and honour…a feast and a good day" (Esth. 8:16, 17, cf Rev. 7:9-14).

Even after separating from the southern kingdom of Judah and joining in the Canaanite religion of Baal, the northern tribes could still be saved, but only by renouncing Baal, leaving their tribes, and coming down to Judah where the blessing of Jehovah still remained. The Israelite northern tribes and Protestants must come back to His Law and the prophets, the seventh-day Sabbath and the truth of the judging advent of the Lord, the sanctuary, and the true state of the dead — a return to the true God as occurred in the days of Hezekiah. (See 2 Chronicles 30; Jeremiah 15:19.)

> Let them return unto thee; but return not thou unto them (Jer. 15:19).

The same principle applied later to the Jews who were "diminished", "cast away", "broken off", "cut off " from God as a nation, because they resisted all efforts that God gave them to believe in their Messiah (see Romans 11:12, 15, 17, 22). "Some" (vs. 14) would still be saved, but only individually or as small groups by accepting their divine judgment from their God (see verse 22), and the gentle correction and tenderhearted invitation from the abhorred Jewish sect following the Messiah (see verse 31, 32). Accordingly, individual Protestants would still be saved, but only by leaving their churches and joining with the despised sabbatarian Adventists who they have branded, under Vatican influence, as a cult. And, soon, thousands of our long-sought Protestant brethren will daily join in the 144,000 of the Advent movement, then full of faith and obedience, to do the work of evangelism that Christ originally gave us all.

Similar to Isaiah's call to his prophetic ministry (see Isaiah 6:6-8), the *"much incense"* of Revelation 8:3 with the coals, that were in Jesus' heavenly censer, indicates an extraordinary gift of the Holy Spirit poured out at this time upon the Advent movement. It would be, as Isaiah had received, the same commissioning with the gift of prophecy for the sanctification of his people.

As the "censer full of burning coals" and the two hands-full of incense were used only for the Day of Atonement, the first trumpet's burning, heaping double portion of the Spirit comes to humanity in the most abundance ever known since Adam. Humanity must have access to the clearest prophetic guidance and condemnation of sin, in order to prepare itself for the antitypical Day of Atonement, during the great investigative judgment. Thus, we see from the first Revelation trumpet an affirmation of the Spirit of Prophecy given to Ellen Harmon White as the last day prophet. This gift came at the start of the Advent movement, as revealed in the beginning of the seven trumpets.

The special dispensation parallels the action of high priest Aaron as he prepares to cleanse the earthly sanctuary. Aaron's sacrifice wasn't only for himself, but also "for his house." Leviticus' parallel being typical then, John's introductory vision to the trumpets indicates that Christ must prepare Himself and His Advent family of disciples before beginning to cleanse the heavenly sanctuary at large, as Aaron made the first entrance for himself and his family. John 13:33, John 17:6-9, John 21:5, and Hebrews 2:11, 13 make it evident that Christ's disciples are His children. He loved them as His own and shared His oil of joy among His fellows.

> There I beheld Jesus, a great High Priest, standing before the Father. On the hem of His garment was a bell and a pomegranate, a bell and a pomegranate. Those who rose up with Jesus would send up their faith to Him in the holiest, and pray, "My Father, give us Thy Spirit." Then Jesus would breathe upon them the Holy Ghost. In that breath was light, power, and much love, joy, and peace *Early Writings*, p. 55.

Our "everlasting Father" (Isa. 9:6) does not work to save the world without the involvement of a human agency. The Revelation chapter 8 intro was Jesus' preparing Himself for the final work of the heavenly sanctuary atonement. Thus, He received from His Father the abundant gift of prophecy. And through the first trumpet He poured out the special dispensation of His Spirit upon young Ellen Harmon, for the movement that would grow the sealed 144,000 firstfruits.

Given all the clues of the seventh seal introductory scene, we can therefore conclude that Revelation chapter 8's 1844 sanctuary scene speaks of Christ's *preparatory phase* of entering the Most Holy Place that year to prepare for a *later* cleansing of the heavenly sanctuary for the world. *But*, He must first enter in to make atonement for the uncleanness of His Adventist household and for the past saints of all time. He must give His living family a special sanctification before they can preach the gospel to every nation, kindred, tongue, and people. He must free them from the power of sin and seal them in victory over sin before He can use them to lead His children around the globe to also get the victory. This the trumpets accomplish. After the sixth trumpet closes then the investigation of the sealed 144,000 and great, innumerable multitude will be complete as the judgment of the living will then also have finished.

The second trumpet blows (see Revelation 8:8, 9). Mount Sinai, the great representation of the holy Law of God (see Exodus 19:18; Isaiah 64:1-3), was cast out of the churches as the Sabbatarian Adventists began to promote the seventh-day Sabbath, and Sunday Protestants realized the emptiness of their profession to keep the Ten Commandments.

> In the 58th chapter of Isaiah, the work of those who worship God, the Maker of the heavens and the earth, is specified: "They that shall be of Thee shall build the old waste places: thou shalt raise up the foundations of many generations." God's memorial, His seventh-day Sabbath, will be uplifted. Isaiah 58:12-14.

> The history of the church and the world, the loyal and the disloyal, is here plainly revealed. The loyal, under the proclamation of the third angel's message, have turned their feet into the way of God's commandments, to respect, to honor and glorify Him who created the heavens and the earth. The opposing forces have dishonored God by making a breach in His law, and when light from His Word has called attention to His holy commandments, revealing the breach made in

the law by the Papal authority, then, *to get rid of conviction, men have tried to destroy the whole law* [emphasis supplied]. But could they destroy it? No; for all who will search the Scriptures for themselves will see that the law of God stands immutable, eternal, and His memorial, the Sabbath, will endure through eternal ages, pointing to the only true God in distinction from all false gods. Satan has been persevering and untiring in his efforts to prosecute the work he began in heaven, to change the law of God. He has succeeded in making the world believe the theory he presented in heaven before his fall, that the law of God was faulty, and needed revising. A large part of the professed Christian church, by their attitude, if not by their words, show that they have accepted the same error. But if in one jot or tittle the law of God has been changed, Satan has gained on earth that which he could not gain in heaven. He has prepared his delusive snare, hoping to take captive the church and the world *Manuscript Releases*, vol. 1, p. 45.

The Jewish nation could have repented at Christ's preaching and would have avoided the dread prophecy against them from Daniel 9:24-27. Had they complied with the high standard of Daniel 9:24 then God would have chosen the whole nation to take the gospel to the world. And what a powerful presentation the nations would have heard! But, Satan was able to get his pride and delusions into their minds, and obstruct the great apostolic revival that he feared. Nevertheless, God's word does not return to Him void, but accomplishes the thing He needs. Those few Jews who did accept the Messiah became the core of a solid, long lasting movement.

History repeats itself over and over; and, once again, a test came. The last phase of the Christian dispensation, Protestantism, was offered to remain the reigning earthly representatives of heaven. Would the Protestant churches accept the final message that God gave them to give to the world? Or, would they choose the homage of the world? Had they accepted the message of William Miller and repented of their departure from the Reformation, the Lord would have accepted them all and would have given them the great call to prepare the world for Judgment Day. Satan, however, attracted their hearts to the abundance of the New World, and their glazed-over minds could not perceive the convictions of the Bible to fear God. This left them unready for the big decision to prepare for the return of Jesus in power. The fourth commandment truth became another test, which the Protestants also failed to pass.

Their protesting against Rome could only be farcical, since they would not surrender the Sun Day, which Satan inspired the papal church to borrow from paganism in order to deny God full obedience. By this counterfeit Sabbath the devil had a base upon which to claim ownership of the entire Law of God, to secret it away and then use God's people to cast boastful, daring blasphemies at God (see Revelation 13:11-14). The denominations took a downward step after rejecting the biblical message of Christ's literal return with destructive power. And because of this, unless repentant they would naturally take a second step deeper into apostasy by justifying their unbiblical worship of God.

This decision to depart further from the Bible wasn't made because a new condition of apostasy suddenly appeared in the mainstream churches. The Reformation departure came over two centuries, capitulating to the Counter-Reformation terrors, and slowly losing the original Reformation principles of reform and of total self-sacrifice, the Reformation itself divinely modeled after the apostolic church. Failing the test of the fourth commandment only revealed the lack of real spirituality in the early 19th century Protestant churches, and their lack of obedience to the Holy One. And as the Jews sold their souls to maintain their public image before Imperial Rome rather than to please God (see John 19:15, cf John 12:43), now the Sunday Christian churches followed the same pattern before the Vatican.

By their refusal to admit to error, or to accept shame and guilt, especially when corrected by the insignificant handful of Sabbatarian Adventists, our Protestant brethren accepted an unbiblical doctrine that had been floating around their theological community. This doctrine, which they accepted, taught that Christ abolished the Ten Commandments when He died on the cross. Now, their fear of the Lord was fully quenched as they plunged Mount Sinai into the lawless sea. From that day forward, they would have no barrier against Satan's insidious machinations. Without the Law to convict and its overwhelming condemnation to humble the inherent, innate pride of sinners, they could feel no dire need for a Saviour from sin; they would eventually lose all ability to choose to return to their Creator. (See Romans 7:9-8:1; Galatians 3:23, 24; Psalm 119:126; 2 Peter 2:9-15.) The Advent band had the Law, through the correction, reproof, instruction, and doctrinal insight of Ellen

White. And to the extent that some Adventists would not hear the Law from the Testimony of Jesus, they too have had no discernment or barrier against Satan's insidious machinations.

With the second trumpet the Protestants rejected this second conviction from the Holy Spirit, and now their hope of God's grace could only be an empty profession. In John's vision, the denominations now were classed as the lawless Gentile sea; and the sea turning to blood signified the denominations' spiritual death and their blood-guiltiness that resulted from the loss of many Protestant descendants who dove into presumptuous irreverence toward the God of their fathers.

> They that forsake the law praise the wicked: but such as keep the law contend with them (Prov. 28:4).

The affect of abrogating the Law of God on the American multitudes and on the nations of the world who would follow the American Protestants' example has caused world-wide Protestantism to lose its holy standing in the world, as the third trumpet would show. Glorious navies and decadent yachts — the pride of the ancient nations, proudly daring heaven to contest them — this vision uses to describe the pride of all the Protestant Americans who were cut off from God at this time. (See Isaiah 2:11-13, 16; 43:14; Ezekiel 27:1-10, 27, 36; Revelation 18:3, 10-19.) Protestant America would eventually lose its former humility and holiness, and slowly turn into the world's premier aggressor nation, roaring like the dragon (see Revelation 13:11).

The third trumpet sounds (see Revelation 8:10, 11). Satan gained final access to minds and hearts of most of the Protestant leadership with their congregations by a bitter poison of wormwood because they rejected the truth of God's Judgment Day and the authority of His Law. Protestantism imbibed the spells of the ancient serpent when they rejected His Law, and they could no longer say to the Lord, "all my springs are in thee" (Ps. 87:7). Their "well of water springing up into everlasting life" (John 4:14) from Jesus dried up, and now their springs flowed from Satan. No spring can produce "sweet water and bitter" (Jas. 3:11), and neither can the Spirit's sweet fruits share hearts that cannot hear the voice of Him who sent it. Satan now begins to poison their spiritual fountains with his twisting of biblical doctrines, leavening the denominations with his mold, so that many of them carry on intoxicated with an emotion-based gospel, and empty of real salvation.

> Lest there should be among you man, or woman, or family, or tribe, whose heart turneth away this day from the LORD our God, to go and serve the gods of these nations; lest there should be among you a root that beareth gall and wormwood; and it come to pass, when he heareth the words of this curse [the warnings against forsaking God's statutes and commandments (Deuteronomy 28:15-68)], that he bless himself in his heart, saying, I shall have peace, though I walk in the imagination of mine heart, to add drunkenness to thirst (Deut. 29:18, 19).

"The law was our schoolmaster to bring us unto Christ" (Gal. 3:24). "All that the Father giveth me shall come to me" (John 6:37), Jesus said. That is, God is a Spirit; and He uses His instructive, condemning Law to open our resistant hearts to the invitation of His Messiah. But, without the sinner accepting the conviction of the Father, that sinner can never repent and realize the grace of God's dear Son. By denying God's authority to reprove through His Law and to baptize His Protestant and Adventist children in guilt, they can never be shamed and humbled. And, thus, every professed servant of God who ministers to sinners but disdains the conviction of the Law is illegitimate, and a worker of iniquity (see Matthew 5:19; 12:36, 37; Luke 13:24-27; Hebrews 12:8).

> The law and the gospel go hand in hand. The law without faith in the gospel of Christ cannot save the transgressor of law. The gospel without the law is inefficient and powerless. The law and the gospel are a perfect whole.... The two blended — the gospel of Christ and the law of God — produce the love and faith unfeigned *The Ellen G. White 1888 Materials*, p. 783.

Without the Law of God, we all naturally are like the Zidonians, "careless...quiet and secure; and there was no magistrate in the land, that might put them to shame in any thing" (Jdg. 18:7). Without the Law to humble the human race (see Romans 3:19), our naturally proud hearts become intoxicated with unbridled pride, the poisonous wine that brings horrible gall and wormwood to our alienated hearts.

We must bow to the power of God's word to convict our conscience, or we can never need a Saviour and receive His repentance. Submission to the reprimanding Law of God — especially as seen from the Testimony of Jesus — prepares our soul for submission to

His merciful-kindness. Only when God has humbled our uncircumcised hearts are we meek. When we are broken and mourning He offers us the beauty of holiness, the oil of joy, and the true garment of praise. We must surrender to the powerful authority of God's Law; only then are we given the powerful authority of His grace and peace that reconciles us to Him. Only then do we have the ability to claim Romans 8:33, 34 and Isaiah 43:9-12; only then can we have His powerful workmanship "to be conformed to the image of his Son" (Rom. 8:29). Only then do we have certainty of His salvation. Go to the zealous Spirit of Prophecy and there drink in the tonic truth that sets your teeth on edge and ultimately comforts the heart with a peace that passes all understanding.

> If they shall confess their iniquity, and the iniquity of their fathers, with their trespass which they trespassed against me, and that also they have walked contrary unto me; and that I also have walked contrary unto them, and have brought them into the land of their enemies; if then their uncircumcised hearts be humbled, and they then accept of the punishment of their iniquity: *then* will I remember my covenant with Jacob, and also my covenant with Isaac, and also my covenant with Abraham will I remember; and I will remember the land (Lev. 26:40-42).

> The Spirit of the Lord GOD is upon me; because the LORD hath anointed me to preach good tidings unto the meek; he hath sent me to bind up the brokenhearted, to proclaim liberty to the captives, and the opening of the prison to them that are bound; to proclaim the acceptable year of the LORD, and the day of vengeance of our God; to comfort all that mourn; to appoint unto them that mourn in Zion, to give unto them beauty for ashes, the oil of joy for mourning, the garment of praise for the spirit of heaviness; that they might be called trees of righteousness, the planting of the LORD, that he might be glorified (Isa. 61:1-3).

Accepting His gracious scourging from the Spirit of the Law, we can become the children of God and heirs of the promise. "My son," Jesus says to us, "despise not the chastening of the LORD; neither be weary of his correction: for whom the LORD loveth he correcteth; even as a father the son in whom he delighteth" (Prov. 3:11, 12). *But,* "if ye be without chastisement, whereof all are partakers, then are ye…not sons" (Heb. 12:8). "The Spirit of Christ" (Rom. 8:9, cf John 14:15-21) is the Stone we fall on and break (see Matthew 21:44; Luke 2:34). Without His humiliation, we are "none of his" (Rom. 8:9, cf John 13:8). Said, the prophet,

> I will bear the indignation of the LORD, because I have sinned against him, until he plead my cause, and execute judgment for me: he will bring me forth to the light, and I shall behold his righteousness (Mic. 7:9).

No sooner do we submit to His conviction than He moves in with His blessing of mercy and comfort.

> I will pray the Father, and he shall give you another Comforter, that he may abide with you for ever; even the Spirit of truth; whom the world cannot receive, because it seeth him not, neither knoweth him: but ye know him; for he dwelleth with you, and shall be in you. I will not leave you comfortless: I will come to you (John 14:16-18).

> For his anger endureth but a moment; in his favour is life: weeping may endure for a night, but joy cometh in the morning (Ps. 30:5).

> Shall not God avenge his own elect, which cry day and night unto him, though he bear long with them? I tell you that he will avenge them speedily (Luke 18:7, 8).

"The law was our schoolmaster to bring us unto Christ" (Gal. 3:24). No longer alienated from God by surrendering to His Law, our nature is calmed and at peace; our "flesh also shall rest in hope" (Ps. 16:8, 9). The Law of God as schoolmaster, in the skillful hands of the Lord God, did its job to humble our proud hearts. Then faith came; and likewise our justification, as we cried out for a Deliverer from sin (see Romans 7:24, 25). Afterwards, the Law is no longer needed *as a schoolmaster* because now we love the Law; He has written it in our heart. The whipped conscience, the wounds and bruises and putrefying sores from the Spirit of truth are bound up by the same Comforter, mollified by the Balm of Gilead; the heart and mind robbed of peace are a thing of the past (see Hebrews 10:16-18). "Blessed are the poor in spirit: for theirs is the kingdom of heaven" (Matt. 5:3). (See also Psalm 119:97; Hebrews 8:10-12; Hebrews 10:22; Jeremiah 31:2). Under the supervision of our merciful High Priest the balanced spirit and letter of the Law are not bondage. On the contrary, together they abide in us forever and are perfect freedom in love.

> Then said I, Lo, I come (in the volume of the book it is written of me,) to do thy will, O God (Heb. 10:7).

> I delight to do thy will, O my God: yea, thy law is within my heart (Ps. 40:8).

Our natural separation from God causes exhausting restlessness (see Isaiah 57:5, 10, 21). Only Christ's chastening and then His comforting Spirit of truth can bring us to repentance and motivate us out of that unconverted, unsettled, and irritable state. "Let him take hold of my strength, that he may make peace with me; and he shall make peace with me" (Isa. 27:5). Our health, physical and mental, needs both the Law and the gospel, both the Testimonies for the church and Righteousness by faith.

> Lest there should be among you a root that beareth gall and wormwood; and…he bless himself in his heart, saying, I shall have peace, though I walk in the imagination of mine heart, to add drunkenness to thirst (Deut. 29:18, 19).

Moses warned of disregarding God's covenant and His laws and statutes yet imagining that everything was right with God. This warning to the Hebrews given from Moses shows a connection between serving the other gods (Baal and Ashtoreth) — spiritualism (see Psalm 106:36-38) — and rejecting God's authority to strike terror against sin in the soul. If we proudly reject the correction of God through His Law and prophets, then we open ourselves wide to Satan's rebellious familiar spirit and lawlessness (see 1 Samuel 15:22, 23; 2 Peter 2:10, 15, 17). The churches, then, denying God His Law and its condemnation yet calling themselves blessed, by default came under the spiritualistic enchantments of Lucifer.

> He that turneth away his ear from hearing the law, even his prayer shall be abomination (Prov. 28:9).

> If I regard iniquity in my heart, the Lord will not hear me (Ps. 66:18).

The once holy Protestant religion came more and more under the devils' insinuating sway, some denominations becoming conduits for the supernatural, and others for humanistic philosophies. And, there the Sunday churches have remained his unsuspecting slaves. As Ellen White writes,

> As spiritualism more closely imitates the nominal Christianity of the day, it has greater power to deceive and ensnare. Satan himself is converted, after the modern order of things. He will appear in the character of an angel of light *The Great Controversy*, p. 588.

> With every rejection of truth the minds of the people will become darker, their hearts more stubborn, until they are entrenched in an infidel hardihood. In defiance of the warnings which God has given, they will continue to trample upon one of the precepts of the Decalogue, until they are led to persecute those who hold it sacred. Christ is set at nought in the contempt placed upon His word and His people. As the *teachings of spiritualism* [emphasis mine] are accepted by the churches, the *restraint imposed upon the carnal heart is removed* [emphasis mine], and the profession of religion will become a cloak to conceal the basest iniquity. A belief in spiritual manifestations opens the door to seducing spirits and doctrines of devils, and thus the influence of evil angels will be felt in the churches *Ibid.*, p. 603.

The "teachings of spiritualism" remove the Law's "restraint imposed upon the carnal heart". But, today this warning trumpet is also for Seventh-day Adventists, by their unprecedented and growing acceptance of the Vatican's celebration movement and its Spiritual Formation. In these spiritual disciplines, contemplative prayer and celebration worship solely focus on the nice things Jesus gave us through the Bible and the Spirit of Prophecy. Meanwhile, it purposely avoids the instructive principles and corrective reproofs in the Spirit of Prophecy which expose sin and rightfully cause our pride to tremble before God.

Spiritual Formation bypasses God's work as Spirit of truth and accepts only His work as Comforter. This false gospel, stealing its way into Adventism by this unique Spirit of Prophecy genre, accomplishes the same design as does the Jesuit Spiritual Exercises that originated in eastern mysticism. It releases the conscience from strong conviction, which our Sunday brethren have been adopting, and is identical to Baal and Ashtoreth worship. "They [the prophets of Baal and Ashtoreth] have healed also the hurt of the daughter of my people slightly, saying, Peace, peace; when there is no peace" (Jer. 6:14).

Condemnation-dodging Spiritual Formation will never lead a soul to be subject to the Law of God and His peace. It will only mock God's authority, perpetuating man's natural born pride and his natural accumulation of wormwood bitterness and death. Spiritual Formation is the abomination that the whole world worships and makes the whole world desolate.

> ...the testimony of the True Witness has not been half heeded. The solemn testimony upon which the destiny of the church hangs has been lightly esteemed, if not entirely disregarded. This testimony must work deep repentance; all who truly receive it will obey it and be purified *Early Writings*, p. 270.

Heeding the True Witness of Revelation 3:14, letting its high standard work deep repentance in the heart, obeying the testimony, and being purified by the truth, altogether will fortify our minds to stand through the last great conflict. To facilitate our special work of purification in order to stand in the chaotic day that Jesus returns, the power that Jesus has given us in the Spirit of Prophecy challenges our rebellion and slays our Laodicea peace.

> Before the seed of the gospel could find lodgment, the soil of the heart must be broken up. Before they would seek healing from Jesus, they must be awakened to their danger from the wounds of sin.
>
> God does not send messengers to flatter the sinner. He delivers no message of peace to lull the unsanctified into fatal security. He lays heavy burdens upon the conscience of the wrongdoer, and pierces the soul with arrows of conviction. The ministering angels present to him the fearful judgments of God to deepen the sense of need, and prompt the cry, "What must I do to be saved?" Then the hand that has humbled in the dust, lifts up the penitent. The voice that has rebuked sin, and put to shame pride and ambition, inquires with tenderest sympathy, "What wilt thou that I shall do unto thee?" *The Desire of Ages*, p. 103, 104.

"As many as I love, I rebuke and chasten: be zealous therefore, and repent" (Rev. 3:19). The Spirit of truth is the Comforter; the True Witness is faithful, and faithful is He that calls you. Even if His chastening doesn't always make the Christian feel good, God and His Law, as our Schoolmaster, have only one end: our peace. "That we might be justified by faith" (Gal. 3:24) and "have peace with God through our Lord Jesus Christ" (Rom. 5:1). Peace with God is what Jesus wants for us; but, His peace and His power to overcome happen only through our wrestling under His conviction and condemnation of sin, and our accepting His arrows of shame and humiliation. He doesn't afflict happily; our mischievous duplicity forces Him to afflict. But, the wounds of the best Friend work on the heart and are the most faithful. (See Lamentations 3:33; Proverbs 27:6).

Our sin natures, our distrust of reproof, have made it difficult for us to bow to correction and reproof.

> Now no chastening for the present seemeth to be joyous, but grievous: nevertheless afterward it yieldeth the peaceable fruit of righteousness unto them which are exercised thereby (Heb. 12:11).
>
> Then the LORD answered Job out of the whirlwind, and said, Who is this that darkeneth counsel by words without knowledge? Gird up now thy loins like a man; for I will demand of thee, and answer thou me. Where wast thou when I laid the foundations of the earth? declare, if thou hast understanding (Job 38:1-4).
>
> Gird up thy loins now like a man: I will demand of thee, and declare thou unto me. Wilt thou also disannul my judgment? *wilt thou condemn me, that thou mayest be righteous?* (Job 40:7, 8).

The Lord is saying that if we don't allow His Law the authority to reprove and correct us, then we have declared *ourselves* righteous and have no need of God's necessary, heavy rectifying. We condemn God for correcting our self-acclaimed righteous nature. We recuse ourselves from judgment. We excuse ourselves from God's judgment on us because we have already made our own. We have self-made righteousness; we are self-righteous. If we excuse ourselves from the uncomfortable work of reproof by the Comforter, then Satan has convinced us that we are bigger and wiser than God. We magnify ourselves even to the Prince of the host. We stand up against the Prince of princes (see Daniel 8:11, 25) when we refuse to stand before the righteousness of God. We say, "I...shall see no sorrow" (Rev 18:7).

Ye shall be as gods (Gen. 3:5).

If we utilize our own limited self-made punishment in order to avoid God's much more painful consequences for our sin, then we save ourselves. But, if we patiently wait for God to bring us all the way out of the troubles He sends, then He is the cause of our salvation. He is our Saviour from sin and we have certainty of His salvation.

If we don't think we deserve His condemnation, then we condemn God for His lack of good judgment to scourge us and chastise our peace (See 1 John 1:8). This lesson is for even the most austere commandment-keepers (as Job was). Those strong statements from Jesus through Ellen White, which make us sweat, are really blessings in disguise. Like nothing else can, the Law will shake us out of the proud, yet fatal, self-management of our faulty habits and addictions, and bring us to a deathly need of divine mercy and help. Then, the prayer is sincere, "God *be merciful* to me *a sinner*" (Luke 18:13), and opens the ear of the Almighty.

> Job answered the LORD, and said,... Hear, I beseech thee, and I will speak: I will *demand* of thee, and *declare* thou unto me. I have heard of thee by the hearing of the ear: but now mine eye seeth thee. Wherefore *I abhor myself*, and repent in dust and ashes (Job 42:1, 4-6).

Once Job humbled himself and repented before God and His Law, then he was justified and at peace, and lived a happy, long life (see verses 10-17).

When God has chastised us, and we've abhorred ourselves and confessed to Jesus our great need for Him, then He will immediately give us the faith that boldly takes us straight through the veil to God's mercy seat and surrenders our will to His holiness. (See 1 John 1:9; Romans 12:3; Hebrews 4:16; 10:19, 20; Luke 18:7, 8.) Desperate faith in His gracious authority justifies us and makes us whole. But, such desperate faith and surrender are born out of God's threatening curses against our sins, filtered by the warm, gracious humanity of Jesus who died to deliver us from self-will. Beside the strong Law and humbling Saviour there can be no other way back to God's paradise. The straight Testimony of Jesus ultimately gives us a solid faith, a faith which we know God has moved in our behalf to give us.

> He brought me up also out of an horrible pit, out of the miry clay, and set my feet upon a rock, and established my goings (Ps. 40:2).

> The law of the LORD is perfect, converting the soul (Ps. 19:7).

"*Look* upon Jesus... Father, *impute* His life unto me... *Cover* with His life, whiter than snow" (*Cover with His life, Seventh-day Adventist Hymnal*, # 412. Emphasis mine.) *Yes, in the form of a command, strong need makes bold requests for God's mercy and acceptance. And strong need obtains His strong mercy at the throne of grace. There is no stronger argument before God than great need.*

> Lord, I believe; **help** thou mine unbelief (Mark 9:24).

> God be merciful to me a sinner (Luke 18:13).

These bold, helpless demands are the faith of Jesus, the only faith that God accepts (see Galatians 2:16; Romans 3:22). Without this kind of faith it is impossible to please Him.

> *I will not let thee go, except thou bless me* (Gen. 32:26).

> *Give him no rest*, till he establish, and till he make Jerusalem a praise in the earth (Isa. 62:7).

He commands us to give Him no rest until He helps. That is His command. But, we can only speak so strongly *when He has humbled us by His Law and we are ready to come in line with His will*. And His Law is the reproving Testimony of Jesus (see Revelation 19:10; 12:17) given at this last hour to facilitate the fullest surrender of the Seventh-day Adventists. Before the father in Mark 9:24 could have that bold helplessness, Jesus had to rebuke him. "If thou canst believe, all things are possible to him that believeth" (Mark 9:23). Through His strong rebuke Christ gave repentance to the man, and forgiveness.

Once surrendered to the reproof of God's Law, we are like the focused toddler when it realizes mommy and daddy are missing, and our cries reach all the way to His throne. "Our great need is itself an argument and pleads most eloquently in our behalf" *Steps to Christ*, p. 95. The humbling and great need have purified our demands, and we take hold of His strength. Surrendered to the Law of God, we become susceptible to the cross of Christ. In the shadow of the cross, we are divinely born again and become little people in a kingdom where the least are "great" and the weak "strong" (Isa. 53:12, cf Joel 3:10).

If we've been humbled by the Law or by the consequences for disobeying it, and are brought to the goodness of Jesus, then we are "in Christ", in His family, under His parenting and the molding influence of His eternal words. Divine reprimand drove into us the need for a Saviour from sin, and we searched for Jesus with all our heart until we found Him (see Jeremiah 29:14). We prove that His Law still has omnipresent authority and we have every right to God's eternal home (see Romans 3:31; Revelation 22:14; Matthew 5:17-19).

> To turn aside the right of a man before the face of the most High, to subvert a man in his cause, the Lord approveth not (Lam. 3:35, 36).

Thus, in His spiritual Petri dish of sins rightfully condemned, God's heated testing solidifies the substance of our hope into faith. We receive the "faith of Jesus" (Rom. 3:22), the "power to become the sons of God… which were born, not of blood, nor of the will of the flesh, nor of the will of man, but of God" (John 1:12, 13). Submitting to both His merciful furnace of offense (see Isaiah 48:10) and then His cool waters of life "that go softly" (Isa. 8:6, cf Ps. 23:2), comforted by His staff after His rod has removed our self-will, we are transformed into new and living foot soldiers to do battle for the Lord, His "exceeding great army" (Eze. 37:10). We will remember the pit of sin from which we were saved and will remain humbled by the memory (see Isaiah 51:1; Deuteronomy 9:1-6).

Sweet faith does not come easily. The Lord makes His newborns suck it from His reproving stone Law. That way He births extraordinarily healthy dynamos.

Sweet faith does not come easily. The Lord makes His newborns suck it from His reproving stone Law. (See Deuteronomy 32:13.) That way He births extraordinarily healthy dynamos. God's children today who will wrestle with and surrender to His Law will become a host of Samsons for His last great work. (See Isaiah 8:18; Psalm 18; Zechariah 12:10, 6-8, 3.) After knowing the great offenses of the offensive Law of God against our sins, nothing else can offend us! (See Psalm 119:165.)

> It is God that girdeth me with strength, and maketh my way perfect. He maketh my feet like hinds' feet, and setteth me upon my high places. He teacheth my hands to war, so that a bow of steel is broken by mine arms. Thou hast also given me the shield of thy salvation: and thy right hand hath holden me up, and thy gentleness hath made me great (Ps. 18:32-35).

> Blessed be the LORD my strength, which teacheth my hands to war, and my fingers to fight: my goodness, and my fortress; my high tower, and my deliverer; my shield, and he in whom I trust; who subdueth my people under me (Ps. 144:1, 2).

Only those who wrestle with God's condemnation and overcome it with surrender receive the new name of Israel. They become part of the true apostolic succession and possess heaven's spiritual authority. (See Genesis 32:28; Philippians 3:3; Galatians 6:16; Matthew 16:18, 19; Mark 16:17, 18; John 20:23.)

The account of Job shows us that God's word must come on strong (see Job 38:1-3; 40:6-8). This is not because He loves to overpower the sinner but because that's the only way to shut down our Goliath pride. Leviathan, the towering Old Testament Dragon-like beast, which Revelation borrows to represent the great destroyer Apollyon (see Isaiah 27:1; Daniel 7:25; 8:10; Revelation 12:3, 9; 13:1, 6; 9:11; 11:7), is "king over all the children of pride" (Job 41:1, 34). Without God's chastising, humbling truth, we will remain forever captives of our natural born arrogance, shut away from Christ and forever shut out from sweet faith (see Galatians 3:23). "Thou hast rebuked the proud that are cursed, which do err from thy commandments" (Ps. 119:21). But "Christ…[was] made a curse for us" (Gal. 3:13, 14) and has absorbed all of God's rebukes, so that the blessing of Abraham may come to us, and we can receive the promised reconciled Spirit of our Father.

Remember the burning Gethsemane and Golgotha experience of Jesus. He endured all of God's hatred of our sinfulness in order for us to be willing to have our stubborn resistance washed away and make us able to live by the standard of holiness. "It is as high as heaven; what canst thou do? deeper than hell; what canst thou know?" (Job 11:8). Yes, it is a standard high, deep, and broad; and only Jesus' humbling can help us fulfill it. That high standard is given to Protestantism today to enable us to stand in the day of God (see Psalm 1:4, 5; Revelation 6:17; 7:2; Isaiah 8:16). Beauty and divine love are in the pages of the Spirit of Prophecy counsels once we have surrendered to them. Surrendering to God's Law through the Spirit of Christ is the great triumph of life; surrendering is the victory that leads us to Jesus and then on to all other victories (see Psalm 1:2, 3; James 2:21, 22; Deuteronomy 32:47; Romans 4:20-22; Genesis 18:19; 22:6-13; John 8:56; Hebrews 10:36; 1 John 5:4). Surrender to the Law is the very first work (see Romans 7:25). It demands effort; it's not easy. *But it's the gift that keeps on giving*; it is "everlasting life" (John 4:14). "Great peace have they which love thy law" (Ps. 119:165).

Be strong and of good courage before the Testimony of Jesus, and dare to look at the powerful language of truth found in the law of His mouth (see Joshua 1:7, 8). Continue therein (see James 1:25; John 8:31) and "let patience have her perfect work, that ye may be perfect and entire, wanting nothing" (Jas. 1:4). Trust the Lord to reward all of His children with gleams of His acceptance and love. As their hardened, unwilling hearts begin gradually to give way they finally bow their resistance, born into faith and righteousness, wisdom and confidence (see Proverbs 4:18; John 3:21; Galatians 3:24-26).

> He that hath my commandments, and keepeth them, he it is that loveth me: and he that loveth me shall be loved of my Father, and I will love him, and will manifest myself to him…. If a man love me, he will keep my words: and my Father will love him, and we will come unto him, and make our abode with him (John 14:21, 23).

Love from Jesus present in our soul is an overpowering incentive for keeping His commandments. But, turning away our ear from hearing His Law means we have new-modeled the true religion from Jesus (see *The Great Controversy*, p. 385.1). That leaves us with a religion empty of His Spirit of truth, a religion of pure emotion that will be blown away in the rapidly advancing winds of strife and the soon catastrophic day of His coming when the heavens fall. New-modeling the cause of truth is what Satan wants; and, either God's immutable truth or Satan's remodeling the truth presides over our receiving the sealing or the mark.

Say No to Spiritual Formation which purports to offer the goodness of God, but has no power to humble proud hearts and sanctify into true, natural obedience. *No* to that new-modeled religion, even of today's smooth Adventist variant, because it is not authorized by the Bible (see Romans 2:13; 3:19; 3:31; 2 Timothy 4:2). The Adventist variant of Spiritual Formation is still the same old eastern mystical gift of the gods, which our Reformation and Advent fathers never knew. Its refusal of reproof and correction fits the identical template of the iniquitous, smooth and lustrous Baal religion and every other spiritualistic religion and worship since the beginning of time. It gradually leads its adherents to work lawlessness (see Jeremiah 6:14-16; 19:5; 23:13, 14, 32; John 16:2; Revelation 17:4-6). Spiritual Formation is spiritualism, the abomination of desolation. It is the gall of the third trumpet that came after the denominations rejected the Law from Mount Sinai. Spiritual Formation is the ancient seed of the "infidel hardihood" and "basest iniquity", quoted above from *The Great Controversy*, p. 603. As it soothes the conscience it slowly usurps the conscience. To the Spiritual Formation votives Jesus says, Why do you call Me Lord and not do the hard things I say? I never knew you. Depart from Me, all of you workers of iniquity. (See Luke 6:46; John 6:60, 61; Matthew 7:21-23; Matthew 5:19; John 15:14.)

The fourth trumpet blows. Now that Satan had control of our Reformation brethren's doctrine and hearts, their light went out (see Revelation 8:12). They no longer carried the biblical torch of truth.

> Thus saith the LORD concerning the prophets that make my people err, that bite with their teeth, and cry, Peace; and he that putteth not into their mouths, they even prepare war against him. Therefore night shall be unto you, that ye shall not have a vision; and it shall be dark unto you, that ye shall not divine; and the sun shall go down over the prophets, and the day shall be dark over them. Then shall the seers be ashamed, and the diviners confounded: yea, they shall all cover their lips; for there is no answer of God (Mic. 3:5-7).

The Bible makes much less sense to the popular denominations as they intensely contradict the solid truth that God has given the Seventh-day Adventists. All the Protestants can still be saved as could all the Jews in Paul's day, but not by stubbornly remaining in their synagogues of Satan. They must come out individually or as congregations, and throw their allegiance with the heavenly light which the Adventists have received from the first trumpet during this present investigative judgment period. They must endure the "burning and … shining light" (John 5:35) of the Spirit of Prophecy.

At a meeting of the presbytery of Philadelphia, Mr. Barnes, author of a commentary widely used and pastor of one of the leading churches in that city, "stated that he had been in the ministry for twenty years, and never, till the last Communion, had he administered the ordinance without receiving more or less into the church. But now there are *no awakenings*, *no conversions*, not much apparent growth in grace in professors, and none come to his study to converse about the salvation of their souls. With the increase of business, and the brightening prospects of commerce and manufacture, there is an increase of worldly-mindedness. *Thus it is with all the denominations.*" *Congregational Journal*, May 23, 1844 *The Great Controversy*, p. 376.

In the month of February of the same year, Professor Finney of Oberlin College said: "We have had the fact before our minds, that, in general, the Protestant churches of our country, as such, were either apathetic or hostile to nearly all the moral reforms of the age. There are partial exceptions, yet not enough to render the fact otherwise than general. We have also another corroborated fact: the almost universal absence of revival influence in the churches. The spiritual apathy is almost all-pervading, and is fearfully deep; so the religious press of the whole land testifies.... Very extensively, church members are becoming devotees of fashion, — join hands with the ungodly in parties of pleasure, in dancing, in festivities, etc.... But we need not expand this painful subject. Suffice it that the evidence thickens and rolls heavily upon us, to show that the *churches generally are becoming sadly degenerate*. They have gone very far from the Lord, and He has withdrawn Himself from them Ibid., p. 377.

Thou sayest, Because I am innocent, surely his anger shall turn from me. Behold, I will plead with thee, because thou sayest, I have not sinned. Why gaddest thou about so much to change thy way? thou also shalt be ashamed [because] of Egypt, as thou wast ashamed [because] of Assyria. Yea, thou shalt go forth from him, and thine hands upon thine head: for the LORD hath rejected thy confidences, and thou shalt not prosper in them (Jer. 2:35-37).

Their copying Catholic Europe and having forgotten the fear of God, He would let the Protestants' new nation humble them as the papal persecutions had.

Those who had great light from the Reformation had become lackadaisical in their land of refuge. The Reformation descendants "waxed fat, and kicked" (Deut. 32:15). Like Israel of old, their faith had become spoiled by God's provisions and protection. "When they knew God, they glorified him not as God, neither were thankful" (Rom. 1:21, cf Col. 3:15). They lost the power of His Spirit which had attended the Reformers and the generation that had faced the terrorism of the Counter-Reformation. The children of the martyrs lost the willingness to die to self. The Protestant fervor had cooled and their religion turned into formality and mere respectability. Without the power of faith in God's grace through His Law, they could not stand up before the power of testing biblical truth.

Each individual among the Sunday churches who continued to fight the message of Christ's second coming and to smear the Seventh-day Adventist cause, was searing his conscience toward Bible truth, and the Spirit of truth permanently departed from that Protestant. God's Spirit cannot strive forever against rebellion. So, although individual Protestants may today still come out and receive the blessing of His Spirit, the Lord's protection had expired for the denominations as institutions. After a couple of centuries of uninterrupted departing, they stumbled over the Lord's seventh day Sabbath stumblingstone and the door of mercy finally went shut on Protestantism. The door of God's truth went forever shut on the Protestant denominations, as organized bodies, and opened to the Advent movement. (See Isaiah 8:14-16; 1 Samuel 15:23, 26-29; Luke 13:24, 25; Revelation 3:7-9; Romans 11:32.) Now there was little sunlight to rule the day or moonlight to rule the night for the Protestant churches. "Let their eyes be darkened, that they may not see, and bow down their back alway" (Rom. 11:10). "If therefore thine eye be single, thy whole body shall be full of light. But if thine eye be evil, thy whole body shall be full of darkness. If therefore the light that is in thee be darkness, how great is that darkness!" (Matt. 6:22, 23). However, those Protestants who lived by all the light they received could still say, "Thou wilt light my candle: the LORD my God will enlighten my darkness" (Ps. 18:28).

The fourth trumpet judges that at this point in the trumpets prophecy, the leadership of the Protestant churches were brought under the power of the prince of darkness, as many within Protestantism rejoiced in the new delusion of an abolished moral Law. The new celebration was the opening that Satan desired for his entrance. The Law of God is perfect, converting the soul; and the lawlessness of the devil is corrupt, perverting the soul. Therefore, the Protestant denominations were no longer useable by heaven, any more than God could use the Jews after their Judaism had for centuries clung to the influence of Babylon (see Malachi 2:11).

> God hath not cast away *his people which he foreknew*....
>
> Even so then at this present time also there is *a remnant according to the election of grace*....
>
> What then? Israel hath not obtained that which he seeketh for; but *the election hath obtained it*, and *the rest were blinded*....
>
> If by any means I may provoke to emulation them which are my flesh, and might save *some of them*.
>
> For if the casting away of them be the reconciling of the world, what shall the receiving of them be, but life from the dead?...
>
> For I would not, brethren, that ye should be ignorant of this mystery, lest ye should be wise in your own conceits; that *blindness in part* is happened to Israel, until the fulness of the Gentiles be come in....
>
> For God hath concluded them all in unbelief, that he might have mercy upon all (Rom. 11:2, 5, 7, 14, 15, 25, 32).

The Lord had permanently cast away the nation of Israel as a group (see Matthew 21:43; John 9:39-41; Daniel 9:27), yet He had preserved His "remnant of Jacob" (Isa. 10:21, cf Isa. 59:20; Rom. 9:27; 11:26, 27), as He had promised (see Genesis 17:11-7; 22:16-18; 26:3-5; 28:13-15; Deuteronomy 32:43; Leviticus 26:41; Jeremiah 31:21, 33-37). His elect "whom I reserve" (Jer. 50:20, cf Isa. 65:9; Rom. 11:7; John 15:16-19) would be chosen for *their willingness to be corrected and humbled*, and to accept His faithful, self-sacrificing love (see Isaiah 26:1-4; Jeremiah 31:28, 33; Leviticus 26:41; Proverbs 6:20-23). Today, the Lord's policy has not changed for His church. And, has not Adventism begun to follow the Sunday Protestants' course of avoiding heaven-sent reproof and instruction? How can He accept this wrong direction of His remnant if He would not accept the Jews' copying the corrupted northern Israelites? Or Protestantism returning to papal grace-based lawlessness? (See Jeremiah 3:6-10.) He cannot accept it, and will soon punish us with neo-Babylon as He did the Jews of Jeremiah's day.

Therefore, that same judgment in which the Sunday denominations failed goes out to test the rest of a world partaking of heaven's freedoms and prosperity through the Protestants. "My Spirit shall not always strive with man, for that he also is flesh: yet his days shall be..." (Gen. 6:3). Humanity's days would be numbered, during which a remnant out of it would be gleaned. (See Isaiah 6:10-12; 10:23.)

Although God had many, many of His true children in the Sunday churches, the denominations *as institutions* were coming under another Dark Age of ignorance concerning God's character. They were fully preparing to be influenced by Satan to enforce his favorite tool of enslavement — ignorance of the Bible, and the union of religion and state (see Revelation 13:11-15). John sees an angel flying in the midst of heaven, crying out, "Woe, woe, woe, to the inhabiters of the earth by reason of the other voices of the trumpet of the three angels, which are yet to sound!" (Rev. 8:13). The first four trumpets affected the early American Protestants who still looked holy, at least compared to Europe, but who the soul searching God had prejudged, tested, and found deficient. (See Revelation 3:1.) He saw them as the rotted bow of a tree that seemed healthy until the wind blew hard. Then, it came down; "and great was the fall of it" (Matt. 7:27, cf Isa. 10:33, 34).

At this point in Revelation's prophetic drama the desolating work of Satan goes out to affect the whole world which today still lives under divine beneficence granted to the Reformation. These blessings to the nations come by God through America's Protestant Constitution of civil and religious liberty, its Republicanism, freedoms, and civil peace, and their by-products in creativity and invention. The world owes everything to the Lord for this age of light which He has provided it through His liberating religion of Law-loving Protestantism, the Protestant Bible, and His Constitution that provides a refuge for it. Yet, even at an early stage of American history, by 1844 the Protestants had set their God aside, they had neither recognized nor praised Him from hearts of unfeigned faith. They would not bow their pride to His humbling Law. Our forbearing Creator was not even believed to exist by many among the Reformation descendants who were carelessly enjoying His land that flowed with milk and honey and His showers of blessings, unthankful and unmindful of His great generosity.

And now, generations later, the full fruition of their 19th century apostasy is such that the children of this Protestant nation have completely lost their Reformation heritage. No differently than did the northern Israelites, ten thousand times ten thousand and thousands of thousands of Protestant Americans live their lives oblivious of God's handiwork around them, and of their place in His family tree. "Behold, this was the iniquity of… Sodom, pride, fulness of bread, and abundance of idleness was in her" (Eze. 16:49). Multitudes have no faith but in a secular god and its molten images; others, in the churches, have lost their Protestantism and their justification truth, and have returned to mother Rome for her soothing sorceries. Protestantism within the denominations has been scattered to the winds. Today, almost all the Protestants are feeding on husks because they cannot admit the powerful conviction of their Bible's Law. God's Law is disallowed and set to the side by the new Protestant doctrine. Glory to God is negligible in America, even in the churches, because "the carnal mind is enmity against God: for it is not subject to the law of God, neither indeed can be" (Rom. 8:7). Carelessness reigns, and the great Judge calls to many among Protestant America today, "Shall I not visit for these things? saith the LORD: and shall not my soul be avenged on such a nation as this?" (Jer. 5:9).

The trumpets of the final three angels call out a loud warning to the world — "Woe", "woe", "woe", "to the inhabiters of the earth" (Rev. 8:13), to "every nation, and kindred, and tongue, and people" (Rev. 14:6)! The last trumpets' call brings the final test to Americans and then spreads out to encompass the world. The human advocates of God's word are disqualified, and God puts them aside. He sets up the courtroom and lays out the evidence for the final conviction upon Protestantism. The verdict: "I looked, and there was none to help; and I wondered that there was none to uphold: therefore mine own arm brought salvation unto me; and my fury, it upheld me. And I will tread down the people in mine anger, and make them drunk in my fury, and I will bring down their strength to the earth" (Isa. 63:5, 6).

> Jeshurun waxed fat, and kicked: thou art waxen fat, thou art grown thick, thou art covered with fatness; then he forsook God which made him, and lightly esteemed the Rock of his salvation.
>
> They provoked him to jealousy with strange gods, with abominations provoked they him to anger.
>
> They sacrificed unto devils, not to God; to gods whom they knew not, *to new gods that came newly up, whom your fathers feared not.*
>
> Of the Rock that begat thee thou art unmindful, and hast forgotten God that formed thee.
>
> And when the LORD saw it, he abhorred them, because of the provoking of his sons, and of his daughters.
>
> And he said, I will hide my face from them, I will see what their end shall be: for they are a very froward generation, children in whom is no faith.
>
> They have moved me to jealousy with that which is not God; they have provoked me to anger with their vanities: and I will move them to jealousy with those which are not a people; I will provoke them to anger with a foolish nation.
>
> For a fire is kindled in mine anger, and shall burn unto the lowest hell, and shall consume the earth with her increase, and set on fire the foundations of the mountains.
>
> I will heap mischiefs upon them; I will spend mine arrows upon them.
>
> They shall be burnt with hunger, and devoured with burning heat, and with bitter destruction: I will also send the teeth of beasts upon them, with the poison of serpents of the dust.
>
> The sword without, and terror within, shall destroy both the young man and the virgin, the suckling also with the man of gray hairs.
>
> I said, I would scatter them into corners, I would make the remembrance of them to cease from among men:…
>
> For they are a nation void of counsel, neither is there any understanding in them.
>
> O that they were wise, that they understood this, that they would consider their latter end!

How should one chase a thousand, and two put ten thousand to flight, except their Rock had sold them, and the LORD had shut them up?

For their rock is not as our Rock, even our enemies themselves being judges.

For their vine is of the vine of Sodom, and of the fields of Gomorrah: their grapes are grapes of gall, their clusters are bitter:

Their wine is the poison of dragons, and the cruel venom of asps.

Is not this laid up in store with me, and sealed up among my treasures?

To me belongeth vengeance, and recompence; their foot shall slide in due time: for the day of their calamity is at hand, and the things that shall come upon them make haste.

For the LORD shall judge his people, and repent himself for his servants, when he seeth that their power is gone, and there is none shut up, or left.

And he shall say, Where are their gods, their rock in whom they trusted, Which did eat the fat of their sacrifices, and drank the wine of their drink offerings? let them rise up and help you, and be your protection.

See now that I, even I, am he, and there is no god with me: I kill, and I make alive; I wound, and I heal: neither is there any that can deliver out of my hand.

For I lift up my hand to heaven, and say, I live for ever.

If I whet my glittering sword, and mine hand take hold on judgment; I will render vengeance to mine enemies, and will reward them that hate me.

I will make mine arrows drunk with blood, and my sword shall devour flesh; and that with the blood of the slain and of the captives, from the beginning of revenges upon the enemy.

Rejoice, O ye nations, with his people: for he will avenge the blood of his servants, and will render vengeance to his adversaries, and will be merciful unto his land, and to his people (Deut. 32:15-43).

Judgment first began with the house of God, and a small Adventist Remnant of the Reformation was handed the torch of truth (see 1 Peter 4:17, 18). But, will that Remnant fend off Baal (*Ba'al*, "the Lord") through the Remnant's own period of probation and testing (see Jude 5; Ezekiel 9:4-10)?

O generation, see ye the word of the LORD. Have I been a wilderness unto Israel? a land of darkness? wherefore say my people, We are lords; we will come no more unto thee? Can a maid forget her ornaments, or a bride her attire? yet my people have forgotten me days without number (Jer. 2:31, 32).

All the promises and mental pictures of Jesus that we have gathered up in the previous chapters will need to be soundly stored in our minds, and reflected on again. The next chapter is even heavier with bad news, but the beautiful promises from Jesus will carry us through its long, dark tunnel and then on to the glories of chapter 10, on the other side.

Chapter 6
Revelation Chapter 9: The Strong Delusion

The fifth trumpet sounds. By the choice of His own Protestant children, the Lord can no longer restrain their enemy. They have chosen another master. Satan, the great star fallen from heaven which poisoned the Sunday churches during the third trumpet, is now given the key to the abyss (Gr. *abussos*). No longer fettered by God, Satan opens the bottomless pit and out comes his influence, the blackest, densest smoke, let loose to scourge the earth with his spiritualistic charms.

> Hell hath enlarged herself, and opened her mouth without measure (Isa. 5:14).

Pillars of darkness escaping hell's gaping mouth immediately begin to eclipse faith in God all over the earth (see Revelation 9:2). After Satan's billowing demonic agencies follow his Beast's servants (see Revelation 9:3; 11:7). The agents of the Beast gradually grow into an uncountable army, and unaccountable to anyone except Satan. Millions of his demon and human hosts, and their temptations and deceptions, are sent to lead Protestantism and their global dominion to depart from the God of Abraham, completely and forever. Are they not all deceiving spirits sent forth to delude those who will be heirs of damnation?

The Protestants of the United States will be foremost in stretching their hands across the gulf to grasp the hand of spiritualism; they will reach over the abyss to clasp hands with the Roman power; and under the influence of this threefold union, this country will follow in the steps of Rome in trampling on the rights of conscience *The Great Controversy*, p. 588.

The Bible declares that before the coming of the Lord, Satan will work "with all power and signs and lying wonders, and with all deceivableness of unrighteousness;" and they that "received not the love of the truth, that they might be saved," will be left to receive "strong delusion, that they should believe a lie." 2 Thessalonians 2:9-11. Not until this condition shall be reached, and the union of the church with the world shall be fully accomplished throughout Christendom, will the fall of Babylon be complete. The change is a progressive one *Ibid.*, p. 389.

Satan's purpose is to lead Protestants to become a persecuting power (see Revelation 13:11), imitating his Papacy from which they had fled three centuries earlier. The Protestant apostasy would repeat the progression of the papal power which the destroyer had built out of the once pure apostolic church — to remove them from the powerful Law of God and true grace of Jesus. Then they can never know the rest and peace of salvation, until the lack of peace consumes them and they seek retribution upon those they deem unbelieving or heretical. God grants Satan's voracious locust-like agencies, spirit and human, permission to devour every individual in whose heart the love of this world has supplanted faith in his Creator. In their demon driven domination of the earth, the locusts consume the knowledge of Jehovah's character in everyone enjoying the blessings He has given the world through His biblical, peacemaking laws to Protestantism. The only exceptions of this overspreading of abominations are those who fear God, their Father in heaven. They obey Him, in humility give Him glory, and receive His Seal in their forehead. This sealing of the forehead, which we saw in the Revelation chapter 7 account, prepares a group to stand in the tumultuous day of God. (See Revelation 7:3 and 9:4.)

> And I saw another angel ascending from the east, having the seal[G4973] [Gr. *sphragis*, "signet", "stamp", "fencing"] of the living God: and he cried with a loud voice to the four angels, to whom it was given to hurt the earth and the sea, saying, Hurt not the earth, neither the sea, nor the trees, till we have sealed[G4972] [Gr. *sphragizō*, "to stamp", "to attest"] the servants of our God in their foreheads (Rev. 7:2, 3).

> Just as soon as the people of God are sealed in their foreheads — it is not any seal or mark that can be seen, but a settling into the truth, both intellectually and spiritually, so they cannot be moved — just as soon as God's people are sealed and prepared for the shaking, it will come. Indeed, it has begun already; the judgments of God are now upon the land, to give us warning, that we may know what is coming *Maranatha*, p. 200.

And what is the Seal in their forehead? It is the gift of Christ's perfect communion and His character being implanted *permanently* in the mind and heart of God's people, during the investigative judgment. The Seal is the Spirit of Christ given in special abundance to the needy ones for obedience to all of God's commandments during this hour of trumpet temptations (see Deuteronomy 6:8; Revelation 3:10; Ephesians 1:13,14). So, in the end God can say, "He that is holy, let him be holy still" (Rev. 22:11).

Sphragizō ("to attest") is related to G3140 *martureo* ("to testify", "to bear witness/record"); G3141 *marturia* ("testimony", "witness", "record"); G3142 *marturion* ("to be testified", "testimony", "witness"); G3144 *martus* ("a witness"). *Marturia* is used by John whenever he speaks of both the witness of the Spirit and the Testimony of Jesus, which he also called the "spirit of prophecy" (Rev. 19:10, cf Rev. 1:9). So, there is a connection between the Seal of God stamped in their forehead and the Testimony of Jesus, which is the gift of prophecy. The Spirit of Christ impresses the Seal of God — His approval and authority and wisdom — deeply upon their characters, inscribing His word line upon line into their surrendered consciences. It is the work exclusive to His Spirit to fortify their consciences with an exceptional abhorrence of sin through the Law, exceptional convictions from His self-sacrificing life and death, and thereby they receive an exceptional consecration and reward of grace and love. The exceptional conviction comes through the light for this special time, shining from the Bible and the writings of Ellen White. Every soul who will go there will know the clearest biblical descriptions of right- and wrong-doing. Those who will not refuse the reproofs and counsels of Ellen White are brought to a deep need for a Saviour from sin, deeper than in all previous earth's history. Surrendering to the especially strong instruction and correction, only they receive authentic, especially strong grace from heaven at this time, the blessing that Jacob received under the same conditions (see Genesis 32:24-29).

More than in preceding ages, they can purify themselves, *"even as [Jesus] is pure"* (1 John 3:3), so that "when he shall appear, we shall be like him; for we shall see him as he is" (1 John 3:2). Once surrendered to the special condemnation of sin, their crucified Redeemer then controls their heart, their tastes, their intellect, and their will. "The expulsion of sin is the act of the soul itself" *The Desire of Ages*, p. 466. They have a natural affinity to Jesus and so a natural avocation to heed His words. Thus, the Law of His mouth works itself out in their life. Faith works out the conviction that is in them; the Law is worked out by Jesus who is the source and the object of their faith, the focus of their love.

He hath done all things well (Mark 7:37).

They have come to Jesus for His shielding intercession from the condemnation of God. They need His help to overcome their inherited and cultivated tendencies to sin, made clear by the letter of God's Law and by the Spirit of Christ's blood. Jesus' grace from His sanctuary has extended all the way to their heart; and His grace has strengthened their faith which can reach all the way to His presence. He has changed their heart; their conversation is on heaven. What they hated before, now they love; what they loved they now hate. The vain and supercilious become serious and unobtrusive. They have a joy to listen and learn from Him, so that His teachings efficiently enter the conscience, the will, and the faculties of the memory and intellect. Therefore, they imitate Him naturally, easily, spontaneously, at will (see Mark 7:37; Philippians 2:12, 13; Matthew 11:29; 1 Samuel 18:5; Psalm1:3; Hebrews 10:9, 10).

> His delight is in the law of the LORD; and in his law doth he meditate day and night.
>
> And he shall be like a tree planted by the rivers of water, that bringeth forth his fruit in his season; his leaf also shall not wither; and whatsoever he doeth shall prosper.
>
> The ungodly are not so: but are like the chaff which the wind driveth away (Ps. 1:2-4).

Little by little Jesus increasingly ingrains His Father's Law into this group throughout the progression of the fifth and sixth trumpet sealing. But, competing with the testimony of Jesus is the almost overwhelming confusion of faith that Satan brings upon the world to shake the people of the Lord. Satan is determined that everyone who can be shaken will be shaken. Simultaneous with the Lord growing His 144,000, the demonically driven locusts and smoke play their role in creating a grand delusion to prevent His Spirit from sealing the whole of humanity (see Revelation 9:4). In the darkness, the holy people — the people of the Book — must stretch all their powers to see the Saviour's compassion and to be certain of His care for them.

> These are they which came out of great tribulation, and have washed their robes, and made them white in the blood of the Lamb (Rev. 7:14).

Over time, even over generations, the faith of this group lodges so solidly in Jehovah that it can never be removed. Those who continue to receive Christ and His conviction during the coming days of trouble receive the Seal of God and become the people "having his Father's name written in their foreheads" (Rev. 14:1). Their sealing is greater than that which the apostolic church received, even as the Day of Atonement was a higher Sabbath than Pentecost.

They don't lose the first love. God's true character is "written" or impressed into their softened hearts. He is all that they can think and talk about. These convicted and converted ones strive for and keep unbroken faith and communion with their Lord (see 2 Timothy 4:7). The Seal results in such genuine, lasting change of heart toward God that Jesus' life and His words fasten forever into their minds (see John 14:15, 21, 23).

> While the investigative judgment is going forward in heaven, while the sins of penitent believers are being removed from the sanctuary, there is to be a special work of purification, of putting away of sin, among God's people upon earth *The Great Controversy*, p. 425.
>
> Beloved, now are we the sons of God, and it doth not yet appear what we shall be: but we know that, when he shall appear, we shall be like him; for we shall see him as he is. And every man that hath this hope in him purifieth himself, even as he is pure (1 John 3:2, 3).

Once sealed by constant faith, perfectly reproducing Jesus' seal (see John 6:27; Job 1:1, 10), they are mercifully hedged in, "fenced in" by the Spirit of God and the holy angels, and protected from the gross atheism/unbelief darkening the land (see Isaiah 42:19, 20). "The angel of the LORD encampeth round about them that fear Him, and delivereth them" (Ps. 34:7). During the fifth trumpet, and later more so in the sixth trumpet, Jesus would accomplish this special work of purification to prepare a people for translation on the day of His return. As time would advance throughout the remaining three trumpets, Jesus would raise the standard higher and higher, from faith to faith, grace to grace, and glory to glory, leading His captivity captive so that He could grace them with the fruits and the gifts of His Spirit. Concurrently, Satan would step up the insinuating temptations of his spirit..

This fifth trumpet's work is to bring the Protestant world to a decision. Although Jesus is our merciful Saviour, only the condemnation of sin through the strong words from God, or the longer, more difficult consequences for disregarding His strong words, can humble us and bring us to the saving need of an Intercessor before God. "Now we know that what things soever the law saith, it saith to them who are under the law: that every mouth may be stopped, and all the world may become guilty before God" (Rom. 3:19). Strong condemnation and conviction from the Law alone can lead them to the only valid need of an Advocate for every sin. During the investigative judgment this age-old process is magnified and compressed for the final sealing.

> The law of the LORD is perfect, converting the soul (Ps. 19:7).

Because Protestantism follows Satan in denying God's Law the authority to condemn and convict of sin, God must allow Satan to lay his claim on the many denominations and torment them with his evil presence (see Revelation 9:5; Hebrews 12:8; Isaiah 8:20-22).

In His testimony God has His indisputable, tough commandments. After our submitting to His infinite convictions, He gives us to Jesus (see John 6:37; Galatians 3:24). The ministry of Christ echoes that strong language to a lesser degree and mixes it with His strong yearning for our heart. Jesus' truth and grace, and the justice and forbearance resident in His Father's Law, provide us the only environment to accept our guilt and drive us to receive the panacea peace from our Lord that heals every physical malady. It's a peace that makes us wise to discern Satan's cunning devices against us. Although God's Law majors on truth and justice, and though it minors on grace and forbearance, He well knows the undetectable leavening power of self-exaltation in the hearts and minds of His corruptible children. So He provides us a strong message of correction because He knows we need it for our repentance and our only salvation from Judgment Day.

As the northern tribes of Israel were relatives of Judah in the south, the Protestant denominations and the Adventists come from the same spiritual, biblical stock; and we are beloved brethren (see 1 Chronicles 11:1; 1 Kings 12:24; 1 Kings 22:4; Ezekiel 23:4). We are "kinsmen" (Rom. 9:3), "fellowheirs [of God in Christ Jesus], and of the same body, and partakers of his promise in Christ by the gospel" (Eph. 3:6). The Protestant Reformation brought back from the apostolic church the message of God's grace to the sinner; and Adventism brought back the truth of Christ's coming, superadding to the gospel the powerful need for Judgment Day purification through a powerful Spirit of Prophecy. But, by making it a doctrine to reject the Law of God, the denominations deceived themselves and brought their own destruction. The Lord permitting Satan new freedom of control fulfills Paul's prophecy, "For this cause God shall send them strong delusion, that they should believe a lie: that they all might be [judged] who believed not the truth, but had pleasure in unrighteousness" (2 Thess. 2:11, 12). The apostle, no doubt, based his judgment of "strong delusion" and "pleasure in unrighteousness" on Isaiah's prophecy. "Behold, the name of the LORD cometh from far…to sift the nations with the sieve of vanity: and there shall be a bridle in the jaws of the people, causing them to err" (Isa. 30:27, 28, cf Isa. 66:4). Unrestrained pride has much to do with the Lord's final, strong delusion. The Law's tough language, an ax laid deeply at the roots of vanity, is the only escape for the last great delusion of Protestantism and of all mankind.

In the fifth and sixth trumpets symbolism the deluding destroyers take advantage of a Protestantism they have weakened, swooping in with well-planned tactics; and Protestantism capitulates. In the Lord's fifth trumpet we again see Babylon's subjugation of the ancient apostolic church, and even earlier against the nation of Israel, this time perpetrated upon the Reformation church.

> Lo, I raise up the Chaldeans, that bitter and hasty nation, which shall march through the breadth of the land (Hab. 1:6).

> An host was given him against the daily sacrifice by reason of transgression, and it cast down the truth to the ground; and it practised, and prospered (Dan. 8:12).

> And he exerciseth all the power of the first beast before him [in his sight, under his purview], and causeth the earth and them which dwell therein to worship the first beast, whose deadly wound was healed (Rev. 13:12).

> And there came out of the smoke locusts upon the earth:… And to them it was given that they should not kill them, but that they should be tormented (Rev. 9:3, 5).

There is no stopping the spiritual locusts of the fifth trumpet. Their work is to torment, doing that of which the third angel of Revelation 14 warns the whole world with respect to involvement with idolatrous worship. The locusts torment by a form of worship that doesn't heed the Law of their fathers' God (see Deuteronomy 29:18-20, 25, 26; 28:45-47; Daniel 11:37). The Sunday churches receive the bitter effects of departing from their Father and Lawgiver. The same apostasy happens to the

Chapter 6 Revelation Chapter 9: The Strong Delusion

denominations which before resulted in Satan's many possessions of ancient Israel through Baal worship and later his ownership of the apostolic dispensation by the blasphemous, vile king who lorded over the church (see Daniel 11:21-24).

All the Protestants who refuse that their sinful self-will should be grinded upon by the convicting Spirit of truth will remain uncertain of their salvation, impatient, unnerved, infected with the devouring doctrines of devils, and unable to know peace and rest. Until they surrender to heaven's monolithic mountain of Law, they are driven by an unseen force, to do and speak lawlessness, and ultimately, to do unimaginable harm. They will not hear the God-given conviction of justice and mercy from the Advent movement. So they receive the bitter effects of endless disconnection from heaven and the torment from the loss of the "holy Spirit of promise" (Eph. 1:13). They have "dimness of anguish" and are "driven to darkness" (Isa. 8:22).

Those Protestants are cut off from Jesus; they live apart from Him, from His words of life and from His blessed rest. That restful blessedness comes only by surrender to His Father's Law, then surrender to His offering on the cross. But, like their father Cain, most do not allow the condemnation of a broken Law and the dying lamb to afflict their souls. Therefore, the denominations become the Dragon's instruments to restore the headship of their old adversary from the Dark Ages.

> His power shall be mighty, but not by his own power: and he shall destroy wonderfully…and shall destroy the mighty and the holy people… and by peace shall destroy many (Dan. 8:24, 25).

> They had a king over them, which is the angel of the bottomless pit, whose name in the Hebrew tongue is Abaddon [G3 *Abaddōn*, "a destroying angel"], but in the Greek tongue hath his name Apollyon [G623 *Apolluōn*, "a destroyer"] (Rev. 9:11).

> Through spiritualism, Satan appears as a benefactor of the race, healing the diseases of the people, and professing to present a new and more exalted system of religious faith; but at the same time he works as a destroyer *The Great Controversy*, p. 589.

Shortly before this at the third trumpet's horrible wormwood bitterness (see Revelation 8:11), Satan had urged Protestant leaders to pour contempt upon Jesus'

earnest testimony through Ellen White. In exchange for the pure principles of the Bible, they led Protestant America into the excitement of spiritualistic freedom from law (see Jeremiah 23:15; 51:7; 25:27; Deuteronomy 29:18; Isaiah 51:17). Now the Protestants imbibe all that religion and the world offer to inebriate the suffering conscience and heart, and thus come to think like the tormented king of pride, called Wormwood and Apollyon (see Revelation 8:11; 9:11; Deuteronomy 32:17, 32, 33; Job 41:34).

> For thus saith the LORD God of Israel unto me; Take the wine cup of this fury at my hand, and cause all the nations, to whom I send thee, to drink it (Jer. 25:15, cf Rev. 14:8-11).

The bitterness of gall and wormwood are the churches' fruit for declining the Bible standard and serving the adversary, who gives the Protestants light and much power, but no sweet love, joy, and peace. Instead of serving God and His Law with all their heart and receiving the deep, settled rest and health that come from faith in God's beneficence, their serving the fallen angels' delusions and being captivated by temptations from Protestantism's spiritual and human antagonists are the fifth trumpet's darkness and locust torment.

> Astonishment hath taken hold on me. Is there no balm in Gilead; is there no physician there? why then is not the health of the daughter of my people recovered? (Jer. 8:21).

> They [the prophets of Baal and Ashoreth] have healed also the hurt of the daughter of my people slightly, saying, Peace, peace; when there is no peace (Jer. 6:14).

The fifth and sixth trumpets' acrid smoke and locusts are the origin of Revelation 14's third angel's message of torment and fire, brimstone and smoke.

The fifth and sixth trumpets' acrid smoke and locusts are the origin of Revelation 14's third angel's message of torment and fire, brimstone and smoke (see Revelation 9:5, 17). During this time, God warned His Protestant people of the severe results of those debilitating plagues if they would continue to reject His sound counsels from the Advent movement.

> And it was commanded them that they should not hurt the grass of the earth, neither any green thing, neither any tree; but only those men which have not the seal of God in their foreheads. And to them it was given that they should not kill them, but that they should be ***tormented***…: and their ***torment*** was as the [fiery] ***torment*** of a scorpion, when he striketh a man.… By these three was the third part of men killed, by the ***fire***, and by the ***smoke***, and by the ***brimstone***, which issued out of their mouths (Rev. 9:4, 5, 18).

> If any man worship ***the beast and his image***, and receive his mark in his forehead, or in his hand, the same shall drink of the wine of ***the wrath of God***, which is poured out without mixture into the cup of his ***indignation***; and he shall be ***tormented*** with ***fire*** and ***brimstone*** in the presence of the holy angels, and in the presence of the Lamb: and the ***smoke*** of their ***torment*** ascendeth up for ever and ever: and they have no rest day nor night, who worship the beast and his image, and whosoever receiveth the mark of his name (Rev. 14:9-11).

> Behold, the name of the LORD cometh from far, ***burning with his anger***, and the burden thereof is heavy: his lips are full of ***indignation***, and his tongue as a ***devouring fire***: and his breath, as an overflowing stream, shall reach to the midst of the neck, to sift the nations with the sieve of vanity: and there shall be a bridle in the jaws of the people, causing them to err (Isa. 30:27, 28).

Bringing all of this together, a Deuteronomy text earlier quoted is now expanded upon to show the everlasting, spiritual nature of the third angel's warning message given from Moses in the Old Testament:

> Lest there should be among you man, or woman, or family, or tribe, whose ***heart turneth away this day from the LORD our God, to go and serve the gods of these nations***; lest there should be among you a root that beareth ***gall and wormwood***; and it come to pass, when he heareth the words of this curse, that he bless himself in his heart, saying, I shall have ***peace***, though I walk in the imagination of mine heart, to add ***drunkenness*** to thirst: the LORD will not spare him, but then the ***anger*** of the LORD and his ***jealousy*** shall ***smoke*** against that man, and all the curses that are written in this book shall lie upon him, and the LORD shall blot out his name from under heaven. And the LORD shall separate him unto evil out of all the tribes of Israel, according to all the curses of the covenant that are written in this book of the law: so that the generation to come of your children that shall rise up after you, and the stranger that shall come from a far land, shall say, when they see the ***plagues*** of that land, and the sicknesses which the LORD hath laid upon it; and that the whole land thereof is ***brimstone***, and salt, and ***burning***, that it is not sown, nor beareth, nor any grass groweth therein, like the ***overthrow*** of Sodom, and Gomorrah, Admah, and Zeboim, which the LORD overthrew in his ***anger***, and in his ***wrath*** (Deut. 29:18-23).

The concise version of this ancient, eternal warning:

He that believeth on the Son hath everlasting life: and he that ***believeth not the Son*** shall not see life; but the ***wrath*** of God abideth on him (John 3:36).

A comparison of the above quoted John 3:36, Revelation 9:4, 5, 18, Revelation 14:9-11, and Deuteronomy 29:18-23 reveals that the locusts' bitterness and torment upon the Protestants come from distrusting Christ, and rather trusting in the gods to give them peace, that is, serving Satan through his seemingly timeless, one false religion in the world. (***See Appendix A.***) Therefore, turning from obedience and service to the Father in preference to worshiping His usurper is the warning of the third angel's message and that of the fifth and sixth trumpets.

The Protestants pretended to rejoice that the God of fatherly love and the God of all comfort would never condemn them or punish them for disobedience because they had been saved; for they were already holy in their heart. They were church members; they would often read from their Bibles and do many wonderful works. Therefore they assumed that they must be in the kingdom of God. But regardless, if Jesus cannot humble them, He says, "Thou hast no part with me" (John 13:8). Their new experience was not faith, because it was not founded upon His Law or His word. "Faith cometh by hearing… the word of God" (Rom. 10:17); and, "the word of God is quick, and powerful, and sharper than any twoedged sword, piercing even to the dividing asunder of soul and spirit, and of the joints and marrow, and is a discerner of the thoughts and intents of the heart" (Heb. 4:12). The word of God to the denominations was not powerful and sharp and cutting their conscience to the quick; therefore, their "new heart" experience was not faith and did not come from above. It was earthly, sensual, devilish.

In the second trumpet the churches rejected the fourth commandment and thereby disallowed the convicting power of God's whole Law (see Revelation 8:8; James 2:10). Those who refused the bright light of God's present truth through the Spirit of Prophecy, because it corrected them, were plagued by the fifth trumpet's burning torment, and were receiving the mark [Gr. *charagma*, "a scratch" or "etching"] of the Beast in their hardened hearts. The same is true for every Seventh-day Adventist who rejects that same bright light. They do not have a love of the truth.

> I have seen an end of all perfection: but thy commandment is exceeding broad. O how love I thy law! it is my meditation all the day (Ps. 119:96, 97).

> Unless thy law had been my delights, I should then have perished in mine affliction (Ps. 119:92).

The newly remodeled Protestantism rejected God's Law until the dark forces from the abyss could help them change gospel doctrine to suit papal dogma. It was not faith leading to the strong obedience of the Reformers. Rather than faith, the second trumpet's new Protestantism was the ancient theology of make-believe. It was rebellion in church clothing, leading to enervating spiritualism (see 1 Samuel 15:23). It resulted not in peace, but in *imagined* peace, away from self-deception which Moses tried to warn Israel: "*…I shall have peace, though I walk in the imagination of mine heart*" (Deut. 29:19). This Old Testament third angel's message (see Deuteronomy 29:18-28) and the fifth trumpet warning have the same result: "The anger of the LORD and his jealousy shall smoke against that man" (vs. 20). Surrender of the human heart was created for the Godhead. Surrendering to Satan arouses God's protective rage. The Protestants' new doctrine didn't resolve the Lord's burning anxiety in their souls, but drove them to accept Satan's age-old, easier, pagan counterfeit. Thus, the new power from the bottomless pit, which had ever been behind the ancient forms of Spiritual Formation, kept its followers from the humbling Law of Him who is a consuming fire to sin (see Hebrews 10:31; 12:27). Therefore, the fifth trumpet locusts were the vile prince over the workers of iniquity and the king over the children of pride that was empowering the new form of Protestantism (see Daniel 11:21; Matthew 7:21-23; Job 41:1, 34; Revelation 12:9). During the delusion's progress, Satan's mark on them would become more and more widely assured.

Under the influence of lawless religion, Protestants could never be sealed. And all the while their "chastisement of…peace" (Isa. 53:5), that "root of bitterness" (Heb. 12:15), causing "sorrow of heart" (Lev. 26:16), would fester into delusional, spiritual madness (see Isaiah 8:19, 20, 22; 50:11; Jeremiah 25:15, 16; 51:7-9). Having added "drunkenness to thirst" to quench their dreadful separation from God, they would one day become a persecuting power through the furious "wine of the wrath of [Babylon's] fornication" (Rev. 14:8, cf Rev. 17:4, 6). The "vine of Sodom", the "grapes of gall", "the cruel venom of asps" (Deut. 32:32, 33) would buy their place in hell (see Matthew 24:48-51). Their deadly thirst would be fed lies through Spiritual Formation and the Mass. And their agitated, unrested souls would end in their aggravated assaults upon everyone who would have peace and rest and faith from above. False prophets' mesmerizing spirit of lawlessness has ever been the cause of the nations' slide into ruin and cruel perdition.

> I have seen also in the prophets of Jerusalem an horrible thing: they commit adultery, and walk in lies: they strengthen also the hands of evildoers, that none doth return from his wickedness: they are all of them unto me as Sodom, and the inhabitants thereof as Gomorrah. Therefore thus saith the LORD of hosts concerning the prophets; Behold, I will feed them with wormwood, and make them drink the water of gall: for *from the prophets of Jerusalem is profaneness gone forth into all the land*. Thus saith the LORD of hosts, Hearken not unto the words of the prophets that prophesy unto you: they make you vain: they speak a vision of their own heart, and not out of the mouth of the LORD (Jer. 23:14-16).

> If a man walking in the spirit and falsehood do lie, saying, I will prophesy unto thee of wine and

of strong drink; he shall even be the prophet of this people (Mic. 2:11).

For from the least of them even unto the greatest of them every one is given to covetousness; and from the prophet even unto the priest every one dealeth falsely. They have healed also the hurt of the daughter of my people slightly, saying, Peace, peace; when there is no peace (Jer. 6:13, 14).

The children gather wood, and the fathers kindle the fire, and the women knead their dough, to make cakes to the queen of heaven, and to pour out drink offerings unto other gods, that they may provoke me to anger. Do they provoke me to anger? saith the LORD: do they not provoke themselves to the confusion of their own faces? Therefore thus saith the Lord GOD; Behold, mine anger and my fury shall be poured out upon this place, upon man, and upon beast, and upon the trees of the field, and upon the fruit of the ground; and it shall burn, and shall not be quenched (Jer. 7:18-20).

For Jerusalem is ruined, and Judah is fallen: because their tongue and their doings are against the Lord, to provoke the eyes of his glory.… As for my people, children are their oppressors, and women rule over them. O my people, they which lead thee cause thee to err, and destroy the way of thy paths. The Lord standeth up to plead, and standeth to judge the people. The Lord will enter into judgment with the ancients of his people, and the princes thereof: for ye have eaten up the vineyard; the spoil of the poor is in your houses. What mean ye that ye beat my people to pieces, and grind the faces of the poor? saith the Lord God of hosts (Isa. 3:8, 12-15).

True peace comes from wrestling with God through His mandates and His mercy, until surrender happens. Then come the longed for reconciliation with God and His justification peace. And faith works in us happiness and goodness, as peace with God "is shed abroad in our hearts by the Holy Ghost which is given unto us" (Rom. 5:5, cf vs. 1). However, disdaining the condemnation of the Law and its humbling fear of God end in confusion of face.

The end [result] of the commandment is charity out of a pure heart, and of a good conscience, and of faith unfeigned: from which some having swerved have turned aside unto vain jangling; desiring to be teachers of the law; understanding neither what they say, nor whereof they affirm (1 Tim. 1:5-7).

By evading the sobering requirements of the Law and the Spirit of Prophecy books, the Protestants' imagined peace was the very wine of Babylon, adding drunkenness to their already tormenting thirst. That thirst resulted from the natural separation from God into which we are all born, and which is magnified by attempting to be righteous without submitting to God's Law (see Romans 7:9-11). To attempt this is to serve humanism and the father of humanism, the devil. Thus, Protestantism could not know real surrender and the sealing without forsaking their modern Baal and Ashtoreth worship, and coming under the powerful tonic of the beautiful exaltation of God's Law given by Ellen White. The torment and burning jealousy of God would grind their soul to powder.

But if ye will not hearken unto me, and will not do all these commandments; and if ye shall despise my statutes, or if your soul abhor my judgments, so that ye will not do all my commandments, but that ye break my covenant: I also will do this unto you; I will even appoint over you terror, consumption, and the burning [fever], that shall consume the eyes, and cause sorrow of heart… (Lev. 26:14-16).

They would have no rest, day nor night.

Among these nations shalt thou find no ease, neither shall the sole of thy foot have rest: but the LORD shall give thee there a trembling heart, and failing of eyes, and sorrow of mind: and thy life shall hang in doubt before thee; and thou shalt fear day and night, and shalt have none assurance of thy life. In the morning thou shalt say, Would God it were even! and at even thou shalt say, Would God it were morning! (Deut. 28:65-67).

And upon them that are left alive of you I will send a faintness into their hearts in the lands of their enemies; and the sound of a shaken leaf shall chase them; and they shall flee, as fleeing from a sword; and they shall fall when none pursueth (Lev. 26:36).

The wicked flee when no man pursueth (Prov. 28:1).

The ungodly… are like the chaff which the wind driveth away (Ps. 1:4).

On the contrary,

The righteous are bold as a lion (Prov. 28:1).

He that dwelleth in the secret place of the most High shall abide under the shadow of the Almighty.

I will say of the LORD, He is my refuge and my fortress: my God; in him will I trust.

Surely he shall deliver thee from the snare of the fowler, and from the noisome pestilence.

He shall cover thee with his feathers, and under his wings shalt thou trust: his truth shall be thy shield and buckler.

Thou shalt not be afraid for the terror by night; nor for the arrow that flieth by day;

Nor for the pestilence that walketh in darkness; nor for the destruction that wasteth at noonday (Ps. 91:1-6).

Rest could only be found by each individual who was humbled and converted by the strong Law of God. Each one must accept a child's disposition toward authority, he must surrender to the Creator, and then be brought to His Son for mercy. And with his rest of body and mind and soul would come his prosperity, spiritually, mentally, physically, and temporally.

His delight is in the law of the LORD; and in his law doth he meditate day and night.

And he shall be like a tree planted by the rivers of water, that bringeth forth his fruit in his season; his leaf also shall not wither; and whatsoever he doeth shall prosper (Ps. 1:2, 3).

My son, forget not my law; but let thine heart keep my commandments:

For length of days, and long life, and peace, shall they add to thee.

Let not mercy and truth forsake thee: bind them about thy neck; write them upon the table of thine heart:

So shalt thou find favour and good understanding in the sight of God and man.…

So shall thy barns be filled with plenty, and thy presses shall burst out with new wine (Prov. 3:1-4, 10).

All that the Father giveth me shall come to me; and him that cometh to me I will in no wise cast out (John 6:37).

For thus saith the Lord GOD, the Holy One of Israel; In returning and rest shall ye be saved; in quietness and in confidence shall be your strength (Isa. 30:15).

The humbled would be the greatest; the last would finish first. The nobodies become somebodies. The boy shepherd of a few sheep who was ordered around and scolded by his hard-hearted brothers, a "stripling" (1 Sam. 17:56) brought out of the sheepcote to the throne, bursted forth with new wine,

By thee I have run through a troop; and by my God have I leaped over a wall.

As for God, his way is perfect: the word of the Lord is tried: he is a buckler to all those that trust in him.

For who is God save the Lord? or who is a rock save our God? (Ps. 18:29-31).

I will never forget thy precepts: for with them thou hast quickened me… (Ps. 119:93).

Bless the LORD, O my soul: and all that is within me, bless his holy name.

Bless the LORD, O my soul, and forget not all his benefits:

Who forgiveth all thine iniquities; who healeth all thy diseases; who redeemeth thy life from destruction; who crowneth thee with lovingkindness and tender mercies;

Who satisfieth thy mouth with good things; so that thy youth is renewed like the eagle's (Ps. 103:1-5).

Connecting Revelation 7:3, 9:4, the third angel's message, and the warnings of the Lord through Moses listed above, we can understand that the mark of the Beast and the Seal of God both ***were being*** distributed throughout the period of the fifth and sixth trumpets. The court of heaven has been deciding for or against Protestants during the investigative judgment since shortly after 1844, following the first four trumpet judgments. Long before a national Sunday law has ever come into force, all who preferred to cut God off by refusing the commanding voice of His Law to the conscience have failed out of the sealing and have not remained green (see Revelation 9:4; Jeremiah 17:5, 6). Long before the counterfeit revival appeared, every Christian who would not suffer the Law's grinding upon his soul, the scourging (see Hebrews 12:6) that comes from not having the presence of God's Spirit of blessing, and all who thus chose to not know God's everlasting love *have been* receiving the mark of the Beast which is taking shape in their hearts and minds. And, rarely have any of them recognized this divine judgment upon them.

> O LORD…thou hast stricken them, but they have not grieved; thou hast consumed them, but they have refused to receive correction: they have made their faces harder than a rock; they have refused to return [to repent and be converted] (Jer. 5:3, cf Isa. 6:9, 10; Eze. 3:7-9; 2 Cor. 4:3, 4).

The mark goes to many of the churched and unchurched Protestants who refuse to let God make His way into their trust and conscience by way of His strong, fatherly voice from His written page. They have resisted His character. Multitudes have received the mark in the forehead because they have chosen a counterfeit doctrine that released them from obedience to God's true religion of Law and grace. They have "turned aside unto vain jangling" (1 Tim. 1:6) and they have only the "sounding brass, or a tinkling cymbal" (1 Cor. 13:1) of loveless, Christless religion.

Generally, the unchurched, secularized Protestants have been receiving the mark in their hand because they care nothing about God or the Bible. The unchurched Protestants will make a token gesture in favor of the new totalitarian religion in order to keep their bank accounts, retirement, house, or other possessions. Meanwhile, the churched throw themselves into the celebration ecstasy of imagined, fanatical peace that is taking place within Christianity today; and they later resort to legislated force and persecution toward anyone opposed to their furious, self-indulgent religion (see Revelation 13:11-15). In the first case as much as the second, those descendants of the Reformation are completely absented of genuine faith in Jesus and full obedience to God.

The name "Israel" in its Genesis 32:28 context is interpreted, "the man who wrestles/fights with God and overcomes (self)." All who have wrestled with their doubts about the righteous demands and love of the great Lawgiver as Jacob wrestled with Christ *have been* receiving the blessed Seal of God and power to replicate the character of Christ in themselves and in others. They came to terms with God, surrendering to the severity and goodness of His correction which they found in His straight testimony, or surrendering to the consequences that come from abhorring His straight testimony. "The foundation of God standeth sure, having this seal, The Lord knoweth them that are his. And, Let every one that nameth the name of Christ depart from iniquity" (2 Tim. 2:19).

Placing the third angel's message next to the other fifth trumpet related scripture warnings, we see that both Seal and mark have to do with more than the true or false *day* of worship, but also with the *whole* Law and testimony of prophets, including Ellen G. White. All who will study and obey the Testimony of Jesus through all of His prophets, *wrestling with it until they see and know Jesus*, will be His disciples indeed and will love His appearing (see John 8:31; Matthew 10:40; Luke 10:10-12; 2 Timothy 4:8).

> As many as received him, to them gave he power to become the sons of God, even to them that believe on his name: which were born, not of blood, nor of the will of the flesh, nor of the will of man, but of God (John 1:12, 13).

> He that hath received his testimony hath set to his seal that God is true (John 3:33).

> Because he hath set his love upon me, therefore will I deliver him: I will set him on high, because he hath known my name (Ps. 91:14).

The investigative judgment extends from 1844 until the final cleansing of the sanctuary in heaven and of the church on earth in the days preceding the seventh trumpet. As it goes forward, individuals' decisions for or against obedience to Jesus have been deciding their own cases for the sealing or the mark in the Supreme Court of heaven. They have cooperated with one of the two great powers contending for the supremacy of man. Depending on whether or not they receive the tonic Testimony

Chapter 6 Revelation Chapter 9: The Strong Delusion

of Jesus and find that God is true, they have had a part to act for setting the Seal or the mark in their own forehead.

> *The shew of their countenance doth witness* against them; and they declare their sin as Sodom, they hide it not. Woe unto their soul! for they have rewarded evil unto themselves. Say ye to the righteous, that it shall be well with him: for they shall eat the fruit of their doings. Woe unto the wicked! it shall be ill with him: for the reward of his hands shall be given him (Isa. 3:9-11).

The cleansing of the sanctuary in heaven coincides with us here exposing our minds to the invigorating Law of God, especially as expressed in the Spirit of Prophecy, striving against it until finally falling at Jesus' feet, and finding rest and wonderful refreshment in the Saviour (see Galatians 5:17; Matthew 16:25; John 3:21; Galatians 3:24; Romans 7:7-25). Or, a gradual decrease of striving will ultimately lead to avoiding Him at all cost, in spite of the resulting tremendous nerve-wracking anxiety of an existence apart from the Creator (see Leviticus 26:16; Deuteronomy 28:28). And, such anxiety causes cancer and every other pestilence, which must be drowned by intoxicating human philosophies and theologies, cultivated habits and inherited traditions, and destructive pharmaceuticals and substances. The fifth trumpet's torment is simply the gospel invitation/warning from Jesus, "Whosoever shall fall on this stone shall be broken: but on whomsoever it shall fall, it will grind him to powder" (Matt. 21:44).

There is a time prophecy associated with the fifth trumpet — five prophetic months, or 150 literal years.

> To them it was given that they should not kill them, but that they should be tormented five months (Rev. 9:5).

Regrouping after the Great Disappointment in 1844, as the first four trumpets were blowing, some of the Millerites again studied the Scriptures. They needed to know what the Lord meant by the gospel and prophecy-centered revival that had thrilled them through William Miller's widespread American movement. The "Sabbath conferences" started in 1848 and at these small gatherings the people studied with all of their hearts, their minds and consciences keener and settled after the '44 Disappointment. They began to see more clearly what the Bible was saying in its truths. They better comprehended the truth of a heavenly sanctuary (see Hebrews 8:1-3). They understood the condition of the dead, that "the dead know not any thing, neither have they any more a reward; for the memory of them is forgotten" (Ecc. 9:5, cf Job 14:20, 21). Rachel Oaks, a Seventh-day Baptist, unveiled to them the seventh-day Sabbath fourth commandment, which they quickly accepted in full repentance and faith. The movement had already received the gift of prophecy, and, of course, the newly revived and riveting sense of coming judgment and the blessed hope of the second advent of Jesus.

Simple farmers and other commoners were qualified to hammer out the Bible's core truths because they had been shaken and humbled before God through His 1844 Disappointment. The Disappointment had harshly tested their faith in the Bible and, under the fire of the first trumpet, had solidified their faith and made it stronger. During the conferences they experienced the biblical principles of Isaiah 28:9, 10 and Matthew 6:22, of which a conference attendee later wrote:

> Many a portion of Scripture which learned men pronounce a mystery, or pass over as unimportant, is full of comfort and instruction to him who has been taught in the school of Christ. One reason why many theologians have no clearer understanding of God's word is, they close their eyes to truths which they do not wish to practice. As understanding of Bible truth depends not so much on the power of intellect brought to the search as on the singleness of purpose, the earnest longing after righteousness *The Great Controversy*, p. 599.

The disappointed, but faithful Adventists, desperate and thrilling to know God's will for them, finished this work of studying the Bible in 1850. They realized that they were servants in a real apocalyptic movement of providence, under the direct guidance of High Priest Jesus, Himself. Now the movement of destiny was prepared for the great race to the finish when the heavenly sanctuary would be cleansed *and Jesus would truly return in power and glory.*

In the middle of the Sabbath conferences the fifth trumpet began to blow. Gold was discovered in 1848, but not until 1849 was it proclaimed.

Almost simultaneously, a crisis arose within the still weakened beast power.

> The Jesuits were restored in 1814, by Pope Pius VII; but not to their persecuting power. In the different countries of Europe since that time the Order has been expelled and restored several times, and even by the Papacy once. But Pius IX, after his return from Gaeta *in 1849, gave them its entire confidence till the day of his death*, and in his Vatican decrees is seen the crowning triumph of Jesuit Ultramontanism
>
> The new head of the Roman Church learned what was his desire to be a moderate pope by allowing political liberty to the Italian states, a liberty which the people were violently striving to obtain, would soon end in their outcry for freedom of religion. But religious liberty was not Pio Nino's to allow. A strong stance toward any and all liberty to the Italian people, therefore, arose as he sought guidance in the precarious imposition of his office. Closing in on him were libertarians dangerous and angered by his resistance toward political freedom or capitulation toward any freedom, as he was stolen away from the Vatican by night to a castle hideaway in Gaeta *The Signs of the Times*, Vol. 12 August 12, 1886, "The End of the Tribulation of Those Days" 12, 31, p. 487, *Ellen White Comprehensive Research Edition*, Copyright 2010. [Emphasis supplied]

In the middle of the Sabbath conferences the fifth trumpet began to blow. Gold was discovered in 1848, but not until 1849 was it proclaimed. During this time, the denominations continued to fight the messengers of biblical prophecy and the message of Christ's literal coming in power and destruction. They continued to resist the warning to Laodicea and of heaven's door that had finally gone shut to them, a door that only the Lord could re-open on an individual basis upon surrender to His present truth (see Revelation 3:7).

Thus, the fifth trumpet blew in 1849, "Gold in California!" as no other announcement. Like the breaking of a dam, every descendant of the Reformation not firmly rooted in Christ was swept up in lethal currents of hopes and dreams of earthly treasures. The California Gold Rush wholly transformed the face of Protestantism. Until then we were, by appearance, a docile, quiet people, upholding the Ten Commandments and the Bible respectably, as relatively proper and well-behaved children of the Reformation. But, Jesus doesn't come to call the righteous, but sinners to repentance.

The Lord had given the American continent to the early Protestants for a refuge from papal persecution (see Revelation 12:15, 16) and as a gift for their obedience to the Reformation. The land was for them to enjoy and to rejoice in before the Lord their God. But, the descendants of the Pilgrim Fathers allowed the glorious land to steal their hearts away from their holy faith in God. Total faith in the Bible, which their Reformation forefathers died to give them, had waned more and more throughout the 17th, 18th, and early 19th centuries, never to be reclaimed (see Revelation 13:11-16). The Reformation descendants heeded not the warnings and injunctions of their Bibles,

> I know thy works, that thou hast a name that thou livest, and art dead. Be watchful, and strengthen the things which remain, that are ready to die: for I have not found thy works perfect before God. Remember therefore how thou hast received and heard, and hold fast, and repent. If therefore thou shalt not watch, I will come on thee as a thief, and thou shalt not know what hour I will come upon thee. Thou hast a few names even in Sardis which have not defiled their garments; and they shall walk with me in white: for they are worthy (Rev. 3:1-4).
>
> I know thy works, that thou art neither cold nor hot: I would thou wert cold or hot. So then because thou art lukewarm, and neither cold nor hot, I will spue thee out of my mouth. Because thou sayest, I am rich, and increased with goods, and have need of nothing; and knowest not that thou art wretched, and miserable, and poor, and blind, and naked: I counsel thee to buy of me gold tried in the fire, that thou mayest be rich; and white raiment, that thou mayest be clothed, and that the shame of thy nakedness do not appear; and anoint thine eyes with eyesalve, that thou mayest see. As many as I love, I rebuke and chasten: be zealous therefore, and repent (Rev. 3:15-19, cf Lev. 18:28).

Neither could these Protestant Americans appropriate the fearful biblical lesson from the northern kingdom of Israel,

For so it was, that the children of Israel had sinned against the LORD their God, which had brought them up out of the land of Egypt, from under the hand of Pharaoh king of Egypt, and had feared other gods,

And walked in the statutes of the heathen, whom the LORD cast out from before the children of Israel, and of the kings of Israel, which they had made.

And the children of Israel did secretly those things that were not right against the LORD their God, and they built them high places in all their cities, from the tower of the watchmen to the fenced city.

And they set them up images and groves in every high hill, and under every green tree:

And there they burnt incense in all the high places, as did the heathen whom the LORD carried away before them; and wrought wicked things to provoke the LORD to anger:

For they served idols, whereof the LORD had said unto them, Ye shall not do this thing.

Yet the LORD testified against Israel, and against Judah, by all the prophets, and by all the seers, saying, Turn ye from your evil ways, and keep my commandments and my statutes, according to all the law which I commanded your fathers, and which I sent to you by my servants the prophets.

Notwithstanding they would not hear, but hardened their necks, like to the neck of their fathers, that did not believe in the LORD their God.

And they rejected his statutes, and his covenant that he made with their fathers, and his testimonies which he testified against them; and they followed vanity, and became vain, and went after the heathen that were round about them, concerning whom the LORD had charged them, that they should not do like them.

And they left all the commandments of the LORD their God, and made them molten images, even two calves, and made a grove, and worshipped all the host of heaven, and served Baal.

And they caused their sons and their daughters to pass through the fire, and used divination and enchantments, and sold themselves to do evil in the sight of the LORD, to provoke him to anger.

Therefore the LORD was very angry with Israel, and removed them out of his sight: there was none left but the tribe of Judah only....

For he rent Israel from the house of David; and they made Jeroboam the son of Nebat king: and Jeroboam drave Israel from following the LORD, and made them sin a great sin.

For the children of Israel walked in all the sins of Jeroboam which he did; they departed not from them;

Until the LORD removed Israel out of his sight, as he had said by all his servants the prophets. So was Israel carried away out of their own land to Assyria unto this day (2 Ki. 17:7-18, 21-23).

Generations later, the liberated and landed Protestant Americans were unwittingly distancing themselves from the cutting truth of the Bible, the book they professed to strictly uphold. So, as He had given a hard message to the Israelites through Isaiah, Christ, in mercy to His Reformation church and to cleanse His holy name, sent to the Protestant churches a bold, strong preaching of His Second Coming and of Judgment Day. The Protestants, however, had so blinded themselves by the cares and treasures of this world that they refused to understand the destructive return of Christ as anything other than a metaphorical coming to the heart of the believer at conversion. To them, only fanatics and cults could believe that the world should be destroyed, though in complete disregard of 2 Peter 3:6-10. And there they have remained until this day, held captive by the cords of that error.

Be not mockers, lest your bands be made strong (Isa. 28:22).

They were reliving the threatening message to ancient Israel.

And he said, Go, and tell this people, Hear ye indeed, but understand not; and see ye indeed, but perceive not. Make the heart of this people fat, and make their ears heavy, and shut their eyes; lest they see with their eyes, and hear with their ears, and understand with their heart, and convert, and be healed (Isa. 6:9, 10, cf Matt. 13:11-15).

Since the denominations rejected the truth about the fiery and destructive Second Advent, they were open to one of Satan's boldest delusions of this time. In his secret rapture doctrine, the Protestants misunderstand the fiery and furious "**DAY** *of the Lord*" (2 Pet. 3:10, cf 1 Thess. 5:2, 4; Rev. 3:3; 16:15; Matt. 24:43; Luke 12:39) which comes as a thief in the night to wake up the world; and the deceiver ingeniously made them believe that *"the Lord"* will come as a thief in the night, invisibly and in the blink of an eye. And then he convinced the denominations to expect a peaceful return of Jesus to this evil world seven years later, in which he will give the earth only a makeover. He will keep the corrupted and enslaving religious, political, and commercial systems in place. The Bible teaches, however, that the "day of the Lord" as a "thief in the night" return of Jesus comes at the end of the seventh plague's global hailstorm of 90 pound stones (see Revelation 16:15-21; 6:12-16). Scriptures teach that we are to watch and wait for *the day* of the Lord every day, morning, noon, and night. For too many things could entice us to be asleep (see Matthew 24:37-39, 43, 44, 48-51; Luke 13:24). When the true Jesus does come, He will call forth from their graves the righteous sleeping saints, glorified in eternal heavenly bodies, and He will change the vile, corruptible bodies and natures of the living saints. Then He will leave with Earth in *a total and complete shambles*, "blood, and fire, and pillars of smoke" (Joel 2:30, cf Jer. 4:23-26; 1 Thess. 4:14-17; 1 Cor. 15:52-55; Phil. 3:21; 2 Thess. 1:7-10). "The LORD is a man of war: the LORD is his name" (Ex. 15:3). In all the scripture references to His return, *there is only one* second advent of Christ; *and they all show the same destruction.*

Instead of the true second advent of Christ, the Evangelicals will get a peaceful "Jesus" when Satan floats down with millions of shining angels, imitating the Son of God and the clouds of His angelic hosts (see 2 Corinthians 11:14; Matthew 24:24). This "Christ" will speak the grace-only things of Spiritual Formation with a melodious, commanding voice. And, with his undue familiarity, he will bring them under his *inescapable* spell. They must be warned of such a wicked false doctrine and fatal deception which is receiving universal acceptance today.

The 19th century Protestant Americans claimed that the Bible's message of Jesus returning in power was not to destroy this world, but only a religious experience. This was really a subconscious excuse for not wanting this world to come to an end. They claimed to be a holy nation dedicated to God, but His strong Millerite message found them hoping in this world and loving this world, despite their repeated reading of 1 John 2:15-17. After all, in 1849 they owned a brand new country, still having a strong memory of the Revolutionary fathers, many among them having personally known those men: Thomas Jefferson, John Adams, James Madison, and other renowned, historic leaders. The Protestant Americans had a huge expanse of land before them to settle and to provide them with the good life. Nevertheless, as Jesus called Peter at the moment of Peter's greatest catch of fish, requiring the fisher to sacrifice all to follow the Messiah (see Luke 5:4-11), so did Jehovah test the churches during their temporal stay in His land abounding with natural resources.

Now, final decisions must be made.

Who is on the LORD's side? (Ex. 32:26).

Our God shall come, and shall not keep silence: a fire shall devour before him, and it shall be very tempestuous round about him.

He shall call to the heavens from above, and to the earth, that he may judge his people.

Gather my saints together unto me; those that have made a covenant with me by sacrifice....

But unto the wicked God saith, What hast thou to do to declare my statutes, or that thou shouldest take my covenant in thy mouth?

Seeing thou hatest instruction, and castest my words behind thee.

When thou sawest a thief, then thou consentedst with him, and hast been partaker with adulterers.

Thou givest thy mouth to evil, and thy tongue frameth deceit.

Thou sittest and speakest against thy brother; thou slanderest thine own mother's son.

These things hast thou done, and I kept silence; thou thoughtest that I was altogether such an one as thyself: but I will reprove thee, and set them in order before thine eyes.

Now consider this, ye that forget God, lest I tear you in pieces, and there be none to deliver (Ps. 50:3-5, 16-22).

The Protestants knew their Bible and professed to love it supremely. But Christ's words, "What is a man profited, if he shall gain the whole world, and lose his own soul?" (Matt. 16:26), aroused insufficient conviction in most of them. Their response was not that of the disciples, "Lord, is it I?" (Matt. 26:22), so far had they departed from the spirit of the Reformation. They had lost the Reformation's first love and the Holy Spirit, and the true conception of the gospel eluded them. Deception looks so correct.

Therefore we ought to give the more earnest heed to the things which we have heard, lest at any time we should let them slip. For if the word spoken by angels was stedfast, and every transgression and disobedience received a just recompence of reward; how shall we escape, if we neglect so great salvation? (Heb. 2:1-3).

Denial of self, laying down their life for the gospel — the original spirit of the Reformation — had disappeared from the vast Protestant multitudes. In the Lord's land of refuge, the Protestant churchs were repeating the history of Israel's many apostasies and that of the post-apostolic Church.

Would the Advent movement escape the same trap? Yes, it would; but only because of the Lord's mercies and forbearance, and by the power He originally vested into the writings of Ellen G. White. Yet, those holy, biblical counsels even His Remnant largely have ignored, which could have led to their humbling and surrender for the special work of purification that the Lord's messenger continuously called for.

Therefore the LORD was very angry with Israel, and removed them out of his sight: there was none left but the tribe of Judah only. Also Judah kept not the commandments of the LORD their God, but walked in the statutes of Israel which they made. And the LORD rejected all the seed of Israel, and afflicted them, and delivered them into the hand of spoilers, until he had cast them out of his sight (2 Ki. 17:18-20).

Therefore say unto the house of Israel, Thus saith the Lord GOD; I do not this for your sakes, O house of Israel, but for mine holy name's sake, which ye have profaned among the heathen, whither ye went. And I will sanctify my great name, which was profaned among the heathen, which ye have profaned in the midst of them; and the heathen shall know that I am the LORD, saith the Lord GOD, when I shall be sanctified in you before their eyes (Eze. 36:22, 23).

For the name of God is blasphemed among the Gentiles through you, as it is written (Rom. 2:24).

The Lord kept Judah during their inter-testamental period. Even though the empires each left a deeper pagan impress upon the majority of Israel, and the Jews further distanced themselves from Jehovah, He kept them as His chosen people. Their religion grew increasingly corrupted by paganism; yet, still God kept them. He retained them not because they were obedient, but because He loved Israel as He loved the whole human race, and needed to give the Messiah to the world through them as He had promised (see Genesis 49:10-12; Micah 5:2), at least through "some of them" (Rom. 11:14). Therefore, by the time Mary delivered the Messiah, only a "very small remnant" (Isa. 1:9, cf Luke 18:8) of the Jews was still walking by faith (see Matthew 2:1-3; Luke 2:8-18, 25-38).

Many evangelical Christians today are suffering because of the sin of the Protestant American forefathers by their rejection of heaven's messengers, William Miller and Ellen White.

I the LORD thy God am a jealous God, visiting the iniquity of the fathers upon the children unto the third and fourth generation of them that hate me; and shewing mercy unto thousands of them that love me, and keep my commandments (Ex. 20:5, 6).

The way of the Evangelicals is hard. Yet, by surrendering to God through the torment that Satan has brought the Evangelical world, it will be said of repentant Sunday Christians, "Backsliding Israel hath justified herself" (Jer. 3:11, cf 2:19). Many Protestants today are seeking a rest from the harassment of Satan which their 19th century forefathers bequeathed them. Due to the harshness of the atheism and purported peace of the fifth trumpet locusts, soon many will welcome the authority of God to condemn and convict their sin; and they will take up the special work of purification. They will be justified and have a place in the Latter Rain. Great will be that day. Of them it will be said, "He that is holy, let him be holy still" (Rev. 22:11).

> The land of Zabulon, and the land of Nephthalim, by the way of the sea, beyond Jordan, Galilee of the Gentiles; the people which sat in darkness saw great light; and to them which sat in the region and shadow of death light is sprung up (Matt. 4:15, 16).

In preparation for the Lord's final battle with Satan before He could redeem humanity, Providence saw that the only way to salvage His gospel at the end of time was to sever those Protestants who were heeding His Spirit from those who would not. The door opened to the handful of sabbatarian Millerites to become God's privileged conduit of heavenly light to humanity. The same privilege as a conduit went shut to the mainline denominational institutions that rejected His biblical message of judgment (see Revelation 3:7, 8).

Our Creator, "who worketh all things after the counsel of his own will" (Eph. 1:11), who "doeth according to his will in the army of heaven, and among the inhabitants of the earth" (Dan. 4:35), "hath determined the times before appointed" (Acts 17:26). It was providence and fulfillment of the Revelation 9 prophecy that caused the discovery of gold on the West Coast. According to this prophecy, the time had come to judge the world and to distil, first from among Protestantism and then from the nations, all who would honestly serve the living God of righteousness.

Until 1849, the American pioneers were all backed up along the eastern edge of the wide Mississippi. They were fearful to cross the river because of the war-like indigenous peoples in the American West, who were jealous to keep their ancient homeland free of European influence and ownership. But, when gold was discovered, the Protestants readily risked their lives to cross the Great Plains. The western Louisiana Purchase territory, which had rarely seen a European, now found its pristine environment rapidly filling with Protestant Americans, reaping and polluting its natural resources.

The Gold Rush quickly populated the extensive western Louisiana Territory, and connected east and west coasts. Transportation and communication expanded to meet the needs of a unified nation, giving birth to the American continent, and laying the foundation for the modern country and culture of THE UNITED STATES.

Quickly, the descendants of the holy Reformation showed their true character by the hustling, debauchery and prostitution, the greed, and forgetfulness of God that attended the 1849 Gold Rush, the later oil bonanzas, and the even later alcohol and stock market frenzies. Protestant America's profession of righteousness, in defense of their rejection of the Millerite message, had been only a thin veneer. They had been whitened sepulchers, Spiritless, Christless. Hindsight has proven it right for God to test the American Protestants by William Miller. The Protestant response to the message of Christ's second advent exposed the true dearth of their hearts, "having loved this present world" (2 Tim. 4:10). The time had come to permit that for which deluded Protestantism had striven so hard against the Spirit of God; that is, for Providence to lure them completely away from the Reformation holiness by a stronger delusion than had existed in the worldly, pre-Gold Rush era.

> My people are destroyed for lack of knowledge: because thou hast rejected knowledge, I will also reject thee, that thou shalt be no priest to me: seeing thou hast forgotten the law of thy God, I will also forget thy children. As they were increased, so they sinned against me: therefore will I change their glory into shame (Hos. 4:6, 7).

History was repeating.

> And it came to pass, as they journeyed from the east, that they found a plain in the land of Shinar; and they dwelt there.... And they said, Go to, let us build us a city and a tower, whose top may reach unto heaven; and let us make us a name, lest we be scattered abroad upon the face of the whole earth (Gen. 11:2, 4).

> And the LORD said, Behold, the people is one, and they have all one language; and this they begin to do: and now nothing will be restrained from them, which they have imagined to do (Gen. 11:6).

As providence lured Esau to sell the priesthood because his interests lay in this world, so did this land of plenty lure the Protestants away from their role as light to the world. Having removed the denominations from their assumed Reformation birthright, Providence could begin from scratch with a new, last-day apostolic, Bible-based movement.

God's Spirit will eventually stop striving with anyone who continually resists His convictions, which consequently gives Satan permission to take control — and ultimately, full control. As God gave an extra 120 years to the antediluvian world in the days of Noah, so would a delay of Christ's return, an additional period of probation, be given at this time of the final judgment. The delay would not change the direction of the spirit driving the Advent movement or mainline denominations; rather, it would make more and more pronounced the different destinations between the two. Nevertheless, it would allow extra opportunity for Protestants to join in the movement designed to purify itself as "light was… given" and "new duties would be revealed" (*The Great Controversy*, p. 424.4, cf 1 John 3:2, 3). As with the Jews in Paul's day, the only way for the Protestants to be saved would come through their grafting again into living faith in Jesus individually and by leaving their denominations for the Advent movement (see Romans 11:14, 15).

For the next 150 years, during the fifth trumpet, it would be a race to the finish for the acrid sulfur of Satan's lawlessness, and the sweet smelling Spirit from Christ's self-sacrifice and His Father's Law.

> Two great parties are developed, the worshipers of the beast and his image, and the worshipers of the true and living God *Manuscript Releases*, vol. 1, p. 45.

The race would decide who among the Protestants would come to Jesus for peace and then prepare for Judgment Day, or who would fall increasingly deeper into worldliness and service to Satan. This would occur first in America and then in the rest of the world. The next one hundred fifty years of the fifth trumpet following 1849 would determine the success of the unending stream of locust emissaries of the devil, which had been driven out of the abyss by the darkness of spiritualism. Those emissaries would consist of a rapidly growing multitude of Jesuit tempters determined to destroy Protestantism and Protestant America. It would also involve the Protestants who would fall to the Jesuit myriad spiritual deceptions, as an intoxicating analgesic for the dense, satanic smoke of their torment.

> Side by side with the preaching of the gospel, agencies are at work which are but the medium of lying spirits *The Desire of Ages*, p. 258.

The papal locusts' temptations and abominations would also filter out of the denominations the growing three angels' followership (see Revelation 14:1-13), whose fear of God and humbled submission to His Law left them desperately needing a Saviour from sin. To those surviving this 150 year shaking of Protestantism Jesus says, "I will be found of you, saith the LORD" (Jer. 29:14); and His promises are verity and sure, faithful and true. In consequence to receiving Him, they obtain His surrender and victory over their sins. Throughout the next five prophetic months, Protestant America would be providentially forced to prepare their hearts for the mark of the Beast or for the Seal of the living God.

During Protestant America's five prophetic month probation, the exaltation of man — movie stars, sports celebrities, music entertainers, politicians, scientists, the rich and famous — man, man, man — 666 — has blotted from them all recognition of their Creator. "When the Son of man cometh, shall he find faith on the earth?" (Luke 18:8). Increasing ignorance of God's character and disregard for His authority have left a foul rebellion in the daring human nature. The torment of the corrupting Jesuits and pitch black smoke have come to us from their darkening of the truth of God's power and of His fearful Law. This condition was foretold: "Darkness shall cover the earth, and gross darkness the people" (Isa. 60:2, cf Rev. 9:2).

But, to the misery encompassing our atheistic world the Lord simultaneously promised another Great Reformation to everyone humbled by His Law. "Arise, shine; for thy light is come, and the glory of the LORD is risen upon thee…. The LORD shall arise upon thee, and his glory shall be seen upon thee. And the Gentiles shall come to thy light, and kings to the brightness of thy rising" (Isa. 60:1-3).

The Seal of God has been given to all of His children during this time who finally bow to the forceful words of divine reproof. They must hear an extra heaping dispensation of instruction through the Law and the Law's living Testimony of Jesus. Before He can be a pardoning Saviour, Jesus must be a law enforcing Prince.

> Him hath God exalted with his right hand to be a Prince and a Saviour, for to give repentance to Israel, and forgiveness of sins (Acts 5:31).

Only those who submit to the light of the Law will consummate their submission to the power and authority of God's word by laying hold onto Christ's gift of repentance and surrender to His fatherly love (see John 3:33). They find great peace with the King through the ministry of their Friend and High Priest, the King's precious Son. They are justified and adopted into the heavenly family through the Spirit of the Son (see Ephesians 3:15; Galatians 4:4-7; Romans 8:14-17). Peace with God leads to a new life of obedience. Nothing offends them, and they offend no one. As peacemakers, everyone calls them the children of God. They receive the power to become the sons of the living God, and His gentleness in them makes them great. By beholding His glory they have glory.

God authorized the big test of the fifth trumpet; and the effect of allegiance to His coming kingdom — or of treason against it — have been the fifth trumpet's most profound manifestations. This fifth trumpet test will continue into the seventh trumpet, then increasingly manifesting the most Christ-like purity ever witnessed from human history, and also causing its most demonic wickedness.

The forces for heaven and hell are growing, and will, in the end, collide in fireworks that this world has never before seen, even in all of its holocausts or inquisitions. "And there shall be a time of trouble, such as never was since there was a nation even to that same time" (Dan. 12:1). "Many shall be purified, and made white, and tried; but the wicked shall do wickedly: and none of the wicked shall understand; but the wise shall understand" (Dan. 12:10).

The coming revival of holiness can only be had in the environment of the restored Testimony of Jesus. Without strong, thundering conviction of sin from the fiery mountain of God, the proud, willful human nature will never release its hold on inbred rebellion. And without the almost overwhelming need for mercy under the wrath toward our sinfulness as God sees it, we can never obtain the powerful desperation that crystallizes hope into faith and propels the soul all the way to heaven to touch the hem of our heavenly High Priest. Through that touch will come His acceptance, His justification, and His restful peace. But, without the language from a prophet's earnest, reproving voice, the conscience will never come to that superhuman need of a Saviour and His grace.

How can anyone need first aid unless he first received a wound? Healing our boastful indulgence of sin requires deep surgical incisions initiated and carefully overseen by One from outside of ourselves. Our sinfulness requires afflictions which are beyond our control. We will never punish ourselves enough to stanch our immorality; we always restrain self-flagellations from digging deeply enough into our conscience to remove the cancer of sin. We need the almighty Spirit of God to bring our conscience sufficiently acute pain, but who will simultaneously and compassionately reassure us of His equally almighty tenderness and wisdom. The Father's fearful warnings and admonitions make us sting with conviction! But, through "the Spirit of His Son" (Gal. 4:6) breathing life into His promises, we know without any doubt that He desires to heal us and not to destroy us. "For the Son of man is not come to destroy men's lives, but to save them" (Luke 9:56, cf 2 Cor. 5:19), and God was in Christ reconciling the world to Himself.

He says, "I wound, and I heal" (Deut. 32:39). In the context of Deuteronomy 32:39, to wound means to punish. But, will we accept the humiliation that comes with punishment?

Many hate the God of the Bible for His discipline because they choose to not see their big need of correction. We can accept our humbling only when we come to admit that we deserve everything we get, and much more. Whoever can accept that premise will humbly endure painful trials and be thankful for God's loving-kindness throughout all the tragedies He allows. Will we really trust our Shepherd's scourging rod and then His comforting staff? Will we accept all the stumblingblocks that He permits Satan to put in our way? Will Protestantism and Adventism submit to the truth found in His Testimonies for the Church, which grate upon our fallen nature until we collapse on the Stone in perfect surrender? Will we let our self-sufficient heart and self-will be broken into a million pieces? Will we let our heart and will shatter to the extent that only He can put them back together again? Will Protestant Americans let self die? These questions are the issues of God's word since the very beginning, but especially so during the final three trumpet plagues upon America.

> In those days the house of Judah shall walk with the house of Israel, and they shall come together out of the land of the north to the land that I have given for an inheritance unto your fathers.
>
> But I said, How shall I put thee among the children, and give thee a pleasant land, a goodly heritage of the hosts of nations? and I said, Thou shalt call me, My father; and shalt not turn away from me.
>
> Surely as a wife treacherously departeth from her husband, so have ye dealt treacherously with me, O house of Israel, saith the LORD.
>
> A voice was heard upon the high places, weeping and supplications of the children of Israel:

for they have perverted their way, and they have forgotten the LORD their God.

Return, ye backsliding children, and I will heal your backslidings. Behold, we come unto thee; for thou art the LORD our God.

Truly in vain is salvation hoped for from the hills, and from the multitude of mountains: truly in the LORD our God is the salvation of Israel.

For shame hath devoured the labour of our fathers from our youth; their flocks and their herds, their sons and their daughters.

We lie down in our shame, and our confusion covereth us: for we have sinned against the LORD our God, we and our fathers, from our youth even unto this day, and have not obeyed the voice of the LORD our God (Jer. 3:18-25).

We Protestant Americans need the necessary pains of the Law at the skillful hands of our heavenly Chiropractor and Physical therapist. In order to have the restoration He speaks of, the bones of our hearts and lives, which He has fractured, He must reset.

Whosoever shall fall on this stone shall be broken (Matt. 21:44).

Behold, this child is set for the fall and rising again of many in Israel (Luke 2:34).

Make me to hear joy and gladness; that the bones which thou hast broken may rejoice (Ps. 51:8).

Unlike Satan, who wounds to enjoy our unending torment, the Lord doesn't wound just to wound or because He enjoys seeing us suffer (see Lamentations 3:33). Like any good physician, Jesus wounds to *heal and only to heal* (see Proverbs 27:6). Resetting is excruciating agony; but to evade it means a lifetime of endless grinding and misery (see Matthew 21:44).

The Chief Surgeon is jealous for the second phase of His healing program, and demands:

Is there no balm in Gilead; is there no physician there? why then is not the health of the daughter of my people recovered? (Jer. 8:22).

Can we trust Jesus to administer punishment without abusing our hearts and lives? Yes. "He that believeth on the Son hath everlasting life: and he that believeth not the Son shall not see life" (John 3:36). "He looketh upon men, and if any say, I have sinned, and perverted that which was right, and it profited me not"; "then he is gracious unto him, and saith, Deliver him from going down to the pit" (Job 33:27, 24). He will heal us when we've accepted His consequences, admitting our infidelity to Him, crying, "Abba, Father" (Rom. 8:15) for His forgiveness and help. When our "uncircumcised hearts [are] humbled, and [we] then accept of the punishment of [our] iniquity" (Lev. 26:41), then He will give us soaring, unprecedented peace and grace from His mercy seat. Go to the Testimony of Jesus and develop a taste for His unvarnished, testing truth. And see the salvation of the Lord.

By denying the Son's tearing conviction and then His healing grace we remain incurably tormented, especially those who have the look of godliness. Vexation and grinding and gnashing of teeth afflict our souls and encompass our meaningless days. So we automatically and involuntarily seek remedies for our oppressive misery through every legal or illegal, socially acceptable or unacceptable self-indulgence and vice. Thus, both the timeless street and pharmaceutical drug trades, and both the fields of humanistic psychology and psychiatry. "By thy sorceries [Gr. *pharmakeia*] were all nations deceived" (Rev. 18:23). And likewise, the poisonous processed foods and beverages that destroy the physical constitution, and demoralize the mind and soul. "For all nations have drunk of the wine of the wrath of [Babylon's] fornication... and the merchants of the earth are waxed rich through the abundance of her delicacies" (Rev. 18:3).

All of these analgesics can offer only the human attempt to allay the heavy wrath of God against all who will not fall in repentance to Jesus during this His investigative judgment. These humanistic quick-fixes of the fifth and sixth trumpets, these sorceries from Babylon's pharmacy are placebos that preempt and prevent the striving for God's love (see Proverbs 2:1-5, 9), and therefore the true healing from the Spirit of Christ. True healing can only come when we've returned to our Reformation fathers' *God of Law*; then, humbled and repentant, His Spirit of blessedness will give us the true purpose-driven life. We've lived in this Babylon long enough. It's time to come out and accept the straight testimony of Jesus, the faithful and true Witness (see Revelation 3:14-22). It's time to be forgiven "all thine iniquities" and to be healed of "all thy diseases" (Ps. 103:3).

The "time of trouble, such as never was," is soon to open upon us; and we shall need an experience which we do not now possess and which many are too indolent to obtain....

...Not even by a thought could our Saviour be brought to yield to the power of temptation. Satan finds in human hearts some point where he can gain a foothold; some sinful desire is cherished, by means of which his temptations assert their power. But Christ declared of Himself: "The prince of this world cometh, and hath nothing in Me." John 14:30... This is the condition in which those must be found who shall stand in the time of trouble.

It is in this life that we are to separate sin from us, through faith in the atoning blood of Christ. Our precious Saviour invites us to join ourselves to Him, to unite our weakness to His strength, our ignorance to His wisdom, our unworthiness to His merits.... None can neglect or defer this work but at the most fearful peril to their souls *The Great Controversy*, p. 622, 623.

The shaking and strong delusion of 2 Thessalonians 2:9-12 don't begin after the sealing ends. They already started long ago, in 1844 with the rejection of strong Bible truth. Let us now believe the strong accusations of the Law against us, and be healed and sealed (see Galatians 3:24).

If they shall confess their iniquity, and the iniquity of their fathers, with their trespass which they trespassed against me, and [*if* they shall confess] that also they have walked contrary unto me; and that I also have walked contrary unto them, and have brought them into the land of their enemies; *if* then their uncircumcised hearts be humbled, and they then accept of the punishment of their iniquity: ***then*** will I remember my covenant (Lev. 26:40-42).

Like Jacob, when we've had enough of striving against God then our will submits at His feet. Then and only then do we bow to His powerful Law which has been brought up-to-date in the unarguable pages of the Spirit of Prophecy through Ellen White. When we admit to the destitute condition of our own making, then we can receive the true medication for our tormented mind and soul. When we surrender to His humbling condemnation and shame toward all of us, His Protestant children, then and only then will Jesus be pleased to heal us and seal us (see Leviticus 26:39-45).

God's forgiveness and acceptance are very conditional. Our humbling, by accepting His immutable Law, simply must be the condition for His Son's grace and peace. But, *the humbling heals; it's the **sweetest** thing!* Great peace have they who love God's humbling Law! Most beautiful is a soul yielded and still, at peace with God and man and self! The affliction behind us, there is no greater relief. God's punishment cleanses and rests our mind, and His Spirit's peace makes the way open for happily hearing the truth. The mind is free again, even for gaining new aptitudes and skills, gifts and discernment. "No chastening for the present seemeth to be joyous, but grievous: nevertheless afterward it yieldeth the peaceable fruit of righteousness unto them which are exercised thereby" (Heb. 12:11). Face the counsel from the Spirit of Prophecy, or accept the troubles that Providence has laid on you in consequence to disregarding His counsel. Receive His discipline, and find your everlasting Father. Let the Lord humble you, "and he shall lift you up" (Jas. 4:10). Let His commandment slay you, "and your soul shall live" (Isa. 55:3, cf Rom. 7:9-11, 24, 25). The Law of the Lord is perfect, converting the soul.

The ones who receive the Seal of God during these fifth and sixth trumpets are those who sigh and cry and hopelessly die to self. Ellen White's experience of surrender as a twelve year old illustrates the grievous chastisement that leads to Jesus' gift of enduring peace:

While bowed at the altar with others who were seeking the Lord, all the language of my heart was: "Help, Jesus, save me or I perish! I will never cease to entreat till my prayer is heard and my sins forgiven!" I felt my needy, helpless condition as never before. As I knelt and prayed, suddenly my burden left me, and my heart was light. At first a feeling of alarm came over me, and I tried to resume my load of distress. It seemed to me that I had no right to feel joyous and happy. But Jesus seemed very near to me; I felt able to come to Him with all my griefs, misfortunes, and trials, even as the needy ones came to Him for relief when He was upon earth. There was a surety in my heart that He understood my peculiar trials and sympathized with me. I can never forget this precious assurance of the pitying tenderness of Jesus toward one so unworthy of His notice. I learned more of the divine character of

Christ in that short period when bowed among the praying ones than ever before....

My life appeared to me in a different light. The affliction that had darkened my childhood seemed to have been dealt me *in mercy for my good* [emphasis mine], to turn my heart away from the world and its unsatisfying pleasures, and incline it toward the enduring attractions of heaven *Testimonies for the Church*, vol. 1, p. 17, 19. (**See Appendix A** for her complete beautiful testimony.)

Little children can understand heaven's discipline because they trust their parents, and therefore their parents' discipline. They submit to their merciful punishment. They love their parents; so they give up the fight. And after the punishment, they are perfectly settled and happy, reasonable and loving, resealed in their parents' upbringing.

We have our punishing Parent in the heavens. "And I saw heaven opened, and behold a white horse; and he that sat upon him was called Faithful and True, and in righteousness he doth judge and make war" (Rev. 19:11). Will we remain under His righteous warfare against our self-focus, or will we run away? Will we trust our heavenly Parent, and accept His judgments and His Spirit's warfare against our sins? Will we appreciate His rod and His staff, and then know the peace and contentment that follow, His comforting Spirit of truth?

> He looketh upon men, and if any say, I have sinned, and perverted that which was right, and it profited me not;
>
> Then he is gracious unto him, and saith, Deliver him from going down to the pit: I have found a ransom.
>
> He shall pray unto God, and he will be favourable unto him: and he shall see his face with joy: for he will render unto man his righteousness.
>
> He will deliver his soul from going into the pit, and his life shall see the light.
>
> His flesh shall be fresher than a child's: he shall return to the days of his youth:
>
> Lo, all these things worketh God oftentimes with man,
>
> To bring back his soul from the pit, to be enlightened with the light of the living (Job 33:27, 24, 26, 28, 25, 29, 30).

Shouldn't we patiently and trustingly endure His righteous warfare against our sins, and humbly say that we deserve much worse discipline than He gives?

Constant mercy and peace with God, and soundness of mind and body await everyone who finally gives in to the truth of God's righteousness, and who then repents. But, this whole person boon to health will require soul affliction for what we've done to God and to His holy name (see Ezekiel 36:21-23) during this investigative judgment. It will require total humiliation toward Him, a supernatural sorrow and humiliation which we cannot manufacture. However, it is a work which Jesus will implant in us after we "pine away" (Lev. 26:39) under the results of our iniquities. Because of our resistance to trust Him we often pine away for many more years than necessary; yet He works with us and waits for us. Christ made us and has also pined away under our curse. He knows what makes us pine away.

Under Christ's care we must accept His consequences and spiritual punishments which convict us of sin (see 1 Peter 2:20; Romans 7:9-11). Christ has tailored God's discipline just for our eventual whole-hearted repentance (see Romans 7:24, 25). Under the supervision of the almighty Schoolmaster, our unbelief and self-sufficiency necessarily require desperate measures through extreme difficulties that inundate us with shame and sorrow, being "shut up unto the faith which should afterwards be revealed" (Gal. 3:23). This baptism of fire brings us down to our humbling, and then to the great possibility of Jesus' help. Here faith works as we look to Jesus for help, which alone leads to full reconciliation and peace with God. Our Father is eagerly waiting to see our souls thus redeemed; and He rejoices when He finally hears the prayer, "Father, I have sinned against heaven, and in thy sight, and am no more worthy to be called thy son" (Luke 15:21).

> Wilt thou not from this time cry unto me, My father, thou art the guide of my youth? (Jer. 3:4).
>
> Come, and let us return unto the LORD: for he hath torn, and he will heal us; he hath smitten, and he will bind us up (Hos. 6:1).
>
> Many times did he deliver them; but they provoked him with their counsel, and were brought low for their iniquity. Nevertheless he regarded

their affliction, when he heard their cry (Ps. 106:43, 44).

I say unto you, that likewise joy shall be in heaven over one sinner that repenteth, more than over ninety and nine just persons, which need no repentance (Luke 15:7).

I have surely heard Ephraim bemoaning himself thus; Thou hast chastised me, and I was chastised, as a bullock unaccustomed to the yoke: turn thou me, and I shall be turned; for thou art the LORD my God. Surely after that I was turned, I repented; and after that I was instructed, I smote upon my thigh: I was ashamed, yea, even confounded, because I did bear the reproach of my youth (Jer. 31:18, 19).

Is Ephraim my dear son? is he a pleasant child? for since I spake against him, I do earnestly remember him still: therefore my bowels are troubled for him; I will surely have mercy upon him, saith the LORD (vs. 20).

Note from the above Jeremiah 31 text how soon our Lord recognized genuine sorrow for sin. *Immediately.*

I will not contend for ever, neither will I be always wroth: for the spirit should fail before me, and the souls which I have made (Isa. 57:16).

Jeremiah heard the Lord's troubled heart quickly refresh and open again to the wandering northern tribes of Israel. And they did return — centuries later in the days of the apostolic church.

Wherefore remember, that ye being in time past Gentiles in the flesh, who are called Uncircumcision by that which is called the Circumcision in the flesh made by hands; that at that time ye were without Christ, being aliens from the commonwealth of Israel, and strangers from the covenants of promise, having no hope, and without God in the world: but now in Christ Jesus ye who sometimes were far off are made nigh by the blood of Christ. For he is our peace, who hath made both one, and hath broken down the middle wall of partition between us (Eph. 2:11-14).

Today, His thoughts toward us all still echo from His appeal to Israel. He watches over our divinely supervised plight while we suffer under His necessary reproving consequences; and He remains vigilant for signs of our relenting. In the above verses of Jeremiah 31:18-20, we see Him poised and longing to receive us like the father of the prodigal son, and to restore plentifully every bounty that He had removed. His Spirit calls out from His written word to our hearts. Today, won't His wandering Protestant children return to Him and surrender to His Law of liberty? Or, will they continue to suffer the devil's dogmatic rulership? Will they endure his tormenting plagues of restlessness from an unsurrendered "evil conscience" (Heb. 10:22)? Will they live under the fire and brimstone of Satan's presence with which he happily rewards them for their distrust and rejection of God?

Quietly, for the past century and a half, Providence has overseen Satan's subtle work to destroy faith and to scratch the mark of his mind upon the consciences of Protestant America. During this fifth and sixth trumpet period, God has been accomplishing to scatter the power of His holy people by the tormenting emptiness that attends their increasing distance from Him. If they won't research His Law and wrestle with His Law, which "worketh wrath" against the control of Satan (Rom. 4:15), then *in mercy* the Lord sends them the troubles of life to wrestle with. Everyone who patiently pursues these difficult precious providences to their full end — in either God's corrective commandments or in the consequences for despising His correction — he will find them leading him to surrender to God's will, and deliverance from his internal torments.

If his children forsake my law, and walk not in my judgments;

If they break my statutes, and keep not my commandments;

Then will I visit their transgression with the rod, and their iniquity with stripes.

Nevertheless my lovingkindness will I not utterly take from him, nor suffer my faithfulness to fail.

My covenant will I not break, nor alter the thing that is gone out of my lips (Ps. 89:30-34).

The end [*telos*, "goal"] of the commandment is charity out of a pure heart, and of a good conscience, and of faith unfeigned (1 Tim. 1:5).

Christ is the end [*telos*, "goal"] of the law for righteousness to every one that believeth (Rom. 10:4).

Christ brings with Him faith and love, obedience and a healthy conscience.

Through His Law, His Bible, our naturally uncircumcised hearts can be humbled. By His word we can learn to surrender to God's will, as did Isaac, Joseph, Moses, David, Daniel, and especially the Man-child Jesus who was the perfect example of surrender. Through the Spirit of God's word we can mortify the desires and deeds of the flesh (see Romans 8:13). Or, we might opt to learn this greatest lesson of life without the Law or the written word, as it was more harshly learned by Jacob, Samson, King Manasseh, and Peter. Still the promise is, "In all their affliction he was afflicted" (Isa. 63:9). As the raw backs of Samson and Manasseh were also experienced by Jesus under the Roman whip, in the afflictions of us all He is afflicted.

These are the two paths to God, either of which can lead to His perfect gift of salvation. They are truth or consequences: the lighter, easier way to God by reading and believing and heeding His word; or the more difficult, hard row to hoe of rebelling against the word of God.

The way of transgressors is hard (Prov. 13:15).

Thine own wickedness shall correct thee, and thy backslidings shall reprove thee (Jer. 2:19).

Wherefore the Lord brought upon them the captains of the host of the king of Assyria, which took Manasseh among the thorns, and bound him with fetters, and carried him to Babylon (2 Chron. 33:11).

And when he was in affliction, he besought the Lord his God, and humbled himself greatly before the God of his fathers, and prayed unto him: and he was intreated of him, and heard his supplication, and brought him again to Jerusalem into his kingdom. Then Manasseh knew that the Lord he was God (2 Chron. 33:12, 13).

Those who choose to avoid the Bible have misinterpreted God's strong language of reproof to be solely against them. The reality is that, His strong language is against Satan through them. The word goes through them to hit the devil. Once they repent, His adversary is no longer them, but the devil (see Matthew 16:23; 1 Peter 5:8).

The LORD rebuke thee, O Satan; even the LORD that hath chosen Jerusalem rebuke thee: is not this a brand plucked out of the fire?... Take away the filthy garments from him. Behold, I have caused thine iniquity to pass from thee, and I will clothe thee with change of raiment.... Let them set a fair mitre upon his head (Zech. 3:2, 4, 5).

But, by far the easier, less self-destructive path to God is to study into and wrestle with His Law's strong, humbling testimony against sin until it gives us the need for a Saviour in Jesus (see Romans 7:9-8:1; Galatians 3:24; John 6:37). On the way to Christ, being humbled is never easy, the human heart, proud as it is. But, reading and heeding God's word is the much nicer path to God than the much harsher consequences of a wasted lifetime for evading the eventual, ultimate bowing to the truth.

It is only as the law of God is restored to its rightful position that there can be a revival of primitive faith and godliness among His professed people. "Thus saith the Lord, Stand ye in the ways, and see, and ask for the old paths, where is the good way, and walk therein, and ye shall find rest for your souls." Jeremiah 6:16 *The Great Controversy*, p. 478.

Yet, today if we have chosen the hard, time-wasting road, when once humbled by the Law and surrendered to Jesus as our companion in life, He makes the aftershocks of the consequences much easier to handle. The Spirit empowers us with faith, hope, and love; and our rehab may be long, but with His faith, hope, and love the rehab is very doable. So then, with regard to our restoration to heaven we may say,

We are troubled on every side, yet not distressed; we are perplexed, but not in despair; persecuted, but not forsaken; cast down, but not destroyed; always bearing about in the body the dying of the Lord Jesus, that the life also of Jesus might be made manifest in our body (2 Cor. 4:8-10).

John had seen Satan fall to earth during the third trumpet. Now, in a new way via the fifth trumpet, John sees God allowing the fallen destroyer to open to the whole world an overwhelming, never-ending curse. (See Revelation 8:13). Through a dense cloud of satanic influence from hell, inspiring and propelling the human agencies of the devil's favored earthly power, God has increasingly isolated Earth from His benediction.

What have we seen arise during the 150 years that followed the California Gold Rush? Have we not a whole different world than the previous six millenniums? Science exploded, and out of that detonation has come continuously accelerating advancements in every field. The fifth trumpet period has produced one modern miracle after another. How tempting for the Protestant descendants to cut the ties to our Reformation heritage and jump on the exciting train of modernization whizzing by! The beautiful spiritual privileges passed down from the Reformation have been abhorred by most of us! The world given to the care of the Protestants to be reconciled back to God has been almost completely neglected. How far we have fallen!

> We have sinned with our fathers, we have committed iniquity, we have done wickedly (Ps. 106:6).

Today, an intimate faith in God has become more difficult to arrive at than at any other time of Earth's history. By way of millions of the most insidious counterfeits of truth, through thousands upon thousands of inventions and scientific advancements, God is hidden from our sight. And we have loved to have it so. The successes of technology and its resulting life of excess and ease, its appetites and addictions, have created a thick barrier between us and our God. Our absorption into the modern world has hidden His face from us (see Isaiah 59:2), His escapees from the papal Dark Ages. We cannot hear His Spirit without diligence on our part to resolve the torment which He has permitted to get our attention. Will we reconsider our unfounded prejudice against His Bible? Will we wrestle with the Angel as did Jacob until we sorrow for our self-sufficiency and seek Him with our whole heart? (See Genesis 32:24-32.) The whole submission of the heart to the Lord of Sabaoth is the battlefield to be regained from the fifth and sixth trumpet rampaging hosts.

The Spirit of the Lord says to His beloved Protestants,

> Can a maid forget her ornaments, or a bride her attire? yet my people have forgotten me days without number.... Yet thou sayest, Because I am innocent, surely his anger shall turn from me. Behold, I will plead with thee, because thou sayest, I have not sinned (Jer. 2:32, 35).

> If we say that we have no sin, we deceive ourselves, and the truth is not in us (1 John 1:8).

The past century and a half of unrestrained worldly success and never before seen technological progress has brought to Protestant America multitudes of temptations, lies, idolatrous inventions for extravagance and convenience, eating away at the principles of uprightness and duty gained by the Reformation, and eating away at the nation God gave to bless the world. Satan's hosts and human agencies, freed to whisper their hints, have slowly, yet systematically, brought the Protestant maintained world to a civilization boasting perpetual forgetfulness of their Provider, Protector, and Deliverer from the Dark Age persecutions.

The empowered hosts of darkness are tempting the Lord to destroy His people as they did many times to ancient Israel. This Protestant nation is cutting the last strands of the cord that God lowered to us 500 years ago to keep us from falling into Satan's bottomless moral dungeon. Protestant America is soon to reach across the abyss and grasp the deadly hand of this pretended benefactor of the earth. Then will the wrath of our God fall upon us. We have crowded ourselves with multitudes of objects that are designed to lead our thoughts away from God's love and from careful obedience to Him, until at last, if this present time were not shortened, even the very chosen movement of God would be completely deceived and hopelessly corrupted. Do we see the reality and impact of all this?

> Therefore thus saith the LORD, Behold, I will lay stumblingblocks before this people, and the fathers and the sons together shall fall upon them; the neighbour and his friend shall perish (Jer. 6:21).

Riding upon Protestant America's temporal blessings have come ever-increasingly easier ways to forget God. They are everywhere: over the airwaves, on billboards, in books and magazines, under our fingertips, floating past our nostrils, touching every sense. Attracting, attracting, attracting the Reformation children, the temptations keep away any thought upon the warnings and promises of God's word. This condition, though enormously concentrated in the cities, has moved out into the countryside, reaching its tentacles out so far that pure back country is confined to small reserves. The opportunities to see God in His created works are dwindling. Idolatry and corruption are sown broadcast across the nation that was once favored of the Lord. It reaps what it has sown. It has sown the wind; and it is reaping the whirlwind, even within the churches. Dazzling and glamorized and sensational, the good life which Lucifer offers is an attraction that nothing can break except by heeding the invitation calling from above to renounce it all and flee to the God of our Reformation fathers.

> *The fifth trumpet explains the unprecedented rapidity of the transition from stone age to space age over the past 150+ years' race of claiming humanity for the Seal or the mark.*

Today's generation, as never before, lives in pervasive idolatry— a system which is so sophisticated, smooth and soothing, that it is almost inescapable. Paganism, especially in Protestant America, has come and built up a high stairway to heaven. Trapped in her worldly successes are found the souls of many who might have known righteousness. Looking to man's achievements and wisdom is the cause of great torment. Cursed with misery is the person who depends on the accomplishments of man. There is no peace for those who turn their faith away from the principles of God's character, to concentrate on the fruits of this world.

The troubled souls of Americans have thrown out the fear of God, and they find their life to be one bitter disappointment after another. The utmost effort is expended by Protestant America for the pursuit of happiness, upon which every society must be founded. Yet, because they have ignored the authority of their Reformation's Law of God and their accountability to Him, innocent love and trust cannot exist. Therefore, neither can real, abiding happiness be found, no matter how intently they pursue it. This was never God's will for His glorious Protestant Reformation.

The children of Protestantism have forgotten their Saviour and Friend. By turning away from the Ten Commandments, they have been given over to another master, a transition which they have not comprehended. "I will wait upon the LORD, that hideth his face from" "both the houses of Israel" (Isa. 8:17, 14). Protestants, "Israel, part II," are experiencing the torment of living apart from God and being absorbed into the idolatrous world around them; and Adventists, "Judah, part II," are following right on the heels of Protestant Americans (see Jeremiah 3:8). (*See Appendix A.*) The ancient and modern counterparts are different settings, but the very same sorrowful story.

The fifth trumpet explains the unprecedented rapidity of the transition from stone age to space age over the past 150+ years' race of claiming humanity for the Seal or the mark. It confirms what happens when knowledge of good is mingled with evil. It shows how curiosity and science end in another towering Babel whenever they are emptied of fear, faith, and thankfulness to the Creator.

But, this modern Babylon is actually all one thing of two aspects. It is Jehovah's gift of His continuing, plenteous, promised prosperity to His beloved Law and gospel Protestant Reformation for its 16th century acceptance of His relationship covenant. But, it is also Satan's relentless acting to make heaven's wonderful gifts for the self-sacrifice of the Reformers' generation from five centuries ago the strongest source of idolatry and the greatest impediment to Christ's final call for obedience.

> I have forsaken mine house, I have left mine heritage; I have given the dearly beloved of my soul into the hand of her enemies (Jer. 12:7).

As the Lord brought the children of Israel the flocks of quail to satisfy their perverted appetites (see Exodus 16:11-13), so has He opened to the children of Protestantism swarms of earthly things because their hearts were there. Covetousness is where they have "set [their] love" (Ps. 91:14).

> Ye shall not eat one day, nor two days, nor five days, neither ten days, nor twenty days; but even a whole month, until it come out at your nostrils, and it be loathsome unto you: because that ye have despised the LORD which is among you, and have wept before him, saying, Why came we forth out of Egypt?…
>
> And while the flesh was yet between their teeth, ere it was chewed, the wrath of the LORD was kindled against the people, and the LORD smote the people with a very great plague (Num. 11:19, 20, 33).

He led Israel down into Egyptian slavery and later into the Babylonian stream of four heathen empires, to help them see their toying with the adversary's temptations (see Genesis 35:1-4). So has He brought the abundance of luxuries and refined delicacies of the idolatrous world to the lives and mouths of Protestants (see Revelation 18:3) to test their self-denial and soul-affliction in preparation for His soon-coming kingdom. Through the Lord's setting in motion "the hour of temptation, which shall come upon all the world, to try them that dwell upon the earth" (Rev. 3:10), the fifth trumpet has been God's sorrowful letting go of the vast majority of His beloved bride of the 1500s because of her infidelity. The Lord, foreseeing Protestantism's initial rejection of 1844, foreknew her inevitable apostasy to her secret consort from below, the full apostasy which is now taking place. His continued, abundant prosperity to His beloved Protestant America combined with the expected delusive temptation that He permitted her consort to create from it, would be His test for her heart's secret love, and her undoing.

> Then said I, Ah, Lord GOD! surely thou hast greatly deceived this people and Jerusalem, saying, Ye shall have peace; whereas the sword reacheth unto the soul. At that time shall it be said to this people and to Jerusalem, A dry wind of the high places in the wilderness toward the daughter of my people, not to fan, nor to cleanse, even a full wind from those places shall come unto me: now also will I give sentence against them. Behold, he shall come up as clouds, and his chariots shall be as a whirlwind: his horses are swifter than eagles. Woe unto us! (Jer. 4:10-13).

> The Lord is...longsuffering to us-ward, not willing that any should perish.... But the day of the Lord will come as a thief in the night (2 Pet. 3:9, 10).

The Revelation shows that Protestantism would heed the fifth trumpet locust army of false prophets. They would woo her with smooth words and deceptions that depart from the sin-condemning, authoritative Law of a Father. They would glaze over the prospects of her departure's unavoidable punishment. The strong delusion from God would catch almost all in its spell. Imbibing the lying prophecies and the doctrines of Romanism which strike at the Law of God, the Protestant church would become a lighthouse of false prophecy to the world.

> For they prophesy falsely unto you in my name: I have not sent them, saith the LORD (Jer. 29:9).

Today, that restless and violent army of fifth trumpet destroyers has left Protestant America completely devoid of faith in her Creator and Redeemer.

> Now go, write it before them in a table, and note it in a book, that it may be for the time to come for ever and ever: that this is a rebellious people, lying children, children that will not hear the law of the LORD: which say to the seers, See not; and to the prophets, Prophesy not unto us right things, speak unto us smooth things, prophesy deceits (Isa. 30:8-10).

At the end of the prophetic five months of wasting the Protestant faith, another gold rush occurred. The stock market began to rise in 1993 and to accelerate in 1995. Year after year its exponential growth skyrocketed, drawing more and more unwary Protestant Americans and the nations under her care into its dizzying heights for the hope of easy, lush retirement in a world empire that they believed could never end.

The fifth trumpet 150 year prophecy came to its conclusion at the end of 1999. As we moved into the sixth trumpet, the up-surging stock market abruptly leveled off and became rocky and untrustworthy (**see Appendix B**). But, by then the Protestants were afraid to get out of it, atheistically trusting that this world will never end. They thought that America and its global empire must continue forever, and that the market forces are their friend. In accordance with pagan philosophy and far from the stance of their Reformation forefathers, Protestant Americans now believed that the nature of men is basically good and would never hurt them. The enemy was emptying their treasuries, as was prophesied.

> He [the vile King of the north] shall enter also into the glorious land, and many countries shall be overthrown... He shall stretch forth his hand also upon the countries: and the land of Egypt [atheistic United States] shall not escape. But he shall have power over the treasures of gold and of silver, and over all the precious things of Egypt (Dan. 11:41-43).

Protestant Republican America — spiritually called the atheistic Egyptian King of the south and the enemy to all things papal — duped themselves. In the delusive trap that the Lord permitted Satan to lay for them they eventually lost their wealth, their retirements, and, only partially their confidence in man.

Heaven's strong promises to Israel of old the Lord bequeathed to prosperous, abounding, Protestant America:

If thou shalt hearken diligently unto the voice of the LORD thy God, to observe and to do all his commandments which I command thee this day, that the LORD thy God will set thee on high above all nations of the earth:

And all these blessings shall come on thee, *and overtake thee*, if thou shalt hearken unto the voice of the LORD thy God.

Blessed shalt thou be in the city, and blessed shalt thou be in the field.

Blessed shall be the fruit of thy body, and the fruit of thy ground, and the fruit of thy cattle, the increase of thy kine, and the flocks of thy sheep.

Blessed shall be thy basket and thy store.

Blessed shalt thou be when thou comest in, and blessed shalt thou be when thou goest out.

The LORD shall cause thine enemies that rise up against thee to be smitten before thy face: they shall come out against thee one way, and flee before thee seven ways.

The LORD shall command the blessing upon thee in thy storehouses, and in all that thou settest thine hand unto; and he shall bless thee in the land which the LORD thy God giveth thee.

The LORD shall establish thee an holy people unto himself, as he hath sworn unto thee, if thou shalt keep the commandments of the LORD thy God, and walk in his ways.

And all people of the earth shall see that thou art called by the name of the LORD; and they shall be afraid of thee.

And the LORD shall make thee plenteous in goods, in the fruit of thy body, and in the fruit of thy cattle, and in the fruit of thy ground, in the land which the LORD sware unto thy fathers to give thee.

The LORD shall open unto thee his good treasure, the heaven to give the rain unto thy land in his season, and to bless all the work of thine hand: and thou shalt lend unto many nations, and thou shalt not borrow.

And the LORD shall make thee the head, and not the tail; and thou shalt be above only, and thou shalt not be beneath; if that thou hearken unto the commandments of the LORD thy God, which I command thee this day, to observe and to do them:

And thou shalt not go aside from any of the words which I command thee this day, to the right hand, or to the left, to go after other gods to serve them (Deut. 28:1-14).

The early days of Protestant America were a picture of simplicity and beauty and hope. But, today, we're seeing just the beginning of the fulfillment of our choice to so long depart from our living God, as Moses also made clear.

But, it shall come to pass, if thou wilt **not** hearken unto the voice of the LORD thy God, to observe to do all his commandments and his statutes which I command thee this day; that all these curses shall come upon thee, *and overtake thee*:

Cursed shalt thou be in the city, and cursed shalt thou be in the field.

Cursed shall be thy basket and thy store.

Cursed shall be the fruit of thy body, and the fruit of thy land, the increase of thy kine, and the flocks of thy sheep.

Cursed shalt thou be when thou comest in, and cursed shalt thou be when thou goest out.

The LORD shall send upon thee cursing, vexation, and rebuke, in all that thou settest thine hand unto for to do, until thou be destroyed, and until thou perish quickly; because of the wickedness of thy doings, whereby thou hast forsaken me.

The LORD shall make the pestilence cleave unto thee, until he have consumed thee from off the land, whither thou goest to possess it.

The LORD shall smite thee with a consumption, and with a fever, and with an inflammation, and with an extreme burning, and with the sword, and with blasting, and with mildew; and they shall pursue thee until thou perish.

And thy heaven that is over thy head shall be brass, and the earth that is under thee shall be iron.

The LORD shall make the rain of thy land powder and dust: from heaven shall it come down upon thee, until thou be destroyed.

The LORD shall cause thee to be smitten before thine enemies: thou shalt go out one way against them, and flee seven ways before them: and shalt be removed into all the kingdoms of the earth.

And thy carcase shall be meat unto all fowls of the air, and unto the beasts of the earth, and no man shall fray them away.

The LORD will smite thee with the botch of Egypt, and with the emerods [hemorrhoids], and with the scab, and with the itch, whereof thou canst not be healed.

The LORD shall smite thee with madness, and blindness, and astonishment of heart:

And thou shalt grope at noonday, as the blind gropeth in darkness, and thou shalt not prosper in thy ways: and thou shalt be only oppressed and spoiled evermore, and no man shall save thee.

Thou shalt betroth a wife, and another man shall lie with her: thou shalt build an house, and thou shalt not dwell therein: thou shalt plant a vineyard, and shalt not gather the grapes thereof.

Thine ox shall be slain before thine eyes, and thou shalt not eat thereof: thine ass shall be violently taken away from before thy face, and shall not be restored to thee: thy sheep shall be given unto thine enemies, and thou shalt have none to rescue them.

Thy sons and thy daughters shall be given unto another people, and thine eyes shall look, and fail with longing for them all the day long: and there shall be no might in thine hand.

The fruit of thy land, and all thy labours, shall a nation which thou knowest not eat up; and thou shalt be only oppressed and crushed alway:

So that thou shalt be mad for the sight of thine eyes which thou shalt see.

The LORD shall smite thee in the knees, and in the legs, with a sore botch that cannot be healed, from the sole of thy foot unto the top of thy head.

The LORD shall bring thee, and thy king which thou shalt set over thee, unto a nation which neither thou nor thy fathers have known; and there shalt thou serve other gods, wood and stone.

And thou shalt become an astonishment, a proverb, and a byword, among all nations whither the LORD shall lead thee.

Thou shalt carry much seed out into the field, and shalt gather but little in; for the locust shall consume it.

Thou shalt plant vineyards, and dress them, but shalt neither drink of the wine, nor gather the grapes; for the worms shall eat them.

Thou shalt have olive trees throughout all thy coasts, but thou shalt not anoint thyself with the oil; for thine olive shall cast his fruit.

Thou shalt beget sons and daughters, but thou shalt not enjoy them; for they shall go into captivity.

All thy trees and fruit of thy land shall the locust consume.

The stranger that is within thee shall get up above thee very high; and thou shalt come down very low.

He shall lend to thee, and thou shalt not lend to him: he shall be the head, and thou shalt be the tail.

Moreover all these curses shall come upon thee, and shall pursue thee, and overtake thee, till thou be destroyed; because thou hearkenedst not unto the voice of the LORD thy God, to keep his commandments and his statutes which he commanded thee:

And they shall be upon thee for a sign and for a wonder, and upon thy seed for ever.

> Because thou servedst not the LORD thy God with joyfulness, and with gladness of heart, for the abundance of all things;
>
> Therefore shalt thou serve thine enemies which the LORD shall send against thee, in hunger, and in thirst, and in nakedness, and in want of all things: and he shall put a yoke of iron upon thy neck, until he have destroyed thee.
>
> The LORD shall bring a nation against thee from far, from the end of the earth, as swift as the eagle flieth; a nation whose tongue thou shalt not understand;
>
> A nation of fierce countenance, which shall not regard the person of the old, nor shew favour to the young:
>
> And he shall eat the fruit of thy cattle, and the fruit of thy land, until thou be destroyed: which also shall not leave thee either corn, wine, or oil, or the increase of thy kine, or flocks of thy sheep, until he have destroyed thee.
>
> And he shall besiege thee in all thy gates, until thy high and fenced walls come down, wherein thou trustedst, throughout all thy land: and he shall besiege thee in all thy gates throughout all thy land, which the LORD thy God hath given thee (Deut. 28:15-52).

"Can a man take fire in his bosom, and his clothes not be burned?" (Prov. 6:27). We have bitten the hand that was feeding us. "Jeshurun waxed fat and kicked" (Deut. 32:15). The new stock market was a message from God to the children of liberty, that we might have a lot of money, but we won't be able to eat our money.

Because Providence granted it, Protestantism has lost its wealth, which went to their old enemy on the Tiber.

O LORD, thou hast ordained [the Vatican] for judgment (Hab. 1:12).

The warnings from His word should have alerted Protestants to their relation with mammon, and also of His preparations to end their supremacy over the world. God's message to Protestant Americans was, "Make to yourselves friends of [materialism]; that, when ye fail, they may receive you into everlasting habitations" (Luke 16:9).

The good news is that Jesus continues to extend His mercy and to call to everyone who will give up on a world that "decayeth and waxeth old and is ready to vanish away" (Heb. 8:13). This old world is passing away; yet, He is still calling to His Protestant children. Until the bitter and demon-driven Jesuit millions can prohibit preaching Jesus' invitation, and until those corrupting locusts can end all Protestant earnest Bible study and honest interpretation of it, Christ's warnings through Moses and His personal appeal to them will stand.

> Come unto me, all ye that labour and are heavy laden, and I will give you rest (Matt. 11:28).
>
> The grass withereth, the flower fadeth: but the word of our God shall stand for ever (Isa. 40:8).

This world is passing away; but, He will yet receive all who admit to serving the pleasures of this life in disobedience to His Law, and who finally look to Him for something better than this world — a peace that creates powerful, overcoming sons and daughters of God. They receive from the Spirit the whole heart's consecration to faith and love that overcomes the world. Will Americans accept their Lord's social and economic troubles as helpful warnings? Those needed punishments are His providential hand among us! *It's our God.* The punishments are the living, loving work of the God of Protestantism!

> I form the light, and create darkness: I make peace, and create evil [punishing calamity]: I the LORD do all these things. Drop down, ye heavens, from above, and let the skies pour down righteousness: let the earth open, and let them bring forth salvation, and let righteousness spring up together; I the LORD have created it (Isa. 45:7, 8).
>
> And all the trees of the field shall know that I the LORD have brought down the high tree, have exalted the low tree, have dried up the green tree, and have made the dry tree to flourish: I the LORD have spoken and have done it (Eze. 17:24).
>
> Then judgment shall dwell in the wilderness, and righteousness remain in the fruitful field. And the work of righteousness shall be peace; and the effect of righteousness quietness and assurance for ever. And my people shall dwell in a peaceable habitation, and in sure dwellings, and in quiet resting places (Isa. 32:16-18).

His beautiful promises are for us.

> Since thou wast precious in my sight, thou hast been honourable, and I have loved thee: therefore will I give men for thee, and people for thy life.
>
> Fear not: for I am with thee: I will bring thy seed from the east, and gather thee from the west;
>
> I will say to the north, Give up; and to the south, Keep not back: bring my sons from far, and my daughters from the ends of the earth;
>
> Even every one that is called by my name: for I have created him for my glory, I have formed him; yea, I have made him.
>
> Bring forth the blind people that have eyes, and the deaf that have ears.
>
> Let all the nations be gathered together, and let the people be assembled: who among them can declare this, and shew us former things? let them bring forth their witnesses, that they may be justified: or let them hear, and say, It is truth.
>
> Ye are my witnesses, saith the LORD, and my servant whom I have chosen: that ye may know and believe me, and understand that I am he: before me there was no God formed, neither shall there be after me.
>
> I, even I, am the LORD; and beside me there is no saviour.
>
> I have declared, and have saved, and I have shewed, when there was no strange god among you: therefore ye are my witnesses, saith the LORD, that I am God (Isa. 43:4-12).

The above promises are for whoever reads them, wherever they are in the world. "Thou wast precious in my sight… Fear not: for I am with thee." No matter how atheistic and troubled with doubt you may be, all reasonable belief comes from witnessing evidence. So, faith in God comes by hearing the evidence of His promises.

"I make peace, and create evil [punishing calamity]: I the LORD do all these things." To save His beloved people from their sins He permits their master Satan to create their stumbling blocks. And that is all He can do to get their attention because they are not seeking Him in His Bible; and, therefore His hands are tied. But, He purposes Satan's evil stumbling to create their ultimate humbling; for only through stumbling blocks can He deliver the obstinate sinner from sin's monumental pride. Afterward, they can't deny that the Lord has helped them, and they testify of His goodness to them. *They have "received of the LORD's hand double for all [their] sins" (Isa. 40:2)! The goodness of God led them to repentance.* Then, they are His witnesses because they can only "speak [what they] do know, and testify [of what they] have seen" (John 3:11), although many will not receive their witness. Like their loving, earthly parents who have punished them, their *terrible Enemy in the consequences was* their *best Friend all along!*

> As it is written, Behold, I lay in Sion a stumblingstone and rock of offence: and whosoever believeth on him shall not be ashamed (Rom. 9:33).
>
> Therefore will the LORD wait, that he may be gracious unto you, and therefore will he be exalted, that he may have mercy upon you: for the LORD is a God of judgment: blessed are all they that wait for him (Isa. 30:18).

No one hears the good news without first submitting to the bad news; nobody gets the blessing until he has surrendered to the breaking. No one is comforted by the Spirit unless first convicted by the Law. *Nobody.* No one comes to God until he is stumbled and tumbled and humbled (see Romans 3:19).

Don't think you are alone if stumbling over your own sins and being horrifically humbled describes your present circumstances. You are just where He needs you in order to save you if you will trust in His merciful humbling, and will be thankful for His loving involvement. His punishment means that among the multitudes in a perverse and atheistic generation, God hasn't forgotten you; you are called by His name. His eye is upon you. You are the apple of His eye. If you believe you have committed the unpardonable sin, remember that "The last shall be first" (Matt. 20:16); the poor in spirit inherit the kingdom (see Matthew 5:3).

Now is the time for everyone within Protestantism and in the Advent movement to read the Spirit of Prophecy and submit to the stumbling and humbling, and see the Lord's blessing, saving hand in it. If He can't correct us, He can't protect us. *Like the turbulent "floods of great waters", the near future will be too chaotic. The coming anarchy will make it too late* to obtain the time-consuming process of reconciling our pride nature with His humbling hand. By our procrastination, we will have

Chapter 6 Revelation Chapter 9: The Strong Delusion

placed ourselves in His enemy's camp. *This cannot be overemphasized.*

> Blessed is he whose transgression is forgiven, whose sin is covered.
>
> Blessed is the man unto whom the LORD imputeth not iniquity, and in whose spirit there is no guile.
>
> When I kept silence, my bones waxed old through my roaring all the day long.
>
> For day and night thy hand was heavy upon me: my moisture is turned into the drought of summer. Selah.
>
> I acknowledged my sin unto thee, and mine iniquity have I not hid. I said, I will confess my transgressions unto the LORD; and thou forgavest the iniquity of my sin. Selah.
>
> For this shall every one that is godly pray unto thee in a time when thou mayest be found: *surely in the floods of great waters they shall not come nigh unto him* (Ps. 32:1-6).

The coming Babylonian reign of terror is already building around Protestant America the bulwarks for our spiritual and economic besiegement. Are we awake to this?

> O mighty God, thou hast established them for correction (Hab. 1:12).
>
> Behold the mounts, they are come unto the city to take it; and the city is given into the hand of the Chaldeans, that fight against it, because of the sword, and of the famine, and of the pestilence (Jer. 32:24, cf Jer. 6:6).
>
> He is come to Aiath, he is passed to Migron; at Michmash he hath laid up his carriages: they are gone over the passage: they have taken up their lodging at Geba; Ramah is afraid; Gibeah of Saul is fled. Lift up thy voice, O daughter of Gallim: cause it to be heard unto Laish, O poor Anathoth. Madmenah is removed; the inhabitants of Gebim gather themselves to flee (Isa. 10:28-31).

Yet, despite the inroads of Protestantism's primary nemesis at this eleventh hour, Jesus is still working with the hearts of all His Protestant children, which includes all of their Remnant. In order to give mercy in abundance, He must come on strongly and show us our sin. Then, with our pride broken we can see His love for us, and all the mercy that has ever infused His justice. Through the six trumpets He calls to His Protestants, "I am not come to call the righteous, but sinners to repentance" (Matt. 9:13). Whoever will admit to God's disfavor will then cast themselves at His feet for peace and rest. God is calling them. They will be stumbled and humbled, healed and sealed, and will make up His 144,000 Christ-like elite. Submitting to the Spirit of Prophecy and falling broken on Christ will bring the peace and sealing.

> The LORD answered Job, and said, Shall he that contendeth with the Almighty instruct him? He that reproveth God, let him answer it.
>
> Then Job answered the LORD, and said, Behold, I am vile; what shall I answer thee? I will lay mine hand upon my mouth. Once have I spoken; but I will not answer: yea, twice; but I will proceed no further.
>
> Then answered the LORD unto Job out of the whirlwind, and said, Gird up thy loins now like a man: I will demand of thee, and declare thou unto me. Wilt thou also disannul my judgment? Wilt thou condemn me, that thou mayest be righteous? (Job 40:1-8).

After the humbling our beautiful confession will be,

> Against thee, thee only, have I sinned, and done this evil in thy sight: that thou mightest be justified when thou speakest, and be clear when thou judgest (Ps. 51:4).
>
> ...That thou mightest be justified in thy sayings, and mightest overcome when thou art judged (Rom. 3:4).

The Lord sounds so overwhelming toward sinners because that is what it takes for them to back down from their pride and to receive His peace and comfort, as Job learned. But, all too frequently, the strong language doesn't cause the proud hearts to stand down. As it was with King Saul, Satan politely, yet stubbornly, resists God's Spirit and maintains his bitter, self-sufficient stronghold in his human host. "The Spirit of the LORD departed from Saul, and an evil spirit from the LORD troubled him" (1 Sam. 16:14). And although the Lord's strong language too often results in the sinner steeling himself against God, the stubborn, resistant heart's conviction and humiliation and honest surrender must still remain the only true basis for a solid, lasting entrance into the life-giving relationship with God. Can a Creator who wants our total happiness be satisfied with anything less for His children than their total humiliation and full surrender? Agape Love says, "*I will put them through the greatest difficulty in order to reward them with the greatest peace and strength*" (see Revelation 3:19; Hebrews 12:6). Therefore, He must humble fully into the dust those who will glorify Him the most brilliantly in the end. He cannot fail short of our full restoration, and risk the poison to His eternal kingdom which our congenital pride would certainly forever bring it. Clearly, our absolute humiliation must be. Blessed are all they who stay patient in His work of humbling.

Here is the patience of the saints, they that keep the commandments of God and the faith of Jesus. (See Revelation 14:12.) Redemption's courtroom is set up to weigh our humbling and our surrender to the gift of God. The Lord's humbling and the gift of His Spirit are where the Lord's controversy over sinners has been raging among Protestantism's descendants, the churched and the unchurched, and all within Protestantism's sphere of influence the world round. And *here in the humbling* is where the third angel and the investigative judgment have presided to give their sentence upon everyone, for or against the sealing, prior to Jesus' return. The seven trumpets are all about humbling us and sealing the character of Christ into our intellect and heart.

> The lofty looks of man shall be humbled, and the haughtiness of men shall be bowed down, and the LORD alone shall be exalted in that day (Isa. 2:11).

> While the investigative judgment is going forward in heaven, while the sins of penitent believers are being removed from the sanctuary, there is to be a special work of purification, of putting away of sin, among God's people upon earth *The Great Controversy*, p. 425.

Following 9/11, 2008 hit and spelled doom to the American experiment of Republicanism and Protestantism. A scripture which the Reformation forefathers knew very well, their children must now learn the hard way: "Cursed be the man that trusteth in man, and maketh flesh his arm, and whose heart departeth from the LORD. For he shall be like the heath [dry bush] in the desert, and shall not see when good cometh; but shall inhabit the parched places in the wilderness, in a salt land and not inhabited" (Jer. 17:5, 6). 2008 challenged Protestant Americans' unabated adding of drunkenness to their unacknowledged thirst (see Deuteronomy 29:19).

The personal debt and home mortgages that many Protestants had amassed during the roaring '90s turned into a galling yoke of permanent enslavement. The children of the Reformation who rejected the solemn message of the Advent movement had preferred to live on this planet forever in its sinful state rather than go with Jesus to the home that He had gone to prepare for them. Therefore, Providence permitted greater liberty to the devil who has trapped them in their world of sin and self-preservation. The Protestants have laid up treasures on earth, and thieves have broken through and stolen it all.

> Woe unto us! for we are spoiled (Jer. 4:13).

> Your spoil shall be gathered like the gathering of the caterpiller: as the running to and fro of locusts shall he run upon them (Isa. 33:4).

> And they shall come, and shall rest all of them in the desolate valleys, and in the holes of the rocks, and upon all thorns, and upon all bushes (Isa. 7:19, cf Rev. 9:4).

> They shall run to and fro in the city; they shall run upon the wall, they shall climb up upon the houses; they shall enter in at the windows like a thief (Joel 2:9).

The atheistic children of Protestantism, like the ten northern tribes of Israel, may have all forgotten their spiritual roots, but God hasn't; and neither has their adversary, the Vatican (see Revelation 12:15; 13:2). The centuries-old enemy of Protestantism has come back to life and has never lost its sworn vow — to destroy Protestantism, to rid the Earth of it. It all must go — the Protestants' holy Received Text Bible and their holy religion of Law and grace. Forever removed must be Protestant America's civil liberties and America's original lamblike Protestant peacefulness. Forever obliterated must be their Protestant Republican Constitution that has separated church from state, a posture which America had faithfully stood guard to protect and preserve for the world against the despotic plans of Papal Rome. In their places will sit an Edomite dictator who will follow the Babylonian concept that the ruler owns the land, the people, and everything it and they produce. The first Beast of

Revelation chapter 13 was wounded by the Reformation's sword of the Spirit (see Revelation 13:3, 14; Ephesians 6:17). But, that Beast's deadly wound has healed and it must avenge itself on its assailant, Republican Protestantism. Now the whole world is following after Papal Rome (see Revelation 13:3, 4, 15). Since 9/11 the Vatican locusts have made rapid strides at our demolition.

> For the day of the LORD of hosts shall be upon every one that is proud and lofty, and upon every one that is lifted up; and he shall be brought low (Isa. 2:12).

The Medieval Papacy has returned to life. It has attained the trust and authority for global supremacy. After working so long and hard to regain that supremacy, it will not allow any obstacle to prevent its final success. It will return unimpeded to its former glory and persecutions. This is not an understatement.

> It is true that there are real Christians in the Roman Catholic communion….
>
> But Romanism *as a system* [emphasis mine] is no more in harmony with the gospel of Christ now than at any former period in her history. The Protestant churches are in great darkness, or they would discern the signs of the times. The Roman Church is far-reaching in her plans and modes of operation. She is employing *every device* [emphasis mine] to extend her influence and increase her power in preparation for a *fierce and determined conflict to regain control of the world* [emphasis mine], to re-establish persecution, and *to undo all that Protestantism has done* [emphasis mine]. Catholicism is gaining ground upon every side *The Great Controversy*, p. 565.

It is not without reason that the claim has been put forth in Protestant countries that Catholicism differs less widely from Protestantism than in former times. There has been a change; *but the change is not in the papacy* [emphasis mine]. Catholicism indeed resembles much of the Protestantism that now exists, because *Protestantism has so greatly degenerated* [emphasis mine] since the days of the Reformers *Ibid.*, p. 571.

> "The pacific tone of Rome in the United States does not imply a change of heart. *She is tolerant where she is helpless* [emphasis mine]. Says Bishop O'Connor: 'Religious liberty is merely *endured until the opposite can be carried into effect* [emphasis mine] without peril to the Catholic world.'. . . The archbishop of St. Louis once said: 'Heresy and unbelief are crimes; and in Christian countries, as in Italy and Spain, for instance, where all the people are Catholics, and where the Catholic religion is an essential part of the law of the land, they are punished as other crimes.'. . .
>
> "Every cardinal, archbishop, and bishop in the Catholic Church takes an oath of allegiance to the pope, in which occur the following words: '*Heretics, schismatics, and rebels to our said lord (the pope), or his aforesaid successors, I will to my utmost persecute and oppose* [emphasis mine].'"
> --Josiah Strong, Our Country, ch. 5, pars. 2-4 *Ibid.*, p. 565.

Not Jews or Jewish aristocrats, not fundamentalist Muslims, and not American right-wing ultra-conservative extremists proclaiming their Second Amendment liberties, have caused the new reign of terrorism sweeping the nations. Backed by all the hosts of darkness, Rome is the terrorist. With her ingenious multitudinous, multi-national army of Jesuits, her tightly woven network of international bankers, intelligence agencies, and the plethora of her other secret societies "she is employing every device to extend her influence and increase her power". They are all her children, for she is the mother of abominations in the earth.

If you believe the Bible and make it your standard, then you must interpret history and the recent world news in light of the Bible. "The foolishness of God is wiser than men" (1 Cor. 1:25). As if written in 2017, the following statement gives us the true glasses through which we must understand current events.

> The present is a time of overwhelming interest to all living. Rulers and statesmen, men who occupy positions of trust and authority, thinking men and women of all classes, have their attention fixed upon the events taking place about us. They are watching the relations that exist among the nations. They observe the intensity that is taking possession of every earthly element, and they recognize that something great and decisive is about to take place, — that the world is on the verge of a stupendous crisis.

The Bible, and the Bible only, gives a correct view of these things [emphasis mine] *Prophets and Kings*, p. 537.

The Bible says, "Upon her forehead was a name written, MYSTERY, BABYLON THE GREAT, THE MOTHER OF HARLOTS AND ABOMINATIONS OF THE EARTH" (Rev. 17:5). She and all of her secret societies today are the highest echelons of government agencies and the media. My last statement may sound extreme beyond measure until understood from the websites referenced in the next few paragraphs. That Protestantism has an insatiable adversary is biblical and explains the recent, mysterious turnabout in Protestant America's direction, its new religious, economic, political, and the military policies in its zealous aggressions taking place today.

Shortly after the war of 1812 a Holy Alliance among the monarchs of Europe and the Vatican decided that Protestantism and this free nation must be destroyed in order to regain the world for dictatorial oligarchies and their high priest, intolerant religion. Her Jesuits were chosen to covertly do that work. After centuries of experience in fomenting wars, assassinating and creating popular uprisings against "heretical" rulers, and upsetting peaceful societies, the Jesuits were the only candidate for such a large, difficult, deceptive, and unconscionable enterprise.

> For they speak not peace: but they devise deceitful matters against them that are quiet in the land (Ps. 35:20).

> Woe to them that devise iniquity, and work evil upon their beds! when the morning is light, they practise it, because it is in the power of their hand (Mic. 2:1).

The enemy invaders would enter the United States as commoners; they would join companies, denominations, government organizations, financial institutions, publishers and news organs, etc.; and they would rise to the top of them all. Then they would steer those entities by legislation, decree, and corporate decision from the highest positions of leadership. For a fuller story I recommend, *The Secret Terrorists*, by Bill Hughes. The book is a very small, researched, and quick read, that needs to be widely proliferated.

To read it online, go to: *www.pacinst.com/terrorists/chapter1/target.html.*

Another resource is the Jesuit Extreme Oath of Induction found at: *www.ianpaisley.org/article.asp?ArtKey=jesuit.*

(Please read while they are still available on the internet.)

In light of this, it is very conceivable that everything was in place for the Jesuits by 1849 to begin the process of overthrowing Protestantism and civil America under the investigative judgment providences of God. Once Protestant America rejected the truths of the Bible, Providence opened the door for both satanic and holy forces to begin a race. For every Protestant around the globe, the Seal of God or the mark of the Beast would comprise the finish line at the end of the sixth trumpet. The Jesuits created the criminal Nazi SS policing army, and then they formed the CIA, the FBI, the NSA, the FEMA, and the Office of Homeland Security. Papal wickedness runs the highest places of every department, agency, and branch of our Protestant government.

> The king of the north shall come against him like a whirlwind, with chariots, and with horsemen, and with many ships; and he shall enter into the countries, and shall overflow and pass over (Dan. 11:40).

Today, the surprising bloodshed and deaths of innocent Muslim people in order to perpetuate the myths of 9/11 are happening due to the corruption of Protestant America. Satan's mysterious efforts by elitist men and women to erode the American Bill of Rights and to plunder America's wealth are coming to pass because of Protestantism's departure from the Law of God. Already by 1849 at the beginning of the fifth trumpet 150 year prophecy, Protestantism had abandoned its biblical religion of Law and grace that Jesus had once delivered to the Reformers. Today, Americans are soon to reap the whirlwind, and experience the modern counterpart of Israel's Babylonian captivity.

The ancient admonitions and jeremiads forewarning the Babylonian punishment cry out from Protestant scriptures that the same is coming to them today.

> Thus saith the LORD to the men of Judah and Jerusalem, Break up your fallow ground, and sow not among thorns. Circumcise yourselves to the LORD, and take away the foreskins of your heart, ye men of Judah and inhabitants of Jerusalem: lest my fury come forth like fire, and burn that none can quench it, because of the evil

of your doings. Declare ye in Judah, and publish in Jerusalem; and say, Blow ye the trumpet in the land: cry, gather together, and say, Assemble yourselves, and let us go into the defenced cities. Set up the standard toward Zion: retire, stay not: for I will bring evil from the north, and a great destruction. The lion is come up from his thicket, and the destroyer of the Gentiles is on his way; he is gone forth from his place to make thy land desolate; and thy cities shall be laid waste, without an inhabitant (Jer. 4:3-7).

For this gird you with sackcloth, lament and howl: for the fierce anger of the LORD is not turned back from us (Jer. 4:8).

That which the palmerworm hath left hath the locust eaten; and that which the locust hath left hath the cankerworm eaten; and that which the cankerworm hath left hath the caterpiller eaten....

Blow ye the trumpet in Zion, and sound an alarm in my holy mountain: let all the inhabitants of the land tremble: for the day of the LORD cometh, for it is nigh at hand;

A day of darkness and of gloominess, a day of clouds and of thick darkness, as the morning spread upon the mountains: a great people and a strong; there hath not been ever the like, neither shall be any more after it, even to the years of many generations.

A fire devoureth before them; and behind them a flame burneth: the land is as the garden of Eden before them, and behind them a desolate wilderness; yea, and nothing shall escape them.

The appearance of them is as the appearance of horses; and as horsemen, so shall they run.

Like the noise of chariots on the tops of mountains shall they leap, like the noise of a flame of fire that devoureth the stubble, as a strong people set in battle array.

Before their face the people shall be much pained: all faces shall gather blackness.

They shall run like mighty men; they shall climb the wall like men of war; and they shall march every one on his ways, and they shall not break their ranks:

Neither shall one thrust another; they shall walk every one in his path: and when they fall upon the sword, they shall not be wounded.

They shall run to and fro in the city; they shall run upon the wall, they shall climb up upon the houses; they shall enter in at the windows like a thief.

The earth shall quake before them; the heavens shall tremble: the sun and the moon shall be dark, and the stars shall withdraw their shining:

And the LORD shall utter his voice before his army: for his camp is very great: for he is strong that executeth his word: for the day of the LORD is great and very terrible; and who can abide it?

Therefore also now, saith the LORD, turn ye even to me with all your heart, and with fasting, and with weeping, and with mourning:

And rend your heart, and not your garments, and turn unto the LORD your God: for he is gracious and merciful, slow to anger, and of great kindness, and repenteth him of the evil.

Who knoweth if he will return and repent, and leave a blessing behind him; even a meat offering and a drink offering unto the LORD your God? Blow the trumpet in Zion, sanctify a fast, call a solemn assembly (Joel 1:4; 2:1-15).

"Blow the trumpet in Zion"! This is the purpose of the seven trumpets to Protestantism and Adventism. "Both the houses of Israel" (Isa. 8:14) are Zion, "the Israel of God" (Gal. 6:16), children of "the Lord of hosts, which dwelleth in mount Zion" (vs. 18). Zion needs to see its coming desolation.

The fifth trumpet prophesies the amalgamation of locust and human (see Revelation 9:7); that is, satanic agencies incorporated with men. The fifth trumpet prophecy pictures marauding cavalry horses with breastplates of iron (see Revelation 9:7, 9). The iron breastplates signify the Jesuit and Protestant unredeemed hard-heartedness toward God and lack of submission to His Law due to their chosen separation from Him through spiritualistic worship, the pseudo-science of evolution, and a developing technology with all of its self-sufficient, self-reliant, soul hardening by-products. Through the symbolism of iron breastplates Jesus is saying to all of His apocalyptic Protestant denominations, "I knew that thou art obstinate, and thy neck is an iron sinew, and thy brow brass" (Isa. 48:4). Our calloused condition results from our failure to surrender to God's Law, to receive the His Spirit of approbation through His Son, and to be sealed in Their righteousness (see Revelation 9:4; Galatians 3:23; 4:6). Instead, by beholding the carnal wares of the Beast through his duplicitous armies, Protestantism and Adventism — "the mighty and the holy people" (Dan. 8:24, cf Dan. 12:7) — have changed into the same, hardened image of the Beast, from darkness to darkness, the Beast's darkness becoming their darkness.

> They that make them are like unto them; so is every one that trusteth in them (Ps. 115:8).

The locust temptations were instilling fallow, thorny, insolent, hardened foreheads into the Protestant public (see Ezekiel 3:7-9). We had grown mechanical in spiritual things and lost the Reformation's earnest longing for righteousness. Even many of the Adventists were copying the unruly spirit of the children of Evangelicalism, inculcating the lawlessness of Rome. True "pressing together" was rare because we no longer walked in the light as God is in the light (see 1 John 1:7). We had dismissed the reproofs of our prophet of the Lord, and therefore He could no longer justify us. We had left off the special work of purification. Like the Jews of Christ's day, SDAs knew the Bible and some even loved to argue it; but most could not find sanctification by its peace and power.

> The testimony of the true Witness has not been half heeded. The solemn testimony upon which the destiny of the church hangs, has been lightly esteemed, if not entirely disregarded. This testimony must work deep repentance, and all that truly receive it, will obey it, and be purified *Spiritual Gifts*, vol. 1, p. 185.

The little red books from the pen of Ellen White became the little read books. And no differently than the torment of the Protestants who avoided the Law of God in the Bible, Adventists who evaded the Spirit of Prophecy to preempt the convicting Testimony of Jesus, could know only the same Protestant self-manufactured repentance and imitation peace, and the same mental gymnastics and exhausting anguish.

> Through heathenism, Satan had for ages turned men away from God; but he won his great triumph in perverting the faith of Israel. By contemplating and worshiping their own conceptions, the heathen had lost a knowledge of God, and had become more and more corrupt. So it was with Israel. The principle that man can save himself by his own works lay at the foundation of every heathen religion; it had now become the principle of the Jewish religion. Satan had implanted this principle. Wherever it is held, men have no barrier against sin *The Desire of Ages*, p. 35.

This quotation was written to all the descendants of the holy Reformation. All scripture is for our admonition, upon whom the end of the world is come, especially to Adventists.

Today, they've been having no rest, and lots of cancer. The mark of the Beast has been making its way into the consciences of Adventism, the Remnant people of God. But, some will be saved because of these troubles and more, for the Lord is determined to have a last day people to announce His Father's coming kingdom. His prophecies will be fulfilled, whether by few or many.

During the fifth trumpet 150 years, many among the Protestant Remnant were resting on the spirituality of their Advent fathers whom God had lead in our past history. All the while we were clinging to this world and forgetting that the Lord was no respecter of persons or of denominations (see Jeremiah 9:25, 26). No matter how good and moral had been our past, the Almighty's impartiality in His fifth trumpet judgment of torment applied as much to us as to the mainline denominations. How will we stand in the day of our visitation?

> Bring forth therefore fruits meet for repentance: and think not to say within yourselves, We have Abraham to our father: for I say unto you, that God is able of these stones to raise up children unto Abraham. And now also the axe is laid unto the root of the trees: therefore every tree which bringeth not forth good fruit is hewn down, and cast into the fire (Matt. 3:8-10).

> Who may abide the day of his coming? and who shall stand when he appeareth? for he is like a refiner's fire, and like fullers' soap: and he shall sit as a refiner and purifier of silver: and he shall purify the sons of Levi, and purge them as gold

and silver, that they may offer unto the LORD an offering in righteousness (Mal. 3:2, 3).

For the time is come that judgment must begin at the house of God (1 Pet. 4:17).

Protestant and Adventist stubborn resistance against the indefatigable power of God to convert by His perfect Law has completely exhausted us, and we've had no rest day or night.

For the flesh lusteth against the Spirit, and the Spirit against the flesh: and these are contrary the one to the other: so that ye cannot do the things that ye would (Gal. 5:17).

We could sing emotional praise music and we could talk about living under His unmerited favor, but we were celebrating divine acceptance which we only imagined to have. We had no certainty by His Spirit. Our doctrine was, "I shall have peace, though I walk in the imagination of mine heart" (Deut. 29:19). We refused to allow God His authority to condemn sin so that He could truly humble us, and ultimately, give us real happiness. Hand could join in self-righteous hand to build the tallest heaven-scraping temple to *Ba'al*, "the Lord", but Jehovah disdains that outward offering from proud hearts. Read Ezekiel 23 to hear His strong, no-holds-barred jealousy for His beloved, original Protestant and Adventist movements. And understand that Christ's omnipotent wail in verse 20 translates to the abominable Protestant-Adventist Spiritual Formation apostate revival Toronto Blessing from the bowels of the bottomless pit.

"One woe is past; and, behold, there come two woes more hereafter" (Rev. 9:12).

After 1999 comes the final transformation of Protestantism into a fierce demonic force to finalize the Reformation's destruction. It is the Protestant power that completes the fifth trumpet's decimation of the truth and grace throughout all the nations. At this point, the locusts transform to do to Protestant America what heaven had prevented them during the fifth trumpet period (see Revelation 9:5). In the sixth trumpet they can finish the work they began in the fifth; they can "kill" the foreheads that had not been receiving the Seal of God. That symbolism means that they can completely devour the last vestige of faith, sear the consciences, and possess the hearts that they had previously tormented to the point of hardening during the fifth trumpet. A Protestant world, so long resistant to God's high calling given from Ellen White, the army of Satan can bring to full, permanent disconnection from their God. Multitudes among the Protestants and their Remnant are enamored with imagined favor with God without surrender to His authority to correct or to rebuke them, or to "put them to shame in any thing" (Jdg. 18:7).

During the fifth trumpet, hardened resistance to God's Law (see Isaiah 48:1-4; 28:2), symbolized by breastplates of iron, had been considered acceptable alike to both halves of Protestantism: the aloof, reckless, Protestant religious; and the ethical, atheistic Protestant irreligious. But, the sixth trumpet sounds, and the Protestants' probation for their iron hard-heartedness now ends in unexpected severity. This next phase of Satan's desolating Protestant hosts causes hard, legalistic hearts to get his full relief from their great torment. Their relief of torment comes through the self-exaltation and devil-possession by Spiritual Formation, or in symbol, breastplates full of fire and smoke and brimstone (see Revelation 9:17, 18; 14:9-11; Deuteronomy 29:18-23). They are drunken with the wine of the wrath of God.

Thou art wearied in the multitude of thy counsels. Let now the [ordained spiritual guides of Spiritual Formation] stand up, and save thee from these things that shall come upon thee. Behold, [the Protestant-Adventist Spiritual Formation devotees] shall be as stubble; the fire shall burn them; they shall not deliver themselves from the power of the flame: there shall not be a coal to warm at, nor fire to sit before it (Isa. 47:13, 14).

"Enflaming yourselves" (Isa. 57:5) by a forced, fanatical, counterfeit revival, the churched Protestants waste their vitality. Everyone trapped by the apparently harmless name of Spiritual Formation are engulfed in spiritual fire falling upon the altars of their hearts which are full of conversations with so-called "God" through "the Spirit". But, the inviting conversations with the gentle sounding familiar spirits bring them no rest from their torment. Their initial high might feel warm and heavenly, but in the end their souls are chilled and drained, and with increased torment. The familiar spirits give a nice persona, but with zero fear and love for our Father in heaven. The demons offer the worshipers "light and much power, but no sweet love, joy, and peace" *Early Writings*, p. 56. Living off the excitement that "God" revealed "Himself" to them, the worshipers need to meet with "God" again and again, until their souls are as cold as the heart of Satan, with whom they were conversing. The sparks of excitement and emotion leave their spirit dark and hollow. Yet, their proud self-made goodness keeps them drawn to "God", which makes the "only true God" hotly jealous. "Spiritual disciplines" are nothing like God's discipline. He can no more share the same heart of His beloved children with this abominable "God" than He could cohabit a heathen temple with Dagon (see 1 Samuel 5:1-6).

> The sacrifice of the wicked is an abomination to the LORD (Prov. 15:8).

> Who is among you that feareth the LORD, that obeyeth the voice of his servant, that walketh in darkness, and hath no light? let him trust in the name of [Jehovah], and stay upon his God. Behold, all ye that kindle a fire, that compass yourselves about with sparks: walk in the light of your fire, and in the sparks that ye have kindled. This shall ye have of mine hand; ye shall lie down in sorrow (Isa. 50:10, 11).

The Protestant churches have turned away their ears from the Law of God, and their prayers are abomination to Him (see Proverbs 28:9).

> *Satan has offered them a lawless, spiritualistic religion through Spiritual Formation that will not let them surrender to the righteousness of God, and afterward be sealed.*

"To this man will I look, even to him that is poor and of a contrite spirit, and trembleth at my word" (Isa. 66:1, 2). "The prayer of the upright is his delight" (Prov. 15:8). Our humbling and surrender alone pass His inspection and give us the access to His presence, which is His earnest of our inheritance (see Exodus 20:20).

The church still refuses to wrestle with the Law's palpable condemnation of sin. "For she saith in her heart", I will not be humbled and repentant to God, "I sit a queen…and shall see no sorrow" (Rev. 18:7). *Engrossed in celebrating a supposed salvation, they do not afflict their souls during the Lord's final cleansing of His heavenly sanctuary.* Satan has offered them a lawless, spiritualistic religion through Spiritual Formation that *will not let them surrender to the righteousness of God, and afterward be sealed.*

Similar to Israel's apostasy into spiritualism in the days of Jeremiah, by evading the affliction of their souls during this investigative judgment the Protestants permanently cut themselves off from the Spirit of God and from the sealing. Their pain is overwhelming. In a flushed state of mind, they throw themselves into the current carnival atmosphere that shimmers with temptation on every hand. The prophecy shows that many strove against God's Spirit during the fifth trumpet until Satan cuts them off from Him forever in the sixth (see Revelation 9:18; 14:9-11; Leviticus 23:29; 16:31). The spirit of darkness has sent them the smooth intoxicants of Spiritual Formation and celebration worship (see 1 Kings 22:23), which they indulge until the Spirit of Jesus can no longer reprove their consciences and give them merciful correction. *Spiritual Formation causes them to lose **all** capacity to fear God and His discipline.* (See Revelation 14:7). None can need a Saviour from sin. *Spiritual Formation thus dominates their conscience; they cannot be subject to the Law of God.* They cannot give God glory by striving before His humbling truth and hoping in His mercy until "joy cometh in the morning" (Ps. 30:5) because they need no Saviour from sin. But, if tears do not endure over a long, dark night of wrestling with God, the joyful morning never arrives. (See Genesis 32:31.) And many are squandering this privilege during the little time that it is still available. The song of Moses was about this very departure into spiritualism.

> They sacrificed unto devils, not to God; to gods whom they knew not, to new gods that came newly up, whom your fathers feared not.

> Of the Rock that begat thee thou art unmindful, and hast forgotten God that formed thee.…

> And he said, I will hide my face from them, I will see what their end shall be: for they are a very froward generation, children in whom is no faith.

> They have moved me to jealousy with that which is not God; they have provoked me to anger with their vanities: and I will move them to jealousy with those which are not a people; I will provoke them to anger with a foolish nation (Deut. 32:17, 18, 20, 21).

Chapter 6 Revelation Chapter 9: The Strong Delusion

The LORD is in his holy temple, the LORD's throne is in heaven: his eyes behold, his eyelids try, the children of men.

The LORD trieth the righteous: but the wicked and him that loveth violence his soul hateth.

Upon the wicked he shall rain snares, fire and brimstone, and an horrible tempest: this shall be the portion of their cup (Ps. 11:4-6).

The sixth trumpet is this more profound and permanent manifestation of the mark of the Beast than that received during the fifth trumpet. Without knowing it, the vast majority of Protestants commit the unpardonable sin; they have pushed away from the conviction of God's Law too politely for too long.

They were not looking at Jesus in His Law; they were not spending the time and effort to search for the living Stone behind the Law of stone, a Person warm and friendly and earnest to please His Father in every way, from womb to tomb. They did not plug His name into every word of God, seeing the beauty of His holiness, and thus getting life from His life. They did not let the whole scriptures testify of Him, as He taught us to do. For them, the whole volume of the Book was never written of Him. They never went to the scriptures to commune with Jesus; therefore they can't love the Bible. Their souls can never rejoice in the Bible's mortifying statutes and scourging laws. They never avail themselves of Christ's actions exemplifying the Bible's rules, rules that are so blinding to our fallen nature that we need the welding goggles of Christ's life and death. Finally, they resort to Spiritual Formation and communications with the devils for resolution of their tormented souls.

Therefore, they can never take hold of His strength. Their own spiritual resources are all that they can rely upon. And therefore, the non-personable letter of the Law without Christ's Spirit imbuing the Law, the personless stone testimony that cannot be gracious, continues to scourge and quench the last embers of their faith. The constant burning and shining condemnation of God's offensive commands are never shielded by the Spirit from Christ, which He has specially inculcated into His doctrine (see John 6:63; Isaiah 42:2). They would have been drawn to Jesus if only they had searched for Him in His Old Testament words and heard His voice from the Law and prophets.

Every word of Jesus is pure: *He* is a shield unto them that put their trust in *Him*. (See Proverbs 30:5.)

Jesus was never the Word of God to them; *He* was never God's Law made visible and audible. They never came to Him in His word, that they might have life. The word of God always remained an *it*, only letters and words, concepts and information. The Bible never took on the sound of His voice. Like a taskmaster, the Holy Scriptures exacted righteousness as an overseer of drab ideals and laborious duties and hated requirements, things they *should* do, things they *had* to do, things they *had better* do. The Bible never became a living experience of the beauty and courage of Jesus, which would have developed trust and a friendship with Him, and righteousness through that trust and friendship with Him. By the end of the sixth trumpet they are fully possessed of the satanic agencies; their probation is closed. They are forever beyond hope; their case is closed in the books of heaven. He that is filthy, let him be filthy still.

Since 9/11 this scourge has been loosed. It is the final product that King Saul experienced after years of refusing to surrender his envious heart to the gentle, but firm correction of the Lord's Spirit seen in David. His stubborn resistance to God caused him untrammeled susceptibility to the insidious adversary. He would not drive away his dislike toward the Lord's correction through Samuel; and the demon of pride within him laughed off his needed lessons in humility. Not foreseeing his demise, King Saul welcomed his own subtle destroyer. By an endless manhunt for David, Satan filled Saul's heart with his raucous, arrogant presence, and made the king a cage of every hateful spirit. In the terrible ordeal, the Lord had no choice but to give him up to satanic powers at Endor.

The sixth trumpet is Satan's last push to corral the recipients of his painful mark into the final stages of a once holy nation experiencing King Saul's doom. King Saul's defection from the Holy Spirit of life to the spirits of hopeless darkness reveal Protestantism's defection during this period before the seventh trumpet ends human probation.

In mercy to the Protestant peoples, the worst of the desolating winds (see Revelation 7:1-3) has remained held back; but, since the year 1999, Providence has given the command to loose the final desolation (see Revelation 9:14). The atrocities of September 11, 2001 have done much to inaugurate the sixth trumpet and to lay the foundation for the development of religious fundamentalism. Using 9/11 to provoke the Islamic spirit of avenging wrong, today the Jesuit locusts cloak their destructive actions under the guise of protecting freedom from every form of terrorism. On 9/11, sleight of hand and the power of suggestion accomplished many first time illusions with precision. The current spreading of terror in the world is simply more sleight of hand and deception by the same Jesuit power that orchestrated 9/11. As they began the work of delusion, so they have walked in it.

Much evidence indicates that military incendiaries accomplished the destruction of the World Trade Center, that a bomb made the crater outside of Shanksville, Pennsylvania, and that a cruise missile and internal explosives damaged the Pentagon killing all the Navy personnel who were investigating the Army's lost $4 Trillion (simultaneously a decoy empty passenger airliner flew over it, see CitizienInvestigationTeam https://www.youtube.com/watch?v=j5FhQc-LJ-o). Until 9/11, no high-rise building ever collapsed due to fire throughout the history of commercial construction. World Trade Center (WTC) Buildings 1 and 2 had Thermate all through the pulverized concrete that lay around their destruction sites. Thermate is solely manufactured by the military for its explosives. World Trade Center Building 7 (WTC 7) had the same Thermate dust in its debris, the massive skyscraper falling straight down into its basement. Although no airliner crashed into WTC 7, its collapse occurred five hours after the fall of WTC 1 and 2, with only small fires barely seen inside. Even WTC 3, 4, 5, and 6, which were the buildings located at the base of the Twin Towers (WTC 1 and 2), remained standing though sustaining the collateral damage from the falling debris of the Towers, as well as far greater heat than did WTC 7. WTC 7, which stood a football field distance away from WTC 1 and 2, had no reason to free-fall into its basement. The total collapse of WTC 7 points to wickedness in high places in the 9/11 Christian perpetration against America, Protestant America.

Neither the Pentagon nor the site near Shanksville, Pennsylvania left any wreckage — no titanium turbine engines, no steel landing gear, no wings or fuselage. 9/11 sleight of hand and power of suggestion have been very effective. There were only holes at each impact site; and at the Pentagon, April Gallop, an active-duty soldier in the Pentagon testified that at the time of the explosion she smelled Cordite (the distinct fumes from explosives, and — she stated explicitly — *not* diesel fumes from jet fuel). Ms. Gallop made her way out of the Pentagon without seeing any plane sections, major parts, or even seats, and she spoke clearly that no raging fires or high heat existed — proving the claim false that the plane was incinerated inside the Pentagon. If no wreckage could even be possible at the plane crash sites, it would be a first in the history of aviation ground crashes. Aluminum airliners cannot be incinerated by their own jet-grade kerosene, which essentially is low heat-producing diesel fuel. Especially so does melting a plane's titanium turbine engines and steel landing gear require heat much higher than jet-grade kerosene can create. Thus, the whole history of hundreds of located plane crashes has always left the wreckage of major plane sections.

Since the start of this new millennium, Satan maneuvered his top level Jesuit agents, the voracious locusts in his favored earthly agency, to finish their master plans for the Counter-Reformation that had begun in the European Councils of the early 1800s. That plan was to destroy all popular government, Protestantism, and faith in the Bible (the Book which empowered Protestantism and Republicanism, and gave the Papacy a deadly wound). *The Jesuit locusts* orchestrated 9/11's terrorist action against a recently acclaimed "Christian" America, and then laid the blame on the Muslims. As they have done since their inception, today Jesuits are the new group of terror, masquerading as religious extremists for starting a *global* purge of non-Catholic Christendom, while creating a world that hates and fears all Islamists. Muslims, the greatest competition to the Holy Roman Empire and having a culture that is the alter-ego of modern democracy, are being massacred and slandered by the lie that they are the enemy of both, and satanic. And Christian America is doing the slaughtering and slandering.

9/11's purpose was to create a holy war against "Christian America". But, civil America never was "Christian America". As far as religion goes, civil America has always been *Protestant*. And *Bible* Protestantism has never feared competition from other religions. America never was a Christian nation that must insist on government support of religion. We were a civil nation; and the Spirit of God gave our religion, Bible Protestantism, the fortitude to handle the challenges of our nation's secular aspects, and the spiritual confidence to happily cohabit with a government established upon a completely secular foundation. Even while our American nation was forming, the terrorism of the Vatican was still reclaiming its European territory, which the Bible had previously delivered from its tyranny. This was still ongoing in

Chapter 6 Revelation Chapter 9: The Strong Delusion

Europe when our nation's founding fathers saw to it that America would never link itself with the larger umbrella of Christianity, which would thus place it as part of the Christendom of the Old World. It would form its Constitution upon the Protestant principle of self-government, rather than in any way come under submission to the Holy Roman Empire. In every respect, America would separate from the corrupt papal system which they eyed with much suspicion, and would remain staunchly Protestant. In accordance with scripture, the American forefathers said, "Lo, the people shall dwell alone, and shall not be reckoned among the nations" (Num. 23:9). But, the rampant desire among today's Protestant Americans to return to the Church of the Dark Ages says that few there are in America who still hold on to the liberating Protestant principles of the Reformation. They have been tempted away from the only true God, who is also a jealous God.

It is the Beast ascended from the bottomless pit that has conspired to produce the recent string of "terrorist" actions on American soil and to create America's militant aftermath since 9/11.

The truth is that Satan's favored religio-political organization, the Papacy, which has ascended from the abyss, is responsible for all the past aggression against America since it became a nation. It is the Beast ascended from the bottomless pit that has conspired to produce the recent string of "terrorist" actions on American soil and to create America's militant aftermath since 9/11. Satan is quickly moving his favorite world power of the Dark Ages to inspire America to be its military arm and to fight his battles. The Beast's deadly wound is healed (see Revelation 13:3, 12). The war on terror is presently an Inquisition against the Muslim religion; but, soon that holy war will attack all anti-"War on Terror", anti-"Christian nation" and anti-"Union of church and state" sentiment (*see Appendix A*).

The unbiblical Christianity which the Church espouses has been gutted of its convicting truth. Biblical truth wars against her carnal, pagan traditions and enrages her. Long ago she replaced Bible Christianity with Baal worship, which is ancient Babylonian religion, and which is the new lawless Beast driving the fifth and sixth trumpet locusts (see Revelation 11:7). The democracy that she is seeding among the nations today is not balanced with Republicanism. Overhauled and empty of all the Republicanism that our forefathers put into the U.S. Constitution, the Church's democracy is prone to dictatorial decree and mimics the professed republic of Imperial Rome. Through the Church's terrorism against other countries and her new American military arm, she is fomenting the nations' resistance. Then, their assumption of every nation's sovereign right of national defense she calls Islam defending its terrorism. But, the spreading of terrorist cells throughout the world are *her* locust terrorists, for she is the mother of abominations in the earth (see Revelation 17:5). The ruse of an invisible enemy of extremist terrorism opens the way for her to overthrow governments and install leaders who are trained for Satan's agenda to bring about an international lockdown in a worldwide totalitarian state. Ultimately, she will subjugate the world for totalitarianism and spiritualism.

Protestant America has been warned: Let it be remembered, it is the boast of Rome that she never changes. The principles of Gregory VII and Innocent III are still the principles of the Roman Catholic Church. And had she but the power, she would put them in practice with as much vigor now as in past centuries. Protestants little know what they are doing when they propose to accept the aid of Rome in the work of Sunday exaltation. While they are bent upon the accomplishment of their purpose, *Rome is aiming to re-establish her power, to recover her lost supremacy* [emphasis mine]. Let the principle once be established in the United States that the church may employ or control the power of the state; that religious observances may be enforced by secular laws; in short, that the authority of church and state is to dominate the conscience, and the triumph of Rome in this country is assured.

God's word has given warning of the impending danger; let this be unheeded, and the Protestant world will learn what the purposes of Rome really are, only when it is too late to escape the snare. She is silently growing into power. Her doctrines are exerting their influence in legislative halls, in the churches, and in the hearts of men. She is piling up her lofty and massive structures in the secret recesses of which her former persecutions will be repeated. Stealthily and unsuspectedly she is strengthening her forces to further her own ends when the time shall come for her to strike. All that she desires is vantage ground, and this is already being given her. We shall soon see and shall feel what the purpose of the Roman element is. Whoever shall believe and obey the word of God will thereby incur reproach and persecution *The Great Controversy*, p. 581.

I recommend reading the entire chapter of the above quote from *The Great Controversy*, chapter 35, entitled, *Liberty of Conscience Threatened*.

Today the Vatican sows the fear through every available information avenue and communication organ, even in the Evangelical Sunday churches, that Islam must be destroyed or brought to submission through military action. This Christian beast is massacring hundreds of thousands of innocent adults and children, none of whom, throughout the Arab nations, have had anything to do with terrorism in America. Every recent turn of events dismantling Protestant America politically, socially, morally, and religiously has been accomplished by the Vatican's corrupting locust wickedness in the highest places of government agencies, private sector, and of the complicit denominations. Since 1999 a Papal-Protestant plague has broken out, strewing abomination upon the human race.

> Save yourselves from this untoward generation (Acts 2:40).

A foreign organization lurking within the highest levels of the United States government killed the American people on 9/11. However, the most egregious atrocity, which imputes the greatest judgment upon these so-called "Christian" top-level military and political people, comes from their creating the illusion that whole nations are aiding invisible terrorists, and then raining fiery retribution upon these accursed enemies against whom the Christian leaders have spoken all manner of evil falsely. If these Christians would read their Bible and admit the authority of God's Law, they would hear:

> The *doers* of the law shall be justified (Rom. 2:13).

> Be ye *doers* of the word, and not hearers only, deceiving your own selves (Jas. 1:22).

> Blessed are they that *do* his commandments, that they may have right to the tree of life, and may enter in through the gates into the city (Rev. 22:14).

> Thou shalt not bear false witness against thy neighbour (Ex. 20:16).

> Thou shalt not raise a false report: put not thine hand with the wicked to be an unrighteous witness (Ex. 23:1).

> He that saith he is in the light, and hateth his brother, is in darkness even until now (1 John 2:9).

> If a man say, I love God, and hateth his brother, he is a liar: for he that loveth not his brother whom he hath seen, how can he love God whom he hath not seen? (1 John 4:20).

> Be sure your sin will find you out (Num. 32:23).

> Let [the guilt of murder] rest on the head of Joab, and on all his father's house; and let there not fail from the house of Joab one that hath an issue, or that is a leper, or that leaneth on a staff, or that falleth on the sword, or that lacketh bread (2 Sam. 3:29).

> Their blood shall therefore return upon the head of Joab, and upon the head of his seed for ever: but upon David, and upon his seed, and upon his house, and upon his throne, shall there be peace for ever from the LORD (1 Ki. 2:33).

> Let their table be made a snare, and a trap, and a stumblingblock, and a recompence unto them: let their eyes be darkened, that they may not see, and bow down their back alway (Rom. 11:9, 10).

Surely the kings of the earth have committed fornication with the whore that rides this Beast of Revelation (see Revelation 17:1-5; 18:3).

> Hear the word of the LORD, ye rulers of Sodom; give ear unto the law of our God, ye people of Gomorrah.... When ye come to appear before me, who hath required this at your hand, to tread my courts?... And when ye spread forth your hands, I will hide mine eyes from you: yea, when ye make many prayers, I will not hear: your hands are full of blood (Isa. 1:10, 12, 15).

I will make mine arrows drunk with blood, and my sword shall devour flesh; and that with the blood of the slain and of the captives, from the beginning of revenges upon the enemy. Rejoice, O ye nations, with his people: for he will avenge the blood of his servants, and will render vengeance to his adversaries, and will be merciful unto his land, and to his people (Deut. 32:42, 43).

"Verily I say unto you, They have their reward" (Matt. 6:2), Jesus says to the agents of Jesuit terrorism and their Evangelical workers of iniquity. Their successful lawlessness may appear to pay off now, but their fabulous rewards will be short-lived. "Sufficient unto the day is the evil thereof" (Matt. 6:34). Having all that heart could wish until the Day of Judgment is what makes Judgment Day so horrifically bad. This life is all the reward they will ever see; they will miss an eternity of perfect excellence with infinite security and grace and selflessness from their Redeemer.

"That the blood of all the prophets, which was shed from the foundation of the world, may be required of this generation; from the blood of Abel unto the blood of Zacharias, which perished between the altar and the temple: verily I say unto you, It shall be required of this generation" (Luke 11:50, 51). "Behold, your house is left unto you desolate" (Matt. 23:38).

The world of freedom will be dismantled and will fall before global Nazi dictatorship/totalitarian terrorism. In the overthrow no trace of connection with the Vatican will be visible. All that most people will see is a union of all religions and a world coming to peace. For fear of terrible retribution, not a peep of dissent will arise in the new world order. Satan will finally reign supreme.

> Woe to thee that spoilest, and thou wast not spoiled; and dealest treacherously, and they dealt not treacherously with thee! when thou shalt cease to spoil, thou shalt be spoiled; and when thou shalt make an end to deal treacherously, they shall deal treacherously with thee. O LORD, be gracious unto us; we have waited for thee: be thou their arm every morning, our salvation also in the time of trouble. At the noise of the tumult the people fled; at the lifting up of thyself the nations were scattered (Isa. 33:1-3).

The wicked walk on every side, when the vilest men are exalted (Ps. 12:8).

Ye are they that forsake the LORD, that forget My holy mountain, that prepare a table for that troop, and that furnish the drink offering unto that number. Therefore will I number you to the sword, and ye shall all bow down to the slaughter: because when I called, ye did not answer; when I spake, ye did not hear; but did evil before mine eyes, and did choose that wherein I delighted not. Therefore thus saith the Lord GOD, Behold, my servants shall eat, but ye shall be hungry: behold, my servants shall drink, but ye shall be thirsty: behold, my servants shall rejoice, but ye shall be ashamed: behold, my servants shall sing for joy of heart, but ye shall cry for sorrow of heart, and shall howl for vexation of spirit. And ye shall leave your name for a curse unto my chosen: for the Lord GOD shall slay thee, and call his servants by another name (Isa. 65:11-15).

And ye shall tread down the wicked; for they shall be ashes under the soles of your feet in the day that I shall do this, saith the LORD of hosts (Mal. 4:3, cf vs. 1).

To many people today it might seem that these "kings of the earth" and "merchants of the earth" (Rev. 18:3) — government agencies, multinational banks, merged monopolizing corporations, powerful think tanks, and secret societies — have only the exploitation of Middle Eastern and African natural resources for a global economic agenda. But, Jesus' prophecy declares a deeper, more sinister purpose. They have "committed fornication with her" (Rev. 18:3); that is, the Church has bewitched the world's governments and international private sector. For years, the Red Mass has wooed the minds of American lawmakers, justices, and executives. Through that mesmerizing, they are fulfilling her agenda, which is the conquest of the world for her consort from the abyss. Lucifer's purpose for the Church is to restore global dictatorships and totalitarian religion. By corrupting the world culturally and healthfully, and causing political unrest in peaceful nations, her Jesuits are creating in the world a desire for the Papacy's religion that captivates the conscience. Driven by the black smoke from the bottomless pit, the Jesuits' work is to exalt the pope to the topmost position of power over the world's populations. By her Jesuit front men, the Church is winning the world over for her 2017 exaltation. Since medieval Europe, it will be the second recurrence of the woman that rides the Beast; and Lucifer will again give her his spiritual and temporal sovereignty, as the usurped ethical authority in heaven and earth. Already, she has almost regained the old glory of the Dark Ages. This time her exaltation will be on a global scale and humanly impregnable.

"The beast that ascendeth out of the bottomless pit" (Rev. 11:7) is fulfilling Satan's agenda. "The dragon ['called the Devil, and Satan' (Rev. 12:9)] gave him [the Beast, Medieval Christendom] his power, and his seat, and great authority.... And all the world wondered after the beast. And they worshipped the dragon which gave power unto the beast: and they worshipped the beast, saying, Who is like unto the beast? who is able to make war with him?" (Rev. 13:2-4, cf see Rev. 2:12-23).

The symbolic Beast referred to here is the conglomeration of the first three prophetic beasts of Daniel 7:4-6 that represent the ancient world empires of occult Babylon, moralistic Persia, and philosophic Greece. "The Beast" is the last empire of the four that arose out of the turbulent sea of devil tormented pagan nations (see Daniel 7:2, 3, 7, 8; Revelation 13:1, 2; Revelation 17:15). The Beast is the Roman Empire and its heir of unrest, bitterness, control, and persecution, the Holy Roman Empire. Also known as the Papacy, from antiquity she is the descendant of the spiritual center on the seventh hill of ancient Rome. She is *vaticanus*, "relating to, or characteristic of a prophet" with "possessed", "raging" "frenzy", the progenitor of the "faith" (*see Appendix A*). As the self-appointed All-seeing eye and the voice of "God", the See of Rome claims the final say on Earth. The definition of the word Vatican has its roots in the deepest occult. Retention of the ancient name evinces perpetuation of the same spiritualistic system. Satan never gives up any earthly agency that he fully develops. A small minority of individuals have been delivered from Satan through their diligent, personal efforts to get to Jesus. But, throughout human history organizations and nations have never done so; the trend of leadership and their multitudes alike has always and ever been downward.

Before our very eyes this medieval Beast is rising from its deadly wound. And the churched and secular children of Protestantism sit idly by, watching its killing with patriotic hearts. Their consciences and intellects are benumbed by entertainment from the Jesuit controlled media (*see Appendix A*) and from pulpits unable to warn of the impending conflict. "His watchmen are blind: ... they are all [mute] dogs, they cannot bark; sleeping, lying down, loving to slumber" (Isa. 56:10).

In the wake of 9/11, every other act of global terror since has been and will continue to be choreographed by the same secret organizations of 9/11 in order to destroy the liberties which Protestant America has proffered the world. The Vatican-inspired Protestant politicians, combined with the Jesuit forces, have illicitly gutted the U.S. Constitution Bill of Rights one Amendment at a time; and in the end of this covert work, church will overtly unite with state.

When that happens, all the fair laws that have protected rights of person and property will be transformed into laws which protect only the party members of the new regime. To get a clear picture of what lies ahead, read the following description of a society rebuilt upon unjust law.

> If the law were not binding, why should any fear to transgress? Property would no longer be safe. Men would obtain their neighbor's possessions by violence, and the strongest would become richest. Life itself would not be respected. The marriage vow would no longer stand as a sacred bulwark to protect the family. He who had the power, would, if he desired, take his neighbor's wife by violence. The fifth commandment would be set aside with the fourth. Children would not shrink from taking the life of their parents if by so doing they could obtain the desire of their corrupt hearts. The civilized world would become a horde of robbers and assassins; and peace, rest, and happiness would be banished from the earth *The Great Controversy*, p. 585.

As Rome continues to war against Protestant and civil America she increasingly uses America to remove constitutional democracies and to foment strife in the earth. America's freedoms and wealth and its primitive Protestantism will disappear, the Monroe Doctrine a whim of the past. Totalitarianism will spread quickly to every nation not already under such regimes, and dictatorial religion will control the populace along with the violent world of dictatorships which Satan will birth and Rome will christen. Jesus said, "Yea, the time cometh, that whosoever killeth you will think that he doeth God service" (John 16:2).

Scripture describes the destructive force that will drive Satan's final kingdom, Babylon being the Revelation symbol of it.

Thou shalt take up this proverb against the king of Babylon, …he who smote the people in wrath with a continual stroke, he that ruled the nations in anger…that made the world as a wilderness, and destroyed the cities thereof; that opened not the house of his prisoners… (Isa. 14:4, 6, 17).

This says that Satan, the dragon, which torments the world with an evil conscience (see Zechariah 3:1, 2; Revelation 12:10), is the same evil force behind the power, seat, and great authority of Rome (see Revelation 13:2), the symbolic "fourth beast" that "shall be the fourth kingdom upon earth, which shall be diverse from all kingdoms, and shall devour the whole earth, and shall tread it down, and break it in pieces" (Dan. 7:23). The dragon, his beast, and his beast's eldest son proclaim for themselves, "All power and authority are given to me in heaven and in earth."

Since 9/11, the same bitter spirit that possessed ancient Babylon has been raised up to possess the nations because of their forsaking the Law of God and the grace of Christ for victory over sin and for the special work of purification (see Revelation 11:18, cf Hosea 8:7).

A noise shall come even to the ends of the earth; for the LORD hath a controversy with the nations, he will plead with all flesh; he will give them that are wicked to the sword, saith the LORD. Thus saith the LORD of hosts, Behold, evil shall go forth from nation to nation, and a great whirlwind shall be raised up from the coasts of the earth (Jer. 25:31, 32).

Again, the proven facts of 9/11, 1) the three largest buildings of the World Trade Center, WTC 1, 2, 7, achieved the impossible feat of free-falling straight down, perfectly into their already exploded basements, without the buildings tipping over on the way to the ground, and travelling almost at the speed of gravity, a never seen occurrence except for controlled demolitions, 2) the many eye-witness testimonies of explosions in the basements *before* the planes hit (piling up charred cars, and maiming, burning, and killing individuals in the basements), and testimonies of the numerous, rapidly detonating, sequential explosions after the plane impacts as the buildings came down, 3) the total pulverization of the concrete floors, and the footage showing "squibs" (exploding demolition ejecta shooting out from the sides of the Twin Towers) ten to thirty floors below the falling destruction, telling the work of demolition, 4) the yellow, super-heated liquid steel, running down from the upper floors and along channel ways beneath the debris, of the twin towers and WTC 7, and 5) the aftermath of 9/11 in the imperialistic and aggressor actions of America around the world as nations topple, economies collapse, and new-modeled democracies are established. These all cry out to the world that we have entered into the sixth trumpet period when the winds of destruction would be loosed from the spiritual Euphrates as Providence has permitted a complete, though temporary, resuscitation of occult Babylon (see Revelation 7:1; 9:14, 15, cf Jeremiah 47:2). (Reader, please hang on, real good news is just around the corner in the Revelation drama. Revelation chapter 10 will be a turning point from Revelation chapter 9's dark, unsettling scenes. Chapter 10 will bring hope and a future with Jesus overseeing this work in the earth. This is all for sealing His people. The story ends in His servants' favor.)

Thus, Satan's black smoke and his hosts "breathing out threatenings and slaughter against the disciples of the Lord" (Acts 9:1), ultimately will have unlimited capture of the world (see Revelation 17:8, 11-14). A rapid period of fierce restoration of wicked control will bring the human race under world dictatorship and global lawlessness. The tell-tale evidence of Satan's human hosts will be a relentless anger fomented by a tortured conscience, leading directly to a heretofore inconceivable persecution against the Reformation people of the Lord (see Revelation 11:18; Matthew 24:21, 22). The history of Vatican-driven Nazi Germany will be repeated, this time with democratic America as the tool of Rome.

***Nevertheless**, the overthrow of the Lord's Protestant blessing to the world does not warrant anyone arming himself to defend against its modern Babylonian perpetrator.*

Nevertheless, the overthrow of the Lord's Protestant blessing to the world does not warrant anyone arming himself to defend against its modern Babylonian perpetrator. **Why?** Because *our desolation comes from above for our punishment and our preparation for Jesus' return.* All punishment from heaven is always motivated by infinite love and is only for our salvation.

> Moreover the word of the LORD came unto me, saying, Jeremiah, what seest thou? And I said, I see a rod of an almond tree.
>
> Then said the LORD unto me, Thou hast well seen: for I will hasten my word to perform it.
>
> And the word of the LORD came unto me the second time, saying, What seest thou? And I said, I see a seething [boiling] pot; and the face thereof is toward the north.
>
> Then the LORD said unto me, Out of the north an evil shall break forth upon all the inhabitants of the land.
>
> For, lo, I will call all the families of the kingdoms of the north, saith the LORD; and they shall come, and they shall set every one his throne at the entering of the gates of Jerusalem, and against all the walls thereof round about, and against all the cities of Judah.
>
> And I will utter my judgments against them touching all their wickedness, who have forsaken me, and have burned incense unto other gods, and worshipped the works of their own hands (Jer. 1:11-16).

Our destruction comes because, no differently than ancient Israel, we have increasingly taken God's beautiful land without a moment of true thankfulness and childlike, whole-hearted obedience to the Giver. We have pretended to love Him so that we could continue reaping His gifted land. *We have used God.* We have listened to false prophets and have accepted the new gods through lawless Spiritual Formation from the Vatican, instead of accepting the rebuke of God. They have changed our Protestant religion; we have lost the everlasting covenant. We celebrate a pagan justification and an imagined peace with God, and have rejected the special work of purification.

We have lost the original love of self-sacrifice that the Reformers had. We do not love the Bible and cannot lay down our lives for it. Our desolation comes for our not receiving the lessons of falling on the Stone and learning contrition, sanctification, and patient endurance, lessons from which we have long been remiss. All who desire these fruits of the Spirit, but have found them elusive, will welcome the coming tribulation. And everyone who had been learning surrender in the little things during our peacetime fifth trumpet world will appreciate the larger troubles ahead with their potential for deeper faith and stronger communion with Jesus. To them the small gift of God that they have won so far speaks of greater treasures in the near future. The punishing discipline will humble and redeem all who God has reserved.

> All nations shall serve him [Nebuchadnezzar], and his son, and his son's son, until the very time of his land come: and then many nations and great kings shall serve themselves of him. And it shall come to pass, that the nation and kingdom which will not serve the same Nebuchadnezzar the king of Babylon, and that will not put their neck under the yoke of the king of Babylon, that nation will I punish, saith the LORD, with the sword, and with the famine, and with the pestilence, until I have consumed them by his hand. Therefore hearken not ye to your prophets, nor to your diviners, nor to your dreamers, nor to your enchanters, nor to your sorcerers, which speak unto you, saying, Ye shall not serve the king of Babylon: for they prophesy a lie unto you, to remove you far from your land; and that I should drive you out, and ye should perish. *But the nations that bring their neck under the yoke of the king of Babylon, and serve him, those will I let remain still in their own land, saith the LORD; and they shall till it, and dwell therein.* I spake also to Zedekiah king of Judah according to all these words, saying, Bring your necks under the yoke of the king of Babylon, and serve him and his people, and live. Why will ye die, thou and thy people, by the sword, by the famine, and by the pestilence, as the LORD hath spoken against the nation that will not serve the king of Babylon? Therefore hearken not unto the words of the prophets that speak unto you, saying, Ye shall not serve the king of Babylon: for they prophesy a lie unto you. For I have not sent them, saith the LORD, yet they prophesy a lie in my name; that I might drive you out, and that ye might perish, ye, and the prophets that prophesy unto you (Jer. 27:7-15).

Israel could not win against the Lord and His indomitable "hammer of the whole earth" (Jer. 50:23), mighty Babylon. Let this be our warning against battling today's "Babylon the Great" (Rev. 17:5). Prophecy and disciplinary providence have determined that disobedient America and Protestantism must lose all their liberties.

They would not let God's Law convict them of righteousness, and bring them to conversion and sanctification, to happiness and preparation for their Lord's return. Now, for God's people to fight against the corrective armies of modern Babylon is to fight against the Lord's decreed punishment and discipline that can help them stand when He returns in power to destroy sin and its satanic kingdom of the Vatican.

> I am the LORD your God, which brought you forth out of the land of Egypt, that ye should not be their bondmen; and I have broken the bands of your yoke, and made you go upright.
>
> But if ye will not hearken unto me, and will not do all these commandments;
>
> And if ye shall despise my statutes, or if your soul abhor my judgments, so that ye will not do all my commandments, but that ye break my covenant:
>
> I also will do this unto you;…
>
> I will set my face against you, and ye shall be slain before your enemies: they that hate you shall reign over you.…
>
> And I will bring a sword upon you, that shall avenge the quarrel of my covenant: and when ye are gathered together within your cities, I will send the pestilence among you; and ye shall be delivered into the hand of the enemy (Lev. 26:13-17, 25).
>
> For thus saith the LORD, Behold, I will make thee a terror to thyself, and to all thy friends: and they shall fall by the sword of their enemies, and thine eyes shall behold it: and I will give all Judah into the hand of the king of Babylon, and he shall carry them captive into Babylon, and shall slay them with the sword. Moreover I will deliver all the strength of this city, and all the labours thereof, and all the precious things thereof, and all the treasures of the kings of Judah will I give into the hand of their enemies, which shall spoil them, and take them, and carry them to Babylon (Jer. 20:4, 5).
>
> The consumption decreed shall overflow with righteousness. For the Lord GOD of hosts shall make a consumption, even determined, in the midst of all the land (Isa. 10:22, 23).
>
> He shall make it desolate, even until the consummation, and that determined shall be poured upon the desolate (Dan. 9:27).

Individuals and groups have sought Justice Department investigations into 9/11 to find the perpetrators and to bring the truth to light. The Lord has provided His Protestant nation such avenues for preserving and executing justice; and those avenues should be used. But, if those seekers of justice find that legal loopholes and other high power roadblocks are obstructing justice, they should not be too disappointed. These atrocities against Protestant America are happening because Jehovah is bringing His judgments against us. He is prospering the old enemy of Protestantism because we have left the covenant that our Reformation fathers received from Him; we have forgotten the terrors of the Dark Ages. We have accepted the devil's deception that there is no Creator, and we no longer commune with our God and seek help from Him who delivered us from the terrible days of papal bondage and persecution.

The Protestant Reformation is the reason Americans have lived in such a fair land. Yet, rather than study the Law of God and respond in thankful obedience to our Deliverer from papal darkness, we have been having one party after another in honor of Satan. Jehovah will not permit this dishonor to go on any longer. We have departed far from the righteousness that He desires. Obedience to His righteous laws is the reason that He called us His people and has protected us. To depart from the covenant means we no longer deserve the blessed refuge of America and the blessed form of government that He gave us. Therefore, our God has allowed the enemy of Protestantism to punish America. Until their plan is finalized to make war on America, our old enemy will block every effort by Protestants to stop the overthrow of America. We must have war on American soil; Bible prophecy has predestinated it. We must all be punished: the hedonist, the atheist, the secular, the mocker of God's Law, the militias who try to prevent the Lord's punishment, etc. Even those who desire to follow the one true God will be punished, as Daniel and others like him went into Babylonian captivity with all the rebellious Jews, religious and non-religious alike. The God of Protestantism has already made His actions clear; He has laid it out in His Bible for a warning. Per Deuteronomy 28, everything Protestant must go away. The holy people will be punished. The Lord has determined it.

The consumption decreed shall overflow with righteousness. For the Lord GOD of hosts shall make a consumption, even determined, in the midst of all the land (Isa. 10:22, 23).

Therefore thus saith the LORD, Behold, I will lay stumblingblocks before this people, and the fathers and the sons together shall fall upon them; the neighbour and his friend shall perish (Jer. 6:21).

However, in God's mercy, life would yet be accorded to everyone who would choose surrender, submission, humiliation, and enslavement.

He that abideth in this city [to defend it] shall die by the sword, and by the famine, and by the pestilence: but he that goeth out, and falleth to the Chaldeans that besiege you, he shall live, and his life shall be unto him for a prey (Jer. 21:9).

Thus saith the LORD, He that remaineth in this city [to fight for Israel] shall die by the sword, by the famine, and by the pestilence: but he that goeth forth to the Chaldeans [and to captivity] shall live; for he shall have his life for a prey, and shall live.... Then said Jeremiah unto Zedekiah, Thus saith the LORD, the God of hosts, the God of Israel; If thou wilt assuredly go forth unto the king of Babylon's princes, then thy soul shall live, and this city shall not be burned with fire; and thou shalt live, and thine house.... Jeremiah said, They [the Jews' armies] shall not deliver thee. Obey, I beseech thee, the voice of the LORD, which I speak unto thee: so it shall be well unto thee, and thy soul shall live (Jer. 38:2, 17, 20).

Hearken not ye to your prophets, nor to your diviners, nor to your dreamers, nor to your enchanters, nor to your sorcerers, which speak unto you, saying, Ye shall not serve the king of Babylon: for they prophesy a lie unto you, to remove you far from your land; and that I should drive you out, and ye should perish. But the nations that bring their neck under the yoke of the king of Babylon, and serve him, those will I let remain still in their own land, saith the LORD (Jer. 27:9).

For whosoever will save his life shall lose it: but whosoever will lose his life for my sake, the same shall save it (Luke 9:24).

Before the first tribulation comes, we must be praying that we will *not* fight. We must be regular visitors to the throne of Law and grace to receive help at the time the need arises. God's main lesson in the sixth trumpet troubles is our perfect surrender to Christ for the special work of purification, to give up our anger and fighting, and to learn to pray and to trust in divine help. *We must learn surrender.*

When powerful foes were uniting to overthrow the reformed faith, and thousands of swords seemed about to be unsheathed against it, Luther wrote: "Satan is putting forth his fury; ungodly pontiffs are conspiring; and we are threatened with war. Exhort the people to contend valiantly before the throne of the Lord, by faith and prayer, so that our enemies, vanquished by the Spirit of God, may be constrained to peace. Our chief want, our chief labor, is prayer; let the people know that they are now exposed to the edge of the sword and to the rage of Satan, *and let them pray* [emphasis mine]." — D'Aubigne, b. 10, ch. 14.

Again, at a later date, referring to the league contemplated by the reformed princes, Luther declared that the only weapon employed in this warfare should be "the sword of the Spirit." He wrote to the elector of Saxony: "We cannot on our conscience approve the proposed alliance. *We would rather die ten times than see our gospel cause one drop of blood to be shed* [emphasis mine]. Our part is to be like lambs of the slaughter. The cross of Christ must be borne. Let your highness be without fear. *We shall do more by our prayers than all our enemies by their boastings* [emphasis mine]. Only let not your hands be stained with the blood of your brethren. If the emperor requires us to be given up to his tribunals, we are ready to appear. You cannot defend our faith: each one should believe at his own risk and peril." — Ibid., b. 14, ch. 1 *The Great Controversy*, p. 209.

Touching the course of some who had resorted to violent measures in abolishing the mass, Luther said:

"The mass is a bad thing; God is opposed to it; it ought to be abolished; and I would that throughout the whole world it were replaced by the supper of the gospel. But let no one be torn from it by force. We must leave the matter in God's hands. His word must act, and not we. And why so? you will ask. Because I do not hold men's hearts in my hand, as the potter holds the clay. We have a right to speak: we have not the right to act. Let us preach; the rest belongs unto God. Were I to employ force, what should I gain? Grimace, formality, apings, human ordinances, and hypocrisy. . . . But there would be no sincerity of heart, nor faith, nor charity. Where these three are wanting, all is wanting, and I would not give a pear stalk for such a result. . . . God does more by His word alone than you and I and all the world by our united strength. God lays hold upon the heart; and when the heart is taken, all is won. . . .

"I will preach, discuss, and write; but I will constrain none [emphasis mine], for faith is a voluntary act. See what I have done. I stood up against the pope, indulgences, and papists, but without violence or tumult. I put forward God's word; I preached and wrote — this was all I did. And yet while I was asleep, . . . the word that I had preached overthrew popery, so that neither prince nor emperor has done it so much harm. And yet I did nothing; the word alone did all. If I had wished to appeal to force, the whole of Germany would perhaps have been deluged with blood. But what would have been the result? Ruin and desolation both to body and soul. I therefore kept quiet, and left the word to run through the world alone." — Ibid., b. 9, ch. 8 *The Great Controversy*, p. 189, 190.

There must be no long discussions, presenting new theories in regard to the prophecies which God has already made plain. Now the great work from which the mind should not be diverted is the consideration of our personal safety in the sight of God. Are our feet on the rock of ages? Are we hiding ourselves in our only refuge? The storm is coming, relentless in its fury. Are we prepared to meet it? Are we one with Christ as He is one with the Father? Are we heirs of God and joint heirs with Christ? Are we working in copartnership with Christ?--Manuscript 32a, 1896 *Evangelism*, p. 199.

The soon to be reestablished Revelation 17 Babylonian armies, which we see galloping across the landscape in Revelation 9 and which end in our Revelation 18 captivity, represent testing and trying punishment. It will be real punishment, spiritual and temporal, on God's end-time Protestants because they would not love the Lord their God with all their heart and strength. They would not sit at Jesus' feet, learning to trust Him and be transformed by His holy influence. But, it will also be a time of accelerating development of righteousness by faith in those who had begun to learn it during the fifth trumpet and continue to learn surrender into the sixth trumpet captivity.

When He has successfully taught His people to forgo their own battle against self, then they will lay down their weapons against their earthly enemies, as well. Only as they learn to surrender to God's Law and Jesus' cross on the spiritual front will they surrender to Him on life's front to obey the directions from His modern Jeremiah. Will they not let Christ be their wisdom and their righteousness, their shield and their exceeding great reward (see 1 Corinthians 1:30; Genesis 15:1)? This was His lesson to Israel since their very beginning and it will be His lesson to Protestant America through the Babylonian armies, Jeremiah experiencing that very principle.

> The LORD said [to Jeremiah], Verily it shall be well with thy remnant; verily I will cause the enemy to entreat thee well in the time of evil and in the time of affliction (Jer. 15:11).

> Now Nebuchadrezzar king of Babylon gave charge concerning Jeremiah to Nebuzaradan the captain of the guard, saying, Take him, and look well to him, and do him no harm; but do unto him even as he shall say unto thee. So Nebuzaradan the captain of the guard sent, … and took Jeremiah out of the court of the prison, and committed him unto Gedaliah the son of Ahikam the son of Shaphan, that he should carry him home: so he dwelt among the people (Jer. 39:11-14).

A time of desolating trouble, which the sixth trumpet reveals will fiercely drive over us (see Revelation 9:7-10, 17-19, cf Jeremiah 47:2), comes from the providence of God to correct Protestantism and its Remnant for selling His Reformation's treasures of truth and grace for the trinkets of celebration worship and Spiritual Formation. The very presence of Protestantism's old enemy living as a parasite within Protestant America (see Daniel 7:8; 8:9; 11:21-23) declares the Lord's lifting of divine protection. Our tryst with Baal and Ashtoreth, our baptizing the whole world's lawless, loveless pagan religion is the cause of the sixth trumpet captivity, and has been the cause of every subjugation of God's people throughout sacred history. We have ignored the special work of purification and the duplication of Christ's character, in spirit and in truth. This Jesus mandated for His people, through the counsels of Ellen White, in order to give us the sealing and to prepare us to stand when He comes.

And what is the standard of primitive godliness given to us from Christ and His apostolic church? It is to have the perfect surrender to Christ's grace and truth.

"Verily I say unto you, Among them that are born of women there hath not risen a greater than John the Baptist: notwithstanding he that is least in the kingdom of heaven is greater than he." "Blessed is he, whosoever shall not be offended in me" (Matt. 11:11, 6). Rather than following false prophets' advice to defend ourselves, the special work of purification will cause Christ's disciples to lay down their personal rights, and become servants. This is just what the Lord has always been trying to teach His Protestants and especially His Adventists.

We are directed by scripture to serve as servants and slaves, even to our enemies. A slave of the Lord means to do everything Jesus commands us without complaint.

Strong's G1249 *diakonos*, "attendant", "servant".

"If ye continue in the faith grounded and settled, and be not moved away from the hope of the gospel, which ye have heard, and which was preached to every creature which is under heaven; whereof I Paul am made a minister[G1249]" (Col. 1:23).

"Paul, a servant[G1249] of Jesus Christ, called to be an apostle, separated unto the gospel of God" (Rom. 1:1).

Strong's G1401 *doulos*, "slave" "bond-servant".

"Servants[G1401], obey in all things your masters according to the flesh; not with eyeservice, as menpleasers; but in singleness of heart, fearing God" (Col. 3:22).

"Let as many servants[G1401] as are under the yoke count their own masters worthy of all honour, that the name of God and his doctrine be not blasphemed" (1 Tim. 6:1).

"And the servant[G1401] of the Lord must not strive; but be gentle unto all men, apt to teach, patient" (2 Tim. 2:24).

"Exhort servants[G1401] to be obedient unto their own masters, and to please them well in all things; not answering again" (Tit. 2:9).

"In the days of the voice of the seventh angel, when he shall begin to sound, the mystery of God should be finished, as he hath declared to his servants[G1401] the prophets" (Rev. 10:7).

The patriarchs and prophets and kings and apostles were bondservants or slaves to the Lord and to others, as are missionaries and others today who have a testimony of what Jesus did for them, or through them.

Strong's H5650 *'ebed*, "bondman", bondservant".

"I am not worthy of the least of all the mercies, and of all the truth, which thou hast shewed unto thy servant[H5650]" (Gen. 32:10).

"Thus saith the Lord GOD; When I shall have gathered the house of Israel from the people among whom they are scattered, and shall be sanctified in them in the sight of the heathen, then shall they dwell in their land that I have given to my servant[H5650] Jacob" (Eze. 28:25).

"Now after the death of Moses the servant[H5650] of the LORD it came to pass, that the LORD spake unto Joshua the son of Nun, Moses' minister" (Josh. 1:1).

"And Joshua the son of Nun, the servant[H5650] of the LORD, died, being an hundred and ten years old" (Judg. 2:8).

"And the LORD came, and stood, and called as at other times, Samuel, Samuel. Then Samuel answered, Speak; for thy servant[H5650] heareth" (1 Sam. 3:10).

"And David said to Saul, Let no man's heart fail because of him; thy servant[H5650] will go and fight with this Philistine" (1 Sam. 17:32).

"And Saul knew David's voice, and said, Is this thy voice, my son David? And David said, It is my voice, my lord, O king. And he said, Wherefore doth my lord thus pursue after his servant[H5650]? for what have I done? or what evil is in mine hand?" (1 Sam. 26:17, 18).

"Princes also did sit and speak against me: but thy servant[H5650] did meditate in thy statutes. Deal with thy servant[H5650] according unto thy mercy, and teach me thy statutes. I am thy servant[H5650]; give me understanding, that I may know thy testimonies" (Ps. 119:23, 124, 125).

"For I will defend this city to save it for mine own sake, and for my servant[H5650] David's sake" (Isa. 37:35).

"Hear now, O Joshua the high priest, thou, and thy fellows that sit before thee: for they are men wondered at: for, behold, I will bring forth my servant[H5650] the BRANCH" (Zech. 3:8).

"But thou, Israel, art my servant[H5650], Jacob whom I have chosen, the seed of Abraham my friend" (Isa. 41:8).

"And also upon the servant[H5650] and upon the handmaids[H8198] [H8198 *shiphchah*, female slave, bond-woman] in those days will I pour out my spirit" (Joel 2:29).

"Then she fell on her face, and bowed herself to the ground, and said unto him, Why have I found grace in thine eyes, that thou shouldest take knowledge of me, seeing I am a stranger? And Boaz answered and said unto her, It hath fully been shewed me, all that thou hast done unto thy mother in law since the death of thine husband: and how thou hast left thy father and thy mother, and the land of thy nativity, and art come unto a people which thou knewest not heretofore. The LORD recompense thy work, and a full reward be given thee of the LORD God of Israel, under whose wings thou art come to trust. Then she said, Let me find favour in thy sight, my lord; for that thou hast comforted me, and for that thou hast spoken friendly unto thine handmaid[H8198], though I be not like unto one of thine handmaidens[H8198]" (Ruth 2:10-12).

"And the Syrians had gone out by companies, and had brought away captive out of the land of Israel a little maid; and she waited on Naaman's wife. And she said unto her mistress, Would God my lord were with the prophet that is in Samaria! For he would recover him of his leprosy" (2 Ki. 5:2, 3).

Naaman demonstrates the fruits of the Spirit, showing that everyone who is converted will become a humbled servant to others.

"In this thing the LORD pardon thy servant[H5650], that when my master goeth into the house of Rimmon to worship there, and *he leaneth on my hand*, and I bow myself in the house of Rimmon: when I bow down myself in the house of Rimmon, the LORD pardon thy servant[H5650] in this thing" (2 Ki. 5:18).

Jesus, the Son of the Highest, was the Bondservant of bondservants.

"Behold my servant[H5650], whom I uphold; mine elect, in whom my soul delighteth; I have put my spirit upon him: he shall bring forth judgment to the Gentiles.... Who is blind, but my servant[H5650]? or deaf, as my messenger that I sent? who is blind as he that is perfect, and blind as the LORD's servant[H5650]? Seeing many things, but thou observest not; opening the ears, but he heareth not. The LORD is well pleased for his righteousness' sake; he will magnify the law, and make it honourable" (Isa. 42:1, 19-21).

"Behold, my servant[H5650] shall deal prudently, he shall be exalted and extolled, and be very high. As many were astonied at thee; his visage was so marred more than any man, and his form more than the sons of men" (Isa. 52:13, 14).

"Let this mind be in you, which was also in Christ Jesus: who, being in the form of God, thought it not robbery to be equal with God: but *made himself of no reputation*, and took upon him the form of a servant[G1401], and was made in the likeness of men" (Phil. 2:5-7).

"If I then, your Lord and Master, have washed your feet; ye also ought to wash one another's feet. For I have given you an example, that ye should do as I have done to you. Verily, verily, I say unto you, The servant[G1401] is not greater than his lord; neither he that is sent greater than he that sent him" (John 13:14-16).

The standard has been high: service to the Creator and to others from a heart that Jesus has made new. If we will surrender to the Heaven-determined scattering of our power, unlike the response of the northern kingdom of Israel in Isaiah's day and the southern kingdom of Judah in Jeremiah's day, then we will receive the purifying for which Jesus has been waiting all these 170 some years. While we still have time, we must follow His example and the examples of all those who testified of Him as help-meets.

"If we walk in the light, as he is in the light, we have fellowship one with another, and the blood of Jesus Christ his Son cleanseth us from all sin" (1 John 1:7). "If ye be willing and obedient, ye shall eat the good of the land: but if ye refuse and rebel, ye shall be devoured with the sword: for the mouth of the LORD hath spoken it" (Isa. 1:19, 20).

> The LORD hath sent unto you all his servants the prophets, rising early and sending them; but ye have not hearkened, nor inclined your ear to hear. They said, Turn ye again now every one from his evil way, and from the evil of your doings, and dwell in the land that the LORD hath given unto you and to your fathers for ever and ever: and go not after other gods to serve them, and to worship them, and provoke me not to anger with the works of your hands; and I will do you no hurt. Yet ye have not hearkened unto me, saith the LORD; that ye might provoke me to anger with the works of your hands to your own hurt. Therefore thus saith the LORD of hosts; Because ye have not heard my words, behold, I will send and take all the families of the north, saith the LORD, and Nebuchadrezzar the king of Babylon, my servant, and will bring them against this land, and against the inhabitants thereof, and against all these nations round

about, and will utterly destroy them, and make them an astonishment, and an hissing, and perpetual desolations. Moreover I will take from them the voice of mirth, and the voice of gladness, the voice of the bridegroom, and the voice of the bride, the sound of the millstones, and the light of the candle. And this whole land shall be a desolation, and an astonishment (Jer. 25:4-11).

The admonition of the scriptures is to learn to submit and to patiently suffer.

Take, my brethren, the prophets, who have spoken in the name of the Lord, for an example of suffering affliction, and of patience. Behold, we count them happy which endure (Jas. 5:10, 11).

Why do ye not rather take wrong? Why do ye not rather suffer yourselves to be defrauded? (1 Cor. 6:7).

Woe is me.… I have neither lent on usury, nor men have lent to me on usury; yet every one of them doth curse me (Jer. 15:10).

They that hate me without a cause are more than the hairs of mine head: they that would destroy me, being mine enemies wrongfully, are mighty: then *I restored that which I took not away* (Ps. 69:4).

And when they were come to the place, which is called Calvary, there they crucified him, and the malefactors, one on the right hand, and the other on the left. Then said Jesus, Father, forgive them; for they know not what they do. And they parted his raiment, and cast lots (Luke 23:33, 34).

And they stoned Stephen, calling upon God, and saying, Lord Jesus, receive my spirit. And he kneeled down, and cried with a loud voice, Lord, lay not this sin to their charge. And when he had said this, he fell asleep (Acts 7:59, 60).

The meek shall inherit the earth; and shall delight themselves in the abundance of peace (Ps. 37:11).

And unto him that smiteth thee on the one cheek offer also the other; and him that taketh away thy cloke forbid not to take thy coat also.… The disciple is not above his master: but every one that is perfect shall be as his master (Luke 6:29, 40).

The LORD gave, and the LORD hath taken away; blessed be the name of the LORD (Job 1:21).

Why call ye me, Lord, Lord, and do not the things which I say? (Luke 6:46).

Shouldn't our response to persecution and false accusation be without self-defense and the same as our Lord's toward Judas and the rabble? "Jesus said unto him, Friend, wherefore art thou come? Then came they, and laid hands on Jesus" (Matt. 26:50).

Do violence to no man (Luke 3:14).

Vengeance is mine; I will repay, saith the Lord (Rom. 12:19).

Put up again thy sword into his place: for all they that take the sword shall perish with the sword (Matt. 26:52).

How are the mighty fallen, and the weapons of war perished! (2 Sam. 1:27).

Amon trespassed more and more. And his servants conspired against him, and slew him in his own house. But the people of the land slew all them that had conspired against king Amon (2 Chron. 33:23-25).

And God said unto him [Solomon], Because thou hast asked this thing, and hast not asked for thyself long life; neither hast asked riches for thyself, *nor hast asked the life of thine enemies*; but hast asked for thyself understanding to discern judgment; behold, I have done according to thy words: lo, I have given thee a wise and an understanding heart; so that there was none like thee before thee, neither after thee shall any arise like unto thee (1 Ki. 3:11, 12).

Satan delights in war, for it excites the worst passions of the soul and then sweeps into eternity its victims steeped in vice and blood. It is his object to incite the nations to war against one another, for he can thus divert the minds of the people from the work of preparation to stand in the day of God *The Great Controversy*, p. 589.

Friend, we should not heed the voices calling us to fight against our promised discipline from heaven, lest we "be found even to fight against God" (Acts 5:39). Fighting off the punishment of our Father in heaven must result in even severer punishment, as ancient Israel discovered time after time.

> The LORD shall cause thee to be smitten before thine enemies: thou shalt go out one way against them, and flee seven ways before them: and shalt be removed into all the kingdoms of the earth (Deut. 28:25).

> One thousand shall flee at the rebuke of one; at the rebuke of five shall ye flee: till ye be left as a beacon upon the top of a mountain, and as an ensign on an hill (Isa. 30:17).

> Yea, and nothing shall escape them (Joel 2:3).

> Though ye had smitten the whole army of the Chaldeans that fight against you, and there remained but wounded men among them, yet should they rise up every man in his tent, and burn this city with fire (Jer. 37:10).

> Thus saith the LORD God of Israel; Behold, I will turn back the weapons of war that are in your hands, wherewith ye fight against the king of Babylon, and against the Chaldeans, which besiege you without the walls, and I will assemble them into the midst of this city. And *I myself will fight against you with an outstretched hand and with a strong arm, even in anger, and in fury, and in great wrath* (Jer. 21:4, 5).

> In the ninth year of Zedekiah king of Judah, in the tenth month, came Nebuchadrezzar king of Babylon and all his army against Jerusalem, and they besieged it. And in the eleventh year of Zedekiah, in the fourth month, the ninth day of the month, the city was broken up (Jer. 39:1, 2).

> And it came to pass, that when Zedekiah the king of Judah saw them, and all the men of war, then they fled, and went forth out of the city by night, by the way of the king's garden, by the gate betwixt the two walls: and he went out the way of the plain. But the Chaldeans' army pursued after them, and overtook Zedekiah in the plains of Jericho: and when they had taken him, they brought him up to Nebuchadnezzar king of Babylon to Riblah in the land of Hamath, where he gave judgment upon him (Jer. 39:4, 5).

> And they [the children of Israel at Kadesh] rose up early in the morning, and gat them up into the top of the mountain, saying, Lo, we be here, and will go up unto the place which the LORD hath promised: for we have sinned.

> And Moses said, Wherefore now do ye transgress the commandment of the LORD? but it shall not prosper. Go not up, for the LORD is not among you; that ye be not smitten before your enemies. For the Amalekites and the Canaanites are there before you, and ye shall fall by the sword: because ye are turned away from the LORD, therefore the LORD will not be with you.

> But they presumed to go up unto the hill top: nevertheless the ark of the covenant of the LORD, and Moses, departed not out of the camp. Then the Amalekites came down, and the Canaanites which dwelt in that hill, and smote them, and discomfited them, even unto Hormah (Num. 14:40-45).

> We wrestle not against flesh and blood, but against principalities, against powers, against the rulers of the darkness of this world (Eph. 6:12).

The coming punishment is our due. We must learn truth; and speak out and meet deception and error with truth. But, we must not use physical force to defend ourselves against "the northern army" (Joel 2:20) of Babylon that God is sending today. "The LORD shall utter his voice before his [Babylonian] army: for his camp is very great: for he is strong that executeth his word: for the day of the LORD is great and very terrible; and who can abide it?" (Joel 2:11).

If we are to war against anything, let us war against the cause of the Lord's opening the fifth and sixth trumpets' pit of Hades. That cause is us; we, His Protestants, are the reason that all this is coming upon our nation and our world. We would not behold the "beauty of the Lord our God" (Ps. 90:17). We would not surrender to the sealed, childlike Son. We would not let His yearning friendship give us His Spirit that can convict minds that are in rebellion, developing in us His genuine deference and self-sacrificing love. We would not let the restful seventh-day Sabbath, a day with Jesus the Holy One, sanctify our characters in order to help prepare the world for His coming Judgment Day. We would not glorify God in our tragedies and trials. In this golden age of atheism, we would not burden our souls with the difficulties of winning rebellious Protestants to their God and Saviour. Therefore, He allows an increasing wickedness to assist our detachment from the faith-deadening influence of this world, to surrender self, and to ready ourselves and others for Him at His appearing. A numberless multitude must now learn from the Chaldean scourge. They would not go to the Schoolmaster to repent and be converted, and to learn humility and surrender the easier way. So they must learn through this sudden, harsher curriculum. We need the coming punishment. It will be our cross experience that the disciples went through. We need a crisis to wake us up to total faith in Jesus.

> Behold, the days come, saith the LORD, that I will punish all them which are circumcised with the uncircumcised; Egypt, and Judah, and Edom, and the children of Ammon, and Moab, and all that are in the utmost corners, that dwell in the wilderness: for all these nations are uncircumcised, and all the house of Israel are uncircumcised in the heart (Jer. 9:25, 26).

Like the children of Israel, we've been circumspect in the behavior, but not in the heart. We've been stuck in the mode of thinking that character is in the actions only, rather than starting with the heart, requiring the second birth and a new nature. The 1888 Minneapolis conference should have corrected that notion. As a group, we're hot on the outside and cold on the inside. Our self-sufficiency has corrupted our conceptions of God's requirements in the special work of purification. We've not cared to have the deeper things of Christ's faith and love. A dangerous daze is upon us, and like the Jews, we will need their same shocking punishment by Babylon. We, the Protestant denominations, could have prevented our Lord's approaching punishment by making good use of His Testimonies through Ellen White. This would have cooperated with His work of exposing our consciences to the light of His word, and thus letting His Spirit put in us His faith and love, obedience "wrought in God" (John 3:21).

> Let him that glorieth glory in this, that he understandeth and knoweth me, that I am the LORD which exercise lovingkindness, judgment, and righteousness, in the earth: for in these things I delight, saith the LORD (Jer. 9:24).

Protestant America should have known "the grace of the Lord Jesus Christ, and the love of God, and the communion of the Holy Ghost" (2 Cor. 13:14). Instead, the bride expecting the Bridegroom, delved into the search for this world's possessions, which soon will all pass away. By evading God's power in His Law, we made ourselves easily tempted away from His presence. Then we accepted the invitation to rejoice and celebrate an imagined purification of character, and a nonexistent relationship with a God whose rules we had not reconciled with. Now Protestant America is the epitome of atheism/unbelief and corruption. "She hath changed my judgments into wickedness more than the nations, and my statutes more than the countries that are round about her: for they have refused my judgments and my statutes, they have not walked in them" (Eze. 5:6).

> *Many pastors have destroyed my vineyard*, they have trodden my portion under foot, they have made my pleasant portion a desolate wilderness. They have made it desolate, and being desolate it mourneth unto me; the whole land is made desolate, because *no man layeth it to heart*. The spoilers are come upon all high places through the wilderness: for the sword of the LORD shall devour from the one end of the land even to the other end of the land: no flesh shall have peace. They have sown wheat, but shall reap thorns: they have put themselves to pain, but shall not profit: and they shall be ashamed of your revenues because of the fierce anger of the LORD (Jer. 12:10-13).

> O LORD…thou hast stricken them, but they have not grieved; thou hast consumed them, but they have refused to receive correction: they have made their faces harder than a rock; they have refused to return [repent] (Jer. 5:3).

We have been disobedient to our calling. Yet, there remains a little time to recover. But, our weapon must be the sword of the spirit upon ourselves. "If ye through the Spirit do mortify the deeds of the body, ye shall live" (Rom. 8:13).

> (For the weapons of our warfare are not carnal, but mighty through God to the pulling down of strong holds;) casting down imaginations, and every high thing that exalteth itself against the knowledge of God, and bringing into captivity every thought to the obedience of Christ; and having in a readiness to revenge all disobedience, when your obedience is fulfilled (2 Cor. 10:4-6).

Our war should be to quickly overcome our ignorance of God's word, to unite with Jesus against self-love, self-indulgence, and temptation to sin, to pull down all of our strongholds of sin that so easily beset us. Then, our cache of weapons will be the faith of Christ; our protection will be His breastplate of righteousness and His helmet of salvation that come from living under the shadow of His wings. The angels will create a barrier around us and their presence will bring us comfort and joy. The Lord of hosts will be our defense.

> But I will sing of thy power; yea, I will sing aloud of thy mercy in the morning: for thou hast been my defence and refuge in the day of my trouble.

> Unto thee, O my strength, will I sing: for God is my defence, and the God of my mercy (Ps. 59:16, 17).

Ancient Israel's disobedience was the cause of their desolation by violent Assyria and Babylon. Likewise, modern Assyria took away the disobedient Protestants 170 years ago, and modern Babylon's current conquest of Protestant America is due to our, today's Adventists', disobedience. The neglect of our wrestling with the Law for the victory over self through the grace of Christ has forced the God of Protestantism to bring upon us the desolations He brought upon His people of old. Departing from the precepts of the Spirit of Prophecy in exchange for empty, adulterous Spiritual Formation has already been tried, with dreadful results. We learn valuable lessons from the Jews and their smooth prophets. All scripture is for us today.

> They have healed also the hurt of the daughter of my people slightly, saying, Peace, peace; when there is no peace. Were they ashamed when they had committed abomination? nay, they were not at all ashamed, neither could they blush: therefore they shall fall among them that fall: at the time that I visit them they shall be cast down, saith the LORD. Thus saith the LORD, Stand ye in the ways, and see, and ask for the old paths, where is the good way, and walk therein, and ye shall find rest for your souls. But they said, *We will not walk therein*. Also I set watchmen over you, saying, Hearken to the sound of the trumpet. But they said, We will not hearken (Jer. 6:14-17).

Israel's Levites and priests had served the religion of Baal for so long that they could no longer grasp the true character of God's Law and grace. Therefore, they could no longer train up the children of Israel in the ways of God's goodness. When the Jews left the Lord in preference to Babylon's gods and polluted lifestyle, the Lord raised up Babylon to conquer Israel. Then He sent His prophets to teach them His word. But, down to the very last prophet they wouldn't take heed. Will we, His Protestants?

> And now, O ye priests, this commandment is for you.

> If ye will not hear, and if ye will not lay it to heart, to give glory unto my name, saith the LORD of hosts, I will even send a curse upon you, and I will curse your blessings: yea, I have cursed them already, because ye do not lay it to heart.

> Behold, I will corrupt your seed, and spread dung upon your faces, even the dung of your solemn feasts; and one shall take you away with it.

> And ye shall know that I have sent this commandment unto you, that my covenant might be with Levi, saith the LORD of hosts.

> My covenant was with him of life and peace; and I gave them to him for the fear wherewith he feared me, and was afraid before my name.

> The law of truth was in his mouth, and iniquity was not found in his lips: he walked with me in peace and equity, and did turn many away from iniquity.

> For the priest's lips should keep knowledge, and they should seek the law at his mouth: for he is the messenger of the LORD of hosts.

> But ye are departed out of the way; ye have caused many to stumble at the law; ye have corrupted the covenant of Levi, saith the LORD of hosts.

> Therefore have I also made you contemptible and base before all the people, according as ye have not kept my ways, but have been partial in the law (Mal. 2:1-9).

Without the least thought or gratitude while partaking of God's blessings, our cavalier minds and hearts are the cause for all of America's blessings leaving us. We are no better than were the abominable Canaanites. Like the stampeding cavalry of the sixth trumpet, all the troubles rushing toward us mean our rightful judgment and punishment. The lessons of righteousness by faith in God's Law and Jesus' grace have fallen upon deaf ears and double-minded hearts. The readiness for Christ's coming are the lessons given from the Spirit of Prophecy *for the special purification* of His Protestants in the Advent movement. Let us accept the tribulation to come and not listen to the voices that cry, "Defend America's freedoms! Defend yourselves! Fight the foreign and domestic armies!" Never forget that the prophecy against the Beast power is that it would be "broken without hand" (Dan. 8:25); that is, without human hand.

> The LORD spake thus to me with a strong hand, and instructed me that I should not walk in the way of this people, saying, Say ye not, A confederacy, to all them to whom this people shall say, A confederacy; neither fear ye their fear, nor be afraid. Sanctify the LORD of hosts himself; and let him be your fear, and let him be your dread. And he shall be for a sanctuary; but for a stone of stumbling and for a rock of offence to both the houses of Israel, for a gin and for a snare to the inhabitants of Jerusalem. And many among them shall stumble, and fall, and be broken, and be snared, and be taken (Isa. 8:11-15).

> For thus saith the Lord GOD, the Holy One of Israel; In returning and rest shall ye be saved; in quietness and in confidence shall be your strength: and ye would not. But ye said, **No**; for we will flee upon horses; therefore shall ye flee: and, We will ride upon the swift; therefore shall they that pursue you be swift. One thousand shall flee at the rebuke of one; at the rebuke of five shall ye flee: till ye be left as a beacon upon the top of a mountain, and as an ensign on an hill. And therefore will the LORD wait, that he may be gracious unto you, and therefore will he be exalted, that he may have mercy upon you: for the LORD is a God of judgment: blessed are all they that wait for him (Isa. 30:15-18).

We *need* the soon tribulation. It is for our benefit. For our special work of purification the troubles are coming. We have deserved the punishment Jesus is sending us now through the sixth trumpet in order for Him to create a chosen generation, a peculiar people that He has wanted from the Reformation since its inception.

We, Protestants, would not strive to obtain surrender to Jesus and His sealing. Surrender will give us hunger for the things of God, things that Jesus loved. He has graciously given us one last chance to purify our souls, "being born again, not of corruptible seed, but of incorruptible, by the word of God, which liveth and abideth for ever" (1 Pet. 1:23, cf 1 John 3:2, 3). Will we wake up at this late hour and seek the Lord's help to get up to speed for the last, great, tumultuous troubles? Each public shooting, each plane crash, each news report of rampant crime or act of terror, all tell us that we are overdue for our divinely ordained punishment. The Vatican's murderers are already here. Will we learn surrender and be born again, "obeying the truth through the Spirit" (1 Pet. 1:22)?

> When thou art spoiled, what wilt thou do? Though thou clothest thyself with crimson, though thou deckest thee with ornaments of gold, though thou rentest thy face with painting, in vain shalt thou make thyself fair; thy lovers will despise thee, they will seek thy life. For I have heard a voice as of a woman in travail, and the anguish as of her that bringeth forth her first child, the voice of the daughter of Zion, that bewaileth herself, that spreadeth her hands, saying, Woe is me now! for my soul is wearied because of murderers (Jer. 4:30, 31).

> The treacherous dealers have dealt treacherously; yea, the treacherous dealers have dealt very treacherously. Fear, and the pit, and the snare, are upon thee, O inhabitant of the earth. And it shall come to pass, that he who fleeth from the noise of the fear shall fall into the pit; and he that cometh up out of the midst of the pit shall be taken in the snare: for the windows from on high are open, and the foundations of the earth do shake (Isa. 24:16-18).

There will be murderers and marauders on every hand. All our blessings from God that we have taken for granted will be replaced with satanic evils from the master that we preferred. And we will then know what God has thought of our self-righteousness and half-hearted obedience and dead works, "the last to be more than the first" (Rev. 2:19). The bitter and hasty spiritual guides of Babylon who we have loved hate us. They cannot love us; only the Lord of the Bible can love sinners.

> Of whom hast thou been afraid or feared, that thou hast lied, and hast not remembered me, nor laid it to thy heart? have not I held my peace

even of old, and thou fearest me not? I will declare thy righteousness, and thy works; for they shall not profit thee. When thou criest, let thy companies deliver thee; but the wind shall carry them all away; vanity shall take them: but he that putteth his trust in me shall possess the land, and shall inherit my holy mountain; and shall say, Cast ye up, cast ye up, prepare the way, take up the stumblingblock out of the way of my people (Isa. 57:11-14).

During this Investigative Judgment and cleansing of the heavenly sanctuary, we are all either being sealed or marked. We are either softening our hearts to Jesus or hardening them by listening to the nice sounding familiar spirits of the world-wide locust temptation invasion. We are daily either coming to terms with obedience to God's laws and living by every word of God, or we are being hardened in rebellion against Him. He longs to give us a new heart, so that He can dwell with us forever. He wants His cloud to sit upon a mercy-seat which only He can put in our new tabernacles. But, we must learn the lessons of righteousness by faith, to strive to know Jesus by His Spirit in the Law.

> That they should seek the Lord, if haply they might feel after him, and find him, though he be not far from every one of us (Acts 17:27).

> Those that seek me early shall find me (Prov. 8:17).

What we all have needed is a clearer view of Christ in the Law (*see Appendix A*), without which we could not obey the mandate for a special work of purification.

All, who know the experience of righteousness by trusting Jesus through studying Him in His Law, will let Him fight their sins. They will have His peace and contentedness, and will stop fighting flesh and blood. He saved them from pride and from their "cruel venom" (Deut. 32:33), and they have nothing more to drive them to hurt anyone through self-defense. They would rather die than cause the death of their pursuer, oppressor, killer. Thus, all who know the experience of righteousness by faith will be the only ones who will let Him fight Protestantism's earthly enemies. For those whose hearts are faithful to know Him, our God will show Himself strong in their behalf. "The eyes of the LORD run to and fro throughout the whole earth, to shew himself strong in the behalf of them whose *heart* is perfect toward *him*" (2 Chron. 16:9, cf Rev. 5:6). Loving and trusting the Son will be the only defense in the times of trouble ahead. They will come down from sitting in heavenly places with Jesus, their faces calm and their minds clear. They will naturally trust His promise, "The angel of the LORD encampeth round about them that fear him, and delivereth them" (Ps. 34:7). Jesus, who calmly walked through the enemy crowds (see Luke 4:30), will be their model.

> Because thou hast made the LORD, which is my refuge, even the most High, thy habitation;
>
> There shall no evil befall thee, neither shall any plague come nigh thy dwelling.
>
> For he shall give his angels charge over thee, to keep thee in all thy ways.
>
> They shall bear thee up in their hands, lest thou dash thy foot against a stone.
>
> Thou shalt tread upon the lion and adder: the young lion and the dragon shalt thou trample under feet.
>
> *Because he hath set his love upon me, therefore will I deliver him*: I will set him on high, because he hath known my name.
>
> He shall call upon me, and I will answer him: I will be with him in trouble; I will deliver him, and honour him.
>
> With long life will I satisfy him, and shew him my salvation (Ps. 91:9-16).
>
> With whom my hand shall be established: mine arm also shall strengthen him.
>
> The enemy shall not exact upon him; nor the son of wickedness afflict him.
>
> And I will beat down his foes before his face, and plague them that hate him.
>
> But my faithfulness and my mercy shall be with him: and in my name shall his horn be exalted.
>
> I will set his hand also in the sea, and his right hand in the rivers.
>
> He shall cry unto me, Thou art my father, my God, and the rock of my salvation.
>
> Also I will make him my firstborn, higher than the kings of the earth.

> My mercy will I keep for him for evermore, and my covenant shall stand fast with him (Ps. 89:21-28).
>
> I will lift up mine eyes unto the hills, from whence cometh my help.
>
> My help cometh from the LORD, which made heaven and earth.
>
> He will not suffer thy foot to be moved: he that keepeth thee will not slumber.
>
> Behold, he that keepeth Israel shall neither slumber nor sleep.
>
> The LORD is thy keeper: the LORD is thy shade upon thy right hand.
>
> The sun shall not smite thee by day, nor the moon by night.
>
> The LORD shall preserve thee from all evil: he shall preserve thy soul.
>
> The LORD shall preserve thy going out and thy coming in from this time forth, and even for evermore (Ps. 121).

If we have set our love upon Jesus, like David set his love upon Him, then He who never slumbers nor sleeps will more than protect us if it is in God's plan for His people, and we will be more than conquerors through Him who loves us.

> He that hath my commandments, and keepeth them, he it is that loveth me: and he that loveth me shall be loved of my Father, and I will love him, and will manifest myself to him (John 14:21).
>
> I am thy shield, and thy exceeding great reward (Gen. 15:1).

Meshach, Shadrach, and Abednego so fully received the godly love of Christ, and were so settled in His peace, that they could accept death if God so willed it. Contrariwise, if we spend our lives working hard to save ourselves from our sins because we don't learn surrender to God's Law and love, to let Him fight our battles against sin, then we will naturally fight against flesh and blood to save ourselves during the coming trouble. We will fight as did Israel, and reap the harshness of God's penalty against self-defense (see Isaiah 30:15-18; Jeremiah 38:2, 7, 20-23; 39:4-7; Lamentations 1:15). We will fight like Peter in Gethsemane (see Matthew 26:51-56; John 18:10, 11).

The violent juggernaut that is hastening apace is our due because of our negligence to wrestle with the whole Spirit of Prophecy, to develop the faith and obedience of Jesus and to receive His robe of perfect righteousness, having every thought woven by the loom of heaven. His robe is for Protestantism's preparation to meet her long sought Husband at His soon return, and also for them to lead the world to prepare. We need to accept as discipline the approaching marauding storm and be humbled by its relentless fury; we must learn to stop fighting against violent men and to sorrow for our own naturally violent nature. Then, we will fear the Lord, and His angel will deliver us (see Psalm 34:7).

> In those days, and in that time, saith the LORD, the children of Israel shall come, they and the children of Judah together, going and weeping: they shall go, and seek the LORD their God.
>
> They shall ask the way to Zion with their faces thitherward, saying, Come, and let us join ourselves to the LORD in a perpetual covenant that shall not be forgotten.
>
> My people hath been lost sheep: their shepherds have caused them to go astray, they have turned them away on the mountains: they have gone from mountain to hill, they have forgotten their restingplace.
>
> All that found them have devoured them: and their adversaries said, We offend not, because they have sinned against the LORD, the habitation of justice, even the LORD, the hope of their fathers.
>
> Remove out of the midst of Babylon, and go forth out of the land of the Chaldeans, and be as the he goats before the flocks.
>
> For, lo, I will raise and cause to come up against Babylon an assembly of great nations from the north country: and they shall set themselves in array against her; from thence she shall be taken: their arrows shall be as of a mighty expert man; none shall return in vain.
>
> And Chaldea shall be a spoil: all that spoil her shall be satisfied, saith the LORD (Jer. 50:4-10).

When He has fully scattered our power (see Daniel 12:7), when our self-sufficiency has evaporated and we are wholly submitted to heaven (see Leviticus 26:40-42; 2 Chronicles 16:9), then He will raise us up and we will live in His sight (see Hosea 6:1-4; Revelation 11:12). We will be the apple of His eye and He will commission His angels to be a ring of fire around us (see Zechariah 2:8, 5).

If we live for this world, we are on Satan's enchanted ground (see John 3:18). We can only warm ourselves by the sparks of our imagined fire (see Isaiah 50:11). The sixth trumpet cries out to us the need to awaken from our worldly slump and to promptly begin receiving the faith of Jesus for obedience to all of God's commandments. The coming violence that removes from us our idols of gold and selfish gratifications is God's last effort to reach all who have at least a mustard seed grain of faith, but who need the fear and hardship of tribulation to shake them out of their unbelief and apathy, and to give them His genuine obedience. The faith of few will survive the time of trouble who do not now begin to seek communion with God and find in Him a resting place.

> Those who exercise but little faith now, are in the greatest danger of falling under the power of satanic delusions and the decree to compel the conscience. And even if they endure the test they will be plunged into deeper distress and anguish in the time of trouble, because they have never made it a habit to trust in God. The lessons of faith which they have neglected they will be forced to learn under a terrible pressure of discouragement.

> We should now acquaint ourselves with God by proving His promises. Angels record every prayer that is earnest and sincere. We should rather dispense with selfish gratifications than neglect communion with God. The deepest poverty, the greatest self-denial, with His approval, is better than riches, honors, ease, and friendship without it. We must take time to pray. If we allow our minds to be absorbed by worldly interests, the Lord may give us time by removing from us our idols of gold, of houses, or of fertile lands *The Great Controversy*, p. 622.

Therefore shall the Lord, the Lord of hosts, send among his fat ones leanness; and under his glory he shall kindle a burning like the burning of a fire. And the light of Israel shall be for a fire, and his Holy One for a flame: and it shall burn and devour his thorns and his briers in one day; and shall consume the glory of his forest, and of his fruitful field, both soul and body: and they shall be as when a standardbearer fainteth. And the rest of the trees of his forest shall be few, that a child may write them. And it shall come to pass in that day, that the remnant of Israel, and such as are escaped of the house of Jacob, shall no more again stay upon him that smote them; but shall stay upon the LORD, the Holy One of Israel, *in truth* (Isa. 10:16-20).

The remnant shall return [repent and be healed], even the remnant of Jacob, unto the mighty God. For though thy people Israel be as the sand of the sea, yet a remnant of them shall return: the consumption decreed shall overflow with righteousness. For the Lord GOD of hosts shall make a consumption, even determined, in the midst of all the land.... And the LORD of hosts shall stir up a scourge for him [the Assyrian enemies of God] according to the slaughter of Midian at the rock of Oreb: and as his rod was upon the sea, so shall he lift it up after the manner of Egypt. And it shall come to pass in that day, that his [the Assyrian's] burden shall be taken away from off thy shoulder, and his yoke from off thy neck, and the yoke shall be destroyed *because of the anointing* (Isa. 10:21-27, cf Isa. 6:13).

The Lord will fight for us, if we will take up our fight to get and to stay with Him. The battle with our sins is His and only His to command (see Ephesians 6:14-18; Exodus 14:13, 14; 2 Chronicles 20:14-22); while, the fight for His gift of faith is ours and only ours to command (see 1 Timothy 6:12; 2 Timothy 4:7; Luke 10:39, 42). The work of battling our sins we must surrender up to Jesus in His Most Holy Place, and be busy with our work to find the Lord of love in all of His convicting holiness. Our surrender will only come by seeing Christ in every word that has proceeded from the mouth of God (see Isaiah 42:1-4; Matthew 4:4), Christ who took the whole wrath of God and lost His perfect peace, so that we can have His perfect peace. He will then fight for us and in us as our love distills upon Him (see Psalm 91:14; Phil. 2:12, 13; *Maranatha*, p. 200). He can only fight the battle against our sins proportionate to our growth in humiliation before, and surrender to, His Law and love. If we will not choose to engage the fight for a knowledge of Jesus, then He sends us the worsening troubles today that may shake us up to that fight to know Him (see Jeremiah 47:3; Revelation 7:14; Philippians 3:8-10). If we have engaged the Law of God in Christ and surrendered to that Stone Mountain of offense, then Jesus gives us rest and a new capacity to let go of sin today. When we leave the battle of sin to Jesus and trust in Him as He is seen in the Law of God, only then will we stop wrestling with flesh and blood, our own and other enemies'.

> Not one of us will ever receive the seal of God while our characters have one spot or stain upon them. It is left with us to remedy the defects in our characters, to cleanse the soul-temple of every defilement. Then the latter rain will fall upon us as the early rain fell upon the disciples on the day of Pentecost *Christian Experience and Teachings*, p. 189.

All who will spend 100% of their time and effort, poverty and self-denial, fighting for the knowledge of God in Jesus, so that they spend 0% of their time and effort and abstinence fighting their own evil and the evil in the world, will find themselves surrendering to Jesus and afflicting their souls, able to mortify their flesh through His Spirit. Because these folks have cooperated with Him, the Lord can protect only them from the towering tsunami of wickedness in the sixth trumpet, which is racing toward unpreventable world captivity. And, when that evil empire, the Lord's "hammer" (Jer. 50:23), has helped to finish bringing down our mountain of self-sufficient forgetfulness of God, then the Lord will destroy that empire like we never could. (See Psalm 76:5, 6; Psalm 9:15, 16; Proverbs 28:10; Jeremiah 25:11-14; Isaiah 13:17-19; Jeremiah 30:16; Revelation 19:11-21; Revelation 13:10; Deuteronomy 9:1-6.)

We are fast closing in on the final actions of this deceptive, global centralization of power — a united religious, governmental, financial, media, intelligence, and military front. The facts of the past sixteen years all cry out to the world that we have entered into the sixth trumpet period during which the winds of final destruction were to be loosed (see Revelation 9:14; Matthew 24:8). God foreknew this empire of perdition from the beginning of the Revelation 7:3 delay (see Revelation 9:15). He knew His people would be captive in Babylon before He would return. The American experiment of republican democracy has run its providential course. It has accomplished its purpose to protect God's beloved religion of Protestantism and its follow-on, Adventism. Through America God has created a land of Goshen for the Advent movement until we could fully accept Jesus' robe of righteousness upon our natures, and its obedience to all of His commandments in the sealing.

Protestant America will have transitioned into Christian America when the Lord sends His Latter Rain upon "them whom I reserve" (Jer. 50:20). The Latter Rain comes to all who will not be joining in all the irreverent frolic and celebration and occult Spiritual Formation, but who will be distressing and crying for all the abominations sweeping the nations (see Ezekiel 9:4; Numbers 25:1-6). The Roman Empire, as abusive as it was, continued to protect the world from the approaching Papacy (see 2 Thessalonians 2:6, 7) until the church in the wilderness could establish itself in preaching the gospel. Likewise, until now civil America has remained to hold back Christian America in preparation for the scattered flock of the 144,000 to be fully sealed during the coming captivity. In Christ's humility and surrender they will preach to the world one last time a whole Bible gospel of righteousness by God's Law and by Jesus' faith. They will cry out against the surrounding abominations until the finale of Satan's tyrannical mountain of unprecedented wickedness plays out under the purview of an on-looking angelic jury of heaven (see Jeremiah 51:19-24; Revelation 11:12-17; Daniel 4:13, 17; Judges 5:20; 1 Corinthians 4:9; 1 Peter 1:12).

> The sun shall be turned into darkness, and the moon into blood, before the great and the terrible day of the LORD come. And it shall come to pass, that whosoever shall call on the name of the LORD shall be delivered: for in mount Zion and in Jerusalem shall be deliverance, as the LORD hath said, and in the remnant [H8300, "survivor"] whom the LORD shall call (Joel 2:31, 32, cf Isa. 60:2; Jer. 31:1, 2).

> In those days, and in that time, saith the LORD, the iniquity of Israel shall be sought for, and there shall be none; and the sins of Judah, and they shall not be found: for I will pardon them whom I reserve (Jer. 50:20, cf Rom. 11:4, 5).

Revelation Chapters 4 through 11 (KJV)

Revelation Chapter 4

Rev 4:1 After this I looked, and, behold, a door was opened in heaven: and the first voice which I heard was as it were of a trumpet talking with me; which said, Come up hither, and I will shew thee things which must be hereafter.

Rev 4:2 And immediately I was in the spirit: and, behold, a throne was set in heaven, and one sat on the throne.

Rev 4:3 And he that sat was to look upon like a jasper and a sardine stone: and there was a rainbow round about the throne, in sight like unto an emerald.

Rev 4:4 And round about the throne were four and twenty seats: and upon the seats I saw four and twenty elders sitting, clothed in white raiment; and they had on their heads crowns of gold.

Rev 4:5 And out of the throne proceeded lightnings and thunderings and voices: and there were seven lamps of fire burning before the throne, which are the seven Spirits of God.

Rev 4:6 And before the throne there was a sea of glass like unto crystal: and in the midst of the throne, and round about the throne, were four beasts full of eyes before and behind.

Rev 4:7 And the first beast was like a lion, and the second beast like a calf, and the third beast had a face as a man, and the fourth beast was like a flying eagle.

Rev 4:8 And the four beasts had each of them six wings about him; and they were full of eyes within: and they rest not day and night, saying, Holy, holy, holy, Lord God Almighty, which was, and is, and is to come.

Rev 4:9 And when those beasts give glory and honour and thanks to him that sat on the throne, who liveth for ever and ever,

Rev 4:10 The four and twenty elders fall down before him that sat on the throne, and worship him that liveth for ever and ever, and cast their crowns before the throne, saying,

Rev 4:11 Thou art worthy, O Lord, to receive glory and honour and power: for thou hast created all things, and for thy pleasure they are and were created.

Revelation Chapter 5

Rev 5:1 And I saw in the right hand of him that sat on the throne a book written within and on the backside, sealed with seven seals.

Rev 5:2 And I saw a strong angel proclaiming with a loud voice, Who is worthy to open the book, and to loose the seals thereof?

Rev 5:3 And no man in heaven, nor in earth, neither under the earth, was able to open the book, neither to look thereon.

Rev 5:4 And I wept much, because no man was found worthy to open and to read the book, neither to look thereon.

Rev 5:5 And one of the elders saith unto me, Weep not: behold, the Lion of the tribe of Juda, the Root of David, hath prevailed to open the book, and to loose the seven seals thereof.

Rev 5:6 And I beheld, and, lo, in the midst of the throne and of the four beasts, and in the midst of the elders, stood a Lamb as it had been slain, having seven horns and seven eyes, which are the seven Spirits of God sent forth into all the earth.

Rev 5:7 And he came and took the book out of the right hand of him that sat upon the throne.

Rev 5:8 And when he had taken the book, the four beasts and four and twenty elders fell down before the Lamb, having every one of them harps, and golden vials full of odours, which are the prayers of saints.

Rev 5:9 And they sung a new song, saying, Thou art worthy to take the book, and to open the seals thereof: for thou wast slain, and hast redeemed us to God by thy blood out of every kindred, and tongue, and people, and nation;

Rev 5:10 And hast made us unto our God kings and priests: and we shall reign on the earth.

Rev 5:11 And I beheld, and I heard the voice of many angels round about the throne and the beasts and the elders: and the number of them was ten thousand times ten thousand, and thousands of thousands;

Rev 5:12 Saying with a loud voice, Worthy is the Lamb that was slain to receive power, and riches, and wisdom, and strength, and honour, and glory, and blessing.

Rev 5:13 And every creature which is in heaven, and on the earth, and under the earth, and such as are in the sea, and all that are in them, heard I saying, Blessing, and honour, and glory, and power, be unto him that sitteth upon the throne, and unto the Lamb for ever and ever.

Rev 5:14 And the four beasts said, Amen. And the four and twenty elders fell down and worshipped him that liveth for ever and ever.

Revelation Chapter 6

Rev 6:1 And I saw when the Lamb opened one of the seals, and I heard, as it were the noise of thunder, one of the four beasts saying, Come and see.

Rev 6:2 And I saw, and behold a white horse: and he that sat on him had a bow; and a crown was given unto him: and he went forth conquering, and to conquer.

Rev 6:3 And when he had opened the second seal, I heard the second beast say, Come and see.

Rev 6:4 And there went out another horse

that was red: and power was given to him that sat thereon to take peace from the earth, and that they should kill one another: and there was given unto him a great sword.

Rev 6:5 And when he had opened the third seal, I heard the third beast say, Come and see. And I beheld, and lo a black horse; and he that sat on him had a pair of balances in his hand.

Rev 6:6 And I heard a voice in the midst of the four beasts say, A measure of wheat for a penny, and three measures of barley for a penny; and see thou hurt not the oil and the wine.

Rev 6:7 And when he had opened the fourth seal, I heard the voice of the fourth beast say, Come and see.

Rev 6:8 And I looked, and behold a pale horse: and his name that sat on him was Death, and Hell followed with him. And power was given unto them over the fourth part of the earth, to kill with sword, and with hunger, and with death, and with the beasts of the earth.

Rev 6:9 And when he had opened the fifth seal, I saw under the altar the souls of them that were slain for the word of God, and for the testimony which they held:

Rev 6:10 And they cried with a loud voice, saying, How long, O Lord, holy and true, dost thou not judge and avenge our blood on them that dwell on the earth?

Rev 6:11 And white robes were given unto every one of them; and it was said unto them, that they should rest yet for a little season, until their fellowservants also and their brethren, that should be killed as they were, should be fulfilled.

Rev 6:12 And I beheld when he had opened the sixth seal, and, lo, there was a great earthquake; and the sun became black as sackcloth of hair, and the moon became as blood;

Rev 6:13 And the stars of heaven fell unto the earth, even as a fig tree casteth her untimely figs, when she is shaken of a mighty wind.

Rev 6:14 And the heaven departed as a scroll when it is rolled together; and every mountain and island were moved out of their places.

Rev 6:15 And the kings of the earth, and the great men, and the rich men, and the chief captains, and the mighty men, and every bondman, and every free man, hid themselves in the dens and in the rocks of the mountains;

Rev 6:16 And said to the mountains and rocks, Fall on us, and hide us from the face of him that sitteth on the throne, and from the wrath of the Lamb:

Rev 6:17 For the great day of his wrath is come; and who shall be able to stand?

Revelation Chapter 7

Rev 7:1 And after these things I saw four angels standing on the four corners of the earth, holding the four winds of the earth, that the wind should not blow on the earth, nor on the sea, nor on any tree.

Rev 7:2 And I saw another angel ascending from the east, having the seal of the living God: and he cried with a loud voice to the four angels, to whom it was given to hurt the earth and the sea,

Rev 7:3 Saying, Hurt not the earth, neither the sea, nor the trees, till we have sealed the servants of our God in their foreheads.

Rev 7:4 And I heard the number of them which were sealed: and there were sealed an hundred and forty and four thousand of all the tribes of the children of Israel.

Rev 7:5 Of the tribe of Juda were sealed twelve thousand. Of the tribe of Reuben were sealed twelve thousand. Of the tribe of Gad were sealed twelve thousand.

Rev 7:6 Of the tribe of Aser were sealed twelve thousand. Of the tribe of Nepthalim were sealed twelve thousand. Of the tribe of Manasses were sealed twelve thousand.

Rev 7:7 Of the tribe of Simeon were sealed twelve thousand. Of the tribe of Levi were sealed twelve thousand. Of the tribe of Issachar were sealed twelve thousand.

Rev 7:8 Of the tribe of Zabulon were sealed twelve thousand. Of the tribe of Joseph were sealed twelve thousand. Of the tribe of Benjamin were sealed twelve thousand.

Rev 7:9 After this I beheld, and, lo, a great multitude, which no man could number, of all nations, and kindreds, and people, and tongues, stood before the throne, and before the Lamb, clothed with white robes, and palms in their hands;

Rev 7:10 And cried with a loud voice, saying, Salvation to our God which sitteth upon the throne, and unto the Lamb.

Rev 7:11 And all the angels stood round about the throne, and about the elders and the four beasts, and fell before the throne on their faces, and worshipped God,

Rev 7:12 Saying, Amen: Blessing, and glory, and wisdom, and thanksgiving, and honour, and power, and might, be unto our God for ever and ever. Amen.

Rev 7:13 And one of the elders answered, saying unto me, What are these which are arrayed in white robes? and whence came they?

Rev 7:14 And I said unto him, Sir, thou knowest. And he said to me, These are they which came out of great tribulation, and have washed their robes, and made them white in the blood of the Lamb.

Rev 7:15 Therefore are they before the throne of God, and serve him day and night in his temple: and he that sitteth on the throne shall dwell among them.

Rev 7:16 They shall hunger no more, neither thirst any more; neither shall the sun light on them, nor any heat.

Rev 7:17 For the Lamb which is in the midst of the throne shall feed them, and shall lead them unto living fountains of waters: and God shall wipe away all tears from their eyes.

Revelation Chapter 8

Rev 8:1 And when he had opened the seventh seal, there was silence in heaven about the space of half an hour.

Rev 8:2 And I saw the seven angels which stood before God; and to them were given seven trumpets.

Rev 8:3 And another angel came and stood at the altar, having a golden censer; and there was given unto him much incense, that he should offer it with the prayers of all saints upon the golden altar which was before the throne.

Rev 8:4 And the smoke of the incense, which came with the prayers of the saints, ascended up before God out of the angel's hand.

Rev 8:5 And the angel took the censer, and filled it with fire of the altar, and cast it into the earth: and there were voices, and thunderings, and lightnings, and an earthquake.

Rev 8:6 And the seven angels which had the seven trumpets prepared themselves to sound.

Rev 8:7 The first angel sounded, and there followed hail and fire mingled with blood, and they were cast upon the earth: and the third part of trees was burnt up, and all green grass was burnt up.

Rev 8:8 And the second angel sounded, and as it were a great mountain burning with fire was cast into the sea: and the third part of the sea became blood;

Rev 8:9 And the third part of the creatures which were in the sea, and had life, died; and the third part of the ships were destroyed.

Rev 8:10 And the third angel sounded, and there fell a great star from heaven, burning as it were a lamp, and it fell upon the third part of the rivers, and upon the fountains of waters;

Rev 8:11 And the name of the star is called Wormwood: and the third part of the waters became wormwood; and many men died of the waters, because they were made bitter.

Rev 8:12 And the fourth angel sounded, and the third part of the sun was smitten, and the third part of the moon, and the third part of the stars; so as the third part of them was darkened, and the day shone not for a third part of it, and the night likewise.

Rev 8:13 And I beheld, and heard an angel flying through the midst of heaven, saying with a loud voice, Woe, woe, woe, to the inhabiters of the earth by reason of the other voices of the trumpet of the three angels, which are yet to sound!

Revelation Chapter 9

Rev 9:1 And the fifth angel sounded, and I saw a star fall from heaven unto the earth: and to him was given the key of the bottomless pit.

Rev 9:2 And he opened the bottomless pit; and there arose a smoke out of the pit, as the smoke of a great furnace; and the sun and the air were darkened by reason of the smoke of the pit.

Rev 9:3 And there came out of the smoke locusts upon the earth: and unto them was given power, as the scorpions of the earth have power.

Rev 9:4 And it was commanded them that they should not hurt the grass of the earth, neither any green thing, neither any tree; but only those men which have not the seal of God in their foreheads.

Rev 9:5 And to them it was given that they should not kill them, but that they should be tormented five months: and their torment was as the torment of a scorpion, when he striketh a man.

Rev 9:6 And in those days shall men seek death, and shall not find it; and shall desire to die, and death shall flee from them.

Rev 9:7 And the shapes of the locusts were like unto horses prepared unto battle; and on their heads were as it were crowns like gold, and their faces were as the faces of men.

Rev 9:8 And they had hair as the hair of women, and their teeth were as the teeth of lions.

Rev 9:9 And they had breastplates, as it were breastplates of iron; and the sound of their wings was as the sound of chariots of many horses running to battle.

Rev 9:10 And they had tails like unto scorpions, and there were stings in their tails: and their power was to hurt men five months.

Rev 9:11 And they had a king over them, which is the angel of the bottomless pit, whose name in the Hebrew tongue is Abaddon, but in the Greek tongue hath his name Apollyon.

Rev 9:12 One woe is past; and, behold, there come two woes more hereafter.

Rev 9:13 And the sixth angel sounded, and I heard a voice from the four horns of the golden altar which is before God,

Rev 9:14 Saying to the sixth angel which had the trumpet, Loose the four angels which are bound in the great river Euphrates.

Rev 9:15 And the four angels were loosed, which were prepared for an hour, and a day, and a month, and a year, for to slay the third part of men.

Rev 9:16 And the number of the army of the horsemen were two hundred thousand thousand: and I heard the number of them.

Rev 9:17 And thus I saw the horses in the vision, and them that sat on them, having breastplates of fire, and of jacinth, and brimstone: and the heads of the horses were as the heads of lions; and out of their mouths issued fire and smoke and brimstone.

Rev 9:18 By these three was the third part of men killed, by the fire, and by the smoke, and by the brimstone, which issued out of their mouths.

Rev 9:19 For their power is in their mouth, and in their tails: for their tails were like unto serpents, and had heads, and with them they do hurt.

Rev 9:20 And the rest of the men which were not killed by these plagues yet repented not of the works of their hands, that they should not worship devils, and idols of gold, and silver, and brass, and stone, and of wood: which neither can see, nor hear, nor walk:

Rev 9:21 Neither repented they of their murders, nor of their sorceries, nor of their fornication, nor of their thefts.

Revelation Chapter 10

Rev 10:1 And I saw another mighty angel come down from heaven, clothed with a cloud: and a rainbow was upon his head, and his face was as it were the sun, and his feet as pillars of fire:

Rev 10:2 And he had in his hand a little book open: and he set his right foot upon the sea, and his left foot on the earth,

Rev 10:3 And cried with a loud voice, as when a lion roareth: and when he had cried, seven thunders uttered their voices.

Rev 10:4 And when the seven thunders had uttered their voices, I was about to write: and I heard a voice from heaven saying unto me, Seal up those things which the seven thunders uttered, and write them not.

Rev 10:5 And the angel which I saw stand upon the sea and upon the earth lifted up his hand to heaven,

Rev 10:6 And sware by him that liveth for ever and ever, who created heaven, and the things that therein are, and the earth, and the things that therein are, and the sea, and the things which are therein, that there should be time no longer:

Rev 10:7 But in the days of the voice of the seventh angel, when he shall begin to sound, the mystery of God should be finished, as he hath declared to his servants the prophets.

Rev 10:8 And the voice which I heard from heaven spake unto me again, and said, Go and take the little book which is open in the hand of the angel which standeth upon the sea and upon the earth.

Rev 10:9 And I went unto the angel, and said unto him, Give me the little book. And he said unto me, Take it, and eat it up; and it shall make thy belly bitter, but it shall be in thy mouth sweet as honey.

Rev 10:10 And I took the little book out of the angel's hand, and ate it up; and it was in my mouth sweet as honey: and as soon as I had eaten it, my belly was bitter.

Rev 10:11 And he said unto me, Thou must prophesy again before many peoples, and nations, and tongues, and kings.

Revelation Chapter 11

Rev 11:1 And there was given me a reed like unto a rod: and the angel stood, saying, Rise, and measure the temple of God, and the altar, and them that worship therein.

Rev 11:2 But the court which is without the temple leave out, and measure it not; for it is given unto the Gentiles: and the holy city shall they tread under foot forty and two months.

Rev 11:3 And I will give power unto my two witnesses, and they shall prophesy a thousand two hundred and threescore days, clothed in sackcloth.

Rev 11:4 These are the two olive trees, and the two candlesticks standing before the God of the earth.

Rev 11:5 And if any man will hurt them, fire proceedeth out of their mouth, and devoureth their enemies: and if any man will hurt them, he must in this manner be killed.

Rev 11:6 These have power to shut heaven, that it rain not in the days of their prophecy: and have power over waters to turn them to blood, and to smite the earth with all plagues, as often as they will.

Rev 11:7 And when they shall have finished their testimony, the beast that ascendeth out of the bottomless pit shall make war against them, and shall overcome them, and kill them.

Rev 11:8 And their dead bodies shall lie in the street of the great city, which spiritually is called Sodom and Egypt, where also our Lord was crucified.

Rev 11:9 And they of the people and kindreds and tongues and nations shall see their dead bodies three days and an half, and shall not suffer their dead bodies to be put in graves.

Rev 11:10 And they that dwell upon the earth shall rejoice over them, and make merry, and shall send gifts one to another; because these two prophets tormented them that dwelt on the earth.

Rev 11:11 And after three days and an half the Spirit of life from God entered into them, and they stood upon their feet; and great fear fell upon them which saw them.

Rev 11:12 And they heard a great voice from heaven saying unto them, Come up hither. And they ascended up to heaven in a cloud; and their enemies beheld them.

Rev 11:13 And the same hour was there a great earthquake, and the tenth part of the city fell, and in the earthquake were slain of men seven thousand: and the remnant were affrighted, and gave glory to the God of heaven.

Rev 11:14 The second woe is past; and, behold, the third woe cometh quickly.

Rev 11:15 And the seventh angel sounded; and there were great voices in heaven, saying, The kingdoms of this world are become the kingdoms of our Lord, and of his Christ; and he shall reign for ever and ever.

Rev 11:16 And the four and twenty elders, which sat before God on their seats, fell upon their faces, and worshipped God,

Rev 11:17 Saying, We give thee thanks, O Lord God Almighty, which art, and wast, and art to come; because thou hast taken to thee thy great power, and hast reigned.

Rev 11:18 And the nations were angry, and thy wrath is come, and the time of the dead, that they should be judged, and that thou shouldest give reward unto thy servants the prophets, and to the saints, and them that fear thy name, small and great; and shouldest destroy them which destroy the earth.

Rev 11:19 And the temple of God was opened in heaven, and there was seen in his temple the ark of his testament: and there were lightnings, and voices, and thunderings, and an earthquake, and great hail.

Chapter 7
Revelation Chapter 10: Preparation for the Latter Rain

Revelation chapter 10, joined with chapter 11, forms a most thrilling breakthrough and major turning point in the sorrowful trumpet timeline. The Lord is about to do a new thing. Revelation chapters 6, 8, and 9 have shown many tragic, depressing scenes. However, chapters 10 and 11 introduce the Latter Rain of the Spirit of God, the great, revived conclusion to the kingdom that Christ set up by His apostles. "Before the final visitation of God's judgments upon the earth there will be among the people of the Lord such a revival of primitive godliness as has not been witnessed since apostolic times" *The Great Controversy*, p. 464. Satan's successful corruption first overcame the church after the apostles' death. But, Revelation chapter 10's wonderful closing prophecy gives a closer look at the end of chapter 9's difficult subjugation. When we look at this further in Revelation chapter 11, we will see that Satan's subjugation and captivity of God's people will terminate at the future awakening and restart of the Advent movement as we will see in Revelation 11. Their captivity is turned not at the end of the sixth trumpet, but *close to* the end of the sixth trumpet. When the devil finally moves as "son of perdition" throughout the seventh trumpet (see 2 Thessalonians 2:3, 8-12; Revelation 17:8; 11:18), when the harshest difficulties surround the glorious end of the Protestant Reformation, then the original church of the apostles will be completely free again of the post-apostolic apostasy and restored to its original apostolic glory. This will enrage the demonic forces.

Revelation chapter 10, joined with chapter 11, forms a most thrilling breakthrough and major turning point in the sorrowful trumpet timeline.

Revelation 10:1 through 11:10 prepares the reader for that great victory of God and His earnest desire to finish the seals' and the trumpets' work. But, let us backtrack and recap some untouched upon aspects at the end of Revelation chapter 9.

Chapter 9 finished with the sixth trumpet's complete devastation of Protestantism. "The third part" (Rev. 9:18, cf Rev. 5:3; Phil. 2:10), the worst of the children of Protestantism, finally have their consciences seared by the fire and smoke and brimstone of spiritualism, and Protestantism is "killed"; Protestants' consciences are seared. The mark of the Beast rules their forehead; the evil conquest by Spiritual Formation is complete.

The third part are completely won over to the powers of darkness and their hearts are possessed of a fanatical, religious zeal that they hardly believe comes from the devil (see Jeremiah 51:7; 50:7). As Satan always has done, he has inspired his subjects to execute capital punishment on anyone opposed to their service to God, — Satan himself being "God" (John 16:2, cf Isa. 14:12-14). Corrupted and seduced by the locusts and darkened reason, these folks whose faith and love are dead and their consciences seared, are inspired with a driving ambition to unite church and state for the greater glory of "God". They desire to rebuild the medieval Papacy with Christian America as the new papal states, and to create a provincial serfdom that is forced upon the oligarchic dictatorships of every nation in the world (see Revelation 13:11-15).

This yet future change among the third part of Protestant Americans necessitates no obvious psychotic behavior, but, rather a subtle, dark control of their hopeless hearts and mesmerized minds. These abandoned souls could never find refreshment in the Law because they never sought it through the Spirit of Christ in the Law. Therefore, they had no rest for their nagging, mind-numbing anxiety due to their unwillingness to come under the almighty will of God, to overcome their sins, and to serve their Creator and Redeemer with the whole heart. Thus, they were "empty" (Matt. 12:44) of the Spirit of truth, open to deception, and brought to abandon all authority of God's Law. They never found the Spirit of Jesus in the Law that could have quickly led them through the process of conviction and wrestling, surrender and peace. True peace could have been theirs by the mercy they would have seen in Jesus. Their abrogating the Law's essential reproof and its merciful humiliation permanently disconnected them from the Spirit of God. Thus, lacking the blessedness from the Creator caused them to be continually worn down, and with no access to spiritual and emotional rest, they grasped an alternative source of life and peace from Ashtoreth, the Queen of heaven. This "third part" ultimately sought out the easier, counterfeit peace of the Christianized paganism for their tormented souls (see Jeremiah 6:10, 13, 14; 2 Thessalonians 2:4, 9-12). They can never be Schoolmaster-loving, commandment-keeping, powerful "children of God by faith" (Gal. 3:26, cf vs. 23-25; John 1:12).

Through "smooth things", "deceits" (Isa. 30:10), and "fair words" (Jer. 12:6) Baal's ancient Spiritual Formation brought them under his spell. By new-designing biblical doctrine, he stood up against and magnified himself above Jesus, the Prince of the host (see Isaiah 24:5; Daniel 8:11, 25; 11:22). Through his craftiness to promise redemption without the humbling reprimands of the Law, he destroyed many by a counterfeit peace (see Daniel 8:24, 25; Deuteronomy 29:18, 19). Baal thus led the world away from obedience to God's commandments (see Jeremiah 12:10-13). The great familiar spirit led the denominations to worship the sweet-talker from the abyss as their peace-giver instead of the convicting, commanding "Messiah the Prince" (Dan. 9:25, cf Isa. 11:4). In the foremost sense, Satan is the worker of iniquity with his venerated, age-old means of communing with human hearts, Spiritual Formation.

And, as he has done in all ages, the evil one has, far in advance, prepared this "third part" to brand as Arian heretics the protesting dissenters of his wickedness. Those Christian fundamentalist leaders and laymen alike will malign as terrorists anyone who cries out against a fallen church, persecuting the protesters, the world round. "As then he that was born after the flesh persecuted him that was born after the Spirit, even so it is now" (Gal. 4:29, cf Matt. 18:5-10).

As they make their moves to silence God's people, they separate more and more from the Life-giver and unite more and more with the tormenter-destroyer. Every choice to break God's express will by hurting His children (see Matthew 18:6; 2 Kings 21:1-7, 16), leads to increased painful withdrawal of God's life and contentedness from their hearts. The third angel of Revelation 14 speaks of this final forsaking by God and full possession by Satan.

"The third part" (Rev. 9:18) — the Protestant hosts given to the Jesuit invasion — receive the third angel's punishment of consumption by demons (see Revelation 14:9-11; Isaiah 10:23) because, even if unaware of it, they had subtle contempt toward the Law of God, the Law of love (see Romans 8:7). When this sixth trumpet prophecy will be fully accomplished, the consecration of Protestantism has been eaten up by their tempting continent, and the dark jacinth spirit of Satan has tormented them as they have increasingly separated from Jesus by the cares of this world and the deceitfulness of covetousness, "which is idolatry" (Col. 3:5). These Protestants did not strive to seek Jesus in His humbling Law or in His atoning sanctuary. The temptations of atheistic conceptions and man-made objects constantly surrounding them kept them away from their Creator and Redeemer. Finally, they easily fell to the strong delusion of communicating with the spirits. This we learned in the history of Israel, and by comparing the warnings from Deuteronomy 32:15-43, Deuteronomy 29:18-28, and Revelation 14:9-11. The time has arrived for them to be spewed out of their American continent that has flowed with God's milk and honey (see Leviticus 18:25-28).

But, only those trusting in atheistic, lawless religion among the American Protestants — the third part — had their consciences killed. This infers, at this point, that the locust plagues had not yet completed the desolation for which the Lord sent it. There remained other Protestants not ruined by the plagues, although openly rebellious — that is, "the rest of the men which were not killed by these plagues" (Rev. 9:20). Worshiping "the works of their hands," and "devils, and idols of gold, and silver, and brass, and stone, and of wood", not repenting "of their murders, nor of their sorceries, nor of their fornication, nor of their thefts" (Rev. 9:20, 21), describes the unchurched within Protestantism not sealed. But, these "rest of the men" are also not yet marked by the unpardonable sin of "the third part" — the churched Protestants whose consciences in the fullest sense are "alive without the Law" (Rom. 7:9) and have no "delight in the Law of God" (Rom. 7:22, cf vs. 25). "The rest" of the unsealed consciences had not been "killed" and fully ruined by Satan.

"The rest of the men" still have hope for salvation before the Lord executes His judgments. Idolatry and debasement of appetites and of the conscience, however, do hold "the rest" in misery, captives to the evil one (see Ephesians 4:17-19; 2 Timothy 2:26) and on the downward slope to Satan's full control. What we see near the end of the sixth trumpet is that Protestantism, primarily in America, has split between two factions: ultra-conservative religious fundamentalists; and "the rest" — the other half who are ultra-liberal freedom-fighters, who desire only freedom from the compulsions of religion (*see Appendix A*).

"The rest of the men" have not repented; but this verse infers that they were accountable for much evidence needed to do that. The overwhelming sixth trumpet, picturing a plague of Christian fundamentalist terrorism sweeping uncontrollably throughout the globe, should have put fear into "the rest of the men". Yet, they still don't look to God for help, but continue their self-indulgent hedonism, unmindful of eternity. "They did eat, they drank, they bought, they sold, they planted, they builded" (Luke 17:28) with no regard to Judgment Day.

Therefore, the wrath of God is upon them. The sixth trumpet prophecy pictures them on the verge of complete self-destruction. Their description resembles the multitudes who lived "in the days that were before the flood… eating and drinking, marrying and giving in marriage, until the day that Noe entered into the ark" (Matt. 24:38). It's the same picture we see at Belshazzar's debauched party in honor of Satan when "they drank wine, and praised the gods of gold, and of silver, of brass, of iron, of wood, and of stone" (Dan. 5:4). These demoralized multitudes of the Protestant unchurched world, the corrupted victims of Jesuit allurement during the fifth and sixth trumpets, fulfill another repeated scenario,

> And even as they did not like to retain God in their knowledge, God gave them over to a reprobate mind, to do those things which are not convenient; being filled with all unrighteousness, fornication, wickedness, covetousness, maliciousness; full of envy, murder, debate, deceit, malignity; whisperers, backbiters, haters of God, despiteful, proud, boasters, inventors of evil things, disobedient to parents, without understanding, covenantbreakers, without natural affection, implacable, unmerciful: who knowing the judgment of God, that they which commit such things are worthy of death, not only do the same, but have pleasure in them that do them (Rom. 1:28-32).

> And receiving in themselves that recompence of their error which was meet (Vs. 27).

Moses made it clear,

> But it shall come to pass, if thou wilt not hearken unto the voice of the LORD thy God, to observe to do all his commandments and his statutes which I command thee this day; that all these curses shall come upon thee, and overtake thee:…

> The LORD shall make the pestilence cleave unto thee, until he have consumed thee from off the land, whither thou goest to possess it.

> The LORD shall smite thee with a consumption, and with a fever, and with an inflammation, and with an extreme burning, and with the sword, and with blasting, and with mildew; and they shall pursue thee until thou perish….

> Then the LORD will make thy plagues wonderful, and the plagues of thy seed, even great

plagues, and of long continuance, and sore sicknesses, and of long continuance.

Moreover he will bring upon thee all the diseases of Egypt, which thou wast afraid of; and they shall cleave unto thee.

Also every sickness, and every plague, which is not written in the book of this law, them will the LORD bring upon thee, until thou be destroyed (Deut. 28:15, 21, 22, 59-61).

The last quote from Romans 1, however, that describes the wretchedness of western civilization of Paul's day, as desperate as it was, still did not assume that everyone had committed the unpardonable sin. Paul's constant work was to save all who through the painful consequences of their life of sin and a gracious word from above would come to the Son for repentance and forgiveness. Paul's complaint concerning the spitefulness of the then Pharisaical religious leadership against the unclean Greco-Roman populace was, "…forbidding us to speak to the Gentiles that they might be saved, to fill up their [the Gentiles'] sins alway: for the wrath is come upon them to the uttermost" (1 Thess. 2:16).

Paul saw divine retribution already falling on the world, and his burden was to save as many Greeks and Romans as possible. But, Paul saw great potential for God's mercy upon these publicans and sinners. For, they were, like he had been, "a blasphemer, and a persecutor, and injurious: but I obtained mercy, because I did it ignorantly in unbelief" (1Tim. 1:13). He sought to minimize the pestilence of God's wrath as Aaron had; and for those who received the incense of the Spirit of Christ, the apostle "stood between the dead and the living; and the plague was stayed" (Num. 16:48).

And many of the unclean Gentiles clung to Paul (see Acts 17:34; 20:36-38), even within the Imperial palace (see Philippians 4:22). They would have given anything to him (see Galatians 4:15), some even treating him like they would Jesus (see verse 14). There will yet be a repeat of that kind of fellowship when people very distant from God, churched and unchurched, within Christianity and outside of it, press close to Jesus in the final Latter Rain preaching of the gospel (see Isaiah 61:5, 6).

Identical to the demoralized ancient Roman Empire is "the rest of the men" at the end of the sixth trumpet. And our gracious Lord will work to save every last soul (see Luke 13:6-9; Luke 19:10; Revelation 6:2).

For God hath concluded them all in unbelief, that he might have mercy upon all (Rom. 11:32, cf 1 Tim. 1:11-13).

The apostolic church shifted from a majority of Jewish to a church of Gentile Christians. The larger Gentile population of the Early Rain mimicked the innumerable multitude of the Latter Rain seen in Revelation 7:9. This suggests that the 144,000 are the Protestant and Adventist Christians who have become grounded in the Law and the spiritual truth of the Bible, and who are firstfruits to receive the experience of victory over the "sorceries" (Rev. 18:23) of Babylon. Through obedience to the spirit and letter of the Testimony of Jesus they received Him as their Father-friend while He was in the Most Holy Place cleansing His priestly family first. Those Adventists and eleventh hour Protestants within the future Advent movement, who trust in Jesus for the victory over temptation and the tempter, become the 144,000 preachers who evangelize the world. They see the rapid conversion of millions within atheistic, Christianity, and among the world religions; and they witness many victories over sin, addictions, disease, and death.

The Gentiles shall come to thy light, and kings to the brightness of thy rising….

Thy sons shall come from far, and thy daughters shall be nursed at thy side (Isa. 60:3, 4).

Then shalt thou say in thine heart, Who hath begotten me these, seeing I have lost my children, and am desolate, a captive, and removing to and fro? and who hath brought up these? Behold, I was left alone; these, where had they been? (Isa. 49:21).

Other millions come from among the multiplying gay plague, and from the hedonistic unchurched Protestant "rest of the men". Their Jesuit sixth trumpet imposed wretchedness and misery, poverty of love, and spiritual nakedness left them needing a Saviour from sin. The hosts of darkness and Jesuit locusts could not destroy the fear of God in these humbled idolaters of Revelation 9:20, 21, or their deepest need for acceptance from God (see Revelation 9:18).

Thus saith the Lord GOD, Behold, I will lift up mine hand to the Gentiles, and set up my standard to the people: and they shall bring thy sons in their arms, and thy daughters shall be carried upon their shoulders (Isa. 49:22).

The final, gracious preaching (see Matthew 24:14) reaches all of these tormented publicans and sinners who have afflicted their souls, crying out, "O wretched man that I am! who shall deliver me from the body of this death?" (Rom. 7:24). For the first time, "the rest of the men" (Rev. 9:20) will hear the invitation from the Spirit of Christ, "They that be whole need not a physician, but they that are sick.... I am not come to call the righteous, but sinners to repentance" (Matt. 9:12, 13). Many will receive Jesus who will come personally, and repeat the glories of the New Testament.

> As Jesus sat at meat in his house, many publicans and sinners sat also together with Jesus and his disciples: for there were many, and they followed him (Mark 2:15).

> This man receiveth sinners, and eateth with them (Luke 15:2).

These pagan converts to Christ, in the confusion of the Revelation 9 sixth trumpet desolations, have learned submission to God's Law the hard way (see Proverbs 13:15; Jeremiah 2:19). They were all humbled and ready to open their hearts to the gospel, as did their ancient Gentile counterparts who heard Jesus and His apostles teach (see Isaiah 42:1-4; 61:1-3; 8:22-9:7; John 12:20, 21; Ephesians 2:1-6, 14-16; Colossians 1:3-6; 1 Thessalonians 1:4-7;1 Peter 1:1, 2).

These children of the Spirit have struggled with the Law through consequences to disobedience, and will find Christ in the Law a remedy for their body of death, as the Greco-Roman churches did. They will know the "blessedness" of "the promise of the Spirit through faith" (Gal. 4:15; 3:14), "that the blessing of Abraham might come on the Gentiles through Jesus Christ" (Gal. 3:14). Walking with Jesus (see Romans 7:25-8:1), all their "briers and thorns" (Isa. 7:24) will be replaced by "butter and honey" (Isa. 7:15, cf Ps. 18:35; 19:10; 36:8; 63:5; Deut. 32:13, 14), Jesus' sole diet and source of strength. "Instead of the thorn shall come up the fir tree, and instead of the brier shall come up the myrtle tree: and it shall be to the LORD for a name, for an everlasting sign that shall not be cut off" (Isa. 55:13, cf Isa. 8:18).

> In that day shall the deaf hear the words of the book, and the eyes of the blind shall see out of obscurity, and out of darkness. The meek also shall increase their joy in the LORD, and the poor among men shall rejoice in the Holy One of Israel. For the terrible one is brought to nought, and the scorner is consumed, and all that watch for iniquity are cut off.... They also that erred in spirit shall come to understanding, and they that murmured shall learn doctrine (Isa. 29:18-20, 24).

This ends the sixth trumpet recap of Revelation chapter 9, which has completed the moral desolation of the one-time holy Protestant movement. Next, the whole Revelation chapter 10 intermission and last half of chapter 11 explain how God deals with these corrupted souls from Revelation 9:20. God works to reach those among this group, many of whom never fully rejected the authority of the divine, spiritual Law or the merciful influence of His Spirit to give repentance. He had been making His way into their hearts. They had been rejected by the religio-political Christian establishment for their lifestyle that blasphemed the *misrepresented* name of Jesus. They had rejected the World Council of Churches; but, they had not rejected the power of God unto salvation. Their acceptance by God will be a duplicate scenario to the days of Christ's ministry in Judea and Galilee.

This whole chapter 10 is a preliminary to the long expected Latter Rain of the Holy Spirit. Revelation 10 sits interjected between the sixth trumpet in Revelation 9 and the great final revival that will take place prior to the seventh trumpet in Revelation 11. As we continue in this chapter, we will see Jesus in the heavenly Most Holy Place, and hear His command to give the final warning to the world. With a sense of His soon return, the Godhead's evident joy in heaven will wake up the sleeping Adventists in their difficult captivity, who have come to greatly hope in Jesus as their cherished Bridegroom. Wrestling with Jesus in their captivity will have crystallized their hope into faith and will propel their soul all the way to touch the hem of their heavenly High Priest (see Matthew 25:6).

Long before Revelation chapter 10's yet future point in time during the seven trumpets chronology, righteousness by faith by Jesus, our only hope for victory in the Christian life, should have been preached to the world by Christ's holy people of the Book, His Protestants. However, as we will see in Revelation 11, during the fifth trumpet (see verse 7-10) they and their Remnant have given in to the religion of Baal that despises obedience to the special work of purification, and they have been experiencing its torment. They both have been overrun by the sixth trumpet demonic occupation, the powerful scattering of the Lord's people as in the days of Gideon, which the prophets have always given warning (see Daniel 12:7; Leviticus 26:13-46). The failure to preach righteousness by faith in God's Law and Jesus' grace has left the masses of this planet in a spiritual downward tailspin ending with the immoral morass described in Revelation 9:18-21. Without faith in Christ's righteousness there is no barrier against sin. The great need to preach the everlasting gospel, therefore, is the subject when the Revelation chapter 10 scene opens.

So John, acting the part of the still future church of God, receives from Christ — the Angel wrapped in His Father's glory, who appears full of power and joy, and standing resolutely before the Ancient of days — the commission to preach the gospel of righteousness by faith by Jesus. Righteousness by beholding Jesus in the Law needs to go to every person on earth, the billions of our world. "Thou must prophesy again before many peoples, and nations, and tongues, and kings" (Rev. 10:11). This Jesus had earlier foretold, "This gospel of the kingdom shall be preached in all the world for a witness unto all nations; and then shall the end come" (Matt. 24:14).

The word "again" here in Revelation chapter 10 verse 11 above implies that "prophesying" had already happened before in this prophetic chronology. Previous to this point, here at the end of the sixth trumpet prophesying had occurred. When we study Revelation chapter 11 we will see who prophesied and, therefore, who it is that John is vicariously personating in the chapter 10 prophetic portrayal. We will recognize a group that had testified for the truth, but *ceased to testify*, yet who in the end, by means of His merciful punishment, God will again return to its original office as heaven's humbled spokespersons.

But, prior to all of this, an interesting exchange takes place between Christ and His Father, which lifts the curtain of the Revelation chapter 10 drama.

Until this point of the trumpets vision, we last saw Christ during Revelation chapter 8 removing the final seal of God's infinitely bound book. Jesus stood before His Father at the altar of incense in the heavenly sanctuary's Holy Place. (See Revelation 8:3-5.) He was ready to enter into the Most Holy to cleanse the sanctuary, but He first needed to enter to cleanse Himself and His family — His church that was to be sealed, per Revelation 7:1-8 and per the type from Leviticus 16:11.

Now, in the magnificent Revelation chapter 10 setting, we see Jesus glorified. He is no longer a lamb slain from the foundation of the world, as in Revelation chapter 5; nor is He an officiating High Priest, as in Revelation chapter 8. But, as the Lion of the tribe of Judah (see Revelation 5:5, 6; 10:3) and as King of kings, Jesus is ready to wield His whetted, razor sharp, two-edged, "glittering sword" (Deut. 32:41, 42, cf Heb. 4:12; Rev. 1:16; 19:15).

Jesus is transfigured; He is clad in a cloud of innocence and purity, baptized in God's power. An ethereal victory crown of high priestly rainbow colors radiates over the head of Christ like an aurora borealis, indicating that He is now in the Holiest of all. He has received the most holy anointing (see Isaiah 61:1) to give the Latter Rain gospel, His salvation is "ready to be revealed in the last time" (1 Pet. 1:5). He is restored to His original standing with His Father prior to adopting Adam's sinful race. His joy comes from the soon sealing of His Adventist family. They have heeded His testimonies to them. They have made great strides to reproducing His character in themselves, and He will soon finalize the atonement for His family's atonement. He is already tasting the cup of joy that He will yet not enjoy to the full until He drinks it new with His whole redeemed race.

> Thou art fairer than the children of men: grace is poured into thy lips: therefore God hath blessed thee for ever.
>
> Gird thy sword upon thy thigh, O most mighty, with thy glory and thy majesty.
>
> And in thy majesty ride prosperously because of truth and meekness and righteousness; and thy right hand shall teach thee terrible things.
>
> Thine arrows are sharp in the heart of the king's enemies; whereby the people fall under thee.
>
> Thy throne, O God, is for ever and ever: the sceptre of thy kingdom is a right sceptre.
>
> Thou lovest righteousness, and hatest wickedness: therefore God, thy God, hath anointed thee with the oil of gladness above thy fellows (Ps. 45:2-7).

Christ has permitted the sixth trumpet to do its work of scattering the pride and self-sufficiency of His people (see Leviticus 26:41). Now, with self humbled and slain by the sword of the Lord, His soon-to-be-atoned-for priestly family can give the good news of the fourth angel of Revelation chapter 18 to the world for a witness to all nations. His hand holds the same little book which He took from His Father in Revelation chapter 5, but which He could not open until chapter 8, at the removal of the last seal and the commencement of the trumpets.

When chapter 10 begins, Protestantism has been laid waste spiritually, morally, financially, politically, and militarily, overthrown by Rome. Satan's fifth and sixth trumpet armies of Jesuit corrupting influence, now occupy the Protestant churches and the Protestants' new Christian state. Under international despotic Jesuit control, the new religio-political American nation is possessed by all the hosts of darkness. The once holy Protestantism is defunct, considered a consummate failure and is consigned to an unfortunate, misguided history. Five hundred years after separating, the Reformation bride of Christ has returned to Mother. The Advent movement, also, is in a desperate condition, as described in the next chapter: "Their dead bodies shall lie in the street of the great city", "Babylon the Great" (Rev. 11:8; 17:5; 16:19). Yet, though the Protestants and Adventists sleep in their sins (Revelation 11:8), they will hear that the Bridegroom is coming and many will awaken (see Matthew 25:5-7), some to the Latter Rain of the Holy Spirit, ["the Spirit of life from God entered into them, and they stood upon their feet…. And they ascended up to heaven in a cloud" (Rev. 11:11, 12)]. But, others, by uniting with the world and partaking of its spirit, awaken to the horror of divine rejection and everlasting shame.

The Father's book, now completely unsealed and opened with authority in Christ's hand, His face radiant and head beaming with the crown of a resonating rainbow, indicates Christ's imminent triumph over Lucifer's controversy (see Leviticus 16:10). He has almost purified His 144,000 family, and He is about to receive His kingdom (see Daniel 7:9-11, 13, 14; Revelation 11:15). In anticipation that all enemies will soon be put under His feet (see Psalms 110:1-7; Deuteronomy 32:41-43), Jesus glories in His victory over Lucifer's deceptive argument that God's demand of perfection was a standard too high and unfairly condemning, and that His royal Law was not needed because everyone was sufficiently moral. Christ has proven, through His purifying incarnation into fallen humanity, that He could keep a life of perfect obedience under the most austere circumstances of temptation and hardship, torment and death. By educating and testing His predestinated family, Jesus can produce a people who willingly come under the power of His holy influence in order to perfectly obey God's Law, as He did (see Ephesians 1:4, 12-14). Depending upon His Father's gracious and commanding Spirit from His Law, Jesus defeated every charge that Satan brought against the kingdom of God. And, so will His family (see Isaiah 8:18; Romans 3:31). The Father's eternal justification and His redeemed people's are intimately entwined.

"He whom God hath sent speaketh the words of God: for God giveth not the Spirit by measure unto him" (John 3:34, cf Isa. 63:11). His Father's measureless Spirit first dwelled in Christ's divine-human person through His divine birth from His Father. And through the scriptures and prayer, He maintained His Father's eternal Spirit by Their blessed union together. That same "power of the Highest" (Luke 1:35) dwells in us when we surrender to the Father's chastisement, which brings us the need for a Saviour. "All [who] the Father giveth me shall come to me" (John 6:37), Christ said. Having been scourged and humbled by God, we *desire* to come to Jesus. And once we come into His presence by faith and are born again, we gladly spend the effort and time getting better acquainted with Him, and with His Father, while the divine influence from the Spirit of Christ molds our natures. "For…God sending His own Son in the likeness of sinful flesh, and for sin, condemned sin in the flesh". The most perfect obedience for us to behold is Christ in the Law, that by doing so "the righteousness of the law might be fulfilled in us, who walk not after the flesh, but after…the Spirit of Christ" (Rom. 8:3, 4, 9).

When Jesus ascended to take the shut book binding God's reputation, there remained a work for Them to cooperate in until a judgment could clear the Father's name. Greater than in past ages Jesus then heard His Father say, "Sit thou at my right hand, until I make thine enemies thy footstool" (Ps. 110:1, cf Heb.1:13). The next 1,813 years would sweep through, in behalf of His Father the Son of God doing battle with Satan as He removed each of the seven seals from the book. Then in 1844 Jesus could open the book for the Father's exoneration; and the hour of God's judgment began. But necessary court preliminaries of the six trumpets delayed the judgment. Trumpet after trumpet blew; the Father's children must be subpoenaed as evidence for or against Him, their witness being true or false. During those trumpets, the final battle between Christ and Satan would accelerate the evidence for the Father's judgment.

Now, in Revelation 10, the world sets heavily under the dark domain of the sixth trumpet plagues, and we now see that Father and Son have everything ready in order to present Their evidence in the case that Lucifer thought he had closed.

The book, which had been bound up under Lucifer's permanent internment at the beginning of the great controversy (see Revelation 5:1) is open, implying the commencement of final judgment upon the Father's character and His right to reign. Through the Father's provision, Jesus' successful holding onto lost humanity until death swept over Him gave Him the authority to settle this case (see Revelation 5:5, 6). Emboldened and impenitent, Lucifer has usurped Christ as earthly sovereign (see Daniel 7:25; 8:11) and has subjugated Christ's faithful church for 1,260 years by his dictatorial earthly vicar (see Revelation 6:4-11; 12:13-15; 13:5-8; 17:3-6; 18:7). The blasphemy to Christ on the cross and the continued offense to His church in the wilderness more than cleared God of that mastermind's accusations in the hearts of the angelic hosts. But, humanity is not yet unconvinced of the mastermind's complaints against the Father. By 1844, God's reputation and trustworthiness had yet to be fully restored to His church on earth. Christ must complete the work to resolve their misconceptions of His Father's character created by the deceiver. Christ's final resolving His Reformation and Adventist children's trust will ultimately result in their happy obedience to Him, just like Christ did during the Early Rain to the apostolic remnant of the Ezra and Nehemiah revival (see Isaiah 6:13).

The open book in Christ's hand, from which He had removed each seal says that the judgment against God can very soon be fully finalized by the evidence, where our previously recusing God will preside over the court as the Defendant and the Judge (see Daniel 7:9, 10), the Son of man will act as District Attorney and Attorney General (see 1 Corinthians 15:25; Psalms 110:3-5), the angelic hosts and unfallen worlds will be the jury and the bailiffs (see Revelation 14:10; Luke 15:21), Satan and his hosts will be the self-defending criminals as charged (see Genesis 3:15; Leviticus 16:10), and those redeemed people whose hearts and lives Jesus reclaimed from Satan's snares will be His humbled and quiet supporting evidence (see Job 40:4; 42:6). Thus, the Law of the universe will be correctly and perfectly satisfied; six thousand years of the great controversy has been the Father's Gethsemane. After all the damage Lucifer has caused his innocent Creator, when God wins the seemingly impenetrable case that the mighty cherub brought against Him, then the adversarial hosts of Satan will be finally sentenced to eternal destruction. And none shall help him.

We will see in Revelation chapter 10, when viewed from the perspective of Revelation 11:11-13, that this scene of Revelation chapter 10 portrays the joy of Christ over His final earthly group, which remained "green" (Rev. 9:4, cf Jer. 17:7, 8; Ps. 1:3) throughout the first six trumpets. The 144,000 will be the fruit and grain who survive the locust invasion. It won't bother them if their fruit grows from a tree or a bush or a little stalk; Jesus will appreciate their fruit nonetheless. He will put a seal on them because they are the apple of His eye. They have grown in fields and orchards that He kept weeded and cultivated and pest-free. They made good use of every little dew drop that distilled upon them. Then they will ripen under Jesus' Latter Rains. They will be ready for His harvest and will happily lay down their lives as His firstfruits.

Even though the 144,000 have previously loved disobedience, their hearts reconciled with God's discipline, and they were enabled to follow Jesus out of self-reliance and self-indulgence. When the Father is vindicated by the perfect reconciliation and purification of His people, their exoneration of God before the angels and unfallen worlds prepares the way for His justice to blot out their sins from the memory of heaven. Thus happens the fullest sealing and cleansing of His sanctuary that was happening during the six trumpet period.

We will see His sealed servants weaving into the gospel message the Father's acquittal, His proven unselfish and justified character by His overpowering disciplinary role, His justifiably using rejection, condemnation, and even our mortality to assist humanity's surrender of sinful pride. The first time of trouble is instrumental in creating a love for perfect obedience in the 144,000. Through the grace of Christ's Spirit that He breathes in them, they preach this message to the whole world at this time, "having his Father's name written in their foreheads" (Rev. 14:1). This new gospel of God addition to the gospel of Christ will Satan resist and call cultic. The devil fears the power in God's people as God's special justification further galvanizes their loyalty to His Law and their faith in His strong love, results in the special purification, the "putting away of sin, among God's people upon earth" *Great Controversy*, p. 425.

Throughout the Bible, the sea represented the world's tumultuous, unsanctified multitudes. Like a vast ocean, "the isles of the Gentiles" (Gen. 10:5), "the nations which are in the four quarters of the earth" are the great majority of the world population whose fathers had long ago lost a knowledge of God's love. They are ignorant of Jehovah's true character. Constantly harassed by Satan, they can never surrender to God's authority and gracious Spirit. They have congregated together in cities, alliances, and counter-alliances for convenience and safety. They have bumped into each other and harassed each other. They have continually distracted each other from catching the messages of love that their Creator painted across the sky, landscape, and cosmos, and put into the animal kingdom. They eclipsed and blinded their own minds to the great God, who has become the "UNKNOWN GOD" (Acts 17:23). By comparing themselves among themselves and measuring themselves by themselves, their fallen, selfish natures have prevented each other from seeing the only redemptive, self-sacrificing love of God. But, the Lord's constant effort from the beginning of the fall has been to bring the unruly, unsettled hearts of the "sea" to Himself and seal them with His peace on the "earth". The God who finally brought the Gentiles back to Himself during the Early Rain, today is not yet ready to close the door of probation on those in the atheistic world.

> This is a people robbed and spoiled; they are all of them snared in holes, and they are hid in prison houses: they are for a prey, and none delivereth; for a spoil, and none saith, Restore (Isa. 42:22).

He will give the atheistic sea one last invitation to leave the captivity of the carnal, comfortable traditions of ancient Babylon. He will call out "them whom I reserve" (Jer. 50:20) before He overthrows the city whose Goliath captors think themselves great.

> O thou that dwellest upon many waters, abundant in treasures, thine end is come, and the measure of thy covetousness (Jer. 51:13).

> Because thine heart is lifted up, and thou hast said, I am a God, I sit in the seat of God, in the midst of the seas; yet thou art a man, and not God, though thou set thine heart as the heart of God (Eze. 28:2).

"The waters which thou sawest, where the whore sitteth, are peoples, and multitudes, and nations, and tongues" (Rev. 17:15, cf Isa. 57:19-21; 60:5; Matt. 4:15; Jas. 1:6-8). Conversely, the earth, or the land, represents God's holy people, His church (see Psalm 24:1-3; Isaiah 32:15-18; 33:20, 21; Revelation 6:4). Specifically, during the trumpet period of Revelation, the "earth" represents Protestant Americans who have known the one true God and have lived in "the pleasant land" (Dan. 8:9) of God's refuge from papal persecution (see Revelation 12:15, 16; Revelation 13:11). It has been a "glorious land" (Dan. 11:41), a gifted land that has flowed with milk and honey, freedom and joy. But, they have left their pure Protestantism and have returned to the Queen of heaven (see Revelation 13:12; Jeremiah 7:14-19). The Queen of heaven was the shrewish mistress god of the world's one false religion, who lured her devotees into self-pity and pride, anxiety and bitter wrath. She was Ashtoreth to the Canaanites (see Judges 2:11-13, cf 2 Kings 17:8-12, 15-17), Artemis and Athena to the Greeks, Venus and Diana (see Acts 19:23-35) to the Romans; and today, a modern Diana gets the title, Queen of heaven. Many other titles agree for this mystery female deity, throughout her varied locations around the world, from the beginning to the present day.

In biblical times, the right hand side represented favor and the left represented disfavor (see Genesis 48:13, 14; Matthew 25:33, 34, 41; Psalms 16:8; 45:4; 110:1, 5; Isaiah 41:10). Now, in this Revelation vision, Christ's left foot of disfavor sets on the earth, the trees and grain every way devastated by the fifth and sixth trumpet locusts and midnight gloom. This means that He has found Protestantism weighed in the balances and found destitute, primarily in America. Though having adhered to the Bible decreasingly during its post-Reformation colonial days, in the end Protestantism has become ruined by spiritualism, arrogance, and idolatry; it has transformed into a "habitation of devils, and the hold of every foul spirit, and a cage of every unclean and hateful bird" (Rev. 18:2). Spiritual Formation and celebration worship give them "a form of godliness, but denying the power thereof" (2 Tim. 3:5). The Revelation 10 vision shows Protestantism on the side of the Lord's disfavor. Accordingly, the sixth trumpet Reformation generation sees their God's promised curses upon them. Their nation crested its fifth trumpet time of prosperity in the 1990s to start its post-1999 predestinated roller-coaster ride into total confusion and scattering during the sixth trumpet (see Deuteronomy 28:15-52, previously quoted).

> Hell hath enlarged herself, and opened her mouth without measure: and their glory, and their multitude, and their pomp, and he that rejoiceth, shall descend into it (Isa. 5:14).

> The mirth of the land is gone (Isa. 24:11).

> Your covenant with death shall be disannulled, and your agreement with hell shall not stand; when the overflowing scourge shall pass

through, then ye shall be trodden down by it (Isa. 28:18).

Jesus has pleaded with Protestant Americans, but they have not heard Jesus, the Lord God of the Old Testament.

> Hast thou not procured this unto thyself, in that thou hast forsaken the LORD thy God, when he led thee by the way?... Know therefore and see that it is an evil thing and bitter, that thou hast forsaken the LORD thy God, and that my fear is not in thee, saith the Lord GOD of hosts. For of old time I have broken thy yoke, and burst thy bands; and thou saidst, I will not transgress; when upon every high hill and under every green tree thou wanderest, playing the harlot. Yet I had planted thee a noble vine, wholly a right seed: how then art thou turned into the degenerate plant of a strange vine unto me? (Jer. 2:17, 19-21).

The "earth", or the sealed *and* marked churched Protestants, at this point will no longer get His focus. And having already judged America and the free Protestant nations by the fifth and sixth trumpets, Christ's stance will indicate the soon to end culmination of the investigative judgment which, in the vision, will afterward preside over the non-Protestant Gentile sea. The non-Protestant world will also include the unchurched Protestant trees and grain and "any green thing" (Rev. 9:4) thus far spared from the voracious Jesuit locusts — "the rest of the men which were not killed by these plagues" (Rev. 9:20) — all of the church-marginalized secularists, skeptics, and hedonists of Protestantism who as yet will not have fully rejected the sealing Law of God in their heart.

Jesus' right foot, the side of His favor, is upon the sea because the non-Protestant world, "many peoples, and nations, and tongues, and kings" (Rev. 10:11), then get His fullest attention. They all need to hear the truth of God's character and then be judged faithful or not, as the Protestants were given a fair trial and, for the most part, were judged unfaithful in Revelation chapters 8 and 9.

The Angel's earnest, time limited message to them will be,

> Repent ye therefore, and be converted, that your sins may be blotted out, when the times of refreshing shall come from the presence of the Lord; and he shall send Jesus Christ (Acts 3:19, 20).

Christ standing on the sea and land speaks of the missionary activity that will happen around the world quickly in the future. The future Vatican global conquest and punishment of the Laodicean Protestant world by the fifth and sixth trumpet plagues past (seen in Revelation 11:8-10), and the follow-on Latter Rain preaching of the gospel to every nation (seen in Revelation 11:13) will equate directly to the period of time referenced by Revelation 10:11 and 18:1-8.

The finale of the investigative judgment of the living, the world-wide preaching of the full gospel of Law and grace, must occur then. Combined with supernatural events in the heavens, the enemies of the gospel will put forth superhuman effort to stop the truth. Everyone among the nations will choose to follow Jesus with all their heart, or reject Christ's salvation from the depths of their soul. After final decisions are made, the confirmed rebellious multitudes, tongues, and peoples outside the Protestant world, together with the decided hedonists, LGBT community, and atheists among the locust corrupted Protestant nations (see Revelation 13:13, 14) will comprise the great bulk of the world (see Daniel 7:23, 21, 22, 18; Matthew 7:13; Revelation 13:3). Combined with the previously apostate, Spiritual Formation Protestants whose consciences were already killed by the locusts, almost the whole world will war against the approaching kingdom of God. The prophecy will be fulfilled that "all the world wondered after the beast" (Rev. 13:3). The world unmistakably witnesses the restored kingdom of God in the faultless lives of a revived apostolic church, as prophesied in Revelation 11:12, 15 and Revelation 14:5.

During the first six trumpets, the vast majority of Protestants (see 1 Peter 3:20) who constituted the good "earth" (Rev. 7:3; 9:4) gradually transform into "the sea", a worldly flood, a parallel tributary of "the great river Euphrates" (Rev. 16:12, cf 9:14), flowing into "Babylon the great" (Rev. 18:2). The strong delusion from God swept up almost every Reformation descendant, its overflowing scourge reaching to the bridles and steering the people into perdition. The glorious land between the oceans that began the trumpet process is no longer the land of peace and glory. It is denuded of spiritual life and its morality is eroded by the locust plagues. The only exceptions that remain planted in the earth are those men who stand "on the mount Sion" (Rev. 14:1), who have "the seal of God in their foreheads" (Rev. 9:4). Individual decisions throughout the pagan world continue to feed both camps of "earth" and "sea" until all the nations have decided for the health-giving truth, or for

Chapter 7 Revelation Chapter 10: Preparation for the Latter Rain

moral decay. And the unchurched Protestants, "the rest of the men who were not killed" (Rev. 9:20) by the locust plagues, also find their places in either camp, sealed by Jesus or marked by Satan.

The many from the Gentile sea who abandon their vices and atheism, and who join in the peace and righteousness of the "earth" (Rev. 7:3; 9:4) — God's final "chosen generation" (1 Pet. 2:9, cf Ps. 24:6; Gal. 3:19; Jer. 50:20; Rom. 11:4, 5) — take part in a simultaneous sifting and exchange that happens between the members of the "sea" and of the "earth" during the final preaching by the 144,000 Adventist Protestants. These prospective arrivals from the "sea" foreseen in Revelation 10, under which Christ's right foot of favor sets, are the "remnant" in John's next vision who "were affrighted, and gave glory to the God of heaven" (Rev. 11:13). They will obey the message from the 144,000, "Fear God, and give glory to him; for the hour of his judgment is come" (Rev. 14:7, cf Rev. 7:9).

The same preaching of primitive godliness and the reappearance of the straight testimony from the True Witness cause many among God's previous remnant people to abandon their holy religion of Law and grace at this eleventh hour. They had clung to the one true religion without seeking the one true God. As tares among the wheat each has been found "to smite his fellowservants, and to eat and drink with the drunken" (Matt. 24:49). They have made friends with the apostate religions and they easily join with the unbelieving, celebrating and spiritualistic, and abusive Gentile "sea", who gladly receive them into everlasting habitations (see Revelation 16:12-16; 2 Thessalonians 2:8-12; Joel 3:14; Luke 16:9).

At that time, the confirmed rebels of the "sea", the "many waters", "peoples, and multitudes, and nations, and tongues", "the great river Euphrates", "the whole world", "all the world", "the inhabitants of the earth", "all nations", "they that dwell on the earth" "whose names are not written in the book of life of the Lamb slain from the foundation of the world" (Rev. 17:1, 15; 16:12, 14; 17:2; 13:3; 14:8; 17:8; 13:8), will be "cut off" (Lev. 23:29) from the Spirit of God. Everyone from the nations who fully abandoned themselves to Satan, join with the previously confirmed wicked among the Protestants and their Remnant, that is, the Revelation chapter 9 "third part" (Rev. 9:18) whose consciences the locusts had already killed "by the fire, and by the smoke, and by the brimstone, which issued out of their mouths" (Rev. 9:18, cf Rev. 14:9-11).

Every one that is proud in heart is an abomination to the LORD: though hand join in hand, he shall not be unpunished (Prov. 16:5).

Examine yourselves, whether ye be in the faith; prove your own selves. Know ye not your own selves, how that Jesus Christ is in you, except ye be reprobates? (2 Cor. 13:5).

Thus, the sixth trumpet cavalry will end, the second woe past (see Revelation 11:14). God removes His Spirit from the nominal "earth" and "trees" and "grass" (Rev. 7:3; 8:7) because He can no longer compete with their carnal peace from the "other gods" (Deut. 29:26). Sadly, the "Spirit of grace" (Heb. 10:29) must give up the battle for their salvation. He must turn away, concede the loss, and give them to the other gods. The world has no more possibility to return to the one true God. The previous friendly spirits will then manifest their true disposition toward God's favored world. The spirits will punish the whole race with the harsh curse of devil possession. The devils will jump on them, declaring, "They have sinned"! (Jer. 50:7, cf Acts 19:14-16). The unlimited power of Satanic angels rules all who rejected the protection of God's Law. Their hopeless hearts and minds filled with the bitter infection from the Beast's mark of fire, smoke, and brimstone, and then from its never satisfying intoxication of unclean spirits. "They shall look unto the earth; and behold trouble and darkness, dimness of anguish; and they shall be driven to darkness" (Isa. 8:22). Their covenant with death is disannulled, their agreement with hell does not stand; the overflowing scourge passes through, and they are trodden down by it. But, the sealed have their angelic Goshen protecting them from the chaos that is terrorizing the whole world. Now is our salvation nearer than ever; today is the day to find the Spirit of Christ in the Law of God.

Though hand join in hand, the wicked shall not be unpunished: but the seed of the righteous shall be delivered (Prov. 11:21).

Many of the fruit of the 144,000 Protestant-Adventist lay evangelists will have been the most hopeless cases of the "rest of the men which…repented not of the works of their hands" (Rev. 9:20), who were wrongly condemned by the pious religious and ethical atheistic.

Hear the word of the LORD, ye that tremble at his word; your brethren that hated you, that cast you out for my name's sake, said, Let the LORD be glorified: but he shall appear to your joy, and they shall be ashamed (Isa. 66:5).

What shall we say then? That the Gentiles, which followed not after righteousness, have attained to righteousness, even the righteousness which is of faith (Rom. 9:30).

Thousands in a day sprinkled throughout the nations will be drawn out of the corrupted practices and traditions of their fathers, and into biblical truth by the "Spirit of truth; whom the world cannot receive, because it seeth him not, neither knoweth him" (John 14:17).

In their own right, the 144,000 are "mothers of all living", being helpmeets with Christ, sacrificing self and laying down their lives for the salvation of their Gentile children (see Isaiah 8:18; Galatians 4:19). They have oversight of a flock, which are the multitude of Revelation 7:9 who receive the strong message of heaven's good-will toward men and peace on earth (see Revelation 2:26; Isaiah 60:4-10).

> For thus saith the Lord GOD; Behold, I, even I, will both search my sheep, and seek them out.... I will feed my flock, and I will cause them to lie down, saith the Lord GOD. I will seek that which was lost, and bring again that which was driven away, and will bind up that which was broken, and will strengthen that which was sick: but I will destroy the fat and the strong; I will feed them with judgment.... And I the LORD will be their God, and my servant [Jesus] a prince among them; I the LORD have spoken it.... And I will raise up for them a plant of renown, and they shall be no more consumed with hunger in the land, neither bear the shame of the heathen any more.... And ye my flock, the flock of my pasture, are men, and I am your God, saith the Lord GOD (Eze. 34:11, 15, 16, 24, 29, 31).

The 144,000 tenderly shepherd the newborn children of God into green pastures and beside still waters, as the prison houses of that great and fair city, pagan Babylon (see Revelation 18:7; Ezekiel 28:2; Daniel 5:1-4), "fell" (Rev. 11:13, cf Rev. 16:12; 17:16-18; Jer. 25:27).

"After this I beheld, and, lo, a great multitude, which no man could number, of all nations, and kindreds, and people, and tongues" (Rev. 7:9). That mighty group have answered the great call of the 144,000, "Come out of her, my people, that ye be not partakers of her sins, and that ye receive not of her plagues. For her sins have reached unto heaven, and God hath remembered her iniquities" (Rev. 18:4, 5). Escaping the strong spell of the one false religion, the redeemed resist the devil's savory substitutes and holy angels drive him from them forever.

This separating out and shifting between those among the "earth" and the "sea" is a terrible ordeal to the 144,000; nevertheless, it must take place. Long-time friends, family members, spouses, and children have suffered a terrible separation, as Jesus foretold they would (see Matthew 10:21, 37, 38; Luke 12:51-53; Genesis 19:12-16; Numbers 23:9). But, to restore "the first dominion" (Mic. 4:8) is best for everyone among the "earth", for God, and for His heavenly kingdom. Like Lot agonizing over parting from his children in Sodom because they would not flee the city's soon destruction, the 144,000 and innumerable multitude accept with much agony that separation must happen in order for God to end the travesties of a world which demonic hosts have claimed ownership. This is the last opportunity to plead for their loved ones to join the persecuted minority who are denounced as deluded believers in the Bible and Arian heretic terrorists. Michael who stands before God in behalf of the children of His people must ripen His character in this group that He had been growing during the fifth and sixth trumpets' sealing. His final call from heaven to the world also ripens the character of Satan among the group that the devil has come to possess during the sixth trumpet (see Daniel 11:44, 45; Revelation 14:14-20; Joel 3:13).

> I am the true vine, and my Father is the husbandman. Every branch in me that beareth not fruit he taketh away: and every branch that beareth fruit, he purgeth it, that it may bring forth more fruit. Now ye are clean through the word which I have spoken unto you.... If a man abide not in me, he is cast forth as a branch, and is withered; and men gather them, and cast them into the fire, and they are burned. If ye abide in me, and my words abide in you, ye shall ask what ye will, and it shall be done unto you. Herein is my Father glorified, that ye bear much fruit; so shall ye be my disciples (John 15:1-3, 6-8).

Before the "earth" and the "sea" can be judged either for the kingdom of God or the devil's empire, they must all be tested with a full knowledge of God's love, and then accept or reject Him and the laws governing His heavenly country. Where no law is completely explained, no guilt can be fully imputed (see Romans 4:15; 5:13; 14:5;

John 12:47). And until that explanation comes to their conscience, God mercifully tolerates the perpetuation of an evil world. To all who have not heard the appeals of Jesus through His servants, He will say, "If I had not come and spoken unto them, they had not had sin" (John 15:22). He even gives them a grace period, "If any man hear my words, and believe not, I judge him not: for I came not to judge the world, but to save the world" (John 12:47). But, once His Spirit has convicted their conscience of truth by the 144,000, then He will say, "He that rejecteth me, and receiveth not my words, hath one that judgeth him: the word that I have spoken, the same shall judge him in the last day" (John 12:48). The individual responses either to love the truth or to have pleasure in unrighteousness decide for everyone whether Jesus or Satan has their heart (see 2 Chronicles 16:9).

That test will fulfill Christ's yet future standing on the earth and the sea of Revelation 10.

Inside the opened book of God's charges, His character stood guilty until proven innocent. And now, looking forward to the conclusion of judgment on His Father and His Father's kingdom, Christ roars like a lion. This relates back to Revelation 5:5, "the Lion of the tribe of Juda, the Root of David, hath prevailed to open the book, and to loose the seven seals thereof."

The seventh seal loosed and the book open, Christ's stance is a lion's mien. His roar sounds of dominion and victory in anticipation of the soon end of the controversy over His Father. It is a roar of rejoicing for His Father; but, it is also a warning call to Satan whose kingdom is about to fall. And, how Satan will shudder when he hears that cry!

The Lamb, anticipating the soon close of His High Priest ministry of mercy, He is about to don the King's garments of vengeance.

> For I lift up my hand to heaven, and say, I live for ever.
>
> If I whet my glittering sword, and mine hand take hold on judgment; I will render vengeance to mine enemies, and will reward them that hate me.
>
> I will make mine arrows drunk with blood, and my sword shall devour flesh; and that with the blood of the slain and of the captives, from the beginning of revenges upon the enemy.
>
> Rejoice, O ye nations, with his people: for he will avenge the blood of his servants, and will render vengeance to his adversaries, and will be merciful unto his land, and to his people (Deut. 32:40-43).
>
> I will tread down the people in mine anger, and make them drunk in my fury, and I will bring down their strength to the earth (Isa. 63:6).

Following Christ's roar, the unseen Ancient of days, who is greater (see John 14:28, cf Daniel 7:9, 13) and who is above Him, complements His Son's voice by ear-splitting thunders of august agreement at the glad tidings and long-held desire for the return of righteousness and trust and peace to His kingdom.

This majestic rejoicing by the Godhead indicates Their forward look to the termination of the reign of sin and the exoneration of the Father by an obedient remnant of Adam's children. It is Their divine expectation of a soon end of the controversy between satanic hosts and the pouring of Their Spirit upon a special group "who are kept by the power of God through faith" (1 Pet. 1:5).

The victory cries of Son and Father also demonstrate Their preemptive nature. Their thorough work of preparation looks confidently ahead to final outcomes, despite ages of Satan's machinations against Them and Their people. The character of Their example of wisdom and patience helps us to prepare for our big work ahead and inspires us by Their confidence in the sure result.

Now, an omnipotent declaration: Christ lifts His strong, righteous right hand (see Isaiah 41:10; 62:8) to heaven and swears by His Father (see Deuteronomy 32:40), "him that liveth for ever and ever, who created heaven, and the things that therein are, and the earth, and the things that therein are, and the sea, and the things which are therein, that there should be time no longer" (Rev. 10:6). This last phrase, "there should be time no longer" more accurately reads, "there should be no more delay".

The original Greek literally reads, "Delay no shall be longer; but in the days of the voice of the seventh angel, when he is about to sound [the] trumpet, also should be completed the mystery of God, as He did announce the glad tidings to His bondmen the prophets" (Rev. 10:6, 7) *Interlinear Greek-English New Testament*.

The delay refers to Revelation 7:3 and it was an act of God's mercy to give one last chance for obedience by His sin-loving children from every kindred, tongue, and nation. It was an unmerited favor for Christ, through the gift of prophecy, to call back from Laodicea the remnant of His Protestants who were scattered from biblical truth, their apostolic refuge, and then to seal His character in them. The delay also gives time for Satan to fully develop the permanent mark of his character in his kingdom of the world's Law-despising populations.

The delay that began in Revelation 7:3 would be extended until Christ could clear the mystery charges against His Father by His evident ability to create a translatable seed that will have come. He would make the wise more precious than fine gold and blot out their sins, as the prophecies of Daniel and others had foretold. The delay ended says that all the evidence will have accrued that can ever weigh in on the final trial between God and Satan (see Isaiah 14:13, 14; Revelation 13:6). As well, all the evidence will also be gathered that can discern between "saints" at rest in the faith of Jesus (1 Cor. 1:2; Rev. 14:12, 13) versus those tormented by serving Satan, fully in rebellion against God and His holy love, and without rest (see Genesis 3:15; John 3:36; Revelation 14:11; Jeremiah 51:58, 64).

> Delay no shall be longer; but in the days of the voice of the seventh angel, when he is about to sound [the] trumpet, also should be completed the mystery of God (Rev. 10:6, 7) *Interlinear Greek-English New Testament.*

John's Revelation, though certainly inspired by God and perfectly in line with Daniel's visions, was a book difficult to accept by the church when it first circulated. Maybe this is partly due to the little reference to Jesus and even the obvious exaltation of God preeminently over His Son. Revelation shows Christ as a servant swearing by God, God who alone "liveth for ever and ever" (Rev. 10:6, cf Rev. 4:8-10; 5:14; 1:4, 6; 11:17), the grandfatherly "Ancient of days" (Dan. 7:9) who alone has immortality. Revelation shows God sitting on the throne unaccompanied, with Christ "in the midst of the throne" (Rev. 5:6) among the twenty-four elders and the four beasts (see Revelation 5:6; Psalm 45:7), ministering to His Father (see Revelation 5:7; 6:1, 3, 5, 7, 9, 12; 8:1-4). In the days of the pagan insurgency of *homoousia*, the many references to the Father's special reverence and towering greatness over His subordinating Son (see Revelation 4:10, 11; 5:13; 10:3; 11:16, 17), and Christ's sworn testimony of God as eternal Creator (see Revelation 10:6) rather than Himself also as such, must have presented a real quandary to the carnal, apostatizing Church fathers. Christ is very God manifest in the flesh (see 1 Timothy 3:16), but He is also very dependent and supportive; and so are His children (see Genesis 2:18; Isaiah 9:6; Hebrews 2:13, 14; Mark 10:24; John 13:33; 21:5).

The apparent difference between Revelation and the rest of the New Testament with regard to the vast dissimilarity of Father and Son, and Revelation's focus on the Father's greatness must have created a tangible tension in the late apostolic church, which was already bucking for inclusion with the pagan world (see 2 Thessalonians 2:7).

But, in the wisdom of God the difference between the centrality of Christ in the gospels and epistles, and the Father's later exaltation in Revelation, must be. With exception to Revelation, the New Testament gospels and epistles served to necessarily exalt Christ, as He would present His sacrifice to His Father in the Holy Place of the heavenly sanctuary until 1844. The purpose of The Revelation, however, was to articulate "the times of restitution of all things" (Acts 3:21, cf Dan. 7:13, 14), the great event occurring in the heavenly sanctuary (see Hebrews 8:1, 2; 9:11, 12, 28) after 1844. After that year, Christ would begin the move into the "Holiest of all" (Heb. 9:3) next to His Father to cleanse the heavenly sanctuary (see Daniel 8:14), prefigured for Israel annually on the tenth day of the seventh month (see Leviticus 16:1-34; 23:27-32). And the Ancient of days would begin His restoration to the central focus of heaven and earth.

> In the days of the voice of the seventh angel, when he is about to sound [the] trumpet, also should be completed the mystery of God, as He did announce the glad tidings to His bondmen the prophets (Rev. 10:7) *Interlinear Greek-English New Testament.*

The mystery of the judgment on God completed will cause an announcement of "glad tidings" (Gr. *evaggelisen*) before Jesus returns. The Latter Rain, the great controversy preaching with Christ at the center and His Father at both ends as we saw in Revelation 4 and 5, the "glad tidings" of God's soon-coming acquittal are the mystery of God finished. As part of their message, those who preach the Latter Rain at the end will weave in the good news of the completion of our Father's exoneration. The last book is the Revelation of God, and of His great controversy. While the gospels and epistles concerned the gospel of Christ, the book of The Revelation is the gospel of God the Father and His Law.

God, who is the central focus of The Revelation, was revealed in this last book because not only Jesus and His cross, but especially Jehovah and His Law, would at the end of time embody the glad tidings of the gospel to be preached. The full reconciliation to the King would come to His children — thus the greatest exaltation of His Law after 1844 through the counsels of the Spirit of Prophecy. The exaltation of His Law and of Judgment Day would bring His children to Himself through His mediating Son. This said, neither Revelation would be understood, nor would the Law be expounded fully, until after 1844. Thus, the greatest bulk of the Bible's last book would focus on the final battle between the Advent movement carrying the torch of prophetic and gospel truth, and Satan's ultimate work to deceive the humanity with damning falsehoods and sleight of men (see 2 Thessalonians 2:9-12; Ephesians 4:14; Revelation 13:13, 14).

In the final book of the Bible, we see the work involved in restoring the Father to undisputed rulership. Then, we see Him restored to His original throne of peace, as was David after Absalom's rebellion. Thus, God can again "be all in all" (see 1 Cor. 15:26), a never-ending sequel of the eternal picture that we saw in Revelation chapter 4 before the controversy began.

Representing His King, Prince Michael dealt justice with mercy during the Old Testament world. And He has dealt grace with reproving truth for the church thus far during His perfect administration of the new dispensation. Throughout His faithful governance of Earth, and especially against Satan's usurping of the New Testament church seen in the last five seals of Revelation 6, the Son has clarified His Father's actions against Lucifer when arraigning him for his disloyalty and then ordering him cast out of His grace (see 2 Peter 2:4; Job 4:18). The life and death of Messiah the Prince forever has revealed the character of God and of Satan, and reclaimed the full loyalty of the angelic hosts and unfallen worlds (see John 12:31; Revelation 12:7-9).

However, in order for mankind to eternally appreciate the work of the Lamb who had been slain, the proud nature and mind of man would need to suffer and be humbled under the long foretold, extraordinary wickedness of the Roman Papacy, through both its phases Medieval (see Revelation 13:1-7) and New Age (see Revelation 13:11-17). "The times of the Gentiles" (Luke 21:24, cf Rev. 11:2) — a period of freedom for Satan to reveal his deep hostility toward Christ was fulfilled when the adversary's Papacy clearly exposed itself as the virulent enemy of the gospel. By its unrelenting, furious warfare against Christ's wilderness church the deceiver made known his unwillingness to concede the victory of Christ's eternal act of self-sacrificing love, until 1798 when Christ could stop the Papacy's wicked blood spilling.

Then, Christ's exaltation of the Law and His promised forgiveness of sinners, together with troublous times would reconcile hearts back to God. Especially the final troubles would forever harden His people's conviction to hate sin, His good news of peace working in tandem with the bad news of trouble (see Isaiah 45:7; Hosea 6:1; Jeremiah 31:15-17).

As Jehovah made Abraham the remnant of the Hebrew descendants of Noah, and as He made the Jews the remnant of Abraham's descendants (see Isaiah 40:1, 2), He must make a remnant for the gospel. Christ's Church showed itself to fail the new dispensation, as Abraham's Hebrews had the Old. Therefore, a remnant out of the Church — Protestantism — would be reconciled to God and be given the glorious land between the seas. The Protestant resolve against sin which Jesus established in the apostolic church, and His atonement which Satan had withstood during the Dark Ages, would need to be reaffirmed by His New Testament Israel in a final trial. This reaffirmation would be composed of the Reformation from the 16th century with the delay period of Revelation 7:3 for cleansing His Father's holy name by a Remnant of the Reformation, beginning in 1844. The final trial would produce a part II of the original church.

> So will I make my holy name known in the midst of my people Israel; and I will not let them pollute my holy name any more: and the heathen shall know that I am the LORD, the Holy One in Israel (Eze. 39:7).

Our High Priest will cleanse the church of every misrepresentation of Jehovah's holy name and of every Protestant spiritualist who will not turn from following devious Baal and Ashtoreth (see Malachi 3:5). Christ would most fully accomplish this cleansing through the fifth and sixth trumpets' final gleaning of those who would be humbled by the Testimony of Jesus and would submit to His authority. More intensely than ever prior to this time, He would give special chastisement to their conscience, for the greater glory of His Father's exoneration (see Revelation 14:1). During the six trumpets' delay, the outcome of the special humbling would bring the Adventists to "receive the promise of the Spirit" (Gal. 3:14) through the blessedness that Abraham received. That is, in a special measure, the promised Spirit of Christ in the Law would exceptionally shield and deliver them from the humbling, extraordinary condemnation of the instructive and corrective Spirit of Prophecy. In a deeper way than the apostles received in the Early Rain, the Adventists would be specially justified and "sealed with that holy Spirit of promise" (Eph. 1:13). Those who stand before the holy God without their Mediator will be the heirs of the greatest dispensation of Law and grace ever committed to men. In the fullest sense, they will be the seed that should come to whom the promised Spirit was made. The Father would also make use of the accuser of the brethren, loosed and empowered by the fifth and sixth trumpet corrupting and tormenting plagues to distance all from God, except the *very* elect. The accuser would also work to accentuate the chastisement of God against sin (see Revelation 12:10; Zechariah 1:13-15; Isaiah 47:6).

Through this work of His enemy, the Lord would test His 144,000 firstfruits with the same test that His Father gave Him in Gethsemane. [Firstfruits were the sweet, first ripened, and the sacrificed grain, and they promised an abundant future harvest. Would you like to be a first fruit? Would you be a spotless, living sacrifice, not conformed to this world? Will you let the Spirit of Christ in the Testimony of Jesus transform you by the renewing of your mind and provide for an abundant Latter Rain ingathering? Will you hold on in the anxious dark, like your Master who has walked in your steps, until light most assuredly comes in the morning (see Isaiah 50:10; 60:1)?] Thus, the 144,000 follow the Lamb everywhere He goes. "For it became him, for whom are all things, and by whom are all things, in bringing many sons unto glory, to make the captain of their salvation perfect through sufferings", "and being made perfect, he became the author of eternal salvation unto all them that obey him" (Heb. 2:10; 5:9, cf Luke 6:46).

As peacetime could never accomplish, bringing the 144,000 through "an horror of great darkness" (Gen. 15:12) will press out of them what Jesus had pressed into them — His likeness that cannot be removed (see 1 Corinthians 3:10-15). All their comeliness would turn into corruption as they see Jesus more clearly. The end of the delay will produce in them the full yearning of Paul, "That I may know him…and the fellowship of his sufferings, being made conformable unto his death" (Phil. 3:10). They are His predestinated last generation, the eternal vanguard of which He prophesied (see Revelation 7:15).

The end of the investigative judgment, the Day of Atonement will find God's people being established, strengthened, settled, and sealed, through "Jesus the mediator of the new covenant" and His "blood of sprinkling" (Heb. 12:24). By the final tarrying in the midnight darkness Christ, our High Priest, seen in Revelation 8:3-7, will have Adam's family ready for Him to return with power to end their many millennia-long eviction from Eden and captivity by Satan's craftiness. Then upon a fully wicked world the Father can safely exterminate sin in the final display of wrath that He had brought down upon His own Son at Calvary (see Isaiah 13:11-13; Revelation 20:9). In the end, God will have wisely and patiently and righteously restored His full trust in His family of heaven and earth, and their full trust in Him. God's Day of Judgment will have eternally removed all confusing distrust and will have eternally vulcanized His whole kingdom into His righteousness.

No more delay to which Revelation 10:6 referred means that the finalizing of the last test to humanity will end soon after this announcement by Jesus in the Most Holy, a postponement caused by the trumpets' sealing period that began in 1844 (see Revelation 7:1-3; 9:4, 5). Yet, within the next verse we see more precisely when Christ actually means to end this Revelation 7:3 interruption of His 1844 Revelation 6:17 Second Coming.

The conjunction, "**But**," conjoins Revelation 10 verse 6 with verse 7, and more accurately clarifies the end of the delay — "But, in the days of the voice of the seventh angel, when he shall begin to sound, the mystery of God should be finished, as He hath declared to his servants the prophets" (Rev. 10:7). "Delay no shall be longer; but in the days of the voice of the seventh angel, when he is about to sound [the] trumpet, also should be completed the mystery of God, as He did announce the glad tidings to His bondmen the prophets" (Rev. 10:7) *Interlinear Greek-English New Testament.*

The Angel speaks of the last gospel preaching near the close of the sixth trumpet. The mystery of God is finished when the seventh trumpet begins to sound. The glorified Christ enshrouded by Most Holiness will then cleanse the whole temple of heaven and earth while the antitypical scapegoat reveals himself as the Son of God in a counterfeit revival, but without the sacrifice of self. God's greater righteousness composes the glad tidings of this special time, simultaneous with the gathering of multitudes to Christ during the Latter Rain. Jesus long foretold this exciting final revival through Moses (Genesis 3:15), Hosea (6:1-3), and Micah (7:16-20), by Isaiah (4:1, 2; 32:15-18; 40:9; 49:13; 52:7; 60:1-5; 61:1-62:12), by Zephaniah (3:9- 20), Joel (2:21-3:2, 13, 14), Ezekiel (34:26, 27), by Daniel (7:13, 14, 22; 12:7, 9, 10), and by Zechariah (4:3-6, 14; 12:10, 11). The Daniel 11:44 tidings speak of the great gospel harvest, the final glad tidings preached just before Michael their great Prince stands up from within the Holiest of all.

The sixth trumpet trouble has tested the 144,000 until they are walking after the Spirit without any confidence in the flesh. Michael stands ready to receive to Himself His 144,000 and His earthly kingdom. The glad tidings from Jesus brighten up the nations. Then the earthly abomination of desolation stands in Michael's place and the mystery of God Latter Rain is finished in the most holy exemplification of His character in His people. The seventh angel sounds and human probation closes. The Father's temple is cleansed and there is a great time of trouble such that never was when Michael leaves the heavenly sanctuary. He was the only one from the beginning restraining God from destroying this planet (see Matthew 24:13-24; Daniel 11:45-12:1; Revelation 16:12-14).

Thus, before the seventh trumpet fully sounds and probation closes, God can give the world its last chance to hear the truth of His character and to see His holiness perfectly resting in His servants. And as we will find in the next chapter, when the Advent movement's revival and God's final appeal fells Babylon, then He concludes His gracious delay since 1844 and the nations become wildly angry. War and chaos break out everywhere as Satan makes his last short-lived and desperate push to claim all of humanity under his delusions.

The big picture presented, let us turn to an aspect of the delay that some may find unwelcome. Foreseen from their beginning, the Adventists' lack of preparedness for Christ's coming in power and glory would necessitate the fifth trumpet preparation delay.

> The history of ancient Israel is a striking illustration of the past experience of the Adventist body. God led His people in the advent movement, even as He led the children of Israel from Egypt. In the great disappointment their faith was tested as was that of the Hebrews at the Red Sea. Had they still trusted to the guiding hand that had been with them in their past experience, they would have seen the salvation of God. If all who had labored unitedly in the work in 1844, had received the third angel's message and proclaimed it in the power of the Holy Spirit, the Lord would have wrought mightily with their efforts. A flood of light would have been shed upon the world. Years ago the inhabitants of the earth would have been warned, the closing work completed, and Christ would have come for the redemption of His people.
>
> In like manner, it was not the will of God that the coming of Christ should be so long delayed and His people should remain so many years in this world of sin and sorrow. But unbelief separated them from God. As they refused to do the work which He had appointed them, others were raised up to proclaim the message. In mercy to the world, Jesus delays His coming, that sinners may have an opportunity to hear the warning and find in Him a shelter before the wrath of God shall be poured out *The Great Controversy*, p. 457, 458.

Could Christ have returned in 1844 or shortly thereafter? Yes, He could have *if* certain conditions had been satisfied. He could have returned if the Remnant of the Reformation had exceeded their forefather's desire for salvation by faith and the Reformers' serving God in self-sacrifice. Yes, if they had had the faith of Jesus and His primitive godliness on a par greater than had been seen in the martyrs of the Dark Ages. Yes, if they had prepared themselves with the special work of purification as the Testimony of Jesus continually implored of them. Yes, if they had been through the "great tribulation, such as was not since the beginning of the world to this time, no, nor ever shall be" (Matt. 24:21).

Why these conditions? The final snapshot from Daniel 12:10 and Revelation 19:6-8 show a vastly better spiritual condition of the 144,000 than existed among the Millerites or in the Advent movement. The Adventists could have been sanctified as they took up Christ's mandated work to prepare the world, but they wouldn't do the work. Therefore, they must face the worse option of their choice. The tribulations of Matthew 24:5-8 indicate birth contraction intensity increasing and intervals decreasing between contractions, leading to the climax of a whole wicked world caught in travail. This was not the case in the early 1840s. Morality was declining in America during the time of the Millerite movement, but not to the extent that existed in the days before Noah's flood and that we now see coming to the world.

The final time of trouble in this digital age will be a tribulation that could not have been faced in 1844. An expanding fleet of CIA drones that can shoot laser-guided, video game style, over-the-horizon weaponry, with an ever-growing satellite 3-D mapping of the Earth, massive computer databases that hold precise coordinates, and the recent gathering of coordinate information for every residence, will test the faith of the 144,000 to the utmost. Daily, science in America seeks to create ever newer unconscionable capabilities in order to one day surveil and lock down the world's societies. More than all of this a new, fierce world governance will aid the efforts of the adversary to intimidate, without a second of thought, every soul whose mind is not *perfectly* fortified by the Spirit and letter of the Bible. Without a wall of angelic protection by faith in Jesus' promises firmly anchored to the halls of the memory, no one will live to see Him come (see Matthew 24:21, 22). The great troubles will drive the unprepared into joining the final war against the struggling members of the kingdom of God. "The sinners in Zion are afraid; fearfulness hath surprised the hypocrites…. Thou shalt not see a fierce people, a people of a deeper speech than thou canst perceive; of a stammering tongue, that thou canst not understand" (Isa. 33:14, 19). Is the above description the world that God foresaw hosting the "time of trouble, such as never was since there was a nation" (Dan. 12:1)? It does match Daniel's description better than the safe haven, undeveloped early 19th century world of William Miller.

Those who have surrendered to God's Law and to all of His crucibles, examining, interrogating, and afflicting their own souls to know if they could ever betray Jesus (see Matthew 26:21, 22), will be the only exceptions to fleeing from their faith in Him because the odds are completely and utterly against them. God's elect will be saved because they will have surrendered to the Lamb and to His "army of heaven" (Dan. 4:35), and will have received the power to become the sons of God. Intense fear will cut off from God the bulk of the church, trapping them into uniting with the Beast and receiving the full mark of his character, because they did not prepare their hearts during our current time of peace.

Christ could have finished His work in the mid-1800s and have permitted the time of trouble at that time. But, if by their unbelief in His power to keep His commandments His remnant people would choose to turn down the invitation to go home 150+ years ago, then a later alternative would not be easier than Civil War technology. Everything that we would not do in times of much lesser capability back then we will have to do in incomparable perplexity and unparalleled difficulty in the future. Technology's juggernaut and the impossibility of resisting it will forge in His sanctified group the unrivaled dependence on God (see Judges 6:5, 6) that can stand in the great day of the Lord, as described in Bible prophecy. In order to prepare the last generation for the greatest event of history — "the day of the LORD…cruel both with wrath and fierce anger, to lay the land desolate" (Isa. 13:9) — the blast furnaces of affliction that will "make a man more precious than fine gold" (Isa. 13:12) must then be advanced technological circumstances that did not exist in Miller's post-colonial, agrarian age.

Jesus was ready to return in 1844; but, who could have stood before their Maker in all His power and glory? No one. Revelation 7:1-3 make it clear that the trumpets' sealing delay readies His people for translation. The above statement from *The Great Controversy*, combined with Revelation 7:1-3, show us that the moral and spiritual condition within the earthly movement going to the heavenly Canaan made it impossible for anyone at that time to stand at Christ's Second Advent. Without an extra period of mercy and patience by God, a special work of purification through cooperation with the Spirit of Jesus in His Most Holy Place, and a nightmarish final trouble, no flesh would have been saved the day the King will arrive. The "delay" specified in Revelation 10:6 is the "coming of Christ…so long delayed" written in *The Great Controversy*, quoted above. His Adventist family would themselves need much time for "much" (Rev. 8:3, Lev. 16:11, 12) cleansing before they could join His work of cleansing His worldwide bride (see Leviticus 16:16; Revelation 8:3-5; 19:7-9).

The children of Israel should have entered Canaan within a year. They might have, but in reality they couldn't. "They could not enter in because of unbelief" (Heb. 3:19), with exception of two men and the impressionable, younger generation. That meant essentially the whole adult generation who were delivered from slavery died without seeing the land that flowed with milk and honey, faithful Israelites receiving the punishment with the majority which was hardened in ignorance and unbelief. Their complaining and fighting, their hearts never losing the thorns and briers, they could not have cleansed Canaan with "justice and judgment" (Ps. 89:14).

Fourteen hundred years after their Egyptian deliverance, another avoidable, conditional prophecy was fulfilled. Gabriel had promised the Jews, "Seventy weeks are determined upon thy people and upon thy holy city, to finish the transgression, and to make an end of sins, and to make reconciliation for iniquity, and to bring in everlasting righteousness, and to seal up the vision and prophecy, and to anoint the most Holy" (Dan. 9:24). Doesn't that itemize the special work of purification mandated to the Advent movement?

Israel could have prevented Gabriel's determination against them. The prophecy inferred that tremendous blessings were in store for the nation if it would look upon Messiah the Prince whom they had been piercing (see Zechariah 12:10; Psalm 22:16). The dread calamity might not happen if they would receive Him and His Spirit of sorrow for sin.

Nevertheless, the Lord God six centuries in advance saw that the national unrelinquished sins of their past would continue to so weaken their moral strength by indulgence of pride and passions that He would have to reject most of them. They had not been surrendering before His Law, and they would continue in the same vein (see Romans 10:3). Therefore, as their nation would continue to rebel against their Prince and be noxious to man (see Malachi 3:13-15; 4:1; 1 Thessalonians 2:15, 16; Ephesians 2:14, 15), the whole would be swept away. "The end thereof shall be with a flood, and unto the end of the war desolations are determined…even until the consummation, and that determined shall be poured upon the desolate" (Dan. 9:26, 27).

Daniel's beloved Israel could have received grace to obey the principles of God's Law from hearts circumcised by faith. But, because they accepted Satan's temptation to refuse surrender to the blessedness of abiding in the Anointed One, they would become so corrupted that He would be forced to do to His people as Moses and the prophets had long before forewarned them.

> The land is defiled [by Baal and the Canaanites]: therefore I do visit the iniquity thereof upon it, and the land itself vomiteth out her inhabitants. Ye shall therefore keep my statutes and my judgments, and shall not commit any of these abominations; neither any of your own nation, nor any stranger that sojourneth among you: (for all these abominations have the men of the land done, which were before you, and the land is defiled;) that the land spue not you out also, when ye defile it, as it spued out the nations that were before you (Lev. 18:25-28).

> And they rejected his statutes, and his covenant that he made with their fathers, and his testimonies which he testified against them; and they followed vanity, and became vain, and went after the heathen that were round about them, concerning whom the LORD had charged them, that they should not do like them. And they left all the commandments of the LORD their God, and made them molten images, even two calves, and made a grove, and worshipped all the host of heaven, and served Baal. And they caused their sons and their daughters to pass through the fire, and used divination and enchantments, and sold themselves to do evil in the sight of the LORD, to provoke him to anger. Therefore the LORD was very angry with Israel, and removed them out of his sight: there was none left but the tribe of Judah only. Also Judah kept not the commandments of the LORD their God, but walked in the statutes of Israel which they made. And the LORD rejected all the seed of Israel, and afflicted them, and delivered them into the hand of spoilers, until he had cast them out of his sight (2 Ki. 17:15-20).

> Yea, all Israel have transgressed thy law, even by departing, that they might not obey thy voice; therefore the curse is poured upon us, and the oath that is written in the law of Moses the servant of God, because we have sinned against him. And he hath confirmed his words, which he spake against us, and against our judges that judged us, by bringing upon us a great evil: for under the whole heaven hath not been done as hath been done upon Jerusalem (Dan. 9:11, 12).

In light of this, the Advent movement and mixed multitude could have avoided our long delay and have prepared for the Day of Judgment quickly after the passing of 1844. Yes, we could have; but we didn't. We should have; but, we haven't. And the Beast from the bottomless pit has encouraged our unbelief. We have had a long problem of doing no differently than our brethren of the Sunday churches as Judah copied their Israelite brethren (see Jeremiah 3:7-11). Therefore, couldn't the Godhead have foreseen this and the need for 170+ years to strengthen us against increasing temptations and unbelief in the testimonies, even for the strictest among us? Yes. And, couldn't Christ have predicted the need for another prophetic time period after 1844? Yes.

Did the Son of God need the experiences of Israel not going directly into their promised land, and also the remainder of the nation's 1,500 year history in order to know the future Protestant slowness of heart to believe His promised return? No. Did the Lord God need any or all of Israel's histories to know that the Jews would require an extra 500 years, even after the lessons they learned from the Babylonian captivity (see Nehemiah

13:6-31), in order to prepare for their Messiah? No. Did His omniscience need recorded history to foreknow that He would have only a very small remnant from the nation not ruined by Babylonian paganism (see Malachi 2:11-13), that would keep their Messianic hope alive until He could send John the Baptist? No, the Lord didn't need any of these. He knew human nature; all along He knew what they would do. "He knew all men, and needed not that any should testify of man: for he knew what was in man" (John 2:24, 25).

Likewise, our omniscient Intercessor did not need those histories to know that it would take "five months" (Rev. 9:5), or 150+ literal years and many generations for the Advent movement to prepare a group to stand in the day when He would finally destroy Satan's work on earth. "For he knoweth our frame; he remembereth that we are dust" (Ps. 103:14). This does not excuse our reticence to believe God; but, it does magnify His abundant forbearance and foreknowledge. We could have done differently than Israel, and have hastened Christ's second coming. A speedier work by us would have prevented the greater tribulation that now must come. But, the delay was prophesied in Revelation 7:3, 9:5, and 10:6 because the Lord knew His last movement from beginning to end, "declaring the end from the beginning, and from ancient times the things that are not yet done" (Isa. 46:10). He knew the weakened, fallen natures of His beloved witnesses traveling down through the last 170+ years.

If then the Angel foreknew our need for a 170+ year delay, as the fifth and sixth trumpets indicate, why did He give His servant the words she wrote on pages 457 and 458 in *The Great Controversy*, quoted above? Here lies the mystery of "him who worketh all things after the counsel of his own will" (Eph. 1:11), whose "purposes know no haste and no delay" *The Desire of Ages*, p. 32. So much of His actions have seemed incomprehensible. Even if His work takes a mercifully long, circuitous route to achieve His ends, He is never early or late. He speaks time into being. He writes the schedule that includes an optional late completion; and it stands fast, wonderful in beauty.

> My counsel shall stand, and I will do all my pleasure (Isa. 46:10).

> So shall my word be that goeth forth out of my mouth: it shall not return unto me void, but it shall accomplish that which I please, and it shall prosper in the thing whereto I sent it. For ye shall go out with joy, and be led forth with peace: the mountains and the hills shall break forth before you into singing, and all the trees of the field shall clap their hands (Isa. 55:11, 12).

The Lord confidently commanded His word to Israel. Yet, the fulfillment of His will must rely on the faith and desire of His people to "go out with joy, and be led forth with peace." If that generation wouldn't desire His beautiful will, maybe their children would. Out of love He gave and gave His best gifts. He gave the gifts of life to men, but they snuffed and grumbled at them.

> And I gave them my statutes, and shewed them my judgments, which if a man do, he shall even live in them. Moreover also I gave them my sabbaths, to be a sign between me and them, that they might know that I am the LORD that sanctify them. But the house of Israel rebelled against me in the wilderness: they walked not in my statutes, and they despised my judgments, which if a man do, he shall even live in them; and my sabbaths they greatly polluted: then I said, I would pour out my fury upon them in the wilderness, to consume them (Eze. 20:11-13).

All the way from Egypt to Kadesh, the Lord foreknew Israel's 40 year wandering, though, prior to that wandering He sternly protested their complaining and lack of faith, a bad combination that could only end in disaster. He then gave them direction to enter right in (see Numbers 13:2). He commanded them to be His holy nation and His kingdom of priests. However, it would take a big departure at the base of Sinai before they could see their filthy rags and begin to comprehend the magnitude of His expectations of holiness.

At the end of the wilderness period, He foresaw many future backslidings after Moses' and Joshua's death; and yet, wrote a song to forestall those apostasies, if not to prevent them altogether.

> And the LORD said unto Moses, Behold, thou shalt sleep with thy fathers; and this people will rise up, and go a whoring after the gods of the strangers of the land, whither they go to be among them, and will forsake me, and break my covenant which I have made with them. Then my anger shall be kindled against them in that day, and I will forsake them, and I will hide my face from them, and they shall be devoured, and many evils and troubles shall befall them; so that they will say in that day, Are not these evils come

upon us, because our God is not among us? And I will surely hide my face in that day for all the evils which they shall have wrought, in that they are turned unto other gods. Now therefore write ye this song for you, and teach it the children of Israel: put it in their mouths, that this song may be a witness for me against the children of Israel. For when I shall have brought them into the land which I sware unto their fathers, that floweth with milk and honey; and they shall have eaten and filled themselves, and waxen fat; then will they turn unto other gods, and serve them, and provoke me, and break my covenant. And it shall come to pass, when many evils and troubles are befallen them, that this song shall testify against them as a witness; for it shall not be forgotten out of the mouths of their seed: for I know their imagination which they go about, even now, before I have brought them into the land which I sware (Deut. 31:16-21, cf Rom, 9:22, 23).

We needed to hear those stinging words from *The Great Controversy* in order for Christ to manage the movement's insubordination to His testimonies through Ellen White and to stave off apostasy until He has prepared the generation of the 144,000. Her song will testify against us as a witness and many will realize the love for us in the Lord's prophet and will receive a "spirit of grace and supplications" (Zech. 12:10). The heart rending of Mother White's many other similar exhortations throughout the Spirit of Prophecy will one day go out to all the holy seed sprinkled among the nations who will heed her words when they see Christ in her words, preached from His 144,000.

So shall they fear the name of the LORD from the west, and his glory from the rising of the sun. When the enemy shall come in like a flood, the Spirit of the LORD shall lift up a standard against him. And the Redeemer shall come to Zion, and unto them that turn from transgression in Jacob, saith the LORD (Isa. 59:19, 20).

The stinging words above from 1888 will prepare that final generation for those same requirements in the future. When the sleeping saints will awaken and trim their lamps, some will gladly receive the conviction of the Spirit. They will look for Jesus in the Bible and Spirit of Prophecy as the gospel requires. They will come to love the testimonies, and will loathe themselves (see Ezekiel 36:31) as the disciples did after their Master ascended to His Father. The same pressing together with Jesus and each other, as occurred among the apostles (see Acts 1:10-14; 2:1), will result in the same "supply of the Spirit of Jesus Christ" (Phil. 1:19) in the Latter Rain. They will have eternal rest, as the greatest "refreshing shall come from the presence of the Lord; and he shall send Jesus Christ" (Acts 3:19, 20, cf Rev. 14:12, 13). The Lord God will again walk among His church.

It seems that only under the heat of failure and remonstrations can the Lord's Adventists and Protestants adhere to the letter and spirit of His high standard. It's not impossible that Jesus knew we would repeat the history of the Israelites, who turned away from the Edenic land that flowed with milk and honey, and went into the oppressive wilderness to wander and wander and wander. Why should it sound far-fetched to apply this to the movement that is advancing with trepidation to the heavenly Canaan?

By prophesying the five month delay after 1844, Jesus must have anticipated our loss of first love and venture into Laodicea. Yet, He has remained the faithful and true Witness behind the Spirit of Prophecy counsels to patiently seal the movement that He has ordained. Like the laws of Moses bringing Israel to Christ, this time the Advent movement under the testimonies from Mrs. White has repeated a similar scenario. "Before faith came, we were kept under the [Spirit of Prophecy], shut up unto the faith which should afterwards be revealed. Wherefore the [Spirit of Prophecy] was our schoolmaster to bring us unto Christ, that we might be justified by faith" (Gal. 3:23, 24). That 2,000 year old architecture is *identical* to ours today, therefore Galatians 3 and the Early Rain are excellent news to the Advent movement. Now, we know where we are in the divine plan, and what direction to go to get the gift of God that the apostolic church received. We need to wrestle with the Schoolmaster and His Testimonies for the church. We need to disdain the gods of Spiritual Formation and receive Lord's blessed presence by faith from His written word. Then we will have a faith that will light up the world. "And they [will] not [be] able to resist the wisdom and the spirit by which [we speak]" (Acts 6:10).

The weak nature of man necessitates a repetition of lessons, correction after correction, instructing and reproving. Ultimately, after the passage of time, even over generations, God has a seed that should come, a humbled and surrendered, predestinated and chosen generation (see Galatians 3:19; Ephesians 1:10, 11; 1 Peter 2:9; Exodus 19:6), travailing to give birth to the Son (see Revelation 12:1). Finally, He gets the kingdom of priests and holy nation that He wanted many years before (see Psalm 24:6). And according to Revelation 10:3, Father and Son both are happy to have the long-awaited generation.

> Jesus has never forgotten His Advent movement. The Watcher on the shore has seen His fear-stricken men and women battling with the tempest. Not for a moment has He lost sight of His followers. With deepest solicitude His eyes have followed the storm tossed ship with its precious burden; for these people are to be the light of the world. As a mother in tender love watches her child, so the compassionate Master has watched over His Adventists. When their hearts are subdued, their unholy ambition quelled, and in humility they have prayed for help, it will be given them. (Adapted from *The Desire of Ages*, p. 381.)

> If they shall confess their iniquity, and the iniquity of their fathers, with their trespass which they trespassed against me, and that also they have walked contrary unto me; and that I also have walked contrary unto them, and have brought them into the land of their enemies; if then their uncircumcised hearts be humbled, and they then accept of the punishment of their iniquity: then will I remember my covenant with Jacob, and also my covenant with Isaac, and also my covenant with Abraham will I remember; and I will remember the land (Lev. 26:40-42).

And that final, chosen Adventist-Protestant generation of the 144,000 will never forget that "years ago" the Lord was ready to end the controversy. Humbled before God and with a new willpower driven by the gift of strong repentance, they will "trust to the guiding hand that has been with them in their past experience", they will "receive the third angel's message and proclaim it in the power of the Holy Spirit", "laboring unitedly in the work"; "the Lord will work mightily with their efforts", "a flood of light will be shed upon the world"; "the inhabitants of the earth will be warned, the closing work completed, and Christ will come for the redemption of His people." (See *The Great Controversy*, p. 457.)

Now that the delay is coming to an end, with delight we can more distinctly see that all along the Lord's hand was heavy; but thankfully, it was *always* on His closing movement. *According to Revelation 7 through 11, the Reformation and the Advent movements are still on His radar. Wonderful. Precious promise. Theme for the most profound meditation!* "As the heaven is high above the earth, so great is his mercy toward them that fear him" (Ps. 103:11). "For God hath concluded them all in unbelief, that he might have mercy upon all" (Rom. 11:32). "So then it is not of him that willeth, nor of him that runneth, but of God that sheweth mercy" (Rom. 9:16). As we consent, He will make us more precious than fine gold. His grace upon His closing movement grows clearer throughout Revelation chapters 7-11, especially chapter 11.

However, anyone who thinks he need not respond now and can extend this delay is gravely mistaken. All around the world we are seeing the same bulwarks going up around us that Jeremiah's Jerusalem saw. We're already tasting of "the sword, and of the famine, and of the pestilence".

> Behold the mounts, they are come unto the city to take it; and the city is given into the hand of the Chaldeans, that fight against it, because of the sword, and of the famine, and of the pestilence (Jer. 32:24).

> Son of man, what is that proverb that ye have in the land of Israel, saying, The days are prolonged, and every vision faileth?... Therefore say unto them, Thus saith the Lord GOD; There shall none of my words be prolonged any more, but the word which I have spoken shall be done, saith the Lord GOD (Eze. 12:22, 28).

This time, the Advent movement is going through, and the 144,000 will not fail, until Jesus returns in power. This next revival of Righteousness by Faith *will* catch on. It *must* catch on in you, my friend. It will be the Latter Rain which *will not* fade like all the previous revivals throughout sacred history; it simply will not. And the tribulation will make sure of that. Everyone who misses this next revival and reformation — or catches on, *but lets it slip away* — will do so at his eternal loss. The last great revival is coming. Prepare your heart and mind and body. The Latter Rain *will* come and go, with or without us. "We are not safe unless we are waiting and watching" *Last Day Events*, p. 42.

Chapter 7 Revelation Chapter 10: Preparation for the Latter Rain

If we had understood, in the 1848 Sabbath conferences, that heaven would give us 150 years in the fifth trumpet to prepare, would we have made good use of that time? We would have made terrible use of it. We would have "turned aside quickly out of the way which the LORD had commanded" (Deut. 9:16). Thank the Lord for His wisdom and mercy by not revealing the true interpretation of the fifth trumpet.

The Advent movement would be much different than it now is. The Papacy's Baalpeor lawless celebration and Spiritual Formation possibly would have entered the Remnant movement a century ago (see Judges 2:10, 11). Instead, our loving Saviour spared us those plagues until just recently, thanks to the constant intimations from the inspired commentary on the Bible, that though His movement of destiny was the object of His supreme regard, He had great concern over the path it would take. Christ could not reveal the 150 year delay, knowing the havoc that such knowledge would have brought into His beloved bride.

Revelation chapter 9 reveals the extra patience and lovingkindness of God in the 150 years and more, which the final group would need for the special work of purification and sealing. His people didn't want to leave this old world, as ancient Israel didn't want to leave the Egyptian and Babylonian captivities. Unbelief has held us here. We profess to believe that Jesus is coming. But, are we making plans for an extended stay here in spite of all the current wars and rumors of wars? Or, do we remind each other of His return and the Latter Rain? In conversation do we raise the subject of the sealing, or of the time of trouble?

> Then they that feared the LORD spake often one to another: and the LORD hearkened, and heard it, and a book of remembrance was written before him for them that feared the LORD, and that thought upon his name. And they shall be mine, saith the LORD of hosts, in that day when I make up my jewels; and I will spare them, as a man spareth his own son that serveth him. Then shall ye return, and discern between the righteous and the wicked, between him that serveth God and him that serveth him not (Mal. 3:16-18).

Are our hymns of praise to Him filled with the excitement for His soon return, which our forefathers had? Or, are they sung out of tradition just to relive our history? Do our songs mimic the joyful, robust singing of Elder White in his hope to be with Jesus for eternity? Is our music sung from the heart "as in the night when a holy solemnity is kept; and gladness of heart, as when one goeth with a pipe to come into the mountain of the LORD, to the mighty One of Israel" (Isa. 30:29)?

Is ours the deep gratitude to God and wholehearted worship that spontaneously happened when Moses first declared the word of the Lord to deliver captive Israel (see Exodus 4:30, 31)? Do we long to see Jesus as the apostles longed to see their resurrected Lord (see John 20:20)? To see Him return? (See Matthew 28:20; 1 Thessalonians 4:13-17; 2 Thessalonians 2:1; 1 Peter 1:3-5, 8; 5:4; 2 Peter 2:16; 3:12, 13; John 14:1-3; 1 John 3:2.)

So, the question remains, Are we anxious to hear that the Bridegroom is coming? Have we taken advantage of this gracious delay of the fifth and sixth trumpets for the return of the holy God, to purify ourselves "even as he is pure" (1 John 3:3)? Why are we waiting for Him to draw close to us through Spiritual Formation when He's already drawn close in the requirements of the Bible and the Spirit of Prophecy, and is waiting for us to make the next move to come to Him there in spirit?

At the end, through His long-suffering mercy, and under compounding difficulties, God will have a people who stand in the mayhem of the last great day, and with shining faces say, "Lo, this is our God" (Isa. 25:9). His bride will have made herself ready in His perfect character, "clean and white" (Rev. 19:8, cf Dan. 12:3, 10).

And because of His gracious forbearance and delay, no one will have anything for which to blame God if He has lost many of His unprepared children in the final shaking. The accuser will be silenced by God's merciful, long-suffering delay. Because of God's foresight and forbearance by His wise willingness to "lead on softly, according as the…children be able to endure" (Gen. 33:14), His grace will be sufficient forever. The accusations of the great controversy will never be voiced with regard to the last generation. But, let's not be among those shaken out; and let's patiently and caringly work to prevent others from doing the same. The six trumpets' delay that began in 1844 finishes the judgment on God's character in His Adventist saints. It declares that, for their sake, He tenderly and unweariedly waited for the truth to settle into them intellectually and spiritually. Simultaneously, the delay bides the time for a final and full development of the man of sin and "the hour of temptation, which shall come upon all the world, to try them that dwell upon the earth" (Rev. 3:10, cf 2 Thess. 2:8-12).

Revelation 10's "no more delay", spoken of in the prophetic context of the sixth trumpet/second woe period (between Revelation 9:21 and 11:14), points to some time after the five month time prophecy of the fifth trumpet that ended in 1999. At the end of the sixth trumpet, the second woe will be past, the seventh trumpet will begin to blow, which will finish the ripening process for both harvests of weeds and wheat (see Matthew 13:38-40), of the grapes and the grain (see Revelation 14:14, 18), and of the sea and the earth (see Revelation 10:2).

The expiration of the delay's first six trumpets and the transitioning into the seventh trumpet completes the whole period of final probation that was granted this world in 1844. That final offer of probation started when Jesus opened the seventh seal (see Revelation 6:17-7:3; 8:1). Then the trumpets began the delay to mercifully warn of Judgment Day and to provide for the necessary preparation to stand through the last great crisis when Jesus returns. The six trumpet probationary delay will close when the seventh will begin to sound before God (see Revelation 10:7; 11:15).

Let us clarify an important note in this part of the vision: Christ's sworn vow from Revelation 10:6 and 7 was not that there would be no more time or time prophecies after 1844. The message of His vow was that there would be no more *delay*, the "no more time" pronouncement that is yet to be made at the end of this present sixth trumpet. His "no shall be longer..." vow concerned the delay of Revelation 7:3 for accomplishing the investigative judgment and waiting for the glad tidings of God's soon-coming acquittal. It meant that *at the Latter Rain, just before the seventh trumpet blows (see Revelation 10:7), then* no more time would be given for sealing the Lord's people (see Revelation 7:3, 9; 9:4; 14:1). Then no more time would be granted to give God glory in preparation for His judgment (see Revelation 14:7). At the end of the delay only those sealed during the delay would be the wise virgins who would pipe and dance and rejoice that the Father's kingdom is restored to Him. No more time would be granted for the sealing and for becoming a wise virgin.

> *The concept of a fifth trumpet 150 year prophecy after 1844 does not contradict Ellen White's statements.*

The concept of a fifth trumpet 150 year prophecy after 1844 does not contradict Ellen White's statements from *Last Day Events*, as every compilation statement needs its context. Pages 35 and 36 of that book, entitled, *No Time Prophecy Beyond 1844*, has left a misconception in the minds of many. It must be read in the context of its pages 32-36, which deal with various persons' misuse of prophetic calculation. Ellen White wrote:

> I plainly stated at the Jackson camp meeting to these fanatical parties that they were doing the work of the adversary of souls; they were in darkness. They claimed to have great light that probation would close in October, 1884. I there stated in public that the Lord had been pleased to show me that there would be no definite time in the message given of God since 1844 [*Selected Messages*, bk. 2, p. 73 (1885)].

> Our position has been one of waiting and watching, with no time-proclamation to intervene between the close of the prophetic periods in 1844 and the time of our Lord's coming [*Manuscript Releases*, vol. 10, p. 270 (1888)].

> The people will not have another message upon definite time. After this period of time [Revelation 10:4-6], reaching from 1842 to 1844, there can be no definite tracing of the prophetic time. The longest reckoning reaches to the autumn of 1844 [*SDA Bible Commentary*, vol. 7, p. 971 (1900)].

When one looks closely at her statements from *Last Day Events*, pages 32-42, and their contexts from *Manuscript Releases*, volume 19 page 320, *Testimonies for the Church*, volume 4 pages 307-308, *Selected Messages*, book 2 page 73, and *Manuscript Releases*, volume 10 pages 268-270, he sees Ellen White writing that the uses people made of "tracing" "definite time" for "time-proclamation," such as William Miller gave, were in the way of "time-setters" and living upon "time excitement." They were using Bible prophecy as a crystal ball, predicting future events, living by thrill and emotion instead of by faith in Jesus' self-sacrificing love and obedience to God's Law.

Fulfillment of definite time prophecies, however, has always been discovered *after* the fact; and this holds true even for the correct event of William Miller's longest 2300 year prophetic proclamation. An interpretation of the fifth trumpet as a 150 year period beginning

Chapter 7 Revelation Chapter 10: Preparation for the Latter Rain

in 1849 does not break this rule, since this study *looks backward* to an overlooked, past fulfillment of prophetic time, rather than *predicting* a future prophetic event. Therefore, the conflicts disappear. Mrs. White's above statements agree perfectly with the connecting together of Revelation 7:3 and 9:4 which results in an interpretation of the fifth trumpet 150 year prophecy occurring after 1844.

> …the search is to be continued. Hitherto very much of the treasure found has lain near the surface, and was easily obtained. When the search is properly conducted every effort is made to keep a pure understanding and heart. When the mind is kept open and is constantly searching the field of revelation, we shall find rich deposits of truth. Old truths will be revealed in new aspects, and truths will appear which have been overlooked in the search. Ms 75, 1897, p. 3 *Manuscript Releases*, vol. 1, p. 37.

When we prayerfully overlay Revelation 7:3 and 9:4, setting aside prejudices and undue protectionism for the Lord's messenger, then we will not mishandle the word of God, but will place the Bible in its true supremacy. Mrs. White is an inspired commentator on the Bible, not over the Bible (see Daniel 9:2; 1 Corinthians 14:32); and she never once thought differently toward that stance. I don't write this lightly. I prize the Testimony of Jesus as the guiding light for these last days. But, we should heed all of Mrs. White's counsel as our duty — to let the Bible and the Bible alone be its foremost interpreter, interpreting scripture by line upon line, precept upon precept. And, newer interpretations must not undermine the older platform of truth. Isaiah 28:9, 10 mandates that God's children accept the plain understanding which comes from following the rule: *The Bible interprets itself; the Bible is its own expositor.*

This is not an appeal to set aside any of the above quotations from Ellen White. But, it does ask the Lord's people to understand them correctly, especially in light of the obvious statements of scripture. Understood correctly, Sr. White's messages in *Last Day Events* align perfectly with an interpretation that the seven trumpets take place after 1844, which accords with the typical Feast of trumpets that immediately preceded the typical Day of Atonement.

Even if the subtitle above those quotations were an honest mistake because the Trustees misunderstood her statements, the subtitle wording has still been greatly misleading. But, this misunderstanding on the part of the EGW Estate is reasonable in that the prophetic 5 month period was not completed in 1992 when the Trustees compiled *Last Day Events* and those quotations could not have been understood in their correct light until 1999 (see Deuteronomy 29:29).

Clearly, Revelation 7:3 and 9:4 both deal with the Seal of God in the forehead. They plainly speak the same wording; unmistakably, they are both telling of the same event. The former verse introduces the subject of the seal in the forehead, showing its commencement, and the latter warns the reader of the mighty obstacles to receiving it. Then comes the time period associated with the seal in the forehead: the fifth trumpet's five months. As honest Bible students in a holy and prophetic movement, how can we not correlate the two verses and apply their related prophetic five month time period to the delay called for in Revelation 7:1-3 and repeated in Revelation 10:6? The 150 year delay relating to the sealed book that is open in the hand of the Christ is the most pivotal theme within this core storyline of Revelation and is utmost vital for us today. The fifth trumpet shows us that the Advent movement is still on our Father's prophetic radar and it teaches the remnant church how to remain on His radar.

To knowingly disregard the obvious comparison of Revelation 7:3 and 9:4 in order to protect the church's historic interpretation of this prophecy is to silence the Spirit of truth. It is to attempt the work of sheltering the church's reputation that Christ will do without our help. We need to accept the truth when He gives it and counsel together concerning what we have learned — even with its raw vulnerability and initially unpalatable results. We should candidly record truth as truth "because it is right, and leave consequences with God" *The Great Controversy*, p. 460. "Christ's ambassadors have nothing to do with consequences. They must perform their duty and leave results with God" *The Great Controversy*, p. 609. This is what Daniel did (see Daniel 7:28; 8:27; 12:8-10; 1 Peter 1:10-13). And, do we not expect honest inclusion of all the evidence from nature and archeology by the scientific community, which would lead it to recant and to accept catastrophism and creationism? We need to do the same with all scriptural evidence regarding the light from the seven trumpets; and we will see the salvation of the Lord.

> New occasions teach new duties,
>
> Time makes ancient good uncouth;

They must upward still and onward,

Who would keep abreast of truth

Once to every man and nation, Seventh-day Adventist Hymnal, #606.

Fear of the unknown should not prevent researching new light from the Bible. God will protect His Advent movement and build it on a firmer foundation. He knows the way that His movement takes, and when He has tried it, it will come forth as gold.

John Robinson, pastor of the embarking Pilgrims implored them,

> "For my part, I cannot sufficiently bewail the condition of the reformed churches, who are come to a period in religion, and will go at present no farther than the instruments of their reformation. The Lutherans cannot be drawn to go beyond what Luther saw; ...and the Calvinists, you see, stick fast where they were left by that great man of God, who yet saw not all things. This is a misery much to be lamented; for though they were burning and shining lights in their time, yet they penetrated not into the whole counsel of God, but were they now living, would be as willing to embrace further light as that which they first received." — D. Neal, History of the Puritans 1:269 *The Great Controversy*, p. 292.

"I am very confident the Lord hath more truth and light yet to break forth out of His holy word.... Remember your promise and covenant with God and with one another, to receive whatever light and truth shall be made known to you from His written word; but withal, take heed, I beseech you, what you receive for truth, and compare it and weigh it with other scriptures of truth before you accept it; for it is not possible the Christian world should come so lately out of such thick antichristian darkness, and that full perfection of knowledge should break forth at once." — Martyn, vol. 5, pp. 70, 71 *The Great Controversy*, p. 291, 292. (**Read full statement in Appendix C.**)

What did Ellen White understand about the trumpets prophecy? In the *Ellen G. White Estate Research Documents* from the *Ellen G. White Writings Comprehensive Research Edition CD, 101 Questions on the Sanctuary and on Ellen White, F — Allegations of Errors and Mistakes, Question 55* we find this statement from EGW Estate researchers on the prevalence of Mrs. White's discussion of the seven trumpets.

55. Revelation 9 and Josiah Litch

[On the basis of his interpretation of Revelation 9:15 Josiah Litch predicted in 1838 that the Ottoman power would be broken in 1840.]

… Did Mrs. White say much about the seven trumpets?

No. This is the only known reference to Revelation 9 in all of Ellen White's writings and it appears, not in connection with an exegetical study of the Bible, but as part of her description of the Millerite movement…

In this commentator's view, Ellen White's statement (from *The Great Controversy*, p. 334, 335) was not an exegetical interpretation with respect to the seven trumpets, although she did refer to it as "another remarkable fulfillment of prophecy". For the full document from the Ellen White CD on this question, ***see Appendix A***.

And there is her one other statement on the trumpets.

> Solemn events before us are yet to transpire. Trumpet after trumpet is to be sounded; vial after vial poured out one after another upon the inhabitants of the earth. — 3SM 426 (1890) *Last Days Events*, p. 238.

That is taken from the following larger text.

> The battle of Armageddon will be fought. And that day must find none of us sleeping. Wide awake we must be, as wise virgins having oil in our vessels with our lamps. The power of the Holy Ghost must be upon us and the Captain of the Lord's host will stand at the head of the angels of heaven to direct the battle. Solemn events before us are yet to transpire. Trumpet after trumpet is to be sounded; vial after vial poured out one after another upon the inhabitants of the earth. Scenes of stupendous interest are right upon us and these things will be sure indications of the presence of Him who has directed in every aggressive movement, who has accompanied the march of His cause through all

the ages, and who has graciously pledged Himself to be with His people in all their conflicts to the end of the world. He will vindicate His truth. He will cause it to triumph. He is ready to supply His faithful ones with motives and power of purpose, inspiring them with hope and courage and valor in increased activity as the time is at hand *Selected Messages*, bk. 3, p. 426.

The above phrase, "scenes of stupendous interest" correlates to her statement from *Prophets and Kings*, page 537, "The present is a time of overwhelming interest to all living…. The Bible, and the Bible only, gives a correct view of these things." Other than Ellen White's above "trumpet after trumpet" statement from *Selected Messages*, the Spirit of Prophecy said nothing of the seven trumpets prophecy of Revelation. But, if Mrs. White fully endorsed Josiah Litch's explanation of the sixth trumpet, why, writing in her 1890 statement from the above quotation in *Selected Messages*, would she refer to other *trumpets* (plural). At a minimum, this would then total to eight trumpets, literally speaking, if Sr. White whole-heartedly believed the sixth trumpet was fulfilled in 1840. Otherwise, the above statement was not meant to refer to the Revelation trumpets.

Her statement above gives the impression that all the trumpets have yet to sound, and that that future event is in connection with the last plagues. She seems to make this statement in a literal sense, not interpreting the symbolic seven trumpets. Mrs. White may have been referring to the trumpet that Israel sounded at the close of the Day of Atonement on the Jubile year (see Leviticus 25:9) and which correlates with "the trump of God" 1 Thessalonians 4:16 and "the last trump" of 1 Corinthians 15:52. Therefore, her "trumpet after trumpet" was a general statement, not commenting on the seven trumpets of Revelation that follow Revelation 7:3 and of the sealing time of Revelation 9:4 during the remaining fifth and sixth trumpets.

Concerning Mrs. White's understanding of the symbolic seven trumpets, I can only give my best guess based on the very limited amount of her references to it. Her near dead silence on the seven trumpets prophecy leads me to conclude that concerning them she received no light from Jesus, and could not understand the details of the prophecy. She profusely published warnings and exhortations from Revelation chapter 7 and 14 that correctly concerned the sealing. But, she wrote essentially nothing on the sealing trumpets with regard to Revelation 9:4. She might have found the trumpets incomprehensible because of Revelation 9 verses 4 and 5 with their reference to the sealing and their inconceivably long time period. And, without confirming light from Christ on such a distant future time of possible fulfillment, silence was her rule of wisdom.

Based on her above statement from *Selected Messages*, book 2, page 73, as published in *Last Day Events*, pages 35 and 36, my thought is that Jesus withheld the light of the seven trumpets until the fifth trumpet would finish, as He has done to Bible students until the end of every other prophetic time period. "And now I have told you before it come to pass, that, *when it is come to pass*, ye might believe" (John 14:29). Now that the fifth trumpet has passed, we can look back and understand the fifth trumpet meaning and also its implications regarding our unfaithfulness to both righteousness by faith and to the spirit of our special work of purification. The worldwide events of late in this sixth trumpet time clearly point to the soon coming of the Latter Rain and, afterward, the chaos and satanic possession of the seventh trumpet period (see Revelation 11:18). Understanding the previously incomprehensible timeframe, and the issues of Revelation 8 and 9, we can have greater confidence and comfort in the validity of Bible prophecy, and of the written word of God in general. And this conclusion does no damage to Ellen White's gift of prophecy when we correctly understand inspiration. Her silence concerning a future prophecy authenticates her gift of inspiration and enhances her honest handling of the Holy Writ.

If Ellen White had understood the prophecies, why would she leave the major prophecy of the Revelation trumpets barely touched upon and not have lifted up her voice like a trumpet on its third angel connection? Why did Uriah Smith have much to say on the seven trumpets prophecy, but she had essentially nothing to say? And, why would she admonish us to continue to study Revelation for new light and truth to shine from it? Why her following statement?

> Sharp, clear conceptions of truth will never be the reward of indolence. Investigation of every point that has been received as truth will richly repay the searcher in finding precious gems. In closely investigating every jot and tittle which we think is established truth beyond controversy, in comparing Scripture with Scripture, searching to see if there is no flaw in their interpretation, *errors may be discovered* [emphasis mine].

Christ would have the searcher of the Scriptures sink the shaft down deeper into the mines of truth. If the search is properly conducted, precious jewels of inestimable value will be found. The word of God is the mine of the unsearchable riches of Christ. — Manuscript 143, 1897 *Manuscript Release,* vol. 16, p. 125.

Ellen White did not comprehend the seven trumpets prophecy correctly, and I must surmise that she knew that neither did our prophecy experts.

Despite the rarity and obscurity of her trumpets explanation, I have found Mrs. White's other inspiring, inspired statements, listed in this book's introduction, to be wonderfully and fearfully true. We need a kinship with her, but should tremble before her words. If we are reconciled to God and humbled by surrender to His Law and by the redemptive death of His Son, and we continue to study the prophecies, we will find precious new light still shining from them. In other words, the previous three Ellen White quotations from *Last Day Events*, which many folks use to say that there can be no time prophecies after 1844, and her other wise counsel *cautioning* the acceptance of new light, all need to be balanced with her statements from *Counsels to Writers and Editors*, chapters four and five. These chapters give positive guidance for testing new light, and they put forward advice for not outright prohibiting new light because it is new or creates controversy.

Especially do Revelation's seven trumpets show us prophetically where we are today and the nearness of the final movements of Satan and of the Lord, and both of their earthly agencies. More than any other Bible prophecy, the trumpets reveal spiritually related details of "the great final scenes in the history of our world".

The prophecies which the great I AM has given in His Word, uniting link after link in the chain of events, from eternity in the past to eternity in the future, tell us where we are today in the procession of the ages, and what may be expected in the time to come. All that prophecy has foretold as coming to pass, until the present time, has been traced on the pages of history, and we may be assured that all which is yet to come will be fulfilled in its order.

Today the signs of the times declare that we are standing on the threshold of great and solemn events. Everything in our world is in agitation.

Before our eyes is fulfilling the Saviour's prophecy of the events to precede His coming: "Ye shall hear of wars and rumors of wars.... Nation shall rise against nation, and kingdom against kingdom: and there shall be famines, and pestilences, and earthquakes, in divers places."

The present is a time of overwhelming interest to all living. Rulers and statesmen, men who occupy positions of trust and authority, thinking men and women of all classes, have their attention fixed upon the events taking place about us. They are watching the relations that exist among the nations. They observe the intensity that is taking possession of every earthly element, and they recognize that something great and decisive is about to take place, — that the world is on the verge of a stupendous crisis.

The Bible, and the Bible only, gives a correct view of these things. Here are revealed the great final scenes in the history of our world, events that already are casting their shadows before, the sound of their approach causing the earth to tremble, and men's hearts to fail them for fear *Prophets and Kings*, pp. 536, 537.

"In the days of the voice of the seventh angel, when he shall begin to sound, the mystery of God should be finished, as He hath declared to his servants the prophets" (Rev. 10:7). In light of the trumpets scenario up to this point by the correctly understood present sixth trumpet and past fifth trumpet which finished at the end of 1999, we can see from the prophecies of Revelation that terrible troubles are soon to break upon us and the world.

Let us now examine the extraordinary similarity between Revelation 10:7 and Daniel 12:7 and their bearing on the trumpets' prophecy.

And one said to the man clothed in linen, which was upon the waters of the river, How long shall it be to the end of these wonders? And I heard the man clothed in linen, which was upon the waters of the river, when he held up his right hand and his left hand unto heaven, and sware by him that liveth for ever that it shall be for a time, times, and an half; and when he shall have accomplished to scatter the power of the holy people, all these things shall be finished (Dan. 12:6, 7).

Chapter 7 Revelation Chapter 10: Preparation for the Latter Rain

The question Daniel heard: When will all these distressing visions of the desolation of God and His people be fulfilled, and come to an end? This question must refer, at the least, to the prophecy that he just witnessed in Daniel 11, which is an expanded version of the Daniel 8 vision. The first answer: "...a time, times, and an half". That is: when God gives the Dark Ages "mystery of iniquity" (2 Thess. 2:7, cf Dan. 7:23-26) a period to develop Satan's real poison against Christ's redemption of man (AD 538-1798), finishing at verse 39 of Daniel's chapter 11 prophecy. And, *then*: "...when he shall have accomplished to scatter the power of the holy people." In other words, the second part of "these wonders" of Daniel 12:6 occurs near the close of Daniel 11, when the desolating Papal supremacy spiritually decimates Christ's end-time holy religion and its people (see Daniel 11:40-43). "Scattering the power", the standard scripture phraseology of decimation, historically has always come to the holy people because they fully accept the temptation to disregard God's laws and to follow after other gods. It has often been repeated. This decimation fulfills the warning of Leviticus 18:24-30. While permitting Satan to decimate us may sound unloving of the God of love, it accords with His jealous punishments listed in Leviticus 26 and Deuteronomy 28, 29, and 32. He never sends pain "above that ye are able" (see 1 Cor. 10:13, cf 2 Cor. 12:9, 10); yet He will send pain that all can bear who are seeking Him (see Job 42:6; 1 Corinthians 13:7; Hebrews 12:6-11).

John's chapter 10 vision supplements the answer Daniel heard in his vision centuries earlier.

> And the angel which I saw stand upon the sea and upon the earth lifted up his hand to heaven, and sware by him that liveth for ever and ever, who created heaven, and the things that therein are, and the earth, and the things that therein are, and the sea, and the things which are therein, that there should be time no longer: but in the days of the voice of the seventh angel, when he shall begin to sound, the mystery of God should be finished, as he hath declared to his servants the prophets (Rev. 10:5-7).

Placing both of the above Daniel and Revelation verse seven texts line upon line, we see them speaking of the same end-time event, simply in different language. They then give a fuller meaning when blended. Collating them together, we get this picture of God's final work: "When He shall have accomplished to scatter the power of the holy people" "in the days of the voice of the seventh angel" "when he shall begin to sound" his trumpet, then "all these [wonders]", i.e. "the mystery of God" — "shall be finished", "as He hath declared to His servants the prophets." In *Appendix A* we have previously explained who are the holy people of Revelation.

The words "wonders" and "mystery" mean the same and superimpose each other. The wonders shown to Daniel and John, and later revealed to Ellen White, are the repeated vision of the heavenly great controversy, but re-played on earth during the fourth empire that followed the Babylonian (see Daniel 2:41-44; 7:8-26; 8:8-12, 14, 23-25; 11:21-39; Revelation 12:4; 13:1-10). Then, they are played out on earth a third time just prior to Jesus standing up to end the controversy (see Daniel 11:40-12:1; Revelation 13:11-17).

In verses 7 of both Daniel 12 and Revelation 10, the wonders seen by Daniel and the mystery of God revealed to John are that same Daniel 8:8-12 theme bound in the book sealed with seven seals, Satan's mysterious character assassination of God which only the desolation of Christ could unveil (see Revelation 5:5, 6). The Revelation chapter 10 un-openable mystery book of Daniel's "wonders" is fully unsealed at the removal of the Revelation 8:1 seventh seal in 1844, and is the book later open in the hand of the Angel clothed with a thick cloud of incense and glory, rapt in the joy of the Holy Ghost. His description indicates that at that time Christ will be standing inside the most holy precincts with His Most Holy Father. With the mystery charges resolved by Christ's crucifixion, and His people's humbling and sealing, They will both be finalizing the Most Holy atonement (see Revelation 10:1, 2; Leviticus 16:2, 13; Hebrews 9:28). They both are involved in the investigative judgment (the book of the God's great controversy being opened for investigation and Jesus' character in greatest abundance being specially imparted to His overcoming people to exonerate His Father). (See Revelation 5:1-5). From the beginning of our fall into sin, the Son's redemption of our race has worked toward the Father's acquittal; but the last generation's full acquittal of God will finalize that of all previous generations, so that their exoneration "without us should not be made perfect" (Heb. 11:40). Therefore, since the beginning of the seven trumpets, the open scroll in the Angel's hand has been revealing a God of love and righteousness to His humbled and repentant final generation on earth.

The mystery of God is the book that had bound up His reputation of unselfishness and credibility arising from Satan's charges against His Law (His character).

The mystery of God also includes His strange behavior of expelling Lucifer from his high position and quarantining him on Earth, and the invidious reaction by Lucifer toward his King's judgment against him.

The language of Revelation 10:5-7, compared with Daniel 12:5-7, confirms that the book which had infinitely bound God in Revelation chapter 5 relates directly with Daniel's visions of the great controversy between Michael and Satan. Prior to Earth's creation Lucifer had worked in heaven as he worked behind Babylon in the Old Testament and would later work behind the two phases of the little horn power (see Daniel 11:21-39, 40-45; Revelation 13:1-10, 11-17). He deceived into transgression a large share of the heavenly hosts, casting them down from heaven, and he stood up against Michael the great Prince of princes in heaven. (See Daniel 8:10-12; 11:21-23; 12:1, cf Revelation 12:4, 13-15.) Therefore, the Revelation 10 scene teaches us that the book in God's hand at the beginning of the Revelation (see Revelation 5:1) was not the book of Daniel; rather, it signified the mystery of God, i.e. the great controversy, veiled in the visions of Daniel, revealed in symbolism by the prophecies of John, and communicated even more clearly and abundantly by Ellen White after 1858.

The beautiful promise through Isaiah helps us understand God's "accomplished" scattering of "the power" of His "holy people".

> Comfort ye, comfort ye my people, saith your God. Speak ye comfortably to Jerusalem, and cry unto her, that *her warfare is accomplished*, that her iniquity is pardoned: for she hath received of the LORD's hand double for all her sins (Isa. 40:1, 2, cf Zech. 1:13-15).

"…for a time, times, and an half; and when he shall have accomplished to scatter the power of the holy people…" (Dan. 12:7). Isaiah 40:1, 2 and Daniel 12:7 have a common theme. The promise of completed scattering from Daniel 12:7 alludes to all the prophets' many prophecies of warfare and scattering, captivity and repentance, pardon and restoration.

> And the LORD saith, Because they have forsaken my law which I set before them, and have not obeyed my voice, neither walked therein;
>
> But have walked after the imagination of their own heart, and after Baalim, which their fathers taught them:
>
> Therefore thus saith the LORD of hosts, the God of Israel; Behold, I will feed them, even this people, with wormwood, and give them water of gall to drink.
>
> I will scatter them also among the heathen, whom neither they nor their fathers have known: and I will send a sword after them, till I have consumed them (Jer. 9:13-16).
>
> Then the LORD said unto me, Out of the north an evil shall break forth upon all the inhabitants of the land.
>
> For, lo, I will call all the families of the kingdoms of the north, saith the LORD; and they shall come, and they shall set every one his throne at the entering of the gates of Jerusalem, and against all the walls thereof round about, and against all the cities of Judah.
>
> And I will utter my judgments against them touching all their wickedness, who have forsaken me, and have burned incense unto other gods, and worshipped the works of their own hands (Jer. 1:14-16).
>
> Therefore will I scatter them as the stubble that passeth away by the wind of the wilderness.
>
> This is thy lot, the portion of thy measures from me, saith the LORD; because thou hast forgotten me, and trusted in falsehood (Jer. 13:24, 25).
>
> Because my people hath forgotten me, they have burned incense to vanity, and they have caused them to stumble in their ways from the ancient paths, to walk in paths, in a way not cast up;
>
> To make their land desolate, and a perpetual hissing; every one that passeth thereby shall be astonished, and wag his head.
>
> I will scatter them as with an east wind before the enemy; I will shew them the back, and not the face, in the day of their calamity (Jer. 18:15-17).
>
> Thus saith the LORD God of Israel; Behold, I will turn back the weapons of war that are in your hands, wherewith ye fight against the king of Babylon, and against the Chaldeans, which besiege you without the walls, and I will assemble them into the midst of this city.

And I myself will fight against you with an outstretched hand and with a strong arm, even in anger, and in fury, and in great wrath.

And I will smite the inhabitants of this city, both man and beast: they shall die of a great pestilence (Jer. 21:4-6).

And I will scatter toward every wind all that are about him to help him, and all his bands; and I will draw out the sword after them.

And they shall know that I am the LORD, when I shall scatter them among the nations, and disperse them in the countries (Eze. 12:14, 15).

O Lord, righteousness belongeth unto thee, but unto us confusion of faces, as at this day; to the men of Judah, and to the inhabitants of Jerusalem, and unto all Israel, that are near, and that are far off, through all the countries whither thou hast driven them, because of their trespass that they have trespassed against thee....

Yea, all Israel have transgressed thy law, even by departing, that they might not obey thy voice; therefore the curse is poured upon us, and the oath that is written in the law of Moses the servant of God, because we have sinned against him.

And he hath confirmed his words, which he spake against us, and against our judges that judged us, by bringing upon us a great evil: for under the whole heaven hath not been done as hath been done upon Jerusalem.

As it is written in the law of Moses, all this evil is come upon us: yet made we not our prayer before the LORD our God, that we might turn from our iniquities, and understand thy truth (Dan. 9:7, 11-13).

For thus saith the LORD, That after seventy years be accomplished at Babylon I will visit you, and perform my good word toward you, in causing you to return to this place.

For I know the thoughts that I think toward you, saith the LORD, thoughts of peace, and not of evil, to give you an expected end.

Then shall ye call upon me, and ye shall go and pray unto me, and I will hearken unto you. And ye shall seek me, and find me, when ye shall search for me with all your heart.

And I will be found of you, saith the LORD: and I will turn away your captivity, and I will gather you from all the nations, and from all the places whither I have driven you, saith the LORD; and I will bring you again into the place whence I caused you to be carried away captive (Jer. 29:10-14).

The accomplished scattering (see Jeremiah 25:27; Deuteronomy 32:32, 33) which Daniel heard would occur following his previously repeated 1,260 year papal subjugation of the church (see Daniel 7:25; 12:7; Revelation 11:2, 3, 7; 12:6, 14), must therefore relate to a Church Age, second captivity after 1798 as seen in Revelation 11. This scattering God would, at the very end, bring upon His holy people, His remnant Protestant and Adventist peoples — the people of the Book.

God has children, many of them, in the Protestant churches, and a large number in the Catholic churches, who are more true to obey the light to the very best of their knowledge than a large number among Sabbathkeeping Adventists who do not walk in the light. The Lord will have the message of truth proclaimed, that Protestants may be warned and awakened to the true state of things *The Ellen G. White 1888 Materials*, p. 377.

Additionally, the backdrop of Daniel's chapter 12:5-7 prophecy also has much in common to Revelation's chapter 10:1-7 vision. Daniel's vision must be a preview of John's. Daniel's vision of Christ standing on water and swearing by heaven in regard to God's accomplishment for scattering the power of His people must preview John's vision of Christ's left foot on the land and holding open in His hand the unsealed book, His opening and investigation of which had caused the desolations of the first six trumpets upon God's people, scattering His Protestants and, at last, sealing a remnant of them in their forehead. "My people hath forgotten me", says the Lord, and He has sent them a strong delusion to cause "them to stumble in their ways from the ancient paths, to walk in paths, in a way not cast up" (Jer. 18:15, cf Isa. 30:28) — lawlessness, spiritualism. He has shown many of His Protestants "the back, and not the face" (vs. 17), fed them "with wormwood, and [given] them water of gall to drink" (Jer. 9:15, cf Deut. 32:32-40; 29:20-28;

Rev. 14:7-11). He cannot lift up His countenance of blessing upon them.

[Both prophets saw Jesus. Enshrouded by a bright cloud was John's Angel, whose face shone like the Sun (see Matthew 17:2). Clothed in linen was Daniel's Man, no doubt whose "raiment was white and glistering", "shining, exceeding white as snow; so as no fuller on earth can white them" (Luke 9:29; Mark 9:3). The prophets' readiness to uphold the Mosaic priesthood, linen clothing was the best description Daniel could find to describe Christ's glory; likewise did Ezekiel (see Ezekiel 9:2, 3, 11; 10:2, 6, 7). Thus, both Daniel and John equally describe the glorious, shimmering (see also Ezekiel 1:7, 13) frame and resplendent countenance of Jesus, when the victorious Son, in behalf of His reconsecrated family, is fully purified and restored to His Father's presence in the Most Holy.

Thus, due to the close likeness between Daniel 12 and Revelation 10, we must understand their messages to be the same. Daniel's prophecy will have accomplished its determination to fully scatter and ultimately to blot out the sins of the end-time New Testament children of Israel. When Christ will have finally dealt with His Protestants at His closing work for investigating the opened book of God's mystery then their scattering will end (see Revelation 11:8-10) and their faith in Jesus resurrected (see verse 11, 12) to preach to the world. The people of God sprinkled throughout the nations will fear Jehovah and their lives will exonerate Him, like the purified remnant will. Then the kingdom of this fallen world will be received again into the kingdom of God (see Revelation 11:15). That investigation, or the measuring of the two witnesses, closes contextually near the final days of the sixth trumpet (see Revelation 11:14). Just prior to that, He will have those purified Adventist Protestants who He needs to "prophesy again" and bring the Latter Rain to the world (see Revelation 11:11-13). Then He will close up the investigative judgment upon His people throughout the world, after He has cleansed the heavenly sanctuary for those peoples. When He has cleansed the character of His extended family in the world, then the mystery investigation upon God's character will be complete. If this interpretation is not yet clear to the reader, it will be reanalyzed in the next chapter as we there look at the relation of Revelation 10:7 to Revelation 10:11 and 11:11-15.]

Judah's and Israel's "warfare...accomplished" and "iniquity...pardoned" from Isaiah's prophecy lays over Daniel's "accomplished", full scattering of the Adventist and Protestant churches' power, post-1999 (see Isaiah 40:2; Daniel 12:7). Isaiah 40 verses 1 and 2 help interpret Daniel 12 verse 7 to be an unexpectedly lengthy and doubly punishing captivity, first spiritually and then nationally. "She hath received of the LORD's hand double for all her sins" (Isa. 40:2). They left the covenant of obedience to their Lord. So He must war against His two religious movements, in order to let "their uncircumcised hearts be humbled", so that they can "then accept of the punishment of their iniquity" (Lev. 26:41) and receive the promised comfort of His blessed Spirit.

> When thy judgments are in the earth, the inhabitants of the world will learn righteousness (Isa. 26:9).

> They provoked him with their counsel, and were brought low for their iniquity. Nevertheless he regarded their affliction, when he heard their cry (Ps. 106:43, 44).

Extra punishment will be the dire but necessary conditions in the first time of trouble (see Revelation 11:11), which alone can result in God humbling His apocalyptic new covenant peoples, doing for them what they cannot do it for themselves. It will lead them to a real justification. As He did with the Jews and the Gentile world, only under a great and violent subjugation can He uproot the Protestants' stubborn pride and purify the springs of their hearts, giving faith and repentance to a renovated Israel of God which will lead to the Latter Rain of His Holy Spirit.

> The Spirit of the Lord GOD is upon me; because the LORD hath anointed me to preach good tidings unto the meek; he hath sent me to bind up the brokenhearted, to proclaim liberty to the captives, and the opening of the prison to them that are bound; to proclaim the acceptable year of the LORD, and the day of vengeance of our God; to comfort all that mourn; to appoint unto them that mourn in Zion, to give unto them beauty for ashes, the oil of joy for mourning, the garment of praise for the spirit of heaviness; that they might be called trees of righteousness, the planting of the LORD, that he might be glorified. And they shall build the old wastes, they shall raise up the former desolations, and they shall repair the waste cities, the desolations of many generations (Isa. 61:1-4).

The comfort to Israel from Isaiah 40:1, 2 speaks of a previous humbling punishment. This humbling is that which *brought Israel to the meekness* expressed in Isaiah 61:1 and in Leviticus 26:41. No one can be meek without getting humbled because no one is born with a meek human nature. Thus, the conquest of the northern Hebrew tribes by Assyria (see Isaiah chapters 36, 37) would be followed by real repentance among the Israelites and then a real divine pardon (see Jeremiah 3:11; 31:20, 27-34). And this prophecy from Isaiah 40 in the next verses tells of a later and bigger such humbling, repentance, and heavenly blessing after the Jews were dominated by four empires. At that time, those Jews from Judea and Galilee who sought out John the Baptist — and only they (see Luke 7:29, 30) — had been sufficiently humbled by the six centuries of pagan captivity that had scattered the pride of Jewish power.

> Like as I pleaded with your fathers in the wilderness of the land of Egypt, so will I plead with you, saith the Lord GOD (Eze. 20:36).

This long captivity we see as a Messianic prophecy by Isaiah foretelling of John the Baptist standing up to prepare the decimated and humbled people for the Messiah (see Isaiah 40:3-5). Next, Isaiah's Early Rain prophecy continues on to describe the Messiah's blessing to Israel and then to the nations:

> O Zion, that bringest good tidings, get thee up into the high mountain; O Jerusalem, that bringest good tidings, lift up thy voice with strength; lift it up, be not afraid; say unto the cities of Judah, Behold your God! Behold, the Lord GOD will come with strong hand, and his arm shall rule for him: behold, his reward is with him, and his work before him (Isa. 40:9, 10).

> For Zion's sake will I not hold my peace, and for Jerusalem's sake I will not rest, until the righteousness thereof go forth as brightness, and the salvation thereof as a lamp that burneth.... Behold, the LORD hath proclaimed unto the end of the world, Say ye to the daughter of Zion, Behold, thy salvation cometh; behold, his reward is with him, and his work before him (Isa. 62:1, 11).

> How beautiful upon the mountains are the feet of him that bringeth good tidings, that publisheth peace; that bringeth good tidings of good, that publisheth salvation; that saith unto Zion, Thy God reigneth! (Isa. 52:7).

Paul quotes from Isaiah 52:7 when he writes, "How beautiful are the feet of them that preach the gospel of peace, and bring glad tidings of good things!" (Rom. 10:15). The fulfillment of Isaiah 40 Paul relates to the work of the Messiah's church, the Early Rain of the Holy Spirit. And, in conjunction with Daniel 12:6 and 7, we will study its complementary Latter Rains when we later compare Revelation 10:11 and 11:11.

Using the help of Revelation 10 and 11 to describe the case of the Lord's last day people, Daniel's chapter 12:5-10 eschatological vision must then be born out of a subjugating captivity, a captivity that comes after the 1,260 year papal supremacy, and just before Jesus returns. "All these [Daniel 2, 7, 8, and 11 visions] shall be finished" after "a time, times, and an half" (Dan. 12:7, cf Dan. 7:25; Rev. 12:14) *and* "when he shall have accomplished to scatter the power of the holy people" (Dan. 12:6). The two phases of the Daniel 12:5-7 vision are also described individually in Daniel chapter 11 verses 21-39 and 40-44, in Revelation 13:1-10 and 11-18, and Revelation 11:3-6 and 7-10. Each second phase aligns with God's scattering of the holy people after 1798.

Today, the enemy of the Reformation has desolated us and we are moving increasingly deeper into bondage. Protestant America's faith and peace are being scattered by the trumpet locusts, though not yet completely desolate. The providentially driven warfare by modern Babylon, which has been underway for the past 168 years, will soon be fully accomplished. The Beast's and its locust army's present warfare in the Middle East is only the beginning of sorrows.

Following, then, the pattern of Isaiah 40's wonderful promises for the Diaspora Jews (the genuine revival under Ezra and Nehemiah, and later under Christ and the apostles), likewise the captivity predicted for Protestantism and its Remnant must be a time of hostile, divinely awarded judgment upon us, as revealed in Daniel's chapter 12:7 vision. This captivity must immediately precede a necessary, final exaltation of the Law from a second John the Baptist straight testimony movement and then a second manifestation of the Holy Spirit of God similar to the apostolic Early Rain, as seen in the verses above. Isaiah 40, Daniel 12, and Revelation 10 therefore speak to us of a revival of primitive godliness, the shaking, and the great and exciting Latter Rains. The Lord's grievous judgment is for our sake; Jesus' salvation means mercy *and* justice. If we don't want His justice, we don't get His mercy. And the corollary to that rule is, that the Lord can make good out of any bad thing (see Genesis 50:20).

> I will bear the indignation of the LORD, because I have sinned against him, until he plead my cause, and execute judgment for me: he will bring me forth to the light, and I shall behold his righteousness (Mic. 7:9).

Judgment is our friend. Its discipline and offense is for the ultimate good of the group of predestinated wise virgins who prepared beforehand by letting the counsels of Ellen White afflict their souls, leading them to need grace and repentance. Only they will not be cut off from the Advent movement. But, those unwise virgins who will be shaken out of the movement by Jesus' judgments will not be persuaded now to humble themselves before Him. Though many were to rise from the dead and urge them to do so, they will not whole-heartedly prepare by reading and heeding the Spirit of Prophecy, and be given genuine heart repentance. They aren't interested, or they think of it all as a farce. They must be made aware that the peaceful good times of today will end very suddenly, "with blinding force" *Maranatha*, p. 182. In the end a great gulf will separate the wise and the fooled (see Luke 16:26, 31).

"There should be time no longer" (Rev. 10:6). The conclusion of the Lord's trumpet plagues delay and His humiliation of the church will be the cause of the expectant joy at the heavenly throne (see Revelation 10:3). The trumpet tormenting plagues of Revelation chapter 9 have been God's work which, when fully accomplished, will produce a wicked world that proves that all the good works of human nature are only rottenness and filth (see Isaiah 40:6-8; Jeremiah 13:1-9). The holy people's self-revelation of their naturally unholy condition, together with the violence filling the earth, will facilitate the humbling that creates "the meek" (Isa. 61:1, cf Lev. 26:41; Eze. 9:4) among the remnant Protestants and Adventists. Their own power scattered, being humbled and meek, now God can give them His power. When viewed through the Daniel 12:7 glasses, the Protestants and Adventists are the current object of the Isaiah chapters 40, 52, 62 promises quoted above, and those holy people will give the Loud Cry with the fourth angel of Revelation 18.

> In all their affliction he was afflicted, and the angel of his presence saved them: in his love and in his pity he redeemed them; and he bare them, and carried them all the days of old.... As a beast goeth down into the valley, the Spirit of the LORD caused him to rest: so didst thou lead thy people, to make thyself a glorious name (Isa. 63:9, 14).

> We have this treasure in earthen vessels, that the excellency of the power may be of God, and not of us. We are troubled on every side, yet not distressed; we are perplexed, but not in despair; persecuted, but not forsaken; cast down, but not destroyed; always bearing about in the body the dying of the Lord Jesus, that the life also of Jesus might be made manifest in our body (2 Cor. 4:7-10).

The conglomerate Daniel 12-Revelation 10-Isaiah 40 punishing prophecy precedes Christ's promise that "his reward is with him" (Isa. 40:10, cf Rev. 22:12). "The Lord GOD will come with strong hand" (Isa. 40:10, cf Acts 3:19-21). By the scattering, doubled punishment passing upon the last day holy people, they are doubly humbled. In the mighty and humbling power of His Spirit "his work" can be "before him", as His people will then be quickened to take the gospel work to the ends of the earth.

"His arm shall rule for him" over His family by righteousness by faith by seeing Jesus in the Law and coming to Him.

> The LORD hath made bare his holy arm in the eyes of all the nations; and all the ends of the earth shall see the salvation of our God. Depart ye, depart ye, go ye out from thence, touch no unclean thing; go ye out of the midst of her; be ye clean, that bear the vessels of the LORD. For ye shall not go out with haste, nor go by flight: for the LORD will go before you; and the God of Israel will be your rereward [rearguard] (Isa. 52:10-12).

The promises will be new again:

> This is the covenant that I will make with them after those days, saith the Lord, I will put my laws into their hearts, and in their minds will I write them; and their sins and iniquities will I remember no more (Heb. 10:16, 17).

Thus saith the LORD, In an acceptable time have I heard thee, and in a day of salvation have I helped thee: and I will preserve thee, and give thee for a covenant of the people, to establish the earth, to cause to inherit the desolate heritages;

That thou mayest say to the prisoners, Go forth; to them that are in darkness, Shew yourselves. They shall feed in the ways, and their pastures shall be in all high places.

They shall not hunger nor thirst; neither shall the heat nor sun smite them: for he that hath mercy on them shall lead them, even by the springs of water shall he guide them (Isa. 49:8-10, cf Rev. 7:14-17).

Sing, O heavens; and be joyful, O earth; and break forth into singing, O mountains: for the LORD hath comforted his people, and will have mercy upon his afflicted (Isa. 49:13).

And he shall sit as a refiner and purifier of silver: and he shall purify the sons of Levi, and purge them as gold and silver, that they may offer unto the LORD an offering in righteousness.

Then shall the offering of Judah and Jerusalem be pleasant unto the LORD, as in the days of old, and as in former years (Mal. 3:3, 4).

His discipline fulfilled in the end time 144,000 and having accomplished their humbling and surrender, His comfort can at that point be recommenced by a second apostolic revival. Thus, Daniel's "scattering" by providence working behind world events since 1849 must be appropriated by God's people in these closing days of Earth's history. Especially do the events since 1999 provide them a guiding light in preparation for the difficult, full scattering of their civil and religious freedom and economic might, all of which today are just over the horizon. Everything that can be shaken will be shaken. The storm will come with blinding force. We must, therefore, be trained in godliness, which "is profitable unto all things" (1 Tim. 4:7, 8), and that includes "bodily exercise" and the other seven laws of health. "They that wait upon the Lord shall renew their strength" (Isa. 40:31, cf vs. 29, 30) a waiting which desires physical fitness, and which invites physical exercise as well as spiritual and mental. Let us be fasted and prayed, practiced and perfected and prepared, busy at His gospel work when the Latter Rain comes before the abomination of desolation stands in the holy place (see Matthew 24:14, 15). At this urgent time in the investigative judgment, employment simply for the sake of working and paying bills God has *strictly* forbidden (see Leviticus 23:25-32). We must be about our Father's business in our occupations.

Behold, I come quickly (Rev. 22:12).

Evidently, the Latter Rain will be a short period, spoken of as happening "quickly" (Rev. 11:14), "in one hour" (Rev. 18:10, 17, 19), before probation closes during "the days" (Rev. 10:7) that commence the seventh trumpet — "the days of the voice of the seventh angel, when he is about to sound [the] trumpet" (Rev. 10:7) *Interlinear Greek-English New Testament*. The delay of the seventh seal finished is that which the Most Holy Angel rejoiced over with His Father in Revelation 10:1-3.

> "...a short period just before they [the seven last plagues] are poured out, ... trouble will be coming on the earth.... At that time the "latter rain," or refreshing from the presence of the Lord, will come, to give power to the loud voice of the third angel" *Early Writings*, p. 85.

This short period foretells the full settling in and sealing of the character of Christ in His troubled children around the world. "Christ in you, the hope of glory" (Col. 1:27) completely clears God of all charges. His judgment has come and He is justified by their acceptance of humiliation and its perfect work of reproducing His character in them. The 144,000 have permitted Christ to purify them and by faith they can serve Him in His temple. Because of the perfected faith and life of Jesus in them God can then cleanse His sanctuary in toto. The beautiful promise from Jeremiah and repeated in Hebrews will be seen again in the Latter Rain.

> For this is the covenant that I will make with the house of Israel after those days, saith the Lord; I will put my laws into their mind, and write them in their hearts: and I will be to them a God, and they shall be to me a people.... For I will be merciful to their unrighteousness, and their sins and their iniquities will I remember no more (Heb. 8:10-12, cf Jer. 31:31-34).

The work of righteousness shall be peace; and the effect of righteousness quietness and assurance for ever (Isa. 32:17).

Precious, very precious promises.

"...in the days of the voice of the seventh angel, when he shall begin to sound..." (Rev. 10:7).

> And it shall come to pass in that day, that the great trumpet shall be blown, and they shall come which were ready to perish in the land of Assyria, and the outcasts in the land of Egypt, and shall worship the LORD in the holy mount at Jerusalem (Isa. 27:13).

> In that day shall the branch of the LORD be beautiful and glorious, and the fruit of the earth shall be excellent and comely for them that are escaped of Israel. And it shall come to pass, that he that is left in Zion, and he that remaineth in Jerusalem, shall be called holy, even every one that is written among the living in Jerusalem: when the Lord shall have washed away the filth of the daughters of Zion, and shall have purged the blood of Jerusalem from the midst thereof by the spirit of judgment, and by the spirit of burning (Isa. 4:2-4).

Christ in Revelation 10:7 speaks of an outstanding time for His church even though spiritualistic lawlessness and carnal vice then fills Satan's church of the sixth trumpet. This we will see again in Revelation chapter 11. These happy days come just prior to the end of God's sixth trumpet's woe and seventh trumpet's worldwide close of probation. From the beginning, through His many prophets, God predestinated this long-awaited time, "as He hath declared to his servants the prophets" (Rev. 10:7). The fruition of the Latter Rain, the future gospel harvest of the final ripening, is "the days" over which the majestic Godhead rejoiced in Revelation 10:3. The sealed believers will be walking in all the light from heaven. They will enjoy a communion with heaven and a fellowship with one another that has not been seen since apostolic times. Their regeneration of faith in the only true God, their genuine disinterested love will show that they are Christ's children, and they will draw many to trust Jesus.

> He brought me up also out of an horrible pit....

> And he hath put a new song in my mouth, even praise unto our God: many shall see it, and fear, and shall trust in the LORD (Ps. 40:2, 3).

> They continued stedfastly in the apostles' doctrine and fellowship, and in breaking of bread, and in prayers. And fear came upon every soul: and many wonders and signs were done by the apostles. And all that believed were together, and had all things common; and sold their possessions and goods, and parted them to all men, as every man had need. And they, continuing daily with one accord in the temple, and breaking bread from house to house, did eat their meat with gladness and singleness of heart, praising God, and having favour with all the people. And the Lord added to the church daily such as should be saved (Acts 2:42-47).

> If we walk in the light, as he is in the light, *we have fellowship one with another*, and the blood of Jesus Christ his Son cleanseth us from all sin (1 John 1:7).

> Behold, I and the children whom the LORD hath given me are for signs and for wonders in Israel from the LORD of hosts, which dwelleth in mount Zion (Isa. 8:18).

That which was made glorious in the Early Rain had no glory in this respect, by reason of the glory that will excel in the Latter Rain.

The ancient prophecies to Israel will be fulfilled as they were at Pentecost and in the apostolic church by a second revival of primitive godliness not seen since the days of the apostles. To those who will have the Son, who will be "strengthened with might by his Spirit in the inner man" (Eph. 3:16), multitudes of needy, weakened souls will cling, as many did to Paul. They will be freed from the reproach of God, His rebuke brought on by their involvement in Baal's one world religion of fifth trumpet gall and wormwood. The punishing subjugation sent from the Lord in the first time of trouble, and His true people's resulting humility and consecration will allow Him to rejoin in His movement on earth, again wafting upon them His Spirit in their soul. And they will reap an abundant harvest as every one of them eschews worshiping and praying to the Holy Spirit, and gathers around Jesus.

> The LORD will create upon every dwelling place of mount Zion, and upon her assemblies, a cloud and smoke by day, and the shining of a flaming fire by night: for upon all the glory shall be a defence. And there shall be a tabernacle for a shadow in the daytime from the heat, and for a place of refuge, and for a covert from storm and from rain (Isa. 4:5, 6).

Chapter 7 Revelation Chapter 10: Preparation for the Latter Rain

Therefore the redeemed of the LORD shall return, and come with singing unto Zion; and everlasting joy shall be upon their head: they shall obtain gladness and joy; and sorrow and mourning shall flee away (Isa. 51:11).

LORD, thou hast been favourable unto thy land: thou hast brought back the captivity of Jacob.

Thou hast forgiven the iniquity of thy people, thou hast covered all their sin. Selah.

Thou hast taken away all thy wrath: thou hast turned thyself from the fierceness of thine anger.

Turn us, O God of our salvation, and cause thine anger toward us to cease.

Wilt thou be angry with us for ever? wilt thou draw out thine anger to all generations?

Wilt thou not revive us again: that thy people may rejoice in thee?

Shew us thy mercy, O LORD, and grant us thy salvation.

I will hear what God the LORD will speak: for he will speak peace unto his people, and to his saints: but let them not turn again to folly.

Surely his salvation is nigh them that fear him; that glory may dwell in our land.

Mercy and truth are met together; righteousness and peace have kissed each other.

Truth shall spring out of the earth; and righteousness shall look down from heaven.

Yea, the LORD shall give that which is good; and our land shall yield her increase.

Righteousness shall go before him; and shall set us in the way of his steps (Ps. 85).

The delay of our redemption has ended, "in the days of the voice of the seventh angel, when he is about to sound [the] trumpet" (Rev. 10:7) *Interlinear Greek-English New Testament*. Humanity has divided into two classes — the holy and the unholy, the peaceful and the angry, the happy and the hateful, the righteous and the unrighteous, the just and the unjust, the grossly filthy and the brightly cleaned. (See Revelation 22:17; 19:8; Daniel 12:10.) This division occurs just prior to the seventh trumpet peal in heaven.

Until the spirit be poured upon us from on high, and the wilderness be a fruitful field, and the fruitful field be counted for a forest (Isa. 32:15).

That fullest revelation of God through the holy love, purity, and mercy of His children resulted in the fourth angel of Revelation 18, a human cooperation with the Lord which brought down Babylon. As we saw when we overlaid Revelation 10:7 with Daniel 12:7, the great controversy of sin and Satan cannot end until God has fully scattered the pride of His people (see Leviticus 26:19), planting them together with Christ in humiliation, and raising them up again in newness of life. Protestant Christianity will suffer through the first time of trouble both for punishment and discipline. This suffering is the necessary prerequisite for the predestinated Advent movement (see Ephesians 1:11; Romans 8:29; 11:26; Revelation 19:3-8; Genesis 3:15; Galatians 3:19) that gives the call to the world, "Come, come out of Babylon". Then, the whole church of Christ, sprinkled around the planet, will be ready to meet her Lord. And so all Israel shall be saved, as it is written.

And the Redeemer shall come to Zion, and unto them that turn from transgression in Jacob, saith the LORD. As for me, this is my covenant with them, saith the LORD; My spirit that is upon thee, and my words which I have put in thy mouth, shall not depart out of thy mouth, nor out of the mouth of thy seed, nor out of the mouth of thy seed's seed, saith the LORD, from henceforth and for ever (Isa. 59:20, 21, cf Rom. 11:26, 27).

The Redeemer's scattering of the power of the holy people would result in their fall and rising again, His comfort and untold blessing upon them.

However, the Daniel 12:7 scattering by the desolation which God had warned He would bring upon Israel must be understood, not if but *when* they would leave Him and His just, and good covenant and laws — after all that He had done to deliver, protect, and provide for them (see Deuteronomy 30:1-3; Deuteronomy 31:16-18; Acts 20:28-31). The inevitable scattering would come to them due to their inevitable following after another god and his spiritualistic worship that had depraved the heathen world. (See Leviticus 18:24-28; Jeremiah 7:29-34; 9:1-16.)

I will give peace in the land, and ye shall lie down, and none shall make you afraid: and I will rid evil beasts out of the land, neither shall the sword go through your land.

And ye shall chase your enemies, and they shall fall before you by the sword.

And five of you shall chase an hundred, and an hundred of you shall put ten thousand to flight: and your enemies shall fall before you by the sword.

For I will have respect unto you, and make you fruitful, and multiply you, and establish my covenant with you.

And ye shall eat old store, and bring forth the old because of the new.

And I will set my tabernacle among you: and my soul shall not abhor you.

And I will walk among you, and will be your God, and ye shall be my people.

I am the LORD your God, which brought you forth out of the land of Egypt, that ye should not be their bondmen; and I have broken the bands of your yoke, and made you go upright.

But if ye will not hearken unto me, and will not do all these commandments;

And if ye shall despise my statutes, or if your soul abhor my judgments, so that ye will not do all my commandments, but that ye break my covenant:

I also will do this unto you; I will even appoint over you terror, consumption, and the burning ague [fever], that shall consume the eyes, and cause sorrow of heart: and ye shall sow your seed in vain, for your enemies shall eat it.

And I will set my face against you, and ye shall be slain before your enemies: they that hate you shall reign over you; and ye shall flee when none pursueth you.

And if ye will not yet for all this hearken unto me, then I will punish you seven times more for your sins.

And I will break the pride of your power... (Lev. 26:6-19).

As we have said, today Protestants and their Remnant are the holy people — the people of the Book. We, the Reformation Protestants are all the ones spoken of in Daniel's chapter 12:5-8 vision who, after the 1,260 year period of papal supremacy, would partake of the privileges of the apostolic church. The houses of Israel and of Judah, the two former recipients of heaven's blessings, failed in this mission throughout the Old Testament era. They failed according to the prophetic song of Moses in Deuteronomy chapter 32 by involving with worship to false gods. And according to Daniel 12 and Revelation 11, for the same reason would the Protestant Reformation and the Advent movement fail. Protestantism's cause of failure was rebellion against the wonderful statutes of the Lord and involvement with the self-exalting worship of Baal. Adventism's cause of failure is copying the pattern set by the Protestant churches. Therefore, God must scatter the Protestant and Adventist power and pride, so that on the day of Christ's Second Advent, "no flesh should glory in his presence" (1 Cor. 1:29).

The vision of Daniel chapter 12 and repeated by John in Revelation chapter 10 and 11, especially when laid over the histories of the two houses of ancient Israel, say that the Sunday denominations and Sabbatarian Adventism would both lose their hold on Christ, even if they would keep up the external appearance of loyalty to the truth given them. The everlasting gospel would suffer. It says that righteousness by faith would disappear from both groups; self-sufficiency would bear sway; a works based religion from Babylon would sneak in. And, celebration of empty presumption would prevail instead. This fallen condition would make their evangelism and victory over sin negligible, and eventually inspire them with persecution upon the obedient, small remnant.

> The prophets shall become wind, and the word is not in them (Jer. 5:13).

> They have healed also the hurt of the daughter of my people slightly, saying, Peace, peace; when there is no peace (Jer. 6:14).

> Behold, I am against them that prophesy false dreams, saith the LORD, and do tell them, and cause my people to err by their lies, and by their lightness (Jer. 23:32).

> For there shall be no more any vain vision nor flattering divination within the house of Israel (Eze. 12:24).

Is not my word like as a fire? saith the LORD; and like a hammer that breaketh the rock in pieces? (Jer. 23:29).

There were false prophets also among the people, even as there shall be false teachers among you (2 Pet. 2:1).

All the denominations' celebration, the "peace and prosperity, and the…feasting and merrymaking," (*Patriarchs and Prophets*, p. 103) break God's commandment during this judgment time of Earth's history. We are in the antitypical Day of Atonement, and in that period of time God commands His people to be examining themselves and mortifying their carnal natures through the Spirit of His Law and grace (see Leviticus 23:27, 29; 2 Corinthians 13:5; Romans 7:25-8:13).

This is a time of holy *solemnity* to ensure that the Spirit of Prophecy has humbled us (see Deuteronomy 31:1-7; Isaiah 30:29). The Testimony of Jesus has been our schoolmaster, to bring the Protestant movement to Christ that we might surrender and be sealed by faith. In this awful time of human experience we are to fear before God in love. We are not only to be called, but chosen; and not only to be chosen, but to be faithful to the end (see Revelation 17:14; Hebrews 3:14; Matthew 24:13). We must remember the lesson of temperance given to Gideon's men, or we will miss the big event of the Latter Rain. We must remain sober even when partaking of heaven's special bounties upon Protestantism today. We are to be "they that use this world, as not abusing it: for the fashion of this world passeth away" (1 Cor. 7:31, cf vs. 29, 30) (see Judges 7:1-7). We are to "fear God, and give glory to him; for the hour of his judgment is come" (Rev. 14:7).

At other similar days of judgment, prior to His visitations God required the same sober frame of mind, laying stringent guidelines to be strictly heeded. Such requirements had to be obeyed lest the wrath of the Lord break out upon the nation. Those self-denying principles echo down to our day.

And they shall eat the flesh in that night, roast with fire, and *unleavened* bread; and with *bitter* herbs…. And thus shall ye eat it; with your loins girded, your shoes on your feet, and your staff in your hand; and ye shall eat it in haste: it is the LORD's passover. For I will pass through the land of Egypt this night, and will smite all the firstborn in the land of Egypt, both man and beast; and against all the gods of Egypt I will execute judgment: I am the LORD (Ex. 12:8, 11, 12).

And the LORD said unto Moses, Go unto the people, and sanctify them to day and to morrow, and let them wash their clothes, and be ready against the third day: for the third day the LORD will come down in the sight of all the people upon mount Sinai. And thou shalt set bounds unto the people round about, saying, Take heed to yourselves, that ye go not up into the mount, or touch the border of it: whosoever toucheth the mount shall be surely put to death: there shall not an hand touch it, but he shall surely be stoned, or shot through; whether it be beast or man, it shall not live: when the trumpet soundeth long, they shall come up to the mount. And Moses went down from the mount unto the people, and sanctified the people; and they washed their clothes. And he said unto the people, Be ready against the third day: come not at your wives (Ex. 19:10-15, cf 1 Cor. 7:29-31).

Escape for thy life; *look not behind thee neither stay thou in all the plain*, escape to the mountain, lest thou be consumed (Gen. 19:17).

And so, since the start of "the hour of temptation, which shall come upon all the world" (Rev. 3:10), the message from Revelation to all living has been one of unmistakable, emphatic warning. "Woe, woe, woe, to the inhabiters of the earth…!" (Rev. 8:13). Affliction of soul, self-examination, genuine surrender to the requirements of God are mandatory; lawless, grace-only gospel and celebration are forbidden.

I will take from them the voice of mirth, and the voice of gladness, the voice of the bridegroom, and the voice of the bride, the sound of the millstones, and the light of the candle. And this whole land shall be a desolation, and an astonishment (Jer. 25:10, 11).

Yes, we are called to rejoice in the Lord.

Mercy rejoiceth against judgment (Jas. 2:13).

Ye shall rejoice before the LORD your God, ye, and your sons, and your daughters, and your menservants, and your maidservants, and the Levite that is within your gates (Deut. 12:12).

> Rejoice in the Lord alway: and again I say, Rejoice (Phil. 4:4).

> The love which Christ diffuses through the whole being is a vitalizing power…. It implants in the soul, joy that nothing earthly can destroy, — joy in the Holy Spirit, — health-giving, life-giving joy *Ministry of Healing*, p. 115.

And,

> Although the fig tree shall not blossom, neither shall fruit be in the vines; the labour of the olive shall fail, and the fields shall yield no meat; the flock shall be cut off from the fold, and there shall be no herd in the stalls: yet I will rejoice in the LORD, I will joy in the God of my salvation (Hab. 3:17, 18).

But, while perfect love casts out all fear of man and Satan (see 1 John 4:18; Hebrews 13:6), genuine agape love will never allow rejoicing in the Lord to be done *at the expense* of its fear of the Lord.

> Serve the LORD with fear, and rejoice with trembling (Ps. 2:11).

> Like as a father pitieth his children, so the LORD pitieth them that fear him (Ps. 103:13).

Fearing the Lord creates no torment, but rather it creates confidence in the perfect right to the peace and joy of abiding under His wings (see Psalm 103:17; Philippians 4:4, 5; 2 Corinthians 7:1, Hebrews 4:1; 10:27-31; 12:9, 21, 25-29; 1 Peter 5:8). We must ever keep our eye single to His strong Law while we rejoice in His strong grace (see Isaiah 30:27-30). And this agape love the Spirit of God alone can accomplish, so long as we hold fast to the Son.

> Kiss the Son, lest he be angry, and ye perish from the way, when his wrath is kindled but a little. Blessed are all they that put their trust in him (Ps. 2:12).

We must put faith in the Law-enforcing Prince (see Psalm 99:4; Proverbs 16:10, 15; 20:2; 22:11) who is also a comforting Saviour. If we trust in His mercy and He has justified us before God, we then would love God and be reconciled to His Law, His Bible, His Spirit of Prophecy. We would love the loving reproofs, instructions, and corrections of our new Prince and Saviour, as much as we love our Prince and Saviour (see John 14:15; 3:33; 8:31).

Whoever rejects the Prince's strong testimony, that person does not know Him and discern His true love. Such a person is still alienated from the Son, His Law, and His strong love (see Isaiah 11:1-6; 8:3-11; John 7:24; 3:20, 21; 13:8). If that person is not accepting His strong testimony, then his rejoicing is empty. He is not rejoicing in the Law-enforcing Prince; he is not in the Spirit, and retains his old nature. And, without the "Spirit of Christ" (Rom. 8:9) he is "none of his" (Rom. 8:9).

Jesus was "full of grace and truth" (John 1:14), as His Father is full of justice and mercy. Loving-kindness and judgment, reverential fear toward His Father filled Christ (see Isaiah 11:2), even on His deepest subconscious level. His was not horse laughter or holy giggling or confusion in worship. He was the Prince of peace and the Author of peace. His custom was to reverence His Father's sanctuary and to keep the Sabbath holy (see Luke 4:16; Leviticus 19:30). Like David (see Psalm 18:35) and like Paul (2 Corinthians 5:14), Christ did as agape love does. Joined to His Father at conception, Jesus was filled with His Father's Spirit; and with joyful obedience He served His Abba, His God, His Saviour (see Luke 1:47; Titus 2:10). So will His reconciled children when filled with all the fullness of God — from His Law, His gospel, and His Spirit.

Let us turn away from the insurgence of celebration in the Advent movement. Mutually exclusive — poles apart — the special work of purification by the church sober and militant is in opposition to celebration of empty presumption by a church assuming itself already victorious.

Likewise is Spiritual Formation the mutual enemy of the Spirit of Prophecy. Spiritual Formation remains aloof from humbling reproof, correction, and instruction in righteousness (see 2 Timothy 3:16), that so largely make up the inspiration of Ellen White and every prophet of the Bible. The Law worketh wrath in the unconverted host of Spiritual Formation until he surrenders to the heavy hand of God (see Psalm 1:4; 32:4). Otherwise, he stands before a jealous God without a union with His Son. Spiritualism won't allow that soul to be commanded and condemned by the Law of God because subtle, satanic pride fuels the Spiritual Formation discipline as demons weave their rebellion into the disciple's character. By the biblical standards of 2 Timothy 3:16-4:4, 7, 8 the last days stand-off goes in favor of the Spirit of Prophecy and plainly condemns Spiritual Formation. That medieval mystical escape reinvented by Ignatius Loyola is being perpetuated by his modern army of Baalim prophets from the abyss. Spiritual Formation is the original false prophet. All who leave the Testimonies that came from Jesus and go to this strong delusion of a grace-only good news will do so to their eternal ruin. The true spokesperson for the Lord will mix into his good news the strong news of a Law that has been put aside and in need of restoration.

> It is no marvel that the church is not vivified by the Holy Spirit's power. Men and women are setting aside the instruction Christ has given. Anger and covetousness are gaining the victory, and the soul temple is full of wickedness, so that there is no room for Christ. Men, unheeding the words of the Saviour, follow their own perverse ways. They take themselves into their own hands, rejecting reproofs and warnings, until the candlestick is moved out of its place, and spiritual discernment is confused by human ideas. Men set the law of God aside to follow the light of their own imagination. All who love Jesus will search the Scriptures, that they may know and do his will. In God alone is our strength. In quietness and forbearance we shall conquer. Those who reveal the patience of Christ will obtain deliverance. They will share in the triumph of their Master. "Blessed are they that do his commandments, that they may have right to the tree of life, and may enter in through the gates into the city" *Southern Watchman*, January 1, 1907 par. 10, 11.

Many mistake the sensual, spiritualistic exercises of Spiritual Formation for the spirituality and moral guidance of the Spirit of Prophecy. To them, these two diametrically opposed guiding lights look similar. Yet, appearances can be deceiving.

> The track of truth lies close beside the track of error, and both tracks may seem to be one to minds which are not worked by the Holy Spirit, and which, therefore, are not quick to discern the difference between truth and error *Selected Messages*, bk. 1, p. 202.

> As truth and error appear so near akin, minds that are not guided by the Holy Spirit will be led to accept the error and, in so doing, place themselves under the power of Satan's deceptions. In thus leading people to receive error for truth, Satan is working to secure the homage of the Protestant world *Christ Triumphant*, p. 324.

The person we worship determines the very character of worship. Likewise, the character of worship indicates the person we seek to please and worship, as we saw in the vain celebration in honor to Jehovah at the base of Mount Sinai. True worship of the "blessed and only Potentate, the King of kings, and Lord of lords" (1 Tim. 6:15) accepts His Law's powerful, fatherly reproof and correction, to the people and to the leaders, alike (see Psalm 40:8-10). As the labor pangs of Christ's return are growing stronger and closer together, true and false worship will most assuredly become the issue of these last days of the three angels' messages (see Revelation 14:7).

Not every kind of worship in Jehovah's name is acceptable to Him. "God is a Spirit: and they that worship him must worship him in spirit and in truth" (John 4:24). Spirited worship alone is not acceptable to the holy God if it is dodging the truth about sin. Whether to those inside the church or outside of it, the Holy Spirit of God is no respecter of persons. "When he [the Comforter] is come, he will reprove the world of sin, and of righteousness, and of judgment" (John 16:7, 8). Genuine, humbled worship appreciates God's full authority to condemn sin. Genuine, humbled worship loves the high standard that He sets (see Psalm 2:11, 12). True reverential worship hangs on every word of biblical truth preached.

"This is the condemnation, that light is come into the world, and men loved darkness rather than light, because their deeds were evil. For every one that doeth evil hateth the light, neither cometh to the light, lest his deeds should be reproved. But he that doeth truth cometh to the light, that his deeds may be made manifest, that they are wrought in God" (John 3:19-21). Spiritual Formation does not allow the Law of God to rebuke sin, and it ends in the condemnations of Revelation 18:2. Spiritual Formation and celebration are worship to Satan, the son of treachery and deception (see Daniel 11:21-23; 8:25). By his flattering peace he destroys many. The celebrator of vanity "bless[es] himself in his heart, saying, I shall have peace, though I walk in the imagination of mine heart, to add drunkenness to thirst" (Deut. 29:19). Therefore, such worship is lawless and abominable to God (see Proverbs 28:9).

Even though Aaron invoked the name, "the LORD" as authorization to celebrate at Sinai, the characteristics of Baal worship — the flattering and celebrating of other gods, the immodesty, and drunkenness — told of its satanic origin (see Deuteronomy 12:29-32). "And when Aaron saw it [the golden calf he had just fashioned], he built an altar before it; and Aaron made proclamation, and said, To morrow is a feast to the LORD [Heb. Y*ᵉhôvâh*]" (Ex. 32:5).

Could Jehovah accept the golden calf, the nakedness, and the partying at His feet, because it was done in His name? "They did flatter him with their mouth, and they lied unto him with their tongues" (Ps. 78:36). The Lord made plain His reaction for all future attempts to repeat a similar apostasy.

> And the LORD said unto Moses, Go, get thee down; for thy people, which thou broughtest out of the land of Egypt, have corrupted themselves: they have turned aside quickly out of the way which I commanded them.... Now therefore let me alone, that my wrath may wax hot against them, and that I may consume them.... And it came to pass, as soon as [Moses] came nigh unto the camp, that he saw the calf, and the dancing: and Moses' anger waxed hot, and he cast the tables out of his hands, and brake them beneath the mount (Ex. 32:7, 8, 10, 19).

Who we worship directly affects whose character we develop. All who worship and love Jehovah receive His humble and happy character and His indelible seal in their forehead. All who worship and love Baal receive his character and his mark. The Lord God will not long forbear with His people to serve lord Baal alongside of Himself (see 1 Samuel 5:1-5; Ezekiel 8:6-18). Neither can we involve ourselves with Spiritual Formation and with empty, emotion-based celebration worship, and remain in the principle-based and redemptive Advent movement. Everyone who will cling to Spiritual Formation rather than afflict his soul before the Spirit of Prophecy will cut himself off from Jehovah.

> If thou do at all forget the LORD thy God, and walk after other gods, and serve them, and worship them, I testify against you this day that ye shall surely perish (Deut. 8:19).

> When thou shalt beget children, and children's children, and ye shall have remained long in the land, and shall corrupt yourselves, and make a graven image, or the likeness of any thing, and shall do evil in the sight of the LORD thy God, to provoke him to anger: I call heaven and earth to witness against you this day, that ye shall soon utterly perish from off the land whereunto ye go over Jordan to possess it; ye shall not prolong your days upon it, but shall utterly be destroyed (Deut. 4:25, 26).

As He had done through Moses, Jesus worked strongly through Ellen White to ensure that the smooth and glossy abomination of Spiritual Formation would never desolate His movement. She clearly understood the mandate of Moses and Paul,

> Preach the word; be instant in season, out of season; reprove, rebuke, exhort with all longsuffering and doctrine. For the time will come when they will not endure sound doctrine; but after their own lusts shall they heap to themselves teachers, having itching ears; and they shall turn away their ears from the truth, and shall be turned unto fables (2 Tim. 4:2-4).

Hear her warning to the Spiritual Formation preachers:

> Saith the Lord: "They have healed the hurt of the daughter of My people slightly, saying, Peace, peace; when there is no peace." "With lies ye have made the heart of the righteous sad, whom I have not made sad; and strengthened the hands of the wicked, that he should not return from his wicked way, by promising him life." Jeremiah 8:11; Ezekiel 13:22.

> "Woe be unto the pastors that destroy and scatter the sheep of My pasture!... Behold, I will visit upon you the evil of your doings." "Howl, ye shepherds, and cry; and wallow yourselves in the ashes, ye principal of the flock: for your days for slaughter and of your dispersions are accomplished;... and the shepherds shall have no way to flee, nor the principal of the flock to escape." Jeremiah 23:1, 2; 25:34, 35, margin.

> Ministers and people see that they have not sustained the right relation to God. They see that they have rebelled against the Author of all just and righteous law. The setting aside of the divine precepts gave rise to thousands of springs of evil, discord, hatred, iniquity, until the earth became one vast field of strife, one sink of corruption. This is the view that now appears to those who rejected truth and chose to cherish error....

> ... Unfaithful pastors have prophesied smooth things; they have led their hearers to make void the law of God and to persecute those who would

keep it holy. Now, in their despair, these teachers confess before the world their work of deception. The multitudes are filled with fury. "We are lost!" they cry, "and you are the cause of our ruin;" and they turn upon the false shepherds. The very ones that once admired them most will pronounce the most dreadful curses upon them. The very hands that once crowned them with laurels will be raised for their destruction *The Great Controversy*, page 655.

Mrs. White prevented every approach by the Spiritual Formation enemy of the gospel, no matter how distant it was. So far as possible, she closed every avenue by which Satan could enter. Her spiritual perceptions were clear; she had developed strength and decision of character, and through the aid of the Holy Spirit she was able to detect Satan's approaches, and to resist his power. Spiritual Formation subtly wars against Christ's sealing message from the Spirit of Prophecy. The kingdom of God has its foundation in the Law of God. The science of salvation begins with the science of humbling the proud heart. Reproof, correction, and instruction in righteousness are an offense to Spiritual Formation, which concentrates on feeling and offers a sensual presence of "God". It requires no faith that works without sight and has no need of a Saviour from the wretchedness of exceedingly sinful sin. But, if Jesus will not be received as a Saviour from exceeding sinfulness, He will be no Saviour at all. "If I wash thee not, thou hast no part with me" (John 13:8).

No less did Israel's eloping with Baal's worship of familiar spirits war against the Lord's statutes and laws through Moses. Those statutes and laws alone could teach the children of Israel the faith and discipline needed for an endless relationship with Jehovah and possession of Canaan.

They made a calf in Horeb, and worshipped the molten image.

Thus they changed their glory into the similitude of an ox that eateth grass.

They forgat God their saviour, which had done great things in Egypt;

Wondrous works in the land of Ham, and terrible things by the Red sea.

Therefore he said that he would destroy them, had not Moses his chosen stood before him in the breach, to turn away his wrath, lest he should destroy them.

Yea, they despised the pleasant land, they believed not his word:

But murmured in their tents, and hearkened not unto the voice of the LORD.

Therefore he lifted up his hand against them, to overthrow them in the wilderness:

To overthrow their seed also among the nations, and to scatter them in the lands.

They joined themselves also unto Baal-peor, and ate the sacrifices of the dead.

Thus they provoked him to anger with their inventions: and the plague brake in upon them.

Then stood up Phinehas, and executed judgment: and so the plague was stayed (Ps. 106:19-30).

Both celebrations at Sinai and at Baalpeor produced such grave results as should never be forgotten by the Advent movement. On the very border of the land of promise Satan interposed to tempt Christ to destroy the Exodus movement by bringing the women of Moab to tempt the men of Israel into worshiping "devils" (Deut. 32:17). Yet, with this lesson put brightly before us through sacred history, will the Advent movement repeat the same perilous blasphemy on the borders of our heavenly Canaan, by copying the celebrations inspired by devils and accepted by the fallen denominations surrounding us? Will we blindly obey these Spiritual Formation modern priests of Baal who are following the error of the house of Judah, and say with them, "The LORD seeth us not; the LORD hath forsaken the earth" (Eze. 8:12)?

What did the Lord command with regard to those agents of Baal worship?

Vex the Midianites, and smite them: for they vex you with their wiles, wherewith they have beguiled you in the matter of Peor (Num. 25:17, 18, cf 2 Ki. 9:30-37).

If we want to be among the 144,000 we must remember their description that says, "These are they which were not defiled with women" (Rev. 14:4). The Baalpeor Ashtoreth worship also helps interpret the symbolic locusts of the fifth trumpet having seductive "hair as the hair of women" (Rev. 9:8).

From *Healthy Living*, 1169-1173, p. 280, 281

The Modern Church Repeating the History of Ancient Israel. The trials of the children of Israel, and their attitude just before the first coming of Christ, illustrate the position of the people of God in their experience before the second coming of Christ *Review and Herald*, 1890, No. 7.

Satan's snares are laid for us as verily as they were laid for the children of Israel just prior to their entrance into the land of Canaan. We are repeating the history of that people *T., No. 31*, p. 156.

Their history should be a solemn warning to us. We need never expect that when the Lord has light for his people, Satan will stand calmly by and make no effort to prevent them from receiving it. Let us beware that we do not refuse the light God sends, because it does not come in a way to please us.... If there are any who do not see and accept the light themselves, let them not stand in the way of others *T., No. 33*, p. 256.

"I call heaven and earth to record this day against you, that I have set before you life and death, blessing and cursing; therefore choose life, that both thou and thy seed may live; that thou mayest love the Lord thy God, and that thou mayest obey his voice, and that thou mayest cleave unto him; for he is thy life, and the length of thy days; that thou mayest dwell in the land which the Lord sware unto thy fathers, to Abraham, to Isaac, and to Jacob, to give them."

This song was not historical but prophetic. While it recounted the wonderful dealings of God with his people in the past, it also foreshadowed the great events of the future, the final victory of the faithful when Christ shall come the second time in power and glory *Patriarchs and Prophets*, p. 467.

The apostle Paul plainly states that the experience of the Israelites in their travels has been recorded for the benefit of those living in this age of the world, those upon whom the ends of the world are come. We do not consider that our dangers are any less than those of the Hebrews, *but greater* [emphasis mine] *T., V. III*, p. 358.

The Lord permitted His church in the wilderness to rejoice. However, as Revelation chapter 11 will show, those Christians worshipped in sackcloth. That is, the constant persecution suffered by the church in the wilderness naturally checked any possibility of antinomian fanaticism, imaginary holiness, and righteousness by emotion. But, because the beast has ascended from the bottomless pit, because the devil knows his time is short, and because the investigative judgment has begun, Jesus needs to rein in our rejoicing as His Father reined in His during His earthly ministry and in Gethsemane.

I have a baptism to be baptized with; and how am I straitened [*sunechō*, "afflicted"] till it be accomplished! (Luke 12:50).

The true celebrations of the church victorious won't come until *after* the earth is destroyed by Jesus' return and we live before the throne of God (see Revelation 7:15-17). Until then, we are cast down but not destroyed, persecuted but not forsaken. We are still the solemn church militant. We are still on the battlefield — not sad and morose, but thankful for the Law's solidifying faith and justification. We suck honey and olive oil out of the stone Law. Christ's honey and olive oil makes us satisfied to be "sober" and "vigilant" (1 Pet. 5:8), denying self and giving God praise by obeying His high moral standard, which is given to us from the Bible and the Spirit of Prophecy. We must be witnesses "clothed in sackcloth" (Rev. 11:3), content in whatever our condition. We must afflict our souls — mortifying the flesh through the Spirit (see Romans 8:13, 9) until we obtain righteousness from the God of our salvation (see Galatians 3:19; 5:5; Isaiah 30:18; Hebrews 10:36; Psalm 24:3-6). Beholding the character of Christ through His Law, we continually gain a deeper loathing of our fallen nature (see Romans 8:23, 10; Ezekiel 36:26). Our nature Jesus must remake through His divine influence during this delay awaiting the next phases of this sixth trumpet experience: the time of humbling trouble; the Latter Rain of God's Spirit; the great time of trouble; and the time of Jacob's trouble. With His Spirit in us as we bow before His strong, humbling, sealing Testimonies, the coming troubles will all be doable.

After Christ's announcement of no more delay, Christ gives John the book of God's judgment for his consumption (see Revelation 10:8, 9). This book written on all its surfaces is the same communiqué that Moses received from Sinai and that Ezekiel was given in vision. Testing, unvarnished truth would be joyous in his mouth, but dismal in his stomach. Like Ezekiel (see Ezekiel 2:6-3:7), John here dramatizes the scroll's effect upon every prophet who the Lord chooses.

As the sure result of wrestling with the Law, the prophets truly believe the promise, "I will be merciful to their unrighteousness, and their sins and their iniquities will I remember no more" (Heb. 8:12, cf Isa. 6:5-7; Hab. 2:4). They receive "the promise of the Spirit through faith" (Gal. 3:14, vs. 23). The conscious forgiveness of sin and acceptance with God leaves a depth of peace that surpasses anything this world offers.

Being "made partakers of the Holy Ghost," the prophets have "tasted of the heavenly gift," (Heb. 6:4), "their sins and iniquities" remembered no more. "Remission of these", and therefore "no more offering for sin" (Heb. 10:17, 18) is sweeter than honey and lighter than manna. Their "hearts sprinkled from an evil conscience", they have "a good conscience" (1 Tim. 1:5), and their actions "washed with pure water" give them a whole new start on life. Now, having "a true heart in full assurance of faith" (Heb. 10:22) and "no more conscience of sins" (Heb. 10:2) the servants receive such wonderful health-giving blessings, mentally and physically, that they want everyone to have the same (see Psalm 103:2-4; John 4:29). "The remission of sins that are past, through the forbearance of God" (Rom. 3:25) is their life's burden to assist others to secure.

> As I knelt and prayed, suddenly my burden left me, and my heart was light.… One of the mothers in Israel came to me and said: "Dear child, have you found Jesus?" I was about to answer, "Yes," when she exclaimed: "Indeed you have, His peace is with you, I see it in your face!" Again and again I said to myself: "Can this be religion? Am I not mistaken?" It seemed too much for me to claim, too exalted a privilege. Though too timid to openly confess it, I felt that the Saviour had blessed me and pardoned my sins (*Testimonies for the Church*, vol. 1, p. 17, 18).

After surrendering to the Law's censures, the refreshing acceptance and abiding presence of the Comforter is naturally a joyful occasion to the prophet, and much to be coveted. However, later the prophet must set the condemnation of the Law before others. There can be no peace between God and the sinner until He first makes war with our natural born self-sufficiency (see Romans 7:7-12, cf Isaiah 45:7; Revelation 19:11). No flesh can glory in Christ's presence. In order to arouse the need for forgiveness in the sinner, sin must be condemned. Once surrendered to His condemnation, as young Ellen finally did, then that one too can receive the life-giving, invigorating, transforming grace of God.

With great mercy, that new messenger of the Lord requires of others nothing differently than the burden of the Lord's condemnation, which he or she had suffered before submitting to it, and which ended in perfect peace and health-giving rest. They view condemnation of sin, spoken in love, as an absolute essential for good order and discipline, it possessing the greatest potential for redemption and blessing. Once pride has been humbled, the anointing of the Spirit will bring new life and strength to the heart and mind.

> Those who take Christ at His word, and surrender their souls to His keeping, their lives to His ordering, will find peace and quietude. Nothing of the world can make them sad when Jesus makes them glad by His presence. In perfect acquiescence there is perfect rest *The Desire of Ages*, p. 331.

This duty, however, falls back on the prophets in cruel aggressions, which weigh heavily on their softened heart.

> After I came out of vision, everything looked changed; a gloom was spread over all that I beheld. Oh, how dark this world looked to me. I wept when I found myself here, and felt homesick. I had seen a better world, and it had spoiled this for me. I told the view to our little band in Portland, who then fully believed it to be of God. That was a powerful time. The solemnity of eternity rested upon us. About one week after this the Lord gave me another view and showed me the trials I must pass through, and that I must go and relate to others what He had revealed to me, and that I should meet with great opposition and suffer anguish of spirit by going. But said the angel, "The grace of God is sufficient for you; He will hold you up." *Early Writings*, p. 20.

> I have attended to my business given me of God. I have injured no one. I have spoken to the erring the words God has given me. Of course, I could not compel them to hear. Those who had the benefit of Christ's labors were just as enraged against Him as the enemies are against me. I have only done my duty. I have

spoken because compelled to speak. They have not rejected me, but Him who sent me. He has given me my work.... I am watched, every word I write is criticised, every move I make is commented upon.... I leave my work and its results until we gather about the great white throne. Do you see the Spirit of Christ in this watching, in these suspicions, in these conjectures, these suppositions? What right have they to suppose, to conjecture, to misinterpret my words? to misstate me as they do? *Selected Messages*, bk. 3, p. 351.

I...journey from place to place, meeting cold hearts, distant looks and severe speeches *Spiritual Gifts*, vol. 2, p. 128.

Despite the belligerent reactions, the Spirit drives His prophets to give His messages in power. Under the hand of God, "fire proceedeth out of their mouth, and devoureth their enemies" (Rev. 11:5, cf Zech. 12:5, 8). Of the Holy One, the Prince of mercy and Servant of grace, Isaiah foretold: "With righteousness shall he judge the poor, and reprove with equity... He shall smite the earth with the rod of his mouth, and with the breath of his lips shall he slay the wicked" (Isa. 11:4). "Out of his mouth went a sharp twoedged sword" (Rev. 1:16). "Christ was a faithful reprover" *Education*, p. 79.

Jesus did not suppress one word of truth, but He uttered it always in love. He exercised the greatest tact and thoughtful, kind attention in His intercourse with the people. He was never rude, never needlessly spoke a severe word, never gave needless pain to a sensitive soul. He did not censure human weakness. He spoke the truth, but always in love. He denounced hypocrisy, unbelief, and iniquity; but tears were in His voice as He uttered His scathing rebukes. He wept over Jerusalem, the city He loved, which refused to receive Him, the way, the truth, and the life. They had rejected Him, the Saviour, but He regarded them with pitying tenderness. His life was one of self-denial and thoughtful care for others. Every soul was precious in His eyes. While He ever bore Himself with divine dignity, He bowed with the tenderest regard to every member of the family of God. In all men He saw fallen souls whom it was His mission to save *Steps to Christ*, p. 12.

Full of grace and truth, Jesus' work to save was always balanced. The Prophet of prophets reproved in order to pardon. The Physician of physicians wounded, but only to heal. He was a Wonderful Counselor, and a convicting Comforter. As Prince of peace He would slay sin "with the rod of his mouth" (Isa. 11:4). Yet, as our faithful High Priest who reads the mind and is never insensitive to our sorrows, Jesus would never overdo His discipline. "Faithful are the wounds of a friend" (Prov. 27:6); and Jesus is a friend, the best kind of friend. Yet, notwithstanding the exalted demeanor of His transparent motives, His obvious compassion and His affection, His divine character and His holy message, Jesus was dogged. He was trapped, and finally incriminated because of His strong, pure expressions from the mouth of God.

Like their Master, the hope of each spokesperson for the Lord is that the people will humble themselves before God and will then surrender to the strong conviction from Christ's high standard (see 2 Samuel 2:7-13). The prophet speaks strongly to the mind and heart of the people in order to repeat the powerful language that had weighed upon the prophet before his surrender to the Lord (see Isaiah 6:1-7). The messenger of conviction only desires them to have the same conviction that brought him to Jesus (see Galatians 3:23, 24; John 6:37), for them to know the eternal peace with God which he has come to possess.

> For the hurt of the daughter of my people am I hurt; I am black; astonishment hath taken hold on me (Jer. 8:21).

The prophet's "obedience is fulfilled," therefore he has "a readiness to revenge all disobedience" (2 Cor. 10:6). He loves his neighbor as himself, and, in obedience to Leviticus 19:17, his surrender to the God of Law drives him to spare the erring one from the sure results of transgression. He desires to give the gift of God to the erring, the panacea for all of human ills.

Sanctified of all self-exaltation and hard-heartedness, the love of Christ constrains the servant of the Lord to reprove sin so that the sinner need no longer suffer from sin's destructive grip, and neither need his loved ones suffer from his sin.

The conflict between the softened heart of the Lord's messenger and the required message of tough love for the people, creates a nausea in his sorrowful soul. This combination of new-born joy and then the later message-bearing is what we are seeing represented when

John eats the opened scroll. The merciful spokesperson for God cries continually within,

> But if ye will not hear it, my soul shall weep in secret places for your pride; and mine eye shall weep sore, and run down with tears, because the LORD's flock is carried away captive (Jer. 13:17).

> Oh that my head were waters, and mine eyes a fountain of tears, that I might weep day and night for the slain of the daughter of my people! (Jer. 9:1).

Yet, this deeply tensioned soul gives the perfect picture of God's disposition toward sin. Fearing divine judgment on sinners, the conflicted messenger is exactly who the righteous Judge can trust to not carelessly mix pride or unnecessary pain into the loving message to warn His people away from their sins and from eternal destruction. The prophet balances the bitter message with compassion from the honey of Christ's Spirit. He or she reproves with an aching heart; tears are blended with their voices, light and much power mixed with sweet love, joy, and peace.

> *For rebellion is as the sin of witchcraft, and stubbornness is as iniquity and idolatry. Because thou hast rejected the word of the LORD, he hath also rejected thee from being king.... And Samuel said unto him, The LORD hath rent the kingdom of Israel from thee this day, and hath given it to a neighbour of thine, that is better than thou. And also the Strength of Israel will not lie nor repent: for he is not a man, that he should repent.... And Samuel came no more to see Saul until the day of his death: nevertheless Samuel mourned for Saul* (1 Sam. 15:23, 28, 29, 35).

In spite of the prophet's much internal conflict from the terrible ordeal, the message is mingled with audible, earnest hope for the rebel. Yet, the reality is that most of the people hear from the prophet only what they think to be selfish anger — the evil spirit that rules their heart.

> Evil men understand not judgment: but they that seek the LORD understand all things (Prov. 28:5).

Thus, to protect his domain, the evil one influences the rebels to ignorantly wage war against the precious condemnation that would bring them to need God's goodness and receive His precious Holy Spirit. So the rebels work to silence the messenger, magnifying his or her angst. They destroy the credibility and authority of the spokesperson. They malign and smear his character and his assumed personal agenda.

> It is enough for the disciple that he be as his master, and the servant as his lord. If they have called the master of the house Beelzebub, how much more shall they call them of his household? (Matt. 10:25).

"The words of a talebearer are as wounds, and they go down into the innermost parts of the belly" (Prov. 26:22). The soul of the Lord's servant is ground upon day and night by the unbelieving, vengeful, earthy-minded multitudes, who he only longs to see reconciled and happily at peace with God, with His righteousness and love reigning over the earth. This explains the sweetness in John's mouth and his dyspeptic stomach.

> Blessed are ye, when men shall revile you, and persecute you, and shall say all manner of evil against you falsely, for my sake. Rejoice, and be exceeding glad: for great is your reward in heaven: for so persecuted they the prophets which were before you (Matt. 5:11, 12).

Jeremiah had the whole sweet to bitter experience that came from John's similar dramatization.

> The LORD put forth his hand, and touched my mouth. And the LORD said unto me, Behold, I have put my words in thy mouth (Jer. 1:9).

> Thy words were found, and I did eat them; and thy word was unto me the joy and rejoicing of mine heart: for I am called by thy name, O Lord God of hosts (Jer. 15:16).

> For, behold, I have made thee this day a defenced city, and an iron pillar, and brasen walls against the whole land, against the kings of Judah, against the princes thereof, against the priests thereof, and against the people of the land. And they shall fight against thee; but they shall not prevail against thee; for I am with thee, saith the Lord, to deliver thee (Jer. 1:18, 19).

He faithfully delivered the divine message,

> Hear ye the word of the LORD, O house of Jacob, and all the families of the house of Israel: Thus saith the LORD, What iniquity have your fathers

found in me, that they are gone far from me, and have walked after vanity, and are become vain? Neither said they, Where is the LORD that brought us up out of the land of Egypt, that led us through the wilderness, through a land of deserts and of pits, through a land of drought, and of the shadow of death, through a land that no man passed through, and where no man dwelt? And I brought you into a plentiful country, to eat the fruit thereof and the goodness thereof; but when ye entered, ye defiled my land, and made mine heritage an abomination. The priests said not, Where is the LORD? and they that handle the law knew me not: the pastors also transgressed against me, and the prophets prophesied by Baal, and walked after things that do not profit. Wherefore I will yet plead with you, saith the LORD, and with your children's children will I plead. For pass over the isles of Chittim, and see; and send unto Kedar, and consider diligently, and see if there be such a thing. Hath a nation changed their gods, which are yet no gods? but my people have changed their glory for that which doth not profit. Be astonished, O ye heavens, at this, and be horribly afraid, be ye very desolate, saith the LORD. For my people have committed two evils; they have forsaken me the fountain of living waters, and hewed them out cisterns, broken cisterns, that can hold no water (Jer. 2:4-13).

Thy way and thy doings have procured these things unto thee; this is thy wickedness, because it is bitter, because it reacheth unto thine heart. My bowels, my bowels! I am pained at my very heart; my heart maketh a noise in me; I cannot hold my peace, because thou hast heard, O my soul, the sound of the trumpet, the alarm of war. Destruction upon destruction is cried; for the whole land is spoiled suddenly are my tents spoiled, and my curtains in a moment (Jer. 4:18-20).

And they would not surrender. Yet, wave after wave of loving appeals continued to come from Jeremiah.

How shall I pardon thee for this? Thy children have forsaken me, and sworn by them that are no gods: when I had fed them to the full, they then committed adultery, and assembled themselves by troops in the harlots' houses. They were as fed horses in the morning: every one neighed after his neighbour's wife. Shall I not visit for these things? saith the LORD: and shall not my soul be avenged on such a nation as this? Go ye up upon her walls, and destroy; but make not a full end: take away her battlements; for they are not the LORD's. For the house of Israel and the house of Judah have dealt very treacherously against me, saith the LORD. They have belied the LORD, and said, It is not he; neither shall evil come upon us; neither shall we see sword nor famine: and the prophets shall become wind, and the word is not in them: thus shall it be done unto them. Wherefore thus saith the LORD God of hosts, Because ye speak this word, behold, I will make my words in thy mouth fire, and this people wood, and it shall devour them. Lo, I will bring a nation upon you from far, O house of Israel, saith the LORD: it is a mighty nation, it is an ancient nation, a nation whose language thou knowest not, neither understandest what they say. Their quiver is as an open sepulchre, they are all mighty men. And they shall eat up thine harvest, and thy bread, which thy sons and thy daughters should eat: they shall eat up thy flocks and thine herds: they shall eat up thy vines and thy fig trees: they shall impoverish thy fenced cities, wherein thou trustedst, with the sword (Jer. 5:7-17).

For if ye throughly amend your ways and your doings; if ye throughly execute judgment between a man and his neighbour; if ye oppress not the stranger, the fatherless, and the widow, and shed not innocent blood in this place, neither walk after other gods to your hurt: then will I cause you to dwell in this place, in the land that I gave to your fathers, for ever and ever. Behold, ye trust in lying words, that cannot profit. Will ye steal, murder, and commit adultery, and swear falsely, and burn incense unto Baal, and walk after other gods whom ye know not...? (Jer. 7:5-9).

Thus saith the LORD; Execute ye judgment and righteousness, and deliver the spoiled out of the hand of the oppressor: and do no wrong, do no violence to the stranger, the fatherless, nor the widow, neither shed innocent blood in this place (Jer. 22:3).

Then came the persecution against the messenger.

> Therefore the princes said unto the king, We beseech thee, let this man be put to death: for thus he weakeneth the hands of the men of war that remain in this city, and the hands of all the people, in speaking such words unto them: for this man seeketh not the welfare of this people, but the hurt (Jer. 38:4).

> And the LORD hath given me knowledge of it, and I know it: then thou shewedst me their doings. But I was like a lamb or an ox that is brought to the slaughter; and I knew not that they had devised devices against me, saying, Let us destroy the tree with the fruit thereof, and let us cut him off from the land of the living, that his name may be no more remembered (Jer. 11:18, 19).

> Then took they Jeremiah, and cast him into the dungeon of Malchiah the son of Hammelech, that was in the court of the prison: and they let down Jeremiah with cords. And in the dungeon there was no water, but mire: so Jeremiah sunk in the mire (Jer. 38:6).

Jeremiah could not sit or lay down without suffocating, and he almost died of dehydration and hunger. Finally, after the Lord delivered Jeremiah from the dungeon, their mean bitterness became overwhelming to Jeremiah, and he was tempted to give up his holy commission of calling the nation back from destruction. He wanted seclusion.

> Woe is me, my mother, that thou hast borne me a man of strife and a man of contention to the whole earth! I have neither lent on usury, nor men have lent to me on usury; yet every one of them doth curse me (Jer. 15:10).

> O LORD, thou knowest: remember me, and visit me, and revenge me of my persecutors; take me not away in thy longsuffering: know that for thy sake I have suffered rebuke.... Why is my pain perpetual, and my wound incurable, which refuseth to be healed? wilt thou be altogether unto me as a liar, and as waters that fail? (Jer. 15:15, 18).

> I was a derision to all my people; and their song all the day. He hath filled me with bitterness, he hath made me drunken with wormwood (Lam. 3:14, 15).

And the Lord had to admonish His servant to return to his role as messenger to the nations.

> Therefore thus saith the LORD, If thou return, then will I bring thee again, and thou shalt stand before me: and if thou take forth the precious from the vile, thou shalt be as my mouth: let them return unto thee; but return not thou unto them (Jer. 15:19).

> As for me, I have not hastened from being a pastor to follow thee: neither have I desired the woeful day; thou knowest: that which came out of my lips was right before thee. Be not a terror unto me: thou art my hope in the day of evil (Jer. 17:16, 17).

David, too, knew the bitter-sweet role of the Lord's servant.

> I waited patiently for the LORD; and he inclined unto me, and heard my cry.

> He brought me up also out of an horrible pit, out of the miry clay, and set my feet upon a rock, and established my goings.

> And he hath put a new song in my mouth, even praise unto our God: many shall see it, and fear, and shall trust in the LORD.

> Blessed is that man that maketh the LORD his trust, and respecteth not the proud, nor such as turn aside to lies (Ps. 40:1-4).

> I delight to do thy will, O my God: yea, Thy law is within my heart.

> I have preached righteousness in the great congregation: lo, I have not refrained my lips, O LORD, thou knowest.

> I have not hid thy righteousness within my heart; I have declared thy faithfulness and thy salvation: I have not concealed thy lovingkindness and thy truth from the great congregation (Ps. 40:8-10).

> Be pleased, O LORD, to deliver me: O LORD, make haste to help me.

> Let them be ashamed and confounded together that seek after my soul to destroy it; let them [the adversarial hosts] be driven backward and put to shame that wish me evil (Ps. 40:13, 14).
>
> …mine enemies…are ever with me (Ps. 119:98).
>
> They that hate me without a cause are more than the hairs of mine head: they that would destroy me, being mine enemies wrongfully, are mighty: then I restored that which I took not away (Ps. 69:4).
>
> Deliver me, O LORD, from the evil man: preserve me from the violent man;
>
> Which imagine mischiefs in their heart; continually are they gathered together for war.
>
> They have sharpened their tongues like a serpent; adders' poison is under their lips. Selah.
>
> Keep me, O LORD, from the hands of the wicked; preserve me from the violent man; who have purposed to overthrow my goings.
>
> The proud have hid a snare for me, and cords; they have spread a net by the wayside; they have set gins for me (Ps. 140:1-5).
>
> Mine enemies would daily swallow me up: for they be many that fight against me, O thou most High.
>
> What time I am afraid, I will trust in thee.
>
> In God I will praise his word, in God I have put my trust; I will not fear what flesh can do unto me.
>
> Every day they wrest my words: all their thoughts are against me for evil.
>
> They gather themselves together, they hide themselves, they mark my steps, when they wait for my soul.
>
> Shall they escape by iniquity? in thine anger cast down the people, O God.
>
> Thou tellest my wanderings: put thou my tears into thy bottle: are they not in thy book?
>
> When I cry unto thee, then shall mine enemies turn back: this I know; for God is for me (Ps. 56:2-9).
>
> Give ear to my prayer, O God; and hide not thyself from my supplication.
>
> Attend unto me, and hear me: I mourn in my complaint, and make a noise;
>
> Because of the voice of the enemy, because of the oppression of the wicked: for they cast iniquity upon me, and in wrath they hate me.
>
> My heart is sore pained within me: and the terrors of death are fallen upon me.
>
> Fearfulness and trembling are come upon me, and horror hath overwhelmed me.
>
> And I said, Oh that I had wings like a dove! for then would I fly away, and be at rest.
>
> Lo, then would I wander far off, and remain in the wilderness. Selah (Ps. 55:1-7).

The god of this world blinds the unconverted minds to the glory that they could possess through humility and righteousness. "Every soul that refuses to give himself to God is under the control of another power. He is not his own.… He is not allowed to see the beauty of truth, for his mind is under the control of Satan" *The Desire of Ages*, p. 466. If they would attend to the message of the Lord to cease living for this world, they would get glimpses of the true beauty of holiness until they could clearly see the blessing that the prophet is working to bring to them.

The bitterness in John's bowels also describes the power of the Spirit driving His messengers to strongly convict sinners.

> And Samuel said to Saul, Thou hast done foolishly: thou hast not kept the commandment of the LORD thy God, which he commanded thee: for now would the LORD have established thy kingdom upon Israel for ever. But now thy kingdom shall not continue: the LORD hath sought him a man after his own heart, and the LORD hath commanded him to be captain over his people, because thou hast not kept that which the LORD commanded thee (1 Sam. 13:13, 14).
>
> And Samuel did that which the LORD spake, and came to Bethlehem. And the elders of the town trembled at his coming, and said, *Comest thou peaceably?* (1 Sam. 16:4).

After eating the scroll, Ezekiel reveals a similar heated bitterness in the powerful gift of prophecy.

Behold, I have made thy face strong against their faces, and thy forehead strong against their foreheads. *As an adamant harder than flint have I made thy forehead*: fear them not, neither be dismayed at their looks, though they be a rebellious house…. So the Spirit lifted me up, and took me away, and I went in *bitterness, in the heat of my spirit*; but the hand of the LORD was strong upon me. Then I came to them of the captivity at Telabib, that dwelt by the river of Chebar, and I sat where they sat, and remained there astonished among them seven days. And it came to pass at the end of seven days, that the word of the LORD came unto me (Eze. 3:8, 9, 14-16).

The strong and hard spirit from the sin-loving rebels necessitates the stronger, harder Spirit of God from the Law-loving prophet. "With the merciful thou wilt shew thyself merciful; …with the froward thou wilt shew thyself froward" (Ps. 18:25, 26). Moses, too, was given the same righteous indignation.

> Notwithstanding they hearkened not unto Moses; but some of them left of it until the morning, and it bred worms, and stank: and Moses was wroth with them (Ex. 16:20).

> And it came to pass, as soon as he came nigh unto the camp, that he saw the calf, and the dancing: and Moses' anger waxed hot, and he cast the tables out of his hands, and brake them beneath the mount (Ex. 32:19).

And Jeremiah also,

> And I will make thee to pass with thine enemies into a land which thou knowest not: for a fire is kindled in mine anger, which shall burn upon you (Jer. 15:14).

> I sat not in the assembly of the mockers, nor rejoiced; I sat alone because of thy hand: for thou hast filled me with indignation (Jer. 15:17).

Isaiah demonstrated both the sweet honey of the prophet's commission and the bitter gall of the prophet's work.

> Then said I, Woe is me! for I am undone; because I am a man of unclean lips, and I dwell in the midst of a people of unclean lips: for mine eyes have seen the King, the LORD of hosts. Then flew one of the seraphims unto me, having a live coal in his hand, which he had taken with the tongs from off the altar: and he laid it upon my mouth, and said, Lo, this hath touched thy lips; and thine iniquity is taken away, and thy sin purged. Also I heard the voice of the Lord, saying, Whom shall I send, and who will go for us? Then said I, Here am I; send me (Isa. 6:5-8).

> The Lord GOD hath given me the tongue of the learned, that I should know how to speak a word in season to him that is weary: he wakeneth morning by morning, he wakeneth mine ear to hear as the learned. The Lord GOD hath opened mine ear, and I was not rebellious, neither turned away back. I gave my back to the smiters, and my cheeks to them that plucked off the hair: I hid not my face from shame and spitting. For the Lord GOD will help me; therefore shall I not be confounded: therefore have *I set my face like a flint*, and I know that I shall not be ashamed. He is near that justifieth me; *who will contend with me? let us stand together: who is mine adversary? let him come near to me* (Isa. 50:4-8).

The bitterness within the soul of the prophet was not a response to the attacks by rebellious people. It was not revenge (see Leviticus 19:18). His bitterness was toward the sin, not the sinners, even if they couldn't see it that way.

"Bind up the testimony, seal the law among my disciples" (Isa. 8:16). In the vision that Jesus had given Ezekiel to begin his prophetic office, He spread out a scroll for Ezekiel to eat, as He did John, which gave Ezekiel the same effects that John received. Then He commanded Ezekiel to go with a forehead newly sealed with the stone hard Law of God. He drove His servant to speak against the Jews' service to the ancient rebellion of Nimrod, the worship of Baal (Tammuz) and Ashtoreth (Queen of heaven) (see Ezekiel 3:4-9; 8:1-18, cf Jeremiah 7:18; 44:25; Judges 2:10-19). In Isaiah's case, and after a long period of probation (see Exodus 34:6; 2 Peter 3:9), failing to inspire Israel with His prophets' testimony, God would finally rein in the light of His words, bind in bundles all who chose not to be His disciples, and then He would become their enemy (see Isaiah 6:9-13; 63:10; 2 Kings 17:20; Exodus 34:7; Deuteronomy 32:19-43; 2 Peter 3:10). But, a remnant would set their hearts on Jehovah and He would seal them in preparation for the distress that would come upon "both the houses of Israel" (Isa. 8:14).

Similarly, during the trumpets delay the Angel was sealing the Law in His 144,000 disciples. Now, in Revelation chapter 10 John acts vicariously for all future preachers of Christ. In them He will finish the sealing at the close of the sixth trumpet in Revelation 11:11-13 and during the opening days of the seventh trumpet. In Revelation 10:8-10, John's actions look forward to the sweet and bitter battle of the sealed 144,000 preachers, after the sealing trumpets' delay. "I looked, and, lo, a Lamb stood on the mount Sion, and with him an hundred forty and four thousand, having his Father's name written in their foreheads…. And I saw another angel fly in the midst of heaven, having the everlasting gospel to preach unto them that dwell on the earth, and to every nation, and kindred, and tongue, and people" (Rev. 14:1, 6). The condemnation of the Law is the foundation of their gospel that "shall be preached in all the world for a witness unto all nations" (Matt. 24:14). Therefore, Jesus commands John, "Thou must prophesy *again* before many peoples, and nations, and tongues, and kings" (Rev. 10:11).

The fulfillment of the Revelation chapter 10 scene must take place between the sixth trumpet bleak destruction of Protestant America portrayed by chapter 9 and the brilliant light to the world from the Latter Rain in Revelation 11, verses 11 through 14. The commission must result in the resurrection scene of Revelation 11:11, where the killed witnesses resurrect to life (see also Joel 2:23, 28-32). This pouring out of God's Holy Spirit is also magnified in Revelation 18:1-8. Thus, the Lord shows us by John's commissioning by the book that at the opening of this chapter 10 intermission the gospel had ceased to be preached. But, judging by the Angel's use of "again", a former worldwide effort *had been made prior to this time.*

However, we have thus far read of no former prophesying. Does not this command of Revelation 10:11 dictate an earlier prophesying somewhere in the previous seal/trumpet drama? "You must prophesy *again.*" But, using scripture to interpret scripture, where is that prophesying during the first 10 chapters of Revelation? We don't see it. Since the seal/trumpet drama began in chapter 4 until chapter 10 no prophesying has been mentioned. Due to no mention of prophesying throughout the entire previous Revelation great controversy pageant, do we find prophesying spoken of anywhere within this seven seal series? Yes, we do. One is described in the next chapter, Revelation chapter 11. Thus, that word "again" must refer to a scene occurring in that chapter. And thus, Revelation 11 gives a large view of John's future, one that encompasses Revelation chapters 5 through 10.

You must prophesy again… *the word "again" is the key to the correct positioning of Revelation chapter 10.*

The word "again" is the key to the correct positioning of Revelation chapter 10; that is, after the first prophesying that occurs within chapter 11 during verses 3 through 6. As we will see when we look at Revelation chapter 11, the "prophesying again" refers to the time following when the two witnesses come back to life after being "killed" (see verses 7-12) and then shake up "their enemies" (see verse 13, cf verse 5) — "the people and kindreds and tongues and nations" (verse 9) of the world. Therefore, the prophesying "again before many peoples, and nations, and tongues, and kings" must pinpoint Revelation 11:11 as its yet future fulfillment. There the two servants of God "stood upon their feet" (verse 11) humbled and in perfect faith, justified, and sanctified in Jesus. They once more stand "before the God of the earth" (verse 4, cf Jer. 15:19) and receive His constant supply of grace. This last quote is a reference to righteousness by faith (see Zechariah 4:14, 6), which God's true people have always had.

The witnesses' prophesying again, and their symbolic resurrection and ascension all point to the Latter Rain. This is similar to the Early Rain, it also, having translated the children of God, letting them sit in heavenly places in Christ (see Colossians 1:13; Ephesians 2:6; Revelation 11:12). It shows God's humbling punishment awarded to His servants for departing from His three angels' messages, a humbling and love which leads to genuine surrender and repentance, and which mobilizes them to new heaven-imbued talents for Him. It speaks of their preaching to a world that doesn't know the one true God and the real Lord Jesus Christ, neither one of whom are found in the Christianized mysticism of Spiritual Formation. It points to the reclaiming of many tormented, yet faithful, souls among the hedonistic Protestant "rest" of the multitudes of Revelation 9:20, 21. "They shall come which were ready to perish in the land of Assyria, and the outcasts in the land of Egypt, and shall worship the LORD in the holy mount at Jerusalem" (Isa. 27:13).

Chapter 7 Revelation Chapter 10: Preparation for the Latter Rain

The witnesses' prophesying again also points to those among the corrupted masses throughout the continents of the world under Protestant America's care. It points to the three angels' wise virgins waking up from their spiritual sleep (see Matthew 25:6), to give the fourth angel's message (see Revelation 18:1-8), testifying in sackcloth "again". It's no wonder that the crowned Angel roared and the Glory of heaven thundered.

> The lion hath roared, who will not fear? the Lord GOD hath spoken, who can but prophesy? (Amos 3:8).

> As for me, this is my covenant with them, saith the LORD; My spirit that is upon thee, and my words which I have put in thy mouth, shall not depart out of thy mouth, nor out of the mouth of thy seed, nor out of the mouth of thy seed's seed, saith the LORD, from henceforth and for ever (Isa. 59:21).

Chapter 8
Revelation Chapter 11: The Final Victory

The *Ellen G. White Estate Research Documents from the Ellen G. White Writings Comprehensive Research edition CD, 101 Questions on the Sanctuary and on Ellen White, F — Allegations of Errors and Mistakes, Question 56* reads,

> 56. Revelation 11 and the French Revolution
>
> Was Ellen White wrong in her *Great Controversy* explanation of Revelation 11?...
>
> In *Testimonies for the Church*, Volume 4, Page 594, Ellen White is not giving an exegesis of Revelation 11. She is simply using the language of Revelation 11:3 as a matter of convenience. In *The Great Controversy*, pages 265-288 she discusses Revelation 11 in considerable detail and gives the impression that she is really telling her readers what that chapter means....
>
> Although certain minor historical points needed revision, this can hardly be used as an argument against the basic exposition itself. No better or more satisfactory interpretation of Revelation 11 has been written than that found in *The Great Controversy*. (**See Appendix A** for the full research document.)

I don't like to speak contrary to Mrs. White. Nor do I desire to compete with Dr. Ford, against whom the above research document was formulated. However, due to a new understanding of the trumpets, I see a different picture developing in Revelation 11 via its context in the core theme of Revelation chapters 4 through 11.

When chapter 11 opens chapter 10 has already shown that it is time to bring to a close the final scenes of the difficult sixth trumpet of Revelation chapter 9 and to prepare for the church's glorious end at the seventh trumpet. It is time to raise up again the devastated church that will stand when Jesus returns, "whose house are we, if we hold fast the confidence and the rejoicing of the hope firm unto the end" (Heb. 3:6). This is the church which Christ built (see Zechariah 6:12; Hebrews 3:1-6; Revelation 12:6), but which, at last, is overrun by the locust hordes of Revelation 9. It is the church which must be judged to see if Christ must give it up to the desolating uncircumcised Gentiles, as He had judged Israel (see Jeremiah 9:25, 26; Daniel 9:24-27; Matthew 21:43; Romans 11:11-14).

Revelation 10 has shown that the Revelation 7:3 delay is about to end. The Godhead is ready to finalize the investigative judgment. The Adventist children of High Priest Jesus are humbled and atoned for. They are commissioned to preach the gospel in the Latter Rain for a witness to all nations, kindreds, and tongues.

The story of the woman in Revelation 12 is ancillary to the story of Revelation 11. It was given as a parallel to the two witnesses of Revelation 11, a comparison of the two chapters which adds to the whole picture of the church of Christ under satanic attack since its birth. Like the woman in chapter 12, the two witnesses represent the holy people that have played so centrally in the war since the start of unsealing the mysterious book of God until the end of the sixth trumpet. The two witnesses courageously prophesy and preach, but then they stop their God-given work and die. Later still, they are a humbled and revived holy people who prophesy and preach a second time, "again".

Therefore, a judgment is in order, a measuring of the final church, an investigation in light of an overview of church dispensation history concluding at the end of the sixth trumpet, with the angelic orders looking on (see Revelation 11:15, 16). Can the angelic court say that the church was really Christ's? Or, by its final failure, does it belong to Satan? By the church's description in Revelation 17:3, it certainly looked like the great red Dragon of Revelation 12:3. Was she persecuted or the persecutor? Who within the church is worthy of the kingdom that God seeks to reinstate at the end of Revelation 11? Who was actually converted and filled with God's Spirit living up to all the light they had or had access to? These are the issues of the concluding segment of the seals and trumpets prophecy.

These issues need resolving because it seems that the commonly repeated thread in every revival since Adam has been that within the people of God the majority — "an host" — "was given" (Dan. 8:12, cf Rev. 11:2, 9; Matt. 7:13, 14) to false religion and false worship, the tares growing up and almost completely overtaking the wheat (see Matthew 13:24-30). Therefore, the investigation involves more than inspection, it first involves testing. Through trial and examination Christ filters out from His people the character of those in the church "which say they are apostles, and are not" (Rev. 2:2, cf 2 Cor. 11:13), and others "which say they are Jews, and are not, but are the synagogue of Satan" (Rev. 2:9). They travel the broad way to destruction instead of seeking the strait gate, entering it, and remaining in the narrow way "unto the end" (Heb. 3:14). So, the investigation and sanctuary cleansing must take away (see Matthew 13:30; Luke 17:34-37) the "host…given [Satan] against the daily sacrifice [the redeeming crucifixion of Christ]" (Dan. 8:12, cf Isa. 14:13). A host, that is, who desire nothing from the cross of Christ except His name to cover their lack of renounced sins.

But, Jesus is no respecter of persons. Simultaneous to judging the apostates, He must also judge His church of the wilderness. His obedient church must also be arraigned, and an investigation must ensue to judge it by using Christ's on-looking Revelation 11 satellite as it replays the video of the church's loyalty and treason throughout the new dispensation, from the apostles to the last generation. Christ must visit and judge those within the church who profess Him but please men, rather than confessing Him from a born-again heart. When His people grow unfaithful, He brings a determined punishment against them as He did to Israel (see Isaiah 10:22, 23). Afterward, they will again be humbled and faithful children (see Psalm 89:31-37; Jeremiah 25:9-12).

Thus, beginning at its apostolic start, a history of the church will run as Christ builds the group that must carry the everlasting gospel to every nation before His return. His people will work hard for their successes while they are fully dependent on their Lord through righteousness by faith. But, they will also have their failure near the end when they disconnect from Jesus and lose His gospel of righteousness by faith. Like Abraham becoming disillusioned after waiting for the son of promise, so does the faith of the church in the wilderness die in the end after they wait for the promised Son to "appear the second time" (Heb. 9:28, cf Matt. 25:5). They indulge Babylonian self-sufficient religion, by which they are given spiritualism and all this world's goods, which leaves them needing nothing from heaven. Then Christ raises up the punishing Chaldeans from the bottomless pit.

In the final analysis by the heavenly council, the true church's dispensation will terminate with the full restoration of the witnesses to the everlasting gospel of righteousness by faith by Jesus (see Revelation 11:11-13). The sealed 144,000 and innumerable multitudes of the last generation will receive the blessing of the angelic court for an abundant entrance into the heavenly kingdom with their Saviour Jesus (see Revelation 11:15, cf Psalm 24:7-10) once He has cleansed the sanctuary of their disloyalties and uncleanness.

> Whereby are given unto us exceeding great and precious promises: that by these ye might be partakers of the divine nature, having escaped the corruption that is in the world through lust….

For so an entrance shall be ministered unto you abundantly into the everlasting kingdom of our Lord and Saviour Jesus Christ (2 Pet. 1:4, 11).

The full restoration and purification of Christ's priestly family (see Leviticus 16:11; Malachi 3:3, 4) by the everlasting gospel of Law and grace as seen in Revelation 11:11-13 will prepare Jesus for the final atonement in the heavenly sanctuary. By His priestly family's special work of purification through the Spirit of Prophecy's strongest reproofs of sin and Christ's equally strong Most Holy ministry of mercy, the two witnesses will ultimately put the headstone upon the roof of the church shouting to it, "Grace, grace" (Zech. 4:7). The eternal Spirit purges their conscience of dead works to serve the living God. By the blood of Christ sprinkling their evil consciences of the past, and their characters washed with the pure water of His Spirit, they can minister before Him in the wicked environment of the dark sixth trumpet locusts and the closing of probation. Their full victory over sin in Christ during the Latter Rain will exonerate the Father and validate His new covenant provisions.

The outpouring of His Spirit that will follow the past 170 years of locust moral darkness is the same "sure mercies of David" (Isa. 55:3) that the Spirit of Christ had given David following the period of the judges. The long dark time after the judges resulted from everyone doing what is right in his own eyes instead of keeping the laws and statutes of Moses, and being dominated by the Moloch-worshiping Canaanites. Likewise, the heavenly outpouring that Israel received through David is what the apostolic church received after the long dark 600 year subjection to the four world empires. Pentecost's liberty in the Spirit that overcame the world was the Early Rain blessing to those who lived long under the sophisticated Imperial lawlessness and the condemning silence from above (see Galatians 3:23; Deuteronomy 28:15ff).

> And these all, having obtained a good report through faith, received not the promise: God having provided some better thing for us, that they without us should not be made perfect (Heb. 11:39, 40).

The promised Latter Rain will bring the fullest downpours of any previous Davidic certainty of salvation and victory over the world.

Now that Christ, in Revelation 10, is in the Most Holy clothed in a cloud of incense and glory, it is time to finalize the investigative judgment that began when the removed seventh seal permitted the book of the great controversy to open in 1844 (see Revelation 8:1). So, John measures the church, starting after the apostolic church's falling away during the first to the fourth centuries. "Little children, it is the last time: and as ye have heard that antichrist shall come, even now are there many antichrists; whereby we know that it is the last time" (1 John 2:18). The measuring "time is at hand" (Rev. 1:3) and the vision sweeps across centuries in one scene. Similar to Ezekiel's vision (see Ezekiel 40:3), Jesus gives to John a reed of a cubit length to measure the condition of the church of God, their gospel, and their "worship" (Rev. 11:1). That is, the church of wheat and tares — the champions who have not entangled themselves with the affairs of this life, and the majority who have; all who stand in the presence of Jehovah (see Ephesians 3:16-21) and who will face the hazards from the wily foe within the church. The measuring instrument represents judging, examining, testing to find deviations from the divine blueprints of Christ's character, which would pose as dangers of church structural failure from seducing prophets' "untempered morter" (Eze. 13:10) of Ashtoreth's imaginary peace.

> Because, even because they have seduced my people, saying, Peace; and there was no peace; and one built up a wall, and, lo, others daubed it with untempered morter: say unto them which daub it with untempered morter, that it shall fall: there shall be an overflowing shower; and ye, O great hailstones, shall fall; and a stormy wind shall rend it (Eze. 13:10, 11, cf vs. 8-21; Jer. 6:8-14).

> Evil men and seducers shall wax worse and worse, deceiving, and being deceived (2 Tim. 3:13).

Even while the church shows much "labour" with "patience" and "canst not bear them that are evil" (Rev. 2:2), Christ commands John to pass judgment on the purity of the church using a measuring reed. Will the temple of truth retain its holiness, or be tempted and desecrated by false religion and false worship? Judgment and testing are a common theme throughout scripture, such as the counsel to examine ourselves daily to make our calling and election sure. (See 2 Corinthians 13:5; 1 Corinthians 11:31; 2 Peter 1:10.)

> Judgment also will I lay to the line, and righteousness to the plummet [plumb bob] (Isa. 28:17).

Thou art weighed in the balances, and art found wanting (Dan. 5:27).

Search me, O God, and know my heart: try me, and know my thoughts: and see if there be any wicked way in me, and lead me in the way everlasting (Ps. 139:23, 24).

I the LORD search the heart, I try the reins, even to give every man according to his ways, and according to the fruit of his doings (Jer. 17:10).

Judge me, O LORD; for I have walked in mine integrity: I have trusted also in the LORD; therefore I shall not slide. Examine me, O LORD, and prove me; try my reins and my heart (Ps. 26:1, 2).

John's judging the faithfulness of the church requires examining the whole replay of the Christian dispensation.

When we interpreted Revelation 8 trumpets, we used the general historicist definition and placed the trumpets prophecy after the first six seals and only during the time of the end, that is, from 1844 onward. We said this because we saw the first trumpet attached to the removal of the seventh seal and integrated into the Revelation chapter 8 sanctuary cleansing commencement scene.

There in chapter 8 we saw verse 7, which featured the first trumpet, *caused by*, *resulting from* verse 5 of the sanctuary scene, as the contents of the censer, which Christ cast down one minute, the next minute fell from the sky onto the earth. Therefore, the first trumpet was integral to the Revelation chapter 8 heavenly sanctuary scene — the seventh seal scene which also signified 1844 since it immediately followed the prophetically paused, unfinished sixth seal Millerite movement of Revelation 6:14-17. Then we concluded that the succeeding six trumpets, which chronologically follow the first trumpet, all fulfilled their prophecies post-1844. The unfinished question and mandate of the sixth seal are finished by the seventh seal, as the sealing and power to stand when Christ returns, which are called for by Revelation 6:17 and 7:3, are accomplished by the seven trumpets after Revelation 9:4.

Chapter 11, however, undoubtedly starts at the very beginning of the church era. The chapter 11 historical background briefly recaptures the historical scenes of Revelation chapter 6. The first seal's conquering white horse (see Revelation 6:2) compares with the two witnesses' valiant protection and preservation of the gospel.

The two witnesses also detail those Christians of the third seal who keep the oil and wine which are the "righteousness, and peace, and joy in the Holy Ghost" (Rom. 14:17), and who are not hurt by the spiritual besiegement that afflicts the masses of the Church (see Revelation 6:6). We see the two witnesses, clothed in sackcloth, again pouring out their souls under the altar in the fifth seal, this signifying their heavy persecution, yet their maintaining Christ's plagues upon all who try to hurt their possession of His Spirit (see Revelation 6:9-11). In life or in martyrdom, the witnesses control who receives the new heart. During their 3 ½ year mission, "whose soever sins [they] remit" (John 20:23) through the gospel, the Spirit rains upon those grateful fields of harvest. But, upon all whose sins are retained because they reject the witnesses' gospel of Christ, His Spirit does not rain. Rather "the wrath of God abideth on [them]" (John 3:36). They trust in a human priesthood and in humanistic wisdom, and they are "like the heath in the desert, and shall not see when good cometh; but shall inhabit the parched places in the wilderness, in a salt land and not inhabited" (Jer. 17:6).

The chapter 11 pageant includes the whole 1,260 year period of papal supremacy, and even previous to the papal period due to the prophecy's mention of the temple court's exclusion. The exclusion of the court represents the end of the Old Testament ceremonial economy as "a shadow of good things to come" (Heb. 10:1). Paul wrote, "Christ our passover is sacrificed for us" (1 Cor. 5:7). At 31 AD, when Messiah the Prince was cut off, the sacrificial system ceased (see Daniel 9:27). All of those sacrifices created a mammoth mountain of evidence for their faith and ours. The millions of animals were slain and burned upon the altar of sacrifice for four millennia. That altar, which was the centerpiece of the temple court, prefigured the Son of God whose heart our hands had pierced and upon whose head had poured His Father's hatred of our iniquities.

At the Passover of 31 AD, Jesus would pour out His soul under the hot, full wrath of God's immolation of our sins. Christ's love for us would allow the scourging for the whole world upon His bloated body, overwhelmed mind, and darkened soul. He was made to be the most repugnant sin and treated with the repugnance that we deserve. Jesus would assume all of the weeping and gnashing of teeth that our entire race has experienced during its temporal existence, and will experience later at Judgment Day. Only by offering His soul could we be forgiven and comforted, justified and released from the Father's curse of judgment that we had been tasting day by day. Even more, Jesus the everlasting Blessing, would take our curse so that He could give us His greatest of all blessings, the blessedness of His Father's reconciled Spirit. To the ten-billionth degree, He would take God's "chastisement of our peace" (Isa. 53:5, cf Gen. 2:17), which has been causing disease and death in each one of the human family. Christ has freed the whole world to repent, and can now start a new life in Him, under His shadow, without any more of the tormenting chastisement of peace. And one day we will receive His blessedness to the ten-billionth degree — His Spirit without measure — when this corruptible puts on incorruption.

The Old Testament sanctuary courtyard had prefigured the first of three dispensations of Christ's grace, the first being His redemptive work since the fall of man. The Son of God was "the Lamb slain from the foundation of the world" (Rev. 13:8). During that long 4,000 year Old Testament period, spotless and innocent year old animals died on the altar of sacrifice to represent the incomparable death of the final Passover Lamb "once for all" (Heb. 10:10, cf 9:28) at His death in Gethsemane and at Golgotha.

After each sacrifice, the Levitical priest washed at the laver to be clean before he entered through the first veil into the tabernacle. This typified Christ's resurrection from the dead where our faith was curiously wrought in the lowest parts of the earth. It represented the "Mother of all living" postpartum exclusion from heaven (see Leviticus 12:2-4), His forty day rest from the agonies of pouring out His soul for our second birth, while He nurtured His infant church (see Acts 1:3), the first seven days of which He was untouchable (see John 20:17, 26). Then the priest's walk from the laver to the veil prefigured Christ's cleansed ascension to His Father's right hand.

The sacrifices of the Mosaic temple courtyard represented the preincarnate ministry of the Lamb of God throughout the Old Dispensation until Pentecost. Similarly, the Aaronic Holy Place and Most Holy Place ministries would represent the last two dispensations of Messiah the Prince (see Hebrews 8:1, 2; 9:2, 3, 11, 12, 28). Those last two sanctuary ministries in the Old Testament temple represented the two periods of the Christian age that High Priest Jesus oversaw, which spanned AD 34 to 1844 and 1844 to His Second Advent, respectively.

Once within the veil, the priest's work in the earthly sanctuary initially prefigured Christ's victorious reunion with His Father at Pentecost (see Isaiah 53:12; John 7:37-39), and the work of keeping His truth instilled in His followers. As the priest sprinkled the blood day by day within the first compartment of the Mosaic sanctuary before the second veil, the priest's work typified Jesus' ministry for the next 1,813 years. During that era He reconciled His people to His Father's Law, justifying and sanctifying their hearts and lives (see Leviticus 10:17, 18; Hebrews 6:19; 9:2; 7:25), and giving them the desire to make known to others the precious Friend they had found in Jesus.

Later, on the Day of Atonement at the end of the ceremonial year, the high priest would enter through the second veil twice to cleanse the sanctuary (see Leviticus 16:2, 11, 15, 16, 30; Hebrews 9:3, 7, 28).

In the Most Holy Place Aaron would re-sanctify his family and then the nation of all the uncleanness that they all had built up in the sanctuary during the preceding twelve months. This signified Christ's work after 1844 to first cleanse His Adventist family, using His high standard given them by His Spirit of Prophecy. There their goal was mandated, "While the investigative judgment is going forward in heaven, while the sins of penitent believers are being removed from the sanctuary, there is to be a special work of purification, of putting away of sin, among God's people upon earth" *The Great Controversy*, p. 425. Later still, it typified Christ entering the Most Holy the second time to cleanse the larger host of His people sprinkled throughout the world populations.

This cleansing by the special dispensation of the Spirit of truth would include a special condemnation and conviction through the counsels from Jesus to Ellen White by His "much incense" (Rev. 8:3) given to His Advent movement. The special condemnation and conviction and repentance would result in a special justification for His people by a special dispensation of His "blood" (Rev. 8:7) of sprinkling upon their abundant uncleanness. That special justification would also empower their diligent efforts for a special sanctification by His present Spirit that came with the special justification. Special difficulties against them in the first and second times of trouble of the sixth and seventh trumpets, combined with the special sanctification, would work to produce the special sealing. This would make them so solid in justification and sanctification that they can never move from the truths of the Bible during Jacob's troubles. Thus, with their sins blotted out they would be special conquerors in the battle with evil, prepared for their High Priest's second coming.

So Christ was once offered to bear the sins of many; and unto them that look for him shall he appear the second time without sin unto salvation (Heb. 9:28).

All the while during this investigation and purification of His Adventist family after 1844, Christ would pass judgment upon all professors of loyalty to His kingdom from the time of Adam to those living at the close of human probation. The cleansing of the heavenly sanctuary was an ancient concept from the days of Moses to Daniel's day to our day. The investigation would decide whether or not God's people died to sin with the Lamb and were filled with the fullness of God. It would determine who among His people held "the beginning of [their] confidence stedfast unto the end" (Heb. 3:14), or who ended with only empty professions, as with Ham and Cush, Balaam and Judas, the grass of the third field of the Matthew 13 parable, et cetera. In connection with that, the investigation also signified the final deposition of guilt against Azazel, or Satan, and against all who have assisted the devil to lead people into error and sin. Especially is this judgment against all who throughout the ages have tempted the children of God's kingdom to leave their heavenly present truth for Baalpeor parties. The evils that Azazel and his hosts have done to Christ's children have also pierced Christ (see Matthew 25:41; 24:29, 30; Jude 11-13; Revelation 1:7; 18:6).

Finally, the Day of Atonement destruction of the scapegoat in the blazing desert demonstrated Christ casting into the lake of fire the Dragon, the Beast, and the false prophet. Once Christ's Adventist-Protestant 144,000 and innumerable multitude receive a special dispensation of His Spirit, then the records of their sins can all be blotted out, the books could be closed, and the investigative judgment ended.

Azazel, or Satan, was the power and authority behind the desolating little horn in Daniel's visions. Spiritualism, cloaked as blessed religion, gave strength to this pretentious force for evil. "Marvelous in her shrewdness and cunning is the Roman Church" *The Great Controversy*, p. 580. By means of Azazel's little horn in which was supernatural intelligence — "eyes like the eyes of man" (Dan. 7:8) — yet "not by his own power" (Dan. 8:24), the ancient adversary from beneath wreaked havoc on Christ's redemption and on the church that Christ was redeeming in His sanctuary. God is justified in the atonement through the supporting evidence of all those who receive His seal in their forehead. Simultaneously with the Beast's little horn, Azazel is condemned in the atonement by the haughty nature of his final collection of souls who receive his Beast's mark. (See Leviticus 16:8-10; Deuteronomy 25:1; Matthew 25:41-46.) Atonement for God is, in a sense, made by Azazel and all the wicked when, their delusions removed, they all clearly see the libel that they brought against the King's love for them, and then they all bow their knee and willingly accept God's executive judgment upon them. The eternal, atoning judgment sentence is upon Azazel and upon his great treason against God, against His Son, and against Their kingdom (see Philippians 2:10, 11). (**For more on Azazel, see Appendix A**).

To reiterate more succinctly, the courtyard typified the truth given through the old covenant from the days of Adam until the crucifixion of Christ, the light from heaven and power to redeem given through His Holy Spirit and the animal sacrifices. All those spotless animal victims, as "a shadow of good things to come" (Heb. 10:1), typified Christ's living condemnation of sin and His loving, selfless propitiation on the cross. Christ's work to save us would come through His better offering — the pouring out of His soul on Calvary — and then, upon ascension, applying His self-sacrifice before His Father in the Holy Place of the heavenly sanctuary to shield His believers from all condemnation of sins past. By Christ's all-powerful gift of His Spirit (see Revelation 5:6; Romans 8:9), dispensed through Him from His reconciled Father, and working with the church's personal effort to know Him and to gain a clearer view of the character of God's holy love for humanity, the Christian's salvation is certain day by day until Jesus returns. They purify themselves, striving to be as pure as Jesus is (see 1 John 3:3), as they part company with their idols (see Isaiah 30:15, 22) opting for their Saviour's full-time presence (see Romans 8:1; Psalm 16:4, 5, 11).

Although John was told to exclude the temple courtyard, the old courtyard was a needed reminder in the examination of the two witnesses' temple because Israel's economy and spirituality had been conquered by Jehovah's uncircumcised enemy, *and the same would happen to the two witnesses*. John is commanded to inspect the Christians' stewardship of the gospel and their ability to cooperate with Christ to lead sinners to God. By measuring the two witnesses' *worship* in the temple of God, the true person of worship would come to light, either "him that made heaven, and earth, and the sea, and the fountains of waters" (Rev. 14:7) or Baalim, the imposter "vicar" of God. John must judge the church's new dispensation and its Christians. Do they remain "as lively stones" (1 Pet. 2:5) in God's spiritual house, "built upon the foundation of the apostles and prophets" (Eph. 2:20), patriarchs and kings, so that the faithful Old Testament Hebrews without the faithful New Testament Christians "should not be made perfect" (Heb. 11:40)? Would Jesus Christ remain the church's chief cornerstone? Or, do they lose their first love for Him, and find their lamps go out?

John's New Testament church already well established upon an accomplished sacrificial system, the angel therefore commanded him to ignore measuring the Old Testament courtyard. John was to concentrate on the New Testament church, judging its successes and loyalty. The apostle was to focus on the church's work of protecting the Law of God's holy condemnation of sin and the gospel of Christ's holy mercy. The church was also to present to the world their Friend's work of truth and grace in the heavenly temple as He administers His justifying virtue to convert and to cleanse on earth. Jesus justifies and makes worthy of eternity everyone in the church who are drawn to His Spirit of friendship from every letter of His word (see Romans 8:1, 2; John 1:9; 8:12, 30).

So, inclusive of the earthly sanctuary economy, the Revelation 11 prophecy extends far beyond the 42 prophetic month, 1,260 year period, both before that central period as well as after it. In total, the prophecy provides a concise gospel continuum, from beginning to end of the great controversy, from the antediluvian Adamites to the Adventists. It looks far backward past the holy Protestant Reformation, through the Dark Ages and the persecuted wilderness church, to the apostolic era (see verses 3-6); and, by "the court" (vs. 2), it alludes to even further back through the embattled Hebrews to the first sacrifice for the fallen pair in Eden.

> The solemn events which are now taking place belong to a series of events in the chain of history, the first link of which is connected with Eden *Seventh-day Adventist Bible Commentary*, vol. 7, p. 985.

The holy Hebrew religion was constantly menaced by its satanic counterfeit, Baalim, until Judaism so deeply imbibed the sophisticated spirit of the world's one religion that Providence gave the Hebrews' holy religion "unto the Gentiles" (Rev. 11:2, cf Dan. 9:26, 27; Deut. 32:45; Isa. 10:23; 63:6; 65:1; Matt. 21:42, 43; Luke 16:9). Finally, the Lord could circumcise the old covenant, bringing forth the new covenant's more perfect science of salvation (see 2 Timothy 1:10; Hebrews 7:11-28; 8:6, 7; 9:14, 15, 23; Philippians 3:3, 8-10; Romans 2:28, 29). But, the church abandoned its new power for transforming hearts and characters in exchange for the primeval system of Babylonian gods, priesthood, and sacramental temples. Satan usurped the church's infinite offering of Christ and changed His unchangeable heavenly priesthood of reconciling rebellious man to God (see Hebrews 7:24; 8:1, 2). He stole away from them Christ's Spirit of grace and truth, of which apostasy Daniel had prophesied (see Daniel 8:11; 11:30-32). Determined to receive into church fellowship all the popular pagan philosophies and festivals, the Christian fathers purposely deafened themselves to scriptural reproof. Only a couple of decades after the apostle John the earliest Waldensian reformers brought the first rebuke against these errors from antiquity. Then, the original church separated from the reprobate post-apostolic, as that church departed purposely, determinedly, and increasingly from biblical truth until their synagogue of Satan would wage war against the holy original church (see 1 Peter 4:1; 2 Peter 3:15).

The Revelation 11 prophecy also looks forward beyond the 1,260 year period and the Reformation, to the Puritanical and popular Protestant churches until the Remnant of the Reformation appears (see verse 7). Then, it shows the Latter Rain falling (see verse 11, 12). And the whole gospel dispensation concludes then with the church humbled, fully obedient to its calling. They take back the holy city, and fill it with the righteousness and glory of God, clean and bright (see Revelation 19:7, 8, margin). The heavenly temple is cleansed and human probation closes (see verse 15-19).

So, the Revelation 11 history represents Christ's work for those who have carried the torch of truth since the beginning of time: the ancient holy Hebrew religion of Adam, Noah, Eber, and Abraham, of Moses, David, and the major and minor prophets; and the holy apostolic era church, the Waldensian Christians and other groups of the church in the wilderness during the unholy Dark Ages (see Revelation 12:6, 12-14; *Truth Triumphant*). The two witnesses continue their prophesying, symbolizing the Reformers and the Puritan denominations (see Revelation 12:15, 16); and lastly, they represent the group that carries the present truth into the end of time, the Advent Movement (see Revelation 12:17).

Revelation 11 gives us the true apostolic succession on earth that has carried the light of truth by the grace of God through Christ — the unofficial church, "being defamed, …made as the filth of the world, and…the offscouring of all things unto this day" (1 Cor. 4:13, cf Heb. 11:37, 38).

Contrast those faithful people to the popes and prelates, "which are gorgeously apparelled, and live delicately…in kings' courts" (Luke 7:25). The papal hierarchy masqueraded as holy men of God, but had disqualified themselves from the kingdom of God by beating their fellowservants, and daily eating and drinking with the drunken (see Matthew 24:48-51; Deuteronomy 32:32-34, 43).

All the while, the men, women, and children who were valiant for the truth (see Daniel 11:32) "suffered the loss of all things" (Phil. 3:8), and counted it all but dung, that they might win Christ. They knew the fellowship of His sufferings.

Here are they that keep the commandments of God, and the faith of Jesus; hence, Satan's intense persecution to overthrow them by his Church. He usurped Christ's name in order the more readily to deceive, and to furiously protect and advance antinomian Ashtaroth and Baalim bitter enslavement. Adventism, as reformers and protesters of the Church, holds the highly privileged place of finalizing this prophecy of the whole great controversy played out on earth, Revelation chapter 11.

It's the everlasting gospel and the church that God must judge by His prophet in this Revelation 11 vision. Satanic forces take away the redemption of Christ from the apostolic church. The indolent church did not repent of her platonic relationship with Jesus (see Revelation 2:4, 5), and therefore the church is conquered by spiritualism (see Revelation 11:8; 2:13) which had so often troubled Old Testament Israel (see Isaiah 52:1-5; Daniel 9:7). Henceforth, hope in Christ's heavenly intercession is lost to the vast church majority as satanic forces "tread under foot" "the holy city" (Rev. 11:2, cf Dan. 8:11; Dan. 11:21-23; 2 Thess. 2:3, 4; Acts 20:29-31; 1 Tim. 3:13; Phil. 3:18, 19; 1 John 2:18; 4:1-3). Every desire for His Spirit and His righteousness devils and their human hosts indefatigably "devoured" and "stamped" (Dan. 7:7), so that "both the sanctuary and the host" are completely "trodden under foot" (Dan. 8:13). The Lord's two spokesmen must defend the apostolic Christianity against Satan's lying spirits. Those spirits which inspire the pagan "people and kindreds and tongues and nations" (Rev. 11:9) already occupy spiritual Jerusalem and the temple courtyard, as twenty years previous to John's vision Jesus had cut off Judaism, the Babylon-corrupted Jewish religion, due to Judaism's "overspreading of abominations" (Dan. 9:27, cf Jer. 16:13; Mal. 2:11-13; John 19:15).

Revelation 11:2 shows that Satan holds the old covenant temple mount, but he lusts to also take the sanctuary of strength fortified with righteousness by faith by Jesus. "As a cottage in a vineyard, as a lodge in a garden of cucumbers, as a besieged city" (Isa. 1:8, cf Dan. 8:12), the gospel refuge for the two witnesses is surrounded by their greatly outnumbering enemies of righteousness. The enemy's pagan influence was enveloping and neutralizing the apostolic church, as Assyria had done to the northern kingdom of Israel. These new dispensation forces of Baal are the very same pagan invaders that ever sought to intrude into the sacred precincts of God's holy Law. The Old and New Testament churches have the very same enemy. Satan's religion of Baal never changes, except for its name, seeking to simulate the Lord's strategy who also never changes His religion, except for its name (see Malachi 3:5, 6; Hebrews 13:8).

As Jesus, the one true Lord Jehovah Elohim, imparts to His servants His peace and righteousness and health and life, likewise the one false lord Baal imparts to his slaves his fatal bitterness. All who depart from Jehovah to serve this god know only continual torment and restlessness, disease and a living death that must be drowned with intoxicants (see Psalm 16:4; Revelation 17:4, 6; Deuteronomy 29:18-23). Unless they imbibe Ashtoreth's multitudinous opiates, they have no rest day or night (see Isaiah 47:12-14; Jeremiah 51:58, 64), each worshiper squandering his whole 80 year opportunity to be humbled and surrendered. Satan, who offers no merciful relief for the guilt of any sinner, eventually imparts his evil to the heart of each devotee.

Baal (the same Molech, Dagon, and Beelzebub, who was the god of the primordial deep and of atheistic confusion), blistering with wrath toward every seeker for peace, blocks all efforts by Jesus to sprinkle His cleansing Spirit upon hearts suffering from "an evil conscience" (Heb. 10:22). This conscience is not evil in the sense that it is demonic, but that it is constantly under condemnation from the God of righteousness. It fears to flee to Christ for an advocate (see John 3:36; Hebrews 12:6), and its soul disturbance is exacerbated by its incumbent master, Satan. The Spirit is preserved in Christ's words as the principle of life is in the seed. Whenever the holy word enters to deliver the soul from Satan the battle between the Spirit of Christ and spirit of Satan causes compounded grief. Unrest consumes the soul day and night until surrender to Jesus can happen (see Galatians

5:17; Mark 9:20), if the troubled one determines to battle against the selfish lusts of the flesh owned by Satan's spirit, and look for selfless love, the selfless Spirit of Jesus draws him to Himself. Salvation is assured for every soul that will patiently endure while he looks for Jesus to let His Spirit do battle in his behalf (see Luke 8:15; 5:39; Isaiah 30:18).

But, the soul who refuses Christ's Spirit of life, which is housed in His written word and is seen in nature, gives up the fight for faith with God. Human promises of peace woo the seeker away from needing peace with God, as Satan offers his earthly benefits to gradually displace every need for God's acceptance.

> Every soul that refuses to give himself to God is under the control of another power. He is not his own. He may talk of freedom, but he is in the most abject slavery. He is not allowed to see the beauty of truth, for his mind is under the control of Satan. While he flatters himself that he is following the dictates of his own judgment, he obeys the will of the prince of darkness *The Desire of Ages*, p. 466.

Eventually, the absence of Christ's Spirit of life grinds the soul to powder, and the soul, intoxicated by Satan's opiates, ultimately unites with Baal to persecute all who are seeking peace with their Redeemer.

Thus the committed servant of Baal bristles at obedience to righteousness and faith; he grinds at innocence and genuine goodness and meekness. His wrath is especially intense in the presence of those who know the salvation of the one true God. He despises those who possess the Lord's purity which he hates. And their peace and soundness of mind, which he so much covets, disturbs him greatly. He may tower over Christ's servants intellectually, but the wisdom of love is His children's forté, and they "though fools, shall not err" from the love Christ gives them (Isa. 35:8, cf Job 28:28; Ps. 119:97-100).

God's true religion, that through His constant grace empowers the soul to victory over both the extremes of legalism and lawlessness, has ever been under attack by Satan. The tenacious enemy of everything good has made it his permanent challenge to rob from Jehovah's people His holy gift of a new heart, obedience to His good laws, His freedom, and His blessedness. Lucifer's successful scheme has, since the days of Cain, worked to subtly substitute God's true, holy religion with his own, bringing the Lord's people down into the world's religions of spiritual dearth, self-serving corruption, and depression — the kingdom over which he has ruled with a seductive and fierce hand (see Daniel 7:25; 8:10-12).

Revelation chapter 11 depicts this war that Satan would bring against the New Testament church. This chapter also portrays the true church's fall near the end, but its ultimate restoration and redemption. The defense of the gospel those two prophets courageously and effectively accomplish from the earliest times (see Revelation 11:3-6; 2:2, 9, 13, 24-29; 3:4). During the apostolic and post-apostolic periods, and during the 1,260 year papal supremacy, the church in the wilderness has the beloved Bible in their popular languages. For 1,260 years the persecuted prophets in the wilderness are fed manna by the sparrows of heaven. Therefore, they have the powerful authority and Spirit of God behind them for protection against Satan's onslaught of truth in the world. (See 1 John 2:18, 19; 1 Timothy 1:19, 20; 1 Corinthians 5:5; 2 Corinthians 2:6-8.)

"These are the two anointed ones, that stand by the Lord of the whole earth" (Zech. 4:14, cf Jer. 15:19). The two witnesses for Jehovah have the testimony of Jesus. They have the anointing of faith and they know the experience of dependence on Him, "Not by might, nor by power, but by my spirit, saith the LORD of hosts" (Zech. 4:6). "These are the two olive trees, and the two candlesticks standing before the God of the earth" (Rev. 11:4, cf 1 Ki. 17:1; 2 Ki. 5:16). To understand Revelation 11:4 we must look closely at the prophecy of Zechariah chapter 3. In that prophecy we hear this clue, "Thus saith the LORD of hosts; If thou wilt walk in my ways, and if thou wilt keep my charge, then thou shalt also judge my house, and shalt also keep my courts, and I will give thee places to walk among *these that stand by*. Hear now, O Joshua the high priest, thou, and thy fellows that sit before thee: for they are men wondered at: for, behold, I will bring forth my servant the BRANCH" (Zech. 3:7, 8).

From the book of Zechariah we glean that Joshua and the twenty-four priests who surrounded him were the apple of God's eye (see Zechariah 2:8). Small in the world and vulnerable, upon whom all heaven was watching, these men were an earthly representation of the heavenly throne room, high priest Joshua typifying High Priest Christ (see Zechariah 6:11-13). And not only that, but if these faulty earth-bound men and their nation, together with Joshua, would continue in sanctification after having their past unfaithfulness forgiven and justified (see Zechariah 3:1-5; Jeremiah 31:33, 34), then they could all have the heavenly experience of the sealed apostolic church, "I will give thee places to walk among these that stand by." By faith, they would sit in heavenly places in Christ, the Lord God of Israel (see Ephesians 1:3; 2:6). Five hundred years in advance He could have exalted them in the earth.

This last conditional promise to walk among those who stand by the Lord referred to those heavenly chief priest-princes on thrones and their hosts who surrounded the Lord. In other words, the promise to Joshua referred to the twenty-four elders and the cherubim we saw in Revelation chapter 4. Thus, as the apostles and the church later did, high priest Joshua and his elders could receive of the heavenly power and give it to lighten the scattered nation of Israel, the faithful Gentiles, and to the whole world. "It is a light thing that thou shouldest be my servant to raise up the tribes of Jacob, and to restore the preserved of Israel: I will also give thee for a light to the Gentiles, that thou mayest be my salvation unto the end of the earth" (Isa. 49:6). If the Israelite priests and Joshua should cooperate with the Lord, depending on His Spirit for strength, His power would run through the length and breadth of the earth (see Zechariah 3:9; 4:10; Revelation 5:6). They would see the Lord and His salvation, and in joy would stand beside Him by faith. This is the very experience of the Revelation 11 church in the wilderness as they defend the faith once given to the saints (see Revelation 11:5, 6). Their powerful message to many a burdened soul lost in that long age of darkness:

> Oh, the unspeakable greatness of that exchange, — the Sinless One is condemned, and he who is guilty goes free; the Blessing bears the curse, and the cursed is brought into blessing; the Life dies, and the dead live; the Glory is whelmed in darkness, and he who knew nothing but confusion of face is clothed with glory. — D'Aubigne, London ed., b. 12, ch. 2 *The Great Controversy*, p. 212

Righteousness by faith instills power for the witnesses of Revelation 11 to love and obey the Bible, and so fills their hearts with the character of God that they speak at will and God moves in their favor (see Revelation 11:6, cf 1 Kings 17:1; Matthew 16:18, 19; Jeremiah 1:9, 10). At peace with God and sanctified by the scriptures, they are living examples of Christ's divine insight, "If ye abide in me, and my words abide in you, ye shall ask what ye will, and it shall be done unto you. Herein is my Father glorified, that ye bear much fruit; so shall ye be my disciples" (John 15:7, 8). This arouses Satan's vehement rage; so, his official state religion redoubles its efforts to destroy them.

The sacrificial church in the wilderness rules the earth with a rod of iron. As with Elijah, the word of God resides in their heart, and by Spirit of the Lord conviction shoots out of the missionaries' and leaders' mouths, and overcomes the enemies of God's Law (see Revelation 11:5; 2 Kings 1:10). They rebuke the corruptions of the official Church, and fearlessly face the deadly repercussions. The apostolic church and its descendants in the wilderness speak the truth with the help of heavenly agencies; and devils tremble, along with their human hosts.

> Their blameless deportment and unswerving faith were a continual reproof that disturbed the sinner's peace. Though few in numbers, without wealth, position, or honorary titles, they were a terror to evildoers wherever their character and doctrines were known. Therefore they were hated by the wicked, even as Abel was hated by the ungodly Cain. For the same reason that Cain slew Abel, did those who sought to throw off the restraint of the Holy Spirit, put to death God's people *The Great Controversy*, p. 46.

They prove what Satan claims is impossible — keeping the commandments of God through the faith of Jesus. Their expulsion of sin from the church the Gentiles within Christianity ceased to do (see Jeremiah 6:29). But, overcoming sin comes as naturally as their own volition; and God protects these early Waldensians and the later Reformers.

> He that overcometh, and keepeth my works unto the end, to him will I give power over the nations: and he shall rule them with a rod of iron; as the vessels of a potter shall they be broken to shivers: even as I received of my Father (Rev. 2:26, 27).

Finally, the Advent movement picks up the torch of heavenly light and marches forth when the seven trumpets begin (see Revelation 11:7). All through the centuries since Christ ascended, the two witnesses prosper, because God is with them. He wrote the Law into their hearts; and, grateful to receive that greatest desire of their heart, they call themselves by His name. They have power to endure the rigors of maintaining the high standard, even while the Gentile forces work relentlessly to discourage them and to wear out their faith in Jesus. This long, sacred history is comprehended in the eleventh chapter of Revelation.

All of these champions of God's truth reign as kings and priests as their godly lives and teachings "tormented them that dwelt on the earth" (Rev. 11:10). Their reign continued from the apostolic church down to the Advent movement — that is, to those humbled Protestants who adhered to the leadership of Ellen White.

The world's torment came from the absence of the Spirit of truth in the heart and through their full acceptance of error, while their religion and philosophy had been partially drowning them in empty emotional zeal. But, the presence of the Law and grace lived out in the children of God awakened the wicked to their already aggravating torment. The blinding light of self-denying love brought to life their burning misery. The Waldensians' determined obedience to God through Jesus reacting against sin's rebellious power in the unbelievers provided the water of life to the enemies of God. But, every merciful conviction from the Spirit heaped coals of fire on their unbelieving heads (see Proverbs 25:21, 22). It was the experience of Paul, as he breathed out threatenings and slaughter against the believers. "I was alive without the law once: but when the commandment came, sin revived, and I died" (Rom. 7:9). The same occurred every time Jesus came face to face with a demoniac. And the same still happens every time one who is disaffected from Jesus meets a soul who is surrendered to Him.

"These have power to shut heaven, that it rain not in the days of their prophecy: and have power over waters to turn them to blood, and to smite the earth with all plagues, as often as they will" (Rev. 11:6). By the power vested in them, these followers of Jesus fulfill His promise,

> I will give unto thee the keys of the kingdom of heaven: and whatsoever thou shalt bind on earth shall be bound in heaven: and whatsoever thou shalt loose on earth shall be loosed in heaven (Matt. 16:19).

By their response to the witnesses' appeals in life and in death, the people made their eternal decisions for heaven or for hell (see 1 Timothy 1:20).

> Whose soever sins ye remit, they are remitted unto them; and whose soever sins ye retain, they are retained (John 20:23).

> Verily I say unto you, Whatsoever ye shall bind on earth shall be bound in heaven: and whatsoever ye shall loose on earth shall be loosed in heaven. Again I say unto you, That if two of you shall agree on earth as touching any thing that they shall ask, it shall be done for them of my Father which is in heaven (Matt. 18:18, 19).

> Behold, I have put my words in thy mouth. See, I have this day set thee over the nations and over the kingdoms, to root out, and to pull down, and to destroy, and to throw down, to build, and to plant (Jer. 1: 9, 10).

They have faith as a grain of mustard seed, and command evil to be plucked up and cast into the sea; and it obeyed them. Like Davids to their Goliaths and Israel to their captors, they say, "Who art thou, O great mountain? before Zerubbabel thou shalt become a plain" (Zech. 4:7). And, often enough, in the place of wickedness in high places, a mountain of "Grace, grace" (verse 7) descended from above.

> Ye are my witnesses, saith the LORD, and my servant whom I have chosen: that ye may know and believe me, and understand that I am he: before me there was no God formed, neither shall there be after me. I, even I, am the LORD; and beside me there is no saviour. I have declared, and have saved, and I have shewed, when there was no strange god among you: therefore ye are my witnesses, saith the LORD, that I am God (Isa. 43:10-12).

From His throne in the temple of His Father's pure presence, Christ preserves the faith of Waldensian, Albegensian, Celtic, Syrian, St. Thomas, and other witnesses around the world. All the while, they are under the constant threat of persecution by those who hate the truth, whose religion of Baal keeps them from conviction of sin and peace with God.

For "forty and two months" (Rev. 11:2), "a time and times and the dividing of time", wicked hosts "wear out the saints of the most High" (Dan. 7:25) — the unrecognized, beleaguered church of Christ (see Revelation 11:2; Daniel 7:21, 25; 8:10). The witnesses threaten the kingdom of Satan, being living proof of victory over sin, contradicting what the devil has convinced his humanistic crusaders is not possible. Therefore the faithful wilderness church arouses Satan's utmost wrath. He waits his opportunity to strike his revenge on their living faith; *and he succeeds.*

Thus it is, even after the witnesses' long, exciting partnership with the Lord — prophesying for more than "a thousand two hundred and threescore" (Rev.

11:3) years, while the truth they have protected is being trampled under unholy feet by the recognized Church until 1798 — that the two witnesses' effectiveness finally wanes. As the Beast of Revelation 13 ascends out of the bottomless pit at the start of the fifth trumpet (see Revelation 11:7, cf Revelation 13:15; 9:1), and is let loose to overwhelm the world to preempt the final redemption at Christ's return, the devil and his premier earthly agency make war against the remnant of the Lord's witnesses, who have preached the new truth of the three angels' Judgment Day messages.

> The dragon was wroth with the woman, and went to make war with the remnant of her seed, which keep the commandments of God, and have the testimony of Jesus Christ (Rev. 12:17).

Throughout the Dark Ages, this prophecy shows Christ's ability to withstand everything that Satan could bring against His gospel movement; but when the brightest light to the world comes to His church, He must retreat. Why must Christ retreat? The Lord must fall back today as He has done many times throughout sacred history whenever His own people grow weary of loving service to their Lord and of the self-sacrifice that serving Him requires. As one mourned,

> I am filled with sadness when I think of our condition as a people. The Lord has not closed heaven to us, but our own course of continual backsliding has separated us from God. Pride, covetousness, and love of the world have lived in the heart without fear of banishment or condemnation. Grievous and presumptuous sins have dwelt among us. And yet the general opinion is that the church is flourishing and that peace and spiritual prosperity are in all her borders.
>
> The church has turned back from following Christ her Leader and is steadily retreating toward Egypt. Yet few are alarmed or astonished at their want of spiritual power. Doubt, and even disbelief of the testimonies of the Spirit of God, is leavening our churches everywhere. Satan would have it thus. Ministers who preach self instead of Christ would have it thus. The testimonies are unread and unappreciated. God has spoken to you. Light has been shining from His word and from the testimonies, and both have been slighted and disregarded. The result is apparent in the lack of purity and devotion and earnest faith among us *Testimonies for the church*, vol. 5, p. 217.

We have turned away from Jesus, desiring the Egyptian good life; we have "believed not the truth, but had pleasure in unrighteousness" (2 Thess. 2:12). Is that an exaggeration? The precedent for this departure we have seen clearly in the post-apostolic church apostasy. Will the Remnant heed the principle that history repeats itself, and no less does sacred history? Shouldn't the following testimony, given to the post-Reformation denominations and also to their Remnant, cause the Remnant to fear that we could also have similarity to the backsliding late-apostolic church in the early Dark Ages? If we've seen an intended prophecy upon the churches of Protestantism in the next two statements of apostolic history, can't we also see those statements as a warning directed to the denominations' Remnant today?

> The great adversary now endeavored to gain by artifice what he had failed to secure by force. Persecution ceased, and in its stead were substituted the dangerous allurements of temporal prosperity and worldly honor. Idolaters were led to receive a part of the Christian faith, while they rejected other essential truths. They professed to accept Jesus as the Son of God and to believe in His death and resurrection, but they had no conviction of sin and felt no need of repentance or of a change of heart. With some concessions on their part they proposed that Christians should make concessions, that all might unite on the platform of belief in Christ.
>
> Now the church was in fearful peril. Prison, torture, fire, and sword were blessings in comparison with this. Some of the Christians stood firm, declaring that they could make no compromise. Others were in favor of yielding or modifying some features of their faith and uniting with those who had accepted a part of Christianity, urging that this might be the means of their full conversion. That was a time of deep anguish to the faithful followers of Christ. Under a cloak of pretended Christianity, Satan was insinuating himself into the church, to corrupt their faith and turn their minds from the word of truth *The Great Controversy*, p. 42.

Little by little, at first in stealth and silence, and then more openly as it increased in strength and gained control of the minds of men, "the mystery of iniquity" carried forward its deceptive and blasphemous work. Almost imperceptibly the customs of heathenism found their way into the Christian church. The spirit of compromise and conformity was restrained for a time by the fierce persecutions which the church endured under paganism. But as persecution ceased, and Christianity entered the courts and palaces of kings, she laid aside the humble simplicity of Christ and His apostles for the pomp and pride of pagan priests and rulers; and in place of the requirements of God, she substituted human theories and traditions. The nominal conversion of Constantine, in the early part of the fourth century, caused great rejoicing; and the world, cloaked with a form of righteousness, walked into the church. Now the work of corruption rapidly progressed. Paganism, while appearing to be vanquished, became the conqueror. Her spirit controlled the church. Her doctrines, ceremonies, and superstitions were incorporated into the faith and worship of the professed followers of Christ *Ibid.* p. 49.

"The thing that hath been, it is that which shall be; and that which is done is that which shall be done" (Ecc. 1:9). "And an host was given him [the resurrected little horn power (see Revelation 13:11-15; 2 Thessalonians 2:9-12)] against the daily sacrifice [Christ pouring out His soul on the cross and the daily ministering of His Spirit from His sanctuary] by reason of transgression [the mass departure of His people for the little horn and its Baal worship], and it cast down the truth to the ground; and it practised, and prospered" (Dan. 8:12). So different to the ardor of the Reformers compared the 19th century Protestants' dry spiritual condition (see Revelation 3:1). Protestantism's mingling the practices and spirit of Catholic Evangelicalism into the gospel, and surrendering to abundant worldly prosperity, is precisely the reason the Lord is letting the Papacy rise up again before delighted, but benighted Protestant eyes. In all the pages of sacred history, whenever the people of God joined in the religion and pastimes of the surrounding nations, the Lord raised up those nations to punish His people by their subjugation (see Judges 2:10-23; 3:5-15; 4:1, 2; 6:1-6; 13:1; 2 Kings 17:7-20; Isaiah 10:5, 6; Jeremiah 1:14-16; Amos 6:14; Habakkuk 1:6). The same is happening again today to the Protestant American Evangelical denominations and to the Protestant American Advent movement.

We should never copy the methods and practices of the devil, even in competing with him for souls. Competing with Satan by using his methods leads to conceding to Satan. This error is how the post-apostolic church of Revelation 13:1 and 17:3 came to look so much like the devil in Revelation 12:3. We should leave the warfare against the devil to God, and follow the methods and example of Jesus. Jesus is our tree of life; He is our wisdom. Patterning our evangelism and worship methods and practices after anyone other than Jesus is eating from the forbidden tree.

> Hell hath enlarged herself, and opened her mouth without measure: and their glory, and their multitude, and their pomp, and he that rejoiceth, shall descend into it. And the mean man shall be brought down, and the mighty man shall be humbled, and the eyes of the lofty shall be humbled: but the LORD of hosts shall be exalted in judgment, and God that is holy shall be sanctified in righteousness (Isa. 5:14-16).

While Mrs. White lived and counseled, kept our faith alive; while she patiently pleaded with us and prayed for us and grieved over our worldly-mindedness, Satan must remain at bay. Yet, however the devil's claim on the Advent movement was restrained, his war was on. Then after Mrs. White's passing, by the confusion of world wars, by the surrounding atheistic and spiritualistic delusions, and by the tempting train of modernization, the spirit from the abyss that had already been captivating the Sunday denominations worked relentlessly to overcome sabbatarian Adventism.

> When they shall have finished their testimony, the beast that ascendeth out of the bottomless pit shall make war against them, and shall overcome them, and kill them (Rev. 11:7).

Protestant Americans and Adventists have departed from preaching the three angels' warnings and the high calling of Jesus. Our history of dodging the tough love from the Testimony of Jesus is the reason that we see in Revelation 11 the once-faithful messengers of the Lord killed and laying in the streets of the unholy city — the paganized Church — "which spiritually is called Sodom and Egypt" (Rev. 11:8, cf Isa. 1:10; Dan. 11:40-43).

Therefore thus saith the LORD of hosts; Because ye have not heard my words, behold, I will send and take all the families of the north, saith the LORD, and Nebuchadrezzar the king of Babylon, my servant, and will bring them against this land, and against the inhabitants thereof, and against all these nations round about, and will utterly destroy them, and make them an astonishment, and an hissing, and perpetual desolations. Moreover I will take from them the voice of mirth, and the voice of gladness, the voice of the bridegroom, and the voice of the bride, the sound of the millstones, and the light of the candle.... For many nations and great kings shall serve themselves of them also: and I will recompense them according to their deeds, and according to the works of their own hands.... And the peaceable habitations are cut down because of the fierce anger of the LORD. He hath forsaken his covert, as the lion: for their land is desolate because of the fierceness of the oppressor, and because of his fierce anger (Jer. 25:8-10, 14, 37, 38).

Having rejected the special work of purification, now we are delving into the occult through the mesmerizing "voice", the whispering, "low" "speech" (Isa. 29:4) of Spiritual Formation. By "apostasy, spiritualism, free-lovism" from a "concealed" lawless, Christless brand of quasi-righteousness by faith in Spiritual Formation we are coming under a unique "strain of spiritualism" that will lead many "to give heed to seducing spirits, and doctrines of devils" *Manuscript Release*, vol. 8, p. 304. We are whole-heartedly joining in the mirth and gladness of the imagined victorious Evangelical denominations. By our taking part in their pagan celebration of life we are flaunting our refusal to turn to the Lord's standards, which have been so clearly laid out before us by Mrs. White. And the Lord is leaving our dead souls in endless torment.

O Jerusalem, which hast drunk at the hand of the LORD the cup of his fury; thou hast drunken the dregs of the cup of trembling, and wrung them out. There is none to guide her among all the sons whom she hath brought forth; neither is there any that taketh her by the hand of all the sons that she hath brought up. These two things are come unto thee; who shall be sorry for thee? desolation, and destruction, and the famine, and the sword: by whom shall I comfort thee? Thy sons have fainted, they lie at the head of all the streets, as a wild bull in a net: they are full of the fury of the LORD, the rebuke of thy God (Isa. 51:17-20).

Her gates are sunk into the ground; he hath destroyed and broken her bars: her king and her princes are among the Gentiles: the law is no more; her prophets also find no vision from the LORD....

All that pass by clap their hands at thee; they hiss and wag their head at the daughter of Jerusalem, saying, Is this the city that men call The perfection of beauty, The joy of the whole earth?

All thine enemies have opened their mouth against thee: they hiss and gnash the teeth: they say, We have swallowed her up: certainly this is the day that we looked for; we have found, we have seen it....

The young and the old lie on the ground in the streets: my virgins and my young men are fallen by the sword; thou hast slain them in the day of thine anger; thou hast killed, and not pitied (Lam. 2:9, 15, 16, 21, cf Deut. 29:18-28).

The "people and kindreds and tongues and nations" (Rev. 11:9) of Satan's hosts during the fifth and sixth trumpets have attacked the eternal realities and replaced them with temporal and spiritualistic non-realities. Now, our faith is killed, righteousness by faith is dead. We rarely speak of the Latter Rain and many push Christ's Second Advent off into the distant future. In our hearts we have said, "The days are prolonged, and every vision faileth." "The LORD hath forsaken the earth, and the LORD seeth not" (Eze. 12:22; 9:9).

The Son of God should be our standard *as presented from Ellen White*, not the Jesus from the Evangelical denominations (see 1 Peter 2:21). Christ, who was so dedicated to His Father's Law, is far removed from the things that we hope for and love. And the faith of Christ which comes in the power of His Spirit and, by which we are justified in the Spirit (see Romans 2:13; James 2:21, 22; Luke 18:8), is desolated. The movement's special work of purification (see *The Great Controversy*, p. 425) has ended. The standard is much higher than we have thought or striven for. "For my thoughts are not your thoughts, neither are your ways my ways, saith the

LORD" (Isa. 55:8). The aim is deeper, broader, and more distant than we have been willing to conceptualize. We have abandoned the standard: "Ye shall be holy: for I the LORD your God am holy" (Lev. 19:2). "Be ye therefore perfect, even as your Father which is in heaven is perfect" (Matt. 5:48). The special gift of prophecy should have brought us to a special, deep need of Jesus' merits and to that special work of purification. But, Jesus was never seen in the high standard, and thus never inspired us.

"Godliness — godlikeness — is the goal to be reached"; the object to achieve "includes everything good, and pure, and noble" *Education*, p. 18. But, for too long we've balked at the high standard. Like ancient Israel, we've said **No** to God too many times, and He is allowing confusion to make inroads into His movement. Our works and worship have been up, but simple faith has been down. The work of righteousness by faith has become only work, for Jesus has been lost sight of and left out of the fight for grace. By turning away from the Lord's correction and instruction, the collage where we could have seen Jesus, we are blind to Him. Missionary zeal has spread the message of Christ's return and the importance of the Sabbath, the truths about the state of the dead and the prophecies. But, overcoming, victory over sin through the "terror" (2 Cor. 5:11) of God's judgment and the "constraint" of Christ's love (see verse 14), has not materialized. Neither has the smoke of our torment been quenched with the water of life, the Spirit of Christ Jesus in the Law. And we are in danger of doing to the second refreshing from the presence of the Lord what the Jews did to the first (see John 12:19; 11:46-51).

Denying the work of the Spirit, generation after generation have forced obedience into our lives, "until now the kingdom of heaven suffereth violence" (Matt. 11:12). And the result of such exhausting duress has left discouragement, depression, and finally doubt that the Lord can keep us from falling under temptation. Satan has taken full advantage of our forced frame of mind and has driven love for the word of God far from our children, who want Hollywood instead of the holy God, and basketball instead of the Bible.

The Ordinance of humility has ceased for many, and our communion services rarely are a thoughtful hour of remembering the closing scenes of the Saviour's life. Many arrive late to Sabbath school or struggle into the worship service, and then look forward to the end of a Sabbath tradition in order to get on with life as usual. For others, the Sabbath has become a day only for human fellowship and no longer for communion with Jesus. A name on a baptismal certificate assumes a title to heaven, and membership in the church is assumed to mean a conversion of the heart. Examination of the soul is rare. Our pride has not bowed low before the righteousness of God; we remain stiff-necked before the Testimony of Jesus.

When the Son of man cometh, shall he find faith on the earth? (Luke 18:8).

Who may abide the day of his coming? and who shall stand when he appeareth? for he is like a refiner's fire, and like fullers' soap: and he shall sit as a refiner and purifier of silver: and he shall purify the sons of Levi, and purge them as gold and silver, that they may offer unto the LORD an offering in righteousness (Mal. 3:2, 3).

That I may know him, and the power of his resurrection, and the fellowship of his sufferings, being made conformable unto his death; if by any means I might attain unto the resurrection of the dead (Phil. 3:10, 11).

Jesus will come down in the Latter Rain (see Acts 3:19, 20; Genesis 11:5), whether we are ready or not. He will cleanse His earthly temple a second time as He did when He walked among the Jews. There is no heavenly temple cleansing without an earthly temple cleansing also. Removing the idols and false religion always precedes the return of Jesus to His covenant (see Joshua 24:14, 15; 1 Kings 18:21). Shouldn't we be trembling that the Advent movement has come to a generation that has forgotten the way that the Lord has led us and His teachings in our past history? Aren't we now empty of His Spirit, and primed for everything that our modern Baal and Ashtoreth are offering us from the rest of the world religions, Spiritual Formation and celebration? Can't we see ourselves through biblical history? Or, is biblical history just a nice bedtime story?

And also all that generation were gathered unto their fathers: and there arose another generation after them, which knew not the LORD, nor yet the works which he had done for Israel. And the children of Israel did evil in the sight of the LORD, and served Baalim: and they forsook the LORD God of their fathers, which brought them out of the land of Egypt, and followed other gods, of the gods of the people that were round about them, and bowed themselves unto them, and provoked the LORD to anger. And they forsook the LORD, and served Baal and Ashtaroth. And the anger of the LORD was hot against Israel, and he delivered them into the hands of spoilers that spoiled them, and he sold them into the hands of their enemies round about, so that they could not any longer stand before their enemies (Jdg. 2:10-14).

We are deceived, self-satisfied, and asleep in our sins. The love of many has waxed cold. How can we continue to applaud ourselves for a job well done? Shouldn't we appropriate the scripture condemnations to ourselves? Shouldn't we search out where it was that the Advent movement left the Lord, instead of plodding along trying to mend our ephod that is threadbare and "marred" (Jer. 13:7)?

> The line of distinction between professed Christians and the ungodly is now hardly distinguishable. Church members love what the world loves and are ready to join with them *The Great Controversy*, p. 588.

Just as the Protestants and we ourselves have turned to the false gods that are today driving Spiritual Formation and emerging church worship, the houses of Israel and Judah would not cease from working to redeem themselves through the worship of false gods. Therefore they could not give Jesus their whole heart. And if they would never submit their heart to His conviction and blessing, the Lord could not remove their thorny hearts and abrasive characters. So, His hard words fell on their ears. He would cease to restrain His vengeance. He would send them unbeatable enemy empires. He would "proclaim…the day of vengeance of our God" (Isa. 61:2).

> The LORD shall bring upon thee, and upon thy people, and upon thy father's house, days that have not come, from the day that Ephraim departed from Judah; even the king of Assyria.
>
> And it shall come to pass in that day, that the LORD shall hiss for the fly that is in the uttermost part of the rivers of Egypt, and for the bee that is in the land of Assyria. And they shall come, and shall rest all of them in the desolate valleys, and in the holes of the rocks, and upon all thorns, and upon all bushes….
>
> And it shall come to pass in that day, that every place shall be, where there were a thousand vines at a thousand silverlings [pieces of silver], it shall even be for briers and thorns. With arrows and with bows shall men come thither; because all the land shall become briers and thorns (Isa. 7:17-19, 23, 24, cf Rev. 9:3-5).

> Behold, the days come, saith the LORD, that I will punish all them which are circumcised with the uncircumcised; Egypt, and Judah, and Edom, and the children of Ammon, and Moab, and all that are in the utmost corners, that dwell in the wilderness: for all these nations are uncircumcised, and all the house of Israel are uncircumcised in the heart (Jer. 9:25, 26).

Because they would not look into the humbling, condemning Law of God and rest in Jehovah's power to give them His righteousness, He had to raise up Assyria to route the northern kingdom out of His presence. [Likewise, He did to the Protestants.] A century afterward, Judah had also lost the heart work of *Jehovah-tsidskenu*. [Likewise, Adventism has done.] So Jehovah had to raise up Babylon to successfully communicate to the house of Judah His condemnation of their idolatry. [Likewise, He is on the verge of doing to Adventists and Protestant Americans.] Don't we see ourselves in the following?

> The LORD said also unto me in the days of Josiah the king, Hast thou seen that which backsliding Israel hath done? she is gone up upon every high mountain and under every green tree, and there hath played the harlot. And I said after she had done all these things, Turn thou unto me. But she returned not. And her treacherous sister Judah saw it. And I saw, when for all the causes whereby backsliding Israel committed adultery I had put her away, and given her a bill of divorce; yet her treacherous sister Judah feared not, but went and played the harlot also. And it came to pass through the lightness of her whoredom, that she defiled the land…. And yet for all this her treacherous sister Judah hath not turned unto me with her whole heart, *but feignedly*, saith the LORD (Jer. 3:6-10).

One hundred years later, the Jews had not corrected this problem.

Then came the word of the LORD of hosts unto me, saying, Speak unto all the people of the land, and to the priests, saying, When ye fasted and mourned in the fifth and seventh month, even those seventy years, did ye at all fast unto me, even to me? And when ye did eat, and when ye did drink, did not ye eat for yourselves, and drink for yourselves? (Zech. 7:4-6).

Still, another century later, the Jews had fallen back into the same empty, feigned, emotional and spiritualistic religion. What about us today?

Judah hath dealt treacherously, and an abomination is committed in Israel and in Jerusalem; for Judah hath profaned the holiness of the LORD which he loved, and hath married the daughter of a strange god. The LORD will cut off the man that doeth this, the master and the scholar, out of the tabernacles of Jacob, and him that offereth an offering unto the LORD of hosts. And this have ye done again, covering the altar of the LORD with tears, with weeping, and with crying out, insomuch that he regardeth not the offering any more, or receiveth it with good will at your hand (Mal. 2:11-13, cf Jer. 9:13-18; Eze. 8:13, 14; Mark 5:38, 40).

Behold, I will send my messenger, and he shall prepare the way before me: and the Lord, *whom ye seek*, shall suddenly come to his temple, even the messenger of the covenant, *whom ye delight in*: behold, he shall come, saith the LORD of hosts. But who may abide the day of his coming? and who shall stand when he appeareth? for he is like a refiner's fire, and like fullers' soap: and he shall sit as a refiner and purifier of silver: and he shall purify the sons of Levi, and purge them as gold and silver, that they may offer unto the LORD an offering in righteousness. Then shall the offering of Judah and Jerusalem be pleasant unto the LORD, as in the days of old, and as in former years (Mal. 3:1-4, cf Amos 5:18).

For most, the profuse emotion and the feigned delight for the Messiah would continue to His first advent. And He would not accept the spiritualistic flattery. They were completely unprepared for the Messiah and the Spirit of truth. Are we prepared for the mighty Cleaver of truth at the head of His Latter Rain?

And I will come near to you to judgment; and I will be a swift witness against the sorcerers, and against the adulterers, and against false swearers, and against those that oppress the hireling in his wages, the widow, and the fatherless, and that turn aside the stranger from his right, and fear not me, saith the LORD of hosts (Mal. 3:5).

Then shall ye begin to say, We have eaten and drunk in thy presence, and thou hast taught in our streets. But he shall say, I tell you, I know you not whence ye are; depart from me, all ye workers of iniquity (Luke 13:26, 27, cf Matt. 20:20).

We need to groan and travail in pain for the lack of Christ in us like the apostolic church did. "For in this we groan, earnestly desiring to be clothed upon with our house which is from heaven: if so be that being clothed we shall not be found naked" (2 Cor. 5:2, 3). We need to love both dispositions of divine love: strong mercy and strong conviction. We need to surrender to not only the tender goodness of Christ, but also to His terrible severity; not only His severity, but also His abounding goodness (see Isaiah 7:9-13). Then, God can send His commandment-keeping Protestants and Adventists the Spirit of His Son, putting into our hearts the humbled cry, "Father" (Gal. 4:6). He can be our everlasting Father and wonderful Counselor only if we fear Him and His Law (see Psalm 103:13; Hebrews 12:5-8). Then, through the Spirit attending His Law He will abide with us.

But, this kind of repentance cannot come from our self-sufficient hearts without a terrible punishment that will precede the Latter Rain. The proud Protestant American economic and political power must be totally destroyed. We are repeating Weimar Germany of the 1920s, and soon will repeat its similar 1930s horrific depression and chaotic transition to a Third Reich. 2017 may be the year that the final 1929 stock market collapse recurs. The 1929 collapse took place only months after the Vatican's return to power that year and first shook the pride of Protestant power after the Great War had drained Protestant America's coffers. Protestantism will officially end at its 500th anniversary in 2017, and nothing will stop Protestantism's old enemy to regain its violent dominance over the world.

When that second market collapse comes, after the Vatican has ascended to power, most Americans will give up their Protestant Constitution in exchange for the restoration of their idolatrous, perverted diets and addictive substances. Protestant Americans will sell their Reformation birthright to regain the good life as they know it now. They will beg the retired pope to return to the Vatican to pray for another year of mercy. And they will accept the conditions that he will bring with his prayers — to receive the religion of ancient Rome and to pass Sunday legislation. Americans will fill the Sunday churches of the land, where Spiritual Formation already introduces Ashtoreth to them for her lawless grace, and where they receive "the Holy Spirit" of Ashtoreth, Queen of heaven.

The economic collapse and religious revival will finish Satan's war over Protestantism's holy doctrines and self-government, and over the Protestant heart. "Multitudes will exult that God is working marvelously for them, when the work is that of another spirit. Under a religious guise, Satan will seek to extend his influence over the Christian world" *The Great Controversy*, p. 464.

In our tryst with Evangelical worship, Adventism is fast repeating the final end of ancient Israel's history, when only "a remnant shall be saved" (Rom. 9:27). The response of Israel's remnant, who received John the Baptist and the Messiah, and to whom He gave power to become the sons of God, needs to be our response now while the last troubles and the Latter Rain are yet forestalled. We need to receive our John the Baptist by the Law in the Spirit of Prophecy; and we need to receive our Messiah by His Spirit of life in the Spirit of Prophecy. Then the same blessedness upon the remnant Jews will come to the Advent movement's 144,000; and they will give it to the world as those remnant Jews gave it.

> ...they shall confess their iniquity, and the iniquity of their fathers, with their trespass which they trespassed against me, and that also they have walked contrary unto me; and that I also have walked contrary unto them, and have brought them into the land of their enemies... (Lev. 26:40).

We have turned from the doldrums of Laodicea to the excitement of Midianite worship. While we should have been sealed long ago, we are now drunken with the wine of our Ashtoreth Spiritual Formation "false prophet."

We have turned from the doldrums of Laodicea to the excitement of Midianite worship. While we should have been sealed long ago, we are now drunken with the wine of our Ashtoreth Spiritual Formation "false prophet" (Rev. 19:20, cf Rev.13:13, 14; Mal. 2:11; 1 Ki. 18:26). Jesus' concerned, stern look is upon His Advent movement. But, when His holy people will have come to total heart surrender by His strong testimony, or when they surrender through the consequences He sends due to their evading His Testimonies, *when* our power has been fully scattered by God (see Daniel 12:7), and *when* He has banished our pride and ridden from Adventism all self-sufficiency and atheism, *then* God will raise up His mighty and holy movement again.

Won't we please hear the warning that we have previously read concerning the denominations? Won't we to apply it to ourselves?

In the *Congregational Journal* of May 23, 1844 Professor Finney of Oberlin College said:

> We have had the fact before our minds, that, in general, the Protestant churches of our country, as such, were either apathetic or hostile to nearly all the moral reforms of the age. There are partial exceptions, yet not enough to render the fact otherwise than general. We have also another corroborated fact: the almost universal absence of revival influence in the churches. The spiritual apathy is almost all-pervading, and is fearfully deep; .... Very extensively, church members are becoming devotees of fashion, — join hands with the ungodly in parties of pleasure, in dancing, in festivities, etc.... But we need not expand this painful subject. Suffice it that the evidence thickens and rolls heavily upon us, to show that the *churches generally are becoming sadly degenerate*. They have gone very far from the Lord, and He has withdrawn Himself from them *The Great Controversy*, p. 377.

We have forgotten to stretch for the mark of the high calling of God in Christ Jesus. Says our John the Baptist to us:

> Who may abide the day of His coming? and who shall stand when He appeareth? for He is

like a refiner's fire, and like fullers' soap: and He shall sit as a refiner and purifier of silver: and He shall purify the sons of Levi, and purge them as gold and silver, that they may offer unto the Lord an offering in righteousness. Malachi 3:2, 3. Those who are living upon the earth when the intercession of Christ shall cease in the sanctuary above are to stand in the sight of a holy God without a mediator. **Their robes must be spotless** [emphasis mine], their characters must be purified from sin by the blood of sprinkling. Through the grace of God and their own diligent effort they must be conquerors in the battle with evil. While the investigative judgment is going forward in heaven, while the sins of penitent believers are being removed from the sanctuary, there is to be a special work of purification, of putting away of sin, among God's people upon earth....

When this work shall have been accomplished [emphasis mine], the followers of Christ will be ready for His appearing. "Then shall the offering of Judah and Jerusalem be pleasant unto the Lord, as in the days of old, and as in former years." Malachi 3:4. Then the church which our Lord at His coming is to receive to Himself will be a "glorious church, not having spot, or wrinkle, or any such thing." Ephesians 5:27. Then she will look "forth as the morning, fair as the moon, clear as the sun, and terrible as an army with banners." Song of Solomon 6:10 *The Great Controversy*, p. 425.

Christ is waiting with longing desire for the manifestation of Himself in His church. When the character of Christ shall be perfectly reproduced in His people, then He will come to claim them as His own.

It is the privilege of every Christian not only to look for but to hasten the coming of our Lord Jesus Christ, (2 Peter 3:12, margin). Were all who profess His name bearing fruit to His glory, how quickly the whole world would be sown with the seed of the gospel. Quickly the last great harvest would be ripened, and Christ would come to gather the precious grain *Christ's Object Lessons*, p. 69.

The Lord can do nothing toward the recovery of man until, convinced of his own weakness, and stripped of all self-sufficiency, he yields himself to the control of God. Then he can receive the gift that God is waiting to bestow. From the soul that feels his need, nothing is withheld. He has unrestricted access to Him in whom all fullness dwells. "For thus saith the high and lofty One that inhabiteth eternity, whose name is Holy; I dwell in the high and holy place, with him also that is of a contrite and humble spirit, to revive the spirit of the humble, and to revive the heart of the contrite ones." Isaiah 57:15 *The Desire of Ages*, p. 300.

When "the seed should come to whom the promise was made" (Gal. 3:19), when that "chosen generation" (1 Pet. 2:9, cf Ps. 24:6) has assumed the posture of meek children before the Spirit of Prophecy counsels and has seen the vision of Jesus exemplifying and personifying His own testimonies, then He will renumber the hosts of the Adventist 144,000, restarting the movement, and will give us the Latter Rain.

If then their uncircumcised hearts be humbled, and they then accept of the punishment of their iniquity: then will I remember my covenant with Jacob, and also my covenant with Isaac, and also my covenant with Abraham will I remember (Lev. 26:41, 42).

Until we personally admit to the failure of our movement to obey the counsels of Sr. White and individually confess that transgression to Jesus, we cannot be trusted with the Latter Rain. We cannot be trusted any more than the remnant of Israel could be trusted with entrance into Canaan until they had reconciled themselves to the laws of Moses while they were in the wilderness. Without recognition and admission to our failure of the Advent mission, God's Spirit cannot resurrect us to His purpose to warn and to prepare the world for His return (see Revelation 11:11, 12). Abundantly more is needed than praying for the Latter Rain twice every day. Without surrender to the Testimony of Jesus and to Jacob's repentance He cannot entrust to us the final preaching to the whole world any more than the Jews could receive the Early Rain without acknowledging God's punishment for their departure from Him (see John 8:33), and then falling on the Anointed One sent to them (see Luke 2:34). Won't we appropriate the Lord's profitable rebuke, that we are repeating the history of Judah, as our Protestant brethren have repeated that of the northern kingdom of Israel? Won't we look forward to these promises?

> For, lo, the days come, saith the LORD, that I will bring again the captivity of my people Israel and Judah, saith the LORD: and I will cause them to return to the land that I gave to their fathers, and they shall possess it (Jer. 30:3).
>
> In those days, and in that time, saith the LORD, the children of Israel shall come, they and the children of Judah together, going and weeping: they shall go, and seek the LORD their God (Jer. 50:4).
>
> They shall come with weeping, and with supplications will I lead them: I will cause them to walk by the rivers of waters in a straight way, wherein they shall not stumble: for I am a father to Israel, and Ephraim is my firstborn (Jer. 31:9).

Overrun by satanic hosts and fallen under corrupting temptations from Ashtoreth Spiritual Formation and Baalpeor celebration, the two witnesses lay slain in the streets of Jerusalem (see Revelation 11:8-10) (the city being an extension of the temple court and under uncircumcised, unsanctified, enemy occupation).

> There is none to guide her among all the sons whom she hath brought forth; neither is there any that taketh her by the hand of all the sons that she hath brought up. These two things are come unto thee; who shall be sorry for thee? desolation, and destruction, and the famine, and the sword: by whom shall I comfort thee? Thy sons have fainted, they lie at the head of all the streets, as a wild bull in a net: they are full of the fury of the LORD, the rebuke of thy God (Isa. 51:18-20).

Protestantism has completely capitulated, and the Advent movement is dragged out of the heavenly temple, its three angels' commission is slain. We lay in the aisles of the church, dead of righteousness by faith, and dead in trespasses and sins. We sold our judgment call and three angels' roots in exchange for acceptance into the World Council of Churches, and its empty celebration liturgy. And we sold out to the good life which this world offers, very short-lived, though it be. It's been a slow progression, but, according to this chapter 11 prophecy, the saints at the end would be finally empty of the anointing (see Revelation 11:8). The people of faith are dead in slumber and sleep (see Revelation 11:7; Isaiah 26:18).

According to Revelation 11:7, when let loose from his divinely imposed restraint as seen in Revelation chapter 9, Satan's whisperings and his 150+ year blitz of luxury and spiritualistic religion, have finally killed the beautiful, ancient heritage of the apostolic dispensation of Law and grace. And according to the trumpets prophecy, the Beast's lethal attack did not come during the 1,260 year period. As the fifth and sixth trumpets are briefly seen in Revelation 11:7, it came during the sealing; it happened on Adventism's watch.

> Church members love what the world loves and are ready to join with them, and Satan determines to unite them in one body and thus strengthen his cause by sweeping all into the ranks of spiritualism *The Great Controversy*, p. 588.
>
> In those churches which [the enemy of souls] can bring under his deceptive power he will make it appear that God's special blessing is poured out; there will be manifest what is thought to be great religious interest. Multitudes will exult that God is working marvelously for them, when the work is that of another spirit. Under a religious guise, Satan will seek to extend his influence over the Christian world *The Great Controversy*, p. 464.

Just as Judah copied the northern kingdom in its Baalim adultery before Jehovah, Adventism has copied their Protestant brothers' departure from Bible purification by stopping their ears to the holy calling of the Spirit of Prophecy. Therefore, Jehovah cannot protect them from worldliness and from the modern incursion of "Christian" sorcery through involvement with Spiritual Formation.

The newly empowered papacy and its open-hearted welcome to apostatized Protestantism leads to their final rejection by their God. Historically, temporal punishment from above has always accompanied the spiritual chastisement upon the people who would no longer walk in Jehovah's Law. But, He delays the temporal enslavement and mortality, refraining from His strange act until His truth loses all power to the draw of spiritualism in His people's hearts, the people that He was raising up to be His holy kingdom of priests.

But, the day finally arrives when divine patience has reached its limit for Protestant America, and God's restraints are removed. At that time the Vatican will collapse Protestantism's beloved stock market, as it did in 1929. Civil unrest will bring unsympathetic, hostile armies from the United Nations onto American soil. And every Protestant American and Adventist will lose his life who, against the impossible odds, will attempt to fight the divinely imposed punishment.

> For I will be unto Ephraim as a lion, and as a young lion to the house of Judah: I, even I, will tear and go away; I will take away, and none shall rescue him. I will go and return to my place, till they acknowledge their offence, and seek my face: in their affliction they will seek me early (Hos. 5:14, 15).

> They shall die of grievous deaths; they shall not be lamented; neither shall they be buried; but they shall be as dung upon the face of the earth: and they shall be consumed by the sword, and by famine; and their carcases shall be meat for the fowls of heaven, and for the beasts of the earth. For thus saith the LORD, Enter not into the house of mourning, neither go to lament nor bemoan them: for I have taken away my peace from this people, saith the LORD, even lovingkindness and mercies. Both the great and the small shall die in this land: they shall not be buried, neither shall men lament for them, nor cut themselves, nor make themselves bald for them (Jer. 16:4-6).

> Then will I cause to cease from the cities of Judah, and from the streets of Jerusalem, the voice of mirth, and the voice of gladness, the voice of the bridegroom, and the voice of the bride: for the land shall be desolate (Jer. 7:34).

> The palaces shall be forsaken; the multitude of the city shall be left; the forts and towers shall be for dens for ever,…a pasture of flocks; until the spirit be poured upon us from on high, and the wilderness be a fruitful field, and the fruitful field be counted for a forest. Then judgment shall dwell in the wilderness, and righteousness remain in the fruitful field (Isa. 32:14-16).

There will be nowhere to hide. The survivors will be abused. God will humble His Reformation children. But, His punishment will reveal those who can be humbled by the Lord and will prepare them to take His everlasting gospel to a world suffering under Satan. Once America and the nations of the world have experienced enough misery, they will cry to the pope for another year of mercy. When he grants their requests (through Mary, the mother of mercy), and when his Jesuits restore the stock market, then the unsuspecting multitudes' loyalty will gravitate from their national leaders to the Holy Father of Christendom.

The whole world will wonder after him. For the first time since the Dark Ages, "arms shall stand on his [the Vatican's] part, and they shall pollute the sanctuary of strength [with the Vatican's Spiritual Formation turning the Protestant churches into houses of spiritualism], and shall take away the daily sacrifice [the redemption through Christ], and they shall place the abomination that maketh desolate" (Dan. 11:31, cf Matt. 24:15). The whole world is on board the train of spiritualism.

> As spiritualism more closely imitates the nominal Christianity of the day, it has greater power to deceive and ensnare. Satan himself is converted, after the modern order of things. He will appear in the character of an angel of light. Through the agency of spiritualism, miracles will be wrought, the sick will be healed, and many undeniable wonders will be performed *The Great Controversy*, p. 588.

> Papists, who boast of miracles as a certain sign of the true church, will be readily deceived by this wonder-working power; and Protestants, having cast away the shield of truth, will also be deluded. Papists, Protestants, and worldlings will alike accept the form of godliness without the power, and they will see in this union a grand movement for the conversion of the world and the ushering in of the long-expected millennium *Ibid*.

But, there is hope for the slumbering saints. All who arouse to repentance and surrender to Jesus because of His punishment will see His salvation. Living in the reality of fulfilled prophecy, the faith of Jesus will stay in their hearts, for which they had been striving.

With the Protestant protected world still shaky from the global economic distress, Satan can then commence his final delusion.

> For they are the spirits of devils, working miracles, which go forth unto the kings of the earth

and of the whole world, to gather them to the battle of that great day of God Almighty (Rev. 16:14).

Unmanned drone airliners, which had been developed over the decades, fall out of the sky. Remotely controlled trains collide or derail. Buses crash and ships sink. Many passengers die. Led by the spirit world, the Jesuit-controlled media quickly broadcast to the masses the propaganda of the sudden disappearance of millions.

> He shall cause craft [H4820 "deceiving", "fraud", "false", "feigned", "guile", "subtilly", "treachery"] to prosper in his hand (Dan. 8:25).

> And he shall destroy wonderfully, and shall prosper, and practise, and shall destroy the mighty and the holy people (Dan. 8:24).

The Evangelical multitudes at that time are beholden to believe the falsehood that they missed the unbiblical secret rapture of Christ. Even the unchurched Evangelicals who had left their faith rally behind the doctrine that they had learned earlier in life. They all believe that they must endure the terrors of a wicked, evil-minded "Antichrist" about whom they have read in unscriptural novels that were originated from the Vatican. The secret rapture falsehood was the devil's complex disinformation scheme to point the Lord's finger of accusation away from Rome, the true Antichrist. When the rapture fraud is pulled off minds confused and tormented will be horrified and resentful that Christ rejected them at His invisible second advent, despite all of their church-going and good living. They were all prayed up, all tithed up, all tracted up, all Bible studied up. They were full of good works. What went wrong? Classic cases of righteousness by works (see Matthew 7:22, 23), now they are terror-stricken and petrified in self-preservation at the thought of torture from an Asian demon.

Frozen in hysteria, their only consolation is the belief that they have a second chance of seven short years to afflict their souls and to reform their lives the best they can. They believe that they must make themselves repent lest they fail in the return of Jesus seven years later and end up in the everlasting fires of hell. In order to please "God" they mentally prepare themselves to do anything the religious leaders require of them. The Secret Rapture hoax now empowers the unified Evangelical half of America to take political ascendency over the reigning anti-religion half, and the resulting civil strife leaves the Vatican-led Evangelicalism in religio-political control, making policy for the world's premier nation. A united Papal-Evangelical power dominates Christian America, dubbing the United States the new eldest son of the Church and its militant right arm. Already prepared Sunday legislation is rushed into law and the secular, religion-hating half of the population are forced to concede. The day of papal vengeance has arrived and the Vatican-installed U.S. president announces the need for cleansing from America all religious and secular dissidents. The cleansing will especially target all Bible-believing "cults" that dissent the global unification of all religions through the United Nations.

> Therefore thus saith the Lord GOD of hosts, O my people that dwellest in Zion [the 144,000], be not afraid of the [Jesuit]: he shall smite thee with a rod, and shall lift up his staff against thee, after the manner of Egypt. For yet a very little while, and the indignation shall cease, and mine anger in their destruction (See Isa. 10:24, 25, cf Rev. 19:20).

Together with the absence of peace with God in the hearts of Protestant America, the terrible economic collapse has afflicted Protestant bodies and minds and their temporal needs. Only those who were being sealed during the fifth and sixth trumpets will receive heaven's desired effect from this punishment — *yearning for Jesus' acceptance, repentance* humbled and deep, and a willing submission to the Bible and Spirit of Prophecy. The drying up of the world's wealth will test to the maximum the faith and endurance of the children of God, whether churched or unchurched. It will make life very difficult, **but** it also will open the door for the "kings of the east" (Rev. 16:12, cf Rev. 5:10; Dan. 11:44) to unite with the desolated and repentant 144,000 to overthrow the rejoicing city, triumphant Babylon the Great. "*The gates shall not be shut*" (Isa. 45:1). Nothing will prevent the King of kings' bombardment of Babylon and the deliverance of His humbled children. Therefore, despite this tragic scene in Revelation 11:8-10, the wayward Advent and Protestant movements have hope. The Spirit will be poured upon them from above.-

> Therefore hear now this, thou afflicted, and drunken, but not with wine: Thus saith thy Lord the LORD, and thy God that pleadeth the cause of his people, Behold, I have taken out of thine hand the cup of trembling, even the dregs of the cup of my fury; thou shalt no more drink

it again: but I will put it into the hand of them that afflict thee; which have said to thy soul, Bow down, that we may go over: and thou hast laid thy body as the ground, and as the street, to them that went over (Isa. 51:21-23).

According to Revelation 11:11, God has vowed to yet use a humbled Protestant Remnant. Borrowing from Ezekiel chapter 37 Jesus shows us what will happen to the Advent movement. "And he said unto me, Son of man, can these bones live?" (Eze. 37:3). Protestant, Adventist, is your heart as dried up as a bleached bone under the furious sun? If you are thirsty, then you need a well that is very deep, you need the shade of a big Rock. You need Christ's faithful love that will not let you go. You need good news from His Father's house.

> As cold waters to a thirsty soul, so is good news from a far country (Prov. 25:25).

> Make me to hear joy and gladness; that the bones which thou hast broken may rejoice (Ps. 51:8).

"Son of man, can these bones live?" From the Lord come the same earnest tones that we hear from Job and from many millions around the world, "If a man die, shall he live again?" (Job 14:14). Yes, is the rhetorical answer from Job. The dead in Christ shall be raised incorruptible. And, *Yes*, according to Revelation 11, our humbled Protestant and Adventist hearts will live again, too.

The bones that Ezekiel saw were not only dry, they were "very dry" (Eze. 37:2) under the jealous wrath of God. Yet, the humbled descendants of the Reformation have the invitation from Jesus, "If any man thirst, let him come unto me, and drink. He that believeth on me, as the scripture hath said, out of his belly shall flow rivers of living water" (John 7:37, 38). Why were those bones so dead and so dry? Because both Israel and Judah had sought the world's one atheistic religion of Baal, and the empty rejoicing and lawless, brazen celebration of "happy" Ashtoreth. That happiness and celebration was Satan himself, *sitting within God's own children*, deviously laughing at God and at His condemning Law. His Remnant has been under the wrathful frown of the Lord, and He will cause us to be laid out under His hot displeasure, according to Revelation 11:9 (see also Jeremiah 8:2; Numbers 25:4).

> I will take from them the voice of mirth, and the voice of gladness, the voice of the bridegroom, and the voice of the bride, the sound of the millstones, and the light of the candle. And this whole land shall be a desolation, and an astonishment (Jer. 25:10, 11, cf Deut. 29:19-23).

> For my people have committed two evils; they have forsaken me the fountain of living waters, and hewed them out cisterns, broken cisterns, that can hold no water (Jer. 2:13).

By the Gentile Baal worship Israel added drunkenness to their already tormenting thirst for peace with God. They lost the ability to suck the honey and olive oil of God's grace out of His firm Law given through Moses. They could not see the Anointed one in the Law, so they turned to lawless Ashtoreth. And, precisely no differently do we Protestants turn to the modern Ashtoreth today who have not found the grace of Jesus in His Father's stone Law or in the Spirit of Prophecy. We have sought out carnal, pagan celebration worship and Spiritual Formation. These ancient, empty delusions have always counterfeited the prophets' admonitions in the tough, strong love of God heard from His Law. Righteousness by faith, *born from the Lord God's powerful testimony to us*, is what we need. It was to assuage our tormenting thirst from our alienation to God's Law that *Jesus reconciles us to the Law by His Spirit*.

Protestantism is defunct; all the Protestant daughters have returned to their Mother. The Adventists and Mrs. White's heritage of convicting counsel no longer torments the world with the truth (see Revelation 11:10, cf Romans 4:15; 3:19). Therefore the world's pagan religions and the Beast exult in their victory over Protestantism and the Advent movement.

> All thine enemies have opened their mouth against thee: they hiss and gnash the teeth: they say, We have swallowed her up: certainly this is the day that we looked for; we have found, we have seen it (Lam. 2:16).

The World Council of Churches reached out its pitying, Baalpeor arms to help us escape Ellen White's "harsh" and "legalistic" testimonies that condemn sin, and the Council substituted the world's ancient, lawless, smooth Spiritual Formation. But, Spiritual Formation and celebration can only fake the real salvation found in the Adventism's original tenets of surrendering to the righteousness of God and then to the grace of Christ. Although Spiritual Formation can come under other names, its earmark is the absence of and resistance to biblical reproof, correction, and instruction in righteousness.

Those unholy intruders, Spiritual Formation and celebration, were the very subject of Jeremiah's warnings to Judah and, as we have seen from Deuteronomy 29:18-28, they have been the subject of the third angel's damnation warning to us today. Yet, we are prostrating ourselves before these gods of the heathen religions. Therefore, the Lord has already been humbling us; and He has yet much more humbling, grievous humbling to send us in a difficult but beneficial time of trouble that contributes to the great shaking and the Latter Rain.

> And it shall come to pass, that he that is left in Zion, and he that remaineth in Jerusalem, shall be called holy, even every one that is written among the living in Jerusalem: when the Lord shall have washed away the filth of the daughters of Zion, and shall have purged the blood of Jerusalem from the midst thereof by the spirit of judgment, and by the spirit of burning (Isa. 4:3, 4, cf Isa. 51:21-23).

By now in Revelation 11, the fifth and sixth trumpet plagues have stripped the remnant Adventists and the eleventh hour Protestants of self-sufficiency. The marauding locust armies left them desolated by pillaging Protestants' faith and love, and plundering their earthly wealth. All that the 144,000 can see in their desolate lives is ransacked ruins, "blood, and fire, and pillars of smoke" (Joel 2:30). But, the trumpet plagues were predestinated participants in God's strategy for bringing the predestinated 144,000 to Jesus for His grace and truth. Incubating under Christ's protective providences — *even though their faith slumbered and slept* — He was developing the 144,000 into stalwart servants for His gospel work, full of His Spirit. They have come to terms with their great apostasy and unbelief.

In their shame they tremble before God; and His words speak to them,

> Comfort ye, comfort ye my people, saith your God. Speak ye comfortably to Jerusalem, and cry unto her, *that her warfare is accomplished, that her iniquity is pardoned*: for she hath received of the LORD's hand double for all her sins (Isa. 40:1, 2).

> For your shame ye shall have double; and for confusion they shall rejoice in their portion: therefore in their land they shall possess the double: everlasting joy shall be unto them (Isa. 61:7).

> Rejoice not against me, O mine enemy: when I fall, I shall arise; when I sit in darkness, the LORD shall be a light unto me. I will bear the indignation of the LORD, because I have sinned against him, until he plead my cause, and execute judgment for me: he will bring me forth to the light, and I shall behold his righteousness. Then she that is mine enemy [Jezebel typifying the religions of Ashtoreth, ancient and modern] shall see it, and shame shall cover her which said unto me, Where is the LORD thy God? mine eyes shall behold her: now shall she be trodden down as the mire of the streets [see 2 Kings 9:33]. In the day that thy walls are to be built, in that day shall the decree be far removed. In that day also he shall come even to thee from Assyria, and from the fortified cities, and from the fortress even to the river, and from sea to sea, and from mountain to mountain (Mic. 7:8-12).

In the end, the imperious, Baalpeor, prostituting religions of Christendom cannot defile the 144,000, for they are fully humbled and sealed in justification. Their repentance was for a host of sins, and also for their sinfulness as a whole; and their justifying forgiveness from above is in total and free. Because of a valid justification rooted in strong conviction and humiliation, and sprouting up in strong faith in His mercy, God declares His witnesses to never have been unfaithful. "*They are virgins*" (Rev. 14:4). The highest authority has declared them so. *Great is their reward in heaven*. Once justified, *they were never impure*. By their repentance God has reconciled with them and given them rest from their fifth and sixth trumpet tormented conscience. His rest fortifies them to mortify all of their inherited and cultivated tendencies to evil. And, through a humbling and painful conviction hardened by their excursion into Laodicea and Baalpeor, ever afterward they remain humbled, obedient, and pure.

> Let us draw near with a true heart in full assurance of faith, having our hearts sprinkled from an evil conscience, and our bodies washed with pure water (Heb. 10:22, cf Num. 19:19).

> Unto him that loved us, and washed us from our sins in his own blood, and hath made us kings and priests unto God and his Father; to him be glory and dominion for ever and ever. Amen (Rev. 1:5, 6).

Not until the Lord razed Solomon's temple did the Jews wake up to their abominable standing before Him. Likewise, Revelation 11 shows that He must raze the Advent movement before He can raise it up again in newness of life. God, providentially through His compounded consequences, and spiritually through His greatly magnified Law, brought the 144,000 to Christ to be glorified by faith. The Spirit from Christ sprinkled their vociferous consciences, comforting and purifying each one. Jesus' sprinkling energized their diligent effort to overcome their evils "by his Spirit in the inner man" (Eph. 3:16, cf Rom. 8:9). The expulsion of sins became the act of their new heart. They are "children of God by faith in Christ Jesus" (Gal. 3:26). "As newborn babes" (1 Pet. 2:2) they purified their "souls in obeying the truth through the Spirit" (1 Pet. 1:22). Jesus washed their bodies clean from the idolatry of their former self (see Ezekiel 16:9; Ephesians 5:25-27). They had been afflicting their souls and were not cut off from God.

God has accomplished His warfare against them; He has fully scattered their self-sufficiency.

> Hear the word of the LORD, O ye nations, and declare it in the isles afar off, and say, He that scattered Israel will gather him, and keep him, as a shepherd doth his flock. For the LORD hath redeemed Jacob, and ransomed him from the hand of him that was stronger than he (Jer. 31:10, 11).

Only true virgins with abundance of oil make it all the way through to the end. As His little lambs, they learn to eat of Jesus' spotless human nature and drink the life pouring down from His self-sacrifice. They learn to suck honey and oil from the holy Law. They learn to see their beautiful Jesus in the Bible and hear His voice from the Spirit of Prophecy. Because of the Spirit of Jesus the stony Law tastes like sesame seed candy, mildly sweet and very nutritious. They overcome worldliness and the dead works of stony dedication to the Lord. They have a distaste for the laughing daughters of "happy" Ashtoreth, and the brutal sons of "Lord" Baal (see Numbers 25:1; Judges 3:7). Rather, their simple heart's surrender to the genuine gift of repentance, revival, and reformation is the possession of these 144,000 sealed, Protestant Seventh-day Adventist servants of God.

> Hearken unto me, ye that know righteousness, the people in whose heart is my law; fear ye not the reproach of men, neither be ye afraid of their revilings. For the moth shall eat them up like a garment, and the worm shall eat them like wool: but my righteousness shall be for ever, and my salvation from generation to generation…. Awake, awake, stand up, O Jerusalem, which hast drunk at the hand of the LORD the cup of his fury; thou hast drunken the dregs of the cup of trembling, and wrung them out (Isa. 51:7, 8, 17).

The Gift of God is finally to arrive — "the blessing of Abraham…the promise of the Spirit" (Gal. 3:14). The Father is about to regain His previous perfect reputation within His kingdom's hearts, as seen in Revelation 10:1-3, 7. The glorious days that close the sixth trumpet are about to be fulfilled when once more He can send "the Spirit of Christ" (1 Pet. 1:11). The Saviour's presence to them will be all of heaven in one gift and His pardon and eternal acceptance will impart the atmosphere of heaven to His people. Partaking of His ever present Spirit they taste the "powers of the world to come" (Heb. 6:5). The final Pentecost is experienced, "Repent ye therefore, and be converted, that your sins may be blotted out, when the times of refreshing shall come from the presence of the Lord; and he shall send Jesus Christ" (Acts 3:19, 20).

Many Protestants and Adventists have surrendered to the punishing, God-given anxiety, and their repentance to His Spirit brings them immediate healing. Revelation 7:3 is fulfilled in these two groups within Protestantism. They open to Jesus; they genuinely give Him their whole heart. They are the final seed that "should come to whom the promise was made" (Gal. 3:19).

> I will call them my people, which were not my people; and her beloved, which was not beloved. And it shall come to pass, that in the place where it was said unto them, Ye are not my people; there shall they be called the children of the living God (Rom. 9:25, 26).

The majority of the Protestant world in bondage is swept into the ranks of religious lawlessness, which is spiritualism. They would never submit to the hewing by Jesus through His last day prophet. Satan has seared their consciences; they are his "dead" (Eph. 2:1) captives, "spirits in prison" (1 Pet. 3:19), and ready to "be judged" (Rev. 11:18).

The land shall be desolate because of them that dwell therein, for the fruit of their doings (Mic. 7:13).

Thou hast multiplied the nation, and not increased the joy (Isa. 9:3).

In contrast, the oppressions from Satan's dead have humbled Christ's last day living (see Deuteronomy 32:43). The humbling made the 144,000 teachable, the wicked actually contributing to their "good conscience" (1 Tim. 1:5; 1 Pet. 3:21). The Adventist schoolhouse that trained them to fight for their inheritance in the heavenly Canaan was the harsh trumpets experience, its tormenting high standard and wrestling, its hot wandering and its delay, during which they endured a denuded, "great and terrible wilderness, wherein were fiery serpents, and scorpions" (Deut. 8:15), poisonous water, consuming locusts, enemy armies, and seductive Baal-peor spiritual exercises. (The above symbolisms in Revelation 8:10, 11; 9:3-5, 8, 19 taken from Numbers 21:6; Exodus 15:23; Deuteronomy 28:42; Exodus 17:8-16; Numbers 21:1-3, 23, 24; Numbers 25:1.) All of their wanderings in the hard path of infidelity have taught them to return to the reality that the Spirit of life is in the Son and that His truth is in God's Law, with which now they humbly and happily desire to comply. Insubordination in the Adventist ranks is non-existent.

Wretchedness and violence are seen in the new counterfeit Christianity, but the 144,000 are not discouraged. Their old prejudices against the Law found in the Spirit of Prophecy counsels now completely removed by the aggravated cruelty around them, they discover new worth in the Law's primitive holiness. By the Son of God manifested to them through His gracious Spirit bound in His word they hear His voice, and they find Jesus in the Law a most precious gem, a diamond full of fire.

Riches and honour are with me; yea, durable riches and righteousness (Prov. 8:18).

For the commandment is a lamp; and the law is light; and reproofs of instruction are the way of life (Prov. 6:23).

Bind them continually upon thine heart, and tie them about thy neck. When thou goest, it shall lead thee; when thou sleepest, it shall keep thee; and when thou awakest, it shall talk with thee (Prov. 6:21, 22).

Come, and let us return unto the LORD: for he hath torn, and he will heal us; he hath smitten, and he will bind us up. After two days will he revive us: in the third day he will raise us up, and we shall live in his sight. Then shall we know, if we follow on to know the LORD: his going forth is prepared as the morning; and he shall come unto us as the rain, as the latter and former rain unto the earth. O Ephraim, what shall I do unto thee? O Judah, what shall I do unto thee? for your goodness is as a morning cloud, and as the early dew it goeth away. Therefore have I hewed them by the prophets; I have slain them by the words of my mouth: and thy judgments are as the light that goeth forth (Hos. 6:1-5).

Now the sealed Christians love the principles of God's Law. Ultimately, the church will return to its holy apostolic condition seen in Revelation 11:3-6 when as living testaments of Christ, its fidelity to God's Law had tormented the children of disobedience during the church's first prophesying of Revelation 11. And this had created the deadly reaction of the world (see Revelation 11:10; 2 Corinthians 3:2, 3; Revelation 14:9-11).

The people that walked in darkness have seen a great light: they that dwell in the land of the shadow of death, upon them hath the light shined.... They joy before thee according to the joy in harvest, and as men rejoice when they divide the spoil. For thou hast broken the yoke of his burden, and the staff of his shoulder, the rod of his oppressor, as in the day of Midian. For every battle of the warrior is with confused noise, and garments rolled in blood; but this shall be with burning and fuel of fire. For unto us a child is born, unto us a son is given: and the government shall be upon his shoulder: and his name shall be called Wonderful, Counsellor, The mighty God, The everlasting Father, The Prince of Peace. Of the increase of his government and peace there shall be no end, upon the throne of David, and upon his kingdom, to order it, and to establish it with judgment and with justice from henceforth even for ever. The zeal of the LORD of hosts will perform this (Isa. 9:2-7).

This is that which was spoken by the prophet Joel; and it shall come to pass in the last days, saith God, I will pour out of my Spirit upon all flesh: and your sons and your daughters shall prophesy, and your young men shall see visions, and your old men shall dream dreams: and on my servants and on my handmaidens I will pour out in those days of my Spirit; and they shall prophesy (Acts 2:16-18).

Their love has set upon Him, they lay hold of the great Promise-maker (see Revelation 19:11; 1 Thessalonians 5:24; Isaiah 27:5). Loving His image in the Law, they are content with few earthly needs; they can take them or leave them. Their mind is: Take the world, but give me Jesus; all its joys are but a name.

> Then shalt thou delight thyself in the LORD; and I will cause thee to ride upon the high places of the earth, and feed thee with the heritage of Jacob thy father: for the mouth of the LORD hath spoken it (Isa. 58:14).

They are humbled and they are happy. They have deeply repented of living apart from Jesus and the careless life to which that led. God has wholly pardoned their infidelity to Him and touched their souls with His approbation. Behind every earthly thing Jesus is all they see. They serve Him with their whole heart, mind, and body. They see His rainbow and hear His harpers. And He reassures them that they are His children.

> They shall be mine, saith the LORD of hosts, in that day when I make up my jewels (Mal. 3:17).

By their acceptance of the Son His Spirit liberates their minds with relief and rest. They had set their heart on Him and He gives them the desires of their heart— to be like their Master. Rapid sanctification has developed in them a fortitude that will withstand an offended world's fiercest opposition, waiting in the winds.

The words of David express where they have laid up for themselves treasures. "*The law of thy mouth* is better unto me than thousands of gold and silver" (Ps. 119:72). The justice of God and the mercy of Christ compel them to invite others to their new-found Friend and strong Father. The saving and sanctifying truth cannot be shut up in their heart. Trust in the Creator and Redeemer gives them a new spirit; divine acceptance empowers them to accept any amount of reproach and persecution. No adversary is too offensive for them to refuse prayer to God in their behalf. God is their Saviour, and Jesus is their new song.

> I waited patiently for the Lord; and he inclined unto me, and heard my cry.
>
> He brought me up also out of an horrible pit, out of the miry clay, and set my feet upon a rock, and established my goings.
>
> And he hath put a new song in my mouth, even praise unto our God (Ps. 40:1-3).

"The Spirit of life from God entered into them, and they stood upon their feet; and great fear fell upon them which saw them" (Rev. 11:11).

The popes, their Jesuits, and all the hosts of Christendom have a woeful surprise coming. According to this Revelation 11 vision, the Reformation rises again. When His people are humbled and repentant, their God will awaken among them "as one out of sleep, and like a mighty man that shouteth by reason of wine" (Ps. 78:65, cf Ps. 106:44; Jer. 25:12-14). And all the powers of hell, spirit or human, smoke and locust, cannot prevent the fulfillment of Revelation 11:11.

> For the oppression of the poor, for the sighing of the needy, now will I arise, saith the LORD; I will set him in safety from him that puffeth at him (Ps. 12:5).

> *The popes, their Jesuits, and all the hosts of Christendom have a woeful surprise coming. According to this Revelation 11 vision, the Reformation rises again.*

He put them to a perpetual reproach (Ps. 78:66).

Now will I rise, saith the LORD; now will I be exalted; now will I lift up myself. Ye shall conceive chaff, ye shall bring forth stubble: your breath, as fire, shall devour you. And the people shall be as the burnings of lime: as thorns cut up shall they be burned in the fire. Hear, ye that are far off, what I have done; and, ye that are near, acknowledge my might…. Who among us shall dwell with the devouring fire? who among us shall dwell with everlasting burnings? He that walketh righteously, and speaketh uprightly; he that despiseth the gain of oppressions, that shaketh his hands from holding of bribes, that stoppeth his ears from hearing of blood, and shutteth his eyes from seeing evil (Isa. 33:10-15).

The third Great American Awakening arrives because of the final anointing. The devils begin to tremble again, and their human counterparts exceedingly fear and quake. The denominations have filled their doctrines with spiritualism and have been absorbed into the world, but God has always had His eye on His Remnant Adventists and eleventh hour Protestants.

> Awake, awake; put on thy strength, O Zion; put on thy beautiful garments, O Jerusalem, the holy city: for henceforth there shall no more come into thee the uncircumcised and the unclean (Isa. 52:1).

> So I prophesied as I was commanded: and as I prophesied, there was a noise, and behold a shaking, and the bones came together, bone to his bone. And when I beheld, lo, the sinews and the flesh came up upon them, and the skin covered them above: but there was no breath in them. Then said he unto me, Prophesy unto the wind, prophesy, son of man, and say to the wind, Thus saith the Lord GOD; Come from the four winds, O breath, and breathe upon these slain, that they may live. So I prophesied as he commanded me, and the breath came into them, and they lived, and stood up upon their feet, an exceeding great army (Eze. 37:7-10).

The Reformation is reborn through the powerful Testimony of Jesus. The remnant, "being with child" has "cried, travailing in birth, and pained to be delivered" (Rev. 12:2). Now, the Mother of all living has made them mighty leaders like Paul, as they "travail in birth until Christ" (Gal. 4:19) is born in the world. With minds fortified by the words of truth, and hearts humbled and surrendered to Christ's mercy, the strait testimony of the True Witness returns to God's people from whom, many generations before, fire had proceeded out of their forefathers' mouths and had devoured the Lord's adversaries, spirit and human alike.

> Before the final visitation of God's judgments upon the earth there will be among the people of the Lord such a revival of primitive godliness as has not been witnessed since apostolic times. The Spirit and power of God will be poured out upon His children. At that time many will separate themselves from those churches in which the love of this world has supplanted love for God and His word. Many, both of ministers and people, will gladly accept those great truths which God has caused to be proclaimed at this time to prepare a people for the Lord's second coming *The Great Controversy*, p. 464.

> Would God that all the LORD's people were prophets, and that the LORD would put his spirit upon them! (Num. 11:29).

They mix into their message a warning about the corruption of free governments which have united in unholy alliance with the universal Church, with her unholy United Nations, and her wicked international bankers. They also give a strong warning against the movement of spiritualism within the denominations, and the final judgment that will go in favor of their Father's acquittal in the Most Holy Place (see Revelation 18:2-8; 14:7-11). Most of all, they cheerfully proclaim to the furthest points of the globe that they have "received of the LORD's hand double" (Isa. 40:2) for all their sins! His hand of discipline is very special to them. His involvement remains very precious to them.

> Though the number of the children of Israel be as the sand of the sea, a remnant shall be saved: for he will finish the work, and cut it short in righteousness: because a short work will the Lord make upon the earth (Rom. 9:27, 28).

Only those who were being sealed during the fifth and sixth trumpet plagues, and who take part in this wondrous and powerful revival and reformation, will be victors over the vindictive, satanic maelstrom that follows, and they will leave with Jesus at His return in destructive retribution upon Satan's wretched kingdom.

The remnant within the denominations complements the remnant Adventist majority of the 144,000, all of whom had been faithful to heed all the light they had.

> And it shall come to pass in that day, that the Lord shall set his hand again the second time to recover the remnant of his people, which shall be left, from Assyria, and from Egypt, and from Pathros, and from Cush, and from Elam, and from Shinar, and from Hamath, and from the islands of the sea. And he shall set up an ensign for the nations, and shall assemble the outcasts

of Israel, and gather together the dispersed of Judah from the four corners of the earth (Isa. 11:11, 12).

The envy also of Ephraim shall depart, and the adversaries of Judah shall be cut off: Ephraim shall not envy Judah, and Judah shall not vex Ephraim. But they shall fly upon the shoulders of the Philistines toward the west; they shall spoil them of the east together: they shall lay their hand upon Edom and Moab; and the children of Ammon shall obey them. And the LORD shall utterly destroy the tongue of the Egyptian sea; and with his mighty wind shall he shake his hand over the river, and shall smite it in the seven streams, and make men go over dryshod.

And there shall be an highway for the remnant of his people, which shall be left, from Assyria; like as it was to Israel in the day that he came up out of the land of Egypt. And in that day thou shalt say, O LORD, I will praise thee: though thou wast angry with me, thine anger is turned away, and thou comfortedst me. Behold, God is my salvation; I will trust, and not be afraid: for the LORD JEHOVAH is my strength and my song; he also is become my salvation. Therefore with joy shall ye draw water out of the wells of salvation (Isa. 11:13-12:3).

In that day shall the branch of the LORD be beautiful and glorious (Isa. 4:2).

The Adventists and their Protestant complement see eye to eye as they go strong to take back the holy city of righteousness by faith through the Law of God.

Thy children shall make haste; thy destroyers and they that made thee waste shall go forth of thee (Isa. 49:17).

How beautiful upon the mountains are the feet of him that bringeth good

tidings, that publisheth peace; that bringeth good tidings of good, that publisheth salvation; that saith unto Zion, Thy God reigneth! Thy watchmen shall lift up the voice; with the voice together shall they sing: for they shall see eye to eye, when the LORD shall bring again Zion. Break forth into joy, sing together, ye waste places of Jerusalem: for the LORD hath comforted his people, he hath redeemed Jerusalem (Isa. 52:7-9).

Stand therefore, having…your feet shod with the preparation of the gospel of peace;

Above all, taking the shield of faith, wherewith ye shall be able to quench all the fiery darts of the wicked.

And take the helmet of salvation, and the sword of the Spirit, which is the word of God (Eph. 6:15-17).

"After three days and an half [*see Appendix A*)] the Spirit of life from God entered into them. And they heard a great voice from heaven saying unto them, Come up hither. And they ascended up to heaven in a cloud; and their enemies beheld them" (Rev. 11:11, 12).

The fire of the Reformation reflashes, super-added with a soon-coming King. The mighty rushing wind comes from heaven's rarefied response to genuine Adventist repentance. His Father's power for their ultra-Reformation catches the Papacy off guard, despite the many Bible and Spirit of Prophecy warnings. The Lord gets the last word, as all the superhuman forces from the bottomless pit cannot prevent the final revival of real godliness, and the simultaneous removal of His people from Babylon. The gates of hell shall not prevail, as the apostolic church resurrects into the new 144,000 Advent movement. The leaner movement with a new yearning and appeal repeats the apostolic translation "into the kingdom of [God's] dear Son" (Col. 1:13, cf Ps. 91:14; 16:11; 18:33; 42:2; 23:6; Hab. 3:19; Deut. 32:13; Isa. 58:14; 62:9; Rev. 1:6; 3:21; 5:9, 10; 15:2-4; 13:6; Dan. 8:10; John 3:5; Rom. 6:10, 11).

By receiving Jesus, this chosen generation receives perfect heavenly mindedness and the earthly mind flees away, never to return. They live godly in Christ Jesus; they are sealed in His faith. "Truth alone was exalted to them" *Early Writings*, p. 271. And, as they walk in the light as God is in the light, the blood of Jesus cleanses all sin from them. To be with their best Friend "in paradise" (Luke 23:43), they ascend to heaven and sit "together in heavenly places in Christ Jesus" (Eph. 2:6).

The new covenant returns in its fullest reality since the days of the apostles. Thorough repentance and renunciation of the traditions of men have prepared them for all the blessings of heaven. God has written His Law into their hearts and He remembers their sin no more. Acknowledging God's hand of judgment upon the Adventists has given their hearts a spirit of burning. His humbling has given them the mind of Christ who "made himself of no reputation" (Phil. 2:7). Willing to do His will becomes their greatest pleasure. The humbling sobered them up; and, their "obedience…fulfilled", they have "a readiness to revenge all disobedience" (2 Cor. 10:6). Their witness follows Stephen's: "[The rulers of the synagogues] were not able to resist the wisdom and the spirit by which he spake" (Acts 6:10). Jesus has taught them truth through His anointing, who is their wisdom and who inspires their prayers to God. God honors these unified Adventist penitents, and signs and wonders follow the believers.

"These are they which follow the Lamb whithersoever He goeth" (Rev. 14:4). He has been in the Most Holy Place since 1844 to purify for Himself a peculiar people. For successfully cleansing "his household" (Matt. 10:25) Jesus has used His providential locust raids and His strait Testimony refuge. Now He can use His newly disciplined army to harvest the world, and the hosts of locusts cannot stand before them. "My people that dwellest in Zion" (Isa. 10:24) by faith enter in with their Lord through the second veil of the heavenly sanctuary and receive the Most Holy Spirit from the Most Holy "atonement" (Lev. 16:16, cf Lev. 4:35). The humbled and contrite ones will have the consecration and faith of their Adventist founders, and even more so. As the fruit of the Elijah message they outshine the generation of 1844, who were first numbered in Revelation 7:4-8 to be purified and prepared for Christ's return.

> And I looked, and, lo, a Lamb stood on the mount Sion, and with him an hundred forty and four thousand, having his Father's name written in their foreheads. And I heard a voice from heaven, as the voice of many waters, and as the voice of a great thunder: and I heard the voice of harpers harping with their harps: and they sung as it were a new song before the throne, and before the four beasts, and the elders: and no man could learn that song but the hundred and forty and four thousand, which were redeemed from the earth (Rev. 14:1-3).

Per the children of Israel as type, numbered at the beginning and at the end of their wandering in the wilderness (see Numbers 1 and 26), the Advent movement has been numbered again and is ready to move under the direct command of Jesus. Though their first numbering in Revelation 7 had a good start in 1844, the first and second woes eventually overran them. Now they are renumbered in Revelation 14 as a detailed expansion of Revelation 11:12, and they are enabled to go forth to avenge the name of Jehovah. The witnesses have abandoned their Evangelical, Baalpeor, work-based worship and atheistic relationship with devils. They have come back to a simple life of obedience to the Spirit of Prophecy, to righteousness by Jesus, and rest for their souls (see Jeremiah 6:16).

Revelation 11:11, 12 point to the great future revival of the Latter Rain that will follow the punishing first time of trouble which scatters their Protestant power, and the Lord's final pardon for our unbelief and hypocrisy. Patience has done her perfect work; the strong delusion and the first humbling time of trouble have worked the indomitable faith of Jesus into the 144,000. They are forgiven and sealed in Christ's divine nature and in His every word from the whole Bible. They are ready to follow the Lamb's Spirit of truth (see Revelation 5:6) wherever it leads. Anywhere with Jesus they know they can safely go.

Overcoming the corruption of the trumpets' cavalry, the 144,000 have received the earnest of their inheritance, the power of the sons of God to drive Apollyon, his darkness, and his locust army out of the holy city.

> Thy children shall make haste; thy destroyers and they that made thee waste shall go forth of thee (Isa. 49:17).

The Adventist revival of the Holy Ghost sent down from Jesus shakes the foundations of Babylon the Great. Like a host of Samsons the 144,000 put to flight the bitter and hasty Chaldean armies of the sixth trumpet enemies of God. The Lion of Judah roaring behind them, they take down the wicked locust cavalry.

> For thus hath the LORD spoken unto me, Like as the lion and the young lion roaring on his prey, when a multitude of shepherds is called forth against him, he will not be afraid of their voice, nor abase himself for the noise of them: so shall the LORD of hosts come down to fight for mount Zion, and for the hill thereof (Isa. 31:4).

> In that day, saith the LORD, I will smite every horse with astonishment, and his rider with madness: and I will open mine eyes upon the house of Judah, and will smite every horse of the people with blindness. And the governors of Judah shall say in their heart, The inhabitants

of Jerusalem shall be my strength in the LORD of hosts their God. In that day will I make the governors of Judah like an hearth of fire among the wood, and like a torch of fire in a sheaf; and they shall devour all the people round about, on the right hand and on the left: and Jerusalem shall be inhabited again in her own place, even in Jerusalem. The LORD also shall save the tents of Judah first, that the glory of the house of David and the glory of the inhabitants of Jerusalem do not magnify themselves against Judah. In that day shall the LORD defend the inhabitants of Jerusalem; and he that is feeble among them at that day shall be as David; and the house of David shall be as God, as the angel of the LORD before them (Zech. 12:4-8).

The occupied city falls before the revival of righteousness by faith through the Spirit of Christ imbuing His Testimony.

> A sword is upon their horses, and upon their chariots, and upon all the mingled people that are in the midst of her; and they shall become as women (Jer. 50:37).

Distant Protestants, far from the Lord, listen to the message of the 144,000. The sanctified Sabbath-keepers remove the dying thirst of the locusts' captives and quench the fiery hearts of "the rest of the men which were not killed by these plagues". "[The truth] had effect" *Early Writings*, p. 271. Their message appeals to hearts and brings hope to life; and the new believers are glad that their flesh profits nothing. Their word is received by multitudes starving for a righteous Friend to trust in, as they throw themselves into the merciful hands of the appetite- and addiction-healing Creator.

> Ye shall defile also the covering of thy graven images of silver, and the ornament of thy molten images of gold: thou shalt cast them away as a menstruous cloth; thou shalt say unto it, Get thee hence (Isa. 30:22).

Signs and wonders follow the believers. Adding to the fire and brimstone plaguing the demon-driven cavalry, the sealed 144,000 execute the captives' deliverance fearlessly, flawlessly casting out demons and everything that exalts itself against the knowledge of God.

> The LORD hath made bare his holy arm in the eyes of all the nations; and all the ends of the earth shall see the salvation of our God. Depart ye, depart ye, go ye out from thence, touch no unclean thing; go ye out of the midst of her; be ye clean, that bear the vessels of the LORD. For ye shall not go out with haste, nor go by flight: for the LORD will go before you; and the God of Israel will be your rereward [rear guard] (Isa. 52:10-12).

"There shall be an highway for the remnant of his people, which shall be left, from Assyria; like as it was to Israel in the day that he came up out of the land of Egypt" (Isa. 11:16). Millions, including pastors, and priests, even Jesuit priests, are obedient to biblical truth. It is a glorious time. The hearts of those who see the beautiful justice and mercy of Christ's character earnestly tell others of both the everlasting Father and everlasting Friend they have found. And "as many as received him, to them gave he power to become the sons of God, even to them that believe on his name" (John 1:12). Under the sheets of heavy, divine and angelic precipitation the world harvest ripens quickly.

> Drop down, ye heavens, from above, and let the skies pour down righteousness: let the earth open, and let them bring forth salvation, and let righteousness spring up together; I the LORD have created it (Isa. 45:8).

At that day shall a man look to his Maker, and his eyes shall have respect to the Holy One of Israel. And he shall not look to the altars, the work of his hands, neither shall respect that which his fingers have made, either the groves, or the images [the religion of Ashtoreth and Baal] (Isa. 17:7, 8).

> It shall come, that I will gather all nations and tongues; and they shall come, and see my glory (Isa. 66:18).

The faith of Jesus ends in rest. "For he that is entered into his rest, he also hath ceased from his own works, as God did from his. Let us labour therefore to enter into that rest" (Heb. 4:10, 11). They "through the Spirit wait for the hope of righteousness by faith" (Gal. 5:5).

> Here is the patience of the saints: here are they that keep the commandments of God, and the faith of Jesus (Rev. 14:12).

They speak the word only, and the Lord's servants among the world religions are healed. The spiritual rest gives the remnant of the nations strength for victory over sin. Thousands in a day sprinkled amongst the nations, "the isles which are beyond the sea" (Jer. 25:22, cf Isa. 49:1), joyfully make the third angel's message their refuge, and they depart from Babylon.

> For ye shall not go out with haste, nor go by flight: for the LORD will go before you; and the God of Israel will be your rereward (Isa 52:12).

> I will walk at liberty: for I seek thy precepts (Ps. 119:45).

> Yet gleaning grapes shall be left in it, as the shaking of an olive tree, two or three berries in the top of the uppermost bough, four or five in the outmost fruitful branches thereof, saith the LORD God of Israel (Isa. 17:6).

> When thus it shall be in the midst of the land among the people, there shall be as the shaking of an olive tree, and as the gleaning grapes when the vintage is done. They shall lift up their voice, they shall sing for the majesty of the LORD, they shall cry aloud from the sea. Wherefore glorify ye the LORD in the fires, even the name of the LORD God of Israel in the isles of the sea. From the uttermost part of the earth have we heard songs, even glory to the righteous (Isa. 24:13-16).

The word goes out and the people flock in. With hearts greatly moved by the global response, the witnesses cry, "Behold, I was left alone; these, where had they been?" (Isa. 49:21).

> And the Gentiles shall come to thy light, and kings to the brightness of thy rising. Lift up thine eyes round about, and see: all they gather themselves together, they come to thee: thy sons shall come from far, and thy daughters shall be nursed at thy side. Then thou shalt see, and *flow together*, and thine heart shall fear, and be enlarged; because the abundance of the sea shall be converted unto thee, the forces of the Gentiles shall come unto thee.... Who are these that fly as a cloud, and as the doves to their windows? Surely the isles shall wait for me, and the ships of Tarshish first, to bring thy sons from far, their silver and their gold with them, unto the name of the LORD thy God, and to the Holy One of Israel, because he hath glorified thee. And the sons of strangers shall build up thy walls, and their kings shall minister unto thee: for in my wrath I smote thee, but in my favour have I had mercy on thee (Isa. 60:3-5, 8-10).

> Thus saith the Lord GOD, Behold, I will lift up mine hand to the Gentiles, and set up my standard to the people: and they shall bring thy sons in their arms, and thy daughters shall be carried upon their shoulders (Isa. 49:22).

> Feed thy people with thy rod, the flock of thine heritage, which dwell solitarily in the wood, in the midst of Carmel: let them feed in Bashan and Gilead, as in the days of old. According to the days of thy coming out of the land of Egypt will I shew unto him marvelous things. The nations shall see and be confounded at all their might: they shall lay their hand upon their mouth, their ears shall be deaf. They shall lick the dust like a serpent, they shall move out of their holes like worms of the earth: they shall be afraid of the LORD our God, and shall fear because of thee (Mic. 7:14-17).

The torrents of the Loud Cry and of the Latter Rain disseminate out, and fully develop the character of Christ in every soul that was distraught yet submitting to the reigning religious, political, and economic despotism. The saints sprinkled around the globe finally lose hope in corruptible man because the wizards and philosophers of Christian Baal and Ashtoreth have proven themselves deceivers and seducers. Their disillusioned lives have fired their thirst for the revelation of Christ's truth and grace. For the two precious commodities of truth and grace they find but one reliable resource, in the majestic excellence of Jesus revealed to them from both Old and New Testaments, and from His newer Testimonies. For the first time, those worldwide candidates for heaven can look wholly to the Lord God of Abraham and to His Law for hope. They tell others of Christ's "blessedness" (Gal. 4:15); they have much to say about the Son of God. "Come, see a man, which told me all things that ever I did: is not this the Christ?" (John 4:29).

> I will set a sign among them, and I will send those that escape of them unto the nations, to Tarshish, Pul, and Lud, that draw the bow, to Tubal, and Javan, to the isles afar off, that have

not heard my fame, neither have seen my glory; and they shall declare my glory among the Gentiles (Isa. 66:19).

The global call to flee spiritual Babylon will involve much service to the nations. Exponential growth of Latter Rain personal evangelism will quickly reach out to every needy soul.

Servants of God, with their faces lighted up and shining with holy consecration, will hasten from place to place to proclaim the message from heaven. By thousands of voices, all over the earth, the warning will be given. Miracles will be wrought, the sick will be healed, and signs and wonders will follow the believers *The Great Controversy*, p. 612.

Many deeply buried in Babylon will break free through the fear and love of God, but, their family and long-time friends will fight to get the newborn children of God back into the world. Their unbelieving companions see in the sober urgency of the 144,000 only religious fanaticism, and they feel that they must save their friends who they believe to be deluded in this strange and apparently dangerous new excitement that seems so embarrassing. But they know not what they are doing. The tremendous spiritual battle of this "great multitude, which no man could number" (Rev. 7:9) requires all the endurance and willpower that they can muster to retain their new-found faith. Like their Master in Gethsemane, once they have expended all of their willpower and have drank the dregs of the cup of temptation that God gives them, then they break free from the earthly grasps, and the full victory is theirs (see *Early Writings*, p. 240-242; *The Desire of Ages*, p. 690.3-694.1).

He that shall endure unto the end, the same shall be saved (Matt. 24:13).

If a man love me, he will keep my words.... He that loveth me not keepeth not my sayings (John 14:23, 24).

Behold my mother and my brethren! For whosoever shall do the will of my Father which is in heaven, the same is my brother, and sister, and mother (Matt. 12:49, 50).

The saints sprinkled in the world have received from the Lord's hand double for all their sins; He has taken captivity captive. The powers that be see innumerable multitudes of their "slaves, and souls of men" (Rev. 18:13) go "out with an high hand" (Ex. 14:8; Num. 33:3). The captives spoil the Babylonians and take back the robbed evidences for faith in the great Creator and Redeemer. "All they...that spoil thee shall be a spoil" (Jer. 30:16).

Whoso causeth the righteous to go astray in an evil way, he shall fall himself into his own pit: but the upright shall have good things in possession (Prov. 28:10).

So shall my word be that goeth forth out of my mouth: it shall not return unto me void, but it shall accomplish that which I please, and it shall prosper in the thing whereto I sent it. For ye shall go out with joy, and be led forth with peace: the mountains and the hills shall break forth before you into singing, and all the trees of the field shall clap their hands. Instead of the thorn shall come up the fir tree, and instead of the brier shall come up the myrtle tree: and it shall be to the LORD for a name, for an everlasting sign that shall not be cut off (Isa. 55:11-13).

Babylon gets her double punishment for all the robbing lies and mental trauma that she had given these newly freed citizens of Christ's kingdom. All that they have heard in the closet they preach from the housetops.

Reward her even as she rewarded you, and double unto her double according to her works: in the cup which she hath filled fill to her double. How much she hath glorified herself, and lived deliciously, so much torment and sorrow give her: for she saith in her heart, I sit a queen, and am no widow, and shall see no sorrow (Rev. 18:6, 7).

This divine vengeance on modern Babylon follows the typical model of its ancient counterpart, the destruction of which gave the 144,000 much guidance and hope from fulfilled promises of the past:

And it shall come to pass, when seventy years are accomplished, that I will punish the king of Babylon, and that nation, saith the LORD, for their iniquity, and the land of the Chaldeans, and will make it perpetual desolations. And I will bring upon that land all my words which I have pronounced against it, even all that is written in this book, which Jeremiah hath prophesied against all the nations. For many nations and great kings shall serve themselves of [Israel] also: and I will recompense them according to their deeds, and according to the works of their own hands (Jer. 25:12-14, cf Jer. 30:10-14, 16; Rev. 13:10).

The renewed Reformation, supplemented with sanctuary cleansing prophecy, dries up Satan's apparent domination (see Revelation 16:12).

A drought is upon her waters; and they shall be dried up: for it is the land of graven images, and they are mad upon their idols (Jer. 50:38).

The Spirit of the "Stone" (Dan. 2:34) explodes Babylon's seemingly invincible bridges into the New Age; and the spiritual Rock turns her skyscrapers of mental idols, her whispering gods, and legislated lawlessness into finely pulverized debris. Multitudes come out of the mesmerizing Spiritual Formation, a construct which bursts into rubble, throwing steel girders and scudding dust.

And "a rushing mighty wind" (Acts 2:2), "sent down from heaven" (1 Pet. 1:12), carries "them away, that no place was found for them" (Dan. 2:35).

The coming King is at the door!

They looked unto him, and were lightened: and their faces were not ashamed (Ps. 34:5).

Israel is a scattered sheep; the lions have driven him away: first the king of Assyria hath devoured him; and last this [Nebuchadnezzar] king of Babylon hath broken his bones. Therefore thus saith the LORD of hosts, the God of Israel; Behold, I will punish the king of Babylon and his land, as I have punished the king of Assyria. And I will bring Israel again to his habitation, and he shall feed on Carmel and Bashan, and his soul shall be satisfied upon mount Ephraim and Gilead. In those days, and in that time, saith the LORD, the iniquity of Israel shall be sought for, and there shall be none; and the sins of Judah, and they shall not be found: for I will pardon them whom I reserve (Jer. 50:17-20, cf Heb. 8:10-12).

Break forth into joy, sing together, ye waste places of Jerusalem: for the LORD hath comforted his people, he hath redeemed Jerusalem (Isa. 52:9).

And it shall come to pass in the day that the LORD shall give thee rest from thy sorrow, and from thy fear, and from the hard bondage wherein thou wast made to serve, that thou shalt take up this proverb against the king of Babylon, and say, How hath the oppressor ceased! the golden city ceased! The LORD hath broken the staff of the wicked, and the sceptre of the rulers. He who smote the people in wrath with a continual stroke, he that ruled the nations in anger, is persecuted, and none hindereth. The whole earth is at rest, and is quiet: they break forth into singing. Yea, the fir trees rejoice at thee, and the cedars of Lebanon, saying, Since thou art laid down, no feller is come up against us (Isa. 14:3-8).

So shall they fear the name of the LORD from the west, and his glory from the rising of the sun. When the enemy shall come in like a flood, the Spirit of the LORD shall lift up a standard against him (Isa. 59:19).

And in that day shall the deaf hear the words of the book, and the eyes of the blind shall see out of obscurity, and out of darkness. The meek also shall increase their joy in the LORD, and the poor among men shall rejoice in the Holy One of Israel. For the terrible one is brought to nought, and the scorner is consumed, and all that watch for iniquity are cut off.... They also that erred in spirit shall come to understanding, and they that murmured shall learn doctrine (Isa. 29:18-20, 24).

The work of righteousness shall be peace; and the effect of righteousness quietness and assurance for ever. And my people shall dwell in a peaceable habitation, and in sure dwellings, and in quiet resting places (Isa. 32:17, 18).

Lord, thou hast been our dwelling place in all generations (Ps. 90:1).

For with thee is the fountain of life: in thy light shall we see light (Ps. 36:9).

Justice and judgment are the habitation of thy throne: mercy and truth shall go before thy face. Blessed is the people that know the joyful sound: they shall walk, O LORD, in the light of thy countenance (Ps. 89:14, 15).

Everyone who has ears for mercy and truth, who hear the 144,000 witnesses preach for a testimony to all nations, "were affrighted, and gave glory to the God of heaven" (Rev. 11:13). They heed the four heavenly messengers,

> And I saw another angel fly in the midst of heaven, having the everlasting gospel to preach unto them that dwell on the earth, and to every nation, and kindred, and tongue, and people, saying with a loud voice, *Fear God, and give glory to him; for the hour of his judgment is come: and worship him that made heaven, and earth, and the sea, and the fountains of waters.*
>
> And there followed another angel, saying, *Babylon is fallen, is fallen, that great city, because she made all nations drink of the wine of the wrath of her fornication.*
>
> And the third angel followed them, saying with a loud voice, *If any man worship the beast and his image, and receive his mark in his forehead, or in his hand, the same shall drink of the wine of the wrath of God, which is poured out without mixture into the cup of his indignation; and he shall be tormented with fire and brimstone in the presence of the holy angels, and in the presence of the Lamb: and the smoke of their torment ascendeth up for ever and ever: and they have no rest day nor night, who worship the beast and his image, and whosoever receiveth the mark of his name* (Rev. 14:6-11).
>
> And after these things I saw another angel come down from heaven, having great power; and the earth was lightened with his glory. And he cried mightily with a strong voice, saying, Babylon the great is fallen, is fallen, and is become the habitation of devils, and the hold of every foul spirit, and a cage of every unclean and hateful bird. For all nations have drunk of the wine of the wrath of her fornication, and the kings of the earth have committed fornication with her, and the merchants of the earth are waxed rich through the abundance of her delicacies.... Come out of her, my people, that ye be not partakers of her sins, and that ye receive not of her plagues. For her sins have reached unto heaven, and God hath remembered her iniquities (Rev. 18:1-5).

The 144,000 are further sanctified by the message that they give. No doubts cloud their minds that Jesus will soon return to claim them as His own and take them to His Father. "They shall be mine, saith the LORD of hosts" (Mal. 3:17). The comfort of His written promise and His Spirit holds them steady during the confusion ahead. Nothing can stop the thunder claps and cataracts of the Most Holy Spirit from the Most Holy God in His Most Holy Place upon His ripened waves of grain. And all whose hearts are not purified in its searching and humbling truth are burned up with rage against the true full gospel.

> The controversy extends into new fields and the minds of the people are called to God's downtrodden law, Satan is astir. The power attending the message will only madden those who oppose it. The clergy will put forth almost superhuman efforts to shut away the light lest it should shine upon their flocks. By every means at their command they will endeavor to suppress the discussion of these vital questions....
>
> As the storm approaches, a large class who have professed faith in the third angel's message, but have not been sanctified through obedience to the truth, abandon their position and join the ranks of the opposition. *By uniting with the world and partaking of its spirit, they have come to view matters in nearly the same light; and when the test is brought, they are prepared to choose the easy, popular side* [emphasis mine]. Men of talent and pleasing address, who once rejoiced in the truth, employ their powers to deceive and mislead souls. They become the most bitter enemies of their former brethren. When Sabbath-keepers are brought before the courts to answer for their faith, these apostates are the most efficient agents of Satan to misrepresent and accuse them, and by false reports and insinuations to stir up the rulers against them.
>
> In this time of persecution the faith of the Lord's servants will be tried. They have faithfully given the warning, looking to God and to His word alone. God's Spirit, moving upon their hearts, has constrained them to speak....
>
> As the opposition rises to a fiercer height, the servants of God are again perplexed; for it seems to them that they have brought the crisis. But

conscience and the word of God assure them that their course is right; and although the trials continue, they are strengthened to bear them. The contest grows closer and sharper, but their faith and courage rise with the emergency. Their testimony is: "We dare not tamper with God's word, dividing His holy law; calling one portion essential and another nonessential, to gain the favor of the world. The Lord whom we serve is able to deliver us. Christ has conquered the powers of earth; and shall we be afraid of a world already conquered? *The Great Controversy*, p. 607, 608, 610.

But not one is made to suffer the wrath of God until the truth has been brought home to his mind and conscience, and has been rejected. There are many who have never had an opportunity to hear the special truths for this time. The obligation of the fourth commandment has never been set before them in its true light. He who reads every heart and tries every motive will leave none who desire a knowledge of the truth, to be deceived as to the issues of the controversy. The decree is not to be urged upon the people blindly. Everyone is to have sufficient light to make his decision intelligently *Ibid.*, p. 605.

The 144,000 and the great multitude live confidently in the blessed hope:

These are they which came out of great tribulation, and have washed their robes, and made them white in the blood of the Lamb. Therefore are they before the throne of God, and serve him day and night in his temple: and he that sitteth on the throne shall dwell among them. They shall hunger no more, neither thirst any more; neither shall the sun light on them, nor any heat. For the Lamb which is in the midst of the throne shall feed them, and shall lead them unto living fountains of waters: and God shall wipe away all tears from their eyes (Rev. 7:14-17).

These are they which follow the Lamb whithersoever he goeth. These were redeemed from among men (Rev. 14:4).

Christian America will then be fully a persecuting power and moral darkness from the trumpet locusts will have corrupted the nations. "And God looked upon the earth, and, behold, it was corrupt; for all flesh had corrupted his way upon the earth. And God said…, The end of all flesh is come before me; for the earth is filled with violence through them; and, behold, I will destroy them with the earth" (Gen. 6:12, 13). The new immoral, oppressive regime will settle a pall of death upon humanity; but, the colder that the moral and spiritual night grows, the warmer and stronger God's stars will shine.

Why do the heathen rage, and the people imagine a vain thing?

The kings of the earth set themselves, and the rulers take counsel together, against the LORD, and against his anointed (Ps. 2:1, 2).

"Behold, the darkness shall cover the earth, and gross darkness the people: but the Lord shall arise upon thee, and his glory shall be seen upon thee" (Isa. 60:2, cf Rev. 16:10, 11). Night possesses every heart and mind, but the 144,000 have the light of Christ's constant presence dwelling in their hearts and minds. In the midst of the spiritualistic movements toward total possession of the human conscience and soul, and the complete centralization of global power, the Latter Rain pours down from heaven upon God's afflicted and humble people. Cells of resistance form against the moral night—not terrorist cells, but cells of Latter Rain recipients. They transform into a mighty, unstoppable medical missionary movement that preaches the Jesus who the apostles loved.

He shall cut off the spirit of princes: he is terrible to the kings of the earth (Ps. 76:12).

All earthly support disappears in the face of religio-political-economic reprisals; yet, the servants of Christ live by faith and move out with His message.

My soul followeth hard after thee: thy right hand upholdeth me (Ps. 63:8).

Christ has been great with glory and incense, roaring with the Father's thunders while They have been sending the Latter Rain of Their Spirit. The delay has been coming to its end and the seventh angel is about to sound its trumpet. The 144,000 and the great harvest of their labors are almost ready for Jesus to return.

But, they still need a difficult tribulation of imprisonment or exposure to the wilderness to completely whiten their robes in the blood of the Lamb (see 1 Peter 5:10). In order to put the blessing of Abraham before the people, part of their warning to the world required unmasking Satan, his earthly agencies, and his mystery methods to deceive. Therefore, the gospel constantly put them in danger. Martyrdom has not been a stranger to this group preparing for eternity (see Revelation 6:11). But, the world-wide missionary work has fortified them for the next wave of trouble.

> Satan also works, with lying wonders, even bringing down fire from heaven in the sight of men. Revelation 13:13. Thus the inhabitants of the earth will be brought to take their stand *The Great Controversy*, p. 612.

Prior to the entrance of Satan, as the full accomplishment of his grand scheme of confusion, his demonic angels bring down fire from heaven — a small taste of the much larger destruction by the angels of the Lord. The evil hosts make a token destruction, but not to end civilization. Yet, the powerful display is enough to mobilize those of secret rapture eschatologies against the Latter Rain.

> Fearful sights of a supernatural character will soon be revealed in the heavens, in token of the power of miracle-working demons. The spirits of devils will go forth to the kings of the earth and to the whole world, to fasten them in deception, and urge them on to unite with Satan in his last struggle against the government of heaven. By these agencies, rulers and subjects will be alike deceived *Maranatha*, p. 210.

Great balls of fire were falling upon houses, and from these balls fiery arrows were flying in every direction. It was impossible to check the fires that were kindled, and many places were being destroyed. The terror of the people was indescribable.

Strictly will the cities of the nations be dealt with, and yet they will not be visited in the extreme of God's indignation, because some souls will yet break away from the delusions of the enemy, and will repent and be converted, while the mass will be treasuring up wrath against the day of wrath *Maranatha*, p. 25.

Warn My people to cease from putting their trust in men who are not obedient to my warnings and who despise My reproof, for the day of the Lord is right upon the world when evidence shall be made sure. Those who have followed the voices that would turn things upside down will themselves be turned where they cannot see, but will be as blind men *Manuscript Release*, vol. 11, p. 361.

To prevent further judgments from God, and to stop the Latter Rain, the newly established Christian America will frantically resurrect the religious cleanse which the nation had earlier enacted. "They shall deliver you up to councils; and in the synagogues ye shall be beaten: and ye shall be brought before rulers and kings for my sake, for a testimony against them.... But when they shall lead you, and deliver you up, take no thought beforehand what ye shall speak, neither do ye premeditate: but whatsoever shall be given you in that hour, that speak ye: for it is not ye that speak, but the Holy Ghost" — it is "the Spirit of your Father which speaketh in you" (Mark 13:9, 11; Matt. 10:20).

> And the woman was arrayed in purple and scarlet colour, and decked with gold and precious stones and pearls, having a golden cup in her hand full of abominations and filthiness of her fornication: and upon her forehead was a name written, MYSTERY, BABYLON THE GREAT, THE MOTHER OF HARLOTS AND ABOMINATIONS OF THE EARTH. And I saw the woman drunken with the blood of the saints, and with the blood of the martyrs of Jesus (Rev. 17:4-6).

Many who disbelieved the third angel's message and disregarded the powerful appeals of the Latter Rain will now try to find God. Telltale danger is around the world. They see Judgment Day coming, and they suffer under the fear that the 144,000 were speaking the truth. They will all now try to connect with the Lord "and shall not be able" (Luke 13:24).

> Many will be lost while hoping and desiring to be Christians. They do not come to the point of yielding the will to God *Steps to Christ*, p. 47.

Wishing for faith and grace is not striving with the hard condemnation of God, and then desperately going to Jesus for His sterilizing conviction of sin. This sorrowing group never yielded to God's will concerning their idols. Too many times, in the face of obvious light pouring down from their High Priest, they spurned Him. They could never mortify the deeds of their body in order to be dependent children of the living God.

Because they had always balked at surrendering their heart and will, they never came to love His blended grace and truth. Caught up with the wide road of the world, they pushed away the pleas of His servants, the pleading of His Law and testimony voice, and His providential troubles, while they pushed away His Spirit. Instead they indulged grace without truth Spiritual Formation. The Spirit of Christ has finally left them. They can never have His comfort and know His presence. As with King Saul, their hearts are now filled with the fire and smoke and brimstone of Satan's presence, because the Spirit is permanently muted to them. Their probation is closing before God, as their Intercessor must step aside.

Now, in their effort to reconcile with God, they can only produce empty, half-hearted wishing, which is all that the deceptively innocuous Spiritual Formation trap allowed. Real justification and peace with God comes by striving under His condemnation for acceptance from Jesus. Christ's robe of righteousness comes by strongly sucking the oil of His Spirit's fullness from the Rock of flinty condemnation, "with patience" (Luke 8:15). The elect have endured the horror of great darkness from the Law, doing more than is humanly possible, so that a trusting personal covenant with the Lord could be made. Thus, "they are worthy" (Rev. 3:4) of God's grace. "Blessed are the dead which die in the Lord from henceforth: Yea, saith the Spirit, that they may rest from their labours; and their works do follow them" (Rev. 14:13). More than the foolish could produce is what the foolish need; but they squandered all the necessary time to learn to trust Jesus for all of His treasured acceptance and His fortifying sanctification. Learning earthly lessons takes time; no less does learning the things of God. "Courage, fortitude, faith, and implicit trust in God's power to save, do not come in a moment. These heavenly graces are acquired by the experience of years" *Christian Experience and Teachings*, p. 188.

Both Spiritual Formation and celebration overlooked and petted darling sins; those two abominations blessed the indulgence of earthly things and worldly pastimes, which Satan had thrust upon the Protestant people by his voracious locust armies (see Jeremiah 23:11-15). And the corrupted holy people "love to have it so" (Jer. 5:31; Dan. 8:12). By multitudinous avenues of counterfeit peace he has destroyed "all the world" (Rev. 13:3). The foolish virgins had chosen their deceptions, they denied the whole counsel of God, and their eternal loss is on their own head (see 2 Timothy 3:1-5; Ezekiel 33:4). The counsel and reproofs of the Spirit of Prophecy that they silenced gave Satan easy access to their minds, which left him unhampered in his subtle work to delude them. The devil twisted the truth of God's character until he entirely blocked all reverence for the way of righteousness. The will of his nominal human hosts is under his complete control. No longer is God's convicting power of truth available to them, and therefore, neither can they obtain His comfort and peace.

The nominal, foolish virgins would not choose to search for Jesus and His peace in the Law or in the Spirit of Prophecy, seeking Him until they found Him. Even though He called them to search the scriptures because His words testify of Him, the procrastinators never came to know Him. The little light that His Spirit gave them they never improved and He has now completely withdrawn it. (See Matthew 13:12; Revelation 2:4, 5.)

Two thousand years of forewarnings of this very moment are now reality; and, horrified, the foolish virgins can only implore human help. "I have sinned: yet honour me now, I pray thee…turn again with me, that I may worship the LORD thy God" (1 Sam. 15:30). They throw themselves at those who fought the hard battle to keep their sealing throughout the long night of darkness and confusion during the fifth and sixth trumpets. They wish to have their same reward for their battles — a beautiful, settled peace with God.

In Christ's parable the foolish beg the wise, "Give us of your oil; for our lamps are gone out" (Matt. 25:8). However, the ungodly hear the sad, but serious tones in reply, "Not so; lest there be not enough for us and you" (verse 9). Trusting the holy God is not naturally the fallen human forté. It takes much time spent talking together and doing things together in order to trust another earthly person. Much more so is there no short-cut in the good fight for trusting our law-enforcing Saviour in the heavenly sanctuary. And neither is mature faith transferable; it must be built up in each heart from the first dawning of the goodness of God's condemning justice upon them. Each person must make the time and effort which trusting requires. We must be striving to obtain constant, perfect faith in Jesus now, talking together with Him, learning of Him, standing on His promises of pardon, and looking for opportunities to share His truth and grace with others. Now is the time; now is the day of salvation. Procrastinating on this has eternal ramifications. Do we hear what the Spirit is saying to us? Will we not today fear and heed this intense parable from Christ?

The foolish virgins grew weary by enflaming themselves with their idol religion (see Isaiah 57:5, 10) and so never desired to expend all they could, through the Law and the cross, to have a personal experience in the things of God. They never needed the Holy Ghost to cleanse their guilt and shame, because seductive false religion excused them, and kept condemnation and repentance away from their thinking. Only Jesus can excuse; and He would have excused them if He had seen them accept His Father's chastisement of their pride. Jesus' words are Spirit and life (see John 6:63); but, His Spirit in His Testimonies never had an opportunity to drive them to His cross for their help to remove thorny character traits. The Testimony of Jesus converts the soul, but they never read His Testimonies. Instead, they played around with country club proprieties and peer approval, and they could never get serious with a right standing before God and His Law (see 2 Corinthians 10:12; Revelation 14:7; Luke 16:15; John 12:43). They would not see Jesus as the pearl of great price and then sell all for a visit with Him, the sure result of faith and surrender. Additionally, like troubled King Saul on his throne, even many holding a high office within the Remnant organization clung to their positions, refusing to heed the call to repentance and conversion from the 144,000 firstfruits (see 1 Samuel 18:29; 20:30, 31; Matthew 3:5-10; Luke 7:29, 30).

The foolish will accost those who wisely fought for surrender to Christ. His Spirit was available during the tormenting and eclipsing fifth and sixth trumpets. During that time the wise virgins invested in Him while the foolish chased after earthly mirages (see Revelation 9:4; Acts 3:19-21; Isaiah 55:6). But, being so late in the Latter Rain, the wise virgins shudder at the request of these panicking professors of religion not knowing when the judgment of the living will conclude. The wise virgins mercifully counsel the desperate ones to waste no time, but do as they had done — *Cooperate with the heavenly agencies to do the simple work of spending the effort and the little remaining time to know Jesus as a Lawgiver and a Friend, and you will be children of the everlasting Father. Even if you enter the kingdom last, at least you entered. Make haste, "go ye...to them that sell, and buy for yourselves"* (Matt. 25:9, cf Rev. 3:18; Matt. 13:46; Isa. 55:1-3).

However, the door of their probation has closed; their case in the judgment of the living has ended. For them the spiritual windows of heaven have closed and the deep wells of spiritually have staunched. For them, not even mercy drops are sensed. The foolish don't even hear Esau's token promise of grace from above (see Genesis 27:39, 40). The little faith, hope, and love has been at last removed from the world, with which the Spirit of God had sometimes blessed their hearts as His incentive for them to seek the full strength of the Latter Rain (see John 1:16). They seared their own conscience. It finds nothing palatable in patiently enduring the rebuke of God until His compassion could be realized. Spiritual Formation's smooth, grace-without-truth false doctrine has left Satan too deeply entrenched in their heart. Spiritualism has left their unexercised, diseased hearts fully rebellious and incapable of enduring even a merciful amount of wrath from an offended God. Their enflamed conscience is completely enervated by empty grace-only doctrines. And now nothing except honest wrestling with the rebukes of the Law, which requires more time than remains, can resuscitate their conscience (see Romans 7:9-23). God was not willing that any should perish; but, they have forced His hand.

> Awake, ye drunkards, and weep; and howl, all ye drinkers of wine, because of the new wine; for it is cut off from your mouth…. The vine is dried up, and the fig tree languisheth; the pomegranate tree, the palm tree also, and the apple tree, even all the trees of the field, are withered: because joy is withered away from the sons of men (Joel 1:5, 12).

> Therefore hath the curse devoured the earth, and they that dwell therein are desolate: therefore the inhabitants of the earth are burned, and few men left. The new wine mourneth, the vine languisheth, all the merryhearted do sigh. The mirth of tabrets ceaseth, the noise of them that rejoice endeth, the joy of the harp ceaseth. They shall not drink wine with a song; strong drink shall be bitter to them that drink it. The city of confusion is broken down: every house is shut up, that no man may come in. There is a crying for wine in the streets; all joy is darkened, the mirth of the land is gone (Isa. 24:6-11).

Satan has completely poisoned their consciences toward the high and holy principles of God's Law, which alone is the narrow way. The Law is the restrictive turnstile to the joy of knowing a merciful and tender Saviour from sin. But now, even their prayers are a constant abomination to God, hopelessly empty of His mediating Spirit. All that God detects from their weeping and howling is the wrath, arrogance, and unholy "holy laughter" of the demons from Spiritual Formation. As much as they seek it now, like destitute King Saul (see 1 Samuel 28:5, 6), their dry souls receive no confirming word from God in their conscience and heart. Despite all their abundant, self-generated, uninspired propitiating of God, their souls receive no water of life. They don't know the Intercessor, and the wrath of God forever abideth on them.

> The sinners in Zion are afraid; fearfulness hath surprised the hypocrites. Who among us shall dwell with the devouring fire? Who among us shall dwell with everlasting burnings? (Isa. 33:14).
>
> Therefore shall the Lord, the Lord of hosts, send among his fat ones leanness; and under his glory he shall kindle a burning like the burning of a fire. And the light of Israel shall be for a fire, and his Holy One for a flame: and it shall burn and devour his thorns and his briers in one day; and shall consume *the glory of his forest, and of his fruitful field, both soul and body*: and they shall be as when a standard bearer fainteth. And the rest of the trees of his forest shall be few, that a child may write them....
>
> For the Lord GOD of hosts shall make a consumption, even determined, in the midst of all the land (Isa. 10:16-19, 23).

It's too late!

> And they shall wander from sea to sea, and from the north even to the east, they shall run to and fro to seek the word of the LORD, and shall not find it. In that day shall the fair virgins and young men faint for thirst (Amos 8:12, 13).

During the powerful and abundant availability of the Holy Spirit, the foolish virgins assumed that the blessed Latter Rain would continue forever. Under the very downpour of Jesus' glorified presence (see Acts 3:19, 20; Revelation 10:1) they carelessly stayed too busy to be a child of God. Jesus personally came to purify the sons of Levi, but these would not admit His sanctifying presence. The abundant Spirit of God through Christ from the Most Holy was spurned and insulted (see John 14:21, 23, 24; Isaiah 7:10-13). Rather than covet and indulge His Spirit which He was giving for the life of the world, and which was springing up into everlasting joy all around them, they contemptuously kept themselves occupied with a career and Babylonian education, with play and sports telecasts. Many even stayed too busy with religious work and the futile burden to be their own ascetic victor over sin. At this most important juncture since the beginning of the great controversy, Jesus was never allowed into their trust to seek Him out for His self-sacrificing love to change their evil nature. And they remained children of wrath, just like the wicked. Much of this sad story can be owed to the counterfeit emerging church deception that caught Christianity by surprise and diverted multitudes from the Latter Rain (see *The Great Controversy*, p. 464).

Likewise, zealots among them, never forgiving or knowing forgiveness from God's Spirit, strategized within their militias for a secular military campaign against Babylon (see 2 Chronicles 20:17). They never stocked up on the promises of Psalm 91 and never read the Lord's prohibitions of self-defense in Jeremiah. They involved themselves in anarchy.

All were too proud to fear that they needed the true victory and testimony of the 144,000, and now they cannot hear a single word of response from the Lord's Spirit despite all their anxious praying (see 1 Samuel 13:7-9; 1 Kings 18:26, 27). They had abandoned the three angels' messages, and instead sought mystery Spiritual Formation and temporal advantages in a world that they only half-believed would ever pass away. They knew to inspect their soul for genuine faith, and to chasten self during the antitypical Day of Atonement (see Leviticus 23:27, 29, 32). But, they lost that conviction because they involved themselves with nothing more than keeping a good job and making a living (see Luke 17:28; Matthew 24:38). This they did in complete disregard toward the Spirit of Prophecy counsels and the commandment to stop working in preparation for Judgment Day (see Leviticus 23:27-32; Hebrews 4:10, 11). "For whatsoever soul it be that shall not be afflicted in that same day, he shall be cut off" (Lev. 23:29).

The foolish virgins never developed faith by exercising a warm relationship with Jesus, and now they seek Him and He cannot be found; they are forever cut off from His life. They would not assemble often together with others seeking renewed favor and Spirit from Jesus, especially as they saw judgment nearing. They lost all discernment to distinguish "between him that serveth God and him that serveth him not" (Mal. 3:18). So they followed the wrong teachers, who sprang up during this time of uncertainty (see 2 Peter 2:1; Matthew 24:24).

They proudly refused to give up the fight with sin and to fall in sorrow on that Stone who alone could break their heart and their self-will. Only He could give them the beautiful, spiritual things of God — rest from the presence and the bitterness of our natural rebellion (see Psalm 16:9). But, they wouldn't make eternal realities supreme over temporal realities. They wouldn't learn the rest and peace that God readily made available for His children if they would lay everything on the altar to trust Him (see Hebrews 4:1-11; Matthew 13:44-46). Jesus must bear the difficult position of telling them the truth that He never knew them. They had been serving the imposter, Baal; and the Lord will never share the same heart with that cunning master.

Now, in the fear of Church retaliation and in their natural distress to save themselves from soon-coming judgment, the procrastinators cannot sit at the feet of Jesus and learn of Him. Try as they might, they can no longer find anything of the biblical love of God or beauty of Jesus which would lead them to repentance. They cannot have that perfect peace and health-giving rest seen in the 144,000. Their light is gone out; the Spirit from Christ has forever left them. They strive to glean salvation from the pages of the Bible, but their study is in vain. Because of their decided indolence and violence toward the pleading of the Spirit, they can never have the joy of knowing Jesus (see Galatians 5:17; Genesis 6:3; Luke 14:24).

The terrible reality seizes them:

The harvest is past, the summer is ended, and we are not saved (Jer. 8:20).

Eternal loss fills their hearts. But, their fear isn't the fear of God, or they would have responded to Him before time ran out. No, their terror is that which comes to those who will know they are lost forever. "For if we sin wilfully after that we have received the knowledge of the truth, there remaineth no more sacrifice for sins, but a certain fearful looking for of judgment and fiery indignation, which shall devour the adversaries" (Heb. 10:26, 27, cf 2 Cor. 5:11).

The foolish virgins knew the truth, but focused on the praise of men instead of God's approval, celebrating their own righteousness in humanistic, celebratory Babylon (see 2 Corinthians 10:12; Revelation 13:18; John 12:43). They had spent their days avoiding a comforting Priest because He was also an intimidating law-enforcing Prince (see Matthew 25:24, 25; Luke 19:21; Acts 5:31). They had remained offended at the holy requirements of the Bible. They had felt affronted at God's wrath with which He had inundated His Son on the cross, because His wrath was a reflection on them. They squandered precious time forcing out a moral character from their own unconverted heart (see Matthew 13:20, 21) to create nothing more than a good public image (see Isaiah 64:6).

Instead of coming to Jesus for His redemptive virtue, they turned down the good fight of faith. Therefore, the bitter roots of their fallen nature now bear the full strength in a bumper crop of briers and thorns, choking out even the love and faith which they had once received (see Matthew 13:22; Mark 4:23-25).

Looking diligently lest any man fail of the grace of God; lest any root of bitterness springing up trouble you, and thereby many be defiled; lest there be any fornicator, or profane person, as Esau, who for one morsel of meat sold his birthright. For ye know how that afterward, when he would have inherited the blessing, he was rejected: for he found no place of repentance, though he sought it carefully with tears (Heb. 12:15-17).

After having half-heartedly waited so long for the marriage of the Bridegroom, the impenitent virgins' voices can be heard in Esau's frantic, high volume prayers still echoing from the past,

Hast thou not reserved a blessing for me?... Hast thou but one blessing, my father? bless me, even me also, O my father" (Gen. 27:36, 38).

Esau had long played around with holy things. Unlike Jacob who received a mustard seed of faith, from childhood Esau never feared God, had no time for Him amidst all of his earthly pursuits, and even subconsciously never gave Him glory. In time, as much as his father Isaac wanted to give him the blessing, it was no longer available. Providence had determined it. And Esau lifted up his voice and wept (see verse 38).

Likewise, among this distraught group arises much weeping and gnashing of teeth, perplexity and agony. So, they turn away to nervously rejoin the world celebrating a universal Spiritual Formation and empty charismatic sensation. They quickly feel at home in Baalpeor and their fears subside. Maybe the Adventist revival was just a fundamentalist cult, after all, as the religious authorities say. The foolish had united with the world and had partaken of its spirit. They chose friends from this temporal world; they made deals with them in the mammon of rebellion. They could no longer come to Jesus to "buy wine and milk without money and without price" (Isa. 55:1).

> Wherefore do ye spend money for that which is not bread? and your labour for that which satisfieth not? hearken diligently unto me, and eat ye that which is good, and let your soul delight itself in fatness. Incline your ear, and come unto me: hear, and your soul shall live; and I will make an everlasting covenant with you, even the sure mercies of David (Isa. 55:2, 3).

Therefore, Jesus must regretfully recommend, "I say unto you, Make to yourselves friends of the mammon of unrighteousness; that, when ye fail, they may receive you into everlasting habitations" (Luke 16:9, cf Ps. 18:26). Those permanent habitations will be inescapable dungeons of devils (see Revelation 18:2; 14:11).

The virgins lose all spirituality as the heavenly messengers from the Word of life leave them and double up around those who had honestly and eagerly sought for more of Him (see Matthew 13:12; Luke 19:24; 2 Peter 2:22). It's too late. The merciful delay has ended. After so long a time of mercy, they are rejected by God, and their names are blotted from the book of life (see Revelation 3:5). God has removed His Spirit of life from them, what little they had.

> And they shall look unto the earth; and behold trouble and darkness, dimness of anguish; and they shall be driven to darkness (Isa. 8:22).

This will be the pitiful experience of "multitudes, multitudes" (Joel 3:14), even of Adventists, who do not today make use of this quickly shrinking period of relative peace left in the sixth trumpet. Before the soon-coming real trouble starts, we all need to meet our Maker at the foot of His Law. The stone Law of love requires love but it never gives love. Therefore, the foolish virgins had left the Law for pleasures from the god of this world, which had put their minds and consciences into deep sleep. They wouldn't fall and break in total helplessness to be loved. If they had, then Jesus would have touched their heart with evidence that He heard their cry (see Psalm 106:44; 1 Samuel 10:26). But, they had never thus found the Prince and Saviour through the condemning Law, the strait gate to life and happiness.

No, the Law doesn't give love because the Law is an it... God has provided us a Friend who does love to love and to be loved.

No, the Law doesn't give love because the Law is an *it*, and *only persons* can give love. **The Law** is not a person; no matter what we make of *it*, the Law cannot be a warm friend. But, *God has provided us a Friend who does love to love and to be loved.* Stone cannot sympathize; letters cannot love or be touched with the feelings of our infirmities. The cold stone of God's Law is the district attorney for the Most High; He has made it so. For the sake of our deceitful, mischievous hearts this has to be. The Law *shouldn't* love, and it *doesn't* forgive. It isn't *designed* to love and forgive us. Yet, *it* alone will give us the terrified, focused need for a living, loving, warm-hearted Saviour who **is** a person like us, who **does** love us, who **is** touched with the feelings of our infirmities, and who **wants to** forgive us. **And,** He also loves the stone Law of love, which He sees as the perfect representation of His Father to mischievous sinners. He loves us and desires all of us to be with both of Them for all eternity. While we can't open our heart to the Law or to the Spirit of Prophecy, we *can* open to our Law-loving, fair, and warm-hearted Friend. Then *He will open our heart to the Law and Spirit of Prophecy*. None of us sinners are good enough to love the Law, and He knows we must have His help.

The Spirit of Prophecy, the Bible, the Law are an *it*. All three are made up of letters, and "the letter killeth" (2 Cor. 3:6). The Spirit of Prophecy, that adamant Law enforcing officer for these last days, has stood staunchly opposed to the innate rebellion of this perverse generation. Yes, surely it has! But it alone could cause us to meet our warm-blooded Saviour at the foot of His cross; and He will advocate for every virgin today who still appears to be foolish (see Daniel 12:1; 1 Corinthians 1:26-29; Isaiah 35:8). He alone can help them love His Father's Law (see *The Great Controversy*, p. 461.1; Galatians 3:24; Micah 7:18), and will yet facilitate His Father's promised blessedness upon them. We must need Someone beyond the requirement of the Law, but who upholds the law. We need to conceptualize such a Person, and then we need to go find that Person. He's not beyond the sea; He is not far from every one of us. *He is in the requirement of the Law*, for the requirement testifies of Him. He is the Law-lover and the Law-liver. And with Him principle is as unbudging as a boulder. That's why He's called the Rock, as in the Citadel. If He did budge our mischievous souls could not be saved. For our sakes He never alters anything that comes out of His mouth (see Malachi 3:6; Psalm 89:34). But, He is also a warm-hearted Lawgiver for everyone who will fall on Him and break.

Isn't God concerned that we today might be too offended at His Law enforcement and turn down His salvation, and remain a foolish virgin? He has sworn an oath that He wants no one to perish, but for all to come to repentance (see Hebrews 6:13-20; 7:20-22; 2 Peter 3:9). And He knows that everyone who honestly searches for Him certainly will be offended. They will be blinded like Daniel was blinded, and they will see their human goodness in all of its corruption (see Daniel 10:8). But they will search for evidences of His love written in His words and in His handiwork, and they will keep seeking His face until they see signs of His longed-for love (see Daniel 10:11, 18, 19).

> Ye shall seek me, and find me, when ye shall search for me with all your heart. And I will be found of you, saith the LORD (Jer. 29:13, 14).

They will reconcile with His requirements. He infinitely desires everyone to be with Him forever "because he delighteth in mercy" (Mic. 7:18). But He cannot allow for a single unconfessed, unrepented of sin to enter His coming kingdom. "Though He was the Prince of Peace, His coming must be as the unsheathing of a sword" *The Desire of Ages*, p. 111. It is disobedience to the laws of God that has brought the human race to the indescribable misery which is driving it to stimulants, intoxicants, and opiates. Sin never pays except in enervation and death. Jesus must make war against every offender of His Father, then we cling to His strength like Jacob did by the ford Jabbok. We sue for peace and He makes peace (see Isaiah 27:5; Hebrews 4:16; Isaiah 26:5).-

> Have I any pleasure at all that the wicked should die? saith the Lord GOD: and not that he should return from his ways, and live?... I have no pleasure in the death of him that dieth, saith the Lord GOD: wherefore turn yourselves, and live ye (Eze. 18:23, 32).

> Say unto them, As I live, saith the Lord GOD, I have no pleasure in the death of the wicked; but that the wicked turn from his way and live: turn ye, turn ye from your evil ways; for why will ye die? (Eze. 33:11).

God must keep the standard as high as heaven is above the earth. In order to get His elect safely through the final delusions of Satan He must present a standard that is infinitely high, higher than every human thought can reach. To be healed of sin must be the last day virgins' chief want. Isn't that fair? Isn't that honest and right? Our Father will not go through another great controversy. This controversy has taken too great a toll upon His Son, and on His family in heaven and earth. He cannot let a second controversy erupt. He has provided all that the world needs to be redeemed. "Thou wilt keep him in perfect peace, whose mind is stayed on thee: because he trusteth in thee" (Isa. 26:3). Looking unto Jesus *everyone* would be saved. But, only those who, with all their heart and soul, want a friend in Jesus will find in Him the truest friend. He has revealed Himself in the Bible, in the natural world, and in the experiences of life. If we will humble ourselves before His Spirit of Prophecy and let the thunders of God rumble against our resistance, then, and only *if* we will struggle to hear Christ's favorite words, will He speak them to us personally: "Be not afraid" (Matt. 17:7); "Be of good comfort" (Matt. 9:22); "Be of good cheer" (John 16:33); "Thy sins be forgiven thee" (Luke 5:23); "Peace, be still" (Mark 4:39); "The Father himself loveth you" (John 16:27).

> I create the fruit of the lips; Peace, peace to him that is far off, and to him that is near, saith the LORD; and I will heal him (Isa. 57:19).

> The Spirit of the Lord GOD is upon me; because the LORD...hath sent me to bind up the brokenhearted, to proclaim liberty to the captives, and the opening of the prison to them that are bound; to proclaim the acceptable year of the LORD, and the day of vengeance of our God; to comfort all that mourn; to appoint unto them that mourn in Zion, to give unto them beauty for ashes, the oil of joy for mourning, the garment of praise for the spirit of heaviness; that they might be called trees of righteousness, the planting of the LORD, that he might be glorified (Isa. 61:1-3, cf Matt. 9:12).

From our first birth, we are born self-centered, angry children. (See Ephesians 2:3; Psalm 39:3, 4; Exodus 16:2, 3.) All of our life we strive against the Law, and against humiliation and correction. Our fallen nature of selfish discontent taints our best intentions, even from infancy. We are screamers before we know how to talk,

Chapter 8 Revelation Chapter 11: The Final Victory

and grumblers and complainers ever afterward. On this issue scripture is clear (see Exodus 16:2, 3; Psalms 51:5; 58:3; Romans 3:10-19). Meanwhile, spiritualism, human philosophy, and the one false religion seek to evade the basic tenet of the Bible that says none of us are inherently good. Without the help that only our Creator can give, even the best humans are all bound for the grossest evils (see 2 Samuel 11; Jeremiah 32:35; Matthew 7:11; 19:17). Without Christ, we are all "by nature the children of wrath", "fulfilling the desires of the flesh and of the mind" (Eph. 2:3). It's only as we can admit this that we begin to remove the sins that beset us.

Many judge themselves "good enough", or "pretty good compared to the next person"; but, the Bible declares that our "pretty good" is not "good enough". Jesus was the only one on this planet born inherently good, the only one to please the most holy God. Jesus was the only one "good enough" to need no repentance; He alone can stand before the Almighty without an intercessor. They both are the same in character — proven infinitely empty of self.

The standard to pass the judgment bar of God is the character of Christ, the perfect life of faith. "And in him is no sin" (1 John 3:5). We have to have the "faith of Jesus" (Rev. 14:12, cf Rom. 3:22; Gal. 2:16). We must be forgiven and justified by His gift of faith, and anointed with His Spirit and *His obedience*. The goal to meet is immaculate princely perfection, as exemplified by the Messiah, the Anointed One (see 1 Peter 2:21-24; 2 Corinthians 5:21). And, although the world strives against His high standard, by His Spirit God wrestles with every soul throughout our lifetime in order to give us His gracious power to change our self-centered heart (see Galatians 5:17; 1 Timothy 1:5; Ezekiel 36:25-27).

But, by joining with Satan's favored religious agency to prevent the final gospel invitation and to persecute the 144,000 who preached it, lost humanity has finally cut itself off from the Holy Spirit. They would have no king but Antichrist. The Spirit of God can no longer wrestle with the conscience of the guilty race. The humanistic, sin-loving world has committed the unpardonable sin by its communication with the spirits which counseled to destroy God's mouthpieces; and human probation closes. God cuts them off from His comfort as they have cut Him off by false religion and worship (see Malachi 2:11, 12; Revelation 14:7). "I will…make them drunk in my fury" (Isa. 63:6, cf Rev. 14:9-11; Jer. 25:14-38; Rom. 1:26, 28). Now, although appearing devoutly religious and pious, the congenital rage within every self-sufficient heart, forever alienated from God, becomes uncontrollable. The whole world is given to Satan, who will drive them to exterminate God's people. Nothing short of genocide will silence the preachers of righteousness.

"*There are those commandment-keeping cultists who refuse to unite with the global religious community!*" Accused as trouble-makers, the redeemed 144,000 had such settled love, joy, and peace, so lively and sweet, which drove them to stand so staunchly for the Bible's high standard, that the finally impenitent multitudes now believe the Beast, which declares that the Antichrist isn't a person. Rather the 144,000 are the charismatic Antichrist that must be destroyed before it makes other commandment-keeping devils. The Adventists' exaltation of the first Amendment separation of church and state has left them buried in suspicion and made them prime candidates for vigilante justice. They are made targets of a great crusade for the final Inquisition.

> The proud have had me greatly in derision: yet have I not declined from thy law (Ps. 119:51).

> Because he hath set his love upon me, therefore will I deliver him (Ps. 91:14).

The ultimate rejection of the Law of God is to destroy His representatives in the name of "God". An all-pervasive, horrible root of bitterness is plaguing the world. Each one is "made to suffer the wrath of God" when "the truth has been brought home to his mind and conscience, and has been rejected" *The Great Controversy*, p. 605. The permanently deceived now suffer under the grinding indignation from a most holy God who has been finally vindicated by the holy characters of His people. The mean, atheistic consciences of the lost, "as a wild bull in a net …full of the fury of the LORD, the rebuke of thy God" (Isa. 51:20), cannot resolve the supernatural rage in their hearts of fire and smoke and brimstone. Possession by demons is the mark of the Beast. The destructive anxiety arises from Satan's lawlessness totally blotting from the conscience the lawful love of God. Nothing else than the perfect, lawful love of God can calm nervous minds and schizophrenic psyches.

> As the restraining Spirit of God shall be withdrawn from men and they shall be under the control of Satan, who hates the divine precepts, there will be strange developments. The heart can be very cruel when God's fear and love are removed *The Great Controversy*, p. 608.

If any man worship the beast and his image, and receive his mark in his forehead, or in his hand, the same shall drink of the wine of the wrath of God, which is poured out without mixture into the cup of his indignation; and he shall be tormented with fire and brimstone in the presence of the holy angels, and in the presence of the Lamb: and the smoke of their torment ascendeth up for ever and ever: and they have no rest day nor night, who worship the beast and his image, and whosoever receiveth the mark of his name (Rev. 14:9-11).

"The beast that was, and is not, even he is the eighth, and is of the seven, and goeth into perdition" (Rev. 17:11). A driving force to do evil — the full mark of the Beast — controls the world. Through self-pleasing Spiritual Formation, they had emptied God's image from their hearts, and spirits of devils have entered their souls in full force. And the success of the turmoil and degradation in the world cause much exultation from the locusts and the demonic black smoke.

Blow ye the trumpet in Zion, and sound an alarm in my holy mountain: let all the inhabitants of the land tremble: for the day of the LORD cometh, for it is nigh at hand; a day of darkness and of gloominess, a day of clouds and of thick darkness, as the morning spread upon the mountains (Joel 2:1, 2).

Satan has substituted himself upon the total expulsion of the Spirit of God from the human race. Through Spiritual Formation he placed the abomination that makes desolate. He set himself as God in the temple of every worshiper (see Daniel 11:31, 45; Matthew 24:15; 2 Thessalonians 2:4), and he quickly sent the worshipers to corrupt the worldlings. Since the start of the fifth trumpet, Satan had gradually set up a global dictatorial government of force just for this occasion. To take advantage of a global government as his medium to direct the worst crimes, he uses his loose freedom from the conscience provided to the world by the wine of lawless centering prayer and the Mass. The Mass' "peace", which is not divine peace (see Isaiah 50:11), causes endless disillusionment that turns into a vengeful urge to make war against everyone who speaks against the pagan mysteries of the Church. Those who have true peace with the God of Abraham will become the objects of intense hatred. All that the anger-filled national leaders need is a hint from the papacy, and those semi-Arian Sabbatarians will be the targets of vicious man-hunts. "Yea, the time cometh, that whosoever killeth you will think that he doeth God service" (John 16:2).

Woe to the multitude of many people, which make a noise like the noise of the seas; and to the rushing of nations, that make a rushing like the rushing of mighty waters! The nations shall rush like the rushing of many waters: but God shall rebuke them, and they shall flee far off, and shall be chased as the chaff of the mountains before the wind, and like a rolling thing before the whirlwind. And behold at eveningtide trouble; and before the morning he is not. This is the portion of them that spoil us, and the lot of them that rob us (Isa. 17:12-14).

The global search begins for Law and gospel sympathizers. But, the children of God are prepared because they have peace through the scriptural vision of Jesus sealed in their minds, and His precious promises of redemption are sealed in their hearts. Cooperating with the Spirit of Christ, the angelic hosts have finished their labors to seal "the servants of our God in their foreheads" (Rev. 7:3). Christ has replaced their sinful character with His perfect character, which further establishes, strengthens, and settles their union with Him.

"The second woe is past; and, behold, the third woe cometh quickly" (Rev. 11:14).

The door of human probation closes and no one can buy or sell faith anymore (see Isaiah 55:6, 7; Revelation 13:17). Fierce Nazi-like Gestapo danger rages all around, and fear to join the 144,000 casts out all possibility of learning perfect faith in God's love (see Psalm 32:6; Matthew 24:9, 10). Because of repeated choices, either for or against the Spirit of Christ, there is a wide, unalterable chasm between all who He has drawn with His everlasting love and those who have rejected His drawing. Not one who is unsealed can be sealed; neither do the sealed ones want to be unsealed, as they dwell in constant close communion with Jesus who they have for so long desired. (See Luke 16:26; Revelation 22:11).

Throughout the fifth trumpet and especially during the sixth trumpet since 9/11, God's providences have permitted Satan and his devouring locusts to prosper unhampered at their work to fully devise a global totalitarian religion and United Nations government. This joint Protestant-Vatican power forces everyone to make their final decisions whether or not to join the brutal persecution against the sanctified, sealed people who are branded as Arian terrorists, and are being declared to speak heresy upon heresy. Everyone must forever be either a persecutor or the persecuted, oppressed or an oppressor. The divide between the two groups becomes impassable.

The sanctifying Spirit of God leaves those hearts that unite in the persecution or who stay with the majority for fear of financial loss, social ostracism and recrimination, or fear of punishment by Satan's newly established religio-political authorities. Only those who were mourning to God for the abominations taking place around them and within their own hearts, during the fifth and sixth trumpets, were receiving the seal of God's Spirit. They alone prepared to withstand the deluding spiritual devices sweeping humanity into spiritualism. Only the 144,000 and innumerable multitude could by faith flee the terrorizing leadership rather than give the nod to persecution.

There is no taking away their convictions. The sealed were sober and vigilant; they feared God during the trumpets' expediting of the investigative judgment. None except these received from Christ's censor the spiritual coals from His heavenly altar. They alone had bent their will to be pure for God, and had found themselves inept to do so. Conviction of their sinfulness ravaged their pride and they conceded the battle to God. They alone looked for a Saviour in His Father's offensive Law and, having found faith in Jesus there, received His power to become sons of God (see Romans 7:9-25). Only they gained the needed spiritual fortitude to stand apart from a unified world and to walk alone through the fiery persecution with Jesus (see 2 Peter 1:4-10; Daniel 3:23-25; Isaiah 43:1-4). Everyone who had procrastinated the special purification during the fifth and sixth trumpets cave in to the present dangers of reprisal (see 2 Peter 1:8-10). When the son of perdition suddenly reappears on his throne of the Dark Ages to "wear out the saints of the most High" (Dan 7:25, cf Ps. 49:14; 2 Thess. 2:8; Rev. 13:15), it will be much to the surprise and shock of many, many nominal Protestants (see Isaiah 33:14).

But, to many multitudes sprinkled among all the nations, tongues, and peoples this will mean joy. They will have only praise to God that prophecy is being fulfilled and that Jesus will return after the great troubles, as He promised He would (see Malachi 3:16-4:2; Isaiah 24:14-16; Matthew 24:29, 30; John 14:1-3). His unerring, living word (see 1 Peter 1:23) and "the Spirit of Christ" (1 Pet. 1:11, cf Rom. 8:1, 2) have guided them to watch for the "stealthy but rapid" formation of the Beast from the Dark Ages. Their eyes have been awake and discerning. Prayer "and the supply of the Spirit of Jesus Christ" (Phil. 1:19) have strengthened them to meet the crisis by having given them many occasions to count the cost of standing at the end. Their trust in Jesus has matured; they have thrown themselves into the work of winning many to Him during the Loud Cry of the Latter Rain, and their communion with Him has deepened. Now they are prepared and the worst winds of destruction can blow. The time of perdition for the ungodly begins, and young and old who never decidedly obtained faith are hopelessly caught up in the confusion (see Psalm 32:6).

Christ's blessedness on the 144,000 and upon all who received their gospel preaching continues to thrill every soul. Perfect unity exists among them and they revel in the fellowship and the pure bond of love and selfless commonality (see Acts 2:42-47, cf Nehemiah 8:10-18; Psalm 40:3-5; Psalm 16:6-11; Esther 8:17; Esther 9:22; Isaiah 61:7; 1 John 1:7; John 13:35; 17:21). This is the beautiful time that fulfills Revelation 10:7; that is, "the days of the voice of the seventh angel, when he is about to sound [the] trumpet," when "should be completed the mystery of God, as He did announce the glad tidings to His bondmen the prophets" *Interlinear Greek-English New Testament*. The second and greater atonement for the Most Holy God has brought a greater and holier blessing than Pentecost saw. All martyrdom prior to probation closing has only added to the gravity and tight fellowship and prophetic vision among the sealed group preparing for translation.

> O God, when thou wentest forth before thy people, when thou didst march through the wilderness; Selah:
>
> The earth shook, the heavens also dropped at the presence of God: even Sinai itself was moved at the presence of God, the God of Israel.
>
> Thou, O God, didst send a plentiful rain, whereby thou didst confirm thine inheritance, when it was weary.
>
> Thy congregation hath dwelt therein: thou, O God, hast prepared of thy goodness for the poor.
>
> The Lord gave the word: great was the company of those that published it....

The chariots of God are twenty thousand, even thousands of angels: the Lord is among them, as in Sinai, in the holy place.

Thou hast ascended on high, thou hast led captivity captive: thou hast received gifts for men....

Blessed be the Lord, who daily loadeth us with benefits, even the God of our salvation. Selah (Ps. 68:7-11, 15-19).

Christ's Adventist-Protestant 144,000 firstfruits and the full harvest of their Spirit-impelled missionary labors — the Lord's sealed, innumerable host throughout the world — are about to be reclaimed for His eternal kingdom. By these sealed disciples God is fully exonerated before the angelic hosts and myriad unfallen worlds. Rapidly has every ear heard the truth. Quickly has the door of human probation closed (see Luke 13:24-30). The Father is satisfied to bring them to Himself.

The grand finale of the investigative judgment and sanctuary cleansing can proceed.

"And the seventh angel sounded" (Rev. 11:15).

Heaven's probation for Earth's populations has ceased. Many have deserted their hedonistic rabble which was left over from the locusts' demolition of Protestantism (see Revelation 9:20, 21). Christ has transformed their old, destructive lifestyles and they have prepared to meet Jesus. Millions from the non-Protestant religions around the globe have also joined the Advent band. *Glad tidings!*

Every mind that was entrenched in sin before the Latter Rains fell has accepted or rejected the gentle truth seen in Christ's character. His sealed and redeemed people throughout the world have responded to the Loud Cry, "casting down imaginations, and every high thing that exalteth itself against the knowledge of God, and bringing into captivity every thought to the obedience of Christ" (2 Cor. 10:5). The Father has redeemed them from the captivity of sin so that they can serve Jesus forever; not one stain remains in their character or on their record. This chosen generation has exonerated the blessed and only Potentate, and there is rejoicing in heaven — "great voices" (Rev. 11:15, cf Luke 15:7). The King has regained full trust from His heavenly kingdom; He has "put down all rule and all authority and power... He hath put all enemies under [Christ's] feet" (1 Cor. 15:24, 25).

Multitudes from heathen religions and no religion have pressed into the movement that the 144,000 have led, and have joined the holy rivalry with the angels. The presence of Jesus has inundated the innumerable hosts with victories over sin and with a love for the Law of His mouth. They have taken the very places of the Adventist and Protestant masses who never surrendered their heart to Jesus as Lawgiver and Sin-forgiver, and who abandoned the Reformation movement in exchange for Protestantism's revival of Ashtoreth. The shaking was a terrible ordeal, nevertheless it had to take place.

The shaken out Adventists and Protestants with all their heart and soul and strength had not sought the new heart and new will; nor did they work out the sanctified life and the fortified mind. They came to view reality in the same light as the world. They would never accept the Lawgiver's method of humbling by His strong reproofs and condemnation of sin. They would not have their sins condemned by His Spirit of Prophecy. Their spirit controlled by the demon of pride could not tolerate trembling, even for a moment, as a hopelessly lost sinner. They failed the first works of the everlasting test. They cannot stand erect and fearless in the presence of earthly monarchs because they had never bowed low before the King of kings (see *The Desire of Ages*, p. 103.3). They never yielded the will to God, and now they cannot stand bravely against the terrors of the great time of trouble.

God has had to work determinedly yet slowly to not scare sinners away. But having rejected God's last sorrowful effort to offer them love, a deceived world has followed the destroyer. Too late and beyond hope, every lost soul has struggled successfully against wave after wave of Christ's Spirit of grace, and their exclusion from God they have earned for themselves. "For the wages of sin is death" (Rom. 6:23). Jesus' angels have gathered "out of his kingdom all things that offend, and them which do iniquity" (Matt. 13:41). Divested of all who resisted the appeals of God's Spirit and clung to the corrupted spirit of Satan, Earth can now rightly be claimed by the Father. The mystery book of the seals and trumpets is finished, and God's great heavenly tribunal has concluded (see Revelation 10:7; Daniel 7:9-11, 13; Revelation 14:7).

At that time shall Michael stand up, the great prince which standeth for the children of thy people (Dan. 12:1).

Behold, one like the Son of man came with the clouds of heaven, and came to the Ancient of days, and they brought him near before him. And there was given him dominion, and glory, and a kingdom, that all people, nations, and languages, should serve him: his dominion is an everlasting dominion, which shall not pass away, and his kingdom that which shall not be destroyed (Dan. 7:13, 14).

There were great voices in heaven, saying, The kingdoms of this world are become the kingdoms of our Lord, and of his Christ; and he shall reign for ever and ever. And the four and twenty elders, which sat before God on their seats, fell upon their faces, and worshipped God, saying, We give thee thanks, O Lord God Almighty, which art, and wast, and art to come; because thou hast taken to thee thy great power, and hast reigned (Rev. 11:15-17).

The Father of all has proven Himself by not sparing His own soul when He spared not His only divine Son; and, neither did He spare His servants of the past who gave up their lives for us to have the Holy Textus Receptus Bible (see Isaiah 43:4; Revelation 6:9-11; 12:13-16). From His Father's sanctuary, the Son's work of vindicating His Father through His children went forward throughout the Christian dispensation and especially during the investigative judgment. Thus, His reward can be with Him when He returns for His people (see Revelation 22:12; 11:18).

This world is His rightful jurisdiction once again, to execute punishment according to His all-wise discretion. When Jesus goes in to His Father alone to acquire His kingdom, then He receives from His Father the commandment to bring His people home. He leaves the throne and speeds to Earth (see Hebrews 9:28; Luke 18:8). His reward is with Him (see Isaiah 40:10; Revelation 22:12). His redeemed family of Earth is His everlasting reward (see Malachi 3:16, 17) and He is theirs.

"And the temple of God was opened in heaven, and there was seen in his temple the ark of his testament" (Rev. 11:19). The sanctuary's atonement is complete. The time has ended for His servants' sins to be fully atoned for, blotted out of existence and out of the memories of His justifying angelic jury. Christ has fully cleansed His sanctuary and restored it as the original haven of rest, a cleansing process which began in 1844.

When ye therefore shall see the abomination of desolation, spoken of by Daniel the prophet, stand in the holy place, (whoso readeth, let him understand:) then let them which be in Judaea flee into the mountains…pray ye that your flight be not in the winter (Matt. 24:15, 16, 20, cf Dan. 11:44, 45; 2 Thess. 2:4).

"…and there shall be a time of trouble, such as never was since there was a nation even to that same time: and at that time thy people shall be delivered, every one that shall be found written in the book" (Dan. 12:1).

And ye shall be hated of all men for my name's sake: but he that shall endure unto the end, the same shall be saved (Mark 13:13).

We shall be able to go to prison trusting in Him as a little child trusts in its parents *Last Day Events*, p. 149.

If the world hate you, ye know that it hated me before it hated you. If ye were of the world, the world would love his own: but because ye are not of the world, but I have chosen you out of the world, therefore the world hateth you (John 15:18, 19).

They shall lay their hands on you, and persecute you, delivering you up to the synagogues, and into prisons, being brought before kings and rulers for my name's sake. And it shall turn to you for a testimony. Settle it therefore in your hearts, not to meditate before what ye shall answer: for I will give you a mouth and wisdom, which all your adversaries shall not be able to gainsay nor resist (Luke 21:12-15).

Satan, who in heaven originally stood up against Michael "your prince", "Messiah the Prince" (Dan. 10:21; 9:25, cf Dan. 12:1; 8:11, 25; Acts 5:31), must forever rid the world of faith and love, which is such a danger to his soon to begin millennium of peace attempt. The great division has taken place on earth. Everyone has either fully made their decision to love their Creator and His righteousness with all that is within them, or, like King Saul and Judas, they have fought the Almighty and His righteousness with all of their stubbornness until His Spirit is fully extinguished in them.

The previous peaceful and firm support from God that had buoyed up the 144,000 is now mingled with His wrath toward the brazen wickedness of possessed humanity. Our High Priest is no longer officiating before God for His chosen. Jesus has left the heavenly sanctuary to come and receive them to Himself (see John 14:1-3; Hebrews 9:28).

Those who are living upon the earth when the intercession of Christ shall cease in the sanctuary above are to stand in the sight of a holy God without a mediator. Their robes must be spotless, their characters must be purified from sin by the blood of sprinkling *The Great Controversy*, p. 425.

Who shall be able to stand? (Rev. 6:17).

The just shall live by his faith (Hab. 2:4).

Upon His Spirit's withdrawal, God completely removed the world's protection against Satan, and the evil one's oppressive and aggressive presence lustfully took full control. Prior to the Latter Rain, the first time of trouble had rooted out the nominal of Protestantism and Adventism, and all potential opposition to Satan's new global pagan-political-commercial-militant empire. God has cut off the global empire, as the world populations have cut Him off from His rightful rulership over them. They have turned their hearts to their varied cultures' spiritualism and superstitions, and to the Vatican's weekly gathering for Spiritual Formation. Human probation has closed, and devil possession darkens every mind and soul.

The last great plagues begin to pour upon a wicked world and the plagues torment their minds immeasurably. In figure modeled after the Egyptian deliverance, where the children of Israel suffered under the first three plagues, but were spared the last seven, God's final people have experienced the first three plagues during the three woes of the investigative judgment period (see Revelation 8:13; 9:20). But, Christ has chosen and sealed them through those plagues' torments (see Revelation 9:4) by His blood of sprinkling and their own diligent effort to work out their own salvation during the locust invasion. Now, Christ's children with the Seal of God are protected from the last seven plagues.

The seals and trumpets did Christ's work upon the hearts of His people to separate those who made themselves His enemies from all who made themselves His friends. The Ancient of Days is rightfully restored as Judge (see Daniel 7:9-11), trusted fully by all of His earthly children who by faith rest in heavenly places (see Revelation 11:15; 15:2; Ephesians 1:3; 2:6).

Through surrender to God's strength, and continued resting in His saving and sanctifying love seen in His Law, the sealed ones are fortified against the Father's oppressive wrath in the plagues, already on the other side of the convulsive tempest. They stand as it were on the Red Sea victorious like the freed tribes of Israel and mixed multitude (see Revelation 15:1-4). Though their certainty of salvation will soon be greatly challenged, it will remain preserved.

And I saw as it were a sea of glass mingled with fire: and them that had gotten the victory over the beast, and over his image, and over his mark, and over the number of his name, stand on the sea of glass, having the harps of God. And they sing the song of Moses the servant of God, and the song of the Lamb, saying, Great and marvelous are thy works, Lord God Almighty; just and true are thy ways, thou King of saints. Who shall not fear thee, O Lord, and glorify thy name? for thou only art holy: for all nations shall come and worship before thee; for thy judgments are made manifest (Rev. 15:2-4).

The sealing was built on a sure foundation; they had obeyed the gospel, and God was right to blot out their sins. They had accepted the strong condemnation from the Testimony of Jesus, which gave them strong conviction and a strong need for a Saviour in Jesus. That strong need gave them a special repentance, and that special repentance secured a special justification and a special blotting out of sin from God. That blotting out of sin gave special power to overcome all addiction to sin, and led to their special work of purification and sanctification. And that special sanctification led them to the sealing and to their perfect reproduction of Christ's character. Surrendering to the justice and mercy of God and receiving His Spirit, they had willed to do God's will with fear and trembling as He worked in them to will and to do of His good pleasure.

None but those who have fortified the mind with the truths of the Bible will stand through the last great conflict *The Great Controversy*, p. 593.

Because he hath set his love upon me, therefore will I deliver him: I will set him on high, because he hath known my name. He shall call upon me, and I will answer him: I will be with him in trouble; I will deliver him, and honour him. With long life will I satisfy him, and shew him my salvation (Ps. 91:14-16).

All who remained intoxicated by Satan's deluding television; all who kept themselves half-hearted toward their Creator by the world's burgeoning objects of worship and idols of fashion, its celebration and New Age spiritualism, now writhe under the last plagues. The wrathful separation from God's love and acceptance is heavy upon them. The Babylonians are drunken with the fury of God. Now that Satan owns them, he replaces his seductively, overly friendly Ashtoreth persona with his true, abusive Baal persona. Those with the mark of the Beast the Father gives over to the Ashtoreth they loved; but, Baal's bitter chastisement of their peace drives them into a constant, aggressive insanity.

> And even as they did not like to retain God in their knowledge, God gave them over to a reprobate mind, to do those things which are not convenient;
>
> Being filled with all unrighteousness, fornication, wickedness, covetousness, maliciousness; full of envy, murder, debate, deceit, malignity; whisperers,
>
> Backbiters, haters of God, despiteful, proud, boasters, inventors of evil things, disobedient to parents,
>
> Without understanding, covenantbreakers, without natural affection, implacable, unmerciful:
>
> Who knowing the judgment of God, that they which commit such things are worthy of death, not only do the same, but have pleasure in them that do them (Rom. 1:28-32).
>
> ...receiving in themselves that recompence of their error which was meet (Rom. 1:27).

They evaded all conviction by the first three plagues during the last three warning trumpets. Now Beelzebub's oppressive chastisement of their peace, as it were "a lake of fire burning with brimstone" (Rev. 19:20), drones on without let-up his scattering confusion and anger in their hateful souls. Babylon is a habitation of demons, the hold of every enslaved soul, and the cage of hawks and vulchers.

> And the smoke of their torment ascendeth up for ever and ever: and they have no rest day nor night, who worship the beast and his image, and whosoever receiveth the mark of his name (Rev. 14:11).

> The wicked shall be turned into hell, and all the nations that forget God. For the needy shall not alway be forgotten: the expectation of the poor shall not perish for ever. Arise, O LORD; let not man prevail: let the heathen be judged in thy sight. Put them in fear, O LORD: that the nations may know themselves to be but men. Selah (Ps. 9:17-20).

> He that believeth on the Son hath everlasting life: and he that believeth not the Son shall not see life; but the wrath of God abideth on him (John 3:36).

They have none of God's comfort or hope of His acceptance. They have chosen their delusions and He must leave them as they belligerently craved. "Yea, they have chosen their own ways, and their soul delighteth in their abominations" (Isa. 66:3). Because they have pushed away His Spirit they are overwhelmed by the hellish vacancy of God's Spirit of life. But, this is only a foretaste of that which they will experience again even more dreadfully on Judgment Day and ending in the second death. Thus already sorely tormented, the catastrophic last plagues and supernatural disasters they must face alone without any hope in their Creator's mercy. Perplexity and anxiety crush heavily upon every soul because they spent their lives despising the truth and peace of Abraham's God and His wise love. They had no time for their Creator. The thick presence of satanic hosts, visible on faces all around, adds to their hopeless misery and internal anguish.

> Joy is withered away from the sons of men. Gird yourselves, and lament, ye priests: howl, ye ministers of the altar: come, lie all night in sackcloth, ye ministers of my God: for the meat offering and the drink offering is withholden from the house of your God. Sanctify ye a fast, call a solemn assembly, gather the elders and all the inhabitants of the land into the house of the LORD your God, and cry unto the LORD, Alas for the day! for the day of the LORD is at hand, and as a destruction from the Almighty shall it come (Joel 1:12-15).

The mental rest promised by Jesuit Spiritual Formation has left only unnerving agitation and unrest. The voices of "God" have inspired the world governments to hand over their sovereignties to the Vatican for its promised duplicitous blessings (see Revelation 17:12-

14). "For God hath put in their hearts to fulfil his will, and to agree, and give their kingdom unto the beast, until the words of God shall be fulfilled" (Rev. 17:17, cf 1 Kings 22:20-23; Isaiah 30:27, 28).

> And I will bring upon that land all my words which I have pronounced against it, even all that is written in this book, which Jeremiah hath prophesied against all the nations. For many nations and great kings shall serve themselves of [God's people] also: and I will recompense them according to their deeds, and according to the works of their own hands (Jer. 25:13, 14, cf vs. 15ff).

The nations have given away all the blessedness from the Protestant Constitution of civil and religious freedom. They had preferred earthly atheism over heavenly faith, and now they have all given themselves to locate and bring to justice those who have spoken out against his holiness, Lord God the Pope. In rapid replay the dark history of the Dark Ages repeats itself.

> Shall the throne of iniquity have fellowship with thee, which frameth mischief by a law?
>
> They gather themselves together against the soul of the righteous, and condemn the innocent blood.
>
> But the LORD is my defence; and my God is the rock of my refuge.
>
> And he shall bring upon them their own iniquity, and shall cut them off in their own wickedness; yea, the LORD our God shall cut them off (Ps. 94:20-23).

> Rejoice, O ye nations, with his people: for he will avenge the blood of his servants, and will render vengeance to his adversaries, and will be merciful unto his land, and to his people (Deut. 32:43).

> The LORD hath sworn by his right hand, and by the arm of his strength, Surely I will no more give thy corn to be meat for thine enemies; and the sons of the stranger shall not drink thy wine, for the which thou hast laboured: but they that have gathered it shall eat it, and praise the LORD; and they that have brought it together shall drink it in the courts of my holiness (Isa. 62:8, 9).

As those trumpeting angels of warning return for their second go-around in the last plagues, the world's celebrating intoxication is swept away (see Isaiah 28:15, 17, 18). All their foolish laughter ends. Like Pharaoh's army, stiffened and open-mouthed, breathless and horrified that the high walls of water were coming down, the wicked have the harsh, sobering reality of sure, soon-coming executive judgment when they will see "the Son of man sitting on the right hand of power, and coming in the clouds of heaven" (Matt. 26:64, cf Isa. 28:18; Jer. 25:27-38).

> Woe unto you that desire the day of the LORD! to what end is it for you? The day of the LORD is darkness, and not light. As if a man did flee from a lion, and a bear met him; or went into the house, and leaned his hand on the wall, and a serpent bit him. Shall not the day of the LORD be darkness, and not light? even very dark, and no brightness in it? (Amos 5:18-20).

No "third" is mentioned in the final plagues. Besides the sealed children of God, no exemptions from the plague judgments are found as they were in the warning trumpets. There are no more "the rest of the men" (Rev. 9:20) who are not affected by this last great woe. The guilty now encompass the whole human race which have made themselves as permanently lost as were the demonic hosts figuratively "under the earth" (Rev. 5:3, cf 2 Pet. 2:4; Phil. 2:10), the third group that could not open the mystery book of God. The last angels pour out scourges that resemble the warning, sealing plagues, yet at last unmixed with mercy toward all, including the previously plagued "third part". The three angels' messages from the fifth and sixth trumpet warning plagues are fulfilled in the fourth angel's message plagues, in full consequence to heaven's warnings rejected.

> There is none to plead thy cause, that thou mayest be bound up: thou hast no healing medicines (Jer. 30:13).
>
> Go up into Gilead, and take balm, O virgin, the daughter of Egypt: in vain shalt thou use many medicines; for thou shalt not be cured (Jer. 46:11).

Babylon is troubled on every side and full of distress.

> Chaldea shall be a spoil: all that spoil her shall be satisfied, saith the LORD.

Because ye were glad, because ye rejoiced, O ye destroyers of mine heritage, because ye are grown fat as the heifer at grass, and bellow as bulls;

Your mother shall be sore confounded; she that bare you shall be ashamed: behold, the hindermost of the nations shall be a wilderness, a dry land, and a desert.

Because of the wrath of the LORD it shall not be inhabited, but it shall be wholly desolate:…

How is the hammer of the whole earth cut asunder and broken! how is Babylon become a desolation among the nations!

I have laid a snare for thee, and thou art also taken, O Babylon, and thou wast not aware: thou art found, and also caught, because thou hast striven against the LORD.

The LORD hath opened his armoury, and hath brought forth the weapons of his indignation: for this is the work of the Lord GOD of hosts in the land of the Chaldeans.

Come against her from the utmost border, open her storehouses: cast her up as heaps, and destroy her utterly: let nothing of her be left (Jer. 50:10-13, 23-26).

The celebrations of vanity all cease; the games are over. The world realizes the fraud, but their only true God will not release them from it. Spiritual Formation's empty refuge of lies and imagined glory are gone, replaced with panic. The King is coming, "whose fan is in his hand, and he will throughly purge his floor, and gather his wheat into the garner; but he will burn up the chaff with unquenchable fire" (Matt. 3:12).

When it shall hail, coming down on the forest; and the city shall be low in a low place (Isa. 32:19).

All who disrespected the Law of God horribly regret their mistake to exterminate the innocent children in whose hearts God had sealed His Law.

Why do the heathen rage, and the people imagine a vain thing?

The kings of the earth set themselves, and the rulers take counsel together, against the LORD, and against his anointed, saying,

Let us break their bands asunder, and cast away their cords from us.

He that sitteth in the heavens shall laugh: the Lord shall have them in derision.

Then shall he speak unto them in his wrath, and vex them in his sore displeasure (Ps. 2:1-5).

Touch not mine anointed, and do my prophets no harm (Ps. 105:15).

The mystery of God is finished by the mystery of godliness fruition in holy Jerusalem and by the full disclosure of Babylonian spiritualism, the whorish mystery behind pervasive iniquity. The kings and the people substituted for convicting truth their vain religious sounding language, the "holy" laughter, glossalalia, and glorying in their self-indulgent diet (see Romans 12:1; 1:32; Luke 7:35). Satan has caught them in a hopeless trap, and their professed unity of humanity unravels.

Upon the land of my people shall come up thorns and briers; yea, upon all the houses of joy in the joyous city (Isa. 32:13).

Thorns and snares are in the way of the forward (Prov. 22:5).

As they seek to torture and kill His innocent elect, God amplifies His traumatic wrath upon the children of Satan. Their genocide is prevented as they writhe under His derision upon them.

For their vine is of the vine of Sodom, and of the fields of Gomorrah: their grapes are grapes of gall, their clusters are bitter:

Their wine is the poison of dragons, and the cruel venom of asps.

Is not this laid up in store with me, and sealed up among my treasures? (Deut. 32:32-34, cf Psalm 2:4).

And, the Lord will say, "Where are their gods, their rock in whom they trusted, which did eat the fat of their sacrifices, and drank the wine of their drink offerings? let them rise up and help you, and be your protection" (Deut. 32:37, 38). "Bind him hand and foot, and take him away, and cast him into outer darkness" (Matt. 22:13).

There shall be weeping and gnashing of teeth. For many are called, but few are chosen (Matt. 22:13, 14).

Babylon suffers the furious and fatal hangover for the self-indulgence with which God permitted them to be tempted, as His first plague's wrath torments humanity throughout the remaining six plagues (see Jeremiah 25:27-31; Isaiah 26:11, 12). But, though the children of God have light and health in all their tabernacles (1 Corinthians 3:16, 17; 6:19, 20), to a large degree their perfect peace feels plagued by His wrath until Jesus arrives. Like the gospel from Isaiah, their beautiful robe of righteousness must again resume sackcloth (see Isaiah 61:10; 20:2; Revelation 11:3).

Jacob's troubles begins with the seven last plagues as God no longer has His Son's beloved communion present to rein in His Father's wrath against the controversy of sin. God's people find their connection greatly cut off from their beloved Intercessor. Communion with Jesus through His precepts and promises has been their only help, and the ongoing relationship with the Son their only hope for peace with God. But this last hour, the time of Jacob's trouble, will be the exception to the rule. They cannot dwell in the house of the Lord forever as they had during the Latter Rain, and all that they sense from their God of love are angry "lightnings, and voices, and thunderings" (Rev. 11:19).

> We have heard a voice of trembling, of fear, and not of peace. Ask ye now, and see whether a man doth travail with child? Wherefore do I see every man with his hands on his loins, as a woman in travail, and all faces are turned into paleness? Alas! for that day is great, so that none is like it: it is even the time of Jacob's trouble; but he shall be saved out of it (Jer. 30:5-7).

Like the Mother of all living in His greatly multiplied Gethsemane sorrows, the children of God suffer as a laboring mother in their waves of spiritual, mental, and physical distress under the wrath of their everlasting Father. "These are they which follow the Lamb whithersoever he goeth" (Rev. 14:4).

> To him that overcometh will I grant to sit with me in my throne, even as I also overcame, and am set down with my Father in his throne (Rev. 3:21).

They don't sense Jesus' person; they can no longer "appear before [Jesus]" (Ps. 42:2). They can no more enter into the holy of holies through "the body of Christ" (Rom. 7:4, cf Heb. 10:19, 20). His promise, "Ye in me, and I in you" (John 14:20) seems no more a reality. They feel blasted away from His sanctuary of their strength, and with tremendous difficulty their hope enters within "the second veil" (Heb. 9:3, cf 6:19). From the perspective of His children, God's immense wrath against sin completely eclipses His mercy for them. The meek cannot see past His anger, which throws them into the disconcerting terror of eternal separation from Jesus, their beloved and strong Convicter, and equally strong Comforter. Who shall be able to stand?

"The temple was filled with smoke from the glory of God, and from his power; and no man was able to enter into the temple, till the seven plagues of the seven angels were fulfilled" (Rev. 15:8). Christ has left the sanctuary to save His trembling people on earth. No one now stands between God and them, and they find themselves immensely anxiety-ridden to stand before the God of Law and justice. They no longer sit joyfully in heavenly places. They no longer feel translated into the Son's kingdom and no longer eat in the paradise of God (see Ephesians 2:6; Revelation 2:7; Exodus 24:10, 11; Luke 23:43). Yet, they had thrilled in the Most Holy second veil experience and are terrified to lose it. The fullness of comfort has vanished as they walk in their Master's Gethsemane distress. So they cling to the Bible truths despite the fearful atheism and anger that surrounds them. They have nothing else to give them hope than every promise that has proceeded from the mouth of God.

> My soul thirsteth for [Jesus], for the living God: when shall I come and appear before [Jesus]? My tears have been my meat day and night, while they continually say unto me, Where is thy [Jesus]?… Why art thou cast down, O my soul? and why art thou disquieted in me? hope thou in [Jesus]: for I shall yet praise him for the help of his countenance…

> The LORD will command his lovingkindness in the daytime, and in the night his song shall be with me, and my prayer unto the God of my life. I will say unto [Jesus] my rock, Why hast thou forgotten me? why go I mourning because of the oppression of the enemy? As with a sword in my bones, mine enemies reproach me; while they say daily unto me, Where is thy God? Why art

thou cast down, O my soul? and why art thou disquieted within me? hope thou in [Jesus]: for I shall yet praise him, who is the health of my countenance, and my God (Ps. 42:2, 3, 5, 8-11).

Unless [Jesus] had been my help, my soul had almost dwelt in silence.

When I said, My foot slippeth; thy mercy, O LORD, held me up.

In the multitude of my thoughts within me thy comforts delight my soul (Ps. 94:17-19).

The power of God's conviction without Jesus conscious to them leaves them overwhelmed by God's desiccating holiness. Similar to Daniel's experience they say, "My comeliness was turned in me into corruption, and I retained no strength…. I stood trembling… neither is there breath left in me" (Dan. 10:8, 11, 17, cf Acts 9:4, 6; 22:7; 26:14). They must stand before an infinitely holy and just God as the children of Israel stood before the Lord of hosts, which "so terrible was the sight, that Moses said, I exceedingly fear and quake" (Heb. 12:21).

And mount Sinai was altogether on a smoke, because the LORD descended upon it in fire: and the smoke thereof ascended as the smoke of a furnace, and the whole mount quaked greatly. And when the voice of the trumpet sounded long, and waxed louder and louder…

God spake….

And all the people saw the thunderings, and the lightnings, and the noise of the trumpet, and the mountain smoking: and when the people saw it, they removed, and stood afar off.

And they said unto Moses, Speak thou with us, and we will hear: but let not God speak with us, lest we die (Ex. 19:18, 19; 20:1, 18, 19).

The living saints must endure their own Judgment Day and do as their Master did, hanging on to every blissful memory that their experiences and prized union with Jesus have left them. When Jesus had been in the Most Holy, they experienced a greater measure than what the apostles had, their spirits united with the Godhead's one Spirit. "Ye shall know that I am in my Father, and ye in me, and I in you" (John 14:20). All of their previous Gethsemanes led to, and prepared for, this final despair. Likewise did all their happy labors during the Loud Cry of the Latter Rain prepare them for this last exertion, the many Sabbaths and mornings resting in communion with Jesus, the memories of so many hearts won to God, and so many lives freed from every kind of Satan's bondage. Truly, "mercy rejoiceth against judgment" (Jas. 2:13).

But, it is in mercy to them that God must now test the strength of their faith in His love (see 2 Chronicles 32:31). Jehovah must give them this utmost test in order to begin their transition to the incorruptible nature directly and eternally in His pristine presence; "holy and reverend is his name" (Ps. 111:9, cf Eze. 1:22). They are to be His special servants. They will stand "before the throne of God, and serve him day and night in his temple: and he that sitteth on the throne shall dwell among them" (Rev. 7:15).

God requires of His children this difficult Gethsemane for the same reason He required it of Israel. "And Moses said unto the people, Fear not: for God is come to prove you, and that his fear may be before your faces, that ye sin not" (Ex. 20:20). Though God has blotted out their sin, He must put His people through this last trial. They must pass through the same terrible ordeal which their Mother of all living endured, by which He brought "many sons unto glory" (Heb. 2:10). Like no other generation before this, they know "the fellowship of his sufferings, being made conformable unto his death" (Phil. 3:10). God seems not to exist; heaven seems not to be real; His deliverance seems no longer imminent; yet Jesus is on the way. In utter hopelessness and dark depression they tread the winepress of the wrath of God alone. Having groaned for the sinless nature, completely unanesthetized and consciously must they experience the extraction of the last roots of sin and death. Having no food or water or any earthly help, they will receive the full redemption of their vile bodies. Who shall be able to stand? Once they survive this trial they will be eternally one with Him — total and forever at-one-ment. Through this mighty work of God upon His special guard contingent, they will help ensure that sin never again comes close to the kingdom.

Meanwhile, Satan imitates the return of Christ in a brilliant display (see Matthew 24:23-27; 2 Corinthians 11:14). With exception to the very small Remnant, the whole world nervously and hopefully flocks to the descending train of this other-worldly being from the cosmos. His face and form have exquisite symmetry and the perfection of beauty. His smooth, clear complexion has the deep luster of a golden calf. He has never known shame or guilt; his countenance shows no marring from chastisement of peace. He is the embodiment of the spirit who the whole world has ever praised and worshipped. Their lawless hearts adore him and they unburden to him all their mental trauma. Will you run into the arms of this "Jesus" and pour out your sorrows when the wrath of God is then heavy upon every conscience? Will you go and have at least one peek along with everyone of that harassed, unrepentant world? This almost overmastering trial will simulate the powerful test brought to the holy pair in Eden. All who come to this lawless "Jesus" are immediately locked into his delusion, and fall down before his handsome presence. He dispels some of their misery and they gratefully worship him.

In accordance with the false secret rapture doctrine, which the prince of deception spread around the globe, seven years after his first invisible return "Jesus" comes down with some supernatural fanfare and splendor. But, contrary to the biblical second advent of Christ, he does not destroy the earth or "the works that are therein" (2 Pet. 3:10). Civilization remains intact. "All the kingdoms of the world, and the glory of them" (Matt. 4:8), continue to bear the corrupted stamp of the god of this world. And the people love to have it so.

"Christ has come! Christ has come!" billions ring out.

> The glory that surrounds him is unsurpassed by anything that mortal eyes have yet beheld.... He lifts up his hands and pronounces a blessing upon them, as Christ blessed His disciples when He was upon the earth. His voice is soft and subdued, yet full of melody. In gentle, compassionate tones he presents some of the same gracious, heavenly truths which the Saviour uttered; he heals the diseases of the people, and then, in his assumed character of Christ, he claims to have changed the Sabbath to Sunday, and commands all to hallow the day which he has blessed. He declares that those who persist in keeping holy the seventh day are blaspheming his name by refusing to listen to his angels sent to them with light and truth *The Great Controversy*, p. 624.

"He shall magnify himself in his heart...: he shall also stand up against the Prince of princes" (Dan. 8:25). The iniquity of the self-righteous, wicked human race is ripe and full. Hundreds of thousands congregate at his appearances. All heaven walks among men again, or is carried about! They now have ears that want to hear and eyes that want to see the imposter, as he promises the nations plenitude of blessing. With his indulgences each may do as he pleases, for all of humanity is declared holy. With confession and renewal through Spiritual Formation there need not be any instruction in righteousness to shame or to define right and wrong. Happiness without Law, and peace without God, is the new world that "Jesus" offers.

The mold of Satan's icy character is permanently affixed in everyone who hated the loving and obedient nature of Jesus, the only true vicar of God. On the other hand, every fiber of the divine nature is likewise forever woven into those who chose to love and be loved by the spotless Prince of heaven. The restless nations sold themselves to honor the Sunday in full disregard to the 144,000's Sabbath commandment which warred upon their consciences. Conviction after conviction of the hallowed seventh day of the week has only hardened their hearts; and now the ultimate hardening comes with the confirmation from "Jesus" that the sabbatarian 144,000 are false prophets. And all the while the Sabbath-keepers with "charity out of a pure heart, and of a good conscience, and of faith unfeigned" (1 Tim. 1:5) are absorbed in supplication and hoping for eternity with Jesus. Transfixed on heaven they stand in a perfect square with Jesus at the center, as if already on the other side of the convulsed persecution.

Simultaneously, Satan, executes his work of rounding up the 144,000 traitors who worked against his proclaimed enrapturing millennium of peace. He promises that Mother Nature's wrath from the plagues will not cease until every keeper of the old Law, and its fourth commandment, is duly punished. But, Jehovah Elohim made the Ten Commandments and the seventh-day Sabbath for all of Adam's family (Genesis 2:1-3; Mark 2:27, 28), and the 144,000 know that the Lord God of the Sabbath will deliver them. The elect also know that when the world will cry, "Peace and safety; then sudden destruction cometh upon them, as travail upon a woman with child" (1 Thess. 5:3).

The Lamb slain from the foundation of the world, the Lion of the tribe of Judah, our High Priest who is touched with the feelings of our infirmities, has left the reverent throne that God for so long had graciously transformed into a triage unit for the redemption of our transgressions. By test after test, the commandment-keepers have cooperated with God to have His Law sealed in their character. Through their own effort, efforts infused with the abundant power supplied by the merits of the Son of God and by His angelic hosts, the people of God have overcome their every flaw and weakness by Christ's grace — which is the only reason that God could be just when He blotted their sins from the books in heaven.

> We are troubled on every side, yet not distressed; we are perplexed, but not in despair;
>
> Persecuted, but not forsaken; cast down, but not destroyed;
>
> Always bearing about in the body the dying of the Lord Jesus, that the life also of Jesus might be made manifest in our body....
>
> For our light affliction, which is but for a moment, worketh for us a far more exceeding and eternal weight of glory;
>
> While we look not at the things which are seen, but at the things which are not seen: for the things which are seen are temporal; but the things which are not seen are eternal (2 Cor. 4:8-10, 17, 18).
>
> We have this treasure in earthen vessels, that the excellency of the power may be of God, and not of us (2 Cor. 4:7).

Surrounded by intense evil and danger, and having no shelter before the infinite God, their minds are whelmed in confusion and harassed by doubts as they struggle to hang on to their hope in His acceptance. Those who pass through this time must endure hunger, weariness, and delay. They must be forgiven and just before God, and survive by their faith. All their life the constant exposure of their sin before the holy Law of God produced in them indomitable faith in Christ and made them patient to wait for His return. Now that they have lost the joy of Jesus' presence they feel crushed by the void, which the wickedness all around them amplifies. But, Christ is rushing to receive them to Himself and tries to get through to them with the reminder,

> Behold, I come quickly: hold that fast which thou hast, that no man take thy crown (Rev. 3:11).
>
> There shall not an hair of your head perish. In your patience possess ye your souls (Luke 21:18, 19).

As wonderfully as they had sat catapulted into heavenly places with their Friend and Saviour, now inversely are they thrust equally deeply into depression without Him. They walk in the disturbing path of their Master who dwelled in heaven through His Father's Spirit without measure, only to have it all taken away, driving Him into hell beyond measure. The 144,000 wrestle under the assault against their once profoundly settled assurances from Jesus. Satan tempts them to feel that there is no God to help them, but that they have brought all of this danger needlessly upon themselves. Yet, they possess enough residual experience with the "Spirit of Christ…sent down from heaven" (1 Pet. 1:11, 12) during their work in the Latter Rain that His Spirit enables them to patiently await the immutable restoration of their permanent peace when He arrives to sweep them up in His arms.

> He shall spread forth his hands in the midst of them, as he that swimmeth spreadeth forth his hands to swim (Isa. 25:11).
>
> Behold, I come as a thief. Blessed is he that watcheth, and keepeth his garments, lest he walk naked, and they see his shame (Rev. 16:15).

The manifest justice of the Father from His immense plagues and Satan's manhunt for them war against their previous close communion with their Master. The warmth of Christ's comfort that had so wonderfully attended them during the Latter Rain is boiled away under God's wrathful disposition toward humanity. Though the saints feel that they can no longer happily stand by faith within the second veil as they previously had (see Revelation 15:8), and though they have no sense that He hears them now, yet Jesus tenderly receives every trembling syllable of their prayers. Christ still remains their Intercessor. Yet His Spirit of grace cannot supersede the greater Spirit of His Father's present disposition of justice; and He understands the necessity of His Father's intense trial upon the recipients of His soon deliverance. As Jesus "who through the eternal spirit" (Heb. 9:14) held on to His Father under Gethsemane's and Golgotha's torments, they must put forth their own imparted superhuman effort to hold on to God. Then they will be heirs of God and joint-heirs with Christ, and stand as Their special guard deputation.

> They are waiting the word of their Commander to snatch them from their peril. But they must wait yet a little longer. The people of God must drink of the cup and be baptized with the baptism. The very delay, so painful to them, is the

best answer to their petitions. As they endeavor to wait trustingly for the Lord to work they are led to exercise faith, hope, and patience, which have been too little exercised during their religious experience. Yet for the elect's sake the time of trouble will be shortened. "Shall not God avenge His own elect, which cry day and night unto Him? . . . I tell you that He will avenge them speedily." Luke 18:7, 8. The end will come more quickly than men expect *The Great Controversy*, p. 630.

The Most Holy Place is open without a High Priest; the power of a vindicated God is felt throughout His infinite realm. (See Revelation 11:19; 15:8.) With all their heart the saints have hungered and thirsted and sought their Father's acceptance during the fifth and sixth trumpet torments, and during the turmoil of the seventh trumpet great time of trouble. Now, Jacob's trouble grinds self to powder so that by the banishment of self, all whom God has called and chosen might receive the promise of eternal inheritance.

> For we are made partakers of Christ, if we hold the beginning of our confidence stedfast unto the end (Heb. 3:14, cf Heb. 10:36; Rev. 2:11).

> These are they which came out of great tribulation, and have washed their robes, and made them white in the blood of the Lamb (Rev. 7:14).

> The remnant of Israel shall not do iniquity, nor speak lies; neither shall a deceitful tongue be found in their mouth: for they shall feed and lie down, and none shall make them afraid (Zeph. 3:13).

Dangers have continually multiplied around the 144,000. No one except Jesus has known their constant intensity and exhaustion. "All thy waves and thy billows are gone over me" (Ps. 42:7). Yet, now and then God gives them relief and renewing rest, and during these moments they cling to the hope that their past is forgiven. By faith they again struggle to stand as it were "before the throne, and before the Lamb, clothed with white robes, and palms in their hands" (Rev. 7:9). They need assurance that God has not forgotten their work to know Him (see Hebrews 6:10). They hope in Jesus' approbation and admonition to John the Baptist, "This is he, of whom it is written, Behold, I send my messenger before thy face, which shall prepare thy way before thee", "and blessed is he, whosoever shall not be offended in me" (Matt. 11:10, 6).

> Though I walk through the valley of the shadow of death, I will fear no evil: for thou art with me (Ps. 23:4).

> Thine eyes shall see the king in his beauty: they shall behold the land that is very far off (Isa. 33:17).

> Look upon Zion, the city of our solemnities: thine eyes shall see Jerusalem a quiet habitation, a tabernacle that shall not be taken down (Isa. 33:20).

Then, another wave of separation from Jesus goes over them, and being in an agony they pray more fervently. Their days and nights are again filled with intense soul searching and fasting to hold on to the reality of Christ's soon arrival. They, like their Lord, are locked in Gethsemane's convulsions of Childbirth (see Revelation 12:2). They tread the press of Gethsemane alone with their Master and are baptized with His fiery baptism. Although their sealed hope spares them the full wrath of God that torments the wicked world, the struggling servants nonetheless feel His hot revulsion toward sin. All that is within them clings to Christ's promises.

> Thus saith the LORD, Even the captives of the mighty shall be taken away, and the prey of the terrible shall be delivered: for I will contend with him that contendeth with thee, and I will save thy children. And I will feed them that oppress thee with their own flesh; and they shall be drunken with their own blood, as with sweet wine: and all flesh shall know that I the LORD am thy Saviour and thy Redeemer, the mighty One of Jacob (Isa. 49:25, 26).

> Let not your heart be troubled: ye believe in God, believe also in me. In my Father's house are many mansions: if it were not so, I would have told you. I go to prepare a place for you. And if I go and prepare a place for you, I will come again, and receive you unto myself; that where I am, there ye may be also (John 14:1-3).

> He which testifieth these things saith, Surely I come quickly (Rev. 22:20).

But the same harassment of mind and heart in the holy ones has troubled the house of the wicked to their breaking point. They are seen in a burning lake of fire (see Revelation 19:20).

> Ye shall conceive chaff, ye shall bring forth stubble: your breath, as fire, shall devour you. And the people shall be as the burnings of lime: as thorns cut up shall they be burned in the fire. Hear, ye that are far off, what I have done; and, ye that are near, acknowledge my might (Isa. 33:11-13).

Like the massive worldwide upheavals of the Genesis flood the natural and economic calamities, a brutal Vatican and United Nations tyranny out of Satan's bottomless pit of devious anger, and his lust for success of his last great empire, agitate the nations of the world and encourage civil wars and international strife. In righteousness Jesus comes to judge and make war against the Dragon and the Beast. He will destroy the locust system that has destroyed all of His Spirit in the earth and He will cast them into the same troubles that they have caused the precious race made in His image.

> The nations were angry, and thy wrath is come, and the time of the dead, that they should be judged, and that thou shouldest give reward unto thy servants the prophets, and to the saints, and them that fear thy name, small and great; and shouldest destroy them which destroy the earth (Rev. 11:18).

> Behold, the name of the LORD cometh from far, burning with his anger, and the burden thereof is heavy: his lips are full of indignation, and his tongue as a devouring fire: and his breath, as an overflowing stream, shall reach to the midst of the neck (Isa. 30:27, 28).

> Then shall that Wicked be revealed, whom the Lord shall consume with the spirit of his mouth, and shall destroy with the brightness of his coming (2 Thess. 2:8).

> Soon our eyes were drawn to the east, for a small black cloud had appeared, about half as large as a man's hand, which we all knew was the sign of the Son of man. We all in solemn silence gazed on the cloud as it drew nearer and became lighter, glorious, and still more glorious, till it was a great white cloud *Early Writings*, p. 15.

With indescribable relief the 144,000 see the small black cloud. The Son of God is literally, visibly here! Prince Michael the Great who has mediated for the child-like people among a proud race! Christ comes for those who love His appearing, His immutable Law, and His immutable grace. He is sent from the one true God and backed by all the heavenly hosts.

> They come from a far country, from the end of heaven, even the LORD, and the weapons of his indignation, to destroy the whole land (Isa. 13:5).

> Moreover the multitude of thy strangers shall be like small dust, and the multitude of the terrible ones shall be as chaff that passeth away (Isa. 29:5).

> Then shall appear the sign of the Son of man in heaven: and then shall all the tribes of the earth mourn, and they shall see the Son of man coming in the clouds of heaven with power and great glory. And he shall send his angels with a great sound of a trumpet, and they shall gather together his elect from the four winds, from one end of heaven to the other (Matt. 24:30, 31).

> Who is this that cometh from Edom, with dyed garments from Bozrah? this that is glorious in his apparel, travelling in the greatness of his strength? *I that speak in righteousness, mighty to save.*

> Wherefore art thou red in thine apparel, and thy garments like him that treadeth in the winefat?

> I have trodden the winepress alone; and of the people there was none with me: for I will tread them in mine anger, and trample them in my fury; and their blood shall be sprinkled upon my garments, and I will stain all my raiment.

> For the day of vengeance is in mine heart, and the year of my redeemed is come (Isa. 63:1-4).

> "Behold, he cometh with clouds; and every eye shall see him, and they also which pierced him" (Rev. 1:7).

> Lo, this is our God; we have waited for him, and he will save us: this is the LORD; we have waited for him, we will be glad and rejoice in his salvation (Isa. 25:9).

Ye shall have a song, as in the night when a holy solemnity is kept; and gladness of heart, as when one goeth with a pipe to come into the mountain of the LORD, to the mighty One of Israel. And the LORD shall cause his glorious voice to be heard, and shall shew the lighting down of his arm, with the indignation of his anger, and with the flame of a devouring fire, with scattering, and tempest, and hailstones (Isa. 30:29, 30).

The daytime sky reveals the new object, dark and growing in size. As it slows to sub-light speed the darkness sheds, revealing the true brilliance of the heavenly entourage. Surely, "the day of the Lord will come as a thief in the night" (2 Pet. 3:10).

> *The daytime sky reveals the new object, dark and growing in size. As it slows to sub-light speed the darkness sheds, revealing the true brilliance of the heavenly entourage.*

Yourselves know perfectly that the day of the Lord so cometh as a thief in the night (1 Thess. 5:2).

Watch ye therefore: for ye know not when the master of the house cometh, at even, or at midnight, or at the cockcrowing, or in the morning: lest coming suddenly he find you sleeping (Mark 13:35, 36).

Moreover ... the multitude of the terrible ones shall be as chaff that passeth away: yea, it shall be at an instant suddenly (Isa. 29:5, cf Isa. 30:13; 47:11; 48:3).

Frowardness is in his heart, he deviseth mischief continually; he soweth discord. Therefore shall his calamity come suddenly; suddenly shall he be broken without remedy (Prov. 6:14, 15, cf Prov. 24:22; 29:1; Ecc. 9:12).

The whole world suddenly sees the Son of God, "sitting on the right hand of power, and coming in the clouds of heaven" (Matt. 26:64). The cosmic cataclysms of Jesus' Second Advent Satan can never duplicate.

For the Son of man shall come in the glory of his Father with his angels (Matt. 16:27).

The Son of man shall come in his glory, and all the holy angels with him, then shall he sit upon the throne of his glory (Matt. 25:31).

Our God shall come, and shall not keep silence: a fire shall devour before him, and it shall be very tempestuous round about him.

He shall call to the heavens from above, and to the earth, that he may judge his people.

Gather my saints together unto me; those that have made a covenant with me by sacrifice (Ps. 50:3-5).

The deceiver and his demonic retinue may float down with a few fiery meteors and destructive winds (see Job 1:16, 19), and he may cause an earthquake or two (not to destroy his kingdom). He can even manifest some glory (see Matthew 24:23, 24; Galatians 1:8; 2 Corinthians 11:14). All these, however, are but sparks compared to the day when the Creator comes near. On that day, "the powers of heaven shall be shaken" (Luke 21:26) as if every human construction and even the elements of nature should disintegrate (see Daniel 2:34, 35, 45).

The great day of his wrath is come; and who shall be able to stand? (Rev. 6:17).

See the collision of Earth by an asteroid, "a stone… cut out without hands" (Dan. 2:34). Behold the bombardment by "great hail out of heaven, every stone about the weight of a talent [averaging 90 lbs.]" (Rev. 16:21) travelling 30,000 miles per hour, demolishing the continents, especially the cities "reserved unto fire against the day of judgment and perdition of ungodly men" (2 Pet. 3:7, cf Jer. 4:23-26; Isa. 14:21; Eze. 28:18). Watch the millions of meteorites and asteroids orbiting between Mars and Jupiter, some the size of mountains, thrust from their regions and pushed ahead of the Creator, impacting our planet's oceans and continents, and adding to the tsunamis and the cataclysmic disturbances of the atmosphere.

But who may abide the day of his coming? and who shall stand when he appeareth? for he is like a refiner's fire, and like fullers' soap (Mal. 3:2).

All the host of heaven shall be dissolved, and the heavens shall be rolled together as a scroll: and all their host shall fall down, as the leaf falleth off from the vine, and as a falling fig from the fig tree (Isa. 34:4).

God came from Teman, and the Holy One from mount Paran. Selah. His glory covered the heavens, and the earth was full of his praise. And his brightness was as the light; he had horns coming out of his hand [bright beams out of his side, margin]: and there was the hiding of his power. Before him went the pestilence, and burning coals went forth at his feet. He stood, and measured the earth: he beheld, and drove asunder the nations; and the everlasting mountains were scattered, the perpetual hills did bow: his ways are everlasting (Hab. 3:3-6).

For my sword shall be bathed in heaven: behold, it shall come down upon Idumea, and upon the people of my curse, to judgment. The sword of the LORD is filled with blood, it is made fat with fatness, and with the blood of lambs and goats, with the fat of the kidneys of rams: for the LORD hath a sacrifice in Bozrah, and a great slaughter in the land of Idumea. And the unicorns shall come down with them, and the bullocks with the bulls; and their land shall be soaked with blood, and their dust made fat with fatness. For it is the day of the LORD's vengeance, and the year of recompences for the controversy of Zion (Isa. 34:5-8).

And they shall go into the holes of the rocks, and into the caves of the earth, for fear of the LORD, and for the glory of his majesty, when he ariseth to shake terribly the earth. In that day a man shall cast his idols of silver, and his idols of gold, which they made each one for himself to worship, to the moles and to the bats; to go into the clefts of the rocks, and into the tops of the ragged rocks, for fear of the LORD, and for the glory of his majesty, when he ariseth to shake terribly the earth (Isa. 2:19-21).

Thou shalt be visited of the LORD of hosts with thunder, and with earthquake, and great noise, with storm and tempest, and the flame of devouring fire (Isa. 29:6).

For thou hast trusted in thy wickedness: thou hast said, None seeth me. Thy wisdom and thy knowledge, it hath perverted thee; and thou hast said in thine heart, I am, and none else beside me. Therefore shall evil come upon thee; thou shalt not know from whence it riseth: and mischief shall fall upon thee; thou shalt not be able to put it off: and desolation shall come upon thee suddenly, which thou shalt not know (Isa. 47:10, 11).

Technologically sophisticated concrete, like "chalkstones" (Isa. 27:9), will hardly stand up against the last plague's asteroids, awaiting their Creator's push into action against a planet in rebellion.

Great balls of fire were falling upon houses, and from these balls fiery arrows were flying in every direction. It was impossible to check the fires that were kindled, and many places were being destroyed. The terror of the people was indescribable *Maranatha*, p. 25.

Bunkers and fortresses miles underground can't withstand meteors travelling 30,000 miles per hour; neither can arson-proof towers stand against the smaller meteorites travelling the same speed. The millions of flaming stones from the sky will cause destruction like bombs as they impact our planet's atmosphere with millions of sonic booms. "Vengeance is mine; I will repay, saith the Lord" (Rom. 12:19). When God displays His power, His holy angels "that excel in strength" (Ps. 103:20) overthrow His wicked enemies. As the high walls of Jericho fell after seven trumpet blasts (see Joshua 6:8, 16), so Babylon's strong prison falls after the seventh plague of the Apocalypse.

And Babylon, the glory of kingdoms, the beauty of the Chaldees' excellency, shall be as when God overthrew Sodom and Gomorrah. It shall never be inhabited, neither shall it be dwelt in from generation to generation (Isa. 13:19, 20).

Shout against her round about: she hath given her hand: her foundations are fallen, her walls are thrown down: for it is the vengeance of the LORD: take vengeance upon her; as she hath done, do unto her.... As God overthrew Sodom and Gomorrah and the neighbour cities thereof, saith the LORD; so shall no man abide there, neither shall any son of man dwell therein (Jer. 50:15, 40).

At the noise of the taking of Babylon the earth is moved, and the cry is heard among the nations (Jer. 50:46).

Rejoice over her, thou heaven, and ye holy apostles and prophets; for God hath avenged you on her (Rev. 18:20).

Judgment also will I lay to the line, and righteousness to the plummet: and the hail shall sweep away the refuge of lies, and the waters shall overflow the hiding place.... For the LORD shall rise up as in mount Perazim, he shall be wroth as in the valley of Gibeon, that he may do his work, his strange work; and bring to pass his act, his strange act. Now therefore be ye not mockers, lest your bands be made strong: for I have heard from the Lord GOD of hosts a consumption, even determined upon the whole earth (Isa. 28:17, 21, 22).

The suddenness of the conflagration comes not only because of His quick disclosure, but because the intoxicated, drugged, and entranced global Christendom was not waiting and watching for its unexpected Lord (see Matthew 24:42-44, 48-51; Mark 13:36, 37; 1 Thessalonians 5:1-3, 6-8; Daniel 5:1, 30).

> The same day that Lot went out of Sodom it rained fire and brimstone from heaven, and destroyed them all. Even thus shall it be in the day when the Son of man is revealed (Luke 17:29, 30).

"The sun was risen upon the earth when Lot entered into Zoar." The bright rays of the morning seemed to speak only prosperity and peace to the cities of the plain. The stir of active life began in the streets; men were going their various ways, intent on the business or the pleasures of the day. The sons-in-law of Lot were making merry at the fears and warnings of the weak-minded old man. Suddenly and unexpectedly as would be a thunder peal from an unclouded sky, the tempest broke. The Lord rained brimstone and fire out of heaven upon the cities and the fruitful plain; its palaces and temples, costly dwellings, gardens and vineyards, and the gay, pleasure-seeking throngs that only the night before had insulted the messengers of heaven — all were consumed *Patriarchs and Prophets*, p. 162.

Our Sun, 96 million miles away, produces solar winds that affect our jet stream and meteorology, causing hurricanes and tornadoes and violent lightning storms. Yet, envision the inexplicable hurricane and tornado and lightning activity the day when the Creator of suns comes close. "The heaven departed as a scroll when it is rolled together; and every mountain and island were moved out of their places" (Rev. 6:14). Think of all the mighty Creator winds He produces, pushing away our atmosphere, and whipping up unimaginably shrieking winds that rape the sea and land, with the wind and the waves roaring.

> Thus saith the LORD; Behold, I will raise up against Babylon, and against them that dwell in the midst of them that rise up against me, a destroying wind; and will send unto Babylon fanners, that shall fan her, and shall empty her land: for in the day of trouble they shall be against her round about (Jer. 51:1, 2).

> I will also make it a possession for the bittern, and pools of water: and I will sweep it with the [broom] of destruction, saith the LORD of hosts (Isa. 14:23).

> Whose fan is in his hand, and he will throughly purge his floor, and gather his wheat into the garner; but he will burn up the chaff with unquenchable fire (Matt. 3:12).

Hear the long and deep and wailing trumpet-like droning that thuds against billions of eardrums, screaming like a free-falling bomb, its deafening roar increasing as the Lord's cosmic speed slows to the frequency range of human hearing.

> The LORD descended...and... the [sound] of the trumpet sounded long, and waxed louder and louder... (Ex. 19:18, 19).

> He shall send his angels with a great sound of a trumpet, and they shall gather together his elect from the four winds, from one end of heaven to the other (Matt. 24:31).

In a moment, in the twinkling of an eye, at the last trump: for the trumpet shall sound, and the dead shall be raised incorruptible, and we shall be changed (1Cor. 15:52).

Amplified by His heavenly host (see Joshua 6:20), He gives a shout that awakens the dead and arrests the death decree for His children, "Lay not your hand upon My children. Touch not Mine anointed! Do them no harm!" The living children of God are instantly cleansed of the nature of sin, while everyone dedicated to evil runs, hoping to be buried by crumbling towers of Babel. Even the devils will fear their extinction.

Who shall stand when he appeareth? (Mal. 3:2).

The Lord shall roar from on high, and utter his voice from his holy habitation; he shall mightily roar upon his habitation; he shall give a shout, as they that tread the grapes, against all the inhabitants of the earth. A noise shall come even to the ends of the earth; for the Lord hath a controversy with the nations, he will plead with all flesh; he will give them that are wicked to the sword, saith the Lord. Thus saith the Lord of hosts, Behold, evil shall go forth from nation to nation, and a great whirlwind shall be raised up from the coasts of the earth (Jer. 25:30-33).

Verily, verily, I say unto you, The hour is coming, and now is, when the dead shall hear the voice of the Son of God: and they that hear shall live (John 5:25).

For the Lord himself shall descend from heaven with a shout, with the voice of the archangel, and with the trump of God (1 Thess. 4:16).

For the trumpet shall sound, and the dead shall be raised incorruptible, and we shall be changed. For this corruptible must put on incorruption, and this mortal must put on immortality. So when this corruptible shall have put on incorruption, and this mortal shall have put on immortality, then shall be brought to pass the saying that is written, Death is swallowed up in victory (1 Cor. 15:52-54).

Picture Jesus' magnetic forces disrupting Earth's tectonic plates, with great rivers flowing backward. Earth's mantle agitates and writhes, and high tsunamis caused by extensive and powerful undersea earthquakes, or pulled up by His gravitation, submerge landmasses far into their coastlines. "There shall be signs in the sun, and in the moon, and in the stars; and upon the earth distress of nations, with perplexity; the sea and the waves roaring; men's hearts failing them for fear, and for looking after those things which are coming on the earth" (Luke 21:25, 26). Would you like to be alive on that great day? Habakkuk didn't.

Was the LORD displeased against the rivers? was thine anger against the rivers? was thy wrath against the sea, that thou didst ride upon thine horses and thy chariots of salvation? Thy bow was made quite naked, according to the oaths of the tribes, even thy word. Selah. Thou didst cleave the earth with rivers. The mountains saw thee, and they trembled [Heb. "writhed in pain"]: the overflowing of the water passed by: the deep uttered his voice, and lifted up his hands on high. The sun and moon stood still in their habitation: at the light of thine arrows they went, and at the shining of thy glittering spear. Thou didst march through the land in indignation, thou didst thresh the heathen in anger. Thou wentest forth for the salvation of thy people, even for salvation with thine anointed; thou woundedst the head out of the house of the wicked, by discovering the foundation unto the neck. Selah. Thou didst strike through with his staves the head of his villages: they came out as a whirlwind to scatter me: their rejoicing was as to devour the poor secretly. Thou didst walk through the sea with thine horses, through the heap of great waters. When I heard, my belly trembled; my lips quivered at the voice: rottenness entered into my bones, and I trembled in myself, that I might rest in the day of trouble: when he cometh up unto the people, he will invade them with his troops (Hab. 3:8-16).

The LORD is good, a strong hold in the day of trouble; and he knoweth them that trust in him. But with an overrunning flood he will make an utter end of the place thereof, and darkness shall pursue his enemies. What do ye imagine against the LORD? he will make an utter end: affliction shall not rise up the second time Nah. 1:7-9).

Watch the satanic and murderous scatter to their subterranean world in terror at the Lord's shocking new reality.

> And the kings of the earth, and the great men, and the rich men, and the chief captains, and the mighty men, and every bondman, and every free man, hid themselves in the dens and in the rocks of the mountains; and said to the mountains and rocks, Fall on us, and hide us from the face of him that sitteth on the throne, and from the wrath of the Lamb: for the great day of his wrath is come; and who shall be able to stand? (Rev. 6:15-17).

> Behold, he cometh with clouds; and every eye shall see him, and they also which pierced him: and all kindreds of the earth shall wail because of him. Even so, Amen (Rev. 1:7).

Feel the heat when the Maker of suns comes near, when "the heavens shall pass away with a great noise, and the elements shall melt with fervent heat, the earth also and the works that are therein shall be burned up" (2 Pet. 3:10).

> The mountains quake at him, and the hills melt, and the earth is burned at his presence, yea, the world, and all that dwell therein. Who can stand before his indignation? and who can abide in the fierceness of his anger? his fury is poured out like fire, and the rocks are thrown down by him…. For while they be folden together as thorns, and while they are drunken as drunkards, they shall be devoured as stubble fully dry (Nah 1: 5, 6, 10).

> And mount Sinai was altogether on a smoke, because the LORD descended upon it in fire: and the smoke thereof ascended as the smoke of a furnace, and the whole mount quaked greatly (Ex. 19:18).

> Oh that thou wouldest rend the heavens, that thou wouldest come down, that the mountains might flow down at thy presence, as when the melting fire burneth, the fire causeth the waters to boil, to make thy name known to thine adversaries, that the nations may tremble at thy presence! When thou didst terrible things which we looked not for, thou camest down, the mountains flowed down at thy presence. For since the beginning of the world men have not heard, nor perceived by the ear, neither hath the eye seen, O God, beside thee, what he hath prepared for him that waiteth for him (Isa. 64:1-4).

> Wherefore glorify ye the LORD in the fires, even the name of the LORD God of Israel in the isles of the sea. From the uttermost part of the earth have we heard songs, even glory to the righteous (Isa. 24:15, 16).

> Come, my people, enter thou into thy chambers, and shut thy doors about thee: hide thyself as it were for a little moment, until the indignation be overpast (Isa. 26:20).

> And to you who are troubled rest with us, when the Lord Jesus shall be revealed from heaven with his mighty angels, in flaming fire taking vengeance on them that know not God, and that obey not the gospel of our Lord Jesus Christ: who shall be punished with everlasting destruction from the presence of the Lord, and from the glory of his power (2 Thess. 1:7-9).

> For, behold, the LORD will come with fire, and with his chariots like a whirlwind, to render his anger with fury, and his rebuke with flames of fire. For by fire and by his sword will the LORD plead with all flesh: and the slain of the LORD shall be many (Isa. 66:15, 16).

> For, behold, the day cometh, that shall burn as an oven; and all the proud, yea, and all that do wickedly, shall be stubble: and the day that cometh shall burn them up, saith the LORD of hosts, that it shall leave them neither root nor branch (Mal. 4:1).

> For, behold, the LORD cometh forth out of his place, and will come down, and tread upon the high places of the earth. And the mountains shall be molten under him, and the valleys shall be cleft, as wax before the fire, and as the waters that are poured down a steep place (Mic. 1:3, 4).

> And the streams thereof shall be turned into pitch, and the dust thereof into brimstone, and the land thereof shall become burning pitch. It shall not be quenched night nor day; the smoke thereof shall go up for ever: from generation to generation it shall lie waste; none shall pass through it for ever and ever (Isa. 34:9, 10).

That Wicked [one]...the Lord shall consume with the spirit of his mouth, and shall destroy with the brightness of his coming (2 Thess. 2:8).

Their flesh shall consume away while they stand upon their feet, and their eyes shall consume away in their holes, and their tongue shall consume away in their mouth (Zech. 14:12).

For our God is a consuming fire (Heb. 12:29).

And out of his mouth goeth a sharp sword, that with it he should smite the nations: and he shall rule them with a rod of iron: and he treadeth the winepress of the fierceness and wrath of Almighty God.

And he hath on his vesture and on his thigh a name written, KING OF KINGS, AND LORD OF LORDS.

And I saw an angel standing in the sun; and he cried with a loud voice, saying to all the fowls that fly in the midst of heaven, Come and gather yourselves together unto the supper of the great God;

That ye may eat the flesh of kings, and the flesh of captains, and the flesh of mighty men, and the flesh of horses, and of them that sit on them, and the flesh of all men, both free and bond, both small and great.

And I saw the beast, and the kings of the earth, and their armies, gathered together to make war against him that sat on the horse, and against his army. And the beast was taken, and with him the false prophet that wrought miracles before him, with which he deceived them that had received the mark of the beast, and them that worshipped his image. These both were cast alive into a lake of fire burning with brimstone. And the remnant were slain with the sword of him that sat upon the horse, which sword proceeded out of his mouth: and all the fowls were filled with their flesh (Rev. 19:15-21).

Only with thine eyes shalt thou behold and see the reward of the wicked (Ps. 91:8).

O thou sword of the LORD, how long will it be ere thou be quiet? put up thyself into thy scabbard, rest, and be still (Jer. 47:6).

At this display of power and catastrophe the deceiver will be showed up for his nothingness. The true event of Christ's return will be Earth-shattering. Even the powers of the heavens will be shaken.

See that ye refuse not him that speaketh. For if they escaped not who refused him that spake on earth, much more shall not we escape, if we turn away from him that speaketh from heaven: whose voice then shook the earth: but now he hath promised, saying, Yet once more I shake not the earth only, but also heaven (Heb. 12:25, 26).

Immediately after the tribulation of those days shall the sun be darkened, and the moon shall not give her light, and the stars shall fall from heaven, and the powers of the heavens shall be shaken (Matt. 24:29).

Behold, the day of the LORD cometh, cruel both with wrath and fierce anger, to lay the land desolate: and he shall destroy the sinners thereof out of it. For the stars of heaven and the constellations thereof shall not give their light: the sun shall be darkened in his going forth, and the moon shall not cause her light to shine. And I will punish the world for their evil, and the wicked for their iniquity; and I will cause the arrogancy of the proud to cease, and will lay low the haughtiness of the terrible. I will make a man more precious than fine gold; even a man than the golden wedge of Ophir: therefore I will shake the heavens, and the earth shall remove out of her place, in the wrath of the LORD of hosts, and in the day of his fierce anger. And it shall be as the chased roe, and as a sheep that no man taketh up (Isa. 13:9-14).

Lo, there was a great earthquake; and the sun became black as sackcloth of hair, and the moon became as blood; and the stars of heaven fell unto the earth, even as a fig tree casteth her untimely figs, when she is shaken of a mighty wind (Rev. 6:12, 13).

This is the real, true, scriptural return of Christ, like the detonation of a million nuclear bombs, a destruction that Satan can never imitate; therefore, that devil replaced the biblical wasting of Earth with a non-destructive, peaceful arrival by his rapture and seven year tribulation blasphemies. And the Protestant protected world has believed the Vatican's rapture lie. Most will join with the enemy of Protestantism to silence the truth concerning this. Which side will you be on? The deceiving or the undeceiving?

> I beheld the earth, and, lo, it was without form, and void; and the heavens, and they had no light. I beheld the mountains, and, lo, they trembled, and all the hills moved lightly. I beheld, and, lo, there was no man, and all the birds of the heavens were fled. I beheld, and, lo, the fruitful place was a wilderness, and all the cities thereof were broken down at the presence of the LORD, and by his fierce anger (Jer. 4:23-26).

> He will make an utter end (Nah. 1:9).

> Who shall be able to stand? (Rev. 6:17).

Take in the power of the Father who, though never leaving His sanctuary across the Milky Way, still shines forth with brilliance greater than Venus at its brightest illumination. "Out of Zion, the perfection of beauty, God hath shined" (Ps. 50:2).

> Through a rift in the clouds there beams a star whose brilliancy is increased fourfold in contrast with the darkness. It speaks hope and joy to the faithful, but severity and wrath to the transgressors of God's law. Those who have sacrificed all for Christ are now secure, hidden as in the secret of the Lord's pavilion. They have been tested, and before the world and the despisers of truth they have evinced their fidelity to Him who died for them. A marvelous change has come over those who have held fast their integrity in the very face of death. They have been suddenly delivered from the dark and terrible tyranny of men transformed to demons. Their faces, so lately pale, anxious, and haggard, are now aglow with wonder, faith, and love. Their voices rise in triumphant song: "God is our refuge and strength, a very present help in trouble. Therefore will not we fear, though the earth be removed, and though the mountains be carried into the midst of the sea; though the waters thereof roar and be troubled, though the mountains shake with the swelling thereof." Psalm 46:1-3 *The Great Controversy*, p. 638.

At the sight of Jesus, the sinful natures of the ravaged waiting ones are instantly and forever changed (see 1 John 3:1, 2, 9). The sleeping saints awaken and arise in the immortal, incorruptible bodies as had been created for Adam and Eve (see Luke 24:39-42; Daniel 12:2, 3). Just like their Saviour departing from His disciples, the redeemed all ascend together up in the air and into space to Jesus, their Deliverer and Friend who truly stayed with them "unto the end of the world" (Matt. 28:20).

> Verily, verily, I say unto you, The hour is coming, and now is, when the dead shall hear the voice of the Son of God: and they that hear shall live (John 5:25).

> For the trumpet shall sound, and the dead shall be raised incorruptible (1 Cor. 15:52).

> We shall be changed (1 Cor. 15:52).

> The dead in Christ shall rise first: then we which are alive and remain shall be caught up together with them in the clouds, to meet the Lord in the air: and so shall we ever be with the Lord (1 Thess. 4:16, 17).

> For we know that if our earthly house of this tabernacle were dissolved, we have a building of God, an house not made with hands, eternal in the heavens.

> For in this we groan, earnestly desiring to be clothed upon with our house which is from heaven:

> If so be that being clothed we shall not be found naked.

> For we that are in this tabernacle do groan, being burdened: not for that we would be unclothed, but clothed upon, that mortality might be swallowed up of life (2 Cor. 5:1-4, cf Phil. 1:6, 10, 23; 3:10, 11).

> Behold, I shew you a mystery; We shall not all sleep, but we shall all be changed,

> In a moment, in the twinkling of an eye, at the last trump:…

> For this corruptible *must* put on incorruption, and this mortal *must* put on immortality.

> So when this corruptible shall have put on incorruption, and this mortal shall have put on

immortality, then shall be brought to pass the saying that is written, Death is swallowed up in victory.

O death, where is thy sting? O grave, where is thy victory? (1 Cor. 15:51-55).

Our conversation is in heaven; from whence also we look for the Saviour, the Lord Jesus Christ: who shall change our vile body, that it may be fashioned like unto his glorious body, according to the working whereby he is able even to subdue all things unto himself (Phil. 3:20, 21).

The deliverance from sin, the removal of all desire to please self, no more guilt, no debilitating shame, no regret, no fear of rejection by God; the pure and pleasant Holy Spirit of our Father without measure, perfect freedom from the influences and temptations from a world of sin, the Lord Jesus who will never again leave their sight; these altogether release from the redeemed a solemn joy that will stay forever.

For the earnest expectation of the creature waiteth for the manifestation of the sons of God.

Because the creature itself also shall be delivered from the bondage of corruption into the glorious liberty of the children of God.

For we know that the whole creation groaneth and travaileth in pain together until now.

And not only they, but ourselves also, which have the firstfruits of the Spirit, even we ourselves groan within ourselves, waiting for the adoption, to wit, the redemption of our body (Rom. 8:19, 21-23).

Sins forgiven, overcome, and forever forgotten by heaven, and having no more hold on their being. At last, **completely** *free from sin, its forbidding of glory to God, and its repelling and separating power from Him!* — The saints have obtained the full, perfect victory for which through the millennia they have longed, and this evokes in them the most holy, sacred joy.

Oh, what a sense of relief and gratitude to God we felt! I heard voices raised in triumphant praise to God. I was happy, perfectly happy *Testimonies for the church*, vol. 2, p. 597.

My heart is fixed, O God, my heart is fixed: I will sing and give praise (Ps. 57:7).

And in this mountain shall the LORD of hosts make unto all people a feast of fat things, a feast of wines on the lees, of fat things full of marrow, of wines on the lees well refined.

And he will destroy in this mountain the face of the covering cast over all people, and the vail that is spread over all nations.

He will swallow up death in victory; and the Lord GOD will wipe away tears from off all faces; and the rebuke of his people shall he take away from off all the earth: for the LORD hath spoken it.

And…in this mountain shall the hand of the LORD rest (Isa. 25:6-8, 10, cf Matt. 26:29).

We will walk in the light of His love, and His name shall forever remain in our foreheads.

No End! *Amen!*

Appendix A:
Comments referred to from main text

From page 38:

The Great Controversy, p. 234, 235:

Throughout Christendom, Protestantism was menaced by formidable foes. The first triumphs of the Reformation past, Rome summoned new forces, hoping to accomplish its destruction. At this time the order of the Jesuits was created, the most cruel, unscrupulous, and powerful of all the champions of popery. Cut off from earthly ties and human interests, dead to the claims of natural affection, reason and conscience wholly silenced, they knew no rule, no tie, but that of their order, and no duty but to extend its power.... The gospel of Christ had enabled its adherents to meet danger and endure suffering, undismayed by cold, hunger, toil, and poverty, to uphold the banner of truth in face of the rack, the dungeon, and the stake. To combat these forces, Jesuitism inspired its followers with a fanaticism that enabled them to endure like dangers, and to oppose to the power of truth all the weapons of deception. There was no crime too great for them to commit, no deception too base for them to practice, no disguise too difficult for them to assume. Vowed to perpetual poverty and humility, it was their studied aim to secure wealth and power, to be devoted to the overthrow of Protestantism, and the re-establishment of the papal supremacy.

When appearing as members of their order, they wore a garb of sanctity, visiting prisons and hospitals, ministering to the sick and the poor, professing to have renounced the world, and bearing the sacred name of Jesus, who went about doing good. But under this blameless exterior the most criminal and deadly purposes were often concealed. It was a fundamental principle of the order that the end justifies the means. By this code, lying, theft, perjury, assassination, were not only pardonable but commendable, when they served the interests of the church. Under various disguises the Jesuits worked their way into offices of state, climbing up to be the counselors of kings, and shaping the policy of nations. They became servants to act as spies upon their masters. They established colleges for the sons of princes and nobles, and schools for the common people; and the children of Protestant parents were drawn into an observance of popish rites. All the outward pomp and display of the Romish worship was brought to bear to confuse the mind and dazzle and captivate the imagination, and thus the liberty for which the fathers had toiled and bled was betrayed by the sons. The Jesuits rapidly spread themselves over Europe, and wherever they went, there followed a revival of popery.

To give them greater power, a bull was issued re-establishing the inquisition.… Notwithstanding the general abhorrence with which it was regarded, even in Catholic countries, this terrible tribunal was again set up by popish rulers, and atrocities too terrible to bear the light of day were repeated in its secret dungeons. In many countries, thousands upon thousands of the very flower of the nation, the purest and noblest, the most intellectual and highly educated, pious and devoted pastors, industrious and patriotic citizens, brilliant scholars, talented artists, skillful artisans, were slain or forced to flee to other lands.

Such were the means which Rome had invoked to quench the light of the Reformation, to withdraw from men the Bible, and to restore the ignorance and superstition of the Dark Ages.

The New Encyclopaedia Britannica, Volume 6 *Micropaedia*, page 542, article, *Jesuit Estates Controversy.*

This article shows the use of backdoor politicking in Constitutional Democracies to undermine the constitutional democratic process and to steer a nation's wealth for the purpose of reviving Rome's agenda in Canada and regaining its control there. It reveals more recently the Church's tenacious efforts to diminish the advancement of biblical teaching in order to prevent, and ultimately to destroy, the spread of freedom and of the institution of Protestantism in North America, as had already been done in Europe. The controversy reveals that, as early as 1842 the age-old aim, and the eventual accomplishment, of the Jesuits was to wield dictatorial power through legislation. The article shows the Vatican's circumventing constitutionally established procedures for national legislation, the sovereignty of nations, and the will of the people.

Jesuit Estates controversy, Roman Catholic-Protestant dispute in 19th century Canada. When the Society of Jesus (the Jesuit order) was suppressed by the papacy in 1773, its extensive landholdings in Canada were transferred to the British government with the stipulation that the revenue derived from them should be applied to educational purposes. The Society was revived early in the 19th century, and in 1842 a number of Jesuits returned to Canada. The idea of granting them restitution was discussed for some time. Finally, by the Jesuits' Estates Act of 1888, they were given $400,000 in compensation for the loss of their estates; at the same time, $60,000 was granted to Protestant educational institutions in the province.

This act aroused anti-Catholic feeling among Protestants in neighbouring Ontario, where in 1889 a motion was introduced into the House of Commons urging the dominion government to disallow the measure on the grounds that its endowment of the Society of Jesus was a threat to civil and religious liberties. The measure did not pass, and the efforts of Ontario's Equal Rights Association to have the Jesuits' Estates Act repealed were also unsuccessful.

A final quote from a recent General of the Jesuit army. It reveals the order's motivation to rapid expansion, which was built into the curriculum. I quote it for the reader to envision an estimate of the potential millions of exponentially reproducing agents today, in places high and low, male and female, working together like a well-oiled machine,

"Jesuit education would consist in the creation of multiplying agents"

From page 70:

Since the apostasy of Cain, there exists and has ever existed but one false religion throughout the world, the second oldest religion in history. And, there has been the oldest, the one true religion, "the everlasting covenant", "the everlasting gospel" (Isa. 24:5; Rev. 14:6) that began before Eden. The one and only true religion is likewise the same through all time (see Malachi 3:6; Hebrews 13:8, 20), with a few added details in the New Testament, and greater power to overthrow strongholds of sin and to obey the Law of God. But, both old and new covenants of the one true religion embody the requirements of God from eternity past and to eternity future — that is, childlike dependence on our Creator, acceptance of His love and redemptive grace, and His empowered, happy, and natural obedience to His laws that are holy and just and good. This is all obtained through a transforming relationship with His Son by receiving His Son's humbling and faith through His Spirit (see Isaiah 41:8; Isaiah 64:8; Romans 7:22-8:9; Galatians 4:6).

The one false religion has been from the beginning. "In process of time it came to pass, that Cain brought of the fruit of the ground an offering unto the LORD" (Gen. 4:3). All the pagan deities have originated from Cain; and after the flood, they were resurrected by Ham, Cush, Nimrod, and Semiramis, who substituted worship of themselves for Elohim. "Cush begat Nimrod: he began to be a mighty one in the earth. He was a mighty hunter before [that is, in place of] the LORD: wherefore it is said, Even as Nimrod the mighty hunter [in place of] the LORD" (Gen. 10:8, 9).

Coming down from time almost immemorial we find "altars" to Baal and "groves" to Ashtoreth (Isa. 17:8). "And it came to pass the same night, that the LORD said unto him [Gideon], ... throw down the altar of Baal that thy father hath, and cut down the grove [Heb. 'ăsherah, derived from "blessed, happy"] that is by it" (Jdg. 6:25). "And Samuel spake unto all the house of Israel, saying, If ye do return unto the LORD with all your hearts, then put away the strange gods and Ashtaroth from among you, and prepare your hearts unto the LORD, and serve him only: and he will deliver you out of the hand of the Philistines. Then the children of Israel did put away Baalim and Ashtaroth, and served the LORD only" (1 Sam. 7:3, 4). Baalim and Ashtaroth are the gods and the groves, respectively. They idolize wealth, ease, and visual beauty. They call out the sensual, the carnal, the devilish. They appeal to religious externals; they cannot reach, they forbid reaching, the human heart. Both Ashtaroth [Hebrew plural for Ashtoreth and Asherah] and Baalim [Hebrew plural for Baal] are still the age-old focus of religion everywhere in the world.

Baalim, under its many aliases, was Satan's impersonation of Jehovah Elohim, the Lord God Creator of the heavens and Judge of all the earth. Baalim means "the Lords", which were the gods concealing Satan and his hosts of darkness. He has stood in the place of the true God; he still does and has "opened his mouth in blasphemy against God, to blaspheme his name, and his tabernacle, and them that dwell in heaven" (Rev. 13:6, cf Dan. 7:8). Ashtoreth is the substitute saviour that stood up against the "Prince of princes" (Dan. 8:25) and "Lord of lords" (Rev. 17:14). Thus impersonating Lord God the Son, Ashtoreth is Antichrist, "who opposeth and exalteth himself above all that is called God, or that is worshipped; so that he as God sitteth in the temple of God, shewing himself that he is God" (2 Thess. 2:4).

Whether it was the original worship of Nimrod and Semiramis at Babel, or Egyptian Osiris and Isis, Canaanite Baal (Moloch, Milchom, Dagon) and Ashtoreth (Asherah, Ishtar, Easter, Eastern Star), Greek Zeus and Athena (Artemis), Roman Jupiter and Venus (Diana), every culture and for all time has had the same two male and female inventions of Satan. And it is even no different today within Christianity, worshiping Nimrod in the Mass over the bones of his "unjustly" executed body, and his wife, Semiramis who claimed for him Sun worship in order to resurrect his effort to overthrow God's kingdom of righteousness in the earth.

Throughout history, the dictatorial male deity "ruled the nations in anger," and "smote the people in wrath with a continual stroke" (Isa. 14:6), while the female god in each tradition, which everywhere was called the great "Queen of heaven" and the mediatorial "mother of God", alone could propitiate the male god's implacable, explosive wrath. In religion, by her niceties, her sex appeal under the innocuous cloak of crop fertility, and her many promises of grace toward all sins, Ashtoreth wooed the worshipers away from the true God of love and righteousness. And once the heart's loyalty was in her possession, Baal became the force of inspiration. Nevertheless, both pagan personalities were united in evil intentions. Satan then used this male figure to transmit his brutality into the hearts of men, women, and children. Baal is the destroyer king over the fifth and sixth trumpet locusts, which have tormented and killed the peace of God in the hearts of Protestants, as seen in Revelation 11:7-12. It is he who has fomented war, and war-like tribes and aggressor nations since the beginning of time (see Genesis 10:8, 9). Baal gives the wrathful result of Ashtoreth's exciting wine (see Revelation 14:8, 10; 18:3). All who have ever accepted Ashtoreth's "nice" side of the departure from the holy God ultimately end in Baal's brutal side of the apostasy in manhunts and murder, assassination and regicide. Baal was the deification of Nimrod, the mighty hunter in the place of God. Baal's crimes will be the result of Spiritual Formation, "the abomination that maketh desolate" (Dan. 11:31).

The many forms of the two mischievous deities, Baal and Ashtoreth, still facilitate the destructive and corrupting work in all who attempt to propitiate the one true God of Abraham for His peace. Having chosen Ash-

Appendix A: Comments referred to from main text

toreth, they then stand before God without an Intercessor in Christ. By refusing the anointed Prince and Saviour of the world, "the chastisement of our peace" (Isa. 53:5) must remain upon them because they do not let it fall upon the Prince. And invariably, they must indulge the many methods and substances of Ashtoreth in order to alleviate the curse of God. A thousand other brands of modern pagan religion are all reproductions of that same ancient system from Ham, Cush, and Nimrod. No differently than Satan had done with the world's religions since the beginning, in Christianity he has paraded God and Christ as King. But, according to the prophecy of Daniel 8:11, he usurps Christ's office as our Intercessor before the Most High. Satan steals away our God of justice and mercy, and His Prince and Saviour Son, replacing each of Them with a Hegelian dichotomy of himself (see Revelation 13:1; 17:3). Practicing his delusion behind the mask of Baal and Ashtoreth, the devil portrayed himself as God and Christ during the old dispensation, and he has done the same with Christ and Mary to Christendom by a New Testament-christened Baal and Ashtoreth. Satan gave the current Christian Ashtoreth power and a throne and great authority as his vicar of bottomless antinomian grace. Thus Mary, that Christian Ashtoreth, is granted the same title(s) that were given to the ancient Ashtoreths, *"Queen of Heaven"*. All the other mother gods— Ishtar, Isis, Ashtoreth, Astarte, Artemis, Diana, and Venus — are one and the same diety-Mediatrix of our great High Priest, Jesus. Thus, via lawless grace, the devil preempts true sorrow for sin and the way to true redemption from our Creator God and His Son (see John 5:21). By this complex scheme Satan obstructs the merciful justice of God the Father and Law-loving grace of Christ to the human race. The deceiver thus confuses, manipulates, and disturbs the hearts and minds of the entire world.

These systems can provide for nothing of God's real redemption. They offer nothing more than creature propitiation, for God and His Son are not the inspiration of repentance. The worshipers' self-manufactured repentance flows from their own prideful, corrupted fountain, of which scripture says, "The heart is deceitful above all things, and desperately wicked" (Jer. 17:9). "Who can bring a clean thing out of an unclean? not one" (Job 14:4). Only an unholy, filthy, and heartless demon would encourage our own unholy, unclean, and un-humbled repentance that needs to be repented of (see 2 Corinthians 7:10).

But, the Father's cry through Jesus to humanity is,

Look unto me, and be ye saved, all the ends of the earth: for I am God, and there is none else (Isa. 45:22).

No one can have peace with God apart from His approved Propitiator — the only Being who loves sinners infallibly and whose immaculate nature is unsurpassed, the Almighty's only begotten Offspring, Messiah the Prince. As much as "the Father himself loveth you" (John 16:27), He cannot accept the presence of Satan who dwells in hearts not reconciled to Himself and His Law. He cannot inhabit the worshipers' praises who will not let His Law inhabit them. He cannot listen to Baal's raucous voice or Ashtoreth's presumptuous rejoicing which inhabit their prayers. Among our fallen race, within Jesus alone did perfection and self-sacrifice feel good in all respects; and likewise did purity and loving-kindness. Therefore, the Anointed One alone needs no mediator before the infinite Judge. Christ is the perfect, innocent, obedient Creator-Lamb, humbled by His Father to an infinite degree. The great Burnt Offering was slain to broker our probation and reconciliation with the great God. He takes away the sin of the world by the sanctifying influence of His inexhaustible determination to save us from sin and to satisfy His Father in our salvation. No one else but the Son has given His Father perfect rest. On the cross, He alone shared the weight of rebellion that the Father had been carrying since sin began. And no one else than Christ in Gethsemane has revealed the agony of God that sin and suffering have caused His infinite empathy since the start of the controversy.

"To him that worketh not, but believeth on him that justifieth the ungodly, his faith is counted for righteousness" (Rom. 4:5). We can't work up enough repentance and propitiation to satisfy the Father's broken heart. Don't even force out sorrow for sin. It has already been tried, and it does nothing to change God's heart (see Malachi 2:13). But, He has made a way for us if we will comply with His conditions. God must and will give us repentance. All we can do is trust in His pre-approved Propitiator who must humble us and work into us His love for Law and righteousness, and a need for His great mercy. Accepting God's invitation to come to His Lamb, trusting in the Lamb is all we can do toward our own salvation.

None but God can subdue the pride of man's heart. We cannot save ourselves. We cannot regenerate ourselves. In the heavenly courts there will be no song sung, To me that loved myself, and washed myself, redeemed myself, unto me be glory and honor, blessing and praise. But this is the keynote of the song that is sung by many here in this world. They do not know what it means to be meek and lowly in heart; and they do not mean to know this, if they can avoid it. The whole gospel is comprised in learning of Christ, His meekness and lowliness.

What is justification by faith? It is the work of God in laying the glory of man in the dust, and doing for man that which it is not in his power to do for himself *Testimonies to Ministers*, p. 456.

> ## *God wants us to accept Him as He is; but we want Him to accept us as we are without any concession on our part. The stalemate has left both parties dying*

We cannot propitiate the holy God; that is, we cannot move Him to accept our selfish characters. We have hated the self-sacrifice and purity that He and all of His Son's inspired messengers have ever stood for. And all the self-centeredness and corruption, which we have ever stood for, the infinite God will never reconcile in His heart. He wants us to accept Him as He is; but we want Him to accept us as we are without any concession on our part. The stalemate has left both parties dying. Even though it strikes at our pride, our Creator does not consider the repentance generated from us good enough to approach Him for His pardon because our repentance comes from our sin-filled heart. We need to surrender up our repentance. The only human who God can receive with a request for our pardon is His Son. And Jesus still says, "him that cometh to me I will in no wise cast out" (John 6:37). The Messiah sent from Jehovah is the same friend today as He was in the past (see Hebrews 13:8). God receives all of Adam's children who come to Him with His Son's interceding Spirit in them, making use of Their provision from Gethsemane and Golgotha.

> Then saith he unto them, My soul is exceeding sorrowful, even unto death: tarry ye here, and watch with me. And he went a little further, and fell on his face, and prayed, saying, O my Father, if it be possible, let this cup pass from me: nevertheless not as I will, but as thou wilt (Matt. 26:38, 39).

> It pleased the LORD to bruise him; he hath put him to grief.... He shall see of the travail of his soul, and shall be satisfied (Isa. 53:10, 11).

> And because ye are sons, God hath sent forth the Spirit of his Son into your hearts, crying, Abba, Father (Gal. 4:6).

> Wherefore he is able also to save them to the uttermost that come unto God by him, seeing he ever liveth to make intercession for them (Heb. 7:25).

Without Christ, we and the infinitely holy God could never co-exist. Thus, we could never have a Father in God; and our Father could never have us for children. His Spirit flowing from His heart would never fill our hearts. This painful, impossibly deep chasm Jesus has bridged. By His acceptable life and victorious death, He paved the way to reunite us to His Father. Both sides looking through Christ, we, humbled and repenting at what Jesus went through for us, can meet with the infinitely meek and already willing to relent Father who suffered together with His Son for us. All three of us together reunited in full acceptance, Their new bond with the human heart is founded upon holiness before the Law. The Father could accept no other method to fix man's problem of sin.

> Looking unto Jesus the author and finisher of our faith; who for the joy that was set before him endured the cross, despising the shame, and is set down at the right hand of the throne of God (Heb. 12:2).

> This is the will of him that sent me, that every one which seeth the Son, and believeth on him, may have everlasting life (John 6:40).

> My little children, these things write I unto you, that ye sin not. And if any man sin, we have an advocate with the Father, Jesus Christ the righteous (1 John 2:1).

"Looking unto Jesus". For the soul who has discovered his total helplessness to accept God and His holiness, or to gain His acceptance, this is very good news. We see Jesus, "a quickening spirit" (1 Cor. 15:45), God manifest in the flesh, during His time with us as a charged

Appendix A: Comments referred to from main text

dynamo of perfect, selfless service to God and man. "I have preached righteousness in the great congregation: lo, I have not refrained my lips, O LORD, thou knowest" (Ps. 40:9). "I had gone with the multitude, I went with them to the house of God, with the voice of joy and praise, with a multitude that kept holyday" (Ps. 42:4). "Thy God, hath anointed thee with the oil of gladness above thy fellows" (Ps. 45:7). In Jesus' uncompromising, infallible, natural obedience to God's Law, flowing out of a warm, human heart, we have Him who relished every moment walking and talking to people. He ever sought to deliver fallen mankind from the grip of Satan and to uplift His people from the destruction of sin. He's a Prince and a Saviour, just and merciful and humble. He did what God desires of us: to do justly, to love mercy, and walk humbly with Him. Jesus is the perfect Mediator between God and man.

As Prince, who bore not His sword in vain, His immutable, unbending integrity to His Father's Law, and, as Saviour, His permanent bond with us from whom He couldn't let go, together give Him the needed credentials and fitness to bridge the wide gulf between a world of sinners and the incomprehensibly holy Almighty. God's own infinite dying that He laid on His Son could not loosen the infinite love for humanity that possessed Jesus, even under His Father's immeasurably intense fires of divine rejection, an insurmountable rejection which the Law demanded of Christ for loving and clinging to the one treasonous world. Through Jesus we see the infinite tension battling in the heart of God since the beginning, whether to create redemption to solve rebellion or leave the kingdom status quo; whether to keep us or His only begotten Son. And, by His Son's willingness to perish in our place, the Father's scale tipped in favor of redemption and in favor of one lost world, deeply hardened in rebellion. Therefore, only the ministry of Christ can close the gap between the holy God and unholy us. Jesus created us and will recreate us, molding each of us individually with His own hands. Except the Father, no one else in heaven is our perfect comforter and helper. Not the holiest, strongest, wisest angel knew us like Him who formed every part of us down to the most yet-undiscovered, microscopic level, "upholding all things by the word of his power" (Heb. 1:3). Hence, no angel understood our sinfulness well enough. The omnipotent One could have entrusted no heavenly being except His Son to love us enough to pass through our eternal rejection. But, Jesus infinitely understood us and His love for us was equal to His infinite knowledge of our worth. And He could not be intimidated by Lucifer like angels could. God sent His best to make our covenant sure and steadfast.

> But thus saith the LORD, Even the captives of the mighty shall be taken away, and the prey of the terrible shall be delivered: for I will contend with him that contendeth with thee, and I will save thy children (Isa. 49:25).

The lack of acceptance and guaranteed grace is traumatic to every child of Adam. Even if the damage from rejection is sedated by substances and entertainment, and even though being unloved escapes the multitudes' notice, their nerves and brains are still tormented and traumatized. Only by knowing an unchanging love toward us settles our nerves and gives us blissful, health-giving rest. But, such all-encompassing, perfect, unchangeable love does not come from any human being other than the Son who has been slain since the foundation of the world.

> Greater love hath no man than this, that a man lay down his life for his friends (John 15:13).

Cursed is the person that trusts in anyone else of this world for unending acceptance. He will find his soul wounded every day of his life. But, blessed is the one who puts his trust in "Messiah the Prince" (Dan. 9:25) who proved His love for us to the very end. He will work into us His truth and grace as we cling to Him through His promises and His reproofs, His refreshing comfort and His strong convictions to our hearts. He will put in us a distaste for our sins and a love for wholesome goodness, putting that in us because we cannot put it in ourselves. But, He can only give us His blessedness in exchange for us yielding up our debilitating willfulness. We must have one or the other; we can't have both. And either we take the quicker, easier way or the longer, harder way; but, ultimately we must accept the will of God as it comes through His Intercessor, Jesus. Through Christ's excellent carefulness working with His Father's corrections, we must hate the sins that pain Him. We must surrender to His convicting and life-giving Spirit. These have ever been His terms.

> Wherefore he is able also to save them to the uttermost that come unto God by him, seeing he ever liveth to make intercession for them. For such an high priest became us, who is holy, harmless, undefiled, separate from sinners, and made higher than the heavens (Heb. 7:25, 26).

Thus, we come forth from the womb of Christ's justifying work humbled and delivered of self-focus. We are peaceful, happy, unimportant little people, and in our right mind. The long trauma of being delivered from Satan's hold is behind us.

The Mother of all living will birth us into new life and carry us (see Mark 1:25; Luke 4:35; Hebrews 2:18). As we earlier stated, in the great controversy we see that the Son of God is the original "mother of all living" (Gen. 3:20). He created Adam kingly and with all earthly power and authority, formed in the spiritual image of His beloved Father (see 1 Corinthians 11:7). And, for the pinnacle and final work of Earth's creation Christ made Eve with His own spiritual characteristics. He also created them both to help better reveal the Fullness of the Godhead bodily before the angelic hosts and unfallen worlds.

> The head of the woman is the man; and the head of Christ is God (1 Cor. 11:3).

As Christ is the Word of God, even so did He give women a voice closer to the frequency range of children and the special gift of communication to teach the children their fathers' will. The mother's reactionary tendency also mimics the Son of God, who could turn into a She-bear if His children were in danger (see Matthew 16:23; Mark 9:16; Luke 19:45, 46; John 2:13-17). As mothers worry perpetually over their away loved ones, so Jesus could not rest until the human race was safe at His home again (see Matthew 26:29). Every woman we see, their natural gentleness, their love and desire to please, surrounds us all with light from the throne of God.

> And they lifted up their voice, and wept again: and Orpah kissed her mother in law; but Ruth clave unto her (Ruth 1:14).

In their tendency to serve and minister in exchange for love and affection, every member of the female gender has revealed the Son of God, causing much joy and inspiration to the heavenly hosts — and also great horror and wrath among the hosts of hell. Were it not for Satan's vehement jealousy of the Son, every woman and girl would have reigned in the earth as queens and princesses, mothers and sisters. But, to efface all evidence of Christ from Earth, the devil has abused and trampled upon, subjugated and excluded from the councils of men, the women's advice of caution and tenderness as a necessary resource of balancing wisdom. Their counsel mimics that of Daniel's Christ-like advice of mercy, spoken in an excellent spirit toward King Nebuchadnezzar's harsh totalitarian measures, "Break off thy sins by righteousness...by shewing mercy to the poor" (Dan. 4:27).

As fathers tend primarily to their long-range needs and enterprises, and mothers tend primarily to the children's immediate needs and character building, likewise have the members of the Godhead. The Father of all has dealt with Earth's rebellion in great justice with some mercy as He is the bedrock of perfection and safety for the whole kingdom. But, He gave provision for His Son to focus on our one world, our needs and issues, often with a strong hand (see Joshua 4:24; Judges 2:15; 1 Samuel 5:6, 9; 7:13; Isaiah 5:25; 9:12, 17, 21; 10:4). Thus, through the Godhead earth's issues have been interwoven with the issues of the rest of the vast kingdom, while we have had the undivided attention of Father and Son, especially the Son. The Son, as with every good mother, has been very close to us, giving instruction and discipline, but also open-hearted compassion and grace. The law of kindness has been in His mouth, and all of His born-again children rise up and call Him blessed.

Thus, by Christ's infinite wisdom and creativity, the Godhead was intended to be displayed by the holy pair in Eden. And their animal kingdom that stretched to the utmost bounds of the everlasting hills, fearing and loving their masters in Eden, revealed the Godhead's universe in a new and living way.

As "God...created all things by Jesus Christ" (Eph. 3:9), so Adam would generate a race through Eve, and that without any pain. But, after sin entered the world, childbirth would mean much agonizing for women. "Unto the woman he said, I will greatly multiply thy sorrow and thy conception; in sorrow thou shalt bring forth children; and thy desire shall be to thy husband, and he shall rule over thee" (Gen. 3:16). Likewise the Son of God, the self-sacrificing "Mother of all living", after His sorrows were greatly multiplied and His strength spent brought us forth to life, "being born again, not of corruptible seed, but of incorruptible" (1 Pet. 1:23).

The Son died in hard labor to give us a new birth of a heavenly order, and life eternal. The consumed and dying Son named us "son of My sorrow", but His victorious Father changed our name to "son of My right hand" (see Genesis 35:18, margin). At that dark, desperate moment of Christ's expiration, His grieving Father could look beyond the loss of His Son; He would "see of the travail of his soul, and...be satisfied" (Isa. 53:11). Through the perfect sacrifice, He could see His Son's perfectly reconciled seed, and He would be able to bring Him back from the tomb (see verse 10). And the Father's plan of our salvation would prosper in the hands of His faithful High Priest, Michael, "the great prince which standeth for the children of thy people" (Dan. 12:1). Because of His hard labor for our delivery from sin, He ever lives for nothing more than to make intercession for His beloved children, to protect us and save us, pulling us out of the fire if necessary. Jesus guaranteed that Eve and all her mothering female offspring could never forget their children because they would suffer so much to give them birth. Likewise, after His overwhelming, substitutionary damnation for our sakes, from Gethsemane to Golgotha, the Son of God will never forget the children of His agonies. Before the great God Christ's proven intercession for us is guaranteed, carved in stone; and when we accept the repentance He gives, our forgiveness through Him is sure. Jesus says to us,

> Can a woman forget her sucking child, that she should not have compassion on the son of her womb? yea, they may forget, yet will I not forget thee (Isa. 49:15).

We behold God spiritually in every man, and Jesus spiritually in every woman. As we see how God exalted His Son after His supernatural labor for our second birth, we should exalt mothers and say that the characteristics of Jesus, the eternal Mother of all living, make all women beautiful. Without discrimination, every female's self-sacrificial traits are wonderfully beautiful, especially the loving mothers.

Our Advocate Jesus, the Lord God, is the real, mothering "desire of all nations" (Hag. 2:7) who also fills heaven.

> Am I a God at hand, saith the LORD, and not a God afar off?... Do not I fill heaven and earth? saith the LORD (Jer. 23:23, 24).

In wonder David prayed to Jesus,

> Whither shall I go from thy spirit? or whither shall I flee from thy presence?
>
> If I ascend up into heaven, thou art there: if I make my bed in hell [the grave], behold, thou art there.
>
> If I take the wings of the morning, and dwell in the uttermost parts of the sea;
>
> Even there shall thy hand lead me, and thy right hand shall hold me (Ps. 139:7-10).

The Mother of all living wars against the Queen of heaven because she is too immaculate to pour out her soul in sorrow (see Leviticus 16:10; Luke 15:7). She can "see no sorrow" (Rev. 18:7). The Son of God, the Mother of all living, is the true omnipresent Monarch of heaven, the focus of universal joy from the beginning (see Isaiah 9:6; Hebrews 1:6).

Striving to see "his star in the east" (Matt. 2:2), by His great starry cloud of witnesses (see Hebrews 12:1; Hebrews 11; John 5:39), we slowly make out the greater constellation of Christ through their characters found in His Bible, and we worship Him through faith in His living word, in spirit and in truth (see Romans 8:1, 2). There is no speech or language where His Spirit is not heard. And He promises to fix us also into His great cloud of witnesses and to keep us from falling from that hall of faith (see Isaiah 40:26; Jude 24). These scriptures expose the counterfeit comforter-mother queen. Contrary to pagan philosophy, all copies of Ashtoreth need to topple, and "her magnificence should be destroyed" (Acts 19:27, cf 1 Sam. 5:3, 4). She has treacherously usurped Christ's office and titles of mediator that are due only to Him. Ashtoreth will only attract you to use you. Far removed from the implacable, wild raging and gross doting of self-promotion, Satan is the deceptively demure "queen of heaven" (Jer. 7:18; 44:18; Dan. 8:11); but, Christ is a Saviour and a Prince, who bore our condemnation and rejection "into the dust of death" (Ps. 22:15), and whose Spirit "filleth all in all" (Eph. 1:23). He always blends His mercy with justice and His truth always with grace. He will faithfully comfort and protect our hearts; but, He will also keep His Father's standard high as He washes away our iniquities. "He will magnify the law, and make it honourable" (Isa. 42:21). In no one better can we put our trust.

> And I, if I be lifted up from the earth, will draw all men unto me (John 12:32).

We can believe Jesus' promise to accept us as we are, self-centered and in desperate need of His help. And we can accept Him as He is, a Prince and a Messiah, a just God and a Saviour. Christ's children are reconciled to Him if they do this much. Jesus says to them, "Let him take hold of my strength, that he may make peace with me; and he *shall make peace with me*" (Isa. 27:5). Then, His grace and truth "are new very morning" (Lam. 3:23, cf Isa. 50:4) as they are studied in His life and death. His children will learn the beauty of His character in every scripture as they see His name and person in every verse (see John 5:39; 15:7). There is power in His name. If they recognize Him as Lord in both the Old and New Testaments and reconcile His roles there, then He can catch their fleeting trust.

> Wherefore seeing we also are compassed about with so great a cloud of witnesses, let us lay aside every weight, and the sin which doth so easily beset us, and let us run with patience the race that is set before us, looking unto Jesus the author and finisher of our faith (Heb. 12:1, 2).

As He fixes their misunderstandings of Him and as they help correct misconceptions of Him in others, then He can keep up the work of their reconciliation with God and the work of their sanctification (see 2 Peter 1:8; Philippians 2:13; 1 John 1:7), carrying them all the way into eternal life with Him (see Philippians 1:6; John 6:37). No one will be able to take His chosen out of His hand unless they cease to see in Him their only Helper. Where there is no vision of Him the people perish. But, beholding Him throughout the Bible, He will keep giving them such powerful conviction and repentance from His image through His Spirit that they will expel all sin from their lives (see *The Desire of Ages*, p. 466; Romans 8:2).

His gentleness will change their will, infusing theirs with His (see Psalm 18:35). They will hate sin for what it does to Him, their best friend, and to everyone around them. All of God's provisions for our redemption are seen in His Son. He breaks us down (see Matthew 21:44) and baptizes us into a new life (see Romans 6:3-7). He translates us, current citizens of His Father's kingdom (see Colossians 1:13; Hosea 6:2; Philippians 3:20; John 6:47, 54; Romans 6:11; Hebrews 11: 27, 16; Revelation 14:1; Psalm 126:1; Zechariah 3:7; 1 John 5:13). And our citizenship is certified by the Son's Spirit in us (see Romans 8:9; 1 John 3:20). Our testimony then is, I was in confusion and Jesus cleared my thoughts; I was hungry, and He filled me; I was needy, and He was good to me; a stranger to God, and He took me in and reconciled me; naked and ugly, and He clothed me with His beauty. I was sick, and Christ healed me; I was lonely, imprisoned in depression and self-indulgence, and He came to me. I want to reciprocate.

The one true religion not only offers reconciliation with God, but freedom from the hated, old life. With the peace that comes through the restored Spirit of God, souls find in Christ's love divine strength to wrestle against inherited and cultivated sin in their thoughts and habits. They receive power to be worthy of the name Christian through the divinely successful warfare against self. The God of peace sanctifies them wholly, helping them pull down mighty, inbred fortresses of un-Christ-likeness. Through the power of Jesus' Spirit from His heavenly ministry (see Revelation 5:6; 3:1), and through the cleansing of His written word (see Ephesians 5:26; John 14:21), they can mortify the old life and break away from the wrong habits learned from the traditions of their fathers. The attraction of their sins grows weaker as, imbued with faith in God's love, their willpower gets stronger and stronger to overcome each horrid aspect of their former self. As their appreciation of Jesus and His goodness grows stronger, the hold that Satan's unrighteousness has had on them melts away. Christ's perfect holiness exalts them among their peers, and everything prospers due to the new Christian life. He has made them kings in the earth. All of these blessed gifts come from Jesus ministering to mankind His truth and grace from His Father's sanctuary.

The one false religion offers none of this. Baal has engineered his religion to *prevent* the humbling, and the new heart and life. In Baal's religion, the sinner must create his own profuse ascetic repentance (see Malachi 2:10-13; 1 Kings 18:26-28), which he can only manufacture from a natural born, corrupt heart. The hopeless sinner must attempt to propitiate God for His mercy, yet he finds only an accuser impersonating God and he can never get past the evil one's insurmountable, adversarial, impersonal, and manipulating barrage of accusations and his power to discourage (see Zechariah 3:1). Baalzebub's legion voices and confusion ensure that his slave can never overcome his sinful past enough to ever hope for mercy. His worship of God is only empty, flattering appeasement and endless, impossible propitiation, "O Baal, hear us" (1 Ki. 18:26). The religionist spends his years serving Baal, never to the satisfying of his soul. He never has peace with Baal's pure justice, his loveless and merciless truth; he never knows the comfort of complete forgiveness that only the true, parental God will give, a God who will not dredge up the past (see Ezekiel 33:16). The great Physician and Counselor who wounds only to heal will never throw back at us the shameful past that we entrusted to Him. He despises it as much as we do. So we know that He is ready to help us overcome the past. He will deal with it faithfully with truth and grace. But, His enemy loves to dredge up our life. So, "choose you this day whom ye will serve" (Josh. 24:15).

Appendix A: Comments referred to from main text

A talebearer revealeth secrets: but Jesus who is of a faithful spirit concealeth the matter. (Adapted from Prov. 11:13, cf Lev. 19:16; Matt. 1:19; John 8:9-11).

The servant of Baal can never learn the trustworthiness of God's love that alone can expel sin from the heart, and bring it peace and rest. Thus, he cannot fall on the Stone and let his pride be broken beyond repair. Though He be not far from every one of us, the redemptive power of the Holy Spirit of God is never available to the worshiper of the one false god in the world, and his impatient and violent religion. "For, lo, I raise up the Chaldeans, that bitter and hasty nation" (Hab. 1:6). Self-sufficiency and self-propitiation, which are naturally occurring at birth, give Satan an effective advantage over them; but the loving, welcoming Spirit from Christ can quickly revive anyone's weakened faculty of humility and hope.

> And the spirit cried, and rent him sore, and came out of him: and…Jesus took him by the hand, and lifted him up; and he arose (Mark 9:26, 27).

> And great multitudes came unto him, having with them those that were lame, blind, dumb, maimed, and many others, and cast them down at Jesus' feet; and he healed them: …and they glorified the God of Israel (Matt. 15:30, 31).

> Then Jesus turned, and saw them following, and saith unto them, What seek ye? They said unto him, Rabbi, …where dwellest thou? He saith unto them, Come and see. They came and saw where he dwelt, and abode with him that day (John 1:38, 39).

Serving Jesus, the perfect Father-Friend who taught His disciples to have faith in His Father God, is what has transformed sinners into saints since the beginning; and it will do the same for all who come see Him today.

From page 84:

Ellen White, "My Conversion":

> In March, 1840, William Miller visited Portland, Maine, and gave his first course of lectures on the second coming of Christ. These lectures produced a great sensation, and the Christian church on Casco Street, occupied by Mr. Miller, was crowded day and night. No wild excitement attended these meetings, but a deep solemnity pervaded the minds of those who heard his discourses. Not only was there manifested a great interest in the city, but the country people flocked in day after day, bringing their lunch baskets, and remaining from morning until the close of the evening meeting.

> In company with my friends I attended these meetings and listened to the startling announcement that Christ was coming in 1843, only a few short years in the future. Mr. Miller traced down the prophecies with an exactness that struck conviction to the hearts of his hearers. He dwelt upon the prophetic periods, and brought many proofs to strengthen his position. Then his solemn and powerful appeals and admonitions to those who were unprepared, held the crowds as if spellbound.

> Special meetings were appointed where sinners might have an opportunity to seek their Saviour and prepare for the fearful events soon to take place. Terror and conviction spread through the entire city. Prayer meetings were established, and there was a general awakening among the various denominations, for they all felt more or less the influence that proceeded from the teaching of the near coming of Christ.

> When sinners were invited forward to the anxious seat, hundreds responded to the call, and I, among the rest, pressed through the crowd and took my place with the seekers. But there was in my heart a feeling that I could never become worthy to be called a child of God. A lack of confidence in myself, and a conviction that it would be impossible to make anyone understand my feelings, prevented me from seeking advice and aid from my Christian friends. Thus I wandered needlessly in darkness and despair, while they, not penetrating my reserve, were entirely ignorant of my true state.

> One evening my brother Robert and myself were returning home from a meeting where we had listened to a most impressive discourse on the approaching reign of Christ upon the earth, followed by an earnest and solemn appeal to Christians and sinners, urging them to prepare for the judgment and the coming of the Lord. My soul

had been stirred within me by what I had heard. And so deep was the sense of conviction in my heart, that I feared the Lord would not spare me to reach home.

These words kept ringing in my ears: "The great day of the Lord is at hand! Who shall be able to stand when He appeareth!" The language of my heart was: "Spare me, O Lord, through the night! Take me not away in my sins, pity me, save me!" For the first time I tried to explain my feelings to my brother Robert, who was two years older than myself; I told him that I dared not rest nor sleep until I knew that God had pardoned my sins.

My brother made no immediate reply, but the cause of his silence was soon apparent to me; he was weeping in sympathy with my distress. This encouraged me to confide in him still more, to tell him that I had coveted death in the days when life seemed so heavy a burden for me to bear; but now the thought that I might die in my present sinful state and be eternally lost, filled me with terror. I asked him if he thought God would spare my life through that one night, if I spent it agonizing in prayer to Him. He answered: "I think He will if you ask Him with faith, and I will pray for you and for myself. Ellen, we must never forget the words we have heard this night."

Arriving at home, I spent most of the long hours of darkness in prayer and tears. One reason that led me to conceal my feelings from my friends was the dread of hearing a word of discouragement. My hope was so small, and my faith so weak, that I feared if another took a similar view of my condition, it would plunge me into despair. Yet I longed for someone to tell me what I should do to be saved, what steps to take to meet my Saviour and give myself entirely up to the Lord. I regarded it a great thing to be a Christian, and felt that it required some peculiar effort on my part.

My mind remained in this condition for months. I had usually attended the Methodist meetings with my parents; but since becoming interested in the soon appearing of Christ, I had attended the meetings on Casco Street. The following summer my parents went to the Methodist camp meeting at Buxton, Maine, taking me with them. I was fully resolved to seek the Lord in earnest there, and obtain, if possible, the pardon of my sins. There was a great longing in my heart for the Christian's hope and the peace that comes of believing.

I was much encouraged while listening to a discourse from the words, I will "go in unto the king," "and if I perish, I perish." In his remarks the speaker referred to those who were wavering between hope and fear, longing to be saved from their sins and receive the pardoning love of Christ, yet held in doubt and bondage by timidity and fear of failure. He counseled such ones to surrender themselves to God, and venture upon His mercy without delay. They would find a gracious Saviour ready to present to them the scepter of mercy, even as Ahasuerus offered to Esther the signal of his favor. All that was required of the sinner, trembling in the presence of his Lord, was to put forth the hand of faith and touch the scepter of His grace. That touch ensured pardon and peace.

Those who were waiting to make themselves more worthy of divine favor before they venture to claim the promises of God, were making a fatal mistake. Jesus alone cleanses from sin; He only can forgive our transgressions. He has pledged Himself to listen to the petition and grant the prayer of those who come to Him in faith. Many had a vague idea that they must make some wonderful effort in order to gain the favor of God. But all self-dependence is vain. It is only by connecting with Jesus through faith that the sinner becomes a hopeful, believing child of God. These words comforted me and gave me a view of what I must do to be saved.

I now began to see my way more clearly, and the darkness began to pass away. I earnestly sought the pardon of my sins, and strove to give myself entirely to the Lord. But my mind was often in great distress because I did not experience the spiritual ecstasy that I considered would be the evidence of my acceptance with God, and I dared not believe myself converted without it. How much I needed instruction concerning the simplicity of it!

While bowed at the altar with others who were seeking the Lord, all the language of my heart was: "Help, Jesus, save me or I perish! I will never cease to entreat till my prayer is heard and my sins forgiven!" I felt my needy, helpless condition as never before. As I knelt and prayed, suddenly my burden left me, and my heart was light. At first a feeling of alarm came over me, and I tried to resume my load of distress. It seemed to me that I had no right to feel joyous and happy. But Jesus seemed very near to me; I felt able to come to Him with all my griefs, misfortunes, and trials, even as the needy ones came to Him for relief when He was upon earth. There was a surety in my heart that He understood my peculiar trials and sympathized with me. I can never forget this precious assurance of the pitying tenderness of Jesus toward one so unworthy of His notice. I learned more of the divine character of Christ in that short period when bowed among the praying ones than ever before. One of the mothers in Israel came to me and said: "Dear child, have you found Jesus?" I was about to answer, "Yes," when she exclaimed: "Indeed you have, His peace is with you, I see it in your face!" Again and again I said to myself: "Can this be religion? Am I not mistaken?" It seemed too much for me to claim, too exalted a privilege. Though too timid to openly confess it, I felt that the Saviour had blessed me and pardoned my sins.

Soon after this the meeting closed, and we started for home. My mind was full of the sermons, exhortations, and prayers we had heard. Everything in nature seemed changed. During the meeting, clouds and rain prevailed a greater part of the time, and my feelings had been in harmony with the weather. Now the sun shone bright and clear, and flooded the earth with light and warmth. The trees and grass were a fresher green, the sky a deeper blue. The earth seemed to smile under the peace of God. So the rays of the Sun of Righteousness had penetrated the clouds and darkness of my mind, and dispelled its gloom.

It seemed to me that everyone must be at peace with God and animated by His Spirit. Everything that my eyes rested upon seemed to have undergone a change. The trees were more beautiful and the birds sang more sweetly than ever before; they seemed to be praising the Creator in their songs. I did not care to talk, for fear this happiness might pass away, and I should lose the precious evidence of Jesus' love for me.

As we neared our home in Portland, we passed men at work upon the street. They were conversing with one another upon ordinary topics, but my ears were deaf to everything but the praise of God, and their words came to me as grateful thanks and glad hosannas. Turning to my mother, I said: "Why, these men are all praising God, and they haven't been to the camp meeting." I did not then understand why the tears gathered in my mother's eyes, and a tender smile lit up her face, as she listened to my simple words that recalled a similar experience of her own.

My mother was a lover of flowers and took much pleasure in cultivating them and thus making her home attractive and pleasant for her children. But our garden had never before looked so lovely to me as upon the day of our return. I recognized an expression of the love of Jesus in every shrub, bud, and flower. These things of beauty seemed to speak in mute language of the love of God.

There was a beautiful pink flower in the garden called the rose of Sharon. I remember approaching it and touching the delicate petals reverently; they seemed to possess a sacredness in my eyes. My heart overflowed with tenderness and love for these beautiful creations of God. I could see divine perfection in the flowers that adorned the earth. God tended them, and His all-seeing eye was upon them. He had made them and called them good. "Ah," thought I, "if He so loves and cares for the flowers that He has decked with beauty, how much more tenderly will He guard the children who are formed in His image." I repeated softly to myself: "I am a child of God, His loving care is around me. I will be obedient and in no way displease Him, but will praise His dear name and love Him always." My life appeared to me in a different light. The affliction that had darkened my childhood seemed to have been dealt me in mercy for my good, to turn my heart away from the world and its unsatisfying pleasures, and incline it toward the enduring attractions of heaven *Testimonies for the Church*, vol. 1, p. 14-19.

From page 89 and 159:

Both movements of Protestantism and Adventism are the last days "holy seed" (Isa. 6:13), the holy people spoken of in Daniel 12:7.

Both movements of Protestantism and Adventism are the last days "holy seed" (Isa. 6:13), the holy people spoken of in Daniel 12:7. As we said earlier, "The Protestant denominations and the Adventists come from the same spiritual, biblical stock; and we are beloved brethren". We are "the Israel of God" that "worship God in the spirit, and rejoice in Christ Jesus, and have no confidence in the flesh" (Gal. 6:16; Phil. 3:3). We believe that Christ died "once for all" (Heb. 10:10). We know we must "keep the commandments of God, and the faith of Jesus"; we know to have "circumcision…of the heart, in the spirit, and not in the letter; whose praise is not of men, but of God" (Rev. 14:12; Rom. 2:29). Our forefathers fled from Satan's papal persecutions (see Revelation 12:6, 14-17). Both of us hallow liberty. We are the people of the Book. Our Sunday schools and Sabbath schools mirror one another wherever the Bible is given authority and studied. And we both compose the group which will preach the gospel in the Latter Rain (see Jeremiah 31:1, 2; Isaiah 11:12-16; Acts 1:8). It is true that Adventist and Protestant doctrines do not agree on everything. Yet, still for many a love of the Bible exists, and minds are still open to the three angels' messages because the Spirit of God has access to them through His word. But, we both are also the Laodicean church awaiting their Lord, and "while the bridegroom tarried, they all slumbered and slept" (Matt. 25:5). Yet, although the holy seed "to whom the promise was made" (Gal. 3:19) lies dormant, the sixth trumpet "torment" and "killing" of the conscience has been guiding those who are sealed among both houses of the gospel to join together for the preservation of obedience to the commandments of God and the faith of Jesus.

Notwithstanding the widespread declension of faith and piety, there are true followers of Christ in *these churches* [emphasis mine]. Before the final visitation of God's judgments upon the earth there will be among *the people of the Lord* [emphasis mine] such a revival of primitive godliness as has not been witnessed since apostolic times. The Spirit and power of God will be poured out upon *His children* [emphasis mine]. At that time *many will separate themselves from those churches* [emphasis mine] in which the love of this world has supplanted love for God and His word. Many, both of *ministers* [emphasis mine] and people, will gladly accept those great truths which God has caused to be proclaimed at this time to prepare a people for the Lord's second coming *The Great Controversy*, p. 464.

According to the above quote, "the people of the Lord", who receive the revival of primitive godliness which will rival the apostolic church, are true followers of Christ still in the Sunday denominations. They and many of their pastors will come out of their churches and join the 144,000 of the Advent movement that will be preparing to battle for the heavenly Canaan land.

I saw that the holy Sabbath is, and will be, the separating wall between the true Israel of God and unbelievers; and that the Sabbath is the great question to *unite the hearts of God's dear, waiting saints.*

I saw that God had children who do not see and keep the Sabbath. They have not rejected the light upon it. [emphasis mine] And at the commencement of the time of trouble, we were filled with the Holy Ghost as we went forth and proclaimed the Sabbath more fully…. This enraged the churches and nominal Adventists,… as they could not refute the Sabbath truth. *And at this time God's chosen all saw clearly that we had the truth, and they came out and endured the persecution with us* [emphasis mine] *Early Writings*, p. 33.

God has children, many of them, in the Protestant churches, and a large number in the Catholic churches, who are more true to obey the light to the very best of their knowledge than a large number among Sabbathkeeping Adventists who do not walk in the light. The Lord will have the message of truth proclaimed, that Protestants may be warned and awakened to the true state of things and consider the worth of the privileges of religious freedom which they have long enjoyed.

This land has been the home of the oppressed, the witness for liberty of conscience, and the great center of Scriptural light. God has sent messengers who have studied their Bibles to find what is truth, and studied the movements of those who are acting their part in fulfilling prophecy in bringing about the religious amendment which is making void the law of God and thus giving ascendancy to the man of sin. And shall no voice be raised of direct warning to arouse the churches to their danger? Shall we let things drift, and let Satan have the victory without a protest? God forbid *The Ellen G. White 1888 Materials*, p. 377.

As we compared in the main text, today the many denominations of Protestantism equate to the many nations within the northern kingdom of ancient Israel. And Adventism equates to the southern kingdom of Judah, which had the sanctuary, the Sabbath, the Spirit of Prophecy, the truth on the state of the dead, et cetera. Protestantism and Adventism are together likened to "both the houses of Israel" (Isa. 8:14, cf Jer. 30:3), respectively. Just as the northern kingdom was taken away first and lost from sacred history, so has Protestantism departed from the Law of God and, *as an institution*, disappeared from the final work of Christ before His return. During the antitypical Day of Atonement, when they would more than ever need the Law of God for the necessary affliction of their souls (see Leviticus 16:29, 31; 23:27, 32), the Sunday denominations cooperated with Satan to abrogate the Law from their religion and from the Protestant conscience. Therefore, the Lord has said to Protestant America,

Hear ye indeed, but understand not; and see ye indeed, but perceive not. Make the heart of this people fat, and make their ears heavy, and shut their eyes; lest they see with their eyes, and hear with their ears, and understand with their heart, and convert, and be healed. Then said I, Lord, how long? And he answered, Until the cities be wasted without inhabitant, and the houses without man, and the land be utterly desolate, and the LORD have removed men far away, and there be a great forsaking in the midst of the land (Isa. 6:9-12).

Yet in it shall be a tenth, and it shall return, and shall be eaten: as a teil tree, and as an oak, whose substance is in them, when they cast their leaves: so the holy seed shall be the substance thereof (Isa. 6:13).

The remnant shall return, even the remnant of Jacob, unto the mighty God (Isa. 10:21-27, cf Isa. 48:17-23).

In those days the house of Judah shall walk with the house of Israel, and they shall come together out of the land of the north to the land that I have given for an inheritance unto your fathers (Jer. 3:18).

And I will make thee exceeding fruitful, and I will make nations of thee, and kings shall come out of thee. And I will establish my covenant between me and thee and thy seed after thee in their generations for an everlasting covenant, to be a God unto thee, and to thy seed after thee (Gen. 17:6, 7).

The above verses gave the Jews hope for the northern kingdom's apostasy, a long apostasy which was due to their following Jeroboam away from Jehovah's true religion (see 1 Kings 12:26-29; Daniel 9:11). The northern kingdom had already, for centuries, stayed on the fringe of consecration and divided their heart's service between Jehovah and the commerce of the Fertile Crescent, and the Fertile Crescent gods. So, through Jeroboam the Lord gave them opportunity to leave His Father and Himself for Baal and Ashtoreth; and the ten tribes quickly apostatized. One temptation by Jeroboam and they were all for the abusive and enabling religion, and the licentious, atheistic, and spiritualistic form of worship.

Likewise, the denominations of Protestantism had become alarmingly distant from the spirit of the Reformation by the time Protestant America fought its first holy war to win its independence from Catholic Europe. The American Protestants had already become greatly influenced by Jesuit corrupted Europe, its deism, its love of fashion, and its humanism, instead of being influenced by their God's simple, understandable, relational, and holy Bible. Living for this world had displaced the American Protestants' need for the God of the earlier

Reformers, putting the Protestants on Satan's enchanted ground. When the denominations later rejected the light of the biblical second coming of Christ and the fourth commandment, and then took hold of the idea that the Law of God lost its authority at the cross, they then accepted the same spiritualistic and empty religion of emotion as had the ten northern tribes of Israel (see Deuteronomy 29:18, 19; Jeremiah 6:14; 2:13). This mistake by the Protestants has led to a gradual searing of the Protestant conscience before the "law of God" (Rom. 8:7, cf Rom. 7:22, 25; 3:31), and a blinding of their understanding to the new covenant requirements, promises, and provisions.

The "weakness and unprofitableness" (Heb. 7:18, cf 8:7, 8) of the old covenant was due to the more limited knowledge of God's love seen by the typical animal sacrifices, which resulted in Israel's lesser ability to comprehend the love of God and thus His purely faith-based salvation (see Hebrews 3:19-4:11; 8:8). Therefore, Israel's more limited relationship with their Redeemer limited His power through the old covenant to overcome their guilt and the power of sin as compared to His greater power to overcome their sin which He had in the new (see 2 Corinthians 3:10, 11).

Until the Messiah should personally come, the old covenant was flawed only by its lesser ability to reveal the Messiah through lambs and kids, bullocks and heifers, and the imperfect priesthood (see Hebrews 7:11-28). These flaws were that of circumstance, for they must wait for Messiah who could not appear until the correct time, according to Daniel's chapter 9 prophecy.

Yet, having said this, *the knowledge of Jesus held by the believers of today is woefully inferior to that of the 500 first generation Jews who followed Christ and saw Him off at His ascension.* The sealing of the first church was an indomitable force behind the Great Commission. The Caesars and kings of the earth could not stand before those first generation Christians' sweep across the Empire, and beyond. The Early Rain was unstoppable. And the Latter Rain will be greater. But, how? How are the final generation of the holy people going to personally know the Anointed One better than the disciples knew Him? By an equally intimate walk with Him. It has to be by doing what they did: trust building as they get better and better acquainted with Him walking and talking with Him, working together with Him in His Father's business; desperate, repentant faith growing as they go with Him through our own gross darkness by a total subjugation of global evil. The science of righteousness by faith by Jesus *in a greater measure than the first church learned it* must be the preparation for receiving the Latter Rain of His Spirit, the greatest refreshing from the presence of the Lord.

The Lamb of God brings a "better" salvation (see Hebrews 7:19; 10:1-4; 11:40) because everyone who "seeth the Son" as a perfectly secure, loving "tender plant", "and believeth on him" (John 6:40; Isa. 53:2) through His Spirit (see Romans 8:9; John 14:18-21), sees much more love and purity and innocence than the Old Testament people could see in the literal spotless, innocent lambs. Moreover, the four successive pagan empires, of Babylon, Persia, Greece, and especially of Rome, further blinded both groups of Jews and Gentiles from the vision of a loving Messiah, driving them into their respective forms of spiritualism (see Isaiah 8:22; Malachi 2:11-13, 17; 3:5; Galatians 4:8-10). Therefore, the greater spirituality from the new covenant, more than from the old, allowed the Lord to rely more upon grace and less upon judgment to correct His people's failings (see Exodus 23:20-22; 2 Corinthians 3:7-9). The new abundance of God's grace upon the church came because His New Testament Israel had "received of the LORD's hand double for all her sins" (Isa. 40:2). By no means, however, is the new covenant free of the disciplining aspect of the Lord's work for the goal of exalting His people and glorifying His name before the world (for example Matthew 16:23; Luke 14:24; 19:27; Acts 5:1-11; Revelation 2:21-23; 3:16-19; Mark 6:45; 2 Corinthians 7:8-12; Jude 23; Hebrews 2:1-3; 4:1; 6:4-6, 8; 10:38).

The old covenant thus was limited in its full gift of the Spirit. The last Jews of the pre-Christian, inter-testamental era who could accept the better salvation that came with Messiah were those who had lived under the double effects of the last of His punishing Gentile empires and God's convicting Law, especially when John the Baptist began to preach it again. And the Lord's old covenant warning that He would humble uncircumcised hearts, to help them repent and to receive His pardon, is still His requirement in order for His last day holy people, Protestantism, to receive the benefits of the better covenant with God (see Leviticus 26:41; Revelation 3:14-19). The everlasting covenant and the everlasting gospel have had the same everlasting requirement for returning to God (see Romans 7:9-25; Galatians 3:23, 24). And that humbling requirement for the denominations, of course, includes Protestantism's Remnant Adventists. "All scripture is…profitable for doctrine" (2 Tim. 3:16). By "all scripture" Paul was referring to the whole Old Testament as God's authority for purifying His New Testament church.

All the mainline denominations and their remnant denomination of Adventism need to accept the easier road of wrestling with the Law of God, for it gives our Friend and Shield better opportunity for Him to gradually take shape in our minds and hearts. Otherwise, we must take the long, hard road of consequence for not wrestling with the Law. Either road ends with the inevitable humbling. No one is exempt from God's scourging, especially those who desperately want to be a son of God (see Hebrews 12:6-11). The Bible is clear, "The scripture hath concluded *all* under sin" (Gal. 3:22), and our God is no respecter of persons. For all the children of Adam, "sin is the transgression of the law" (1 John 3:4). "Now we know that what things soever the law saith, it saith to them who are under the law: that *every* mouth may be stopped, and all the world may become guilty before God" (Rom. 3:19). But, once we surrender to conviction from the authoritative, humbling righteousness of God and cry for His help, He immediately gives us overcoming faith and then His blessing of forgiveness and peace, by His justification through the promised "Spirit of His Son" (Gal. 4:6).

"Before faith came, we were kept under the law, shut up unto the faith which should afterwards be revealed. Wherefore the law was our schoolmaster to bring us unto Christ, that we might be justified by faith" (Gal. 3:23, 24). This statement from Paul is not simply a Jewish history lesson that would mean nothing to us in our twenty-first century world. It's a principle that the humbling has always been and always would be required until Jesus comes to change our vile bodies. Galatians 3:23, 24 says that Jehovah uses His Law and prophets to keep us bound to Him, anchored to a Rock, lest we slip away into the prevailing astral planes and come under hopeless bondage to lawless spiritualism. Will we be convicted by God, corrected, reproved, condemned, shamed and made to accept His punishment for our iniquities? "That every mouth may be stopped, and *all the world* may become guilty before God" (Rom. 3:19) means that even the very spiritual Kings David and Solomon needed the humbling and guilt whenever they would depart from Jesus. It also means that the best Christian pastor, priest, bishop, cardinal, pope, all stand guilty before the Most High. We all need the Law's conviction of Christ's gracious power to overcome our sins. He is the good Shepherd; and we are only the sheep of His pasture.

"Which of you convinceth me of sin?" (John 8:46) is a statement that no one but Christ can make. In order to be subjects of the kingdom of God, Jesus makes us "subject to the law of God" (Rom. 8:7). Only a God of love would require us to be subjects of His Law that is "perfect", and "holy, and just, and good" (Ps. 19:7; Rom. 7:12). And only a kingdom that is perfectly holy, just, and good can endure forever and ever, without end.

The Lord has "concluded [*sugkleiō*, shut up] all under sin" (Gal. 3:22, cf Isa. 8:16; 59:2; Rom. 3:9, 10; 8:20), an accusation which brings our fallen nature great offense and misery. Yet, Jesus has merciful purposes for those who will surrender to His humiliating program of the conviction that His righteousness towers over theirs. He takes captivity captive through the condemnation of His Law so that He can give His rich gifts to those who will fully trust in Him, and even graciously to those who don't yet fully trust (see Psalm 68:18; Romans 9:15, 16; John 1:16; Isaiah 61:3).

Thus, no Protestant or Adventist today has the right to justification and peace with God who will not first come to the blinding light of the perfect, holy, just, and good Law of God (see Psalm 19:7; Romans 7:12), and wrestle with its convicting and pointed requirements (see Romans 7:14-24; Hebrews 4:12). Whether secular unchurched Protestant or religious churched Protestant, all have a duty to bow their pride before the strong tone of the Law's demands. Salvation and heavenly comfort are available to all; and none have gone too far from God to regain His acceptance through Jesus. But all must first look "into the perfect law of liberty, and [continue] therein…being not a forgetful hearer, but a doer of the work" (Jas. 1:25). This very effort, which we saw with Paul in Romans 7:9-11, will call out the rebellion lurking in every Protestant and Adventist heart. Our offended pride will be aroused against God's commanding Law (and Jesus' testimony through prophets) until we become conscious of our natural rebellion, as the commandments did for Paul in Romans 7:13.

The Spirit of God thus notifies us that we aren't yet the good citizens of His kingdom that we thought we were; and that very notification will bring on our wrestling. Genuine faith then comes from our close in, hand to hand combat with our convicting Intercessor. But, once the clinching is over and our tears are shed, then our will submits to His. It is a submission that only Christ could bring us to, and not we ourselves. Our soul yields to righteousness (see Romans 6:14, 16); our heart surrenders to the Law (see Romans 8:7). Jesus wins the bout and we win a new heart, and a blessing from the God of our salvation. "That the promise…might be given to them that believe" (Gal. 3:22, cf Eze. 36:26). His pardon comes, evidenced by His Father's promised Spirit (see Galatians 3:14; Matthew 3:16, 17; John 3:34). Real faith comes only from wrestling with the Lamb who suffered under the eternal fires prepared for our damnation. That wrestling faith has the strength to grasp the pardon from His Father. Out of His belly flows rivers of His living Spirit and we are born a new person, the child of His long angst and His multiplied sorrows.

Now, our disposition toward "*the* Law" (Rom. 8:3, cf Gal. 3:23) is acceptable because it has become "*thy* Law" (Ps. 119:97). Now, our continuing in the Law through the liberty from the Spirit of Christ results in true obedience (see Romans 8:4). "Said Jesus to those Jews which believed on him, If ye continue in my word, then are ye my disciples indeed; and ye shall know the truth, and the truth shall make you free" (John 8:31). Thus, our doing His commandments that we have come to "yield" (Rom. 6:16) to and to "delight in" (Rom. 7:22), ends in "converting the soul" (Ps. 19:7). The heavenly gift of yielding and surrender to the Law results in our "obedience unto righteousness" (Rom. 6:16) that Paul sought for the church. The Spirit of life in Christ Jesus has delivered us from the rulership of our flesh. Jesus has showed Himself strong in behalf of those whose heart became perfect toward Him through the wrestling. Our obedience to our new Lord is natural and happy. "Blessed are they that do his commandments" (Rev. 22:14, cf 2 Pet. 1:8).

The richest gift, His promised Spirit, is the fruit of a previous gift — genuine repentance, a repentance which only comes out of a traumatized conscience from the Law's threatening rebukes. God's Spirit comes to us when we "cry day and night unto him" (Luke 18:8) for help with the "chastisement of our peace" (Isa. 53:5) until He can show us that His Son, our Helper, has been through the same in Gethsemane. Then He can give us repentance and pardon, the long-sought fountain of youth. "The promise by faith of Jesus Christ" (Gal. 3:22) is also called the "holy Spirit of promise" (Eph. 1:13) — the evident token of God's acceptance that only comes by our seeing Jesus' open love toward us in life and in a death under the wages of our sins. This Spirit of holy obedience comes by our surrender to the Law of God and to the "the body of Christ" (Rom. 7:4) on His cross. We witnessed wave after wave of His agony in the garden, His strong cries and tears growing more and more fervent, but never receiving His Father's approbation and relief from the Father's chastisement of His peace. "God left him, to try him" (2 Chron. 32:31), until He sank into a hopeless, eternal death, baptized in the burning anger of God due us for our traitorous rebellion. The glory shining from Jesus' anguished face under the wrath of His damnation gives us power to love God's Law and to obey it (see Romans 6:7, 11-13).

Strong faith, which has accepted His punishment for our iniquities, though still stinging and tender, is humbled and worthy, resting and thankful. Ministering His sacrifice from the sanctuary above, the Mother of all living has coached us through our own Gethsemane, and Christ is born in us today. We are saved in His childbearing (see 1 Timothy 2:15; Jeremiah 30:7). Like our Lord we come back up from the baptism of fire as He arose from the dead by the Spirit of His Father (see Romans 8:11). As He had been at His baptism, the Mother of all living has begotten His Spirit in us. The Law He loves we now love and every sin He hates we hate. Kindness, which is the Law of His mouth, becomes the law of our mouth. God has ruled over us and accomplished His warfare. Our new desire to our Father and the subsiding of His constant, soul-wracking chastisement of our peace has brought us power to obey Him. Once reconciled with God and His Law of righteousness, and Jesus has put our bedeviled evil conscience at rest and peace, we are happily indebted to our heavenly Deliverer-Intercessor to keep all of His Law (see Romans 6:2-6, 13-16; Joshua 1:7). Our new sense of happy obligation to His Law through His Son makes God just to justify us and to reinstate us into His kingdom, giving to us "of his Spirit" (1 John 4:13).

Our surrender to the Law's condemnation of sin is crucial for true justification and liberty in the Spirit, even as the good Shepherd's rod is perfect, converting the soul, rejoicing the heart, and enlightening the eyes. The real blessings in our sanctification come in time from the Spirit of God, and we must patiently wait on Him and cooperate with Him. "For it is God which worketh in you both to will and to do of his good pleasure" (Phil. 2:13, cf John 3:21).

"Now I say, That the heir, as long as he is a child, differeth nothing from a servant, though he be lord of all; but is under tutors and governors until the time appointed of the father" (Gal. 4:1, 2). Not until the heir to any throne has mastered the whole curriculum of state matters and royal etiquette, and takes an oath to keep in line with his training, does the king allow him to rule under him. Likewise, not until we "have done the will of

God", obedient to His Law and gospel (see Psalm 40:8; Hebrews 10:7), do we "receive the promise" (Heb. 10:36), "the promise of the Spirit" (Gal. 3:14).

Not until we have wrestled with God's high standard, and surrendered to its valid jurisdiction over us, do we receive atonement from Jesus who "ever liveth to make intercession for" us (Heb. 7:25). "This man, after he had offered one sacrifice for sins for ever, sat down on the right hand of God" (Heb. 10:12), and out of His belly flowed rivers of His living Spirit. When we have submitted to the heavy hand of God through His Law, then we experience the blessing from God through His Spirit, "Thou art my beloved son, in whom I am well pleased", "I will be merciful to their unrighteousness, and their sins and their iniquities will I remember no more" (Heb. 8:12). "The worshipers once purged…have…no more conscience of sins" (Heb. 10:2, cf Rom. 3:25). Those promises are the "hope we have as an anchor of the soul, both sure and stedfast" (Heb. 6:19), "redemption through his blood, even the forgiveness of sins" (Col. 1:14), "whereof the Holy Ghost also is a witness to us" (Heb. 10:15). "This is the covenant that I will make with them after those days, saith the Lord, I will put my laws into their hearts, and in their minds will I write them; and their sins and iniquities will I remember no more. Now where remission of these is, there is no more offering for sin" (Heb. 10:16-18). The Godhead's death atones for our past grievous rebellion and it settles our hearts into the only real obedience, so "that the righteousness of the law might be fulfilled in us, who walk not after the flesh, but after the Spirit" (Rom. 8:4).

Those needy souls who submit to the Law and grace of God *are the "mighty and the holy people"* (Dan. 8:25); they are the hardy "sons of God" (John 1:12). As He had done to His Only-begotten from everlasting, God will never spoil His children, and neither will He abuse them. But His love is always full of mercy and justice upon His chosen out of the world. "Like as a father pitieth his children, so the LORD pitieth them that fear him" (Ps. 103:13). "As arrows are in the hand of a mighty man", "they shall speak with the enemies in the gate" (Ps. 127:4, 5). Happy is the Lamb whose quiver is full of them. When the Mother of all living has children made innocent and bold by the Law and grace of His Father, then they will delight to do His will. He will have cleansed and sealed His 144,000 house.

"By the which *will* we are sanctified through the offering of the body of Jesus Christ once for all" (Heb. 10:10). How are we sanctified? By what power does the miraculous victory over sin take place? By the combined will of God and the One who just prior to this said, "Lo, I come…to do thy will, O God" (Heb. 10:7). God sanctifies us by His powerful will, like a law harnessing our mind and combating the law of sin. This is "sanctification of the Spirit" (1Pet. 1:2, cf 2 Thess. 2:13). And what is God's will? His will revealed is His doctrine, His truth, His word (see John 7:17; 17:17), His commandments, His testimonies, His precepts, His teachings, His Law (see Psalm 119:97-104). But, God's will is also Jesus' will. "I delight to do thy will, O my God: yea, thy law is within my heart" (Ps. 40:8, cf Rev. 22:14). When we behold Jesus offering Himself to take our damnation, and that He also loved God's will, then our attachment to Him gives us a new disposition toward God's will, His Law. The New Testament covenant was what David had, which was the delightful power given David from knowing that he was loved by God. That allowed David to delightfully obey the Law of God and it allowed God to fight David's battles for him. The Father's love is what the Son of David had on an infinitely greater scale than David, which constrained Him to go so far as to give up His eternal existence so that we could have it.

By being born from the Mother of all living, we will have His delight to do our Father's will. And delighting to do God's Law is about denying self, suffering for Christ's sake, dying to self and yet living. "For even hereunto were ye called: because Christ also suffered for us, leaving us an example, that ye should follow his steps" (1 Pet. 2:21, cf 1 Pet. 4:1 Phil. 1:29; Gal. 2:20). It is the Law of God that we are to follow, as depicted in the example and words of Jesus. Jesus was the Law of God incarnate, the living, walking, breathing Cornerstone (see 1 Peter 2:4-8; Daniel 2:34; 1 Corinthians 3:11), the focus of the heavenly kingdom (see Daniel 2:45, 34, 35). Jesus was the very embodiment of His Father's character, the fullness of the Godhead bodily (see Matthew 21:42, 44; Hebrews 1:3; Col. 2:9). He was the Lawgiver from between God's knees (see Genesis 48:10; John 1:18), the Law of God's mouth from the beginning (see John 1:1; Proverbs 8:23, 30). Once He has humbled His people and written His Law into their melted hearts and moldable minds, then they are sealed and perfectly happy to obey His word, His will, His Testimonies, His Law (see Isaiah 64:1, 4; Revelation 14:1). When we know Jesus obedience becomes our greatest delight.

If we consent, He will so identify Himself with our thoughts and aims, so blend our hearts and minds into conformity to His will, that when obeying Him we shall be but carrying out our own impulses. The will, refined and sanctified, will find its highest delight in doing His service. When we know God as it is our privilege to know Him, our life will be a life of continual obedience. Through an appreciation of the character of Christ, through communion with God, sin will become hateful to us *The Desire of Ages*, p. 668.

The immediate privilege from the new covenant is the cleansing of the conscience, so that it is peaceful and secure in the Father's acceptance. The heart has obtained a new honesty to continually re-assess itself and it no longer has need to feign love to God. The conscience is then subject to the Law and yet free from the abusive accusations and taunts of the evil, old master. "Having an high priest over the house of God; let us draw near with a true heart in full assurance of faith, having our hearts sprinkled from an evil conscience, and our bodies washed with pure water" (Heb. 10:21, 22, cf 1 Tim. 1:5; 1 Pet. 3:16).

Reconciliation with His Law was the vision which the Lord showed Zechariah for projecting to Israel what He wanted to do for them all, especially in the New Testament.

> And he shewed me Joshua the high priest standing before the angel of the LORD, and Satan standing at his right hand to resist him.
>
> And the LORD said unto Satan, The LORD rebuke thee, O Satan; even the LORD that hath chosen Jerusalem rebuke thee: is not this a brand plucked out of the fire?
>
> Now Joshua was clothed with filthy garments, and stood before the angel.
>
> And he answered and spake unto those that stood before him, saying, Take away the filthy garments from him. And unto him he said, Behold, I have caused thine iniquity to pass from thee, and I will clothe thee with change of raiment.
>
> And I said, Let them set a fair mitre upon his head. So they set a fair mitre upon his head, and clothed him with garments. And the angel of the LORD stood by....
>
> Hear now, O Joshua the high priest, thou, and thy fellows that sit before thee: for they are men wondered at: for, behold, I will bring forth my servant the BRANCH.
>
> For behold the stone that I have laid before Joshua; upon one stone shall be seven eyes: behold, I will engrave the graving thereof, saith the LORD of hosts, and I will remove the iniquity of that land in one day.
>
> In that day, saith the LORD of hosts, shall ye call every man his neighbour under the vine and under the fig tree (Zech. 3:1-5, 8-10).

But, after justifying Joshua, what was the next word spoken by the Lord?

> And the angel of the LORD *protested* unto Joshua, saying, Thus saith the LORD of hosts; *If* thou wilt walk in my ways, and *if* thou wilt keep my charge, *then* thou shalt also judge my house, and shalt also keep my courts, and I will give thee places to walk among these that stand by (Zech. 3:6, 7).

In the new covenant, the Lord's requirement of obedience following conversion and justification was no different than what He has always required.

> For, brethren I will hear what God the LORD will speak: for he will speak peace unto his people, and to his saints: but let them not turn again to folly (Ps. 85:8).
>
> For, brethren, ye have been called unto liberty; only use not liberty for an occasion to the flesh, but by love serve one another (Gal. 5:13).
>
> The LORD appeared to Solomon the second time, as he had appeared unto him at Gibeon.
>
> And the LORD said unto him, I have heard thy prayer and thy supplication, that thou hast made before me: I have hallowed this house, which thou hast built, to put my name there for ever; and mine eyes and mine heart shall be there perpetually.
>
> And *if* thou wilt walk before me, as David thy father walked, in integrity of heart, and in uprightness, to do according to all that I have commanded thee, and wilt keep my statutes and my judgments:

Appendix A: Comments referred to from main text

Then I will establish the throne of thy kingdom upon Israel for ever, as I promised to David thy father, saying, There shall not fail thee a man upon the throne of Israel.

But if ye shall at all turn from following me, ye or your children, and will not keep my commandments and my statutes which I have set before you, but go and serve other gods, and worship them:

Then will I cut off Israel out of the land which I have given them; and this house, which I have hallowed for my name, will I cast out of my sight; and Israel shall be a proverb and a byword among all people:

And at this house, which is high, every one that passeth by it shall be astonished, and shall hiss; and they shall say, Why hath the LORD done thus unto this land, and to this house?

And they shall answer, Because they forsook the LORD their God, who brought forth their fathers out of the land of Egypt, and have taken hold upon other gods, and have worshipped them, and served them: therefore hath the LORD brought upon them all this evil (1 Ki. 9:2-9).

By His wisdom, our God of love has always balanced His health-giving justification with reiterating our obligations to Him. All His benefits to us deserve our eternal service to our gracious King. "Afterward Jesus findeth him in the temple, and said unto him, Behold, thou art made whole: sin no more, lest a worse thing come unto thee" (John 5:14). Even though they are balanced with grace, does the Lord give empty warnings? The greater the grace, the greater the obligation to serve "the law of God" (Rom. 7:25, cf 8:7). "Jesus said unto her, Neither do I condemn thee: go, and sin no more" (John 8:11). Therefore, when He blesses us with rest by the removal of a well-worn conscience, this blessing, which brings every other good thing in its wake, automatically obligates us and empowers us to greater service and to a happy, natural obedience to God's Law. To say that after forgiveness and conversion God requires no further humiliation of the conscience by the reproofs of His Law is to accept the greatest presumption and deception invented for mankind, which comes to the world just before Jesus returns (see 2 Samuel 12:7-9; Matthew 16:23; Galatians 2:11; Hebrews 12:7, 8).

That great deception, by the falsehood that the Law of God and His divine condemnation are forever done away with at the cross, lays the foundation for the "strong delusion, that they should believe a lie" (2 Thess. 2:11), which the Lord would send and which He is already sending through Spiritual Formation and its praying to Ashtoreth. It is essentially the age-old papal indulgences that formed the basis for Luther's 95 theses. 2 Timothy 4 verses 2 and 3 agree with this perfectly. The New Testament condemns the idea that we can come to the throne of grace while having evaded the Law's demands and all fear before its condemnation. And now, a newer falsehood called "hyper-grace": that God will not only forgive past sins today, but also give remission of all *future* sins today. That last clause must be wrongly based upon Hebrews 10:10, 12, 14, and 18. Paul was clear that God only gives "remission of sins *that are past*" (Rom. 3:25) because repentance includes the sorrow for and renunciation of sins committed. There is no such thing as renunciation of or sorrow for future sins, and therefore no forgiveness for future sinning.

No better setup than "hyper-grace" can be devised by the arch-deceiver for creating a world deluded and without a conscience. By accepting this error a religious world of unreconciled sinners is damning itself, never again able to wrestle with God by His Law. The sixth trumpet locusts will have finalized their work of destruction. There can be no fear of God under this regime. Humanity, freed from the strivings by the Spirit of God, will live without a knowledge of God's Law. It will be as though they are delivered from all moral accountability, like a whole race of lobotomy patients, the epitome of Judges 18:7 and the fulfillment of Revelation 18:7.

Of Jesus the prophecy said, "He will magnify the law, and make it honourable" (Isa. 42:21), while of Satan another prophecy declared, "The [vile] king shall do according to his will; and he shall exalt himself, and magnify himself above every god, and shall speak marvellous things against the God of gods" (Dan. 11:36). "He shall cause craft [deceit, guile] to prosper in his hand" (Dan. 8:25). The modern freedom from the Law of God simulates the pope's Mass and his indulgences. Because of these pagan custom substitutes, biblical truth is not spoken to the people. Without Christ's convicting truth and love, they cannot receive faith in His power to forgive. Instead, they rely only on a human intercessor.

Thus saith the LORD; Cursed be the man that trusteth in man, and maketh flesh his arm, and whose heart departeth from the LORD (Jer. 17:5).

Therefore, they receive none of Christ's power to bow their will before Him and to receive His Spirit of holiness, the power of the Highest for victory over sin.

He shall be like the heath in the desert, and shall not see when good cometh; but shall inhabit the parched places in the wilderness, in a salt land and not inhabited (Vs. 6).

False church tradition leaves the people feeling good without ever recognizing a Lawgiver offended at their sins. And therefore this unscriptural tradition leaves them unable to hear Him, and He them (see Matthew 15:9; John 8:43; Proverbs 28:9). They may believe that they serve and worship Jesus. But, their blessing from the promised Spirit is imaginary (see Deuteronomy 29:18, 19). They rather worship and serve an unbiblical Jesus, one that does not exist and has never existed (see Deuteronomy 32:17; Psalm 106:37). This explains why people during the Dark Ages could receive the spirit of Cain and Nimrod, being convinced to hunt down and kill everyone who told them that they couldn't find God's forgiveness through absolution of the Mass (see Genesis 10:8-10). The Mass has been simply a mesmerizing of the receivers' minds to accept forgiveness without any conviction from a "hard saying" (John 6:60) through the tough, strong love of God to their soul. Loving rebuke is not an institution of Lucifer's economy, as seen in the Mass and in Spiritual Formation. Spiritual formation having put asunder Protestantism which alone can contest the lawless god of this world, Lucifer will finally succeed to expunge conviction from humanity. The result will be global confusion, anarchy, and satanic possession — "perdition" (Rev. 17:8, 11, cf 2 Pet. 3:7; 2 Thess. 2:3).

Such a state of society will possess Protestant America, not only through the Mass, but worse, through Spiritual Formation, which all the denominations are currently welcoming with open arms. But, "the kisses of an enemy are deceitful" (Prov. 27:6). This metaphor stands opposed to the blessed counterpart of the proverb, "Faithful are the wounds of a friend" (Prov. 27:6). From a true friend we should expect the wounding by correction, and even censure; but never from a cunning enemy who is bent on our destruction. Spiritual Formation is the most deceptive Trojan horse, that is coaxing its devotees into evil habits through the destruction of the conscience. It ends with the destruction of the soul and of all social order (see Jeremiah 23:13, 14; Numbers 25:4-9). Our indolence to wrestle with the strong language of the Lord Jesus is leaving all the denominations wide open to spiritualism. When we know how fundamentally opposite in character unreproving Spiritual Formation and celebration worship are to Ellen White's reproving admonitions, then we will ask, Who is the friend? Is our friend the spiritual guide who trains us in Spiritual Formation which allows us to walk right into "God's" presence without the great need for a converting propitiator in Jesus? Or, is our friend the preacher who ministers to us the tough sounding Bible and Spirit of Prophecy that lovingly grind on our pride and our fallen nature until we receive the strong need for an Intercessor? Will we with Paul in Romans 7:9-12 accept the decimation of our pride, and conclude that the tough humbling is holy and just and good? Is a friend that preacher, that after uplifting the Law of God then preaches Jesus, whose Spirit then brings us humbled, but trusting, into God's presence to touch His scepter, and if we perish, we perish? When we look closely at this unreproving Spiritual Formation and celebration worship to the original Reformation and Advent movements, which one of the two spirits represents an enemy? When we compare Spiritual Formation and celebration worship with Paul's coming to terms with the Law's exceeding condemnation and ultimately finding the Saviour, sucking honey from the stone, which of the two agrees with the word of God? Which gives fraudulent salvation, Spiritual Formation and celebration worship, or the harsh sounding Bible and Spirit of Prophecy?

They have healed also the hurt of the daughter of my people slightly, saying, Peace, peace; when there is no peace (Jer. 6:14).

Her prophets are light and treacherous persons: her priests have polluted the sanctuary, they have done violence to the law (Zeph. 3:4).

Let the heathen be wakened, and come up to the valley of Jehoshaphat: for there will I sit to judge all the heathen round about. Put ye in the sickle, for the harvest is ripe: come, get you down; for the press is full, the fats overflow; for their wickedness is great. Multitudes, multitudes in the valley of decision: for the day of the LORD is near in the valley of decision (Joel 3:12-14).

Appendix A: Comments referred to from main text

The multitudes in Joel's day were sunken in Ashtoreth communication and celebration, oblivious to the punishment clearly warning against it in the Law of Moses. A jealous Jehovah was already preparing His chastising "northern army" (Joel 2:20) for judgment because His nation and their cousin nations were drinking the "cruel venom of asps" (Deut. 32:33) that came from the gods of Babylon. And at the end of probation His people will be drinking the same wine of Babylon, which has a "wrath" (Rev. 14:10) like no drunkard has ever felt. "They shall have no rest day nor night" (Rev. 14:11). It will be satanic panic. "And another angel came out from the altar, which had power over fire; and cried with a loud cry to him that had the sharp sickle, saying, Thrust in thy sharp sickle, and gather the clusters of the vine of the earth; for her grapes are fully ripe. And the angel thrust in his sickle into the earth, and gathered the vine of the earth, and cast it into the great winepress of the wrath of God. And the winepress was trodden without the city, and blood [rejection by God toward unrepented of and unpardoned guilt and sin] came out of the winepress, even unto the horse bridles, by the space of a thousand and six hundred furlongs" (Rev. 14:18-20, cf Isa. 51:21).

> Because, even because they have seduced my people, saying, Peace; and there was no peace; and one built up a wall, and, lo, others daubed it with untempered mortar.... To wit, the prophets of Israel which prophesy concerning Jerusalem, and which see visions of peace for her, and there is no peace, saith the Lord GOD (Eze. 13:10, 16).

> They have chosen their own ways, and their soul delighteth in their abominations. I also will choose their delusions, and will bring their fears upon them; because when I called, none did answer; when I spake, they did not hear: but they did evil before mine eyes, and chose that in which I delighted not (Isa. 66:3, 4).

> I have seen that some, who have been deceived, and led into this error, would be brought out into the light of truth, but it would be almost impossible for them to get entirely rid of the deceptive power of spiritualism. Such should make thorough work in confessing their errors, and leaving them forever.

> I recommend to you, dear reader, the word of God as the rule of your faith and practice. By that Word we are to be judged. God has, in that Word, promised to give visions in the "last days;" not for a new rule of faith, but for the comfort of his people, and to correct those who err from bible truth *A Sketch of the Christian Experience and Views of Ellen G. White*, p. 64.

Jesus... not being seen throughout the Bible... will end with the pendulum swinging to the opposite extreme of apostasy... Jesus in "visions" through Spiritual Formation

Self-made obedience, because God's Law no longer humbles proud natures and Jesus is not being seen throughout the Bible, has been and is currently driving the church into disillusionment and apathy. And, continued departure from the Law of God and from the picture of Jesus in the Bible will end with the pendulum swinging to the opposite extreme of apostasy. "Those who err from bible truth", departing from "the Law and…the testimony" (Isa. 8:20), will finally believe they see Jesus in "visions" through Spiritual Formation, "for a new rule of faith" *Ibid.*. The Law of God and the Spirit of Prophecy which is the Testimony of Jesus, are the Tree of life where Jesus will meet with His children (see Proverbs 3:13-18, 21-24; 6:20-24). Any other spiritual source for meeting God is a forbidden tree. Such a tree allows the worshiper to retain his natural soul temple constantly polluted with the knowledge of evil, rather than the true worship of the holy God which humbles and cleanses the filthy worshiper by the light of the Law's standard of perfection. The humbling permits the soul to enter into God's presence with a repentance gifted from His approved Propitiator. Then he can stand clothed in the purity of his Intercessor's righteousness with clean hands and a pure heart.

Samuel's warning should suffice us.

> Turn ye not aside: for then should ye go after vain things, which cannot profit nor deliver; for they are vain.

> For the LORD will not forsake his people for his great name's sake: because it hath pleased the LORD to make you his people.

Moreover as for me, God forbid that I should sin against the LORD in ceasing to pray for you: but I will teach you the good and the right way:

Only fear the LORD, and serve him in truth with all your heart: for consider how great things he hath done for you.

But if ye shall still do wickedly, ye shall be consumed, both ye and your king (1 Sam. 12:21-25).

All who imbibe the enemy doctrine of Spiritual Formation will not be able to break free from it once the woe of God's displeasure weighs heavily on a world in rebellion, especially after their unlikelihood to believe that all the apparent basking under the smiles of divinity could actually have been their confiding with devils. Psalm 103:13 tells us that love for God with a reverent fear of our Father is what constrains Him to have mercy on us. Reverent love to God "is from above" and "is first pure" (Jas. 3:17). But, proud, irreverent Spiritual Formation is unable to receive God's reproving condemnation of sin, and therefore "descendeth not from above, but is earthly, sensual, devilish" (Jas. 3:15).

> I have seen the results of these fanciful views of God, in apostasy, spiritualism, freelovism. The free love tendencies of these teachings were so concealed that it was difficult to present them in their real character...
>
> There is a strain of spiritualism coming in among our people, and it will undermine the faith of those who give place to it, leading them to give heed to seducing spirits, and doctrines of devils.--Letter 230, 1903, pp. 1, 3, 5. (To Dr. E. J. Waggoner, October 2, 1903.) *Manuscript Release*, vol. 8, p. 304.

The above statement speaks of a worship that looks like love toward God yet circumvents His testimonies; and the author compares it to spiritualism. It is a seductive strain of spiritualism that is very difficult to discern, but leads to accepting the doctrines of devils.

As spiritualism more closely imitates the nominal Christianity of the day, it has greater power to deceive and ensnare. Satan himself is converted, after the modern order of things. He will appear in the character of an angel of light. Through the agency of spiritualism, miracles will be wrought, the sick will be healed, and many undeniable wonders will be performed. And as the spirits will profess faith in the Bible, and manifest respect for the institutions of the church, their work will be accepted as a manifestation of divine power *The Great Controversy*, p. 588.

Those who cannot deny the condemnations of God's Law, who with regrets and remorse still strive to see Jesus and the many tokens of His approbation, will have the fullness of the new covenant. "I will put my laws into their hearts, and in their minds will I write them; and their sins and iniquities will I remember no more. Now where remission of these is, there is no more offering for sin" (Heb. 10:16-18). And that beautiful promise was for the Hebrews after they would accept the six hundred year punishment for their iniquities and their uncircumcised hearts would be finally humbled (see Leviticus 26:41). Today, this blessedness comes to "Jews", "Gentiles", and "unto the uttermost part of the earth" (Acts 1:8) — meaning that it comes to the humbled sabbatarian and the humbled Protestant parishioner, to the humbled unaffiliated Protestants, and to all the humbled converts from the world religions. The humbling from the Law and the crucifixion are mandatory to receive God's blessing. "And it shall come to pass, that whosoever shall call on the name of the Lord shall be saved" (Acts 2:21).

Will we be *thoroughly* accomplished in this experience before we must pass through the big one, when we "see every man with his hands on his loins, as a woman in travail, and all faces are turned into paleness? Alas! for that day is great, so that none is like it: it is even the time of Jacob's trouble; but he shall be saved out of it" (Jer. 30:6, 7). Will this sealing conversion and faith be found in us "when the Son of man cometh" (Luke 18:8)? "Who may abide the day of His coming?" (Mal. 3:2). Will He find in us a faith perfectly surrendered to the righteousness of God? True conversion and genuine faith in the church are even now caving to their final erosion by the spreading abomination of the strongest delusion ever — Baalpeor prostitution through celebration and Spiritual Formation.

All who wrestle with the strong language of the Law survive the strong delusion that God is permitting through lawless Spiritual Formation. Only *those who wrestle with God's Law until they find Christ in the Law* are fortified to endure the increasing birth pangs of the coming trouble. Only they suck "honey out of the rock, and oil out of the flinty rock" (Deut. 32:13). They must endure Jesus leaving His Father's sanctuary to deliver His people, at which time without a Mediator they will bear up under the condemnation of a holy and avenging God. This they can do only because they previously strove before Messiah the Prince under the blistering light of His Father's holy Law, and received the need of a Saviour from sin. Only they receive the blessed salvation from the Lord and His righteousness (see Psalm 24:5). "It is a faithful saying: For if we be dead with him, we shall also live with him: if we suffer, we shall also reign with him" (2 Tim. 2:11, 12). Only those in the last conflict who have suffered with Jesus, "their features, marked with severe internal anguish", will know the experience of the new covenant. "Their features, marked with severe internal anguish, now shone with the light and glory of heaven. They had obtained the victory, and it called forth from them the deepest gratitude and holy, sacred joy" *Early Writings*, p. 270.

"These are they which came out of great tribulation, and have washed their robes, and made them white in the blood of the Lamb" (Rev. 7:14). "*Therefore* are they before the throne of God, and serve him day and night in his temple: and he that sitteth on the throne shall dwell among them" (Rev. 7:15). While everyone else on earth celebrated a presumed salvation, these were struggling under the purifying, perfecting eye of God seen in the unvarnished truth of the Bible and the Spirit of Prophecy. They alone, who wrestled with the condemning righteousness of God, seeking His acceptance and love, are then worthy to be sealed by His Spirit. Therefore, because they submitted to the Testimony of Jesus through His messenger Ellen G. White, the Protestants and Adventists in the Latter Rain — better than even the apostles — will have super-added peace with God, even as a knowledge of God's Law and grace will be more abundant than that of the Early Rain. And their "horror of great darkness" (Gen. 15:12, cf Isa. 60:2) will be greater than that of Abraham when Jesus leaves His exonerated God, speeding from a far country to deliver His people. In proportion to their dark experience will be the greater magnitude of their glory, in which they will be "enlightened" and "made partakers of the Holy Ghost"; they will drink deeply "of the heavenly gift", "the good word of God, and the powers of the world to come" (Heb. 6:4, 5).

> As it is written, Eye hath not seen, nor ear heard, neither have entered into the heart of man, the things which God hath prepared for them that love him (1 Cor. 2:9).

> It shall come to pass, that whosoever shall call on the name of the LORD shall be delivered: for in mount Zion and in Jerusalem shall be deliverance, as the LORD hath said, and in the remnant whom the LORD shall call (Joel 2:32).

Protestantism and Adventism need to reconcile, rejoin forces, and work together for evangelizing the world. We need a renewed revival of the liberties in the gospel along with the high standard and reproof of the Bible, the first of which came through the Reformation movement, and the second of which came through the Advent movement. Neither freedom in the Spirit nor obedience to the Law is bondage. We need to see that both are compatible and have coexisted in the everlasting gospel all along. The uniting of Protestant and Advent forces must be done upon the Reformation's foundation of justification by faith, Sola Scriptura, and priesthood of believers, and under the sabbatarian Adventism's sanctification by faith and its umbrella of distinctive, biblical present truth. There can be no sanctification or right doing without justification and peace with the God of Law.

> Blessed are they that do his commandments, that they may have right to the tree of life, and may enter in through the gates into the city (Rev. 22:14).

Christ will finish what He began many times in the past. During this investigative judgment many Protestants have joined the Advent movement individually, and will continue to join and take part in the 144,000 Remnant of the Latter Rain (see Isaiah 11:13, 14). The Protestant-Adventist 144,000 will be witnesses of Christ in the Law first to the Adventists, and then to the Protestants, the Catholic peoples, and unto the uttermost religions and cultures of the world.

Like a father living for the sole purpose of supporting and raising his children, Paul wrote to the Gentile believers, "All things are yours; whether Paul, or Apollos, or Cephas, or the world, or life, or death, or things present, or things to come; all are yours" (1 Cor. 3:21, 22). This was the work in the Early Rain; and it will be the work in the Latter Rain. Once our reconciliation is done and settled, then the 144,000 can be fatherly missionary support for the Catholic world of genuine searchers for heaven's blessing of sins forgiven. Then the Adventist-Protestant 144,000 offensive drive will continue unto the uttermost part of the earth, as it was in the apostolic church (see Revelation 6:2). The Protestant-Adventist 144,000 will support and train up the world church in the way they should go, so that when the day of Jesus arrives, they will not run away like the spiritualized, careless, and wicked world wholly deluded by Spiritual Formation. All earthly support will be removed from the Adventist-Protestant 144,000, but their few needs will be supplied by the temporal blessings of God upon those in the world who they are leading to the true God and to His science of salvation. The 144,000 will provide spiritual blessings to the nations weakened by sin. They will "give unto them beauty for ashes, the oil of joy for mourning, the garment of praise for the spirit of heaviness; that they might be called trees of righteousness, the planting of the LORD, that he might be glorified" (Isa. 61:3). The promise will be seen again, "Ye shall be named the Priests of the LORD: men shall call you the Ministers of our God: ye shall eat the riches of the Gentiles, and in their glory shall ye boast yourselves" (Isa. 61:6).

From page 105:

Protestant America, as the new military force of the Papacy, can only be perceived in light of the Bible and the real facts of 9/11.

The prophecies of Daniel declare that the great enemy of God is one who breaks its foes covertly, by subterfuge, stealth, and intrigue until it has such control that it can make its moves overtly. Deception and enchantment are its key tactics, using faith and religion as a cloak to hide its nefarious destruction of freedom, a work of destroying without anyone's knowledge that they are being destroyed. It begins with the ruin of truth and faith; but, it ends with mind control, with warfare against the freedom of conscience, and lastly with legislated and militant occupation. Thus, with exception of those who have put their faith in God, none have the capability to overthrow His enemy's perfected spiritualistic road to enslavement.

Using the Strong's concordance number H4581, we learn that this earthly power serves a god "of forces^{H4581}" (Dan. 11:38).

> But in his estate shall he honour the God of forces: and a god whom his fathers knew not shall he honour with gold, and silver, and with precious stones, and pleasant things (Dan. 11:38).

But, H4581 can also be translated "strongholds". [H4581 *mâ'ôz* From H5810 "to be stout, harden, impudent, prevail, strengthen (self), be strong"; a fortified place; figuratively a defence:--force, fort (-ress), rock, strength (-en), (X most) strong (hold).] Therefore, "god of forces" can also mean "god of strongholds". This interpretation agrees with Daniel's *next verse* in which he elaborates on this "vile" king in verse 38, reiterating with H4581: "Thus shall he do in the most *strong holds*^{H4581} with a strange god, whom he shall acknowledge and increase with glory: and he shall cause them to rule over many, and shall divide the land for gain" (Dan. 11:39). The stronghold of this son of perdition is ancient spiritualism.

For the apostate adversary from the book of Daniel that would "destroy wonderfully" (Dan. 8:24) Paul coined the term, "the mystery of iniquity" (2 Thess. 2:7). Paul had clear understanding of Daniel's prophecies (see 2 Thessalonians 2:4; Daniel 11:36, 37, 45). Paul's useage of "temple of God" (2 Thess. 2:4), in which the son of perdition makes his throne, is the heavenly sanctuary (see Hebrews 8:1, 2) which Lucifer aspired to take for his own (see Isaiah 14:13, 14; Daniel 8:11). But, Paul also wrote of the Lord's temple as His home in the tabernacle of His children (see 1 Corinthians 3:16; 6:16-20; 2 Corinthians 5:1-5; 6:16); and he alluded to the heart as the mercy seat upon which His cloud sits (see Romans 5:5). This sealing salvation from our Creator is under relentless warfare by Satan, who desires the human heart to be his seat, with his lawlessness sealed within it. The same vile King of the North who would exalt the god of forces (god of strongholds) and divide the people in order to dominate them, like leaven (see Matthew 16:6) would start small and peaceable before overthrowing not only earth, but also heaven.

> And in his estate shall stand up a vile person, to whom they shall not give the honour of the kingdom: but he shall come in peaceably, and obtain the kingdom by flatteries. And with the arms of a flood shall they be overflown from before him, and shall be broken; yea, also the prince of the covenant (Dan. 11:21, 22).

> And through his policy also he shall cause craft to prosper in his hand; and he shall magnify himself in his heart, and by peace shall destroy many: he shall also stand up against the Prince of princes (Dan. 8:25).

Appendix A: Comments referred to from main text

Thus shall he do in the most strong holds with a strange god, whom he shall acknowledge and increase with glory: and he shall cause them to rule over many, and shall divide the land for gain (Dan. 11:39).

Satan's movements to gain entrance have always been subtle; hence the label, "*mystery* of iniquity". The papacy lays more than a physical serfdom, but also a spiritual enslavement and bondage that the Lord always sought to destroy by His covenant and Law of liberty. By the earnest of His Spirit, He empowers His children with creativity, love of accomplishment, and freedom. It's the silent, craftily laid movements of the ancient serpent wearing a permanent plastic smile that could create the strongholds that Daniel sees in vision. The holy vestments have always made the mystery of iniquity invisible to human investigation and impervious to the governments' resistance to it. The real battles on earth have been spiritual. Looking for the spiritual battle between heaven and hell over the human soul is the only way to understand Bible prophecy; and no other paradigm can most clearly comprehend the movements affecting the world today. Most people use political/economic/military eyes to interpret current news and even Bible prophecies. Laodicean Protestant Americans have lost their spiritual discernment, and thus they are blind to the spiritual forces actuating world events.

Paul gives us the key to understanding the self-exalted northern king's strongholds.

> (For the weapons of our warfare are not carnal, but mighty through God to the pulling down of *strong holds*;) casting down imaginations, and every high thing that exalteth itself against the knowledge of God, and bringing into captivity every thought to the obedience of Christ; and having in a readiness to revenge all disobedience, when your obedience is fulfilled (2 Cor. 10:4-6).

The strongholds for evil from Daniel's prophecies are spiritual, more than they are military. In this scene of Daniel's vision, "the most *strong holds*[H4581] with a strange god" (Dan. 11:39), H4581 was introduced and stood opposed to the "sanctuary of strength", the heavenly Stronghold of the Lord. *The vile king's stronghold is the adversarial substitute for the gospel* seen in the theme repeated all through Daniel and Revelation. Every stronghold that Jesus put into the gospel, which could cast down everything that exalts itself against the knowledge of the great Creator, "holy and reverend is his name" alone (Ps. 111:9), this vile power supplanted with the strongholds of the occult. The vile king is the Roman Papacy. "And arms shall stand on his part [the vile King of the North], and they shall pollute the *sanctuary*[H4720] of *strength*[H4581], and shall take away the daily sacrifice [self crucified with Christ's crucifixion], and they shall place the abomination that maketh desolate" (Dan. 11:31, cf Dan. 8:11-13). The strongholds are the deep mysteries of Babylon, where lawlessness and spiritualism and disinformation about the character of God bind up the body, mind, and soul. These stronghold adversarial substitutes of the heavenly sanctuary's true power for good have been the worship of Christianized Baal and Ashtoreth in Catholicism, or Jesuit Spiritual Exercises, and which today is called, Spiritual Formation. Such disinformation concerning God through the demon voices from Spiritual Formation feed the seeker for peace. Those spirit voices have caused the exponentially multiplying locusts from the stronghold of Satan to do his bidding to destroy every trace of God's truth in the earth, even killing millions of the holy people from the Counter-Reformation to this day. The deep mysteries of "MYSTERY, BABYLON" (Rev. 17:5) arise most fully from Spiritual Formation, the most direct access and most efficient means that satanic forces have to control the minds of their captives. With the strong hopes to be forgiven and accepted by a supernatural mediator, the followers of Spiritual Formation open their hearts to a spirit that the scriptures do not authorize, even if it sounds friendly and comforting.

This mysterious spiritualistic power "shall destroy wonderfully, and shall prosper, and practice ["craft[H4820]" (vs. 25), "deceit, treachery"], and shall destroy the mighty and the holy people." "And his power shall be mighty, but not by his own power" (Dan. 8:24), for "the dragon gave him his power, and his seat, and great authority" (Rev. 13:2). The dragon, who is "called the Devil, and Satan" (Rev. 12:9), and who imbues this earthly power, feels no compunction against forcing his slaves to comply with his evil will, as exemplified in his using an extreme interpretation upon the unintended meaning of Christ's parable as referred to below.

> How demoralizing the influence of the monastic hysteria was may be seen in the transformation wrought in Augustine (354-430 AD). This renowned writer of the church (probably of all Catholic Fathers, the most adored by the

Papacy) was forced by the popular pressure into the views of Jerome, and was in correspondence with him. His complete surrender to the policy of persecution is given at length by Limborch. Augustine, from his episcopal throne in north Africa, gave to the Papacy a deadly weapon; he invented the monstrous doctrine of *"Compel them to come in."* [emphasis mine] Thus he laid the foundation for the Inquisition. Intoxicated with Greek philosophy, he cried out that its spirit filled his soul with incredible fire. He had wandered nine long years in Manichaeism, which taught the union of church and state and exalted the observance of the first day of the week. Augustine found many reasons why the doctrines and practices of the church should be enforced by the sword. The doctrine "Compel them to come in," sent millions to death for no greater crime than refusing to believe in the forms of ecclesiastical worship enforced by the state *Truth triumphant*, p. 73.

The dragon's favorite earthly agency cannot use love to draw the sinner because Satan has no love to provide. The absence of the drawing power of love leaves a dead, platonic church that starves for stimulation. A carnal, lawless religion becomes the church's new, preferred alternative to bring in adherents. This, however, garners only those who receive the mark in their forehead, as they join his ranks willingly and dive headlong into his spiritualism. But, we know in the end that "all the world" will wonder "after the beast" (Rev. 13:3). Therefore, the liberal folks who hate religion, and many of whom will receive his mark figuratively in their right hand, must also be brought under the power of the Church by some other way.

In order to compel the rebel multitudes who refuse religious mind control Satan quickly reverts to his ages-old, intense, violent, military action and the fearful threats of Inquisition by a gestapo regime. With twisted intentions to convert souls, the "Company of Jesus," for almost half a millennium, has consigned multitudes to imprisonment, torture, and death. Thus, John looked on in astonishment when he saw this power "full of names of blasphemy, …drunken with the blood of the saints, and with the blood of the martyrs of Jesus" (Rev. 7:3, 6). "And upon her forehead was a name written, MYSTERY, BABYLON THE GREAT, THE MOTHER OF HARLOTS AND ABOMINATIONS OF THE EARTH" (Rev. 17:5).

Because seduction and force is all that MYSTERY, BABYLON knows, her Jesuits have ingeniously moved today's liberal generation to be indignant toward all religion. The mercenary soldiers of "Jesus" have led many Americans to despise *especially* the Protestantism of their forefathers' who died to give them the Constitution of self-government and the inalienable freedoms that they enjoy. Today, the Jesuits have designed their final thrust against Protestant America by turning all Americans against Protestantism and the only true God. Then, the churched Protestants who accept Rome's charismatic Evangelicalism will ultimately be sufficiently deluded by the new, insidious, spiritual stronghold of Spiritual Formation, and Christian America will "speak like the dragon" (see Revelation 13:11). Through Sunday legislation the spiritualized Evangelical churches of America will declare war on all who stubbornly resist their invitation of peace. "An host was given him against the daily sacrifice by reason of transgression" (Dan. 8:12). By covert Inquisition, they will force the "impenitent" to worship with them. History will repeat, "The doctrine 'Compel them to come in,' sent millions to death for no greater crime than refusing to believe in the forms of ecclesiastical worship enforced by the state" *Truth triumphant*, p. 73.

> Now the true spirit of the papacy was revealed. Said the Romish leader: "If you will not receive brethren who bring you peace, you shall receive enemies who will bring you war. If you will not unite with us in showing the Saxons the way of life, you shall receive from them the stroke of death." — J. H. Merle D'Aubigne, *History of the Reformation of the Sixteenth Century*, b. 17, ch. 2. These were no idle threats. War, intrigue, and deception were employed against these witnesses for a Bible faith, until the churches of Britain were destroyed, or forced to submit to the authority of the pope *The Great Controversy*, p. 62.

Despite her recent, warm appeals to the Pentecostal Protestant community, the Church of Rome has never repented and renounced her wicked spirit to "compel" (Luke 14:23) by fear or death. Thus, she is due to repeat the past horrors. Nevertheless, those who will "be strong" will evangelize and "do exploits" (Dan. 11:32) into the evil kingdom of terror and tribulation. The mighty and holy people will know Jesus; they will constantly see Jesus by His Spirit of life in the Law of God. A greater than Samson will be in their hearts, and the greatness of His gentleness will make them great. "God is our refuge and strength, a very present help in trouble. Therefore will not we fear" (Ps. 46:1, 2). The constraint of love will drive the last gospel preaching.

> In the work of redemption there is no compulsion. No external force is employed. Under the influence of the Spirit of God, man is left free to choose whom he will serve *The Desire of Ages*, p. 466.

Understanding the Holy Writ correctly, seeing the justice and mercy blend of God through His Bible gives peace and goodness to His disciples. The only divine compulsion is the stronghold of love. The love of Christ constrains His disciples and everyone who receives their gospel; and divine love compels others to come in (see 2 Corinthians 5:14). They have a bond that no union of religion and state power can break, though the whole world be joined hand in hand against them.

From page 107:

From *Webster's Third New International Dictionary* definition of *vatic* we understand that the word *Vatican* relates back to the most ancient prophesying and occult practices:

> vat·ic \ 'vad·ik\ adj [L *vates* seer, prophet + E – ic; akin to OIr *fáith* seer, poet, OE *wōth* voice, song, poetry, *wōd* mad, raging, OHG *wuot* frenzy, madness, ON *ōthr*, n., song, poetry, *ōthr*, adj., frantic, mad, Goth *woths* possessed] : of, relating to, or characteristic of a prophet : prophetical, oracular

From page 108:

The New Encyclopaedia Britannica, Volume 6 *Micropaedia*, page 541, article, *Jesuit drama*, below, informs of the Jesuit extensive and effective efforts to reeducate the Protestant populace. We see the highly influential use of polished entertainment and theater as the medium to win the unsanctified heart and reclaim Protestants for Catholicism, first in Europe, then in America, and finally around the world. Today, don't we see the electronic transmissions of their medieval counterpart in the modern movies and sitcoms, the news and sports telecasts, perfected over 450 years, and especially so in the past half century of exponentially developing improvements?

> Jesuit drama, program of theatre developed for educational and propagandist purposes in the colleges of the Society of Jesus during the 16th, 17th, and 18th centuries. Cultivated as a medium for disseminating Roman Catholic doctrine, drama flourished in the Jesuit schools for over 200 years, evolving from modest student exercises to elaborate productions that often rivaled the contemporary public stage in polish and technical skill.
>
> The earliest recorded performance of a Jesuit play was in 1551, at the newly founded Collegio Mamertino at Messina, in Sicily. In less than 20 years, plays were being performed at more than a dozen of the new Jesuit colleges springing up in cities across the continent, including Rome, Seville, Cordoba, Innsbruck, Munich, and Vienna. By the mid-17th century there were nearly 300 Jesuit colleges in Europe, and in almost every one at least one play was given each year.
>
> Originally plays were to be pious in nature, expressing true religious and moral doctrines; they were to be acted in Latin, decorously, and with little elaboration; and no female characters or costumes were to appear. All these rules were relaxed or revised as Jesuit drama evolved. Favourite subjects came from biblical histories, the lives of saints and martyrs, and incidents in the life of Christ, but Jesuit playwrights also drew upon material from pagan mythology, ancient history, and contemporary events, all reinterpreted in terms of Catholic doctrine. Dramas were frequently performed in the national languages or with vernacular prologues that explained the Latin text. Jesuit plays became increasingly elaborate, and their stagecraft kept pace with all the newest technical developments of European theatre.
>
> Music was an important element in most of the plays, ranging from simple songs to works that called for a large orchestra and chorus. The elaborate musical productions of Austria and southern Germany reflected the influence of Italian

opera as well as the long tradition of music in the church. The colleges of France even included ballet in their performances.

The extravagance and luxury of many of the Jesuit productions came under heavy attack. Many of the productions were enormously expensive, and it was charged that students in some colleges did little more than prepare and perform plays. Opponents of the Jesuit order seized upon such charges and made them part of the wave of anti-Jesuit feeling that grew in the mid-18th century. Dramatic performances were prohibited or limited in many areas, and they ceased altogether in 1773, when the Society of Jesus was temporarily suppressed.

From page 120:

Because he hath set his love upon me, therefore will I deliver him: I will set him on high, because he hath known my name (Ps. 91:14).

Righteousness by faith is all about setting our love upon Jesus, a work that we are incapable of producing. Only the Father collaborating with His Son can work that love into us. All we can do is come to Their work. Jesus must reveal Himself through His Father's Law; and the Father oversees the revelation of His Son to us. We must go to that perfect Law of liberty, and look for Jesus there. If we know Jesus today, as can be our great privilege, He will let us sit in heavenly places with Him today. But, the first step in setting us on high is for Jesus to make us stumble and fall through His Father's Law (see Galatians 3:23). This is the bad news that precedes the good news. The gospel of righteousness comes from the power of faith in the grace of Christ by the previous condemnation of God against sin through His Law.

Behold, this child is set for the fall and rising again of many in Israel…that the thoughts of many hearts may be revealed (Luke 2:34, 35).

Whosoever shall fall on this stone shall be broken (Matt. 21:44).

Behold, I lay in Sion a chief corner stone, elect, precious:… And a stone of stumbling, and a rock of offence (1 Pet. 2:6, 8).

He that believeth on him shall not be confounded (1 Pet. 2:6).

We have a big, immovable Cornerstone upon which we must fall. As His Father's representative, Christ is a Prince; He is the Lawgiver and Head of Law enforcement. As our Judge and cornerstone, Jesus will not break or budge; *we* must budge and break — an impossible work for sinners to accomplish. We need to be broken beyond any hope of our repairing ourselves, and then He will bind us up. Whoever chooses to thus lose himself will find himself. As His Father's designated intercessor, Jesus is our Saviour and merciful Messiah and Advocate, our great Physician who never lost a case. He must break us down before He can remake us in His image. Our stumbling Stone is set for the fall and rising again of many within Protestantism. But, whoever bypasses this humbling fall and surrendering up of control to the Creator and Redeemer's will, and seeks to find his peace some other way, will lose eternal life. God considers him a trespasser, a thief and a robber. "Whosoever will save his life shall lose it: and whosoever will lose his life for my sake shall find it" (Matt. 16:25).

However, many have already been humbled by the Law and horrified by their sinfulness, as Paul described in Romans 7:8-24. For some, guilt drives them almost to insanity, as with Martin Luther. For others the consequences sink them into depression; and for others the shame and hopelessness have led them deeper into their miserable lifestyle. But, be of good cheer; only the people who knew they were really bad came to Jesus. Feeling like a "bad" person is the normal reaction to holiness in those who our Lord is calling to be His disciple.

> *They that be whole need not a physician, but they that are sick…. I am not come to call the righteous, but sinners to repentance* (Matt. 9:12, 13).

In fear and trembling, they stand as genuine sinners before the King of righteousness. They duplicate the experience of Daniel and Paul. "Therefore I was left alone, and saw this great vision, and there remained no strength in me: for my comeliness was turned in me into corruption, and I retained no strength" (Dan. 10:8). "I was alive without the law once: but when the commandment came, sin revived, and I died" (Rom. 7:9). "O wretched man that I am! who shall deliver me from the body of this death? I thank God through Jesus Christ our Lord" (Rom. 7:24, 25). While the bad people tremble before His Spirit of truth, they hear a word from the heavenly agencies. "O Daniel, a man greatly beloved, understand the words that I speak unto thee, and stand upright: for unto thee am I now sent" (Dan. 10:11).

They cooperate with Jesus by standing before His piercing testimony until their sins have become exceedingly sinful. Then, these bad ones receive the Romans 7:25 experience — the cross raised, to have reason and conscience connect with the motionless "body of Christ" (Rom. 7:4), the world's truest friend. The Messiah personified the Law by constantly giving His life to win them to His Father. He says to them, "I will very gladly spend and be spent for you; though the more abundantly I love you, the less I be loved" (2 Cor. 12:15). They must catch a glimpse of the tenderness and peace that filled Jesus' heart, and which never once left Him (see Isaiah 53:2); and only guilty, shamed, and hopeless ones have the drive for this vision. Then from the sanctuary, the stumbling Stone will perform the miracle of working His Father's Spirit into their thinking (see Revelation 5:6; Hebrews 8:10). He will give them His peace by bringing them to surrender to His Father's holy Law and then to His proven mercy. "He that believeth on him shall not be confounded" (1 Pet. 2:6).

> He that putteth his trust in me shall possess the land, and shall inherit my holy mountain (Isa. 57:13).

The Bible details the worst cases of a hopeless past, who have been reconciled with God and their hearts remade into His likeness. The former idolaters of Corinth set the new precedence for the sinner's hope in Christ.

> Neither fornicators, nor idolaters, nor adulterers, nor effeminate, nor abusers of themselves with mankind, nor thieves, nor covetous, nor drunkards, nor revilers, nor extortioners, shall inherit the kingdom of God. And such were some of you: but ye are washed, but ye are sanctified, but ye are justified in the name of the Lord Jesus, and by the Spirit of our God (1 Cor. 6:9-11).

Those who the Law has humbled receive full surrender by being driven to Jesus, after studying Him, thoroughly searching out the Law and the grace which Christ displays in Himself. Every page of the Volume was written of Him. We can also find Him in the book of nature, by our experiences in life, and by working with our hands in honest enterprises. We further develop our vision of Jesus by serving with Him; that is, helping others to have confidence in His promises, by undoing their heavy burdens, and letting the oppressed go free. No more perfect environment for receiving the vision of Jesus will come through the future captivity. Gradually, Jesus washes away our self-centeredness and makes service to others enjoyable. Only thus can His Spirit lead us to abandon our angry fighting from hearts naturally filled with scorpion poison (see Ephesians 2:3; Romans 3:13, 14; 2 Peter 1:5-8).

As the Spirit helps us *see* Jesus throughout the Holy Writ, then will our "light break forth as the morning" (Isa. 58:8). His righteousness will appear wonderful to us. Hope will spring up and the possibilities of righteousness will be great; it will be doable. Therefore, *we must see Jesus*.

> This is the will of Him that sent Me, that every one which seeth the Son, and believeth on Him, may have everlasting life (John 6:40).

> We would see Jesus (John 12:21).

> He saith unto them, Come and see. They came and saw where he dwelt, and abode with him that day (John 1:39).

> O taste and see that the LORD is good: blessed is the man that trusteth in him (Ps. 34:8).

> Search the scriptures; …they are they which testify of me (John 5:39).

The New Testament Gospels didn't touch on every beautiful snapshot into Christ's life because He was directing us to the Old Testament for those snapshots. They all testified of Him. Jesus taught us that we can see Him by piecing together the collage of Himself which, through the power of His divine nature, those Bible individuals bore out in their lives and words. *We see Him through them*; for they testify of Him. Teenager Rebecca's happy exertion to help and give water to others described the ever youthful heart of Jesus, the Servant of servants (see Genesis 24:18-28, 58). Go there and drink in all her inner beauty; it testified of Him. Drink in the Master, and the water of life that He offers to everyone reading His Book.

David's love of obedient worship, his beholding Jesus' face by faith (see Psalm 16:8, 11; 23:6), and giving Him thankful praise for His goodness as "the sweet psalmist of Israel" (2 Sam. 23:1) showed us Jesus, the Son of David (see Psalm 63; Matthew 26:30). "Often He expressed the gladness of His heart by singing psalms and heavenly songs. Often the dwellers in Nazareth heard His voice raised in praise and thanksgiving to God" *The Desire of Ages*, p. 73. The close, innocent fellowship between David and Jonathan (see 1 Samuel 18:1-4) speaks volumes of the sensitivity in the heart of Christ for everyone He ever met — and that includes you and me as we watch Him. He has met us in His word through His Spirit. He has called us to the Bible. From His Father's throne His heart has resonated with ours as we loved what we saw in Him there.

The rich, young ruler gives us a backward look to the pure, innocent, brotherly love between David and Jonathan when Jesus first met the princely candidate of discipleship. "Jesus beholding him loved him" (Mark 10:21). It was a perfect millennium throwback to the scene with Jonathan and David, (meaning, "the beloved"). Believing it to be the last time they might see each other, "David arose out of a place toward the south, and fell on his face to the ground, and bowed himself three times: and they kissed one another, and wept one with another, until David exceeded" (1 Sam. 20:41). "Jesus beholding him loved him." Jesus' heart was knit with the ruler who became humbled by the children and mothers crowding Him. But, Jesus' heart was also thrust into the grave when the desperate ruler suddenly remembered a closer friend than Him. The ruler was so close, but did not enter the kingdom.

We can say that we see Jesus treating rich Zacchaeus the same as He did to that 20-something born into wealth. Jesus stopped the procession directly under the little man in the tree, and looked up at Zacchaeus who was desperate to "see Jesus who he was" (Luke 19:3). "Jesus beholding him loved him." And Christ's acceptance thrilled Zacchaeus to no end. Now Zacchaeus was willing to do the same that Jesus had asked of the young ruler — release his death grip on his wealth. Jesus, beholding the world, so loved the world; and that's an understatement. Why else would He die for our second birth? Why else would 5,000 men, together with their families, suffer to hear Him preach? When we see Jesus' loving-kindness toward them, our hungry faith grasps that He is loving and kind to us, too. Under His care we have a joy which the world can't take away. Our response will be Jonathan's. "Jonathan Saul's son delighted much in David" (1 Sam. 19:2). "The soul of Jonathan was knit with the soul of David, and Jonathan loved him as his own soul" (1 Sam. 18:1). And the love of Christ will knit our soul with His, by His love and His righteousness.

Moses' intercession and love for a hard-hearted people who hated him, describes our heavenly High Priest (see Exodus 14:11-13; 15:24, 25; 16:1-3, 8; 17:1-4; 31:18; 32:5, 6, 11-14, 30-32; Numbers 11:1-3; 12:1, 9-13; 14:1-5, 10, 11-20; 16:1-5, 41-48; 20:1-11). But, Christ's steadfast obedience was like Moses', except infinitely greater (see Deuteronomy 18:18; Numbers 12:7; Hebrews 3:1-3). We see Jesus in Elisha. Before healing and converting Naaman, Elisha prefigured the great Physician by his initial humbling, and then by his later gracious treatment toward Naaman. Thus Naaman, with a new heart "joined unto the Lord", in "one spirit" (1Cor. 6:17) with the Lord God of Israel, and no longer having any attraction to idolatry, he could be of service at a pagan temple as a missionary to his beloved master (see 2 Kings 5:10-19, cf Isaiah 11:4, 5). Elisha there showed us the wisdom and the Holy Spirit power of our generous Lord and Lawgiver, Jesus.

Christ is the central focus of the Bible, from its beginning to its end. This has made Satan furious enough to destroy or discredit the Bible in every way.

Solomon's depth of understanding foreshadowed the Master Teacher and the revival that sprung up around Him. "He spake three thousand proverbs: and his songs were a thousand and five. And he spake of trees, from the cedar tree that is in Lebanon even unto the hyssop that springeth out of the wall: he spake also of beasts, and of fowl, and of creeping things, and of fishes. And there came of all people to hear the wisdom of Solomon, from all kings of the earth, which had heard of his wisdom" (1 Ki. 4:32-34, cf Matt. 13:34). Jesus said, "The queen of the south…came from the uttermost parts of the earth to hear the wisdom of Solomon; and, behold, a greater than Solomon is here" (Matt. 12:42).

Jonah's amazingly effective preaching mimicked the even more superior preaching of Christ. "The men of Nineveh…repented at the preaching of Jonas; and, behold, a greater than Jonas is here" (Matt. 12:41). The physical strength and lightning quick agility of Samson speaks of One who was more agile and stronger spiritually than Samson was physically, who could intercept every wily trap of Satan and throw around his host of wickedness hip and thigh, overcoming their storms and death. We also see Jesus in every little lamb with eyes looking up at us longing to be warmly held, and with pursed mouth wanting to be kissed. Each of those loving animals was another testimony of Jesus and of His good things to come (see Isaiah 53:2, 7; Hebrews 10:1).

We see Jesus in His prophets, mediating between God and their people. The Old Testament most often portrays the Lord God (Jesus the Prince) demanding Israel's obedience. This is because, as mediator between God and man, Jesus must represent not only *our*

Appendix A: Comments referred to from main text

position, but also the position of the most holy Ancient of days, Almighty King of the larger kingdom, the God of the eternal Law. Yet, the whole time that He represented His Father we hear His pathos of jealous love for us coming from His prophets. "Turn ye, turn ye from your evil ways; for why will ye die, O house of Israel?" (Eze. 33:11). We see His messengers, filled with and moved by His loving Spirit, laying down their lives to save His people who were bent on destroying themselves and others (see Matthew 23:35-37; Isaiah 43:4; Hebrews 11:36-38; Romans 8:35-39). Christ would wage endless war against the determinedly rebellious and their father, the devil (Ex. 17:16, cf John 8:3-44, 45-59). He would protect the humbled meek and punish the abusive proud (see Deuteronomy 32:43; Isaiah 11:3-5). It was only right.

We see Jesus in His holy ones, because they were His workmanship; they were His handiwork. The work declares its maker; and the house gives glory to the builder/owner of the house (see Hebrews 3:3-6). All find happiness and peace who see the collage of Jesus in the Old and New Testaments, and they rest in His gracious righteousness. Like Abraham, *they find salvation*, the illusive fountain of life. (See Romans 4:1; John 6:40; 15:7, 8; 4:14; Psalm 42:2; 16:8-11.) Jesus says,

> Whoso findeth me findeth life, and shall obtain favour of the LORD (Prov. 8:35).

But, we must search through *both* the Old and New Laws (see Isaiah 42:4) to find Jesus, for He is in the Book from "In the beginning God…. Let us make man" to "our Lord Jesus Christ be with you all. Amen" (Gen. 1:1; Rev. 22:21). He is the Alpha and Omega of the Bible (see Revelation 1:11). As a child, He drank in every word of the scriptures; which is how He could live out every word that He had handwritten into the Law of God. Humbled by the beautiful example of His loving acceptance toward the outcast and downtrodden, and His profound, authoritative expression of the Law, new life surges in our conscience and we receive power to imitate Him. "The Spirit is life because of righteousness" (Rom. 8:10). His Father's Law becomes our delight. Jesus has interceded and reconciled us to God.

> Joyful was Jesus because He walked not in the counsel of the ungodly, nor stood in the way of sinners, nor sat in the seat of the scornful.
>
> But His delight was in His Father's Law; and in His Law did He meditate day and night.
>
> Jesus was a tree planted by the rivers of water, and brought forth fruit in His season; His leaf also did not wither; and whatsoever He did prospered.
>
> The ungodly and demons were not so: but were the chaff which His Spirit drove away.
>
> Therefore the ungodly could not stand before His judgments, nor the devils in the congregation of His disciples.
>
> For the LORD knew the way of the righteous: but the way of the ungodly perished. (See Psalm 1.)
>
> I am joyful because I walk not in the counsel of the ungodly, nor stand in the way of sinners, nor sit in the seat of the scornful.
>
> But My delight is in My Father's Law; and in His Law do I meditate day and night.
>
> I am like a tree planted by the rivers of water, and bring forth My fruit in its season; My leaf also does not wither; and whatsoever I do prospers.
>
> The ungodly and demons are not so: but are like the chaff which My Father's Spirit drives away.
>
> Therefore the ungodly cannot stand before My judgments, nor devils in the congregation of My disciples.
>
> For I know the way of the righteous: but the way of the ungodly shall perish. (See Psalm 1.)
>
> Jesus suffered long, and still was kind.
>
> Jesus envied not.
>
> Jesus exalted not Himself; He was not puffed up.
>
> He did not behave Himself unseemly, He sought not His own.
>
> Jesus was not easily provoked, He thought no evil.
>
> He rejoiced not in iniquity, but rejoiced in the truth;
>
> He bore every burden, believed every sorrowing soul, hoped for every sinner, endured every accusation and discrediting.
>
> Jesus never failed. (See 1 Corinthians 13:4-8.)

As our High Priest, Jesus suffers long with our resistance toward Him, and He still is kind….

Jesus is not easily provoked; He thinks no evil of His children.

He rejoices not in our iniquity, but rejoices in our conviction of the truth;

He bears our every infirmity, believes our every repenting sorrow, hopes in our redemption, endures every one of our sins and shortcomings.

Jesus never fails. (See 1 Corinthians 13:4-8.)

Yes, it is charity that does the above, as the Bible so teaches. We have a duty to love. However, the truth is the most beautiful as it is beautiful in Jesus. We cannot truly have charity without the inspiration that *seeing* Jesus gives us — not only by His confirming treatment of others, but also by His expression of these wonderful actions *to me* as I read of them. If it hasn't yet become natural for me to automatically see Jesus in His Law, I must intentionally *put* Him there. I must plug in His name everywhere in the Bible, for it all testifies of Him. Otherwise, I greatly limit the resource of His Spirit and severely hamper my ability to know Him. I must keep His commandment to search the Book of Himself that He wrote upon Hebrew hearts who would be "read of all men" (2 Cor. 3:2). I must search the Word, His face and His heart. My heart and mind will open to new life when I see Him who so wisely used the lives and words of redeemed people to reveal Himself.

> Then He said unto them, O fools, and slow of heart to believe all that the prophets have spoken…. And beginning at Moses and all the prophets, he expounded unto them in all the scriptures the things concerning himself…. And their eyes were opened, and they knew him (Luke 24:25, 27, 31).

Beholding Jesus throughout the Bible, and knowing Him, calms my reticence, and His example in the Law keeps me converted to Him. Contrariwise, without resting in these visions of Jesus, obedience to righteousness is self-inspired. It is my own work, and I can never drum up the love to get it right. This is the very cause of Laodicea's malaise which afflicts Christendom today. Self-made obedience, because Jesus is not walked with and seen, like the disciples experienced, is currently driving the church into disillusionment. Self-inspired, forced righteousness always leads to a guaranteed, automatic, violent reaction. Because of our fallen nature "the law worketh wrath" (Rom. 4:15) by a violent conscience and resulting in forced obedience. "Until now the kingdom of heaven suffereth violence, and the violent take it by force" (Matt. 11:12). But, getting the vision of Jesus in His written word will free us from our forced morality and lack of peace with God, and will give us "the beauty of the LORD our God" (Ps. 90:17).

> And Jesus said unto them, I am the bread of life: he that cometh to me shall never hunger; and he that believeth on me shall never thirst…. He that eateth my flesh, and drinketh my blood, dwelleth in me, and I in him. As the living Father hath sent me, and I live by the Father: so he that eateth me, even he shall live by me. This is that bread which came down from heaven: not as your fathers did eat manna, and are dead: he that eateth of this bread shall live for ever (John 6:35, 56-58).

> In the last day, that great day of the feast, Jesus stood and cried, saying, If any man thirst, let him come unto me, and drink. He that believeth on me, as the scripture hath said, out of his belly shall flow rivers of living water (John 7:37, 38).

> I am the…truth, and the life (John 14:6).

Bowing to the vision of Jesus in His whole word is the third angel's message. Beholding righteousness any other way leaves our conscience tormented, scratched and rabid by the Beast. Being fruitful in a knowledge of Jesus is "the present truth" (1 Pet. 1:12, cf 1 John 4:23) from Early Rain to Latter Rain.

> Many had lost sight of Jesus. They needed to have their eyes directed to His divine person, His merits, and His changeless love for the human family. All power is given into His hands, that He may dispense rich gifts unto men, imparting the priceless gift of His own righteousness to the helpless human agent. This is the message that God commanded to be given to the world. It is the third angel's message, which is to be proclaimed with a loud voice, and attended with the outpouring of His Spirit in a large measure *Testimonies to Ministers*, p. 91.

Appendix A: Comments referred to from main text

Jesus must win my heart to His life, otherwise the Law will remain only my melancholy, exhausting duty.

Jesus must win my heart to His life, otherwise the Law will remain only my melancholy, exhausting duty. The beauty of holiness is the epitome of lifeless drudgery if the Spirit of truth, as it comes from Jesus, does not take control of me, do it all to me, for me, and in me personally. I must stand in the crowds; with them I must be the recipient of His virtue, joining in the experience of those real folks in the long ago. If Jesus does not minister to me as He did to the other needy people, because my faith doesn't become engrossed in Him through His written word, then the Law is the cause of anger beyond all others. It only adds to my hopeless Laodicean dilemma and later turns me into a beast, as King Saul and the post-apostolic church experienced.

I must see Jesus doing every requirement of the Bible. I must put Jesus in His Law and in His scriptures. Jesus Himself in John 5:39 and 6:40 instructed me to do so. Letters and laws and rules alone cannot provide me enough motivation to do right. But, the Spirit of Christ filled the Old Testament full of action and honest expression that wins me to Him as I see Him there. It gives vivid illustrations of the ways of Christ, which the gospels needed not to duplicate. We must see Jesus, and for that the *whole* Bible is the single best resource.

> Where there is no vision, the people perish (Prov. 29:18).

Paul learned this lesson.

> I [my self-sufficiency, self-will, self-exaltation, etc.] was alive without the law once: but when the commandment came, sin revived, and I died.
>
> And the commandment, which was ordained to life, I found to be unto death.
>
> For sin [his natural resistance to God's shaming holiness], taking occasion by the commandment, deceived me, and by it slew me (Rom. 7:9-11).

Paul is saying that being ignorant of his truly wretched nature, he was satisfied with his morality and believed himself happy — until the Law convicted him of his great sinfulness. Immediately, self rose up in him to declare its own righteousness and to defend his offended self-centered mind, the sudden reaction alarming Paul's conscience. The care-free conscience woke up and Saul's self-satisfied peace was slain. A whole new paradigm rudely presented itself. Through His Law, the Father wiped the Ashtoreth guile out of Paul's mind and her arrogant, self-righteous grin off of his face. Jesus needed Paul's knowledge of himself to exceed his untrained detection of sinfulness, which was as high as heaven is above the earth. His monstrous pride needed to raise its ugly head high above his horizon. Paul's true condition needed to come above his sin radar and be obviously loathsome. "The law entered, that the offence might abound", "that every mouth may be stopped, and all the world become guilty before God" (Rom. 5:20; 3:19, cf Job 40:3-5; 42:5, 6). The Law condemned Paul's fallen nature, and his natural rebellion confirmed the Law's assessment of him. The Law did something supernatural, something that he knew must have been divine. His conclusion: Therefore, the Law must be holy and I had better heed it. After wrestling with the Law of God he was humbled and ready to find Jesus. Paul's dependence on his flesh was finally crushed when he saw the love of God in Christ. That vision permanently branded Jesus in Paul's conscience. And ever afterward he brought Jesus with him when he entered the presence of the Law, the scriptures.

I must have more than the letter of the Law. What I need is the Spirit of the Law which comes to me when my humbled conscience sees Christ in the Law — "as the truth is in Jesus" (Eph. 4:21). We can't give others the truth as it is in Jesus unless we've seen Jesus in the truth. "I am the truth," Jesus says. But, in my own sinful nature I cannot stand before God's convicting righteousness, because my arrogant, fallen nature is utterly belligerent toward a standard infinitely higher than my own; no matter Who or Where it came from. I resist the written requirement because I can't hear any voice inflection and intonation that would indicate a warm, living person with friendship and kindness toward me. I don't naturally know God; and, because of sin, His written instructions don't automatically or effectively communicate His love. And my fallen nature cannot naturally assume that the Prince and Judge is loving and kind, and wanting to help me. My fallen perception cannot discern the law of kindness in His mouth.

For many years already I have looked at the Law of God, and its strong convictions have shamed and finally humbled me. But, now as I read the Bible, Jesus offers me the incomprehensible, unmerited privilege to be in the crowd that followed Him, or David, or Elisha, or any of those holy personalities. I experience the joy of a reprieve from condemnation by simply witnessing Christ's real, loving righteousness and love that I see flow from Him or from His faithful servants. Through the everlasting, divine psychology of His written word, Jesus has mercifully invited me to be a spectator, yes, a third party, safely watching on so that He can win my trust. As a little one carried on my Shepherd's shoulders, or a joey riding in its mother's pouch, He doesn't immediately put me to work on obeying the Law. I am a disciple, looking unto Jesus, and being befriended and changing into His image. I am coming to Jesus and He is giving me rest; I am obeying the gospel. I am seeing the beauty of holiness in Jesus; I am experiencing "the righteousness of Christ in the law." *The Ellen G. White 1888 Materials*, p. 299.

> Come unto me, all ye that labour and are heavy laden, and I will give you rest (Matt. 11:28).

> He shall feed his flock like a shepherd: he shall gather the lambs with his arm, and carry them in his bosom, and shall gently lead those that are with young (Isa. 40:11).

> For I through the law am dead to [the curse of the law (Gal. 3:13], that I might live unto God (Gal. 2:19).

Perfect and perpetual abstinence from all self-indulgence is the Law's immutable demand. I cannot stand before the written Law. It would take a miracle to obey it. I just want a friend, a perpetual friend! I stress out until I can witness and experience unchangeable love! The curse of the Law is the nerve-racking, anxious "chastisement of our peace" (Isa. 53:5) which God rightly lays heavily upon us, but which God's only-begotten Provision assumes upon Himself when our heavy burdens make us needy for Him. Then Christ in the Law shields us from the curse of the Law as we learn to trust Him who became a curse in our place. "Thou wilt not leave my soul in hell" (Ps. 16:10). The Law's heavily layed burden has changed into our exceeding great reward.

> Wherefore, my brethren, ye also are become dead to the law by the body of Christ; that ye should be married to another, even to him who is raised from the dead, that we should bring forth fruit unto God.... Now we are delivered from the law, that being dead wherein we were held; that we should serve in newness of spirit, and not in the oldness of the letter.... That the righteousness of the law might be fulfilled in us, who walk not after the flesh, but after the Spirit (Rom. 7:4, 6; 8:4).

Once the Naaman in me has been humbled by the conviction of my own wretchedness from God's Law, true obedience comes through the trust that Jesus builds in me by His Spirit in **His** Law. Satan knows this, so he tries to get me busy doing what the Law says without first getting that humbling from *the* Law, and then the bond with Jesus as my Friend and Example. But, I've finally learned from my past painful Pauline wrestling. And now to have real obedience I let Jesus move me as I conceive of His love from His inspired accounts. The Spirit of Christ moves upon the confusion of my mind and upon the great darkness of my deep, and says, Let there be light and order and beauty.

> So then with the mind I myself serve the law of God; but with the flesh [my self-sufficient, resistant fallen nature] the law of sin. There is therefore now no condemnation to them which are in Christ Jesus, who walk not after the flesh, but after the Spirit. For the law of the Spirit of life in Christ Jesus hath made me free from the law of sin and death (Rom. 7:25-8:2).

Paul has discovered the principle of righteousness by faith and he teaches it to us. He has rediscovered what Isaiah had learned which allowed Jesus to be a sheltering Rock in his weary land (see Isaiah 32:2). By filling the mind with Jesus through the Law in the holy Bible Isaiah and Paul can obey God without being overwhelmed by the intense justice of God and their constant resistance to it. The struggle of Paul's rebellion left him appreciating the high standard. The pillars of smoke lifted, leaving him longing to own the character it revealed (see Philippians 3:9, 10). In Romans chapter 7, more and more the person of Christ gave Paul delight in righteousness. Now in Romans chapter 8, by Paul seeing Jesus in the requirements of the Law victory over the life of sin could be had, a case against the life of sin which he had been building since Romans chapter 6.

If we be dead with him, we shall also live with him: if we suffer, we shall also reign with him (2 Tim. 2:11, 12).

I have suffered under the Schoolmaster and surrendered to the righteousness of God. So, He gives me a Saviour in the Spirit of His Son (see John 6:37; Galatians 4:6). Because I hold the Law close and love my Saviour who I see in the Law, God counts my relationship with His Son to satisfy His infinitely high standard (see Romans 4:3) and He comes by His Spirit to dwell in me. By Their abiding presence my temple is swept, furnished, and filled with Their presence; and Their Spirit can reside on my new mercy seat (see John 14:21, 23; Romans 5:5). By faith I have entered into Their controversy against sin, I have striven with Christ to the pouring out of my soul against my sin. "I am crucified with Christ" (Gal. 2:20). I have died with Him under the hot displeasure of God's condemnation and suffering because of my sin. Now being a bystander, watching Jesus fulfill the Law keeps me saved. As a fly on the wall watching Jesus in His historical person, I am no longer threatened by the Law's high moral standard. My fly on the wall experience is not self-indulgent, popcorn-eating entertainment because by faith my spirit has fallen on the Father and Son, and has been broken (see Genesis 32:26; Matthew 21:44; Psalm 51:17). I am fixated on Jesus, absorbed in His actions, receiving life from His life. This is my work; I am doing "the first works" (Rev. 2:5). Therefore, my newly surrendered heart toward the Law is susceptible and efficiently absorbs righteousness.

Now with my old stubborn resistance gone, my mind and heart can receive the example of Jesus that fulfilled the Law. I have come to "delight in the law of God after the inward man" (Rom. 7:22) and have fallen on my face before Him. Surrendered to the righteousness of God and seeing the grace of Jesus, "with the mind I myself serve the law of God" (Rom. 7:25) and I soak it in. I abandon the work of keeping the Law by my own efforts, the only method that I knew before I saw the presence of Jesus in His words. My fellowship in His love and mercy, which I see in Him toward others like myself, shields me from further destructive condemnation of the Law's spiritual requirements. By proxy I am the recipient of His earthly ministry to others; I absorb the subtle lessons He brings to life in His past obedience and His present Spirit. I become that leper who hungered for healing so much that nothing could restrain him from Jesus once he caught that first glimpse of the Lord healing others. The blessing became irresistible, the healing a foregone conclusion. My faith becomes the leper's faith which naturally and correctly *assumed* that Jesus' healing was for everyone who needed it! I drink in Jesus' purifying touch and His wonderful reply to me, "I will; be thou clean" (Matt. 8:3).

I am sitting with the disciples when Jesus asks all of us, "Whom say ye that I am?" (Matt. 16:15). In the "press" I hide with the other hungry Bible characters for whom the Son of God had compassion. And my anonymity the Father allows for because my starving focus is on His Son; I have set my love upon Him. Like the happy heavenly hosts that crowded Him in Revelation chapter 4, I am coming to watch and to hear His Son (see John 3:36). Christ's gift of anonymity acts as a giant, cooling rock overshadowing the hot condemnation from the requirements of the Law (see Isaiah 32:2). Having trembled before the Law of God, and still jittery, in Jesus my nerves calm down and I take courage. Through His help to the people written of I find comfort. The Chief Shepherd is carrying me as a lamb while I grow up and learn to imitate Him. He carries me like His Father carried Him "from of old, from everlasting" (Mic. 5:2, cf Prov. 8:22, 30). He fills me with His Spirit of truth and grace, like His Father filled Him with His Spirit of justice and mercy. Thus, I can copy my Mentor, as He could imitate His Father in everything (see John 5:19, 20). Under Jesus' example and influence, my old nature is dead to sin, and my new spirit is alive because I finally witness merciful righteousness (see Romans 8:10). I experience righteousness and receive new power to give it. This was "the blessing to Abraham" (Gal. 3:14).

> This is the rest wherewith ye may cause the weary to rest; and this is the refreshing (Isa. 28:12, cf Acts 3:19, 20).

> This is the heritage of the servants of the LORD, and their righteousness is of me, saith the LORD (Isa. 54:17).

This blessing comes only to those who had previously been humbled by the Law. Now they have fallen on Jesus, Jacob's living, loving Stone (see Genesis 32:26). And their fall is caused by the Law's same powerful convictions and grinding condemnation that Paul had in his Romans 7's frustrations. But now they fall with hope in Jesus' continuing mercies. Therefore, let us all ask, seek, and knock; let us apply our heart, cry after, lift up our voice, for the convicting, grinding, and scourging by the life-giving Law of God. It's all good; that is, holy and just and good. Then our great need will bring our personal Saviour into crystal clear view. "He will bring me forth to the light, and I shall behold his righteousness" (Mic. 7:9). He will catch our love and mold us after His perfect image.

> The true principles of psychology are found in the Holy Scriptures. Man knows not his own value. He acts according to his unconverted temperament of character because he does not look unto Jesus, the Author and Finisher of his faith. He who comes to Jesus, he who believes on Him and makes Him his Example, realizes the meaning of the words "To them gave He power to become the sons of God." *Mind, Character, and Personality*, vol. 1, p. 10.

All who come to Jesus in His word, everyone who "seeth the Son, and believeth on Him", will love the Son of God and it will be in their nature to make Him their example.

The Father wisely brings His hot condemnation against the crowd's sinfulness — the chastisement of their peace — often seen in the Old Testament people. And eventually, so does Jesus imperceptibly and gently, and sometimes strongly, bring His condemnation against the sins of my fly on the wall. Thus, He keeps my faith honest and open to see that in the Bible stories the sins there are also written of me. All whose ears have the privilege of hearing Jesus say, "Thus saith the Lord", morning by morning are enthralled by the witness of Jesus' righteousness and mercy — His life-giving Spirit which the hearers detect in the Law. Jesus' presence in the Law makes them "free from the law of sin and death" (Rom. 8:2). A new spirit comes to life because of righteousness that they witness, which they find refreshing, and which they appropriate and reciprocate (see Romans 8:10). Because of Christ's truth and grace which they see in both Testaments, they become free. They receive a solid relationship with Jesus which began with their own Romans 7 wrestling with the condemnation from a God of love. In Christ they are justified now, and He sanctifies them along the way with His continued presence with them in cooperation with the inspiration of the scriptures that remain a permanent fixture in their mind (see John 15:7; Romans 7:25-8:2). The Son has made them free indeed. No longer servants enslaved to sin, as adopted sons they abide in Christ, addicted to His mercy and truth (see 1 Corinthians 16:15).

I that speak in righteousness, mighty to save (Isa. 63:1).

Through His Spirit in the Law, Jesus, the Lord God of Israel, their Advocate and Protector, abides with His children (see John 14:15-23). Through His Spirit in the written accounts of His love for the world, Christ is being their authorized defense from the Father's fiery darts. His fiery commandments are of the most austere, destructive holiness, and which stand determinedly disavowed and opposed to sin and proud sinners (see Matthew 17:5, 6; Luke 19:22; Revelation 14:10; John 14:6). But, the Father calls them to come into His presence through His powerful representative, the Ten Commandments, only as "the Spirit of Christ" (Rom. 8:9) attends them because they are responding to the Spirit of His Son in "his law" (Isa. 42:4), the scriptures. And the Father, in whose sight they are naked and open, searches their hearts and accepts them for the communion that He sees them having by faith with His Son, and by their agreeableness to His spiritual mindedness. As they "keep" (John 14:23, cf vs. 15, 21) [*tēreō*, "guard from loss"] His words in their soul, the presiding "Spirit of His Son" (Gal. 4:6) makes intercession according to the will of His Father (see Romans 8:26, 27). Thus, through their seeing the beloved Son in the Law, the Son has become their way to God. His shielding demonstration of righteousness as they discerned Jesus in the Law has become His mediation for them before the Law. As a result, they can naturally trust the Son to represent them before God, and to broker their forgiveness and acceptance with Him. They continue in peace with God through their Lord Jesus Christ. As they received the Lord Jesus, so they walk in Him. This is walking after the Spirit; this produces sanctification.

> We through the Spirit wait for the hope of righteousness by faith (Gal. 5:5).

> For what the law could not do, in that it was weak through the flesh [our self-sufficient rebellion], God sending his own Son in the likeness of sinful flesh, and for sin, condemned sin in the flesh (Rom. 8:3).

By His Father sending Him in the likeness of our flesh, His mother's natural rebellion overmastered by His Father's divine nature has left a lasting demonstration to the world that sin can be overcome. And by His condemning sin in the flesh He destroyed our every possible justification for disobedience. But, God's plan for the sweeping removal of all our self-justification includes a Mediator who knows us and will take into account all inherited weaknesses. Better than anyone our Mediator knows just how much we know we do the things we do and why we do them. And He knows how abused we have been by the devil and how strongly we are capable of allying with His Spirit.

He who manifested the fullness of the Godhead came here to *demonstrate before our eyes* all the love that His Father's Law requires. Instead of looking at a requirement, we see the Author of the requirement who makes the requirement visible and audible. We see One who is not all business and demands, not mechanical. We see a high standard, but also communion, sympathy, and someone who will pray for us as He prayed for others back then. Looking at His person, we see someone who we know must understand us, a friend who cares about us. We all can warm up to such a trusted friend, and take delight in the Law that He loves. In the same flesh that we have, Christ condemned sin. In our weakened state, yet through the immeasurable divine nature that Jesus inherited from His Father — Christ's own divine nature — He had perfect victory over sin. Then, by hearing His perfect expression of the mind of His Father and by witnessing His winning ways, we conform to the influence of His Spirit as the disciples did. By being drawn to Christ we can partake of His strong divine nature for His victory in our weak flesh.

> Happy is the man that findeth Christ in the Law, and the man that getteth a knowledge of Jesus.
>
> For the merchandise of His words is better than the merchandise of silver, and the gain His character is more valuable than fine gold.
>
> He is more precious than rubies: and all the things thou canst desire are not to be compared unto Him.
>
> Length of days is in His right hand; and in His left hand riches and honour.
>
> His righteousness results in ways of pleasantness, and all His paths are peace.
>
> He is a tree of life to them that lay hold upon Him: and happy is every one that retaineth Him. (Adapted from Proverbs 3:13-18.)

Our thinking becomes Jesus-centered instead of requirement-centered. Our change enables us to look into Christ's convicting Bible, thankful to Him for designing the Bible stories to be the tabernacle for His Spirit. In His scripture tabernacle He then uses the transformation of biblical personalities to transform us. Our motives and rationale become other-centered rather than self-centered, and we love His wisdom and mercy toward us, a race with a weakened willpower for good and a strengthened willpower for great evil. We are enabled to do the requirements that He demonstrates, because His Spirit has changed our heart toward them. His Spirit, which lives in that great body of written precepts, moves upon me as well as upon His reading audience of multitudes, nations, tongues, and peoples, and leaves a unifying, holy influence upon each reader's spirit.

> He that is joined unto the Lord is one spirit (1 Cor. 6:17).

The Bible stories are the repositories of His presence that our spirit by faith sees and hears Him in His requirements, as the stories emanate His faith and life into every reader that desires to appropriate them.

> Faith cometh by hearing...the word of God (Rom. 10:17).

The Spirit of Christ is in his words; our new spirit of faith recognizes Him by His voice. His presence dwelling in the Bible stories is a mystery that can only happen because we are all made especially in the spiritual image of God. Made in His image, we all have our "own value" *Mind, Character, and Personality*, Vol. 1, p. 10. This ability to resonate with the scripture is what Adam was experiencing through the wonders of the garden. And had we not fallen into sin, we inherently would always spiritually recognize the loving presence of our wonderful Master in the gifts of His requirements and in nature. Paul would need not have said, "If there had been a law given which could have given life, verily righteousness should have been by the law" (Gal. 3:21). Righteousness would have been by the Law because, recognizing Jesus in the Law, our obedience to the Law then would have given life (see John 12:50). That's the way the Law should work — it speaks of holiness and right-doing and goodness, and if we have God's Spirit then we recognize the beauty of it all and plunge right in to obey! But, alas, our fallen natures despise the beauty of perfection. So, we constantly need a perfect Person to win our hearts back to the Father's requirements. And His gift of salvation supplies our natural lack of the personal side of holiness and justness and goodness, a personal element which sin has stolen from our conceptions of the Law. Christ's merciful and just interaction with Bible characters, those historical recipients of His grace, contained the balanced mentoring of His statutes for us. Essentially, the Bible characters contained Him (see Colossians 1:27); therefore their accounts contain His Spirit, the Spirit of truth. And like us, they were common vessels of ore, and subject to corrupting, not gorgeously adorned, pristine, or golden, except as Jesus shone out of them. The Lord was their righteousness, holiness, and goodness, so long as they sat with Him in heavenly places, and continually beheld Him.

> We have this treasure in earthen vessels, that the excellency of the power may be of God, and not of us (2 Cor. 4:7).

The invaluable victories contained in those folks, victories which were gifts from Jesus, become our priceless victories. They walked with Jesus, hanging on to Him and to His overcoming, and they obtained His help for their difficult climb out the pit of deeply ingrained habits. Not Christ through Spiritual Formation, but Christ in the fatherly reproofs of the Law and the Spirit of Prophecy give us the true life, as we suck the honey of His personal example and ministry out of the flinty slabs of condemning commands and reprimands. Causing our greatest happiness, our hearts are humbled by a strong Father who we know must love us if He is willing to convict us and liberate our conscience from miserable self-focus. God, the great Lawgiver, is the great focus of heaven's worship and of His earthly converted children's. Contrariwise, the evasion of conviction built into Spiritual Formation destroys freedom of conscience; its adherents cannot come clean. Therefore, those that bear the vessels of Spiritual Formation can never be clean before the Lord. With our mind having served the Law, and our soul won by Christ's life and sealed by His death, our attitudes change and we take ownership of the Law's requirements. Through Jesus in the Law, we claim God's Law as our best counselor; and God is satisfied. Through His just condemnation in His Law and then through His merciful, Law-loving Propitiator in His Son, God has put His Law into our hearts. And it all happened through Christ in the Law, in the Bible, and in the Testimonies. Do we see why Satan so much fears the rebuke of a loving God in the Bible and in Spirit of Prophecy? Christ in the Law will create the 144,000. The living word of God is very destructive to Satan's kingdom. One little word will fell him. More than our little faith has conceived, the devil knows the deliverance that the Word of God will bring to God's people.

All of this blessedness to the reader comes through the Spirit of the Word rather than a long, abstract list of dos and don'ts, which are often hit or miss guesswork by us. To the unconverted heart, the Law is highly subjectively misinterpreted. Before the Son of God came, humanity didn't have the new advantage of His gracious example attending His life. "The law was given by Moses, but grace and truth came by Jesus Christ." "God sent not his Son into the world to condemn the world; but that the world through him might be saved" (John 1:17; 3:17). Seeing the Son testified to in every word of scripture, all who have lived under the condemnation of the Law will be redeemed from that curse, and will live unto God with open hearts (see Galatians 4:4, 5; 2:19).

[I reiterate, that according to Romans 7, the unbroken heart and unbroken self-will cannot have the privileged liberty in the Lord's Spirit in the Law. Jesus' life-giving, shielding Spirit in the Law comes only to those who have struggled under God's Law and His Bible. They have been ground down by His Testimonies (see Romans 3:19, 20), and then they have fallen on Jesus, their pride and self-will renounced (see verses 21, 22). They have long trembled at His word; they alone do not make void the Law of God. They alone receive a love for Bible truth; they alone will work out their own salvation with fear and trembling.

> Out of Zion, the perfection of beauty, God hath shined.
>
> Our God shall come, and shall not keep silence: a fire shall devour before him, and it shall be very tempestuous round about him.
>
> He shall call to the heavens from above, and to the earth, that he may judge his people.
>
> Gather my saints together unto me; those that have made a covenant with me by sacrifice (Ps. 50:2-5).

The final impediment to the crown of liberty is the cross. Time spent, effort and will-power to find and know Jesus that are driven by the Schoolmaster, must be our investment before He yields the blessing of His Spirit as a comforter to every plagued soul. A hardened self, necessarily pained and slain by the death of the Lamb, goes into a covenant with Christ before His honey comes out of it. His crucifixion slaying our exhausted, self-sufficient heart is our sacrificial offering that consecrates His covenant to dwell in us and to be our God. Before the cleansing of an evil conscience, sinners must have suffered in the flesh. Otherwise they will be led into a euphoric, grace-only mindset and join in the world's Baalpeor spiritualism. Without a covenant made by the death of pride, they will pollute grace by its unworthy assumption into their conscience.

I emphasize this because I want no one to end up disappointed in their efforts to walk in the Spirit. Please do the first works, if you haven't already. Be strong and of good courage, and go to the Bible and Spirit of Prophecy (see Joshua 1:7, 8). Discover a fair, disciplining father in God. He always mixes His powerful threats with His powerful entreaties, His great mountain of justice with His equally great mountain of mercy. Let the Law's grinding do its perfect work of giving the supernatural need of a Saviour from sin. Let the great need from the Spirit send you to the hem of the Anointed One for His virtue. Then, with perfect certainty you will be enabled to say, "Salvation is of the LORD" (Jon. 2:9).]

If we will see the character of Jesus in the Law to be a grace and truth antidote for sin, then we will never fear to stand before the condemning Law *as we read it in light of Jesus*, whether it be the mountainous righteousness throughout the Bible or throughout the Spirit of Prophecy. With the Saviour as adjunct Lawgiver and Judge permanently in our sights, we will rejoice to dwell in the house of the Lord forever. We will be sealed.

David had Paul's experience with victory over sin. And we can be followers of David as he was of Christ.

Lo, I come (in the volume of the book it is written of me,) to do thy will, O God (Heb. 10:7, cf John 5:39).

1)

Jesus was happy and undefiled, because He walked in the law of His LORD.

He was joyful because He kept His Father's testimonies, and sought His Father with His whole heart.

He did no iniquity: He walked in His Father's ways.

Jesus prayed, "Thou hast commanded us to keep Thy precepts diligently.

"O that My ways were directed to keep Thy statutes!

"Then shall I not be ashamed, when I have respect unto all Thy commandments.

"I will praise Thee with uprightness of heart, when I shall have learned Thy righteous judgments.

"I will keep Thy statutes: O forsake Me not utterly."

2)

Jesus' Father was the LORD His God, who kept Him out of the land of Egypt, out of the house of bondage to sin.

Jesus had no other elohim before His Elohim.

Jesus did not make for Himself any graven image, or any likeness of any thing that is in heaven above, or that is in the earth beneath, or that is in the water under the earth: He did not bow down Himself to them, nor serve them.

Jesus was ever careful to not take the name of Jehovah His God in vain; for His Father would not have held Him guiltless if He had ever vainly used His name.

Jesus always remembered the Sabbath day, and kept it holy. Six days did He labor, and do all His work: but the seventh day was the Sabbath of Jehovah His God: in it He did no work, neither He, nor His disciples, nor the multitudes that followed Him.

Jesus honored His earthly parents, Joseph and Mary: that His days might be long upon the land which Jehovah His Father gave Him.

Jesus did not kill.

He did not commit adultery.

He did not steal.

Jesus did not bear false witness against His neighbor, nor was He a talebearer.

He did not covet anyone's house, anyone's wife, nor His neighbor's wealth, nor their material things and possessions, nor anything that was His neighbor's.

3)

Christ loved God His Father with all His heart, and with all His soul, and with all His might.

And the scriptures were always in His heart: He lived by every word of the scripture.

He taught them diligently to His disciples, and spoke of them when they sat in a house, and when they walked by the way, and before they laid down, and when they rose up.

And He bound them in His mind and heart like a sign upon His hand, and as frontlets between His eyes.

4)

Jesus did no unrighteousness in judgment:

He did not respect the person of the poor, nor honor the person of the mighty: but in righteousness did He judge His neighbor. He never went up and down as a talebearer among His people: neither did He stand against the blood of His neighbor: His Father was Jehovah. Jesus loved everyone too much to allow their sin to destroy them: so, in every case He spoke the truth in love. He did not avenge, nor bear any grudge against the children of His people, but He loved them as Himself: He never forgot the holiness of Jehovah His Father.

5)

On the cross Jesus felt like a worm, and not a man; a reproach of men, and despised of the people.

All they that saw Him laughed Him to scorn: they shot out their lip, they shook their head, saying,

"He trusted on God that He would deliver Him: let Him deliver Him, seeing He delighted in Him."

But, Jesus prayed to His Father, "Thou art He that took Me out of the womb: Thou didst make Me hope when I was upon My mother's breasts.

"I was cast upon Thee from the womb: Thou art My God from My mother's belly.

"Be not far from Me; for trouble is near; for there is none to help.

"Powerful people encompass Me: hateful priests and Pharisees have beset Me round.

"They gape upon Me with their mouths, as a ravening and a roaring lion.

"I am poured out like water, and all My bones are out of joint: My heart is like wax; it is melted in the midst of My bowels.

"My strength is dried up like a potsherd; and My tongue cleaveth to My jaws; and Thou hast brought Me into the dust of death.

"For dogs have compassed Me: the assembly of the wicked have inclosed Me: they pierced My hands and My feet.

"I can see all My bones: they look and stare at Me.

"They part My garments among them, and cast lots upon My vesture.

"But be not Thou far from Me , O LORD: O My strength, haste Thee to help Me.

"Deliver My soul from the sword; My soul from the power of the dog.

"Save Me from the lion's mouth: for Thou hast heard Me from the horns of the unicorns.

"I will declare Thy name unto My brethren: in the midst of the congregation will I praise Thee.

"Ye that fear My Father, praise Him; all ye the seed of Jacob, glorify Him; and fear Him, all ye the seed of Israel.

"For He hath not despised nor abhorred the affliction of the afflicted; neither hath He hid His face from him; but when he cried unto Him, He heard.

"My praise shall be of Thee in the great congregation: I will pay My vows before them that fear Him."

The above texts adapted from 1) Psalm 119:1-8; 2) Exodus 20:2-17; 3) Deuteronomy 6:5-8; 4) Leviticus 19:15-18; 5) Psalm 22:6-25.

Appendix A: Comments referred to from main text

In mercy to us Christ has given us everything we need to understand His love. By His Spirit in the Law, all who have wrestled with the Law are enabled to answer and accomplish the question, "WWJD?" And, just what would Jesus do? He would do His Father's Law (see Isaiah 42:21); Jesus would exemplify the goodness that He requires from His children. WWJD? "A bruised reed shall He not break, and the smoking flax shall He not quench: He shall bring forth judgment unto truth…and the isles shall wait for His Law" (Isa. 42:3, 4). Jesus' Law is what His children wait to see and hear in His Father's Law when Jesus exemplifies it in His caring, loving flesh. "Blessed are all they that wait for him" (Isa. 30:18) in the Law. No one can go wrong, and only they can do right, who wait for Jesus to reveal Himself through the scriptures, our only safeguard from Spiritual Formation. They wait for the hope of righteousness by hanging their helpless souls on the Spirit of Jesus that is stirred up in the Law and quickened by Himself in the heavenly sanctuary. He gave the Law, and His Spirit in the Law makes the words glow.

What do we see when we look at Jesus? Every principle of the stone hard Law of God residing in warm human flesh. "In principle firm as a rock, His life revealed the grace of unselfish courtesy" *The Desire of Ages*, p. 68. We see a person constrained to help everyone; we see one who had developed His skills in every way to help others, one who is perfected in all respects, holy and just and good. He was the righteousness of God incorporated in man, God manifest in the human nature and justified in His divine nature. Unified with God and with holy propensities that needed no intercessor, Jesus cooperated with His Father in the work of His perfection, for "God was His instructor" *The Desire of Ages*, p. 70. "He hated but one thing in the world, and that was sin. He could not witness a wrong act without pain which it was impossible to disguise" *The Desire of Ages*, p. 88.

Christ was not only sealed in His forehead, He was sealed from the crown of His head to the soles of His feet. As solid as the great El Capitan, like a boulder broken off of Mount Everest (see Daniel 2:34, 35), He had ever been secure and obedient to His Father. And we can partake of His moral strength by having our conscience and will justified, sanctified, and solidified in loyalty to God and to His commandments "by the spirit of judgment, and by the spirit of burning" (Isa. 4:4). By the Spirit of Christ in His words, through seeing the Anointed One today, we can be anointed by His same, strong convictions. Little by little, memory by memory, principle by principle, the vapid flesh is replaced by the power of the Highest, petrified into the image of Christ by His sealing Spirit.

> My son, keep thy father's commandment, and forsake not the law of thy mother:
>
> Bind them continually upon thine heart, and tie them about thy neck.
>
> When thou goest, it shall lead thee; when thou sleepest, it shall keep thee; and when thou awakest, it shall talk with thee (Prov. 6:20-22).
>
> The words that I speak unto you, they are spirit, and they are life (John 6:63).

By the Spirit of His presence in the Bible, He gives power for pleasing His Father to as many today as will see Jesus and receive Him into their trust. Through the Spirit in the Law of His mouth and in His lifework, Jesus, the *living* Word, will inspire and empower His followers to mortify the deeds of their flesh. Through Him they can afflict their souls in the great finale of this investigative judgment period. His Spirit in the Bible is a mighty weapon for pulling down all their strongholds of sin. The victory comes from desperate, longing faith, needing to hear from Him who their hearts desire, through His written word and from His Father's stone Law. They have stumbled upon a rich Treasure, although it does not possess outward beauty so that the world should desire it.

> Happy is the man that findeth wisdom, and the man that getteth understanding.
>
> For the merchandise of it is better than the merchandise of silver, and the gain thereof than fine gold.
>
> She is more precious than rubies: and all the things thou canst desire are not to be compared unto her….
>
> She is a tree of life to them that lay hold upon her: and happy is every one that retaineth her (Prov. 3:13-15, 18).

God protects these humbled ones who His Law has made contrite. They put all of their time and labor into seeing Jesus, and make ceasefire with the battle against their sins. They fight with all their power to be still every morning, looking into the Law and the Spirit of Prophecy, and knowing the power of the Almighty. The glory of Christ's truth and grace enthralls them, and they let

His Spirit change them. He fights their battles against sin as they surrender up their own rod upon themselves.

They also put down their militant resistance against the locust enemies in the time of trouble. To them the victory is accomplished. They walk vulnerably by faith like Jeremiah walked (see Jeremiah 11:18, 19), with their conversation in heaven, and they continually see the salvation of the Lord (see Jeremiah 15:19-21).

> The swords that were raised to kill God's people broke and fell as powerless as a straw. Angels of God shielded the saints *Early Writings*, p. 284.

> Because he hath set his love upon me, therefore will I deliver him: I will set him on high, because he hath known my name (Ps. 91:14).

Righteousness by Faith by Jesus, Righteousness^3. Righteousness^3 is the science of setting our love upon Jesus. If we know Him today, as it is our high privilege, He will let us sit in heavenly places with Him today. "Today shalt thou be with Me in paradise". But, we need a genuine love that we are incapable of producing, which only God and Jesus can work into us. Therefore, the first step in setting us on high is for the Father to make us stumble and fall at the condemnation of His Law, and His Testimonies.

> Behold, I lay in Sion a chief corner stone, elect, precious: and he that believeth on him shall not be confounded (1 Pet. 2:6).

For twenty wonderful talks on Righteousness by Faith by Jesus, go to: https://www.youtube.com/watch?v=tSkiYTLD8sI&list=PL1356F864B1D83379

From page 133:

The Jesuits have led Protestant Americans to hate Protestantism, which is the only Bible-based, peace-making, and truly voluntary subset of Christianity. Thus, when Rome's time comes to strike and to force religion upon a world of bold, unruly religion-haters, the Protestant-influenced Americans and western world that boast "freedom from religion" will already have potent reservations against their forefathers' Reformation and against its voluntary doctrines of liberty through the Spirit of God. Their hope will not be in their Creator and Redeemer. Therefore, when "the son of perdition", "that Wicked [one]" is suddenly "revealed [unveiled]" (2 Thess. 2:3, 8) and "they behold the beast that was, and is not, and yet is" (Rev. 17:8), then the atheistic secular Protestant Americans will have no Protestant refuge from, and no alternative but to comply with, the violent and compulsory overlord of ancient paganism. And many of these secular Protestants know that the Church has, throughout its history, legislated coercive church policy, attendance, and financial support. She knows what is to be, because the dragon gives the inspiration of her prognostications. The genius of her crafty violence made John marvel (see Revelation 17:6). Since the earliest days of Christianity until now "the kingdom of heaven suffereth violence, and the violent take it by force" (Matt. 11:12, cf 2 Thessalonians 2:7).

The Protestant voices of today proclaiming freedom from religion have their origin in the great deceiver and his fuming Chaldean locusts of the fifth trumpet. And surprisingly, many non-discerning, ecumenized Protestant church-goers are also jumping onto the Jesuits' exciting, do-as-you-please media train of "Just do it". The churched Protestants are copying the corrupted unchurched Protestant Americans. This is evidence that much of the churched Protestants have lost their beautiful holiness which Jehovah always required, and which He bequeathed to His children (see 1 Peter 1:13-16). Protestantism is repeating the pattern of the pre-Constantine apostatizing church spoken of by Daniel. By their abrogation of God's authority to condemn their sins through His Law, the Protestant denominations lost the only means to justification and sanctification. Then, to finish their demise by the Jesuit-driven corruption of the Protestants, the power of Christ's gospel of self-sacrificing love has all but vanished from the holy people. "An host was given him against the daily sacrifice by reason of transgression, and it cast down the truth to the ground; and it practised, and prospered" (Dan. 8:12). Surely our Protestant brethren are fields of grain, bundled and being sifted by the devil (see Isaiah 40:8; Luke 22:31).

The exceptions to this are two groups which ultimately reunite into one: 1) those who, despite the demon and Jesuit darkness that has covered the earth, have continued to love biblical truth taught in their Sunday Schools, Sabbath Schools, and small group Bible studies, and 2) those anti-religion hedonists and freedom fighters who eventually see their flawed rationale to hate the Bible, and come to God during the Latter Rain. Nevertheless, continued corruption is culling out from the Protestant west all the confirmed secularized, atheistic, rebellious Protestants because they are resentful toward the immorality and unethical actions by the Vatican, and the self-righteousness and the foolery plaguing her daughter denominations. Therefore, upon the initiation of Jesuit Inquisitions, when Christian America legislates church doctrine, the rebellious Protestants will find no reason to seek shelter in the Bible and from the God of their salvation.

> The [papal] king of the north shall come against him [the secular, atheistic, Protestant king of the south] like a whirlwind, with chariots, and with horsemen, and with many ships; and he shall enter into the countries, and shall overflow and pass over. He shall enter also into the glorious land, and many countries shall be overthrown: but these shall escape out of his hand, even Edom, and Moab, and the chief of the children of Ammon. He shall stretch forth his hand also upon the countries: and the land of Egypt shall not escape. But he shall have power over the treasures of gold and of silver, and over all the precious things of Egypt: and the Libyans and the Ethiopians shall be at his steps (Dan. 11:40-43).

And Protestant, Constitutional America, the anti-religion King of the south is never heard from again. Money became his god, and his money god was stolen by the vile, religio-political King of the north.

Fear will sweep most of these unwary freedom-loving, church-hating Protestants into Catholicism's ranks. All who the locust tormenters will fully harden against the God of their Reformation fathers, will never again have access to the truly liberating, voluntary, saving, rich, dual religion of the Bible — *Protestantism with its focus on reconciliation with God, superadded by its powerful Judgment Day addition, Seventh-day Adventism.* Tools of the prince of evil, the Jesuits having finally succeeded to overthrow the one holy and pure religion of grace and Law, Protestantism will then forever cease to be available. After exactly five hundred years to the day, the Counter-Reformation will have finally achieved the end of Protestantism and its free nation. The deadline: a big 2017 Halloween party to the Dragon.

> By the rivers of Babylon, there we sat down, yea, we wept, when we remembered Protestant America.
>
> We hanged our harps upon the willows in the midst thereof.
>
> For there they that carried us away captive required of us a song; and they that wasted us required of us mirth, saying, Sing us one of the songs of Protestantism.
>
> How shall we sing the LORD's song in a strange land?
>
> If I forget thee, O Reformation, let my right hand forget her cunning.
>
> If I do not remember thee, let my tongue cleave to the roof of my mouth; if I prefer not the Latter Rain above my chief joy.
>
> Remember, O LORD, the children of Jesuitism during Your revival of Protestantism; who said, Rase it, rase it, even to the foundation thereof.
>
> O Woman who rides the Beast, who art to be destroyed; happy shall he be, that taketh and dasheth thy little ones against the stones.
>
> Happy shall he be, that rewardeth thee as thou hast done to us. (Adapted from Psalm 137).

From page 156:

55. Revelation 9 and Josiah Litch Ford states, "Litch's application of Revelation 9:15 to August 11, 1840, was quite wrong, as he himself admitted in later years." "Ellen White accepted the prophetic conclusions of Josiah Litch regarding August 11, 1840" (Ford, pages 659-660, 584). Did Mrs. White say much about the seven trumpets?

No. This is the only known reference to Revelation 9 in all of Ellen White's writings and it appears, not in connection with an exegetical study of the Bible, but as part of her description of the Millerite movement. On the basis of his interpretation of Revelation 9:15 Josiah Litch predicted in 1838 that the Ottoman power would be broken in 1840. On August 1, 1840, he predicted that it would occur on August 11. What took place on that date confirmed the faith of multitudes in the Millerite interpretation of Scripture and gave the advent movement great impetus.

If Ellen White, in *The Great Controversy*, pages 334-335, means that John the Revelator's prophecy was fulfilled on August 11, 1840, she would be giving support to Litch's interpretation of Revelation 9:15. If she simply means that Josiah Litch's prediction was fulfilled, then she is not necessarily supporting Litch's interpretation of the text.

The Seventh-day Adventist Bible Commentary states, "Generally speaking, the Seventh-day Adventist interpretation of the fifth and sixth trumpets, particularly as touching the time period involved, is essentially that of Josiah Litch" (Volume 7, Page 796). *Ministry* magazine has suggested the dates 1453 to 1844 for the sixth trumpet instead of the period 1449 to 1840 assigned by Litch (*Ministry*, October, 1980, Page 41).

From page 184:

56. Revelation 11 and the French Revolution

Was Ellen White wrong in her Great Controversy explanation of Revelation 11? Ford claims that "it is not possible to support *The Great Controversy* exposition of Revelation 11 either exegetically or historically" (Page 575), and "the application [of the year-day principle] made to the French Revolution is certainly incorrect." He says he prefers the application of Revelation 11 found in *Testimonies for the Church*, Volume 4, Page 594 (*Ford*, pages 575, 326).

In *Testimonies for the Church*, Volume 4, Page 594, Ellen White is not giving an exegesis of Revelation 11. She is simply using the language of Revelation 11:3 as a matter of convenience. In *The Great Controversy*, pages 265-288 she discusses Revelation 11 in considerable detail and gives the impression that she is really telling her readers what that chapter means.

Ellen White did make some minor changes in the 1911 edition of this chapter of *The Great Controversy*. "The great bell of the palace" in the 1888 edition was changed to "a bell" in 1911; "The Word of God was prohibited" became "The Worship of the Deity was abolished." "The decree which prohibited the Bible" was altered to read "the decrees which abolished the Christian religion and set aside the Bible," etc. (See *The Great Controversy*, pages 272, 273, 286, 287.)

These changes did not affect the exposition of the chapter, however, which remained the same in 1911 as it had been in the 1888 edition.

Although certain minor historical points needed revision, this can hardly be used as an argument against the basic exposition itself. No better or more satisfactory interpretation of Revelation 11 has been written than that found in *The Great Controversy*.

From page 189:

Atonement by the scapegoat. Some have misunderstood the truth that Azazel, the scapegoat, correctly represents Satan and his favored earthly organization. They came to the incorrect belief that Azazel represented Christ because they misread Leviticus 16:10. They see the word "atonement" associated with the scapegoat and assume that Christ is typified there. I would like to dispel that error. To clarify it we must look at the annual, Old Testament sanctuary "day of atonement" (Lev. 23:27) and then at the significant Daniel 8:14 prophecy which used that literal, annual, single day ceremony to apply it to the finale of an epoch-spanning apostasy. So first, the annual sanctuary cleansing on the Day of Atonement:

"And Aaron shall cast lots upon the two goats[H8163]; one lot for the LORD, and the other lot for the scapegoat[H5799]" (Lev. 16:8).

"And Aaron shall bring the goat[H8163] upon which the LORD's lot fell, and offer him for a sin offering" (Lev. 16:9).

"But the goat[H8163], on which the lot fell to be the scapegoat[H5799], shall be presented alive before the LORD, to make an atonement with him, and to let him go for a scapegoat[H5799] into the wilderness" (Lev. 16:10).

"And he [high priest Aaron] shall make an atonement for the holy place, because of the uncleanness of the children of Israel, and because of their transgressions in all their sins: and so shall he do for the tabernacle of the congregation, that remaineth among them in the midst of their uncleanness" (Lev. 16:16).

"And when he hath made an end of reconciling the holy place, and the tabernacle of the congregation, and

Appendix A: Comments referred to from main text

the altar, he shall bring the live goat[H8163]: and Aaron shall lay both his hands upon the head of the live goat[H8163], and confess over him all the iniquities of the children of Israel, and all their transgressions in all their sins, putting them upon the head of the goat[H8163], and shall send him away by the hand of a fit man into the wilderness: and the goat[H8163] shall bear upon him all their iniquities unto a land not inhabited: and he shall let go the goat[H8163] in the wilderness" (Lev. 16:20-22).

"And he that let go the goat[H8163] for the scapegoat[H5799] shall wash his clothes, and bathe his flesh in water, and afterward come into the camp" (Lev. 16:26).

Strong's H5799 *'āzâ 'zel* From H5795 and H235; *goat of departure*; the *scapegoat*: — scapegoat.

Strong's H8163 *śâ'iyr, śâ'ir* From H8175; *shaggy*; as noun, a *he goat*; by analogy a *faun*: — devil, goat, hairy, kid, rough, satyr.

The first goat, chosen by lot and sacrificed as a sin offering, took the sins of the people away with his death in order to accomplish the sanctuary's cleansing. We know Christ took our judgment on the cross (see Hebrews 9:12-14, 26; 10:10, 11), therefore the sacrificed goat unquestionably represented the Son of God. Once the sanctuary was cleansed of all the sins of the children of Israel by the blood of the first goat, "reconciling" the whole sanctuary complex (see Leviticus 16:20), all the sins of Israel were loaded upon Azazel (see verse 20, 21). Then the goat, which ceremonially having assumed all the guilt of the nation's sins, was taken into the uninhabitable wasteland to die, as closure to cleansing the sanctuary on the Day of Atonement. Whereas the first goat's blood and blood from every daily sin offering were sprinkled in the sanctuary, the scapegoat's blood never atoned for anyone because its blood was not shed.

Without shedding of blood is no remission (Heb. 9:22).

In contrast to the sympathy evoked by the dying goat where the dying animal gripped and broke impenitent hearts, Azazel disappearing whole and alive called forth no sympathy. Rather, Azazel evoked scorn because it made no covenant with God by sacrifice (see Psalm 50:5), as did the dying goat. "For the life of the flesh is in the blood: and I have given it to you upon the altar to make an atonement for your souls: for it is the blood that maketh an atonement for the soul" (Lev. 17:11). Azazel personified Babylon the Great, who boasted, "I sit a queen, and...shall see no sorrow" (Rev. 18:7); and then burning torment, thirst, hunger, and weariness was her due (see Revelation 17:16; 18:7, 8; Jeremiah 51:58, 64, Isaiah 47:13-15; Amos 8:11, 12). This description had been the subject of the object lesson for God's warning to every nation involved in spiritualism (see Deuteronomy 29:18-27). Therefore, the Lord who created this sanctuary ceremony never intended Azazel to symbolize redemption, but rather retribution and eventual damnation. This ceremonial desert scenario encompasses the Executive Judgment upon Satan. And it judges Satan's one counterfeit religion of spiritualism (see Revelation 19:20), where no dying Saviour ever gripped and broke the impenitent heart, and where no messy blood ever disturbed the petted sensibilities of the wicked. That wilderness judgment upon Azazel is seen symbolically also in Revelation 20:1, 2 where a strong angel with a strong chain binds Satan and restrains him in the bottomless pit while judgment is being passed upon him (see verse 4). This millennium judgment scenario shows that Satan will literally be imprisoned on this barren planet after Jesus burns up its surface and "the works that are therein" with "fervent heat" at His second coming (see 2 Peter 3:10-12; Jeremiah 4:23-27). During that thousand year judgment Satan awaits his full destruction. Thus, Satan is later seen in a lake of fire with the Beast and his false prophet (see Revelation 20:10), both of whom Satan appointed to deceive the whole world (see Revelation 13:2, 3, 11-15). This 2 Peter 3 and Revelation 20 judgment upon the adversary is what played out in miniature year after year by Azazel being bound and abandoned in the shimmering, burning desert.

A kid goat can represent more than a holy Messiah. One of the above definitions of Leviticus 16:8 and 10 scriptures for H8163 *śâ 'iyr*, "goat", is that of Satan. The following verses use goats to represent Satan in the context of pagan false worship.

And he ordained him priests for the high places, and for the devils[H8163] [*śâ 'iyr*], and for the calves which he had made (2 Chron. 11:15).

And they shall no more offer their sacrifices unto devils[H8163] [*śâ 'iyr*], after whom they have gone a whoring. This shall be a statute for ever unto them throughout their generations (Lev. 17:7).

We also know that, as was the hot Sinai desert into which Azazel was taken, likewise the fires of the lake that God has prepared for Satan and his angels (see Matthew

25:41; 2 Peter 2:4; Psalm 90:7-9; Deuteronomy 29:20-23) will be the devil's end.

Another connection between Satan and Azazel is seen in the sanctuary judgment upon the little horn of Daniel 8:14. The little horn represented Satan, seen by comparing the little horn's actions in Daniel 8:10, 11 to those of the great red dragon (Satan) in Revelation 12:4-7 (see also Isaiah 14:12-14 and Ezekiel 28:2, 6).

The little horn power of Daniel 7 and 8 represented Satan's devious work on earth, by the sudden entrance of an apostasy within God's church late in the Roman Empire, "the mystery of iniquity" (2 Thess. 2:7, cf Dan. 8:23, 12; 11:21-23) and would continue until the last days (Daniel 2:40-43; 7:25; 8:17; 10:14; 11:40-12:12; 2 Thessalonians 2:8). Satan has always worked subtly and it was an impeccably subtle work which the Lord permitted Satan to bring to ancient Israel because they repeatedly turned away from His covenant (see Judges 2:20-22; Jeremiah 4:10; 2 Chronicles 36:14-16). Just as Azazel looked identical to the sacrificed goat, Lucifer has sought for his corrupt system of worship to resemble Christ's economy closely enough to fool the unconverted heart, yet to never be redemptive.

Again in Daniel's future, Jehovah would permit the little horn to do another subtle work (see Revelation 17:6-8) by peaceably subjugating the church because the Lord's post-apostolic people would also turn away from Him (see Daniel 8:12; 11:30, 31) as Israel had (see Daniel 9:5-19). Under the Antichrist power during the captivities of the long 1,260 year Dark Ages and the future New Age of light (see Daniel 7:8, 25; Revelation 13:1-10 and 11-17), Satan would have complete control to dominate God's church until Jehovah could recompense upon Satan's head all the departures from salvation into which he had led God's people (see Daniel 7:9-11, 26; 8:25; 11:45). This judgment is also the making of atonement upon him by avenging the terror and death that the adversary waged against the saints of God (see Daniel 7:19-22; Revelation 17:4-6; 19:20, 21; 20:10; Deuteronomy 32:41-43; Jeremiah 25:12-14; 30:16).

In light of the elements of the ceremonial Day of Atonement, altogether it is logical that Azazel should refer to Satan by 1) the actions of high priest Aaron putting the sins of Israel upon the head of scapegoat Azazel *after* atoning for the sanctuary by blood, 2) seeing that the meaning of "goat" was used also to represent Satan, and 3) connecting it with the cleansing of the heavenly sanctuary in Daniel 8:9-14 after the little horn imposed itself against Christ. It overthrew Christ's ministry of His redeeming sacrifice and Spirit, it defiled the sanctuary by substituting his own look-alike system, and led the Lord's host into defiling the sanctuary (also seen in Daniel 11:30-32).

Putting the evidence all together, the scapegoat that was not sacrificed must represent Satan and his attempt to usurp Christ's redemption through His church, that is, to establish the mystery of iniquity.

In short, the first goat represented the *tempted* and the second goat represented the *tempters*. In behalf of the *tempted* people of God, the blood of the sacrificed goat cleansed the sanctuary by making final atonement for all who had repented and had already been atoned for during the preceding year. Christ could cleanse the sanctuary by taking their place in judgment. But, Christ will never do the same for Azazel, Satan and his human agents. Instead, all the sins committed by God's people through Satan's devious temptations will be laid to his account and his full destruction accomplished. And all who never sought Jesus for His atonement (see Luke 13: 25-27; Matthew 25:42-46) will join the tempter in the unquenchable "fire, prepared for the devil and his angels" (Matt. 25:41).

The goat "upon which the LORD's lot fell" (Lev. 16:9), cleared all the resident guilt of the commandment-keepers and saved them from eternal destruction. And the other "on which the lot fell to be the scapegoat", never saw sorrow or pain (see Revelation 18:7), but was "presented alive before the LORD" (Lev. 16:10), summoned before the great Judge for Him to call retribution upon the rebel *tempters* of God and His people (see Daniel 7:9-11; 1 Samuel 15:32, 33; Exodus 17:14-16; Matthew 4:7).

Please, keep in mind that the following pivotal Daniel 8 sanctuary cleansing prophecy that concerned a "little horn, which waxed exceeding great" (Dan. 8:9), was not fulfilled in Antiochus Epiphanes. By a single letter from the Roman Senate in response to Egypt's request for protection, this minor Greek king was forced to turn back from attacking a weak Egypt. The little King Antiochus Epiphanes was exceedingly minor in all respects when compared to Alexander the Great. Alexander's kingdom continued 166 years while Antiochus' kingdom lasted not a dozen. Alexander the Great was termed, "very great" (Dan. 8:8). Yet, this little horn is said to become mightier than the great Alexander. The horn is called, "exceeding great", ascending all the way to the heavenly sanctuary. This corrupting, polluting horn of the pivotal

Daniel 8:14 sanctuary prophecy exceeded the longevity of Imperial Rome, spanning the millennia until Michael resurrects His dead saints and delivers His living (see Daniel 8:25; 11:45; 12:1). Rather than having the horn that stood up higher than Michael, the Prince of princes, representing tiny King Antiochus Epiphanes, this blasphemous power represents Satan, who tempted the holy people to follow after his devils (see Daniel 8:12, 24), and eclipsed Michael's sacrifice and its power of God unto salvation. Satan polluted the heavenly sanctuary (see Daniel 8:10, 11; Isaiah 14:12-14), causing the need for cleansing God's sanctuary of his filth (see Daniel 8:14).

"[Gabriel] said unto me, Understand, O son of man: for *at the time of the end* shall be the vision" (Dan. 8:17). "And the vision of the evening and the morning which was told is true: wherefore shut thou up the vision; for *it shall be for many days*" (Dan. 8:26). "And some of them of understanding shall fall, to try them, and to purge, and to make them white, even *to the time of the end*: because it is yet for a time appointed. And the king shall do according to his will; and he shall exalt himself, and magnify himself above every god, and shall speak marvellous things against the God of gods, and shall prosper till the indignation be accomplished: for that that is determined shall be done" (Dan. 11:35, 36). The little horn/vile king of the north of Daniel's prophecies, who would teach incomprehensible lies against Jehovah, haughtily raising himself up in the minds of Jehovah's people and leading them to look downward upon their God, and who would continue to "the time of the end", was not Antiochus Epiphanes who lived during the third century BC.

The little horn is the earthly manifestation of Satan; it is the visible counterpart of his spiritual kingdom (see 2 Thessalonians 2:9). [Notice that Satan in Revelation 12:4-7 does the same as the little horn did in Daniel 8:10, 11, i.e. casting down stars, and standing up against Michael the great Prince of the host, "Messiah the Prince" (Dan. 9:25, cf 10:21; 12:1).] Thus, Azazel, the little horn power, which will be destroyed by the "cleansed" sanctuary in Daniel 8:14 and Revelation 15:8, is Satan and his favored earthly agency at the time of the end when judgment can be laid against Azazel and atonement made upon him, and not because of him. "He shall also stand up against the Prince of princes; but he shall be broken without [human] hand" (Dan. 8:25). "He shall come to his end, and none shall help him" (Dan. 11:45, cf Isa. 14:16, 17). "But the judgment shall sit, and they shall take away his dominion, to consume and to destroy it unto the end" (Dan. 7:26, cf Rev. 19:19-20:3, 10; Mal. 4:1-3).

Paul understood clearly the Daniel 8 prophecy and its expanded Daniel 11 version, that both were yet to be fulfilled after his lifetime. Writing that the prophecy was still future to Paul's day, Paul commentaries on Daniel 11 verses 36 and 45 in his letter to the Thessalonian church. "Let no man deceive you by any means: for that day [Christ's return] shall not come, except *there come* a falling away first, and that man of sin be revealed, the son of perdition; who opposeth and exalteth himself above all that is called God, or that is worshipped; so that he as God sitteth in the temple of God, shewing himself that he is God" (2 Thess. 2:3, 4). But, Paul also wrote that the little horn, son of perdition, had already begun its work to blaspheme Christ (see verse 7). Therefore, we can conclude that the little horn power would begin its work prior to Paul's death in 67 AD and continue through the centuries until its judgment at Christ's return (see 2 Thessalonians 2:8).

Gabriel showed Daniel that the conclusion of the chapter 8 and 11 visions, which would be "at the time of the end", would actually end at the final time of trouble. "And at that time shall Michael stand up, the great prince which standeth for the children of thy people: and there shall be a time of trouble, such as never was since there was a nation even to that same time: and at that time thy people shall be delivered, every one that shall be found written in the book. And many of them that sleep in the dust of the earth shall awake, some to everlasting life, and some to shame and everlasting contempt" (Dan. 12:1, 2).

This horn that grew bigger and bigger all the way to heaven and that withstood the Lord's redemption sounds identical to the self-exaltation of Satan because it was Satan who breathed life into the little horn earthly power. "And out of one of them [the four winds] came forth a little horn, which waxed exceeding great, toward the south, and toward the east, and toward the pleasant land. And it waxed great, even to the host of heaven; and it cast down some of the host and of the stars to the ground, and stamped upon them. Yea, he magnified himself even to the prince of the host, and by him the daily sacrifice was taken away, and the place of his sanctuary was cast down. An host was given him against the daily sacrifice by reason of transgression, and it cast down the truth to the ground; and it practised, and prospered" (Dan. 8:9-12). Like Goliath, Satan and the little horn have had unlimited self-confidence and power over Christ until their destruction.

How art thou fallen from heaven, O Lucifer, son of the morning! how art thou cut down to the ground, which didst weaken the nations! For thou hast said in thine heart, I will ascend into heaven, I will exalt my throne above the stars of God: I will sit also upon the mount of the congregation, in the sides of the north: I will ascend above the heights of the clouds; I will be like the most High (Isa. 14:12-14).

In the way of the Leviticus 16:10 atonement with Azazel, what do we see in Daniel 8:14?

Then I heard one saint speaking, and another saint said unto that certain saint which spake, How long shall be the vision concerning the daily sacrifice, and the transgression of desolation, to give both the sanctuary and the host to be trodden under foot? And he said unto me, Unto two thousand and three hundred days; then shall the sanctuary be cleansed (Dan. 8:13, 14).

This vision instructs us that the Daniel 8 atonement associated with cleansing the heavenly sanctuary would come, not via sacrificial death, but *by way of ultimate punishment upon* the blasphemous horn power that tried to overthrow heaven and stamp out the saints of the Most High. So, we must not immediately assume that atonement comes only by sacrificial death. Vengeance of the Lord upon His enemy is as much a part of the work of atonement/cleansing as is His grace through the sacrifice of Himself. The horn's atoning/cleansing punishment is indicated more clearly at the end of the vision. "He [the little horn power] shall be broken without hand" (Dan. 8:25). And again, "He shall plant the tabernacles of his palace between the seas in the glorious holy mountain; yet he shall come to his end, and none shall help him" (Dan. 11:45). Of Lucifer's final destruction, we read, "The angels which kept not their first estate, but left their own habitation, he hath reserved in everlasting chains under darkness unto the judgment of the great day" (Jude 6). "For thou hast said in thine heart…I will ascend above the heights of the clouds; I will be like the most High. Yet thou shalt be brought down to hell, to the sides of the pit. They that see thee shall narrowly look upon thee, and consider thee, saying, Is this the man that made the earth to tremble, that did shake kingdoms…?" (Isa. 14:13-16).

We likewise see the same little horn in Daniel 7, judged and destroyed. "I beheld then because of the voice of the great words which the horn spake: I beheld even till the beast was slain, and his body destroyed, and given to the burning flame" (Dan. 7:11). "But the judgment shall sit, and they shall take away his dominion, to consume and to destroy it unto the end" (Dan. 7:26). Similar to the little horn in those burning flames, the scapegoat Azazel is punished with having to suffer in a burning desert without water and protection from the sun, until it slowly dies of dehydration and exposure to heat. This compares with Satan, after being released again from his imprisonment in Revelation 20:7, who, like the little horn, is burned up much longer than anyone else, "unto the end" (Dan. 7:26). "And the devil that deceived them was cast into the lake of fire and brimstone, where the beast and the false prophet are, and shall be tormented day and night for ever and ever" (Rev. 20:10). The symbolic eternal aspect of the Beast's and false prophet's torment expresses the infinite disfavor Jehovah gives them to recompense their coup d'état against His kingdom. They receive all the empty void in the soul from which Christ suffered to shield them when He was in Gethsemane. Their damnation which He took was wasted on them, and now must fall on their souls.

Thus, atoning judgment would need to be made *for* God's heavenly sanctuary and His tempted people. Then judgment would be made *against* the defilement of the sanctuary's redemptive work by Satan's ages-old spiritualistic substitutes under the cloak of the everlasting gospel. A heavenly tribunal must be set up to examine Satan's case for his final destruction (see Daniel 7:9-11). But, judgment must condemn many for joining Satan in defiling "the temple of God, and the altar, and them that worship therein" (Rev. 11:1), and the same judgment would justify those who knew God and fought to preserve His heavenly temple (see Revelation 11:3-13), an investigation to decide whose side each was on, the Lord's or Azazel's.

Through Athaliah, the murderous Ashtoreth worshiper, we preview Satan's demise that will take place away from the heavenly sanctuary. This was the same action taken against the scapegoat, away from the tabernacle of the congregation.

Have her forth without the ranges: and him that followeth her kill with the sword. For the priest had said, Let her not be slain in the house of the LORD. And they laid hands on her; and she went by the way by the which the horses came into the king's house: and there was she slain (2 Ki. 11:15, 16).

In another example, the Lord's atonement with Azazel uses similar language which He used during Israel's deliverance from Egyptian slavery. "I will harden Pharaoh's heart, that he shall follow after them [the children of Israel]; and I will be *honoured upon Pharaoh*, and upon all his host; that the Egyptians may know that I am the LORD" (Ex. 14:4). Pharaoh never honored the Lord by true surrender to Jehovah's commands or by death to self under the heavy hand of the Lord. Pharaoh's desires and actions were of only pride, ease, power, rebellion, and a total lack of compassion. Like Lucifer, Pharoah didn't exonerate the Creator with a heavenly character and self-sacrificing love. He had never known suffering. But Jehovah was honored by Pharaoh *when He executed due justice upon him*. So will He be honored when He executes justice upon Azazel. Thus, the Lord will make atonement with Lucifer, who began as son of the morning and ended as son of perdition.

From page 212:

Obvious similarities exist between Daniel 12:6, 7 and Revelation 10:6, 7. Again, similarities also exist between Revelation chapters 10 and 11 so that those two chapters are tack-welded together at three spots: Revelation 10:11 to 11:1 (the Angel continuing his instructions to John), Revelation 10:7 to 11:15 (the mystery of God finished at the seventh trumpet), and Revelation 10:11 to 11:11 (the holy people prophesying again after being resuscitated from the divine consequences for worshiping other gods). Since Revelation 10 dovetails with Revelation 11, and since Daniel 12:6 and 7 so closely mirror Revelation 10:6 and 7, as we examined in the main text, then may Daniel 12 hide another clue to the composite Revelation chapters 10 and 11 that could help confirm their intimate relationship, and shed light on latter day events?

Something that we notice in Daniel 12 are the two timeframes within Daniel 12:7 that must transpire before "the end of these wonders" (Dan. 12:6) ["the end of these wonders" also expressed as "the mystery of God…finished" (Rev. 10:7)]. When looking at the wonders that Daniel had been given, we can dismiss the false interpretation of Daniel's visions that refer to Antiochus Epiphanes of old Greece. And because the prophecy contains a centuries-long, desolating transgression, we can also dismiss a short, last minute "Antichrist" military attack on modern day Israel, as in the secret rapture-seven year tribulation formula.

This we can nail down by the fact that, as a backdrop to Daniel 12:6, all those "wonders" added up to an overlaid prophecy of great time span, as Gabriel explained in Daniel 8:17, 26, and 10:14, and elaborated in Daniel's chapter 11 vision. This is further understood from Daniel 9's long Messianic prophecy, it being less than a quarter of the larger Daniel 8 vision, Daniel 9's long 490 year vision also being a subset of Daniel 8's much larger vision (compare Daniel 9:21 with Daniel 8:15ff). Those "wonders" reveal the deceptive work of God's one great enemy as the motivating force for world domination at work in all of human history. Daniel's prophecies reveal a work of great systems involving human puppets that mask Satan and his work to destroy humanity, while he and his demonic forces were pulling the strings all along. His earthly power, using the Christian religion as an effective parasite, made its way into world governments divinely established for law and order, destabilizing them for the parasite's ultimate usurpation. Thus did he "weaken the nations" (Isa. 14:12). Specifically, Daniel's visions show this vile parasite to be antithetical to all social order and to just, divinely ordained government for the people. By force and by fraud, it worked above and behind the policies of states and empires. The prophecies show it exceeding the length of every civil dynasty. This vile religious power spanned generations, cultures, and eras far beyond Daniel 9's dissolution of Israel, reaching down to Judgment Day when Messiah the Prince would stand up to deliver His children.

> He said unto me, Understand, O son of man: for at *the time of the end shall be the vision*…. And he said, Behold, I will make thee know what shall be in the last end of the indignation: for *at the time appointed the end shall be*…. And the vision of the evening and the morning which was told is true: wherefore *shut thou up the vision*; for *it shall be for many days* (Dan. 8:17, 19, 26).

> Now I am come to make thee understand what shall befall thy people *in the latter days*: for yet the vision is for many days…. But thou, O Daniel, *shut up the words*, and *seal the book, even to the time of the end*: many shall run to and fro, and knowledge shall be increased (Dan. 10:14; 12:4).

Daniel's "these wonders" (that concerned God and His blasphemous adversary) and John's "the mystery of God" (God who was bound up with seven seals) explain Satan's work behind an earthly power (hateful and bold, having a fierce countenance and a stout look) to ultimately sweep all of humanity into perdition (see Daniel 12:9, 10; 11:21; 7:8; Revelation 13:6-8).

> And I heard the man clothed in linen, which was upon the waters of the river, when he held up his right hand and his left hand unto heaven, and sware by him that liveth for ever that it shall be for a time, times, and an half; and when he shall have accomplished to scatter the power of the holy people, all these things shall be finished (Dan. 12:7).

Each part of the two significant prophecies within Daniel 12:7 precedes the very end before Jesus returns: i.e. 1) the infamous "time, times, and an half", as first given in Daniel 7:25; and, 2) God having "accomplished to scatter the power of the holy people". That significant second prophecy of scattering is a long-standing Old Testament, promised punishment by the Lord, and He spoke it not as a possibility, but as His expectation. (See Leviticus 26:19, 33; Deuteronomy 31:16-19; Jeremiah 9:16; 13:24.) Those Daniel 12:7 prophecies end with the mystery of God finished (see 2 Thessalonians 1:7-9; 2:2-4; Daniel 11:36, 45). The scattering follows the 3 ½ times Dark Ages prophecy, which means that God would accomplish to scatter His holy people after 1798.

Linking the three scripture references in a chain, Daniel 12:7, Revelation 10, and Revelation 11, we see the first of the two events from Daniel 12:7, the "time, times, and an half", occurring twice in the Revelation 11 vision, first as "forty and two months" (Rev. 11:2), and then as "a thousand two hundred and threescore days" (verse 3). In a literary way, the placement of these two identical time prophecies in Revelation 11 has no little significance, in that one immediately follows the other. Nowhere else in scripture does that central prophetic period appear twice, back to back. The close proximity of their repetition equates to emphasis — eye-catching, attention-grabbing emphasis. And it should alert the Bible student to link the combined Revelation 10/11 prophecy with the one that it is interpreting — namely, the end-time prophecy first given in Daniel 7:25 and repeated in Daniel 12:7, which describe the same period of time, not in units of months or days, but in units of years, "time, times, and an half".

Therefore, we can conclude that the Daniel 12:7 mention of papal apostasy and the joint Revelation chapters 10 and 11 have the designed object to help explain each other. This eye-catching emphasis of the 3 ½ year time prophecy is true even though the same prophecy of Daniel 12:7 and Revelation 11:2, 3 come clothed in different numerals and units of time. In fact, the three equivalent time prophecies repeated by their refreshing, non-redundant form of reiteration enhances their readability and connection.

But, that leaves the second event of Daniel 12:7 yet to be seen in the composite Revelation 10 and 11 vision — the Daniel 12:7 scattering of the power of the holy people. Can we see anywhere in the Revelation 11 context this second event, God's inauspicious accomplishment to scatter the power of His people? Is not this scattering the judgment period of "three days and an half" (Rev. 11:9)? In the verses quoted below from Isaiah 51, we see a fulfillment of the scattering Christ promised Israel for involvement with spiritualism. We also see where Christ's Revelation 11 symbolism was derived.

> These two things are come unto thee; who shall be sorry for thee? desolation, and destruction, and the famine, and the sword: by whom shall I comfort thee? Thy sons have fainted, they lie at the head of all the streets, as a wild bull in a net: they are full of the fury of the LORD, the rebuke of thy God (Isa. 51:19, 20, cf Lev. 26:16-39; Jer. 16:4).

Ancient Israel's constant trysts with Babylonian Spiritual Formation and celebration religion are used by the visions written especially clearly in Daniel 8:12 and 11:30, 36 to typify the future work of Satan against the church of Christ during the Dark Ages. This concept Paul confirmed in 2 Thessalonians 2:3-7. Therefore, the many apostasies by the Hebrews form a type of the Beast-led apostasy by New Testament Israel (the church) that would begin during the post-apostolic era. But, far more significant to us today is the prophecy that the end-time people of God would also be spiritually scattered when "their dead bodies shall lie in the street of the great city" (Rev. 11:8). This 3 ½ day scattering is separate and not concurrent with the 3 ½ year time prophecy from AD 538-1798. We can say this because in Revelation 11 the scattering occurs after the 3 ½ year prophecy has successfully finished its mission and the beast arises from the bottomless pit (see verse 7). Therefore, the scattering does not describe the Dark Ages church in the wilderness or the church during the Reformation and the Counter-Reformation. The scattering of God's people takes place after 1798. More specifically, according to Revelation 11:7, it happens during the first six trumpets since the sixth trumpet concludes after the scattering ends when the scattered people of God are resurrected to sit in heavenly places (see Revelation 11:11-13) after the Revelation 7:3 delay ends (see Revelation 10:6, 7) and the Latter Rain revival begins (see Revelation 11:14).

Doesn't the Revelation 11:8 scene of dead bodies laid out in the street even more than closely resemble the divinely determined desolation of ancient Israel when Ezekiel saw their power scattered, symbolized by the very dry bones scattered under the wrathful, burning sun (see Ezekiel 37:1, 2; Jeremiah 8:1, 2; Ezekiel 6:5)? And, doesn't their later resurrection in Ezekiel 37:3-10 describe perfectly that of Revelation 11:11?

From the comparison of the two desolations and resurrections of Jeremiah/Ezekiel and Revelation 11 we can see that the prophetic 3 ½ day period of Revelation 11:9-11 must not be a literal 3 ½ years. Rather the 3 ½ day period must simply imply an indefinite period that describes judgment — the Daniel 12:7 judgment scattering of the power of the holy people who live at the very end of those wonders spelled out in Daniel's visions. And those astonishing visions we have already shown to connect with the mystery of God that is finished at the seventh trumpet. That scattered generation would be the very last in the lineage of the wilderness church's seed, as Revelation 11 and 12 portray it, with whom the dragon would make war by God giving him one last opportunity to re-empower his Beast (see Revelation 11:7; 12:17). The final seed would be those who "keep the commandments of God, and have the testimony of Jesus Christ" (Rev. 12:17, cf Rev. 19:10) not in peacetime, but under the most egregious captivity. They would live at "the end of these wonders" (Dan. 12:6) before Michael stands up (see Daniel 12:1) and they arise out of their stupor of unbelief and spiritual adultery due to "their uncircumcised hearts [being] humbled" (Lev. 26:40). More than Sr. White's commentary of Revelation 11:9-11 in France's Reign of Terror, this interpretation uses scripture to explain scripture. It lets Revelation 10, 11, 12, and Daniel 12 interpret each other. It lets the Bible be its own expositor.

As much as we may not want to hear it, the Daniel 12:7/Revelation 10:7/Revelation 11:9-11 scattering judgment prophecy, similar to the symbolic 3 ½ year judgment of the apostolic church, means a conquest of Protestantism and Adventism, a corrective measure for all who will be humbled by it and converted. Satan having already begun this judgment is becoming increasingly apparent as we are daily seeing bulwarks built up around us economically, socially, religiously, and militarily.

The 3 ½ day prophecy indicates a harsh judgment period consuming unbelief, pride, and worldliness, as 3 ½ was the numeral for judgment established when Elijah reclaimed the hearts of the backslidden Israelites. The Revelation 11:8-13 prophecy must reiterate the Daniel 12:7 scattering of the power of the holy people at the very end before the seventh trumpet blows and the door of human probation closes. Thus, God's Adventists can revive and again give the message of the everlasting gospel to "them that dwell on the earth, and to every nation, and kindred, and tongue, and people" (Rev. 14:6), "they of the people and kindreds and tongues and nations… they that dwell upon the earth" (Rev. 11:9, 10, cf vs. 11, 12). The 3 ½ day prophecy upon the Advent movement is Christ's punishing judgment to purify "a very small remnant" (Isa. 1:9). Then, following the scattering of our power and the revival of righteousness by faith at the Loud Cry, Christ causes a "great earthquake" (Rev. 11:13), which symbolizes the church shaken when Jesus raises the standards of righteousness during the Latter Rain of His Spirit.

> Also I shook my lap, and said, So God shake out every man from his house, and from his labour, that performeth not this promise, even thus be he shaken out, and emptied (Neh. 5:13, cf Isa. 33:14).

> Yet gleaning grapes shall be left in it, as the shaking of an olive tree, two or three berries in the top of the uppermost bough, four or five in the outmost fruitful branches thereof, saith the LORD God of Israel (Isa. 17:6).

> And in that day it shall come to pass, that the glory of Jacob shall be made thin, and the fatness of his flesh shall wax lean (Isa. 17:4).

> And it shall come to pass in that day, that the remnant of Israel, and such as are escaped of the house of Jacob, shall no more again stay upon him that smote them; but shall stay upon the LORD, the Holy One of Israel, in truth. The remnant shall return, even the remnant of Jacob, unto the mighty God. For though thy people Israel be as the sand of the sea, yet a remnant

of them shall return: the consumption decreed shall overflow with righteousness (Isa. 10:20-22, cf Isa. 51:20-23).

Many shall be purified, and made white, and tried; but the wicked shall do wickedly: and none of the wicked shall understand; but the wise shall understand (Dan. 12:10).

That scattering and shaking will result in a new small remnant who the Lord can use to preach the gospel for a witness to all nations and to conquer the overspreading abominations of His enemy, as in the days of Gideon (see Judges 7:2-8). The Early Rain was reminiscent of the future abundant harvest.

The people that walked in darkness have seen a great light: they that dwell in the land of the shadow of death, upon them hath the light shined. Thou hast multiplied the nation, and not increased the joy: they joy before thee according to the joy in harvest, and as men rejoice when they divide the spoil. For thou hast broken the yoke of his burden, and the staff of his shoulder, the rod of his oppressor, as in the day of Midian. For every battle of the warrior is with confused noise, and garments rolled in blood; but this shall be with burning and fuel of fire (Isa. 9:2-5).

Satan has historically decimated Christ's people first spiritually, then temporally; he has never stopped short of both kinds of decimation. Because Christ's earthly kingdom has been a joint, but separated, religious and governmental state, Satan has also always used both in his kingdom. However, in his religio-political, imperialistic, and international kingdom, "they of the people and kindreds and tongues and nations" (Rev. 11:9), he has always united religious and state power to ravenously destroy Christ's presence throughout the earth that works to segregate religion and state. Satan's weakening of the nations had always repeated the same methods of subjugation, beginning with a spiritual approach that removed the divine truth and grace religion given to Adam. Once the corrupted nations became belligerent toward the devils' relentless "evil conscience" (Heb. 10:22), then Satan would change their religion from truth and justice only to lawless grace-only. Finally when the nations were totally corrupted by presumptuous, carnival "grace" from "God's religion", the devil would move in with his totalitarian government and sink the masses into poverty, incapacitating them from rising up to rid themselves of enslavement. Region by region captured, eventually Satan controlled the whole world this way — with exception of a faithful remnant, who lived the divine religion where truth must always be mixed with grace, and grace always mixed with truth. But ever since the beginning with Cain and Abel, all such resistance toward Satan's kingdom of presumptuous grace repeatedly met with his resort to violent force. Again and again, after killing the champions of faith, Satan would have control of Christ's people and the united nations. He had removed all opposition to his kingdom.

The silent, imperceptible movement of a storm front's first thin, leading edge encroaches the cloudless sapphire sky. Eventually, the coming tempest whispers its distant rumbles signaling the approach of a deafening storm. Satan's movements to dominate the world spiritually and legislatively have been indiscernible and pervasively overlooked. Like the serpent's slow slithering, Satan's favored agency in the world goes unnoticed until it is ready to strike. His vile king of the north displayed this characteristic of stealth. "In his estate shall stand up a vile person, to whom they shall not give the honour of the kingdom: but he shall come in peaceably, and obtain the kingdom by flatteries. And with the arms of a flood shall they be overflown from before him, and shall be broken; yea, also the prince of the covenant" (Dan. 11:21, 22). The peace-loving familiarity of the Vatican today has left Protestant America expecting a long future of peace and prosperity. But, behold the iniquity of Protestant America: "Pride, fulness of bread, and abundance of idleness was in her and in her daughters, neither did she strengthen the hand of the poor and needy" (Eze. 16:49). The holy people of the Book have been scattered spiritually, and are soon to be reminded of their militant enemy of the past, the surrogate mother of all living — the seductive, sadistic horn, the queen of dead works who rides the Roman Beast with its "people and kindreds and tongues and nations" (Rev. 11:9).

Appendix A: Comments referred to from main text

Notes

The fact that there is no controversy or agitation among God's people, should not be regarded as conclusive evidence that they are holding fast to sound doctrine. There is reason to fear that they may not be clearly discriminating between truth and error. When no new questions are started by investigation of the Scriptures, when no difference of opinion arises which will set men to searching the Bible for themselves, to make sure that they have the truth, there will be many now, as in ancient times, who will hold to tradition, and worship they know not what *Counsels to Writers and Editors*, p. 39.

There is no excuse for anyone in taking the position that there is no more truth to be revealed, and that all our expositions of Scripture are without an error. The fact that certain doctrines have been held as truth for many years by our people, is not a proof that our ideas are infallible. Age will not make error into truth, and truth can afford to be fair. No true doctrine will lose anything by close investigation *Counsels to Writers and Editors*, p. 35.

Many Gems Yet to Be Discovered. — New light will ever be revealed on the word of God to him who is in living connection with the Sun of Righteousness. Let no one come to the conclusion that there is no more truth to be revealed. The diligent, prayerful seeker for truth will find precious rays of light yet to shine forth from the word of God. Many gems are yet scattered that are to be gathered together to become the property of the remnant people of God. — Counsels on Sabbath School Work, p. 34. (1892) *Counsels to Writers and Editors*, p. 35.

Increased light will shine upon all the grand truths of prophecy, and they will be seen in freshness and brilliancy, because the bright beams of the Sun of Righteousness will illuminate the whole. . . *Manuscript Releases*, vol. 1, p. 40.

Appendix B:
Stock market graph

The nominal stock market chart looks phenomenally high since the first quarter of 2000. However, when adjusted for inflation, it more or less stays level across the peaks of the 1920s, the 1960s and the latest 2000s. Then it struggles to retain the 1999 volume. Even though the Dow Jones has continued to climb outside the graph below, inflation adjusted charts show that it has barely passed the volume of trading when the stock market peaked in the last quarter of 1999. After each high there is a deeper low. Inflated shares do not indicate economic health.

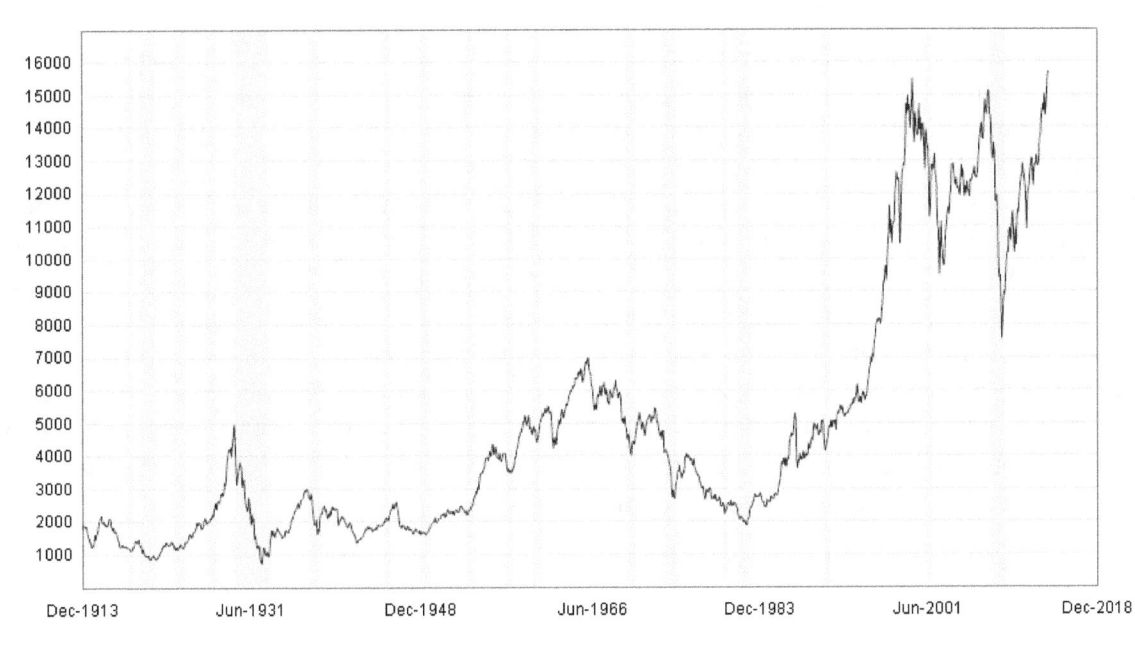

Dow Jones 100 Year Historical Chart

Appendix C:

Statement for scriptural honesty by Pilgrim Pastor John Robinson John Robinson, their pastor, who was providentially prevented from accompanying them, in his farewell address to the exiles said:

"Brethren, we are now erelong to part asunder, and the Lord knoweth whether I shall live ever to see your faces more. But whether the Lord hath appointed it or not, I charge you before God and His blessed angels to follow me no farther than I have followed Christ. If God should reveal anything to you by any other instrument of His, be as ready to receive it as ever you were to receive any truth of my ministry; for I am very confident the Lord hath more truth and light yet to break forth out of His holy word."—Martyn 5:70.

"For my part, I cannot sufficiently bewail the condition of the reformed churches, who are come to a period in religion, and will go at present no farther than the instruments of their reformation. The Lutherans cannot be drawn to go beyond what Luther saw; ... and the Calvinists, you see, stick fast where they were left by that great man of God, who yet saw not all things. This is a misery much to be lamented; for though they were burning and shining lights in their time, yet they penetrated not into the whole counsel of God, but were they now living, would be as willing to embrace further light as that which they first received."—D. Neal, History of the Puritans 1:269.

"Remember your church covenant, in which you have agreed to walk in all the ways of the Lord, made or to be made known unto you. Remember your promise and covenant with God and with one another, to receive whatever light and truth shall be made known to you from His written word; but withal, take heed, I beseech you, what you receive for truth, and compare it and weigh it with other scriptures of truth before you accept it; for it is not possible the Christian world should come so lately out of such thick antichristian darkness, and that full perfection of knowledge should break forth at once."—Martyn, vol. 5, pp. 70, 71 *The Great Controversy*, p. 291, 292.

Conclusion

Until the powerful day that Jesus returns we are to be focused on that day and to remain vigilant against temptation. We are to be sober-minded and watchful that Jesus alone has our heart. The Jesuit army, driven along by forces from below, are bent on the full dissolution of Protestantism and its powerful, infallible Bible. Yet, this is not a call to arms; it is a call to surrender. It's not a call to fight, but a call to stop fighting through the grace of Christ. The Lord has mercifully revealed to us His enemy because we need to know the enemy and the enemy's temptations, so that we might take it all in and "spread it before the LORD" (Isa. 37:14). If we have surrendered to Jesus, He is in our ship and we can rest quiet through the worst storm. If we've surrendered all; we have nothing to lose.

> Behold, I send you forth as sheep in the midst of wolves: be ye therefore wise as serpents, and harmless as doves (Matt. 10:16).

Even though the Jesuits and all the other secret societies have done so much evil to overthrow Protestant America, as well as the world under its protection and dominion, they are not the foremost cause of the soon coming total desolation of everything Protestant. *The cause is us.* Ultimately, we are the reason for our crumbling society and mountainous national debt. **We**, the Protestants, have not taken seriously our Reformation covenant with the God of heaven, or the special work of purification in preparation for Christ's return, in accordance with 1 John 3:3. We have not served Him with the whole heart and mind. We have not heeded the high spiritual standard of the Bible and the Testimony of Jesus which He gave to Ellen White to give to Protestantism, for the time was at hand. Instead, as the modern Israel of God, we've laughed off all condemnation of God, we've tried to giggle and grin away our misery, and celebrate our disobedience, just like the non-Christian world. That is why the Lord promised to sweep away all Israel's celebration and rejoicing in the past. Israel was to blame for God raising up Assyria and Babylon; and we are the reason that Protestantism has died, our old enemy from the ancient seven hills is collapsing constitutional democracies, and freedom in the world is disappearing. We have let the gifts of our land that has flowed with divine love and goodness dissolve our love for the Giver of every good and perfect gift. We have worshipped the gift rather than the Giver. We have not happily responded with the obligation of respectful obedience that little children give their parents, especially when our Parents in the heavens have given nothing but abundant goodness to us. We have not loved God with all of our heart, mind, soul, and strength. We have loved our neighbor with all our heart and mind and strength; and our God as ourselves, if we believed He existed. We have found atheism to be such a cause for disease that we turn to prayer and faith for their health-giving properties. But, who does this atheistic nation pray to? The ceiling? The sky? Other untrustworthy, unfaithful sinners? Blessed are the few who still have faith in the God of the Bible.

Protestant Americans are tuned to the radio signal rather than to the Spirit of their Maker. Their hearts are tuned to the television signal and the video game signal and the movie signal. How can their Redeemer get a word in edge-wise? How can He have communion with His beloved Reformation children for all their personal mountains of CDs and DVDs and their hypnotic gaming? The Protestants gather on their high day called, Thanksgiving. But, to whom is the atheistic nation thankful for all their happiness, creativity, inventiveness, and all the resulting abundance, convenience, and ease? We give a traditional prayer of thanks before we eat that meal. But to whom or to what are we performing that customary prayer? The hypocrisy of it all, after eating every other meal without service and gratitude to our Creator and Father all during the year! Then we dive into idolatrous self-indulgence until we are intoxicated with fat and sugar, rather than to follow the original Thanksgiving, to "rejoice before the LORD your God, ye, and your sons, and your daughters, and your menservants, and your maidservants, and the Levite" (Deut. 12:12). The Thanksgiving ritual is but a shell of the past, empty, very empty of communion with God, the Fount of every blessing. And our atheism has left our souls gutted of purpose and hope. Because we will not afflict our souls in preparation for the day of His visitation, our God must take that work into His own hands, and bring affliction to us. If His Protestant church will not be proactive in preparing a people to meet her Lord at His coming, then He will help her prepare by depriving her of all the blessings that He gave her. Yet, if while their God takes away their goodness, the Protestant Americans would still rather sing and celebrate, party hearty and forget the God who formed them and who delivered them from the past papal persecutions, then they will be unprepared for what's coming — their enemy from the Dark Ages. Free, Constitutional, Protestant America will bring on its own demise. "They have sinned against the Lord" (Jer. 50:7).

The wars that our enemy has fomented, which have caused millions of deaths by Protestants fighting Protestants, and the current Protestant reign of terror against Muslims, are primarily because we left the faith of our Reformation fathers. We refused obedience to the Law of God and what we call worship is service to His adversary. We left off preparing for the Seal of God, which would be placed in our conscience and our heart. We have let idolatry dissolve our yearning for reconciliation with God and for abiding in His peace, an incomprehensible peace possessed by prophets, apostles, and reformers sent from Jesus, the Prince of peace Himself having peace infinitely deep and eternal.

All of the Protestant world's financial woes, its erosion of freedoms and its moral collapse, the pervasiveness of street drugs, the medicated adults and children, and the diseases plaguing us on every hand, every bit of it the Lord warned He would bring upon and watch over us, His holy people, the descendants of the holy Protestant Reformation. And, why? Because of our apostasy from His Bible and from His holy religion of righteousness and peaceful dependence on Him. As He did with Israel, He blames no one except us. **We** left Him; therefore He must let us have our way until the conditions get so difficult that they help us choose to change our disloyalty toward Him again. Having said that, though, He has never forsaken His Reformation movement. We are still on His radar.

> Ye children of Israel, turn again unto the LORD God of Abraham, Isaac, and Israel, and he will return to the remnant of you, that are escaped out of the hand of the kings of Assyria. And be not ye like your fathers, and like your brethren, which trespassed against the LORD God of their fathers, who therefore gave them up to desolation, as ye see. Now be ye not stiffnecked, as your fathers were, but yield yourselves unto the LORD, and enter into his sanctuary, which he hath sanctified for ever: and serve the LORD your God, that the fierceness of his wrath may turn away from you. For if ye turn again unto the LORD, your brethren and your children shall find compassion before them that lead them captive, so that they shall come again into this land: for the LORD your God is gracious and merciful, and will not turn away his face from you, if ye return unto him (2 Chron. 30:6-9).

> If they break my statutes, and keep not my commandments;

> Then will I visit their transgression with the rod, and their iniquity with stripes.

Nevertheless my lovingkindness will I not utterly take from him, nor suffer my faithfulness to fail (Ps. 89:31-33).

A remnant will be saved.

Zion shall be redeemed with judgment, and her converts with righteousness (Isa. 1:27).

Protestants, don't let your enemy from the Tiber take these precious promises away and apply them only to the current nation of Israel. If you love your Bible then you will say that the promises are for you too! Jesus will not "utterly take away His lovingkindness from *you*, nor suffer His faithfulness toward *you* to fail". Beautiful promise! Wonderful hope! We will need as many promises as we can gather up for the trouble ahead. They are divinely tailored to help us to surrender, assisting our heart and self-will to break. Our Redeemer wants to have us with Him forever in the crystal clear, rarefied environment of His kingdom. But, remember that with the promises we must accept His precious fatherly warnings and rebukes. His children must desire to be cleansed from this world's sin-filled miasma. If they seem reluctant to be redeemed, He will use every desperate measure that they can endure. And if our heart is set on Him, He will not give us more than we can endure.

On the other hand Jesus counsels us, "Remember Lot's wife" (Luke 17:32). She chose to cling to the treasures of this world, even while hearing the crashing bedlam of the Lord's displeasure behind her. What more could the Lord do for her? He cannot force us to love and obey Him. He cannot force us to prepare for His judgments; He wants no automatons. But, when His merciful probationary delay runs out, in the crisis we will do only what we have done by repetition and have ingrained into our character.

Much of the Bible makes little sense to most folks today because they are unwilling to take its message to heart. Isaiah 30:15-18, for example. We must ask ourselves, Have we taken this counsel seriously?

> For thus saith the Lord GOD, the Holy One of Israel; In returning and rest shall ye be saved; in quietness and in confidence shall be your strength: and ye would not. But ye said, **No**; for we will flee upon horses; therefore shall ye flee: and, We will ride upon the swift; therefore shall they that pursue you be swift (Isa. 30:15, 16).

> One thousand shall flee at the rebuke of one; at the rebuke of five shall ye flee: till ye be left as a beacon upon the top of a mountain, and as an ensign on an hill. And therefore will the LORD wait, that he may be gracious unto you, and therefore will he be exalted, that he may have mercy upon you: for the LORD is a God of judgment: blessed are all they that wait for him (Vs. 17, 18).

These last verses repeat the warning of Moses from Deuteronomy.

> The LORD shall cause thee to be smitten before thine enemies: thou shalt go out one way against them, and flee seven ways before them: and shalt be removed into all the kingdoms of the earth. And thy carcase shall be meat unto all fowls of the air, and unto the beasts of the earth, and no man shall fray them away (Deut. 28:25, 26).

And there is more.

> If thou wilt not observe to do all the words of this law that are written in this book, that thou mayest fear this glorious and fearful name, THE LORD THY GOD; then the LORD will make thy plagues wonderful, and the plagues of thy seed, even great plagues, and of long continuance, and sore sicknesses, and of long continuance. Moreover he will bring upon thee all the diseases of Egypt, which thou wast afraid of; and they shall cleave unto thee. Also every sickness, and every plague, which is not written in the book of this law, them will the LORD bring upon thee, *until thou be destroyed*. And ye shall be left few in number, whereas ye were as the stars of heaven for multitude; because thou wouldest not obey the voice of the LORD thy God. And it shall come to pass, that as the LORD rejoiced over you to do you good, and to multiply you; so the LORD will rejoice over you to destroy you, and to bring you to nought; and ye shall be plucked from off the land whither thou goest to possess it (Deut. 28:58-63).

All thy trees and fruit of thy land shall the locust consume.

The stranger that is within thee shall get up above thee very high; and thou shalt come down very low.

He shall lend to thee, and thou shalt not lend to him: he shall be the head, and thou shalt be the tail.

Moreover all these curses shall come upon thee, and shall pursue thee, and overtake thee, till thou be destroyed; because thou hearkenedst not unto the voice of the LORD thy God, to keep his commandments and his statutes which he commanded thee (Deut. 28:42-45).

For the day of vengeance is in mine heart, and the year of my redeemed is come. And I looked, and there was none to help; and I wondered that there was none to uphold: therefore mine own arm brought salvation unto me; and my fury, it upheld me. And I will tread down the people in mine anger, and make them drunk in my fury, and I will bring down their strength to the earth (Isa. 63:4-6).

Offensive. Condemning. Making the proponents of Spiritual Formation tremble. Yet, though it is scripture, many keep this strong message tucked away in the history or archeology or fiction vault of their mental library. They will not apply it to themselves. Will we continue that intellectual pursuit until there is no time left to learn strong submission and powerful faith? The above message from Isaiah says that we should not fight to get back all the "good things" we've lost. All of our treasures laid up on earth are leaving us for our good as punishment and discipline from our Father. "If ye be without chastisement, whereof all are partakers, then are ye [illegitimate], and not sons" (Heb. 12:8). Also, our Protestant earthly treasures are leaving because its time for this old Earth to end. Praise the Lord, the saga of sin is almost over! God never intended it to last forever. "When he shall have accomplished to scatter the power of the holy people, all these things shall be finished" (Dan. 12:7).

We must not cling to our possessions as did Lot's wife. Those possessions are now made in wickedness and they poison with unbelief and pride all who possess them. "Shall I not visit them for these things? saith the LORD: shall not my soul be avenged on such a nation as this?" (Jer. 9:9). *Protestants, heaven's temporal blessings will continue to leave you "till thou be destroyed"*. "The stranger that is within thee shall get up above thee very high; and thou shalt come down very low. He shall lend to thee, and thou shalt not lend to him: he shall be the head, and thou shalt be the tail" (Deut. 28:43, 44). God will dispossess us of all the prosperity that He gave us for all the faithfulness of our Reformation fathers.

Thou shalt betroth a wife, and another man shall lie with her: thou shalt build an house, and thou shalt not dwell therein: thou shalt plant a vineyard, and shalt not gather the grapes thereof.

Thine ox shall be slain before thine eyes, and thou shalt not eat thereof: thine ass shall be violently taken away from before thy face, and shall not be restored to thee: thy sheep shall be given unto thine enemies, and thou shalt have none to rescue them.

Thy sons and thy daughters shall be given unto another people, and thine eyes shall look, and fail with longing for them all the day long: and there shall be no might in thine hand.

The fruit of thy land, and all thy labours, shall a nation which thou knowest not eat up; and thou shalt be only oppressed and crushed alway (Deut. 28:30-33).

There is more to life than making money, and much more to eternal life. We will be stripped of hoping in this old, decaying world until we can "come to the point of yielding the will to God" *Steps to Christ*, p. 47. The children of God will finally fall on the Stone and receive the broken heart that they so desperately need, and that Jesus so desperately wants to give them. *Then every spiritual blessing will come in its train* (see Proverbs 8:1, 17-19). Those blessings are eternal realities: peace from God's acceptance, "the heavenly gift", being "made partakers of the Holy Ghost", tasting "the good word of God, and the powers of the world to come" (Heb. 6:4, 5). *Doesn't that sound good! Better than a Lexus or a big house, or the latest toy or game!*

It's only the spiritual blessings of confirmed hope in God's love and its resultant sanctification of character that we will take with us into eternity. By our dispossession of earthly things, Providence is simply facilitating His commandment for His children to lay up for themselves treasures in heaven. He has waited long enough for us to choose the easier path to Him and to proactively take this upon ourselves. Now He must use tragedy and loss to expedite our big decision of whether or not to choose eternal life. We must submit to our dispossession of America; we must lay up for heaven **all** that we treasure.

These are they which came out of great tribulation, and have washed their robes, and made them white in the blood of the Lamb (Rev. 7:14).

Yet, only a very small remnant within Protestantism and Adventism will obey that voice from above. Most among our Protestant nation and the Advent movement will call it insanity to lose the things of Earth.

"Thou wilt…bring down high looks" (Ps. 18:27). He must bring down our self-sufficiency in order for us to know His salvation; when we are weak and emptied of our resources, then we will be strong to suffer for the Lord (see 2 Corinthians 12:10). All that we can bring to heaven from earth is the faith and character of Jesus (see Matthew 6:19-21; Philippians 3:20, 21), the fruits of His Spirit. But, all who will not surrender to His Law and character will find the judgments of God fall on them, grinding them to powder and driving them into Satan's open arms. (See Matthew 21:44; Isaiah 8:21, 22.)

Instead of stockpiling a mountain of ammunition, we must be stockpiling a multitude of admonition. Instead of fighting to prevent our due punishment from Jesus and His help for us to release our death grip on earthly treasures, we should pray to the Lord our God to follow His steps into preparation for His return.

> I say unto you, That ye resist not evil: but whosoever shall smite thee on thy right cheek, turn to him the other also.
>
> And if any man will sue thee at the law, and take away thy coat, let him have thy cloke also.
>
> And whosoever shall compel thee to go a mile, go with him twain.
>
> Give to him that asketh thee, and from him that would borrow of thee turn not thou away.
>
> Ye have heard that it hath been said, Thou shalt love thy neighbour, and hate thine enemy.
>
> But I say unto you, Love your enemies, bless them that curse you, do good to them that hate you, and pray for them which despitefully use you, and persecute you;
>
> That ye may be the children of your Father which is in heaven: for he maketh his sun to rise on the evil and on the good, and sendeth rain on the just and on the unjust.
>
> For if ye love them which love you, what reward have ye? do not even the publicans the same?
>
> And if ye salute your brethren only, what do ye more than others? do not even the publicans so?
>
> Be ye therefore perfect, even as your Father which is in heaven is perfect (Matt. 5:39-48).
>
> I will very gladly spend and be spent for you; though the more abundantly I love you, the less I be loved (2 Cor. 12:15).
>
> Give, and it shall be given unto you; good measure, pressed down, and shaken together, and running over, shall men give into your bosom. For with the same measure that ye mete withal it shall be measured to you again (Luke 6:38).
>
> And every one that heareth these sayings of mine, and doeth them not, shall be likened unto a foolish man, which built his house upon the sand: and the rain descended, and the floods came, and the winds blew, and beat upon that house; and it fell: and great was the fall of it (Matt. 7:26, 27, cf 1 Tim. 3:3; 4:10; 5:22; 6:1-12; 2 Tim. 1: 7, 8; 2:3, 4, 10-12, 24, 25; 3:3, 10-12; 1 Cor. 13:7; 15:30; 2 Cor. 1:5-10; 4:7-12, 17, 18; 11:23-31).

We should expect accusations and offense, but meet them with Jesus' yearning to save every accusing and offensive one, even down to our last hours of life. "[Jesus] said unto them, Why sleep ye? rise and pray, lest ye enter into temptation. And while he yet spake, behold a multitude, and he that was called Judas, one of the twelve, went before them, and drew near unto Jesus to kiss him. But Jesus said unto him, Judas, betrayest thou the Son of man with a kiss? When they which were about him saw what would follow, they said unto him, Lord, shall we smite with the sword? And one of them smote the servant of the high priest, and cut off his right ear. And Jesus answered and said, Suffer ye thus far. And he touched his ear, and healed him" (Luke 22:46-51). "They stoned Stephen, calling upon God, and saying, Lord Jesus, receive my spirit. And he kneeled down, and cried with a loud voice, Lord, lay not this sin to their charge. And when he had said this, he fell asleep" (Acts 7:59, 60).

The battle of Armageddon will be fought. And that day must find none of us sleeping. Wide awake we must be, as wise virgins having oil in our vessels with our lamps. The power of the Holy Ghost must be upon us and the Captain of the Lord's host will stand at the head of the angels of heaven to direct the battle.... **He** [emphasis mine] will vindicate His truth. He will cause it to triumph. He is ready to supply His faithful ones with motives and power of purpose, inspiring them with hope and courage and valor in increased activity as the time is at hand *Selected Messages*, bk. 3, p. 426.

The fifth and sixth trumpets have forewarned us of the harsh times ahead. The current wars and rumors of wars are only the beginning of sorrows; and we see the overt movements of the papacy and the sure involvement of the Jesuits in the abominations taking place today. Yet, we can know that God's church is still on His radar. We can take heart in our Lord's wisdom and watchfulness over His last day people. His ship must meet with great turbulence; but the Watcher on the shore will guide it through the stormy darkness and His angels' hands will hold it steady with its precious cargo. How thankful we can be that He hasn't forgotten us, but prophesied of today's generation back when His Advent movement first began. He watches His precious people who are wending their way down the corridors of fulfilled prophecy. He knows how the great controversy will end because it will end according to His will. If you hold to the Bible and the Testimony of Jesus, you cannot miss the correct side of the conflict.

The difficult first time of trouble will be our last opportunity to learn the powerful lessons of surrender that the Lord has been trying to teach us from His Most Holy Place. Albeit, tomorrow those lessons will be learned under much greater distress than if we will strive to learn them today, reading the Testimony of Jesus, and sharing His goodness with others. We should seek Jesus for the intervention of His providences that can lead us down now into the waters of submission and surrender. With this request He will more than happily comply.

> As a beast goeth down into the valley, the Spirit of the LORD caused him to rest: so didst thou lead thy people, to make thyself a glorious name (Isa. 63:14).

If we set our love upon Him today, then the time of trouble will be easier and its burden much lighter.

> Behold, the name of the LORD cometh from far, burning with his anger, and the burden thereof is heavy: his lips are full of indignation, and his tongue as a devouring fire (Isa. 30:27).

> Deep calleth unto deep at the noise of thy waterspouts: all thy waves and thy billows are gone over me. Yet the LORD will command his lovingkindness in the daytime, and in the night his song shall be with me, and my prayer unto the God of my life (Ps. 42:7, 8).

Let us be praying to be part of the Latter Rain. But, let us also pray and work those prayers to now be part of the Early Rain blessings and primitive godliness. It means beginning now to serve others for the purpose of demonstrating Jesus' true character. It means making things right with enemies, reconciling failed friendships. This means personal involvement in sharing with others the true character of Jesus, not indiscriminately, but appropriately to timing and circumstance. It means the four doables: studying the whole Bible to see the "tender plant" (Isa. 53:2) in Jesus; it means prayer, communing with Jesus about what we are learning from the Bible; it means evangelism, and Christian service, seeking to undo all the misconceptions of the true, self-denying, spotless Lamb of God.

> (For he saith, I have heard thee in a time accepted, and in the day of salvation have I succoured thee: behold, now is the accepted time; behold, now is the day of salvation.)

> Giving no offence in any thing, that the ministry be not blamed:

> But in all things approving ourselves as the ministers of God, in much patience, in afflictions, in necessities, in distresses,

> In stripes, in imprisonments, in tumults, in labours, in watchings, in fastings;

> By pureness, by knowledge, by longsuffering, by kindness, by the Holy Ghost, by love unfeigned,

> By the word of truth, by the power of God, by the armour of righteousness on the right hand and on the left,

> By honour and dishonour, by evil report and good report: as deceivers, and yet true;

> As unknown, and yet well known; as dying, and, behold, we live; as chastened, and not killed;

> As sorrowful, yet alway rejoicing; as poor, yet making many rich; as having nothing, and yet possessing all things (2 Cor. 6:2-10).

Let us come to Him in great need and admission to disloyalty and to disobedience. Let us acknowledge before Him all of our empty religiosity and morality that has been only abominable, polluted rags, the shame of our nakedness, and the cause of our confusion. We should come before Him, not applauding ourselves or celebrating anything; but fearing before Him, mortifying the flesh through the Spirit, purifying ourselves to become like Jesus, and being thankful for His attention. We have only one chance left to prepare for the Hitler-like persecution that is quickly heading our way. It will make or break everyone, and determine who will fear God and be ready to go with Jesus when He returns in power. We must take in earnest the search for Jesus today before the first time of trouble hits with blinding force. We must come out of this Babylon before the nations become uncontrollably agitated and Satan comes down with undisguised fury knowing he has but a very short time reign on earth.

> For I am the LORD: I will speak, and the word that I shall speak shall come to pass; it shall be no more prolonged: for in your days, O rebellious house, will I say the word, and will perform it, saith the Lord GOD.... Son of man, behold, they of the house of Israel say, The vision that he seeth is for many days to come, and he prophesieth of the times that are far off. Therefore say unto them, Thus saith the Lord GOD; There shall none of my words be prolonged any more, but the word which I have spoken shall be done, saith the Lord GOD (Eze. 12:25, 27, 28).

Ezekiel's words came just before Babylon's final destruction of Israel. We stand upon the brink of the final devastation of Revelation's Babylon. There can't be delay much longer. Let us lay claim to Daniel's prayer in Daniel chapter 9, after we have lived too long already serving the gods that will cause our soon-coming Babylonian captivity. If we will pray like Daniel, the Lord will pull us through. When we are weak, then He will be strong.

> Then will I sprinkle clean water upon you, and ye shall be clean: from all your filthiness, and from all your idols, will I cleanse you.
>
> A new heart also will I give you, and a new spirit will I put within you: and I will take away the stony heart out of your flesh, and I will give you an heart of flesh.
>
> And I will put my spirit within you, and cause you to walk in my statutes, and ye shall keep my judgments, and do them.
>
> And ye shall dwell in the land that I gave to your fathers; and ye shall be my people, and I will be your God.
>
> I will also save you from all your uncleannesses: and I will call for the corn, and will increase it, and lay no famine upon you.
>
> And I will multiply the fruit of the tree, and the increase of the field, that ye shall receive no more reproach of famine among the heathen.
>
> Then shall ye remember your own evil ways, and your doings that were not good, and shall lothe yourselves in your own sight for your iniquities and for your abominations.
>
> Not for your sakes do I this, saith the Lord GOD, be it known unto you: be ashamed and confounded for your own ways, O house of Israel.
>
> Thus saith the Lord GOD; In the day that I shall have cleansed you from all your iniquities I will also cause you to dwell in the cities, and the wastes shall be builded.
>
> And the desolate land shall be tilled, whereas it lay desolate in the sight of all that passed by.
>
> And they shall say, This land that was desolate is become like the garden of Eden (Eze. 36:25-35).
>
> And he shewed me a pure river of water of life, clear as crystal, proceeding out of the throne of God and of the Lamb.
>
> In the midst of the street of it, and on either side of the river, was there the tree of life, which bare twelve manner of fruits, and yielded her fruit every month: and the leaves of the tree were for the healing of the nations.
>
> And there shall be no more curse: but the throne of God and of the Lamb shall be in it; and his servants shall serve him:

And they shall see his face; and his name shall be in their foreheads (Rev. 22:1-4).

And he said unto me, These sayings are faithful and true: and the Lord God of the holy prophets sent his angel to shew unto his servants the things which must shortly be done (Rev. 21:6).

Behold, I stand at the door, and knock: if any man hear my voice, and open the door, I will come in to him, and will sup with him, and he with me (Rev. 3:20).

Lord, open our eyes and let this book be the morning star of the Latter Rain
May it start into action forces that cannot be repressed
Let it cause a shaking that swells to a giant tsunami of righteousness. Amen

---

We invite you to view the complete
selection of titles we publish at:

www.ASPECTBooks.com

scan with your mobile
device to go directly
to our website

Please write or email us your praises, reactions, or
thoughts about this or any other book we publish at:

Info@ASPECTBooks.com

TEACH Services, Inc., titles may be purchased in bulk for
educational, business, fund-raising, or sales promotional use.
For information, please e-mail:

BulkSales@ASPECTBooks.com

Finally if you are interested in seeing
your own book in print, please contact us at

publishing@ASPECTBooks.com

We would be happy to review your manuscript for free.

www.ingramcontent.com/pod-product-compliance
Lightning Source LLC
Chambersburg PA
CBHW081347230426
43667CB00017B/2745